ENERGY AND CONFLICT
The Life and Times of Edward Teller

The Life and Times

Energy and Conflict

of Edward Teller

by Stanley A. Blumberg
and Gwinn Owens

G. P. Putnam's Sons
New York

SBN: 399–11551–X

Library of Congress Cataloging in Publication Data

Blumberg, Stanley A.
    Energy and conflict.

    Bibliography: p.
    Includes index.
    1. Teller, Edward, 1908–   I. Owens, Gwinn,
joint author.   II. Title.
QC16.T37B58   623.4'5119'0924 [B]   75–43812

To Berty Blumberg and Joan Owens

Contents

ACKNOWLEDGMENTS

ONE of the unexpected pleasures in writing this biography stemmed from the unusual number of people who went far beyond mere cooperation and volunteered active, time-consuming, and invaluable assistance. It is impossible to rate such generosity on any quantitative scale; our profound gratitude extends to every one of these contributors.

Obviously, in a biography of a living person, the subject himself can be the key to the project. We were fortunate that Edward Teller offered all of his letters, papers, and memorabilia to us exclusively until we were finished. That was, however, the easier part of his involvement. We also demanded of him hundreds of hours of his time, usually coaxing him to talk into a tape recorder. Since he is a peripatetic subject, we often caught him en route to or from the airports around Baltimore and Washington, using a car as a moving sound studio. At no time, despite our probing and difficult questions, did he ever lose patience. On some occasions, when he was returning from some jaunt across the country or the world, he must have been exhausted, but his warmth and good humor never left him. This was all the more remarkable because he never knew how we, as biographers, were going to portray him. He must have sensed that we were going to try to be fair.

Olivette Chinn, Edward Teller's secretary, was practically at our beck and call in rooting out and copying elusive material from his files at Livermore. A similar kindness was rendered by Virginia Walker, administrative aide to the late Lewis L. Strauss. (This was a particularly poignant task for her, because Admiral Strauss died during the course of our work.) Among the more anonymous suppliers of information were the able staff members of the Enoch Pratt Free Library of Baltimore City, the Baltimore County Public Library at Towson, and the Eisenhower Library of the Johns Hopkins University.

Many physicists helped us, but two of them deserve special mention. John A. Wheeler of Princeton reviewed and corrected sections of this book dealing specifically with physics, and Jan Minkowski of Johns Hopkins spent many hours helping us understand and describe quantum theory (if either of these gentlemen did not entirely succeed, the failure is ours, not theirs). We must also give special mention to Alfred Sklar, a colleague of Teller in the 1930s. After submitting to an interview, Dr. Sklar then voluntarily wrote for us his recollections of the scientific accomplishments of the Teller circle of that era. Hans Bethe of Cornell granted a five-hour interview, longer than anyone except Teller himself. Theodore F. Walkowicz, a scientist-engineer, contributed some of the most valuable new information in this book, as well as a number of delightfully detailed anecdotes.

Other scientists who contributed enthusiastically include Frederic de Hoffmann, Eugene P. Wigner, Werner Heisenberg (whom we were able to intercept on a brief visit to the United States from his home in Bavaria), I. I. Rabi, Merle Tuve, Ferdinand Brickwedde, Sterling Hendricks, Raymond Seeger, Herman Mark, Marvin Goldberger, Yuval Ne'eman, Shlomo Gur, Norris Bradbury, Harold Agnew, H. D. Smyth, Robert E. Marshak, Robert Seamans, Herman H. Goldstine, Lowell Wood, Roger Batzel, Morton S. Weiss, Fred Holzer, Stanislaw Ulam, Marshall Rosenbluth, and Maurice Shapiro.

Others who assisted, mainly outside the direct area of science, include General Kenneth Nichols, General Alvin Cowan, Colonel Louis Beck, Dr. James R. Maxfield (Teller's personal physician), Laura Fermi, Richard Hewlett, Bryan F. La Plante, Joseph Volpe, William Liscum Borden, Judge Roger Robb, Robert LeBaron, Vice President Nelson Rockefeller, Manuel Dupkin, Edward Rozek, Arthur Spitzer, Edmund Mroz, Paul W. Wirtz, Pam Peterson, Nancy Milford, and John H. Morse.

Teller, his family, and his close friends having almost entirely vacated their native Hungary, it was particularly difficult to track down those with recollections of his childhood. In this respect we were rewarded by chance and coincidence. Magda Hess Schutz, Teller's governess when he was a small boy, is alive and well and living near Chicago. In a chance conversation with a Hungarian restaurant manager in Baltimore, we discovered that his father-in-law, Miklos Wenczel, had been a Teller school classmate and was now living in Silver Spring, Maryland. Both Mrs. Schutz and Mr.

and Mrs. Wenczel proved to be rich sources of otherwise unavailable information. In addition, we traveled to Israel to talk with Teller's cousin, Ilona Cernat, and her mother, Margaret Dobo, and one of his oldest friends, Ferenc von Körosy.

There is one group of informants to whom we concede some emotional attachment as well professional gratitude. This would be Teller's immediate family. His lovely and devoted wife, Mici, was at first understandably shy after years of enduring the relentless critics of her controversial husband. When she was persuaded of our genuine desire to be objective, she became one of our most gracious interviewees. Teller's son, Paul, a philosophy professor at the University of Illinois, contributed many helpful and amusing recollections, as did Teller's daughter, Wendy Teller Saleski, a mathematician, whose objective and witty view of her father did not conceal a deep affection. Perhaps most remarkable were the anecdotes of Teller's mother, Ilona, a tiny, vigorous great-grandmother, no less than ninety-four years old as we completed this book.

We hold in special affection Teller's older sister, Emmi Kirz, a gentle and generous woman, who has added so much feeling to these pages. She not only talked for hours with us, but uncovered letters, pictures, even diaries, that became priceless sources. Then to supplement her immense contribution, her son, Janos, now a physicist with the State University of New York, told, in minute detail, of the suffering of himself, his mother, and his grandmother under first the Nazis, then the communists in Hungary. Chapter 9 of this book is principally the contribution of Janos Kirz.

Genevieve Phillips, an earlier secretary of Edward Teller, gave us one of the best views of the man at work. Ann Fogle, who did special secretarial work for him, turned up some essential papers, and Tolly Williamson of the Livermore Laboratory supplemented the work of Olivette Chinn. In Baltimore we were ably helped by Ann Chatterton and Marsha McLeod. Dail Gable, of the staff of WJZ–TV, not only transcribed many taped interviews, but applied her considerable literary talent to the constructive review of every chapter.

If there is a literary godfather of the authors, this would have to be Bradford Jacobs, editor of the Baltimore *Evening Sun,* who published our first joint article, and many more thereafter, and cheered from the sidelines as we pushed our way toward publication of this book. George A. Gipe, who has been there himself, gave us some sound advice on getting through the jungle of literary New York and into the hands of the right agent and the right publisher.

Even then we might not have managed without the moral support of a remarkable man, Herbert B. Cahan, area vice-president of the Westinghouse Broadcasting Company in Baltimore. He not only allowed one-half of our team to take time from television chores to write a biography, but actually encouraged our efforts, day by day.

Lastly, we have to pay, not token, but genuine tribute to our wives and families. Berty Blumberg typed literally hundreds of pages of draft after draft and never lost her delightful wit and her infective enthusiasm for the project. Joan Owens applied the expertise of a full-time English teacher to the entire book, while keeping a house full of four children quiet (or reasonably quiet) every evening for two long years. But all the children, Wendy, Ross, Laura, and Paul, were old enough to make their own truly useful contributions, as did their cousin, Alexander H. Owens, a young physics graduate student at Johns Hopkins.

To all these we can honestly say this book is partly their achievement. On the other hand, if the reader should by chance find errors, inaccuracies, or other assorted sins of omission or commission, do not blame our generous sources. The authors alone are responsible for the final product.

STANLEY A. BLUMBERG
GWINN OWENS

Baltimore, Maryland
November 15, 1975

INTRODUCTION

THE most difficult task confronting a biographer is to try to discover and report on the motivations of his subject. The recording of events, of actions, requires only infinite patience and dedication, but the attempt to understand the multiple thought processes that must precede action is a task beyond any but the most skillful analyst.

Of course, a biographer is usually not an analyst, and most subjects have neither the time nor the desire to subject themselves to this long and time-consuming process.

Still, we were fortunate in having a completely honest and cooperative subject. This is not to say that all of our questions were freely answered. They were not. For example, Edward Teller was reluctant and in some cases even refused to discuss some aspects of his early days—of his family or his childhood. In this area of inquiry he referred us to either his sister, his mother, or his governess. His reluctance in this field is difficult to understand. His family ties were close and his relations with his parents were warm and even affectionate.

The conclusions presented in this biography are the result of interviews over a period of more than two years. We traveled the great circle route from Jerusalem to Berkeley, California, in our quest for information and understanding.

In fact, we first met Edward Teller in May 1972 on the steps of the Sheraton Hotel in Tel Aviv. He had been pointed out to us by an old and delightful friend, Shula Lasnitski. This casual, almost brief encounter led to a productive relationship. Teller was and is a man bursting with interesting ideas, and as journalists we felt a deep compulsion to ventilate and expose these flashes of inspiration to the public eye.

We began to view the canvas on which his character had been painted from a different angle, from a new perspective. The stark black and white portrait slowly blended into varying shades of gray. The overly simplistic cubes were seen as the curved lines and rounded forms of a troubled but basically honest human being evolved.

Our first surprise was that this alleged Dr. Strangelove character was opposed to secrecy in science. Moreover, his love affair with openness in science was not a one-night stand, but was a childhood infatuation that ripened into a calm article of faith.

Since we both have a liberal orientation it was more difficult for us to understand Teller's current political conservatism. As biographers we have an obligation to present and explain the motivation for his actions. But we do not always have to agree with Teller. Still, it is interesting that as a result of gathering the material for this book, the degree of our political differences with Edward Teller has narrowed, but it has not been erased. Exposure to new information has a strange effect on the human mind; opinions are subject to change.

It was early in the fall of 1972 when we discovered to our surprise that no one had ever written a biography of Edward Teller. No author had published the story of one of the world's great theoretical physicists, no one had researched in depth the life of this scientist who has been an instrumental, if not *the* crucial advocate for a strong America.

We chided him on this lack. After all, Enrico Fermi had a biography. His old friend Leo Szilard had a biography. What was wrong with Edward Teller? He explained that he had been asked to write an autobiography and had refused. Autobiographies are, in Teller's words, self-serving, and also he did not have the time.

"However," Teller continued, "if you want to do a biography of me, I will place at your disposal, on an exclusive basis, all of my papers and correspondence that are not classified."

This flattering, generous, unexpected offer raised a serious question. And so we responded bluntly, "As you know, Dr. Teller, you are not a popular man and it might be difficult to find a reliable publisher to handle the book. It would be a waste of time and effort to write your biography and then find that only a right-wing publishing house would handle it. [We were wrong.] In this case very few people would read the book and its effect on the public conscience would be minimal."

Teller understood. "You may very well be right, but I am confident that the two of you will find a way to overcome this obstacle. If you decide to write my biography, there is only one promise you must make." We waited for Teller to continue. "You must criticize me, and criticize me violently." Why? we wondered aloud. Clearly Teller's posture was for us to write an objective book with no holds barred, not an "authorized" portrait, not a bloodless account that would sidestep his profound political embroilments. We promised to report the facts as we found them.

It was agreed that we would have complete editorial freedom. Teller would not be shown the manuscript, at least until it was in galley form. The only exception to this would be some scientific material that he would be asked to review for accuracy. All scientific material however, was not reviewed by Teller, so inaccuracies, if any, are the responsibility of the authors. It should be noted, however, that eminent scientists have been generous in vetting our scientific sections.

We asked him, for a list of his friends and his critics. Names were cheerfully supplied. As an aside, Teller commented, "It is a shame that you cannot speak to Oppenheimer [he died in 1967], he was an interesting man."

A large part of this conversation took place during a forty-five-minute drive from Dulles Airport to a flea-bag hotel diagonally across the street from the Greyhound bus terminal in Washington, D.C. Teller usually stayed at fourth-rate hotels in Washington. It was not, we later discovered, that he enjoyed living in oversized closets, but this was all he could afford. The government's per diem allowance was skimpy.

Teller's hotel room was so small that the fine patina of dust on the furniture and walls reduced that area's living space. As we entered this musty cubicle Teller limped around the bed and placed a call to Mici Teller at Berkeley.

We had earlier met Edward's wife in Tel Aviv. This small, wiry, intense woman seemed to divide her time between chainsmoking cigarettes and worrying about the health of her beloved Edward. Teller is not only overweight, but is plagued with the desire for foods that do not agree with his digestive system. We first observed, in Israel, Mici's futile attempts to prevent her husband from consuming chocolate pastry. Whenever Teller violated the restrictions on his diet, his body would rebel and Mici would play nursemaid.

But this night in Washington, Edward was anxious to share the news with Mici. He addressed her in the diminutive form "Mici-cu," and after some endearing words in Hungarian, said, "Stanley and Gwinn are going to do my biography." There appeared to be expressions of alarm and caution on the other end of the line. As we learned later, Mici did not wish to open old wounds. And also, to what degree could two self-confessed liberal writers be objective? Her husband had been pilloried by the press. Why invite another sensational hatchet job?

But perhaps a gamble on the authors' integrity could have a positive effect. History might vindicate or at least explain some of Teller's more controversial actions. After all these years research might reveal facts that could aid in sloughing off old scar tissue.

Edward would not listen to Mici's words of prudent caution or of reasonable restraint. He decided to gamble. In his own mind, at least, he had always played the cards of his own convictions. Perhaps at times he had been guilty of errors of judgment. But if he had, they were honest mistakes. So let the record be written and he would cooperate by making himself available for what turned out to be literally hundreds of hours of interviews.

The files of his unclassified correspondence were made available. And his secretary at Livermore, Olivette Chinn, helped by tracking down long-forgotten material in the files at Livermore and Los Alamos.

The most difficult problem the authors encountered in writing this book was the stifling security restrictions. Some scientists were reluctant to discuss their work freely. They were afraid of violating security even though in many cases they were not aware of what material was still classified. Others were not so restrained.

The Energy Research and Development Administration (formally the Atomic Energy Commission) was helpful in clarifying apparent inconsistencies. And since declassification is a continuing process, additional information became declassified as this book was being written. Still, for mysterious reasons, some material remains classified after twenty-five years. To complicate the reconstruction of the history of this period, apparently there were events so highly classified that even the AEC was not told of them.

We confronted the chief historian of the AEC, Richard Hewlett, with evidence that the Russians had created a thermonuclear reaction before the American thermonuclear experiment took place. This fact was known at the time to a select committee of the U.S.

Air Force, the Secretary of State, and the President. It was, we felt, astounding that Edward Teller, who at that time was not sure that a thermonuclear reaction could occur on the planet Earth, and had the prime responsibility for creating the H-bomb, was not informed of the Soviet success. Hewlett's response was, "It is not a matter of security. I simply have never heard the story of the Soviet prior thermonuclear test."

It was not until early in 1975 that Teller learned from the authors of the Soviets' early success in the thermonuclear field.

With ill-concealed, seething anger Teller expressed his feelings. "I have always told you that I consider scientific secrecy harmful to our national interest. We are not successful in keeping our secrets from the Russians but only from our own scientists. In this case that you mentioned I certainly had 'the need to know.' I was searching for something." We suggested that keeping this information from him was criminal. Teller disagreed with our harsh label and said, "It was certainly irresponsible."

In spite of Teller's abhorrence of secrecy, he lives by the rules. Many a time we would ask a question whose answer might or might not involve classified information. Teller would always respond, "I am not sure if I am permitted to answer your question. Put your question in the form of a letter and I will see if the security people will allow me to answer." In the large majority of cases, the authors' queries were sympathetically considered and answered.

In some cases the records of the AEC differ from the recollections of some of the scientists we interviewed. When this happened, we reported both versions.

In broad terms the life of Edward Teller has been that of a theoretical physicist, an applied scientist, and a political figure. Even though theoretical physics was and remains his first love, Teller has felt compelled to devote his talents to applied science. First, there was the need for weapons design, and later, in recent years, he has been involved in seeking out alternate sources of energy.

This change in his priorities was accomplished by his entrance into the political arena. This is not only understandable but probably was inevitable. Since the beginning of World War II, the funding of research and development work has been primarily the government's responsibility. The decisions to build the atom and hydrogen bombs were political in nature. One of the most fascinating episodes in Teller's career was his political maneuvering that led to President Truman's decision to build the H-bomb.

Teller has been and remains an exciting and controversial figure, but, as biographers, we are faced with the problem of the astrophysicist and the astronomer: because of the space-time relationship and the behavior of light we can never see the present but only the past.

1

The Russians Are Coming

"HE'S a danger to all that's important . . . I do really feel it would have been a better world without Teller." This opinion was expressed by the distinguished Nobel-prize-winning physicist I. I. Rabi in a 1973 interview with the authors. The judgment was political, not personal. Across the spectrum an equally distinguished Nobel Laureate in physics, Eugene Wigner, told us that Teller is "the most imaginative person I ever met—and this means a great deal when you consider that I knew Einstein." But the most lavish tribute of all was expressed for our benefit by Vice President Nelson Rockefeller. "Once in a while," Rockefeller told us, "I have encountered an individual of energy, dedication, and genius so extraordinary as to mark him indelibly on my memory and leave me eternally in his debt for the services he has rendered mankind. One such person is Henry Kissinger. Another is Dr. Edward Teller."

Such are the extremes of the multitude of judgments passed on the Hungarian immigrant who has become one of the most celebrated and controversial physicists of the century. An intense, brooding man, with redeeming moments of joviality, Edward Teller has few detractors when his scientific competence is the issue. But in the political theater, where he has been pursuing his scientific goals, he takes his curtain call before a divided audience, part applauding a hero, part jeering a villain.

Consider that in 1970 University of California students of the radical left branded Teller a "war criminal" and were intercepted by Berkeley police in a march to burn down his house. In 1972 admirers from all over the nation created a postgraduate center at Boulder, Colorado, named in his honor. That Teller later disassociated himself from the center only points up the complexity of the man and the turmoil in his soul. In truth, turmoil, whether in his surroundings or within himself, has been Teller's lot for most of his life. Only in his first six years, and perhaps briefly in his late youth, did he bask in relative tranquillity.

He was six when the guns began to thunder across Europe in August 1914. At such an age he was, of course, unaware of the looming catastrophe, though he was already a thoroughly uncommon youngster. At this stage he would lie in his bed in a modest Budapest apartment and, if he were restless, put himself to sleep by his own method of counting sheep—"60 seconds in a minute, 3,600 seconds in an hour, 86,400 seconds in a day . . ." and perhaps even farther. It was sheer joy to work out complex mathematical calculations in his head.

In the palaces and war offices of Europe the cruel and degrading military capaigns of World War I were being mapped out. The ministers and generals were tragically ignorant of the irrevocable nihilistic forces that would be the century's by-product of their labors. At every stage in his life these forces would confront Edward Teller, and eventually his own genius would bend them in new directions.

That comparatively pleasant Hungarian era that drew to a close with the Great War had begun back in 1867. That was the year that the Hapsburg rulers of the conglomerate Austrian Empire had capitulated to the nationalism of their Hungarian subjects. The empire was split into the dual monarchy, Austria-Hungary, over which Franz Josef ruled as emperor of the former and king of the latter. In domestic affairs the Hungarians had, in theory, won independence, but the peaceful respite in the land of the Magyars lasted less than half a century. Like its native son, Teller, Hungary was usually in turmoil, a situation attributable mainly to an accident of geography. The Magyar people are trapped between Germanic power to the west and Slavic might to the east, and in earlier centuries they were subject to the raids of the foraging Turks from the south.

The peoples under direct Hungarian rule in 1914 included not just the Magyars, but also Slovenes, Czechs, Slovaks, Romanians, Jews, and many others. With the exception of the Jews, Hungary's ethnic minorities nursed national ambitions. Only the economic importance of Budapest and the anachronistic fealty to the Hapsburgs, personified in the aged Franz Josef, held the Hungarian half of the dual monarchy together. Ultimately neither economics nor tradition proved stronger than the fanatic national loyalties unleashed by World War I.

Budapest (actually the twin cities of Buda and Pest) straddles the meandering, multinational Danube River. By 1914 Budapest had acquired that concentration of bureaucratic authority, economic power, and physical grandeur that typified European capitals to the west. These Western characteristics were not accidental. Educated Hungarians revered the spirit and substance of Western civilization, especially its Germanic branch. Budapest emulated Vienna, and not unsuccessfully.

There was, however, a fatal lack of internal fiber in the Hungarian structure. For centuries the political, economic, and cultural leadership of Hungary had been vested in its landed aristocracy. From this mere five percent of the population came intellectual liberals and a spark of enlightened paternalism, but its hard-core outlook was feudal. The peasants who worked the land, nominally free from serfdom since 1848, remained powerless and oppressed for another century.

The machinations of history are strange. The emergence of Edward Teller from the intellectual elite of Budapest is directly related to the aristocracy's unwillingness to make concessions to social change. The burgeoning commercial development of the late nineteenth and early twentieth centuries created a vast need for educated professional and clerical workers. Since these could not arise from the downtrodden peasantry, the vacuum was filled by the two minority groups whose cultural heritage equipped them for the task—the Austro-Germans and the Jews.

The Austro-Germans were Hungarian compatriots under the dual monarchy; their involvement in Hungarian commerce was to be expected. The Jews, including Teller's ancestors, represented a less typical turn of history. A relatively small number of Jews had lived in Hungary under Magyar rule for many centuries. In the eighteenth and nineteenth centuries anti-Semitic pressure in adjacent countries, especially Poland and Romania, forced additional Jews into the traditionally friendlier confines of Hungary. In the historic Hebrew pattern, they tended to cling to a core of cultural and religious traditions, but many of them developed an intense loyalty to Hungary and blended easily into the social landscape. In the nationalist uprisings of 1848, led by superpatriot Lajos Kossuth, the Jews earned the respect of Hungarians for their willingness to fight for the Magyar cause.[1]

The Jewish emergence between 1850 and 1914 was especially notable. In 1850 there were an estimated 350,000 Jews in Hungary. By

1914 their numbers had increased to about a million, out of a total population of twenty million. While this was still only five percent, the disproportionately large number of Jewish professionals was a measure of their intellectual vitality. One the eve of World War I they comprised about a quarter of the journalists, more than half of the physicians in private practice, and about half of the lawyers.[2]

One of these lawyers was Max Teller. As ambitious young men have always been drawn to cities in search of opportunity, Max came to Budapest to study law and become a lawyer. He was born in Ersekujvar, a small town in the Moravian section of Hungary, later ceded to Czechoslovakia in the post-World War I Treaty of Trianon. Max Teller received his secondary education in the Hungarian city of Pozsony, known to its German majority as Pressburg, which was ceded later to the Czechs, who called it Bratislava.

Both of Max's parents died while he was studying law. His character seems to have been formed from an odd mixture of convictions and doubts. When he had received his law degree from the University of Budapest, he wrote in his diary: "A lawyer needs better weapons than I possess to get along in life." And yet he assumed responsibility for three younger sisters, established a successful law practice, and remained a bachelor until all of his sisters were married. Only then, perhaps, did he allow himself to fall in love.

On January 15, 1904, when he was thirty-two, he met Ilona Deutsch at the home of a friend in Budapest. She was striking, only twenty, barely five feet tall, slight, blond, and intense, with determined brows and keen blue eyes. She was already a pianist of near-professional caliber and she spoke, in addition to Hungarian, German, French, Spanish, and Italian.

On January 17, Max spoke his hopes in the silent pages of his diary:

> Now, perhaps, I have found the right one. If the eyes are the mirror of the soul, she is the embodiment of kindness and gentleness. She is as timid as a fawn. In the first five minutes I felt as though we had been friends for a long time, and when I took leave of her I had the feeling that we should never part again. Since I took leave of her I have not done any work. I cannot think while she is away.

Max could not hope to match her in obvious brilliance and beauty. He was short, a little portly, and he played only a second-rate violin. The adjective most often applied to Max by those who knew him then and later is *gentle*. But his professional success seems to evidence subsurface layers of strength and insight, Nor, in his romantic diary entry, had he judged Ilona accurately. She was not "timid as a fawn," but immensely strong-willed. In any case, the mixture of their qualities drew them together. They were engaged on February 1, just sixteen days after they met, and were married on May 29, 1904.

Undoubtedly Ilona's father, Ignac Deutsch, gave serious concern to Max's qualifications. He was a strong, successful banker and cotton mill owner in the city of Lugos in eastern Hungary. He was a heavy, dark man, with a wide forehead and prominent brows. Ilona inherited his character, the forehead, and the brows, but her otherwise delicate features she acquired through her mother, including the clear blue eyes.

There was much in common between Max Teller and his new family of in-laws. Both were Jewish, but both had been assimilated into the general society. Except for ceremonial occasions (Max and Ilona were married by the chief rabbi of Lugos) their heritage was seldom asserted. Both leaned toward Germany in cultural tradition. The Deutsch family usually spoke German, befitting their name, which means *German* and probably indicates an ancestral emigration from Germany.

The newly wed couple had to live in Budapest, where Max maintained his law practice, but for years afterward the Deutsch establishment in far-off Lugos was a retreat and a second home. The Deutsches lived in a large apartment over some shops in the main square of the town. A balcony overlooked the square where the family enjoyed the daily pageant of the townspeople strolling and marketing. Ironically, just as Max's native town was later ceded to the Czechs, Lugos became part of Romania by the terms of the postwar Treaty of Trianon.

Mr. and Mrs. Max Teller chose an apartment at 3 Gorove Street, close to the Budapest law courts and government offices on the Pest side of the Danube. One room of the apartment was used for Max's law office. On November 11, 1905, their first child, Emmi, was born. Max was exceedingly proud of her, and she inherited Ilona's blue eyes. Max accepted the responsibility of parenthood with surprising equanimity, while Ilona was a chronic worrier over the infant Emmi's well-being. At one point Max was moved to comment that if she had a dozen children perhaps she wouldn't worry so much about one.

Two years and two months after Emmi's birth, Edward Teller*
arrived on January 15, 1908. Only a few weeks before the event,
Ilona, heavy with her second child, was walking with a friend
through a nearby park in Pest. She seemed unusually interested in
its corners and vistas. To her friend's puzzled inquiry, she commented: "I have a feeling this time it will be a son, and I'm sure
some day he will be famous, so I'm looking for the best site to build
his monument." It was, perhaps, Ilona's little joke, but it is like insulting the gods to challenge the clairvoyance of an expectant
mother.

Three years later little Edward was famous only in that he had
yet to utter his first coherent word. Emmi had been speaking clearly from a much earlier age and Grandfather Deutsch's concern
was obvious. He tried desperately to coax some words out of his
first male grandchild, but Edward was almost smug in his refusal to
talk. Finally Ignac took it upon himself to prepare Ilona and Max
for the worst. "I think," he said, "that you should face the possibility that you have a retarded child."

Ignac may have been particularly sensitive to Edward's progress,
or lack of it, because the grandson seemed to be growing, in character and features, more like his grandfather every day. He was
dark and stocky, with the forehead and prominent brows that on
Ignac nurtured luxuriant eyebrows and would do the same for Edward when he grew up. There was one mistake in the reproduction
from grandfather to grandson. Ilona, in passing the features along,
had included not her father's brown eyes, but the intense blue
ones that she also bestowed on Emmi.

One day Edward did talk, and it was in sentences, not words, as
if he had been saving the effort until he had something to say. His
family, with its youngest child a participating member, was complete. They were unusually close and harmonious. As Edward became more assertive, Emmi, far from becoming jealous, was proud
of her younger brother and she seemed to sense even before her
parents—and certainly before Grandfather Deutsch—that Edward
Teller was a gifted child.

The politicians of Europe paid little heed to families like the Tellers, who yearned only to live in peace. Fifty million hearthsides
were to be disrupted by the mindless progenitors of violence all

*The Tellers actually named their first son Ede (prounounced "Edda"), the
Hungarian version of Edward. He did not adopt the latter name, the German and
English form, until he went to Germany to study in 1926.

across the continent. Hungary was no exception; the explosive forces building up there were further exacerbated by the disruptions in neighboring states. The hope of Hungarian leaders was that the non-Magyar peoples of Hungary would find sufficient fulfillment of their aspirations through the hegemony in Budapest, but the countermovement of nationalism was running amok. The Romanians in Transylvania, the Croatians, the Slovenes, and the Slovaks were near revolt and, in many cases, justifiably so. The Hungarian suffrage, reflecting the inflexibility of the aristocracy, was rigged against the other nationalities. Their representation in the national parliament was so small as to be negligible—less than one percent for fifty percent of the population.

Meanwhile, in Germany, Kaiser Wilhelm's *Drang nach Osten,* to seek German fortunes in the Middle East, found a willing ally in the leadership of Austria-Hungary and, in this case, only Austrian Emperor Franz Josef was permitted to speak for his Kingdom of Hungary. The dry-rotted Russian Empire was still pugnacious enough to challenge the German drive even while its archaic government was being fatally weakened by the dedicated revolutionaries who would soon pull it down. The Austrian domination of the Balkans had turned into military arrogance. The befuddled Balkan states, witless pawns in the great power tide, had fought three separate wars of their own between 1911 and 1914.

Of course, Europeans had fought Europeans again and again, but the difference in 1914 was that the archaic concept of war as an extension of foreign policy still pervaded the counsels of governments when technology had transformed warfare into physical cataclysm. On June 28, 1914, the Serbian conspirator Gavrillo Princip assassinated the Austrian Archduke Franz Ferdinand during a state visit to Bosnia. When Princip pulled the trigger, the dams of European sanity broke. Austria-Hungary used the archduke's murder as an excuse to launch a war on Serbia. Russian forces were mobilized and the Kaiser, in a panic, sent Germany to war on Russia, then on France, launching his western campaign through Belgium. England declared war on Germany. Russian troops moved against Austria-Hungary, and Hungarian soldiers were dispatched to meet the forces of the czar. For four years the dreadful slaughter raged on. When it was finally over in November 1918, the warped, wounded, and bitter survivors nursed resentments that fed the ambitions of new extremists who would launch another holocaust in just twenty-one years.

Edward Teller grew up in this tortured era between wars. The nations of Central Europe were rife with scarred radicals and hate-filled conservatives, each group seeking to bend Europe to its version of reality; each paranoically distrustful of the middle ground of constitutional democracy. For the Tellers the years of the war itself were only a prelude. They were seldom in real physical danger. They were sometimes cold or hungry, but never freezing or starving. Edward was six, Emmi was eight, when the archduke was assassinated. Max Teller's law practice continued without significant interruption. It was after the war that he began to reveal, in his comments to Edward, his fears for the future of Hungary.

He was by nature a plodder, so he worked hard, building financial security for his family, and placing his highest priority on their proper education. Sixty years later Edward Teller would gratefully recall this contribution, from his grandfather, as well as his father. "What they gave me in a material way," he told the authors, "was one important thing—the means to a good education."

Formal education began for Edward when he was six and was sent to the Mellinger School, a small private institution on the third floor of a nearby apartment house. Informally, he had been educating himself for years, mainly through his self-inspired mathematical games. The custom of putting himself to sleep by testing his ability to compute in his head was apparently a spontaneous effort; he did it because he enjoyed it. Before he started school Edward was thoroughly familiar with addition, subtraction, multiplication, and division. Emmi had been tutored at home when she was school age, then had gone on to the Mellinger School for the second grade. She had been there a year when Edward was enrolled.

Just prior to his venture into formal education, Edward, only six, had run afoul of the law. Someone had given him, or he had acquired, a hand mirror. Sitting in his window, he discovered he could catch and direct the rays of the sun on various targets—a simple experiment in elementary optics. The most attractive target, for a small boy, was the window to the chambers of a learned judge in the government building next door. Edward flashed the merry beam of light through the judge's window, spotting various objects, and finally the judge himself. The honorable gentleman tolerated the blinding intrusion for a while, then became annoyed enough to seek out its source—the Teller apartment.

A short time later there was a knock at the Teller door and a formidable policeman tendered a complaint on behalf of the injured party. Edward was scolded, deprived of his mirror, and warned never to do it again. The agent of the law was satisfied with this probationary punishment and so, apparently, was the judge.

For Edward, however, the experience might have left a permanent scar, as he indicated to the authors. "I think from that point on," he chuckled, "I lost interest in experimental physics." And indeed, Edward Teller became primarily a theoretical physicist, leaving the trappings of the laboratory to those with that inclination.*

If the essential characteristic of a good scientist is to question every assumption, the Tellers' son immediately showed his prowess at the Mellinger School. Religious training was part of the curriculum, and for Jews and Christians alike this begins with "In the beginning God created the heaven and the earth."

"Who created God?" Edward asked a startled teacher and an unsympathetic class. History records only that the question was asked, not how it was answered. And as the study of Genesis proceeded, the teacher told them of the Serpent in the Garden of Eden, punished by God and condemned to crawl on its belly. Again, Edward was skeptical. "How did the Serpent get around before that?" he queried, in honest curiosity. The question has been asked many times, most notably in more recent history by defense lawyer Clarence Darrow of William Jennings Bryan in the famous Scopes evolution trial in Dayton, Tennessee.

Classes in the Mellinger School lasted from nine A.M. to one P.M. The children studied arithmetic, spelling, German music, and reading. The reading fare emphasized fairy tales, especially from the Grimms' collection and Hans Christian Andersen, and there was some delving into poetry. Edward excelled in all of his subjects, though he sometimes annoyed his teachers with too many questions. The classes were small, seldom with more than twenty pupils. Discipline, by current American standards, was strict. Edward was inclined to be a trifle arrogant with friends who were less gifted, to the point where his father worried about it. Emmi still remembers Max's warning to his son: "It's important to have friends in life." The advice may have made an impression because in later and more difficult years, Edward Teller felt an intense need for the support of friends.

*Years later physicist George Gamow, who seldom removed his tongue from his cheek, told a fellow scientist: "It is well known that theoretical physicists cannot handle experimental equipment; it breaks whenever they touch it."

Ilona's concern for her children was not so much for their friendships as for their sheer physical survival. A first cousin of Edward and Emmi, now Mrs. Ilona Dobo Cernat of Tel Aviv, has vivid recollections of her childhood with the Teller children. Known as "Illi," she was the daughter of Ilona Teller's sister, and was seven years younger than Edward.

Illi Cernat remembers Ilona's constant worry about her children's health, their diet, their safety, to the point where Emmi and Edi were unhappy under this constant maternal supervision. For example, Mrs. Cernat told us that they were not allowed to eat anything that wasn't cooked; whipped cream, enjoyed by other children, was considered unsafe by Ilona Teller.

All of the group of friends and relatives enjoyed swimming, mainly in the River Temes, a tributary of the Danube. The beach was well protected, there were lifeguards, and the children took swimming lessons. But this not sufficient for Ilona Teller. She insisted on keeping strings tied to Emmi and Edward, presumably so she could haul them in if there were an emergency. "The string wouldn't really have helped much, but it gave her a feeling of safety," says Mrs. Cernat.

It is difficult for Americans of the late twentieth century to realize that in the early years of the century in Europe almost every middle-class family had several servants. The Tellers were no exception. They generally had a cook and a maid, as well as a governess for the children. The governess—the Tellers had a succession of them—supervised the children all through their waking hours, except when they were at school, although she often delivered them to the schoolroom door and retrieved them there in the afternoons. It was her job to wake the children in the morning, help them get dressed, and escort them to nearby parks and playgrounds in their free hours. She saw that they did their homework and got to bed on time. The wonder is that Ilona Teller, with her excessive concern for the children, would entrust them to a governess. Ferenc von Körosy, an old Teller family friend, agreeing with Illi Cernat, told the authors, "She was afraid they might catch cold, she was afraid they might fall, she was always afraid that something would happen."

When Edward was seven the Tellers' landlord took over their apartment for his own use. Forced to move, Max found a larger apartment in the same neighborhood at 3 Szalay Street. The new apartment had central heating, which was a comparative luxury in those days, and additional space for Max's growing law practice. There were still only two bedrooms, one for the two children, the other for their parents. The governess slept on a daybed in the dining room and used a small room off the front hall as a dressing room.

At about this time, the war, which had had little direct effect on the Tellers' daily routine, was finally threatening Budapest. The Russian army had taken Galicia, the Austrian section of Poland to the north of Hungary. In early 1915 the czar's army was threatening to break through the natural barrier of the Carpathian Mountains and move across the Hungarian plains toward Budapest. Hungary was spared, partly because of pressure of the German army on Russia's northern front, and partly because of a shortage of ammunition and supplies that was blunting the Russian offensive.

Ironically, it was the backwardness of the Hungarian economy that, temporarily, enabled the country to find enough to eat. Its ubiquitous peasants, compared with its relatively insignificant urban population, provided an adequate supply of food for the people of Budapest and other towns and cities. Miklos Wenczel, a Teller classmate, recalls there was some shortage of coal, forcing the Mellinger School to shut down briefly in the winter of 1915. The principal evidence of war in that winter was the coming and going of troop trains, often bringing the wounded to Budapest from the Russian front.

By the summer of 1915 the German, Austrian, and Hungarian armies had thrown the Russians back all along the front and they were forced to retreat almost entirely into their own territory. The threat was removed for a while. The food shortages in Budapest eased and the winter of 1916 was somewhat more comfortable than the previous winter when the Russians had been at the gates of Hungary.

Edward's childhood at this point was surprisingly normal. His mother thought he was brilliant, but years later laughed at herself on the grounds that every mother thinks her son, at seven or eight, is brilliant. Sometimes, however, there were indications that she was absolutely right. Emmi told us of one friend of the Tellers who loved to amuse Emmi and Edward with card tricks. Time and time again Edward would figure out how the trick was accomplished.

The friend, impressed, predicted that Max would someday be best remembered as the father of Edward. He told the dubious father, "He'll be brilliant—but I don't know at what."

If Ilona had had her way the choice would have been music. She wanted him to be a concert pianist. In the custom of wives then (and sometimes now) her own musical career had been sacrificed to her family. She seldom played the piano except when Max asked her. For Edward, however, the door to fame and fortune through music was open. At eight he started piano lessons and was an excellent student, even though his practicing schedule was erratic. In the summer of 1916, when the family went to Lugos for a vacation with the fond grandparents, a local teacher was engaged so that Edward's musical training would not be interrupted. The Lugos teacher, named Willer, became Edward's friend as well, and an inspiration to a small boy with a considerable gift as a musician.

Another significant event of Edward's ninth year was the hiring by his parents of a new governess, Magda Hess. She was from a Hungarian family that had emigrated to the United States and had settled in Chicago. When she was only nineteen both parents died, so Magda returned to Budapest, bringing back with her a proficiency in English. Her employment was on the condition that she teach English to Emmi and Edward, an assignment that she handled competently. When Edward was fourteen, and no longer in need of a governess, she relinquished her task, but remained a friend and helper to the Tellers for many years afterward. She eventually moved back to Chicago, where as Mrs. Magda Hess Schutz, we interviewed her in June of 1973.

Magda, on taking up her task with the Tellers, was impressed with the contrast between Edward's intellectual maturity and his personal immaturity. Helping him dress on her first morning on the job, she was amazed that an eight-year-old expected her even to put his socks on. At the same time he was constantly busy with mathematics problems and had developed considerable skill at chess, usually playing against his father. Emmi was somewhat more independent and easier to manage. Occasionally, when Magda would scold Edward he would protest that she liked Emmi better. As for the English lessons, they soon accepted a rule that neither child could converse with Magda except in English, and both Emmi and Edward made rapid progress.

In the afternoons, when school was out, Magda generally took the children to play in one of the nearby parks, usually a large square adjacent to the Hungarian parliament. Sometimes Edward joined the other boys in a pick-up game of soccer; other times they invented games, the way children do. Magda recalls that he was a good athlete, despite a tendency to be slightly overweight.

In 1917 came the first signs that the war's ghastly deadlock was nearing an end. Emperor Franz Josef had died in November 1916. He was succeeded by his intelligent and well-intentioned grand-nephew, Charles I. The new emperor recognized the futility of the conflict, but his secret peace overtures to England and France were rejected; they now saw victory as a possible and better conclusion. As King of Hungary, Charles also hoped to pacify that country's restive minorities with expanded suffrage. Prime Minister Tisza thought such a reform, in the midst of war, was inopportune. Under pressure from the king, Tisza resigned. He was replaced by Count Mihály Károlyi, who, although a wealthy nobleman, was imbued with Western liberal ideas.

In Russia, the army, hungry and exhausted, had lost the will to fight on. The czar, faced with anarchy and an army revolt, abdicated in favor of a new leader, the enlightened radical Aleksandr Kerensky. In the cities, however, Lenin's Bolsheviks had spread their promise to end the war that had victimized Russian peasants and workers. Successively the Bolsheviks seized power in Petrograd and Moscow, forcing Kerensky to flee in November 1917. One of Lenin's many eager pupils was a disillusioned Hungarian lawyer-journalist, Béla Kun. Kun had already acquired some socialist convictions when he was drafted into the Austro-Hungarian army. He was taken prisoner by the Russians and, after the Bolshevik coup Béla Kun, like many prisoners, was subjected to communist propaganda. What he learned, he liked. Then, much as Lenin had earlier come from Switzerland to Russia to preach revolution, Kun was dispatched to Hungary to fight the holy war of communism in his native country.

In the spring of 1918 Edward completed his four years in the Mellinger School. His parents had to decide where he would go for the rest of his education. Hungarian schools followed the German model, with grades five through twelve in a gymnasium where education was directed primarily toward those who intended to go into business or the professions.

Whether it was the educational system or a particular combination of circumstances during these painful years in Hungary, the flowering of talent from the gymnasia of Budapest is a fascinating field for speculation. An uncanny procession of brilliant men emerged from those troubled classrooms. Most of them were Jewish and many of them made their circuitous way to the United States, where they contributed mightily to American scientific advancement and especially to the development of nuclear physics and the release of nuclear energy. Eugene Paul Wigner, who is now one of the assembly of exceptional physicists at Princeton, won the Nobel prize in 1963. In an interview with us Wigner described the early years of the century in Budapest as a time when "you heard a great deal more erudite conversation than you hear in the United States—people talked more about culture, about art, about literature." These intellectual circles were predominantly Jewish, though Wigner was half Jewish, through his mother. Leo Szilard, also from Budapest, became one of the pioneers in nuclear physics and, in partnership with an Italian, Enrico Fermi, achieved the first controlled nuclear reaction at the University of Chicago in 1942. The capital of Hungary produced, in addition, Theodor von Kármánn, who became one of America's most sophisticated aeronautical engineers, and, most important of all, John von Neumann, the greatest mathematician of the century.

This collective brilliance has given rise to the romantic notion that all of these men were inspired by a single brilliant teacher. It is simply not true. Wigner and von Neumann were stimulated by the same exceptional mathematics teacher in their Lutheran school, and Teller was given some guidance and encouragement by a professor who had also taught von Neumann. Szilard shared no teachers with the others. What all of them did share was the remarkably exhilarating intellectual climate of Budapest, even in the midst of a turbulent and discouraging era. Knowledge was pursued vigorously in the high schools (gymnasia), including the one selected by his parents for Edward Teller, an institution founded by Moritz von Kármánn, father of Theodor.

That gymnasium was called the Minta, roughly translated as "model," which is to say it was a demonstration school for the training of teachers. The decision of Edward's parents to send him to the Minta was made only after rejecting two other possibilities. The first was a school operated by the Catholic Piarist order. It was reputedly an excellent institution, but those who attended were expected to become Christians. This was not as unreasonable a demand as it might seem today. Among the educated in Budapest, religious convictions were relatively casual, and many of its well-assimilated Jews had become Christians. The Tellers, however, though indifferently Jewish, found the Piarist school requirement objectionable. The second possibility was the Lutheran school which included Eugene Wigner and John von Neumann among its students, but both Max and Ilona agreed that the Minta was a better choice for Edward.

That Edward was able to acquire an education during his eight years in the gymnasium is a tribute to the perseverance of his circle in Budapest, because he began in the fall of 1918 when, almost literally, the world was collapsing around them. Russia's newly established communist regime was trumpeting a powerful message around the world: workers arise; the International Soviet shall be the human race! The treaty of Brest-Litovsk, depriving Russia of forty-four percent of its population and creating a new Poland, had humbled the new Soviet state before the Germans; now, in 1918, despite their temporary victory the Germans were finally losing before the supplement of American forces on the Western front. Austria-Hungary was succumbing to the uprisings of its multifarious minorities, encouraged by Point 10 of Woodrow Wilson's Fourteen Points—"The various nationalities of Austria-Hungary to have free development." The war ended on November 11, 1918, but its four-year exploitation of humble people scarred them so deeply that they would never again be the docile pawns of the dynastic and aristocratic societies that had controlled Europe for a millennium.

Nevertheless, in Budapest, the families of the solid middle class, of which the Tellers were a part, pursued their goals as best they could under the uncertain circumstances. Edward went off to the gymnasium a trifle timid, as are most boys when they attend the youngest grade in a new school. He had become an enthusiastic reader, with a particular passion for the vintage science fiction of Jules Verne. In school he enjoyed everything except Latin, which, perhaps because it seemed pointless, he disliked but muddled through. His particular problem, however, was mathematics, toward which, from the start, he was apathetic. Predictably, the cause of the apathy was not ignorance, but boredom. Edward, on his own, and with some help from his father, who had introduced him to basic algebraic concepts, was far ahead of his classmates.

Eventually, the school exempted him from the study of mathematics during his first year, but before this wise decision was rendered, there was considerable hardship for Edward. It is understandable that the ultimate humiliation for a teacher is to be outshone by one of his pupils. That is precisely what happened to Dr. Karl Oberle, who was not only Edward's mathematics teacher but principal of the Minta. Oberle had worked out an algebraic equation on the blackboard to his own satisfaction and presumably to the satisfaction of the forty-odd boys in the class. When he turned around, ten-year-old Edward's hand was raised. "Is there something wrong, Teller?" he asked, sarcastically. Edward suggested there was a better way of doing it. "Then come up here and do it," said the irritated professor. Edward did, and with more dispatch than his teacher. Oberle's response was to the point: "So you are a genius, Teller? Well, I don't like geniuses."*

Some of the pupils didn't like geniuses, either. In Edward's first year he was often bullied and roughed up by schoolmates when he was walking to or from school. His mother was disturbed to the point where she urged Magda Hess, the governess, to escort him. Edward protested that this would only make matters worse. According to Magda, a compromise was reached whereby she would walk across the street so that she could at least come to his aid if the situation became that serious. When she saw him manhandled, his books dumped from his grasp, she did not interfere, but protested to him and to his parents that he should defend himself.

As Magda recalls the story, ten-year-old Edward said, "Don't worry about it. I'm working on a plan." All he asked of his parents was a longer strap for his books. The next day, en route to school, when the same gang approached him, Magda was startled to watch Edward start whirling his books around him at the end of the long strap. Several of the boys were clouted and the others retreated. And Magda Hess insists they never bothered him again.

Before the first year at the Minta was over there was a political upheaval of such massive proportions that life in Budapest would never be the same. The new fear across Europe was Bolshevism. In Hungary, Count Károlyi, with the support of the left-wing Social Democratic party, controlled the government in the midst of the literal dismemberment of his country. His good intentions were no match for the Communist party that Béla Kun had gener-

---

*This incident was related to us by Emmi Kirz (who had heard it from Edward), then was confirmed in detail by Miklos Wenczel, a Teller classmate, who described it some fifty-five years later at his home in Silver Spring, Maryland.

ated in the cities, primarily in Budapest. Meanwhile, the Romanians, fearing a communist revolution in Hungary, and coveting Hungarian Transylvania, occupied eastern Hungary. The Romanian forces had military support from White Russians who had fled from their own country's Bolshevik terror, and moral support from the peacemakers meeting in Paris.

Károlyi, desperate over the breakup of Hungary, sought the support of Kun in the hopes that this would also bring communist Russia to Hungary's aid. In protest against his overtures to the communist leader, Károlyi's cabinet resigned. The prime minister retained the leadership of a coalition only briefly. On March 21, 1919, the coalition collapsed under Kun's pressure, Károlyi resigned, and Béla Kun, doctrinaire communist, became de facto leader of a "workers' and peasants' state" under the Socialist party of Hungary. The Hungarian ruling class was finally dislodged completely from its ancient control of the land of the Magyars.

A distant observer, unaware of human suffering, might have called it a comic-opera revolution. The Kun regime must surely have been one of the most inept in history. His understanding of revolutionary socialism was adopted in such doctrinaire fashion from the Russian model that he seemed totally unaware that the same kind of turnover would not work in Hungary. In *1,000 Years of Hungary*, historian Emil Lengyel reports the story—not verified—that the commissar of finances had to be shown how to endorse a check. By decree, all commerce, industry, and land was transferred to the proletariat—nationalized, in effect. The difficulty was that the "proletariat," which was not even well defined in Hungary, was incapable of wielding its new power. The result was a complete breakdown in the economic system. Services stopped. Goods, including food, did not move to market.

The Tellers shared the desperate circumstances with their neighbors of the middle class. The law was suspended and Max Teller's practice with it. Such food as was in the marketplace soon disappeared. One of the ironies of the revolution was that its greatest opportunity for success—if it had any opportunity at all—should have been in its promise to Hungary's downtrodden peasants. Oddly enough, the peasants, perhaps because of their inbred lack of hope, perhaps because they did not understand it, would have none of it. They would not sell their crops to the revolutionary regime, but they sold them gladly to the thousands of Budapest citizens who, literally, hiked out into the country to barter with the

farmers. The Tellers made numerous such trips because there was
no other way to obtain food. If their parents were alarmed, Emmi
and Edward regarded this new means of acquiring food as an adventure. Magda Hess recalls that at one time no peasants were to
be found and the Tellers took corn from the fields and, in good
conscience, left paper money tied to the stalks. Other citizens, perhaps hungrier and poorer, were not so conscience stricken, and
many peasants had their fields stripped.

The money itself was one of the roots of the problem. The communists had issued new currency, known as "white money." The
peasants, wisely, had no faith in the "white money," but were willing to accept the "blue money" of the pre-communist regime. It
was, in fact, a violation of a governmental decree even to carry out
any transactions in "blue money," but Gresham's law was in full
effect. The citizens hoarded their old currency and used it when it
was necessary.

As the communists realized their hold on the country was weak
and growing weaker, the government reverted to a reign of terror.
There was sporadic street fighting between the revolutionary
forces and the holdouts from the old regime, sometimes remnants
of the defeated Hungarian army. One fusillade killed the son of the
janitor of the Tellers' building. The communists' adherents, such
as they were, came mainly from the urban workers and the urban
poor. Max Teller never knew whether perhaps his cook and serving maid might be communists. "Traitors" were being arrested,
jailed, and sometimes shot every day, though generally the professional families in the Tellers' part of Budapest were not molested.

Nevertheless, Magda Hess recalls, "We were afraid to say a
word." The fear was justified. To make their point that no opposition would be tolerated, the communists hung the corpses of dissidents from lampposts. Edward recalls hearing of these atrocities,
but never saw any corpses himself. The climax, as far as the Tellers
were concerned, came when the revolutionaries billeted two soldiers in their apartment. They occupied Max's two office rooms,
sleeping on couches. They were coolly polite and courteous and
occasionally contributed some food to the family's slim larder.
Their positive offenses included such gaucheries as urinating in
the rubber plant, but it was mainly their presence alone that was
terrifying.

One of their missions apparently was to seek out any hoards of
the "blue money" of the old regime. The Tellers, knowing the

value of this currency, had, like many other families, secreted it in various places. Some they placed in the linings of the covers of several books in the law office. The family watched in horror as the soldiers began shuffling through the books in search of the contraband. They looked between the pages, but not within the linings, to the family's grateful relief. Another time they announced they would need to take over the dining room. It was Magda, according to her recollection, who protested most vigorously (the dining room was also her bedroom) and the soldiers retreated from their demand. Max was alarmed, Magda recalls. "You saved our dining room," he said, "but what do we do if they hang you?"

For the middle-class Jews of Budapest, the darkest aspect of the revolution lay not in its immediate consequences, but in the nature of the revolutionary leaders themselves. Kun was a Jew; so were eight of his eleven commissars in the so-called workers' and peasants' state. The reason for the involvement of Jewish intellectuals is complex, but it certainly stemmed partly from their own historic treatment as outcasts in much of Central Europe. Kun's collaborators had nothing in common with the comfortable middle-class Jews of Budapest as represented by the Tellers. With the rest of their class, the Jewish bourgeoisie resented and rejected the revolution. But by the deposed Hungarian aristocracy and the non-Jewish middle class, including many citizens of German descent, Kun's reign of terror, his inept bungling of a still-functioning state, would be remembered as the product of Jews. Racial resentments, which often lurk just beneath the surface of social behavior, tend to well up in blanket condemnation in times of stress. The fact is that until Béla Kun, the Jews of Hungary, while they endured some quotas and exclusions, were as harmonious with their Christian brothers as any in Europe, but after Kun this harmony disappeared.

Edward sensed that Max Teller, with his quiet insight, was painfully aware of what the revolution meant to Hungarian Jews. Regretfully, as Max watched his son mature into a youth of unusual promise, he began to face the cruel fact that, to realize his talents, his son would someday have to leave Hungary. Ilona nursed no such notions for Edward. She was a possessive mother and she wanted him at her side, but she, too, recognized the consequences of Béla Kun. She confided to Magda, "I shiver at what my people are doing. When this is over there will be a terrible revenge."

One of the ironies of world history is that this pressure to leave

Hungary was felt by those other brilliant Jews, including von Neumann, the mathematician, physicists Szilard and Wigner (who was half Jewish), and von Kármánn, the aeronautical engineer. In response to this pressure they went first to Germany, then the mecca of scientists, only to be driven away by Hitler to eventual sanctuary in the United States. To this extent, Béla Kun can unwittingly take credit for the American preeminence in the development of nuclear energy.

The end of the Kun regime came even more suddenly than its beginning. The entrenchment of a communist government in Budapest was viewed with alarm from England and France as well as from near neighbors such as Austria and Romania. After several abortive attempts to set up a counterrevolutionary government, old-line aristocrats, with help from the Romanian army, put together a working coalition in the eastern Hungarian city of Szeged. The strongest figure in the group was Admiral Miklós Horthy, himself a wealthy landowner and one of the country's few authentic war heroes. He was given the title Commander in Chief of the Army and Minister of War. The cause of the counterrevolutionary forces was given a moral boost by the irrevocable setting up of an independent state of Czechoslovakia. It was made up primarily of Hungarian territory and created a buffer that cut Budapest off from possible help from Russian Bolshevik forces. On August 1, 1919, Bela Kun told his followers, "I have been forced to come to this cold, sobering conclusion: the dictatorship of the proletariat has been defeated economically, militarily and politically."[3]

The Romanian army, unleashed by Kun's admission of failure, marched across Hungary and into Budapest. Kun had fled to Austria. He ultimately returned to Russia, where he worked diligently for the Communist International, only to fall into disfavor with the paranoiac Joseph Stalin, who had Kun shot as a traitor in 1937.

In the summer of 1919 the Teller family, despite the confusion of occupied Budapest, managed to secure permission to send Magda and the children to Lugos to stay with Ilona's parents. Her father's economic power was apparently enough to sustain his influence in the community, even though Lugos was now under Romanian rule, a situation that was to become permanent under the Treaty of Trianon. After the street fighting, the terror, and the food shortages of Budapest, life in Lugos was comparatively secure. The grandparents were always happy to see their grandchildren, Emmi and Edward, now thirteen and eleven.

Magda Hess's assessment of Edward at this time of his life points to a developing assurance, intellectual depth, and athletic prowess. His hesitant early days at the gymnasium were behind him. He had a circle of loyal friends and seemed to be the dominant member of the group. He was always busy, working mathematics problems for fun or playing chess. He was improving at the piano, although seemingly without having to practice a great deal. Some days, according to Magda, he would play the piano for hours, then he might not go near it for a week.

Magda also observed that Edward seemed incapable of speaking anything but the truth in the most literal sense. When the children arrived in Lugos, arrangements were made to have them tutored by the same teacher employed for their two first cousins. One night at dinner, Edward announced, "My tutor is an ass." His grandfather, incensed by this disrespect, demanded that Edward apologize for such a remark.

"I will apologize, but in my mind he is still an ass," said Edward.

Edward's unique and prophetic idiosyncrasy at this time is recalled by Emmi. The family would be sitting around the dinner table when he would announce: "Please don't talk to me—I have a problem." The "problem," according to Edward, was always some mathematical calculation that he was working out in his head for the pure enjoyment of it. Everyone would duly respect his request and isolate him from mundane conversation for the rest of the meal.

Pressure from England, France, and Italy forced the Romanians to withdraw from Budapest in the fall of 1919. Ostensibly the soldiers had been guardians against the restoration of Bolshevism, but they were a typical occupying army in that they had looted and terrorized the city. Meanwhile, from his original base in Szeged, Horthy and the other counterrevolutionary leaders had moved to western Hungary, where they could recruit an army without Romanian interference. On November 16, 1919, he marched into Budapest at the head of a new national army to take charge of his country. Horthy's response to the mayor's address of welcome showed his contempt for Hungary's brief sojourn with communism:

This city disowned her millennial tradition, dragged the Holy Crown
and the national colors in the dust, and clothed itself in
rags. . . . We shall forgive this misguided city if it turns from the
false gods to the love of our fatherland . . . if it reveres the Holy
Crown once more . . . in short, our Hungarian Fatherland and our
Hungarian people.[4]

The pendulum had swung, as it would so many times in the next
forty years. Horthy's summons was to the new superpatriotic rever-
ence for the national state, for the entrenched economic power,
the philosophy that would soon be known as fascism. "Its substance was worship of the nation and punishment for non-con-
formism," writes Lengyel. Max and Ilona Teller's fear of surfacing
anti-Semitism proved to be well grounded. As the counterrevolutionary regime consolidated its power numerous patriotic societies
emerged—some secret, some open, but most of them anti-Semitic
and a sinister threat to all Hungarian Jews.

Edward, who had been distressed and frightened by the excesses
and disruptions of the communists, was equally disturbed by the
changes wrought by the new counterforces. He and his family had
to endure a fascist era that would soon drive him out of Hungary.
Those left behind would endure, successively, Nazi occupation, a
postwar respite of democracy, a reimposition of communism in
1947, and an abortive anti-communist revolution in 1956. The extremes were to become repugnant to Edward and even more so to
Emmi. The idealistic prattle of Béla Kun's communists in 1919
meant also, to the two young Tellers, their first experience with
hunger, the sound of gunfire in the streets, and those stories of the
corpses hanging from the lampposts. Years later, having endured
two communist regimes before her eventual escape to the United
States in 1958, Emmi would say, contemptuously, "We have heard
too much of intellectual communists [in the United States]. They
talk and talk but they don't know what it leads to."

It was an especially cruel trap for the Jewish middle class. They
had no use for Béla Kun in 1919, and yet they were the scapegoats
of Horthy's fascists throughout the 1920s. The Horthy regime proclaimed an era of law and order, but condoned vicious anti-Semitism that forced every Jew to live in a twilight of fear. It is not surprising that Edward Teller later became a profoundly patriotic
American, enamored of the refreshing stability of his adopted

country, which he attributes to conservative capitalism and a strong military establishment. These, to Teller, are the institutions that guarantee stability and fortify the nation against the excesses of the left and the right, and against enemies abroad.

After several months in Lugos, the Tellers finally decided it would be safe to bring Emmi, now fourteen, and Edward, twelve, back to Budapest. The solidifying of the counterrevolutionary government made it possible for Max to resume his law practice and, on the surface, life was closer to normal. The flaring anti-Semitism continued, though it did not often intrude overtly into the tight intellectual circle of Max Teller and his friends. The danger, however, was real enough so that large numbers of Hungarian Jews converted to Christianity. This was not as unusual a phenomenon as it might have been in other countries of eastern and central Europe. The close assimilation of Jewish and non-Jewish professionals and the climate of intellectual sophistication made religion secondary, as it tends to be in similar circles in other countries. Therefore anti-Semitism, when it did come to the surface, was more painful than it might have been in Poland or Romania, where Jews have lived primarily in their own ghettoized society. Edward Teller recalls that "the type of society to which our family belonged was really trying to assimilate."

Nevertheless, Max Teller did not minimize the threat. He decided Edward was old enough to face the facts. "I think this was the first time I was deeply impressed by my father," Edward later recalled. "He said anti-Semitism was coming. To me, the idea of anti-Semitism was new, and the fact that my father was so serious about it impressed me."

There was no anti-Semitic violence against any of the Tellers (Wigner was less fortunate—he was beaten by a mob) but, according to Edward, in school it was made very clear as to who was a Jew and who was not. Some of the teachers were obviously anti-Semitic. One of them sarcastically addressed his class as "Gentlemen, Jews and Pollack" (he wasn't sure if Pollack was Jewish or not). The clearest form of direct discrimination was the imposition of strict quotas on the number of Jews permitted to enter government service or educational institutions. For example, the percentage of Jews admitted to the University of Budapest was limited to their percentage in the total population. This was patently unfair because the proportion of Jews qualified for the university far exceeded the meager five percent that was the Jewish population of Hungary.

The inclination to seek a scapegoat was heightened when the Treaty of Trianon was imposed on Hungary on June 4, 1920. It was named for the remote Trianon Palace of Versailles where it was signed. The massive, multinational prewar state of 125,000 square miles was cut down to a mere 36,000 square miles. Its population was reduced from 21 million to less than 8 million. Slovakia and Ruthenia were ceded to Czechoslovakia, Transylvania to Romania, Croatia and Slavonia to Yugoslavia, and numerous lesser slices to neighboring states. The dismemberment went farther than merely accommodating the national groups. More than 3 million ethnic Hungarians found themselves within the borders of nations other than Hungary. Hungary was deprived of its outlet to the Adriatic Sea, of its historic economic ties to Austria; left a desolate, punished nation. In the face of this adversity, only hope survived, expressed in the fact that in the years of his fascist dictatorship, Admiral Horthy bore the title Regent, implying that his rule was temporary, pending the restoration of the monarchy. Actually, two specific attempts of Charles Hapsburg to resume the Hungarian half of his dual throne were turned aside by Horthy.

As water seeks its level, so the Tellers sought a stable life in the postwar era. Edward continued his studies at the Minta, and Emmi at a girls' gymnasium, called Marie Terezie. Although Emmi was two grades ahead of Edward, he was able to assist her with her algebra, sometimes to the astonishment of their parents. There were beginning signs of friction between Max and his son. Edward's interest in mathematics to the exclusion of more practical subjects seemed to worry Max, who wanted his son to enter one of the established professions. Their relationship was further strained during their occasional attempts to play music together. Edward had become a proficient pianist, devoted to Mozart, Beethoven, Schubert, Brahms. Sometimes Max would tune up his violin and he and Edward would attempt a sonata. It seldom worked. Edward would become impatient with his father's mistakes and suggest they try again. Another try and Edward would give up, leaving his father hurt and perhaps a little ashamed. As a musician, Ilona was in Edward's class, but Max was not.

Once again, however, it was Max who took special pains to see that Edward's suspected talents were recognized. After he had noticed the ease with which Edward tackled his sister's algebra problems, Max decided to seek outside advice. He had a friend, probably also a client, named Leopold Klug, who was a professor of mathematics at the University of Budapest. As a favor to Max, Klug came to the Tellers' and talked with Edward, probing his mathematical ability. Klug was extremely impressed. He suggested that Max buy Edward a copy of Euler's geometry, a standard text based on the work of the eighteenth-century Swiss mathematician Leonhard Euler. Max followed the suggestion and Edward was delighted. "He read Euler as if it were a novel; the way I read love stories," Emmi told the authors. Later Klug gave Edward some geometric theorems to prove. Though he could not prove all of them on the spot, he always worked them out eventually. After a half-dozen visits to see Edward, Klug's conclusion was definite: "Your son is exceptional."

To Edward the sessions with Klug turned out to be more than just a test of his potential. He was impressed with Klug himself—he seemed to be one of the few adults who enjoyed life and enjoyed his work.

Looking back to that time in his life, Teller recalls his dismal view of the future. "I watched the adults around me. Most of them didn't like their work. More and more I was convinced that I didn't want to grow up and become bored like the rest of them. Klug was the exception."

Edward was about fourteen when he completed the sessions with Klug. He was making positive decisions about the direction of his life—decisions that would be distressing to his father. There were other developments that coaxed him onward. He acquired a book on Einstein's special and general theories of relativity. His physics teacher, however, took it away from him and said he wasn't ready for it yet. Edward, after plowing through these theories that many physicists couldn't understand, conceded the teacher was right. Later, after he had completed his course and passed the final exam, the teacher returned the book. "Now you are ready," he said, and once again he was right.

But a boy in his midteens doesn't live by physics alone. Edward had a close circle of friends. Of these five or six youths, the closest was Edward Harkanyi, known as Suki. Teller also had acquired a nickname, Koko.* They were all intensely intellectual students,

*Teller will not reveal the origin or the significance of his nickname. When the authors pressed him on grounds that this mystery could "make or break the book," Teller facetiously answered, "Break the book."

most of them Jewish. Illi Cernat recalls that they "spent summer nights in long walks, discussing philosophy or astronomy for hours and hours."

Eventually, the by-product of Teller's close friendship with Suki would become more important than the friendship itself. Suki had a little sister, Augusta Maria, known as Mici. As a very small child Mici was, according to Magda Hess, rather homely. But as she grew up she blossomed out to become an exceptionally attractive and vivacious young woman. Today Teller doesn't remember when he first met Mici, because they had been vaguely acquainted since their earliest childhood. Their close friendship developed as teenagers attending the various parties in the homes of their friends.

Both of Mici's parents were Jewish, but they were among the many Hungarians who embraced Christianity, so Mici was raised as a Christian. By the time Edward was seventeen and Mici was sixteen there was no question of their devotion to each other.

Teller's cousin Illi, six years younger than Mici, was emotionally stirred by such devotion. As she told us, "He never cared for another girl. He never went out with another girl. He didn't care for being with other girls, for many years all he wanted was her. This made a great impression on me—I knew what it meant to be really, seriously in love. With one girl, not to flirt with anybody else, and for one girl to care only about one boy." Edward and Mici had to wait eight years before they could get married, but neither was ever seriously involved with another person.

The time finally came when Edward and his parents had to reach a decision as to where he would go after his graduation from the gymnasium and what he would study. There was no question in Edward's mind—he wanted to be a mathematician. His father was flatly opposed to this, for two reasons. First, he felt that mathematics would lead only to a professorship which, at best, would be a meager living. Second, as a Jew, Edward would be additionally handicapped in attempting to find an appointment in a system riddled with anti-Jewish quotas. Edward, remembering the example of Professor Klug, protested to his father that he wanted to enter a career he could enjoy, and he was devoted to mathematics. Edward's mother was even less reasonable. Her concern was not only what he would study, but where, and she insisted that he not leave Budapest. She won a temporary victory, but in the long run, as

Teller later recalled, "this was one of the few instances where my mother did not get her own way."

The temporary victory for Ilona found Edward enrolled in the University of Budapest and continuing to live at home. Near graduation time from the Minta he had taken qualifying examinations from the university in physics and mathematics. The mathematics test was administered by Professor Lipot Feher, who had been the principal mentor of the brilliant John von Neumann. Edward was at the top of his class in both examinations. He formally entered the university in the fall term of 1925. But this was what neither Edward nor his father wanted.

The situation resulted in a further compromise that, this time, satisfied Max and spelled defeat for Ilona. Edward would go to the Institute of Technology in the Rhine River city of Karlsruhe in southwestern Germany. He would study chemical engineering, for which Karlsruhe was famous. This would satisfy Max's demand for a "practical" course, but Edward would be permitted to take mathematics as a secondary subject. The decision was also based on Max's painful realization that his son, to succeed, must get out of disillusioned, dismembered, anti-Jewish Hungary.

The opportunity he was offering Edward was one that Max Teller, a generous and intuitive, if limited, man would never seek for himself. He knew that those behind were condemned to a sinking ship. For decades to come, Max, Ilona, and Emmi would endure terrible privations. Edward would return to Budapest often in his university years, but ultimately would escape the horrors imposed on the Jews of Hungary.

But the future hides it secrets, so there was only joy and excitement in Edward Teller's heart as, on January 1, 1926, two weeks before his eighteenth birthday, he boarded the train for Karlsruhe.

2

Birth and Death of a Golden Age

EDWARD TELLER arrived in Kalsruhe at a time when Germany was the center of a scientific revolution. All branches of science flourished in German universities and laboratories, but it was the new discoveries in physics that were to change the course of history. The physicists who studied and taught in Germany in the 1920s were a galaxy of talent such as has rarely been assembled in human history. Some were involved in the broadening implications of the theory of relativity and in the final dramatic discoveries that capped the branch of physics known as quantum theory. These two theories together form the foundation of modern physics. One contributed to a new view of the universe, the other to a new view of the nature of matter. They gave a new picture of reality, in the sense of limiting that which man can observe, measure, and predict with his senses. Behind that different kind of reality lay a new, nonmaterial mathematics. Physics became that which worked, and this was the case with relativity and quantum theory. They worked well enough eventually to produce the nuclear weapons that brought a fiery end to World War II.

The German physicists active when Teller arrived included Max Planck, who laid the foundation for quantum theory, and Albert Einstein, one of the supreme intellects of all time, whose grasp of the universe in the special and general theories of relativity permanently transformed science from the macrocosm of the cosmos to the microcosm of the atom. Closer to Teller were Arnold Sommerfeld, with whom he studied briefly in Munich, and Werner Heisenberg, famous for his uncertainty principle, who awarded Teller his doctorate. There was Erwin Schrödinger, who, like Heisenberg, made fundamental contributions to quantum mechanics, the mathematical systemization of quantum theory. There was Max Born,[4] who, with Heisenberg, produced a different formulation that complemented the world of Schrödinger. Wolfgang Pauli, an

Austrian who worked for a time in Germany, made his contribution through a discovery known as the exclusion principle.

There were, of course, outstanding physicists elsewhere. Among the most important outside Germany in the 1920s was Niels Bohr, head of Copenhagen's famous Institute for Theoretical Physics. P. A. M. Dirac made his contributions from England along with Sir James Chadwick. Prince Louis de Broglie made unique discoveries in France; while in Italy, an outstanding young theoretician (who later switched to experimental physics), Enrico Fermi, was just coming on the scene.

Rating physicists is far more difficult than rating baseball players or movie stars but, excluding Planck and Einstein, who were of an earlier generation, many judges would place Heisenberg and Bohr at the top of the list. It is significant that these were the two physicists who were to exert the strongest influence on Teller.

This golden age of physics began in 1900 with Max Planck's discoveries relating to radiation and energy. It continued at a dramatic pace until 1933, when Hitler's tyranny summarily put an end to it. Many of the physicists were Jews, or had Jewish family connections, and the Nazis, blinded by hate, drove this incalculable wealth of brain power out of the country. One of the ironies was that the United States was to become the principal haven for displaced scientists. Many of them eventually applied their talents to their adopted country and thereby contributed to Hitler's defeat in World War II. Edward Teller was among this gifted corps of Hitler refugees.

By 1926, the year Teller arrived in Germany, Einstein's special and general theories of relativity were no longer very controversial. They had become as generally accepted as the physics of Isaac Newton had once been. For low velocity atomic particles or planets, the predictions of Einstein's relativity agreed with the Newtonian forecasts, and with experience.

Einstein published what is known as his special theory of relativity in 1905. It has many ramifications, but one is especially simple: matter and energy are convertible, almost as if they were two forms of the same thing. The matter that composes this book is something you are holding in your hand. Einstein established that it can become energy, so much energy in fact that if all of it were released it could provide heat for the homes and buildings of a town of ten thousand people for the next hundred years. The energy content of matter is expressed mathematically in what is probably the world's best-known equation, $E=mc^2$, where E is energy, m is mass, and c is the speed of light. The fantastic release of energy in an atomic bomb still taps less than one percent of the energy contained in the atom.

If relativity was old hat by 1926, quantum theory was still controversial, and Teller walked right into the middle of the debate.

What Planck had postulated in 1900 was that radiation (in this case, light of a given color) could not be emitted or absorbed in indefinitely small amounts, but only by a series of steps or discrete packages, which he called *quanta.* It was a strange, almost incomprehensible, emission process. Imagine, for comparison, a water faucet that gives out only one cup of water, or two or three, but never a half a cup and never any other fraction of a cup. This quantization defies common sense, but sensual perception, in the conventional understanding, is a casualty of quantum theory. The theory also defies the classical physics of Isaac Newton, but in the infinitesimal confines of atoms and the nonmaterial world of radiation, different laws apply.

So the quantum physicist had to sweep away the thought processes of man's history and start thinking in mathematical and nonmaterial terms. Quantum theory was further reinforced by Einstein in 1905 when he postulated that light is not a continuous wave, but a series of energy packets, like Planck's radiation packets. The great American physical chemist G. N. Lewis, of Berkeley, California, was the first to call these packets *photons.*

In 1913 Niels Bohr applied the lessons of quantum theory to the motions of electrons around an atom. Most of us are familiar with the representation of an atom as a central nucleus with electrons orbiting around it, like planets around the sun. Once again, this is a convenient material representation of something that, in actuality, cannot be visualized at all. Years later Teller himself expressed this very well when he said, "It is more difficult to convey the idea of an atom by a picture than it is to make a drawing of last night's dream."[1]

For convenience, however, this artificial orbit picture is used. Bohr discovered that the energy of an electron is quantized—when it absorbs energy (in this case, light energy), it jumps to a higher orbit. If it emits energy—for example, in the same amount it previously absorbed—it jumps back to the original orbit. Bohr's quantum orbits and the jumps between them mark the beginning of quantum mechanics.

But why these special orbits? Why not any orbit? In 1925 a young Frenchman, Louis de Broglie, proposed an explanation: Every particle, including the electron, possesses *wave* qualities. Only those orbits exist which allow one, two or three, or some other whole number of waves to fit together around the circuit of the orbit. Again, common sense comes into question. How can something be both a wave and a particle? In 1926 Schrödinger developed de Broglie's wave picture in full mathematical detail.

Meanwhile, what at first looked like an absolutely different theory of the atom was put forward by Werner Heisenberg. He proposed to forget pictures and models and concentrate on the mathematics of what is observable when an electron emits or absorbs light—jumping, for example, from orbit nineteen to orbit eleven, or from orbit seven to orbit six. The numbers ranged in blocks, or matrices. Thus, Heisenberg's approach came to be called matrix mechanics, and was based on the particle theory. Amazingly, however, matrix mechanics yielded exactly the same results as Schrödinger's wave mechanics. As physicist George Gamow later wrote, "It was as if America was discovered by Columbus, sailing westward across the Atlantic Ocean, and by some equally daring Japanese, sailing eastward across the Pacific Ocean."[2]

The most powerful implication of Heisenberg's work, however, was in his insistence that the behavior of atomic particles is random, uncaused, and unpredictable. No one could ever predict how an individual particle might behave. Normally, only when dealing with them in huge quantities was a prediction possible, but then solely in an actuarial sense—the way insurance companies know that a certain number of people of a large group will be dead after a given number of years, but cannot make any predictions in terms of individuals.

This probability aspect of nature upset Schrödinger, who had thought his waves were "real." On a visit to Copenhagen he learned the meaning of Heisenberg's work. "If I had known," he complained, "that wave mechanics would lead to all this jumping around, I would never have had anything to do with it in the first place." But Bohr and the others reassured him of the importance of his wave mechanics.

It was then that Bohr, the father figure for quantum physicists, came up with a profound new concept. He explained that the wave picture of matter and the particle picture are not contradictory, but *complementary!* Depending on the experiment, the electron behaves as a wave or behaves as a particle. It is impossible to fit two experiments in the same space that will permit the physicist to observe at the same time these two complementary aspects of reality. Bohr called the concept *complementarity,* and regarded it as the deeper foundation of Heisenberg's uncertainty principle.

This principle stirred some spirited controversy. If the behavior of particles is random and not part of a chain of causality, then there is an implication that the universe has no basic order; nature is capricious. Einstein, for one, could not accept the uncertainty principle. It offended his sense of the mathematical order of the universe. "God does not throw dice," he insisted and, until his death in 1955, he stood by the belief that quantum mechanics was not the final answer.

It was a stimulating time, not only for physicists, but for philosophers. There were some of the latter who inferred new conclusions about human behavior from the uncertainty principle. If particles, including the atomic constituents of the human brain, are non-determined, perhaps this was proof of free will, a mind liberated from the bondage of cause and effect. Most physicists, however, do not believe any such inference is justified. The relation, if any, between free will and the uncertainty principle or the principle of complementarity has been and continues to be the subject of discussion among physicists, philosophers, and thinkers generally, but the connections, if any, still remain outside the confines of serious science.

These fascinating new concepts in physics excited Edward Teller's interest long before he went to Karlsruhe as an eighteen-year-old. He recalled for us that "my original interest was in mathematics, which is a much more obvious subject for a child. You can become interested in mathematics by playing with numbers, which are available to everyone, but about physics you have to know something. In high school I started to get somewhat interested in physics even though I still wanted to go into mathematics."

At the Institute of Technology, however, his obligation, imposed by his father, was to study chemical engineering. "I studied chemistry under duress," he remembers, "but in fact I cheated and studied chemistry *and* mathematics. My father got what he wanted and I did what I wanted on the side."

Mathematics was still what Teller thought he wanted on his arrival at Karlsruhe, but quantum mechanics soon captivated him. "I got to Karlsruhe in 1926 and I left in 1928. In 1925 and '26 a very remarkable development occurred in physics—quantum mechanics. Such a development reaches the whole scientific community."

Duress or not, Edward was a good chemistry student, and the Institute of Technology may have been the best place in the world for a budding chemical engineer. The institute was sponsored by the huge German chemical combine I. G. Farben. As for the surrounding city of Karlsruhe, it was pleasant, if not exciting. Like many European cities it was built around a grand palace, once the headquarters of the Duke of Baden. Only six miles westward was the Rhine River, and beyond that the province of Alsace, with its mixture of French and German cultures. The older part of Karlsruhe was handsome, but since the late nineteenth century the city had become a burgeoning rail center and was aesthetically marred by the gaunt factory districts of an industrial center.

Max and Ilona accompanied Edward on his inaugural trip to Karlsruhe. Ilona, who didn't like the idea to start with, had made elaborate preparations to protect him while he was away from home. Edward had an acquaintance in Budapest, Ferenc von Körosy, who had already been a student at Karlsruhe for two years. Von Körosy agreed to watch over Edward, but on this occasion, he had not planned to return to Karlsruhe until several days later. So he asked a friend, Erich Landauer, who lived in Karlsruhe, to guard Edward until von Körosy arrived. Within a few days after the Tellers' arrival, von Körosy, still in Budapest, received a letter from Landauer with a cogent comment, based on the fact that "Teller" means "plate" in German. "The two big plates arrived with the little plate," Landauer wrote, "and the big plates are afraid that the little plate will break." (Actually, Teller explains, in physical stature he was, at eighteen, already a big plate.)

In the usual custom of the students at that time, Teller rented a room with a family, after it was inspected and approved by his parents. His mother sought out and found a delicatessen where her son could buy his provisions. Edward reinforced Ilona's fears for his well-being when he wanted to know if, when buying eggs, he should ask for hard-boiled or soft-boiled.

They had no need to fear for his application to his work. Von Körosy, now living in Israel, confirms Edward's claim that "I studied virtually all the time." There were occasional hikes or ski excursions to break the study routine, and short interruptions for a Ping-Pong game or a songfest, but Edward thrived on hard work. Chemistry, with its emphasis on laboratory work, was more time-consuming than mathematics. "I broke a lot of test tubes, cut my fingers, and nearly put my eye out on one occasion," Edward confessed to the authors, "and once in a while I performed a quantitative analysis better than anyone else." He was beginning to show signs of that powerful self-direction that in future years his colleagues would both admire and resent. He found a spectroscope "just standing in the corner and not being used by anyone." At that point he was working on an experiment in which he was to distinguish lithium from other alkalines, a process that was supposed to utilize certain conventional laboratory procedures. But Teller, on his own, used the spectroscope—"there was no rule against it."

In the German university system there was not the clear separation between undergraduate and graduate study that is standard in the United States. The student sought either a teacher's certificate or a degree as a doctor of philosophy. The progress toward either degree was relatively informal and not bound by the time frames of American education. From the beginning Teller sought the Ph.D. The teacher's certificate generally limited the recipient to secondary-school teaching or a minor post in a university.

Teller made a number of close friends at Karlsruhe, including von Körosy and Landauer, another student, Paul Donaph, and two professors, Herman Mark and Peter Paul Ewald. Later, Ewald's daughter would marry Hans Bethe, another top-ranking theoretical physicist. Bethe was a native of Alsace who was trained in Germany, emigrated to the United States in 1935, and became one of Teller's closest friends.

Herman Mark was a brilliant teacher and, in Teller's recollection, "a very wonderful man." Although he was a chemist, he had specialized in physical chemistry and in quantum mechanics. In 1926 I. G. Farben brought him to Karlsruhe to study the potential effect of the new science of quantum mechanics on chemistry and chemical physics. Mark was still only in his late twenties and held the title *privatdozent,* the German designation for a sort of apprentice professor. His ideas intrigued Teller: "It was all so new, and yet it was in the middle of chemistry and mathematics." Quantum mechanics was irresistible and Mark's lectures hardened Teller's determination to desert chemistry for a career in physics.

Mark, who also emigrated to America and eventually became board chairman of Brooklyn Polytechnic Institute, has clear recollections of his eager young student. We interviewed him in May of 1973. "Teller really wasn't a good-looking man," Mark told us. "He was stubby and fat, and always a little pale. But if he wasn't hand-some, he was awfully pleasant, he was always kind. Teller was pop-ular, too, the other students respected him."

The respect came from Teller's obvious grasp of his subjects. Mark recalls that "very frequently, during a lecture, or at the end of a lecture, this young student would say, 'Well, I think that was very interesting, but if you don't mind, I presume what you really wanted to tell us was this . . .' and he'd explain his idea in a Hun-garian accent, and he was always right." Mark was impressed enough to take Teller on a visit to the I. G. Farben laboratories, in nearby Ludwigshaufen, where he could admire the equipment and talk with the physicists.

Von Körosy, looking backward to the days at Karlsruhe, attrib-utes Teller's grasp of physics to Teller himself as much as to Her-man Mark. "I am certain," von Körosy says, "that he learned phy-sics, of course, from books, but mainly from Edward Teller." This was another affirmation of Teller's intense internal drive that had first been manifested in his self-taught mathematics in earliest childhood.

With Christmas and Easter vacations, and the long summer re-cess, Teller continued to spend a large part of his time in Budapest. The principal attraction there was Mici, growing more appealing every day. These were the years when their warm friendship blos-somed into a full-fledged romance. Edward also spent a lot of time with Mici's brother, Suki, and three or four of his old friends.

During these vacations Max Teller became reluctantly aware of Edward's determination to switch from chemistry to physics. De-spite his reservations Max decided, in the spring of 1927, to visit Karlsruhe and talk with his son's professors. They persuaded Max, first, that Edward was an excellent student and, second, that he ought to be allowed to take advantage of his immense enthusiasm for physics. Max was almost convinced but he decided to seek fur-ther advice from a distant relative in Vienna named Ehrenhaft, who was a physics teacher. They visited Ehrenhaft and, after the briefest questioning of Edward, Max was assured by Ehrenhaft that Edward was gifted in physics. Max at last capitulated, insisting on only one concession from Edward, that with physics he contin-ue his pursuit of mathematics. Edward agreed.

The die was cast. Edward Teller was to become a physicist. His choice of an institution was the University of Munich, where the leading professor of physics was Arnold Sommerfeld. By the capriciousness of fate, however, Munich was not where Teller mastered physics, but where he met with disaster.

The sojourn in Munich began routinely enough in the spring term of 1928. Now twenty years old and full of assurance, Teller settled into his new surroundings with much less family fuss than he had endured in Karlsruhe. He was happy to be concentrating on physics at last, and mathematics was an enjoyable second subject. In Sommerfeld he had one of the world-renowned physics teachers, though, to Teller, not an exciting one. "Sommerfeld was not terribly inspiring, but the subject was inspiring," is the way Teller sums it up. It was at Munich where Teller first met Hans Bethe, another student of physics, although their close friendship did not develop until ten years later when both had come to the United States.

Munich, the capital of Bavaria, was a vibrant city, bursting with culture, especially music, all of which pleased Teller. In ominous contrast it had also been the locale, five years earlier, of the first important emergence of Adolf Hitler. In 1923, with his handful of National Socialists, Hitler marched through Munich, demanding revenge on the communists, Jews, international bankers, and other imagined enemies who had "betrayed" Germany. These were the years of the frail, postwar Weimar Republic, which was desperately trying to steer a defeated country to equilibrium. Hitler's Beer Hall putsch in Munich was thwarted and he went to jail, there to refine his Nazi movement into its final, organized plan for the political and military resurgence of Germany.

Edward, at twenty, according to Emmi, was an exceptional athlete, excelling at skiing and tennis. Edward, himself, disputes this, claiming he was an indifferent athlete who excelled only at Ping-Pong. The truth was probably somewhere in between, but there is no doubt that he exulted in physical activity, especially hiking and mountain climbing.

On July 14, 1928, near the end of the first semester at the University of Munich, Teller boarded a Munich streetcar to ride to the railroad station. There he was to join a group of friends for an excursion into the country. He was burdened down with hiking gear, boots, and a rucksack. Riding near the front of a three-section tram, he absent-mindedly failed to notice that the tram had reached the railway station stop. Before he could alight, the tram was under way again.

Without much concern for the danger, Teller simply elected to leap off the streetcar as it accelerated. It was probably going faster than he expected, because as he hit the road he was thrown forward too fast to keep his footing. He fell down, rolled over several times, aware of the wheels rattling close by, and vaguely conscious of a sense of relief when the three rumbling sections of the tram had passed him. He lay on the road, wondering why he was not able to get up. Then, a short distance away, he saw his hiking boot lying beside the track. He recalls thinking, somewhat irrationally, that he could not hike without his boot on. All these thoughts consumed only seconds.

It was not just his hiking boot. It was his entire right foot. The wheels of the tram had severed it just above the ankle. Then the pain struck.

In Budapest Ilona Teller had spent too much of her time worrying about the safety and well-being of of her absent son. When the terrible news arrived from Munich, it was as if her worst fears were realized. A telegram, from a hospital in Munich, said something to the effect that "on account of foot wound your son is confined here." Max Teller put in an immediate call to the clinic, where they were connected with a Dr. von Lossow. The telephone connection was bad, but Max clearly heard the word "amputation." Within hours, Max, Ilona, and Emmi were on a train for Munich.

They found him in the hospital, still dazed and in intense pain. Max was shaken, while Ilona fought back hysteria. It was equally difficult for Emmi. For all of their short lives, Emmi had been motherly and possessive toward her beloved brother, and she was proud of him. "It was terrible, terrible," she recalled many years later, "to see this happen to a happy, active boy of twenty."

Emmi was the only one close enough to learn that Edward soon wrote a letter to Mici suggesting that, because he would be permanently a cripple, their romance should be ended. In effect he was excusing her if she wanted to dissolve any obligations between them. Mici wrote back that nothing was changed. And she was right. Their hearts still didn't miss a beat for each other.

Edward stayed at the Munich hospital for nearly two months, with his mother at his bedside most of the time. He had numerous visitors—his friends from Karlsruhe, and Suki, Mici's brother, who came all the way from Berlin to comfort his best friend. Much comfort came directly from Dr. von Lossow, who was extremely conscientious with his young patient.

There was, however, a conflict in von Lossow's life that, even to-day, Teller cannot fully explain. The doctor happened to be the brother of the Bavarian general who had helped to smash Hitler's Beer Hall putsch. It may be that at this time, 1928, von Lossow already realized that anyone with a record of active opposition to the Nazis was in physical danger. Whatever the reason, in late August or early September, von Lossow suddenly left Munich for self-exile in South America.

Deprived of the reassuring presence of von Lossow, Edward's parents decided to take their son back to Budapest. Installed in a hospital there, he began to suffer more pain than seemed acceptable so long after the accident, and the leg was healing very slowly. After some X rays, the Budapest doctors decided there might be a splinter in the wound, necessitating another operation. The operation proved to be a mistake and only delayed his recovery. Altogether nearly four months passed before Edward finally began to walk on crutches. When he had recovered some strength, he was fitted with an artificial foot and found he could hobble with a cane.

In retrospect, Teller does not believe he ever suffered from any severe depression because of the accident. He rationalized that it would not affect his studies, and he could still engage in two favorite pastimes, the piano and chess. When he got used to the artificial foot he discovered, to his surprise, that he was agile enough to hike and even to play Ping-Pong.

By late fall Edward had recovered sufficiently so that, with his parents' approval, he made plans to resume his studies in Germany. He was free to return to the University of Munich, but Sommerfeld, whose presence had attracted Teller there in the first place, was now on leave of absence. Edward therefore decided to shoot even higher and apply to the University of Leipzig because the towering figure there was Werner Heisenberg.

Heisenberg, though only a few years older than Teller, had already made his basic contribution to the understanding of quantum mechanics, that world-shaking uncertainty principle. This principle held that the movement of subatomic particles was governed by statistical laws, rather than by causality. The position or motion of a given particle could thus not be predicted on the basis of natural laws, but only on the basis of probability. According to Heisenberg's findings, no one can say that a certain particle will behave in a certain way, only that it is *probable* that it will behave in a certain way, a concept that Einstein found "highly disagreeable." [3]

For a young, aspiring physicist, however, there was nothing disagreeable about the prospect of studying with Werner Heisenberg, and Teller was overjoyed when the way was cleared for his admission to the University of Leipzig. Both physically and psychologically he was making remarkable progress in adapting to the loss of his foot. To assume there were no profound effects from the accident on his character or his motivation is, of course, speculative but, objectively, the handicap never seems to have had any marked effect on the order of his life.

Werner Heisenberg, regarded by many as the world's greatest living physicist, was interviewed by the authors when he made a brief visit to Boston in May 1973.* He had abundant recollections of young Edward Teller's student days at Leipzig. Teller subsequently credited Heisenberg as "the one who gave me a start."

On arrival at the university Teller introduced himself to Heisenberg, who asked for the new student's transcripts. "They were excellent, excellent, excellent," Heisenberg recalls. The professor found himself as pleased with his promising protégé as the protégé was with his teacher. "From that time on," says Heisenberg, "he was one of the most interested as well as the most interesting members of my seminary."

Why does Teller credit Heisenberg with giving him a "start"? "Well," Heisenberg recalls, "a brilliant student like Teller would not just sit in the lecture room and listen to what the professor says. The 'start' in such a case is that the professor tells a young man, 'There's a problem I can't solve. Can you solve it?'"

There was just such a problem at hand. Heisenberg had been studying two conflicting papers on the energy levels of hydrogen molecular atoms in a normal state. A group of Danish physicists had published a paper reaching certain conclusions on these energy levels, confirmed by experimental research. Subsequently a group of young British physicists had published a paper challenging the Danish solution, claiming, in effect, that it was in error. The challenge seemed ideal for Teller. "Find out who is right, the Danish or the English group," Heisenberg said, and suggested that Teller then extend his study to calculate the energy levels of the hydrogen molecule in an excited state.

*Heisenberg died in February 1976.

It was a problem of sufficient originality and complexity to justify it as the subject of a doctoral thesis. Heisenberg had thrown down the gauntlet to his brilliant pupil, and Teller had eagerly picked it up. If he could finish successfully, he would be a full-fledged theoretical physicist.

With such a challenge before him, Teller, despite the loss of his right foot, eventually made the Leipzig era one of the happiest of his student life. Along with Heisenberg, he dwelt in a lively community of young scholars, sharing not only long hours of study, but pleasant diversions from the routine of study. Leipzig was perhaps the most imposing city in Germany, with many square miles of sixteenth- and seventeenth-century structures, and a rich history embracing the lives of Martin Luther, Johann Sebastian Bach, Goethe, Leibniz, Schumann, and Mendelssohn.

Most of the students lived in the poor quarters of the town, generally renting a single room from a working-class family. They dined in the cheapest restaurants, though some had been enhanced as the favorites of the luminaries of the past, including the restaurant where Goethe had been a regular customer a century and a half earlier.

"In spite of cheap meals and small lodgings it was an extremely happy life," is the retrospective view of Heisenberg. "We worked hard, but we went on excursions or we met at the swimming pool.

"It was not only a gay life, but a time of great scientific progress, accomplished by very young people, most of them under thirty. They did important work on the theory of metals, the electric conduction of metals, the theory of magnetic behavior, the theory of molecules, and even astrophysical problems. It was an extremely interesting time."

Edward Teller, hobbling on his artificial foot, became a wizard of the Ping-Pong table. His local supremacy was almost unchallenged until Heisenberg left Leipzig for a cruise to the Orient. For weeks aboard ship he played Ping-Pong with the experts from China and Japan, and when he returned, he wrested the crown from his favorite student.

Heisenberg was impressed with the way Teller gradually had conquered his physical handicap. "I could see in the beginning that he really suffered from it, not just bodily but also mentally, but I think he overcame it rather soon. I think, in a year or so, he was quite stabilized in his mind. But still, of course, among the young people he had difficulty—I mean when the young people did their sports, he couldn't participate."

Ping-Pong was, to Heisenberg, symbolic of Teller's determination. "He became an excellent player just because he wanted to become one. There I could see the force in the man. When he was hampered by some outer facts which he couldn't change, he really would try with all his strength to make up for it—and he *did* make up for it."

One of Teller's best friends among the students was Carl F. von Weizsäcker, and Heisenberg enjoyed the vigorous intellectual arguments between two extremely intelligent young men. Their intellectual battles were enhanced by their differences in heritage: Teller, a Jew, from the Hungarian middle class; Weizsäcker, a Christian, from the Prussian aristocracy, the son of an admiral who was to become under-secretary of state in Hitler's government. In their approach to science, Weizsäcker was philosophical, Teller was logical. When Weizsäcker would make philosophical generalizations, Teller would challenge with cold logic. Heisenberg felt Teller usually outpointed his friend—"for such a young man he was so precise and so definite both in questions and answers."

The two friends would subsequently be together again at the University of Göttingen and in Copenhagen. After that the external pressures of politics would force them poles apart but, amazingly, not break their friendship. They stopped corresponding between 1935, the year of Teller's arrival in America, and the outbreak of World War II, but resumed their correspondence after the war.

In the case of Heisenberg, the friendship was even more enduring. Teller last saw his teacher during Heisenberg's visit to America in 1939 on the eve of the war. As soon as the war ended, they immediately restored their old close relationship.

This separation of friendship and professional respect from politics is all the more remarkable when one considers that during World War II Heisenberg and Weizsäcker would be leaders in scientific research for the Nazi government, while Teller and Felix Bloch, Heisenberg's chief assistant at Leipzig, would be engaged in a death struggle against Germany and Japan in the laboratories of Los Alamos.

In 1929, however, most of the students had little interest in politics, and the physics students were probably more isolated from the outside world than any other group. The times were extremely happy, and Heisenberg "would have liked to see them go on forever."

The happiness was soon to end. Ugly forces were at work in Germany and, by 1929, the unrest was reaching the streets of Leipzig. Germany's floundering economy, inflation, and bitterness over the punishment of the Versailles Treaty were fuel for extremist elements. The communist solution was feared by many Germans, who turned for protection to the beguiling promises and the visions of German glory offered by Adolf Hitler. When the communists held rallies in Leipzig, they were often broken up by Nazi hoodlums and, sometimes, vice versa. Jews were the Nazis' primary scapegoats, and anti-semitic poison began to seep into the academic classes of the University of Leipzig.

While politics began inevitably to impinge on his consciousness, the immediate problem for Edward Teller was to win his Ph.D. By late 1929 he had nearly completed work on his thesis. He studied on the ground floor of the physics seminary where, two floors above, Heisenberg dwelt in his bachelor quarters. Sometimes, late in the evening, Teller would take a break and call on his professor. Over cups of tea they would discuss physics or, sometimes, sharpen their minds with the physical activity of a Ping-Pong game. Occasionally, other students would join them. These sometimes included I. I. Rabi, an American, or Lev Landau, a Russian, both of whom would one day win Nobel prizes. They would argue about the new ideas in science with the enthusiasm that most young men reserved only for politics and sports.

Teller had already established what was to be a life-long habit: rising late and working far into the night. In the earliest stages of his work on the thesis he had decided the mathematics of the British paper was incorrect and that the Danish paper had established the proper energy levels for hydrogen molecular ions in a normal state. Now he was engaged in the tedious and exhausting calculation of the energy levels in various excited states.

This stage of the work involved using a primitive calculating machine that clattered and groaned with every pull of the lever. In the cavernous building of the physics seminary, the noisy drums of the infernal machine resounded into the upper floors where Professor Heisenberg was trying to sleep. Teller's story, which Heisenberg refuses to confirm, is that he was awarded his Ph.D. so that Heisenberg could enjoy some uninterrupted sleep. (Both the professor and his student would have appreciated the quiet electronic calculators that appeared forty years later.)

Actually, Heisenberg was unreservedly enthusiastic about his student's thesis, but the final awarding of the degree depended also on his grades in chemistry and mathematics. In chemistry he had no trouble at all, but in mathematics he was up against a Professor Köbe, who replaced a professor preferred by Teller, but who had since left Leipzig. Köbe was conceited and combative. He accused Teller of not knowing anything and then decided the student would have to discuss complex variables and non-Euclidian geometry. Teller, with a few days to prepare, went to Heisenberg in a panic, fearful not of the subjects he was to discuss, but of the apparent vindictiveness of Köbe. Heisenberg offered little comfort. "If I say a word to Köbe, he'll fail you for sure. You'd better just study."

Teller resorted to the time-honored device of learning not about the exam subject, but about the professor. He found out what a student had to do to pass an exam with Köbe. "I didn't study for the subject—which I knew—but for Köbe's exam."

When the time came for the oral examination with Köbe, Teller chose to discuss a particular theorem of complex variables. When the professor asked his student where he learned this proof, Teller coyly told him he learned it in a text. "Well," asked Köbe, "I suppose you know that it was I who proved this theorem first." Teller did know, of course—and he passed.

In the last months at Leipzig, before Teller had been awarded his Ph.D., Heisenberg took about a dozen students on one of several visits to Berlin for a seminar at the Kaiser Wilhelm Institute. This visit was momentous in Teller's life in that it marked his first meeting with Einstein and the beginning of a long friendship with his fellow Hungarian Eugene Wigner, a gentle genius who was six years older than Teller. Through the stormy years that followed, Wigner, who was eventually to win a Nobel prize, was among the minority of scientists who shared Teller's political views and defended him against the onslaughts of the more liberal majority.

"The first time this happened," Teller recalls, "it was to hear a talk by Einstein. He talked about the unified field theory. I listened; I didn't understand a syllable. Afterward a group of us went to the zoo—it was a very good zoo. Wigner was along, and perhaps a few others, students from both Leipzig and Berlin. And I was still upset because I didn't understand Einstein. Eugene came to me and asked, 'What's the matter?'—he saw I was troubled. I very briefly told him. I said, 'I'm very stupid.'

"If Wigner had contradicted me that wouldn't have helped a bit. But he didn't contradict me. He said, 'Yes, that is a general human property.' And that cheered me up. This is a story I have since told my children, so within the family 'a general human property' is synonymous with stupidity."

As Teller was to discover, there is consolation in shared ignorance. Years later when Teller was working with Russian-born physicist George Gamow in Washington, Einstein wrote a book on the unified field theory. A reporter, having interviewed Einstein, called on Gamow to seek other advice on whether Einstein knew what he was talking about. "Why don't you ask Einstein?" Gamow suggested.

"I did," said the reporter. "I asked him if he was sure he was right."

"And what did Einstein say?" Gamow asked the reporter.

"He said come back and ask me in twenty years."

The unified field theory, which so mystified Teller in 1930, was never formulated to Einstein's full satisfaction before his death in 1955. And in 1973 Werner Heisenberg, still energetic and imaginative in his seventies, was trying to conceive a unified field theory in terms of quantum theory.

In his last vacation before leaving Leipzig, at Eastertime in 1930, Teller went for two weeks to Copenhagen with Heisenberg and several other students to hear some lectures by the great Niels Bohr. Bohr, one of the titanic physicists of the century, had described the structure of the atom in terms of quantum theory that laid the foundation for subsequent understanding of the nature of atomic energy. Later he would become Teller's personal friend and counselor.

It was Bohr's custom to have tea with his visiting students. Teller, seated close to the great man at one of these sessions, was thinking that Bohr's theory of the atom—the mechanics—in some important and basic respects contradicts classical mechanics, even common sense. Is an electron a particle or a wave? Then he realized this is the question a good physicist is not even supposed to ask. But he asked Bohr anyhow, a brash query for a physicist just twenty-one with a doctorate for barely a month. Teller, in fact, expounded on the question of basic concepts.

While Teller was holding forth, Bohr's eyelids started to droop. Teller stopped abruptly. Was he boring one of the world's great intellects? For several painful seconds he waited. Then Bohr's eyelids fluttered, and he responded: "You might just as well say we are not sitting here drinking tea, but are only dreaming all this."

What did Bohr mean by such a cryptic statement? All the way back to Leipzig Teller worried about it. Perhaps Bohr was being profound, pointing out that reality does not exist in the conventional sense, as demonstrated by the conflict of waves and particles. This, after all, was a basic belief of the Copenhagen school. But the more Teller thought about it, the more he rejected the notion that Bohr had uttered a careful aphorism, derived from Teller's remarks. The young scientist's conclusion was that he had talked too much. Bohr was just trying to shut him up.

The lure of a longer visit to Copenhagen was to remain in Teller's mind, but the most attractive offer on his departure from Leipzig was an assistantship in physics at the University of Göttingen. The fact that Teller was invited to Göttingen was a measure of his growing reputation, for this medieval Hanoverian town was unsurpassed in the world as a mecca of physicists. The combination of its students, its faculty, and its guest lecturers added up to the greatest names in physics from at least a dozen countries.

It was also to be a symbolic Götterdämmerung of German science. It flourished until Hitler's seizure of power. Then, within a few years, the god-figures of physics had been scattered to the winds.

By the time Teller reached Göttingen, in the fall of 1930, it was no longer possible for anyone in Germany to hide from the realities of politics. The Nazis had elected 107 delegates to the German Reichstag in 1929. The collapse of the American stock market had occurred in October of that same year. These developments were known to Teller, although, as he described it, "I must say that I was much less interested in these facts which now loom so large than I was in trying to find out what was going to happen in the long run."

Along the way he had had occasional enduring exposures to political tides. In 1928, after the accident in Munich, he had shared a hospital room briefly with the son of a Chinese Kuomintang official. He learned a great deal about the emerging power struggle of traditional, moderate, and communist factions in China. At Leipzig one of the most impressive and likable students was the

Russian Lev Landau, who was a confirmed communist. And finally there was Teller's close friend Carl Friedrich von Weizsäcker, who was a colleague in Leipzig, Göttingen, and Copenhagen.

The Teller-Weizsäcker relationship typified the conflict of political and personal relationships where, so often, strong friendships are challenged by external forces. The growth of Nazi power, with its implications of anti-Semitism, was a source of deepening concern to Teller. On the other hand, Weizsäcker, the well-connected Prussian, shared with Teller a fear of the rapid spread of Russian communism. Teller, after all, had known a communist insurrection firsthand in Hungary.

Weizsäcker, though he was critical of many changes the Nazis were forcing, saw as the central point the notion that Hitler was a bulwark against the expansion of communism. The Prussian gentile insisted that "not everything the Nazis are doing is wrong," to which the Hungarian Jew replied, "I disagree—*everything* they are doing is wrong."

It must have been a painful period for two young scientists who were otherwise fast friends. Teller still experienced no anti-Semitism among his intimate friends, though in the early 1930s, Nazi pamphlets condemning the Jews were beginning to appear. Meanwhile, Weizsäcker's father, a former admiral, was acquiring the political stature that would land him in an important post in the Nazi government.*

In the spring of 1932 Teller took a brief leave of Göttingen to join a large gathering of physicists at some seminars with Enrico Fermi at the University of Rome. Teller's participation in the Roman gathering was somewhat of an accident; he was writing a paper with George Placzek, and Placzek was invited by Fermi to come to his laboratory for several weeks. The only way the paper could be completed would be for Teller to tag along. He thus found himself once again in one of those interludes in which an incredible array of the great physicists of the future were all at the same place at the same time. The company included not only Placzek, but Hans Bethe, Rudolf Peierls, and two of Fermi's associates, Emilio Segre

*The elder von Weizsäcker served ultimately as Hitler's under-secretary of state. He was tried and imprisoned as a war criminal, served several years, and died within weeks after his release. Teller believes he was unjustly convicted and in fact was a moderating influence in the Nazi regime. Teller claims it was von Weizsäcker's influence that convinced the Nazis to withdraw their army from Rome without a fight, thereby saving the Eternal City from destruction.

and Franco Rasetti. The magnet was Fermi himself, who was emerging as one of the greatest experimental physicists as well as one of the most admired and beloved figures in science. Ten years later all of these comrades in physics would meet again in the wartime service of the United States.

Before Teller could commit himself to the visit to Rome, he had to find a place to live that would cost little or no money. His pride had reached the point where he could no longer ask for financial help from his father in Budapest. A little investigation turned up the existence of a Hungarian college—Collegium Hungaricum—in Rome where Teller could stay for a few weeks as a nonpaying guest, provided the college received a request for accommodations through Fermi. Fermi responded by inviting Teller to Rome in an extremely formal letter, a copy of which went to the Collegium. Then Fermi sent an informal letter to Teller, apologizing for the official tone of the first letter, but explaining that he had written it to impress the officials of the Collegium. It was Teller's first experience with the relaxed graciousness of Italy's foremost physicist, and the young Hungarian decided Fermi was a man he could like.

Placzek was the dominant figure in the group from Germany. His paper with Teller involved the use of spectroscopy for a study of the structure of molecules. As Bethe recalls those weeks in Rome, they were a mixed blessing for Teller. Placzek, a Czech who grew up in Vienna, was an excellent physicist, but his outlook on life was that of the worldly sophisticate, in contrast to the narrow academic framework in which Teller had been living. "He was a man of the world," Bethe remembers, "much more sophisticated than Teller or I. He had dated girls in large numbers, and he spoke eight or ten languages, all very well, and was well versed in literature and all sorts of things. So he was very impressive to me, at least."

To Bethe, "Placzek was also fundamentally kind and a physicist with tremendously high standards," but he also took great delight in needling Teller.

The Collegium Hungaricum, where Teller lived "with a bunch of crazy Hungarians," was a medieval palace beside the Tiber River. His room was on the top floor and provided just a small table and a very hard bed. A slit of a window gave him a view of the Tiber. Across the river there was some kind of a ceremonial cannon which was fired every day at noon. Teller found the cannon useful—"I used it for an alarm clock." That a noise at noon could be an alarm clock once again reveals the contrast between Teller and most other energetic, productive people. He did not conform to the early-riser stereotype.

It might have been Placzek who dubbed Teller Il Pellegrino (the Pilgrim) because of a hooded raincoat he wore during his weeks in Rome. Placzek seemed to be one of the few people who managed to dominate Teller, and their joint effort at producing an important paper was sometimes a difficult experience for the latter. As Bethe remembers: "The problem was to use a certain discovery in spectroscopy, known as the Raman effect, for the exploration of the structure of molecules. Placzek was merciless with Teller. He always made fun of the things that Teller had found out in the week between his visits [they worked independently and met about once a week to compare notes], and always claimed that 'Well, this isn't much, Teller. . . .' "

Teller took Placzek's ribbing graciously, according to Bethe, and he was very humble to Placzek, "and we used to say he apologized for being alive."

But Teller, in Bethe's opinion, had no reason to be humble. "I thought Teller mostly was quite right. I don't know enough about the detailed arguments to be sure, but what Teller said to me sounded terribly interesting and I don't see why Placzek criticized it so much."

All of the visiting physicists worked under the skilled surveillance of Fermi. To Bethe, "Fermi was a wonderful man. He had such an easy way about him, and everything seemed easy and clear, because he was a wonderful physicist, too. When I think of the physicists I have known, he was the one from whom I learned most, apart from Sommerfeld [who had taught both Bethe and Teller in Munich].

"It was so easy to learn from Fermi. He explained everything so clearly, so quickly, and he made you think in his manner. That really was his great secret—that not only could he do everything so easily, but somehow you learned to do it, too."

While some of the world's best young physicists were gleaning excitement and pleasure from their work with Fermi, the cloud of totalitarianism was building on the horizon. Mussolini, the dictator of Italy, was proud of Fermi, but, in addition to any anti-Semitic tendencies he may have harbored, Hitler's poison was seeping into the land of Il Duce. Fermi was not Jewish, but his wife, Laura, was. So were at least half of the visiting scientists from Germany.

On January 30, 1933, fifteen days after Teller's twenty-fifth birthday, von Hindenburg, the haughty old field marshal who was president of Germany, called on Adolf Hitler to form a government. The president's hand had been forced by inflation, depression, and the resulting political chaos. Less than a month later the Reichstag building in Berlin was destroyed by fire, possibly set by the Nazis themselves. Whatever its origins, the fire provided Hitler with the opportunity to demand emergency powers to cope with the country's "enemies." What William L. Shirer called Germany's "descent into hell" had begun.

Almost immediately the Nazi propaganda machine commenced its assault on Jewish scientists, particularly Einstein. His theories of relativity were scorned. Even a German Nobel Laureate, Philipp von Lenard, publicly declared that "The most important example of the dangerous influence of Jewish circles on the study of nature has been provided by Herr Einstein with his mathematically botched-up theories consisting of some ancient knowledge and a few arbitrary additions."[4]

Students in Berlin turned the great thought of the ages into a funeral pyre of books written by Jews or socialists. Dr. Ernest Krieck was invested as the new rector of the University of Frankfurt with the astounding declaration that "Nowadays the task of the universities is not to cultivate objective science but soldierlike militant science, and their foremost task is to form the will and character of their students."[5]

At this time Teller's most important senior professor was named Eucken, described by Teller as an "old German nationalist." Almost wistfully, Eucken seemed to hope that perhaps Hitler would be good for Germany. His turmoil must have been that of millions of decent Germans. In March 1933 Teller and Eucken took a train ride together, Teller heading home to Budapest, to his parents for a short vacation, Eucken on a skiing trip. Teller mentioned the possibility of moving to England. The old professor was straightforward. "I really want you here, but with this new situation, there is no point in your staying. I would like to help you, but you have no future in Germany."

Teller returned from vacation over his parents' protest. They wanted him to remain in Budapest. Teller agreed that he should not stay in Germany, but he did not see Budapest as the alternative. Ilona Teller, as usual, was the most fearful. "You must not go back. You will be in danger in Germany," she said, in pleading with her son to stay in Hungary.

Edward, remembering the overt anti-Semitism in Hungary, felt that the Hitler evil would spread to his native country.

"In the long run," he told her, "I will be in much greater danger if I stay at home."

When he did return to Göttingen, anti-Nazi or Jewish professors there and in other major universities were resigning in droves. Among the major scientists who had departed Göttingen were physicists James Franck and Max Born.

Most Jews were not yet aware of the danger the Nazis presented to their physical survival. Eucken had a secretary who also did some clerical work for Teller. She was intelligent and lucid. She told Teller that she did not understand how such a wonderful man as James Franck could be so strongly opposed to Hitler. After all, she said, Franck was a good German and should stay. To leave was unpatriotic.

Even the wisest men were deceived. The evening after the Reichstag fire, Teller was visiting a colleague, Walter Heitler, who admitted to socialist leanings. While they were discussing the situation, another physicist, the celebrated Wolfgang Pauli, dropped in. Pauli, a Swiss physicist, was known as one of the great teachers, and for his formulation of the Pauli principle. He had visited Russia and deplored the dictatorship there. But as to the possibility of a dictatorship in Germany? *"Quatsch!* [pure nonsense]," said Pauli. "I have seen dictatorship in Russia. In Germany it just couldn't happen."

Teller subsequently made no claim to clairvoyance. His insistence on leaving Germany was based perhaps on an intuitive feeling of danger, but it was more directly related to the question of progress in his career.

"The hope of making an academic career in Germany for a Jew existed before Hitler came—and vanished the day he arrived. In day-to-day politics I still was hardly interested, except that I wanted to continue my work. It was obvious that I had to leave Germany."

3

The Quantum Jump

THE year Teller spent in Copenhagen "was among the most important and wonderful periods of my life," he wrote to Niels Bohr more than two decades later. It was no wonder that Teller remembered 1934 with such pleasure. He was in the stimulating presence of the patriarch of the new era of quantum mechanics. It was also the year that Teller and Mici were married, after an international comic opera that pitted physicists, including Bohr, against bureaucrats, regulations, and red tape.

Bohr was the founder and the first director of the Institute for Theoretical Physics at the University of Copenhagen. From 1919 until Bohr's death more than three decades later, the institute was a clearinghouse for new ideas. But the climactic period was in the mid 1920s when Bohr was the captain of the international team that fashioned quantum mechanics. Robert Oppenheimer was later to acclaim the revolutionary findings of the era as the "collaboration of scores of scientists from many lands, though from first to last the deep, creative and critical spirit of Niels Bohr guided, restrained, deepened and finally transmuted the enterprise."[1]

To Teller, discussing Bohr in retrospect, "He is one of the very few people who brought about a real change in the course of scientific thought. He started on the right track, explaining the structure of the atom. And it was his students, his school—to which Heisenberg belonged—that brought this development to a successful completion."

In Teller's opinion, atomic theory would have developed with or without Bohr, "but the philosophy that paralleled quantum theory, with the theory of the atom, this was created by Niels Bohr and probably would not have come about without him."

That philosophy was necessary for the accommodation of the new kind of thinking that was intrinsic to quantum mechanics. As Teller explained it to us:

"Prior to Niels Bohr, science, very particularly physical science, stood for strict logic. This is an approach that I would describe as monism. This required a single, straightforward explanation for every scientific fact, systematized and derived from as obvious and consistent an origin as possible. Niels Bohr's contribution, formulated by himself, by Heisenberg and others, was the approach of dualism or *complementarity*.

"This approach says there are things—and atomic structure is one of them—which cannot be understood from a single point of view. These are situations where two complementary points of view are necessary, and by this is meant that you have two points of view which are mutually exclusive and, at the same time, both are necessary if reality is to be represented."

Philosophically, Teller made the analogy with those who would say that a human being cannot be understood without considering both the material and spiritual aspects of his being, of his body and soul. But a nineteenth-century physicist would have said this is not physics but mysticism.

Quantum theory required that physicists no longer think in terms of strict logic and the straightforward explanation, but neither was it mysticism, according to Teller:

"Now we had a dualistic explanation of the atom, where the atom and its constituents must be considered in part as particles, in part as waves, and a clear-cut decision between these two cannot be made without losing an essential part of reality. Bohr may have been inclined to say that there is a real analogy with the human situation, with the materialistic and the spiritual approach, and with many other situations in the world, and in general terms, I agree.

"But there is this particular point; that we have here in physics an occasion for a dualistic approach that is clearly not mysticism, but is a faithful representation of the whole mathematical apparatus by which atoms are actually described. The analogy with the material and spiritual is not so important. What is important is that this is an example of dualism which is strictly scientific, which has not yet been applied in any other field, but may one day."

The seemingly impossible resolution between two versions of reality, of wave and particle theories, was accomplished mainly between 1924 and 1927, with Bohr as the catalyst and Werner Heisenberg achieving the mathematical reconciliation. Heisenberg's uncertainty principle stated that the behavior of atomic particles could not be determined on a cause-and-effect basis, but only on the basis of what probably would happen on a statistical basis. In Teller's terms, "The uncertainty principle limits the accuracy of the observation and states that you cannot push the particle explanation to such accuracies that would get into a direct and demonstrable conflict with the wave theory."

Teller arrived in Copenhagen nearly a decade after the birth of quantum mechanics, but there was still a lot to learn and discover, and just being in Copenhagen was an exciting prospect. His own work, however, was, by his description, "connected with a much more low-brow part of physics." He was not delving into the philosophy of quantum mechanics, but mainly into problems involved with molecular structure.

Before Hitler had seized power, Teller, having visited Copenhagen, was anxious to join Bohr's charmed circle. From Göttingen Teller had made preliminary inquiries into the possibility of winning a Rockefeller Fellowship for a grant to study at the Institute for Theoretical Physics. By the time he had actually applied, the Nazis were in control of Germany. It was obvious that he had to get out. He had no intention of returning to Hungary. In the tense surroundings of the Horthy regime, a Jew couldn't even get a decent job.

In his application to the Rockefeller Foundation in New York, Teller made no secret of his rootlessness. While the Rockefeller officials seemed impressed with his qualifications, he was turned down because he had no home and no permanent source of income. They would not provide a fellowship to an unemployed refugee.

Among those working hardest to assist outcast German scholars were two British scientists, physicist-philosopher Frederick Alexander Lindemann (later Viscount Cherwell) and George Frederick Donnan, a biochemist. The latter was already famous for his formulation of the Donnan Equilibrium, relating to the balance of fluids on each side of a membrane. James Franck had called the attention of both scientists to Edward Teller, and he received invitations from both to work in England. Teller accepted the Donnan offer and departed Germany to become an assistant in physics at University College in London. It was only a temporary assignment, but it provided Teller with the home base he needed to reapply to the Rockefeller Foundation.

In London Teller once again crossed paths with his old friend Hans Bethe. Bethe had also fled Germany, as had Walter Heitler, another comrade from Teller's days at Göttingen. They were now working together at the University of Manchester on a problem involving electrons and gamma radiation. In Bethe's part of the experiment he got a result that Heitler just couldn't believe. They went to London to visit Teller and explained the findings to him.

"Teller immediately grasped the idea of my calculation and very effectively persuaded Heitler that I was right," Bethe recounted for us. "This was, I think, the first time that Teller had participated directly in something I had done. I was very much impressed by his quick understanding and in the way he then explained it. From this time on I had great respect for him."

Though Bethe and Teller had known each other in Munich and in Rome, their close friendship began during this brief time in England. In a period of several months they met two or three times.

In the summer of 1931 Mici, apparently somewhat to Edward's surprise, had made a decision to go to the graduate school of the University of Pittsburgh. Her departure had precipitated their first serious quarrel. She went off to America with no commitments to Edward. "There wasn't even a commitment that there were no commitments," Teller admits. Only under pressure from the authors did Teller, who resists discussing personal affairs, concede that "we had somewhat of a fight before she left." For two years they did not write a single letter.

Now, in the summer of 1933, she was to return to Budapest. When she returned, or shortly after, Teller was in Budapest on vacation. At that time Mici's only possible rival was Edward's young cousin Ilona, "Illi" Dobo. There is strong evidence that the family, especially the patriarch, Grandfather Ignac Deutsch, tried to promote a match between Illi and Edward. Edward, looking back forty years, made it clear that he could not speak for Illi, but that "I might have been interested, except there was Mici."

Apparently, despite their quarrel, and a two-year breakdown in communications, the attraction of Edward and Mici not only survived the separation, but was enhanced by it. Mici had been home only a short time when, in August 1933, they finally did make a commitment. Without any formalities they announced to their families that they were engaged and planned to get married during Christmas vacation. Then, assuming Edward received the Rockefeller grant, they would start their married life in Copenhagen.

Their parents, not surprisingly, insisted the wedding must take place in Budapest, and plans were made for a small but festive gathering.

Alas, it wasn't all that simple. Once again the Rockefeller Foundation dangled its prize just out of Teller's eager reach.

It was a conflict of love and money. The foundation sent Teller a questionnaire, which included the query "Married or Single?" Even for a young man with Teller's mental faculties, the question posed a problem. He could have answered that he was not married, which, of course, was the truth. On the other hand, the fellowship would be effective January 1, 1934, at which time he would be a married man. The weighty problem was taken to Donnan, who had already become a friendly and fatherly counselor. Donnan enjoyed a joke. In fact, Teller recalls, "He was never completely serious."

"That question," Donnan twitted Teller, "is really not properly defined. The Rockefeller Foundation should have given you more alternatives: Single? Married? Widowed? Divorced? Intending to Get Married? Intending to Get Divorced? Intending to Get Widowed? How can you answer with so few choices?"

But Donnan had some practical advice. "Now look. The only thing to do is to put a nice asterisk beside that question and then, on another sheet of paper, explain the situation fully to the Rockefeller Foundation."

Teller followed Donnan's advice exactly, and mailed the letter to the foundation's European headquarters in Paris. In a few weeks he received a wire:

MEETING TO AWARD FELLOWSHIPS TOMORROW. NEED INFOR-MATION IMMEDIATELY ON WHETHER YOU INTEND TO GET MARRIED.

It was obvious that if the marriage question could be resolved, he had won the fellowship. He rushed over to Donnan's office with the telegram.

"I think you have a serious problem," said Donnan. "You'd better take the next train to Paris and talk with them face to face."

As quickly as the schedules permitted, Teller was in Paris and knocking on the door of the mighty Rockefeller Foundation. He was received warmly in his first encounter with American officialdom. Teller explained why he was there, and the functionary's face clouded over.

"Now, Dr. Teller," he began, "I don't want you to get the impression that we in America are opposed to the institution of marriage—" Teller's spirits collapsed.

The official continued in sweet reasonableness, "You see, we've had some problems. There was this Hungarian fellow who, instead of working, got married and went off on a long honeymoon. We do not award Rockefeller Fellowships to send Hungarians off on honeymoons."

Why the emphasis on the mating characteristics of Hungarians? Teller wondered. The message, just the same, was clear. America was a free country. The Rockefeller Foundation believed in freedom; freedom to accept a fellowship or freedom to get married, but not freedom to do both.

Back home in Budapest, Mici received a telegram from Edward advising her that he would telephone at exactly eight o'clock that evening to explain the difficult situation. At the appointed hour she was close to the phone, uneasily awaiting the news. When Edward didn't call her anxiety became acute. He was usually punctual. As the hour of eight receded, her brothers teased her unmercifully, suggesting that her fiancé had forgotten her. By the time the clock struck nine she had all but despaired. Then the phone rang.

It was Edward. He had gotten confused on the time zones and thought he was phoning according to plan. He broke the bad news gently, more or less leaving the decision to Mici. Fighting back tears, she urged him to accept the fellowship. After all, they had waited a long time; they could wait a little longer. Edward agreed, and the December wedding plans were canceled. The decision took a lot of luster away from the projected study in Copenhagen.

But that wasn't the end of the confusion. Early in January, Teller once again packed up and moved, this time to become a Rockefeller Fellow—single—in Copenhagen. Shortly after his arrival he wrote a letter to his old friend and Nobel prize winner James Franck, who had left Göttingen and emigrated to the United States. When Teller had last written to Franck in the fall he had reported the joyful news of his planned Christmastime marriage to Mici. Now he told of his good fortune in winning the Rockefeller Fellowship, but also lamented the conflict that had deferred his wedding.

A few weeks later Teller was surprised by a letter from Franck, who was furious. He told Teller he had never heard of such an outrageous thing as making bachelorhood a requirement for a fellowship. As a matter of fact, Franck continued, he got so angry that he stormed into the Rockefeller Foundation headquarters in New York. There he raised such a colossal fuss that they agreed to change their policy and let Teller get married.

Then Franck made a peculiar request of Teller. "Would you please do this one thing in order to save their face? Write them a letter and tell them you can't stand not being married, that you have to be allowed to get married for the sake of your work. You can be quite sure that you will get a prompt reply permitting you to get married because the decision is already made. But it will help their accounts if you complain accordingly."

To Teller this seemed like a reasonable idea; as a matter of fact, he *did* feel that his work might suffer if he wasn't allowed to get married. So he complied with Franck's suggestion exactly. Then, having finished the letter, "I had a very stupid idea." The idea was that he shouldn't do anything that might jeopardize his standing with the Rockefeller Foundation without first consulting with Niels Bohr. The foundation, after all, was potentially Teller's bread and butter.

A day passed before he could meet with Bohr. Teller showed him the letter. "Hmm," said the Dane, puffing on his pipe. "Let me just study this." Then he turned back to his work, leaving his student in total confusion. Day after day Teller tried to catch up with Bohr, just to find out what had happened to the letter. Bohr seemed to be consciously avoiding Teller. On several occasions when Teller spied him, the teacher quickly ducked out of sight.

Finally, a full two weeks later, Teller cornered Bohr and reminded him of the suspended problem. Bohr agreed to a quick cup of coffee in a little shop adjacent to Bohr's institute, known to the students as The Quantum Coffee Shop. Bohr assumed a paternal role for his uneasy pupil.

"I have always found in my life," he said, "that we must be completely honest. You can't write a letter like this. You know that the Rockefellers will allow you to marry, and yet you ask them to give you this permission that you already have. After all, the Rockefellers have been so nice to us, especially in helping with the refugees from Germany. And this is the worst time to cheat them; you just can't *do* that.

"What you should do," Bohr continued, "is to write to them and tell them exactly what Franck told you."

"I can't do that—Franck asked me *not* to do it.

Bohr shrugged. "Franck is our friend."

"Just because somebody is a friend doesn't mean I can disregard his wishes."

"Then write a letter to Franck."

Teller was getting irritated. "That would mean we wait another two weeks."

"Then send him a wire."

"I can't explain the whole thing in a wire."

Bohr realized finally that Teller was upset. "All right, all right. Let me discuss it with Harald." Harald was Niels's younger brother, a highly respected mathematician. Teller agreed, reluctantly. Another month, he thought, before I know whether I can get married.

But Bohr was quicker this time. The next day he told Teller that Harald thought he could mail the letter, so Niels concurred.

"Mail it," a fellow student suggested, "before Bohr changes his mind."

It was posted, but after it had slid into the mailbox, Teller was suddenly concerned that it was dated two weeks earlier. Would the Rockefeller people conclude that the delay was indicative of some effort to bypass their regulations about marriage? Then Teller consoled himself that perhaps they would conclude only that the discrepancy in dates was merely because a young and timid student took two weeks to make up his mind to confront a powerful foundation.

Only about a week later, Teller nervously tore open an official-looking response from the Rockefeller headquarters. It was utterly confusing and ambiguous—except for the last line.

The letter's first statement was that the foundation had a firm policy that no fellow could be married during his fellowship. The second sentence seemed to say that there were some exceptions. The third sentence said there were never any exceptions; the Rockefeller Foundation never deviates from the policy. The fourth sentence seemed to nullify the third.

"And so it went," said Teller, "like a tennis game, oscillating from sentence to sentence, until the very end of the letter, where it concluded: 'Will you kindly inform us of the date of your wedding?'"

For Teller, the course was clear. "I turned to this mathematical-legal argument: The people who were giving me the fellowship asked me to notify them of the date of my wedding to Mici. Therefore, obviously, I had to marry her."

And he did.

Edward Teller and Mici Harkanyi were united in marriage on February 26, 1934, in the presence of their immediate families and a few friends. It was a civil ceremony performed by a notary public in his office directly across the street from the Teller apartment. The only touch of festivity in the trappings was that for the first time in his adult life Edward wore a hat (at the insistence of his mother-in-law) and the notary, a large, bellowing man, honored the occasion by wearing a red, white, and green sash, the colors of Hungary, around his ample midsection.

The decision in favor of a civil ceremony was based on the almost complete detachment from formal religion on the part of the bride and groom. Near his fortieth wedding anniversary, Teller could quip, "In a religious sense we are still living in sin."

Without a honeymoon, Edward and Mici took the train to Copenhagen. Edward had rented a room in a pension in anticipation of his married state. They lived in the pension for about two months, then moved into a small apartment. This gave Mici her first opportunity to be a housewife and hostess, a situation that threw her into a bride's panic when she learned that their first visitor would be Werner Heisenberg. She managed, however, because Heisenberg obviously enjoyed his dinner. He was Mici's initiation to a lifetime of entertaining Edward's very important friends.

But Teller's most surprising achievement during this time was to produce a scientific paper that proved the Rockefeller Foundation was wrong in its reservations about fellowships for married students. It was, by the objective judgment of his colleagues, the most important paper he had produced to that point in his life. It bore the impressive title "Theory of the Catalysis of the Ortho-para Transformation by Paramagnetic Gases." The co-author was F. Kalchar.

The paths of the great physicists of the era crossed with such regularity that they became something of a family. The casual social gatherings at Copenhagen sometimes included a half dozen Nobel prize winners of the past and future. Teller's professional colleagues became his social friends. Von Weizsäcker was there, continuing the friendship that he and Teller had established in Leipzig.

But the most fruitful friendship for Teller was with George Gamow. A large, brusque, and good-humored man, Gamow was one of the few Russians in the group, a refugee from communism rather than the Nazis. He was four years older than Teller and already had an international reputation that, a few months later, was to win him a full professorship at George Washington University in Washington, D.C.

In Copenhagen, Gamow owned a motorbike. During Easter vacation in 1934 he and Teller went on a vacation all the way across Denmark and back, with Gamow at the controls and Teller clinging on the back. Even though this was a holiday, their discussions finally got around to quantum mechanics. Gamow had been perplexed by a problem about the motion of a particle in a certain kind of field. He asked Teller's help. Teller couldn't solve it, either, but their shared interest established a firm rapport. A year later this rapport would bring the two friends together again in the new surroundings of Washington for a partnership that was to endure for many years.

Bohr, for all his erudition, could be a confusing and erratic teacher, and his foibles sometimes put his students to the test. For a short time Teller collaborated on that first paper with the young Dane, Kalchar. The project was connected with molecular behavior. When they were nearing completion, Bohr asked Teller to report on it before a seminar. The date was set, but at the appointed hour everyone but Bohr showed up. So another date was set and Bohr didn't show up this time either. By this time Teller was assuming the discussion had been more or less forgotten. Then one day Teller wandered into the seminar late and the twice postponed discussion was now taking place with Bohr present. Since Teller hadn't been present when the discussion started, Kalchar was explaining the project, speaking in German. Bohr obviously had preferred that Teller do the talking but he didn't want to hurt Kalchar's feelings by asking him to yield to Teller.

"So he invented a subterfuge—and remember, he was against subterfuges with the Rockefeller Foundation—and he said, when I came in, that he believed it would be better to hear the explanation in English. He turned to me and said, 'Would Dr. Teller continue the discussion in English?' "

Teller had no choice but to go along with the subterfuge, shift gears into another language, and deliver his scientific lecture in

English, all because Bohr wanted to get Kalchar off the floor.

Teller's stature was sufficiently enhanced by the eight months in Copenhagen to insure a return to London to work again with his jovial friend Donnan. In the fall of 1934 he was back at the University of London as a lecturer in the chemistry department. This time he and Mici were ready to accept London as a permanent home. Marriage had radically altered Edward's life-style. As a bachelor arriving in Copenhagen the previous January, his worldly possessions consisted mostly of things he could carry. When he returned to London, a married man, he and his wife had accumulated seventeen pieces of luggage.

They rented makeshift quarters, then, in anticipation of a long stay, set out to find a permanent home. They found a commodious three-room flat in a remodeled old house on Gower Street, so utterly satisfactory that they went out on a limb and committed themselves to a nine-year lease. When the lease was signed, just before Christmas 1934, they vacated their temporary flat and went home to Budapest for Christmas, intending to move into the new residence on their return to London.

In January, this course they had set was suddenly altered by two letters awaiting Teller at the university. One was from Princeton University offering him a lectureship. The other was more startling. It came from George Gamow, who was now established as head of the physics department at George Washington University. The letter, according to Teller, was written in "Gamovian—a very strange dialect of German."

The message, however, was clear. In contrast to the mere lectureship that Teller held at the University of London, or the similar post offered at Princeton, Gamow was tendering a full professorship. For a twenty-six-year-old physicist, it was an offer he could hardly refuse.

But there were problems. Teller had decided reservations about America. In contrast, Mici, who had lived in Pittsburgh for two years, was enthusiastic. Then there was the question of whether it would be fair to leave Donnan so soon. And finally, there was that ridiculous nine-year lease. "Who," Teller wondered, "will live in that house for the next eight years and eleven and three-quarter months?"

With their future status uncertain, there was no point in buying furniture. They moved into the Gower Street flat with nothing but their seventeen pieces of baggage, which included two sleeping bags. It was not the luxury they had planned, but for the present there was no other choice.

Teller was enjoying the London lectureship and that added to his indecision. The routine was enjoyable. Because of Donnan's interest in rescuing refugee scholars, there were many congenial expatriates. Every day at four o'clock, Donnan and his associates had tea. It was a pleasant interlude, and Donnan often conducted the conversation in German to make the refugees feel at home. Eventually, Teller had to broach the subject of the George Washington offer to his kindly host and sponsor. Donnan was surprisingly understanding.

"I'd like you to stay," he said, "but, you know, we have invited more of the refugees than England can really absorb, so if you really want to accept you should feel perfectly free."

The flat proved a thornier problem. If Teller accepted Gamow's offer—which he had made up his mind to do—they would not be leaving London for Washington until August. But somehow they had to divest themselves of that burdensome nine-year lease. Teller attempted to put the whole blame on his wife. "You're the one who wants to go to America," he quipped. "So you find someone to sublet the flat."

In a matter of weeks, she did. Then they had to find still another home to shelter them for the remaining months in London. "We found a nice little flat with a rose garden in the back. Other than that what I remember about the flat was that everything went wrong." That was Teller's recollection from the vantage point of several decades later.

Meanwhile he had written to Gamow, accepting the professorship. He was at last to be an American. Or was he? There was still the problem of getting the visa.

Mici had gotten the passports, then gone to the American Embassy to obtain the visas. Her assumption was that they were eligible for nonquota immigration permits. But she was turned down, flatly. Why? Well, the embassy officials wouldn't say. The hurdle was just enough to dampen Edward's resolve. "Let's forget it," he said, "and stay in England."

But the more they thought about it, they knew the trip to America was their destiny. If a Hungarian seems blocked in pursuit of his destiny, one solution is to seek help from another Hungarian. Back in Budapest Edward had had a friend named Thomas Balogh. Balogh's imperious personality won him a nickname from his play-mates. They called him Sir Thomas.

As a young man, Balogh emigrated to England, where he became a successful economist. Later, his success culminated in knighthood, so that he legitimatized his childhood nickname by becoming a real Sir Thomas. Then he improved his status even farther, accepting an elevation to the peerage and the lofty title Lord Balogh.

In 1935 Balogh was not yet a knight, but he was influential enough to throw some weight around in the American embassy. He found out that the nonquota visa was rejected because it required that Teller have at least two prior years of university teaching, in the field he would teach in in the United States. He had taught for more than a year in London, but the Copenhagen experience was not counted because he was a fellow, and a fellow is not a teacher.

For a time this seemed to be an insurmountable problem, until Balogh discovered that the solution was ridiculously simple. All the effort to extract a nonquota visa from the American officials had been utterly unnecessary. Under the American immigration laws, which allowed immigrants from foreign countries in proportion to the numbers of their nationality in America, there was room for the Tellers on the quota. All they had to do was fill out the papers. So in August 1935, Mr. and Mrs. Teller set sail for the United States, and would remain forever after Americans.

4

The Garfield Street Gang

THE chain of events that brought Teller to America in 1935 had been set in motion several years earlier by Cloyd H. Marvin, president of George Washington University. Marvin was ambitious. His university had a top-bracket law school and a good medical school, but in the basic sciences George Washington was distinctly second-rate. The able scientists elsewhere in Washington and over in Baltimore at Johns Hopkins often referred to GW as "The G Street High School." Marvin wanted to shed this image, as quickly as possible, so he sought the advice of a number of prominent scientists, principally Merle Tuve.

Tuve was the talented director of the Department of Terrestrial Magnetism of the Carnegie Institution of Washington. He was a native of the little town of Canton, South Dakota, a fact that is notable mainly because Canton also produced Ernest Lawrence, the great impresario of cyclotrons at Berkeley. Lawrence and Tuve shared their childhood hours tinkering with primitive radios, and both eventually became high-energy physicists, though Lawrence went west to the University of California and Tuve east to Johns Hopkins and Carnegie.

If money would solve GW's problem, President Marvin was ready. He had acquired about $100,000 to invest in a physics department. But Marvin, as Tuve told it to us, was thinking in terms of experimental physicists, toiling in laboratories resplendent with fancy equipment. Tuve reminded the eager president that if he insisted on experimental physics, he could blow the whole $100,000 on a laboratory before he had hired his first physicist.

Why not hire some top-notch theoretical men, Tuve suggested. "Remember, all they need is pencil and paper, travel money, colleagues, and meetings."

Marvin was impressed. Tuve's next advice was that George Washington University try to hire "a bright young chap named Ga-

64

mow." This struck a responsive chord with Marvin because several years earlier he had met Gamow and Teller during a visit to Copenhagen. Tuve went on to explain that the Russian-born Gamow, who had since moved on to Cambridge, had made a major contribution to quantum mechanics through his formulation of what is usually known as the penetration theory. He predicted from calculations that there is a mathematical probability that a small percentage of subatomic particles can penetrate the electrical barrier around the nucleus even if the barrier has a higher charge than the particle. The theory suggests another example of the way in which quantum mechanics does not coincide with the laws of classical mechanics.

Tuve regarded Gamow's penetration theory as a fundamental achievement of Nobel prize quality, and he predicted that Gamow's name would be conspicuous for at least the next fifty years. Tuve was fairly certain that Gamow was available, especially if Marvin was willing to offer the young Russian a full professorship at a relatively high salary. Tuve even knew how to reach the prospect by cable. Marvin saw the light. "Go get him," he said.

Gamow, in Cambridge, quickly accepted the offer. The genial giant from Russia arrived in Washington in the fall of 1934. According to Teller's recollection, Gamow insisted on two conditions. Both of them, in retrospect, proved to be of epochal importance. The first condition was that he be allowed to organize an annual conference on theoretical physics, modeled after Bohr's meetings in Copenhagen. Second, he was to be free to choose a second theoretical physicist to join him on the George Washington faculty. Apparently Gamow, even before he arrived in Washington, had his eye on his new friend from the motorcycle tour in Denmark.

In a matter of months after he had settled in as GW's full professor of theoretical physics, Gamow was angling to get Teller. He told Tuve: "There's this one man who knows everything, just *everything.*" Tuve recalls that, to Gamow, Teller's appeal was partially that Teller was not just a physicist but a physical chemist who could broaden the expertise of the department. Gamow was given permission to offer Teller a full professorship at a salary comparable to his own.

Thus it was less than a year after Gamow's arrival that Edward and Mici Teller disembarked in the New World. The crossing of the Atlantic was more than a geographical transition. In Europe,

Teller, for all his obvious ability, was still a very young scientist working in the shadow of his great teachers. Now he was to be a full professor among students and colleagues who had not known him before. The burden of his youth had been left in the Old World. He was only twenty-six, but his assurance and his sheer professional competence transformed him very quickly into a leader, counselor, and tutor of his scientific associates. His appearance was another advantage. Teller looked older than his years; he spoke and moved with a mature authority.

Teller also represented a direct link with the already legendary physicists of Europe. He was on a first-name basis with Bohr, Heisenberg, Pauli, Franck, Fermi—the whole remarkable fraternity.

For two such forceful and ambitious men, it is surprising that the Gamow-Teller partnership endured for six fruitful years. They shared an uncanny ability to convey their enthusiasm to colleagues and students. Physicist Raymond Seeger, a onetime junior member of the GW physics department, told us that Gamow was "the best lecturer I ever heard in my life." Eventually, prodded by Teller, Gamow capitalized on his gift and became one of the great popularizers of science, writing nearly a score of books for lay readers.

Gamow was a big man, six-feet-three, blond and shaggy. He had an almost explosive ebullience, a quality that seemed peculiarly Russian. He squinted at the world through small, round eyeglasses, forever in quizzical amusement at his fellow man. Life, to Gamow, seemed to be both a joy and a joke. He savored friends, food, and drink, sometimes too much of the last. He didn't know how to manage money, and often touched his colleagues for a temporary loan.

There was a comparable gusto in Teller's approach to life, but it was balanced by those lapses into moods of solemn contemplation that had recurred since his early childhood. Teller always needed time to think. While Gamow's achievements were often flashes of brilliance, Teller's were based on a thoroughness—an ability to see both the forest and the trees. He, like Gamow, was a good lecturer, but his influence over his students was gained not so much from platform oration as from his ability to challenge them on a one-to-one basis.

When the problems of physics or other weighty matters were laid aside, Teller was gregarious and witty. He was a raconteur of wry and ribald anecdotes and a good listener to the stories of his friends. He would laugh at his own jokes, or at someone else's, with a high-pitched giggle that contrasted with the deep solemnity of his normal voice.

The two scientists made light of each other's competence; this was sort of a running joke. Fundamentally they respected each other. Their work—considering that each had an enormous ego— was carried on with a remarkable complementarity.

Teller recalls the routine of a day that, if not typical, was at least frequent:

"In the morning I would be pulled out of bed by a phone call from Gamow. He would tell me about his latest theory. Now Gamow had a very fertile imagination. He was an exceedingly nice guy and, furthermore, he was the only one of my friends who really believed I was a mathematician. He relied on me for mathematics and for the corresponding checks on his theories. That was the basis of our collaboration.

"Now I'm sorry to say that ninety percent of Gamow's theories were wrong, and it was easy to recognize that they were wrong. But he didn't mind, he was one of those people who had no particular pride in any of his inventions. He would throw out his latest idea, and then treat it as a joke. He was a delightful person to work with.

"So, when I woke up I was—not every day, but frequently—confronted with the latest idea from Gamow. Then we may or may not get together later in the day and work on it a bit. We would prove it or disprove it or work some more on it."

Until he started working with Gamow, Teller's scientific work had involved mainly the applications of atomic physics to molecules. It was Gamow who was largely responsible for shifting Teller's interest to nuclear physics, that is to say, the physics that led to the development of nuclear weapons and nuclear energy and to Teller's eventual prominence in the development of the hydrogen bomb.

With Baltimore only forty miles away, Gamow also lectured at the Johns Hopkins University and many Johns Hopkins students came to Washington to attend lectures by Gamow or Teller. Alfred Sklar, a physicist, was a Hopkins graduate student who first became acquainted with both men during their earliest years in Washington. Sklar remembers that "Gamow was a scream. The Hopkins students used to call him 'goofy Gamow,' but in an endearing way." There was never any question of their genuine respect for Gamow as a nuclear physicist.

Sklar journeyed to Washington for a course with Teller on atomic spectra. He was impressed with Teller's ability to instill enthusiasm in his students. Teller never lectured from notes. He didn't ask questions; he encouraged questions from the students, and he gave them precise answers.

Despite the overlay of humor in Teller's lectures, the sessions were essentially serious and intense. "There was no sympathy sought or given," Sklar recalls. "It was a hard-hitting group. They didn't want sympathy, they wanted knowledge, and they got it. That's why Teller was popular."

On their arrival in Washington the Tellers had briefly lived in a small hotel. Within a few weeks they found a little brown-shingled row house on Garfield Street near Connecticut Avenue, in the shadow of the huge Wardman Park (now Sheraton Park) Hotel. They rented it and eventually lived there for six years. In the restless life of Edward and Mici, this was to be their longest stay in one dwelling until they moved to Berkeley in the 1950s.

During Christmas vacation Gamow and his wife, Loubov, an attractive but highly emotional Russian (they were later divorced), invited Mici and Teller to join them on an automobile trip to Florida.

"By that time we were old friends," Teller recalls. "And while Joe* was a completely unreliable physicist, he was an exceedingly reliable driver. In a way that is quite fitting because mistakes in driving are more irreversible than mistakes in physics."

The trip revealed a quirk in Gamow's nature that might have strained his friendship with Teller, but apparently did not.

"When we arrived in Miami," Teller remembers, "it started to become obvious that Joe was violently unhappy. Well, his wife—it just burst out of her—said Joe was unhappy because there were so many Jews in Miami, because Joe is really an anti-Semite.

"Joe got very red in the face and admitted that this was true. Well, his best friend in Russia was a Jew. The man he invited to be his colleague and collaborator—myself—was a Jew. Yet he was anti-Semitic.

"Since he couldn't take Miami, we moved out and over to the west coast of Florida, where we had a very fine time.

"But the kind of anti-Semite he was is not real, and shouldn't be taken seriously. I sensed that the real part of it was that Gamow

*Some of Gamow's friends called him Joe, possibly from the abbreviation of his name, Geo.

was violently anti-communist and that communism in Russia had been carried out to a great extent by Jews. So the discussion of anti-Semitism within a few minutes became a discussion of what the communists were doing to Russia. I had seen Gamow earlier in Copenhagen when he was just on a visit from Russia, and he was not inclined to talk about what he thought of the communists. This was the first time that we discussed politics, and once he had started, Gamow really let go and told me about all the harassments the physicists had had from the communist philosophers, from the dialectical materialists.

"He talked about censorship, about the lack of freedom, about his attempts to escape from Russia. I had heard a little about this, but never in such detail. And actually this was Christmas 1935 when I was much more worried about the Nazis than the communists."

Gamow, insofar as Teller could discern, was not yet alarmed about the Nazis.

"He didn't know much about them. He was not a politically minded person, except where his own experiences with the communists were involved. So from Gamow I heard that time in Miami and later quite a bit more about what the communists were doing in Russia and that was, in a way, a part of my education."

In those placid depression years, before the world cataclysm of 1939, the scientists of America generally showed little concern with either domestic or foreign political developments. In Europe the ugly fact of Nazi Germany had thrust politics into science, but most of those scientists who escaped to America seem to have yearned only to go back to their laboratories and their calculations. Teller and Gamow, having fled totalitarian repression, appeared to put the experience behind them. Neither Merle Tuve nor Alfred Sklar nor Hans Bethe, despite many hours in Teller's proximity, recalls his having any overt concern with politics.

Within a few years the situation would change, and change violently. Scientists would become both the pawns and the powerful in the world struggle for military supremacy. But the mid-1930s would, in retrospect, be seen as the wistful prelude to a nightmare era. In the broadest sense the time could be compared with Germany in the 1920s—the end of an era when scientists were left alone.

Meanwhile there were some mundane problems facing Gamow and Teller. Despite their extreme youth, they had both been hired as full professors of physics. Their salaries, Seeger recalls, were about $6,000 a year, which was exceptionally high for the depression era. Furthermore, this was about $2,000 better than any of the other scientists, many of whom outranked the two Europeans in experience and age. Seeger, who was at George Washington before Gamow and Teller, recalls the resentment in the university over the special privileges granted the newcomers. Tuve remembers the resentment being especially directed against Gamow because he wasn't asked to bear the burden of teaching freshmen. There was somewhat less concern over Teller's similar perquisites because he volunteered so much of his time to his students. But all of this was exactly what President Marvin intended. He was paying his two stars to delve into theoretical physics and bring glory to George Washington University—and they carried out their assignment.

The first Washington Conference on Theoretical Physics was held on April 21, 1935, five months before Teller's arrival in Washington. It was in accordance with Gamow's plan, but there had already existed a weekly physics colloquium organized by the physicists at the National Bureau of Standards. The colloquium provided a core of interested scientists for the annual conference, which was jointly sponsored by Tuve's Department of Terrestrial Magnetism at Carnegie and George Washington University.

Subsequently the conferences were held every year until the outbreak of World War II. Since there was no other comparable gathering of theoretical physicists anywhere in the United States, the Washington conference flowered into a major attraction. The enrollment was small—seldom more than about two dozen physicists—but they were the top theoretical men in America. Teller, who was present for the second conference and all those that followed, was, perhaps by the nature of his personality, the liveliest participant.

"These conferences," according to Teller, "were in general small and exciting, thoroughly absorbing, and also a little tiring. Somehow, most of the running of the conferences Gamow left to me."

In these Washington years Gamow was becoming increasingly interested in unlocking the secret of energy production in stars. The possibility that the energy from the sun and the stars came from nuclear sources was first suggested in 1928 by English and German physicists. Gamow was then in Russia and reported on these findings at a meeting in Leningrad. As he recounted the story to Teller, the communist officials became very excited about it. Gamow was told that if he could carry out experiments reproducing the process on earth, the government would, if necessary, turn over the whole power supply of Leningrad to him—assuming, of course, that the work could take place at night when the need for power elsewhere was minimal.

Gamow had to advise the communist functionaries that he, or anyone else, was a long way from being able to carry out such an experiment. To Teller, the story was unusual in that it demonstrated the dedication of the Russians to applied science. "They have misdirected it, sometimes violently misdirected it," Teller points out, "but they never have neglected it. At present that is a very particular American sin."

In 1937 Teller and Gamow together pursued their theoretical studies of thermonuclear energy—the energy released when atoms fuse together—and published a joint paper on the subject. It was the first formula giving the rate of thermonuclear reactions as a function of temperature. The theory was that the temperatures in the interior of the sun or the stars were sufficient to sustain the fusion of light nuclei, such as hydrogen, with the release of fantastic amounts of energy.

By 1938 there was enough general interest in the question of thermonuclear energy for Gamow and Teller to make it the principal topic of the annual Washington Conference on Theoretical Physics. The Gamow-Teller paper was one of those on the table. The conference served its purpose, not by providing answers but by posing enough questions to send some of the world's best scientists back to their laboratories and their blackboards to solve the riddle of the energy of the stars.

One of those whose interest was kindled was Hans Bethe, Teller's old friend from his days in Munich, Rome, and London. Bethe was now professor of theoretical physics at Cornell University, and was to become one of the most respected theoreticians in the world. He had studied with Sommerfeld in Munich and with Fermi in Rome. He was teaching at the University of Tübingen when Hitler came to power. The Nazis, with their police-state efficiency, found out that Bethe's mother was Jewish and he was summarily dismissed. Sommerfeld gave him a brief asylum in Munich and then arranged for his former pupil's emigration to England.

In Washington, Bethe and Teller resumed one of the warmest

and ultimately one of the most tragic relationships of Teller's life—a friendship that would later bend and break under the pressures of war and politics.

In 1938 all this heartache was in the future and Teller and Bethe thoroughly enjoyed each other's company. Teller phoned Bethe in an effort to lure him to the conference. Up to that point Bethe hadn't really been interested, but he let Teller persuade him. As a result, Bethe, Teller, and a Teller student, Charles Critchfield, stimulated by the conference, published an important new paper on the theory of energy production in the sun.

The previous year Bethe had made another trip to Washington to attend a meeting of the American Physical Society. There he met an old friend, Rose Ewald, daughter of Peter Paul Ewald, who had been Teller's teacher at Karlsruhe and Bethe's at the University of Stuttgart. When Bethe had last seen Rose, she was only twelve. Now she was nineteen, a refugee in America, studying physics at Duke University. She had approached Bethe in the hope that he could help her father find a job in the United States. Like Bethe, Rose Ewald had a gentile father and a Jewish mother. Up to this point her parents had managed to survive in Germany, but they were anxious to come to America.

What Bethe remembers best is that the conversation with Rose lasted about ten minutes, "but in that ten minutes I fell desperately in love." Bethe usually stayed with the Tellers when he visited Washington, so Edward and Mici took over the role of matchmakers. In the summer of 1937 they invited Hans and Rose to join them on a coast-to-coast vacation. The foursome traversed the United States, using Bethe's car. "It was a happy time for the Tellers and for me," says Bethe.

The trip included several mountain-climbing forays in the Rockies. Bethe recalls his amazement that Teller, with an artificial foot, managed to enjoy so challenging a sport. Only in the snow did Teller become unsure of his footing. When they reached California Enrico Fermi happened to be there on a brief visit to Stanford University. It was a sentimental reunion for three old friends from the days in Rome.

Fermi at this time was still living in Italy, but was disgusted with Mussolini and the ruthless Italian invasion of Ethiopia. He was also alarmed at Mussolini's gradual inclination toward Hitler's anti-Semitism. It was a personal danger to Fermi because his lovely and talented wife, Laura, was Jewish. A year after this visit to Stanford,

Fermi was to win the Nobel prize in physics. Granted permission to travel to Stockholm for the formal award ceremony, Fermi would use the opportunity to effect a dramatic escape from Italy. Once again a great scientist would carry his talents to the United States.

The worsening situation in Europe forced a sad decision on Teller. In 1936, the first year after his arrival in the New World, he and Mici had returned to Budapest for a reunion with their families. It was their intention thenceforth to return to Hungary every other year. By 1938, however, Hitler had annexed Austria, and the Nazi influence was beginning to smother Hungary. Teller was fearful that if he returned he might never be allowed to leave. The Hungarian visit was postponed in favor of a domestic vacation. Teller never saw his father again—Max Teller died in 1950—and he was not reunited with his mother and Emmi until 1958, after a twenty-two-year separation. In the interim, they had undergone unbelievable suffering at the hands of the Nazis and the communists.

In the late 1930s, however, whatever private burdens Edward and Mici bore on behalf of their families in Budapest, their Washington house on Garfield Street was a cheerful haven for scientists visiting Washington as well as the casual drop-ins from the local classrooms and laboratories. To Mici, "Sometimes it seems as if we had company every evening." Bethe recalls, "There were always people in their house—graduate students of his own as well as young chemistry professors who wanted his advice on chemical problems. He had always worked on molecular physics, which borders on chemistry, and he had a very close connection to the chemists in the Washington community."

As Alfred Sklar told us: "In the late thirties, Edward Teller's modest home served as a mecca for a sizable part of those who were thinking about new scientific things in the Washington-Baltimore area. It soon got about in the local community that Teller was interested in the whole gamut of chemical and physical problems, that he was happy to talk about your problems, and that you would come away with some new approach or a new avenue through your scientific maze. Among those who came and went were James Franck, who talked about fluorescence and photosynthesis; Merle Tuve, Larry Hafstad, and Charles Critchfield on nuclear phenomena; F. O. Rice on mechanism of chemical reactions; Herta Spooner, K. F. Herzfeld, and myself on light absorption and molecular spectra; Stephen Brunauer on absorption and catalysis, and a host of specialists from the government bureaus. All relished Teller's 'compenetración,' his quickness in grasping the essence of your problem, and his uncanny ability to make good his half-jest—'I don't understand it, but I will explain it to you.' This was Teller's way of saying that without completely understanding your problem, he could nonetheless offer some ideas which would help *you* understand the problem yourself. This was precisely Teller's forte, his highly developed technique in regard to the mechanism of scientific understanding which, in essence, starts from the perception of obscure interdependence between apparently unrelated concepts, and the construction of speculative models. In later years Edward Teller was to be among the relatively few scientists who appreciated that their scientific technique and method was equally useful and powerful in grappling with problems in nonscientific areas."

Sklar points out one important way in which the world of science has changed: "The modern scientific community has grown so vastly that it is today somewhat difficult to visualize just how intellectually lonely was a specialist's life in those early days, when one might be quite alone with one's interest in a given problem. In those days, Teller was a warmly interested and kindred spirit for the whole scientific community of the area, to all of whom he enjoyed offering his uncanny technique for understanding."

Teller's ability to deal with so many problems meant, according to Sklar, that his scientific friends would end a visit "with a little clearer idea of where to go next."

Mici Teller still insists she enjoyed being a hostess around the clock. "I didn't mind it at all," she says, "because, after all, I didn't have anything else to do." But—according to Bethe—she did mind a little if she had to go into the kitchen during an interesting discussion. "Don't say anything interesting while I'm gone," she would plead, to no avail, as she left the room. When the annual physics conferences were on, Mici sometimes worked almost to exhaustion.

Teller's own scientific work during this period was primarily derived from the basic developments of quantum mechanics by Bohr, Schrödinger, and Heisenberg. Bohr's quantum theory of the atom had been published back in 1913. He established that the mechanical energy of electrons in an atom could exist only in discrete, separate states. This was in contradiction to classical electrodynamics. Bohr showed that the spectra of the atoms rose when the electrons jumped up or down in energy from one another of the steady states, absorbing or emitting the energy difference as light. It was a concept that defied the logic of the conventional mind—how could energy exist at one level or another level but nothing in between?

Bohr's discoveries were amplified over the next decade. For example, it was shown that not all jumps between Bohr's steady states occurred—as if when climbing a flight of stairs a few treads were missing. Some jumps were absent or "forbidden." A set of "selection rules" was developed to predict which jumps would occur in the spectra. It was Schrödinger and Heisenberg who, in 1925, independently formulated the laws of this new concept of quantum mechanics. Their findings initiated a new era by making it possible to calcute, *a priori*, the behavior of atomic systems.

The understanding of quantum mechanics required tedious computations even for the simplest systems. Teller himself made a contribution in his doctoral thesis when he calculated the energy states of the hydrogen molecular ion, the smallest of all molecules. In the middle thirties there were attempts to understand the states of certain larger, organic molecules, especially when it appeared that when such a molecule absorbed light, the atoms in the molecule became less tightly bound together. This implied that quantum mechanics could provide the tools to calculate the states of molecular bonding—a major advance in the science of chemistry. (Teller's contention is that quantum mechanics abolished the dividing line between physics and chemistry.)

It was these problems that were involving Teller at George Washington University, Alfred Sklar and Maria Mayer at Johns Hopkins, and many others who called on Teller at the house on Garfield Street.

In the summer of 1937 Teller, in the most tranquil period of his adult life, caught a fleeting glimpse of his future in the person of J. Robert Oppenheimer. Teller went to Berkeley to address a physics colloquium at the University of California. It was during that visit that he met Oppenheimer. The meeting was casual. As one of the hosts, Oppenheimer took Teller to a Mexican restaurant for dinner. Teller found the plates hot, the spices hot, and Oppenheimer's personality "overpowering."

It was not a surprising reaction to Oppenheimer but, unfortunately, there seems to be no record of Oppenheimer's first reaction to Teller. Perhaps he might have chosen the same word. There was a remarkable similarity between these two future scientific giants, each building a reputation at opposite ends of the country, each moving on a kind of predestined course toward their final, destructive confrontation.

Except that both were Jewish, there was no similarity in their origins. Teller, though protected by his middle-class family, had not been able to avoid the experience of revolution, unrest, political turmoil, and physical threat. Oppenheimer, four years older than Teller, grew up in complete physical security, the son of a German immigrant who became a wealthy fabric importer. His mother was an intelligent, gentle, and artistic woman from a prominent Baltimore family. They wintered in Manhattan and summered in a comfortable cottage at Bay Shore, Long Island. The environment of their home was almost totally intellectual, a milieu of art, music, and books.

Robert Oppenheimer was brilliant and precocious. He had an insatiable enthusiasm for all kinds of knowledge, from languages to mathematics. Philip M. Stern in *The Oppenheimer Case* reports that "at the age of nine or so he was challenging an older girl-cousin to 'ask me a question in Latin and I will answer you in Greek.'"[1]

He had one idiosyncrasy that made him amazingly similar to Teller. From his earliest childhood he was fascinated with mathematics and, like Teller, would work out a problem in his mind and become completely detached from his surroundings. His interest in science began at five when his grandfather gave him a box of minerals. At twelve he delivered a learned paper in the New York Mineralogical Club. He went through Harvard in three years, graduating *summa cum laude*.[2]

When he had settled on physics as a career he went in 1925 to Europe, studying successively at Cambridge, Göttingen (several years before Teller's arrival there), and the University of Leyden in Holland. He had the same kind of quick insight that Teller had into complex problems. He had other qualities that were remindful of Teller. Teller could be arrogant, Oppenheimer was more so; Teller could be impatient, Oppenheimer was more so. On the other hand, Teller was gregarious, Oppenheimer was shy; Teller was witty, Oppenheimer was intense; Oppenheimer was handsome, Teller was not.

At twenty-five, Oppenheimer, whose reputation as a virtual genius had spread through academe, was offered a joint teaching post at Berkeley and at the California Institute of Technology in Pasadena. In a very short time his brilliance as a teacher, especially of other gifted students (he was impatient and intolerant in dealing with slow ones), and the depth and breadth of his intellect turned him into a towering figure at Berkeley. Almost single-handed he made the University of California comparable to Göttingen, Copenhagen, or Cambridge. The students and adherents of Oppenheimer became somewhat of a cult.

Hans Bethe, who knew both Teller and Oppenheimer well, told us that "fundamentally they were very similar. Teller had an extremely quick understanding of things, so did Oppenheimer. Oppenheimer established a great school of theoretical physics at which he discussed absolutely everything with his students, and inspired them. Teller did much the same thing. The difference was that Oppenheimer was concerned with the most profound problems at the frontier of physics—those problems that were mostly not solved and largely not solvable at the time. He worried a great deal about very deep problems.

"Teller's problems were more in the developed parts of physics. They were very largely in chemical physics where the fundamental theory was already understood. Therefore the Oppenheimer school had a much greater influence on the development of theoretical physics in the United States. But their methods were similar. They liked long discussions with their students and with their colleagues, and they both liked to discuss things orally.

"They were also somewhat alike in that their actual production, their scientific publications, did not measure up in any way to their capacity. I think Teller's mental capacity is very high, and so was Oppenheimer's but, on the other hand, their papers, while they include some very good ones, never reached really the top standards. Neither of them ever came up to the Nobel prize level. I think you just cannot get to that level unless you are somewhat introverted."

Teller was certainly not introverted, as Bethe confirms. If there was anything confining about the Tellers and their circle in Washington, it was only that the company was almost exclusively made up of scientists. This is probably why nearly everyone who recalls Edward and Mici at that time emphasizes their lack of concern with politics and in fact with the overall state of the world, except with the underlying fear of Hitler. Mici Teller speculates that she and Edward were too new to the United States to understand it. If they didn't understand it politically, however, they were striving to learn more about its geography in their annual vacations that crisscrossed the continent.

The other common recollection of the Washington era is that despite depression and the threat of war, it was a rewarding time for the scientific community. The United States had become the golden door for the best scholars of Europe, and refugees and native Americans flourished in the sweet air of freedom.

Like the 1920s in Germany, the 1930s in the United States are a nostalgic decade for most scientists because those years represented the end of an era. In Germany in the 1920s the end was signaled by the onset of the Nazi cruelty; in the United States in the 1930s the end came when the demands of war made basic science a defense commodity instead of an academic pursuit. For physicists like Edward Teller or J. Robert Oppenheimer, their lives would never again be so tranquil. The change in eras can be marked by a specific event that occurred on January 26, 1939, in the presence of Edward Teller and other physicists. After that, the nonpolitical scientist became an endangered species.

5

Duty Whispers Low

ON January 16, 1939, John A. Wheeler, a young Princeton physicist, stood on a New York pier and watched the *Drottningholm* edge ponderously into its berth. Wheeler was meeting Niels Bohr, unaware that Bohr was carrying news of a scientific achievement comparable to the discovery of fire. The original reason for Bohr's journey was to lecture and study for several months at the Institute for Advanced Study in Princeton, and to attend the Washington Conference on Theoretical Physics, hosted by Gamow and Teller.

Enrico and Laura Fermi were also there to welcome Bohr. Only three weeks earlier they had arrived in the United States after their breathtaking escape from fascist Italy. Fermi was now on the staff at Columbia University.

When Bohr disembarked he greeted the Fermis and Wheeler warmly but he was obviously weary and tense. Immediately he expressed his fear over the threatening buildup of Nazi power in Europe. Then, while waiting for his baggage to clear customs, he took Wheeler aside and passed along some astounding, but still confidential, information. The atomic nucleus had been split.

Wheeler was awestruck: "I felt like the man who holds a finger out in the painting by Michelangelo in the Sistine Chapel—God had passed the message."

Wheeler was now the seventh person to learn about the event, and the first in the New World. The others were the two German scientists who had accomplished the feat, two émigré colleagues in Copenhagen and Stockholm, Bohr's colleague Leon Rosenfeld (who was also on the *Drottningholm*), and Bohr himself. Wheeler's sense of a majestic moment was not surprising. The very word—atom—is derived from the Greek, meaning that which can-*not* be split. The ancient concept was that a piece of matter could be cut into two parts, those parts cut again and again until the theoretical point where that which remained was so small it could not be divided any more. This was an atom. To go beyond this point was not only a defiance of the word's symbolic etymology, but was accomplishing the "impossible." When it finally happened, man had stepped over a new threshold in his manipulation of nature.

The first observed and confirmed splitting of the atomic nucleus* had taken place only a month before Bohr's arrival in America at the Kaiser Wilhelm Institute (now the Max Planck Institute) in Berlin. Two chemists, Otto Hahn, the institute's chemical director, and Fritz Strassmann, his research associate, had bombarded uranium with neutrons. When the bombarded uranium was chemically analyzed, portions of it had become barium—an entirely different element. The only plausible explanation was that the uranium nucleus had been split, the fractions becoming lighter elements, that is, elements with fewer protons and neutrons in their nuclei than the original uranium. It was the realization of the alchemist's ancient dream of changing one element into another.

The history of the assault on the nucleus went back several decades. The key to nuclear research was radioactivity. The discovery that certain natural elements emit several kinds of radiation gave the scientists a tool with which to bombard various elements in the periodic table of elements from which everything in the universe is constructed. The radioactivity was like a geologist's pick, chipping away the target element to learn more of its nature. The task was made easier by the fact that certain nonradioactive elements, when irradiated, become themselves radioactive.

The acknowledged discoverer of the atomic nucleus was Ernest Rutherford, a New Zealander who worked successively at McGill University in Montreal and at the Cavendish Laboratory of Cambridge University in England. Rutherford used alpha particles, a form of radiation, to bombard various elements. In the course of his experiments he established the basic structure of the atom as a solid nucleus surrounded by electrons.

The chemical elements were found to contain, in the nucleus, protons ranging from one in the atom of hydrogen, the lightest element, to ninety-two in uranium, the heaviest element in the so-called periodic table. Protons have a positive electrical charge and

*The "splitting of the atom" means the splitting of the nucleus of the atom. When the atom's structure was established as a central nucleus surrounded by electrons, there was no mystery in the addition or subtraction of electrons, which is a part of every chemical change.

are balanced by the same number of electrons, of negative charge.

In 1932, James Chadwick, a student of Rutherford, discovered another particle in the nucleus, the neutron. It has the same mass as the proton, but is electrically neutral. The discovery thus not only disclosed a major constituent of the nucleus, but gave scientists a new tool for attacking the nucleus in order to learn more about it. A neutron, fired at the nucleus, penetrates more easily because of its neutral charge, and therefore is more effective in the chipping-away process that yields the secrets of the nucleus.

There was, however, a more ominous aspect of the neutron discovery, and physicist Leo Szilard, in 1934, was apparently the first to recognize it. The particles in the nucleus are held together by powerful binding forces that even today are not understood. If a neutron, fired from an outside source, penetrates the nucleus, might it not, in turn, break the bond holding other neutrons within, sending them, bulletlike, outward to penetrate other nuclei, liberating more neutrons, and creating a chain reaction that would release a cataclysmic amount of energy?

As a practical matter it was discovered that a number of elements—beryllium, for example—could be bombarded with X rays and would then become radioactive and emit neutrons. Beryllium became one of the major sources of neutron supply. A number of scientists, particularly Enrico Fermi, in 1934 when he was still in Rome, methodically fired neutrons at most of the elements in the periodic table.

The most promising targets were the heavier elements, particularly uranium, the heaviest of all. Fermi, however, did not envision that this submicroscopic geologist's pick would split a nucleus asunder. All he expected was a chipping away so as to produce an element just below uranium in atomic weight, or to have the nucleus absorb the neutron and, through a shift in particles, create new, man-made elements which he called *transuranic* (beyond uranium). His expectations were ultimately fulfilled in the creation of neptunium, plutonium (now used in nuclear bombs and potentially as a nuclear power-plant fuel), and a whole succession of man-made elements heavier than uranium.

It is probable that in the course of his experiments Fermi split an atom and didn't realize it. It is almost certain that in France Irene Joliot-Curie and an associate, Pavel Savitch, split an atom, then failed to analyze and interpret their own experiment adequately.

Hahn and Strassmann, on that memorable day in December

1938, carefully analyzed their findings, but still had doubts. Until only a few months earlier, Hahn's principal associate had been physicist Lise Meitner, an Austrian citizen who was Jewish. When the Nazis marched into Austria in the Anschluss of March 1938, all Austrians automatically became German citizens. Meitner, a small, intense and brilliant scientist, knew she was in danger and fled Germany, briefly to Holland and then to the Nobel Institute in Stockholm. Hahn, who had immense faith in Meitner's expertise, wrote to her and outlined what had happened. She wrote back, expressing her excitement over Hahn's findings. Then, by coincidence her nephew, Otto Frisch, another notable refugee physicist, arrived from Denmark for a Christmas visit.

Meitner and Frisch analyzed and reanalyzed the findings of Hahn and Strassmann but, thinking as physicists, recognized a further possibility. If an atom is split, some of its mass is destroyed and transformed into energy in accordance with Einstein's formula, $E=mc^2$. When he went back to Copenhagen, Frisch repeated the Hahn-Strassmann experiment, measuring not only the chemical change in the bombarded uranium, but also the release of energy. The fact of the split atomic nucleus was confirmed. Frisch coined the term "fission" to describe the breaking apart of the nucleus, borrowing the word from biology, where it is used to describe the splitting apart of cells as they multiply.

Frisch passed the news along to Bohr just before he left for his voyage to America, though Bohr departed before Frisch's confirmation of the Hahn-Strassmann findings had been completed. Bohr told his associate Rosenfeld, and then no one else until he met Wheeler at the New York pier on January 16. Otherwise, he had pledged to keep the news a secret until Frisch and Meitner (or Hahn and Strassmann) had published it.

There are a number of versions of how the news finally leaked out to a few scientists in America. Rosenfeld, shortly after his arrival, may have mentioned it to a group of scientists who met at Princeton as the Journal Club. Within a few days Fermi had learned about it.

The fifth Conference on Theoretical Physics was to open on January 26, which was just nine days after Bohr's arrival in America. Bohr went to Washington the day before the conference. From this point on there are more conflicting recollections. Sometime on the afternoon or evening of the 25th, Bohr apparently either heard from Frisch that the atom-splitting story had been published, or received the January 6 issue of the German scientific journal *Die Naturwissenschaften* in which the Hahn-Strassmann findings were revealed.

Late in the evening of the 25th, Teller received an excited call from Gamow (this was not too surprising—Gamow was usually excited).

"That Bohr has gone crazy," Gamow sputtered in his Russian accent. "He says the uranium nucleus splits."

But the next morning, Gamow, who was presiding, postponed the regular agenda and announced that Professor Bohr wished to be heard. The audience could hardly have been more impressive. There were some fifty luminaries from the world of theoretical physics facing the rostrum.

Bohr told them the whole story, of the Hahn-Strassmann experiment and the follow-up confirmation of Lise Meitner and Otto Frisch. There was no room for doubt. A nucleus had been split and, in splitting, released vast quantities of energy.

The conference was thrown into turmoil. Its scheduled topic was low-energy physics. This was momentarily forgotten in the excitement over Bohr's message. The physicists found themselves questioning and arguing the issue. If energy was liberated, how much? According to Alfred Sklar it was Teller who brought up the most far-reaching question. Suppose, Teller theorized, the splitting of the nucleus releases more neutrons and thus sets up a chain reaction?

The remarkable aspect of the Hahn-Strassmann and Meitner-Frisch achievements was that the experiment was a relatively simple one to perform. "It had been lurking under the surface of physics for years, waiting for someone to discover it," said Teller, many years later.

It is probable that, even before Bohr spoke to the Washington conference, at Columbia University's Pupin Physics Laboratory, Fermi's associate John R. Dunning had already accomplished the first splitting of the nucleus in the United States.

Whoever was first, all the scientists at the conference were anxious to repeat the experiment. Baltimore being only forty miles away, a large part of the Johns Hopkins delegation rushed back to their accelerator and had split a nucleus before the afternoon was over. In Washington Merle Tuve dispatched his Carnegie Institution colleague Larry Hafstad back to their laboratory. "Put a new filament in the particle accelerator," said Tuve.

That evening Tuve invited Bohr, Rosenfeld, and Teller to his laboratory in Carnegie's Department of Terrestrial Magnetism.

It was nearly midnight when the small band of physicists arrived in the semi-darkened building and made their way to the particle accelerator. The small uranium target was in place and was soon being blasted with neutrons. The story was told by the green line on the unassuming face of the attached oscilloscope. The line would flutter and then suddenly pulse upward explosively. It was measuring the burst of energy each time a uranium nucleus was split. The epochal event was happening in their presence.

"The state of excitement challenged description," said Rosenfeld.[1] Teller, in contrast, was blasé about the reaction taking place. As a theoretician, he found that the excitement came with the discovery that a particular event was certain to happen. Seeing it happen was an anticlimax. "I just wasn't excited," he says.

Most scientists were, though, and not just in Washington and New York. The word had spread across the country and soon the University of Chicago and the University of California at Berkeley joined the atom-splitting club. Leo Szilard, in bed with the flu at Princeton, did not attend the Washington conference, but on January 25 he wrote to Lewis Strauss: "This is entirely unexpected and exciting news for the average physicist. The Department of Physics at Princeton [where Szilard was a visitor] was like a stirred antheap."[2]

Every scientist who attended the conference remembers the moment that Bohr spoke, the way other Americans who were alive then remember the first news of such events as Lindbergh's flight, or Pearl Harbor, or D-Day. The memory becomes more powerful as, in retrospect, they realize that from that quiet event in a Berlin laboratory came a permanent change in man's place in the world, subsequently emphasized by staggering events—the bombing of Hiroshima, the development of atomic power, the invention of the hydrogen bomb, the nuclear arms race with its balance of terror, and the still wistful hope of abundant energy for all the nations of the earth.

Leo Szilard, who probably foresaw the atomic age before any other physicist,* was on the train to Washington a day or so later to

---

*But not before British writer H. G. Wells, whose 1913 novel, *The World Set Free*, predicted atomic energy and atomic bombs by 1956.

talk the situation over with Teller. Although they were both Hungarians and had known each other since childhood, the paths of Edward Teller and Leo Szilard had not crossed often in subsequent years. From 1939, however, their lives would become increasingly interwoven.

According to Teller, Szilard's involvement began at an inopportune time.

"The conference had run its exhausting course. When the last guest had left Washington, Mici just collapsed into a spacious chair in our living room. She was enjoying the first moments of repose in at least a week when the phone rang."

Edward answered the phone as Mici listened apprehensively.

Then it went something like this:

"Hello."

"Teller, this is Szilard."

"Where are you?"

"At the station—could you come and get me?"

"Just a moment," said Teller, and then, covering the mouthpiece, he turned to Mici. "It's Szilard. He's at the station."

"Oh, God," Mici moaned. "I like Szilard but I've had enough guests for a while. For heaven's sake, don't invite him here."

"All right, I won't, but we'll have to get him and take him to a hotel."

And, according to Teller's version (not entirely corroborated by his wife), they drove to Union Station and met Szilard, whereupon Mici immediately invited him to stay with them. The drive had apparently revived her.

Szilard graciously accepted. Then, when they had arrived at the Tellers' house and he had been shown to his bedroom he ungraciously refused their hospitality. The bed was too hard.

"I've tried to sleep on this bed before," said Szilard. "Where is the nearest hotel?"

"Luckily," said Mici, "we have one in our backyard. In case you've never heard of it, it's called the Wardman Park." The Wardman Park was the largest hotel in Washington.

"So for the next two days," said Teller, "we had Szilard's company in the daytime, but not at night because the bed was too hard."

In 1974 Teller recalled his serious conversations with Szilard while Mici remembered the rejection of their hospitality. Edward chided his wife: "Mici, nuclear fission has its place in history as well as the hardness of your guest-room bed."

Teller knew that Szilard had been one of the first to weigh the possibility of a nuclear chain reaction. In 1934 Szilard had broached the subject to Lord Rutherford at Cambridge but—as Szilard related it to Teller—"I was thrown out of Rutherford's office."

At that time Teller was in London, having just returned from Copenhagen. "Szilard was indignant and then sort of as a measure of revenge, took out a patent [on the nuclear chain reaction] which stood up and turned out to be quite valid. It was sold to the United States government after the Second World War. He got only $20,000 for it; much less than he should have."

What Szilard had done, more than four years before the Hahn-Strassmann breakthrough, was to name the three substances that he thought could be used in producing nuclear energy. They were uranium, thorium, and beryllium. He was—as Teller later pointed out—two-thirds right. He was wrong about beryllium, but that was only because in 1934 some incorrect measurements had been calculated for beryllium.

That was why, in January 1939, Szilard had come to see Teller—to get moral and practical support for his plan to initiate some experimental studies of fission. He had also called upon a third Hungarian, Eugene Wigner, at Princeton. Then he returned to New York to arrange some exploratory experiments with Enrico Fermi, Walter H. Zinn, and others. To Teller there was a key question to be answered by Szilard's experiments, a question that, answered positively, would portend an epochal change in the fortunes of mankind:

If neutrons produce fission, does fission produce neutrons?

This is to say, if a nucleus struck by a neutron in turn releases some of its own neutrons and sends them flying outward to strike adjacent nuclei, and the process keeps recurring, then there would be a chain reaction, as Szilard had envisioned it back in 1934. There would be a sudden release of unprecedented quantities of energy.

The answer was not long in coming.

One evening in March 1939 Teller was at home at the piano, playing a Mozart sonata. Music was still his favorite form of relaxation. To his annoyance, the second movement was interrupted by the harsh discord of the telephone bell. Mici answered; it was Szilard, calling from New York. Teller was reluctant to put the music aside, but in those days long-distance phone calls were usually placed only to convey important news. Szilard, Teller thought, must be calling for a good reason. Teller was right. The message was brief, and "coded" in Hungarian:

"I have found the neutrons."

Teller knew exactly what Szilard meant. The news followed directly from their conversations in January. Everything was adding up. Neutrons had been established, along with protons, as the basic building blocks of the nucleus. Whereas the proton has a positive electrical charge, the neutron, as its name indicates, is neutral. As Hahn, Strassmann, Meitner, Frisch, and their followers had shown, a neutron could be fired against a nucleus without any electrical repulsion and, under certain conditions, split the nucleus. Then what happened?

Szilard's phone call to Teller followed experiments he had carried out with Zinn at Columbia. They exposed beryllium to gamma rays from radium. This made the beryllium radioactive so that it emitted a stream of neutrons. These neutrons were directed at uranium oxide. Normally such neutrons travel at very high speeds (approaching that of light) and are described as *photoneutrons.* Their reaction with a nucleus, however, changes if their speed can be reduced, at which point they are described as *thermal* neutrons. Szilard and Zinn slowed down the neutrons from beryllium by passing them through paraffin. This increased the chance that the neutron would be absorbed or "captured" by the uranium nucleus.

The main question then was whether the uranium nucleus, on capturing the neutron from an outside source, would in turn be split and release additional neutrons, creating the chain reaction.

Szilard and Zinn, using complex laboratory measuring devices, left no doubt of it. During fission, each nucleus emitted at least two neutrons. The chain reaction was a fact. Controlled, it was potentially a beneficent source of energy. Uncontrolled, it was potentially a new concept of the ultimate weapon—a bomb that made the largest conventional bombs mere firecrackers.

Today Teller still remembers that telephone call from Szilard as the starting point of his own internal conflict on the role of this new force in the world.

"All my worries about nuclear energy—the full realization that it was coming, and coming very soon, and that it would be very dangerous—date back to that time in March 1939 when I was interrupted in the middle of a Mozart sonata."

There is an allegorical irony in the interruption of a Mozart sonata by the news of a nuclear chain reaction. Mozart, the supreme genius of a civilized art, of disciplined emotion, was silenced in Edward Teller's living room by the prospect of a force that could obliterate ten million genteel living rooms.

Even without the chain reaction, the obliteration was soon to take place from the conventional bombs of the German Luftwaffe, and then from the air forces of the nations that struck back. But from the start of World War II it was the possibility of the unleashing of nuclear power by Germany that worried so many scientists, including Teller and Szilard. After all, Germany was preeminent in physics; Hahn and Strassmann were Germans. Behind their quiet experiment in the Kaiser Wilhelm Institute was the leering countenance of Adolf Hitler.

If Szilard and his co-workers had established the probability of a nuclear chain reaction, there were still a thousand questions to be answered. One of the most important findings came from the visiting Niels Bohr and his former student, John A. Wheeler. In a paper entitled "The Mechanism of Nuclear Fission," published in the *Physical Review*, Bohr and Wheeler reported that ordinary uranium, U-238, was not fissionable. Fission could be produced only in an isotope of uranium, U-235, which accounted for only one part in 140 of ordinary uranium. In order to produce an explosion this minute quantity of U-235 would have to be separated from U-238, a task that, at the time, seemed next to impossible.

Of course, ultimately, the Manhattan Project did develop a means of extracting U-235 from U-238. It was fantastically elaborate, time-consuming, and expensive, yet necessary. But in 1939 there was a glimmer of hope of developing an entirely new kind of fissionable material. Uranium was element 92 in the periodic table, and was the heaviest material in nature. When uranium 238 captured a neutron, however, it theoretically would become U-239, which, through a series of particle transitions, briefly became a man-made element, number 93 in the periodic table, eventually named neptunium; and neptunium, it appeared, would then transmute itself into element 94, named plutonium. If plutonium turned out to be fissionable, it could provide an alternative to the needle-in-a-haystack extraction of U-235 from U-238. Ultimately both elements were used in the building of atomic weapons, but in 1939 plutonium was just a gleam in the eye of a few theoretical physicists.

Although Bohr and Wheeler, with their vital information on U-235, did pave the way to manufacturing fission bombs, the immediate effect on Bohr of his own work was just the opposite. He all but concluded that the problems involved in the separation of U-235 from U-238 made a bomb project impractical. He told Teller: "It can never be done unless you turn the whole United States into one huge factory." Bohr was not entirely wrong; the size of the ultimate isotope-separation plant in Oak Ridge, Tennessee, could have convinced a visitor that at least a large part of the United States was one huge factory.

As Bohr, Wheeler, Szilard, Fermi, and others contributed rapidly to the store of knowledge about nuclear fission, they, figuratively, looked over their shoulders toward Germany. Most of them, Teller included, felt war with Germany was certain. In September 1938 the appeasement of Hitler through the Munich Pact had proved fruitless. The Nazis were more threatening than ever. In March 1939 Hitler's armies marched into Czechoslovakia, which had already been partly handed over to Germany in the futile Munich agreement. The rest of the unhappy country crumbled without a fight. What Hahn and Strassmann had discovered would be fully appreciated by such brilliant physicists as Teller's former teacher, Werner Heisenberg, or his former colleague, Carl Friedrich von Weizsäcker. It was the beginning of that paradoxical era when men who had been professional colleagues and often intensely close personal friends were girding for mortal combat.

The German threat forced the American scientific fraternity into a policy that most of them intuitively despised—scientific secrecy. All of them had traditionally rejected the idea of science contained within national boundaries, but they were horrified at the thought of nuclear weapons in the hands of Hitler.

The Szilard-Zinn paper and a companion piece by Fermi with H. L. Anderson and H. B. Hanstein were ready for publication in early March 1939. But by this time this small faction that knew the awful potential of their discoveries decided voluntarily not to follow the usual procedure of publication in a scientific journal. It was a difficult decision, concurred in by Szilard and Teller,* but opposed by Fermi. In the last analysis, Fermi went along reluctantly with his colleagues.

The secrecy proposal was set back temporarily when on March 19 the Journal *Nature* carried a paper written by Frédéric Joliot and his co-workers. Independently, Joliot, in France, had reached many of the same conclusions and reported many of the same findings as had the group at Columbia. After some confusion and vacillation the scientists decided the Szilard and Fermi papers might just as well be published. They appeared in the *Physical Review* of April 15, 1939. Thenceforth, papers were published, but only after careful discussion and review of their military consequences. The interesting fact is that at this point the government was not involved at all. The censorship was entirely voluntary and centered mainly around the men at Columbia—Szilard, Fermi, and, most important, George B. Pegram, who was both an outstanding physicist and dean of the graduate schools.

This was a hint of the change that was to come about for a majority of America's best physicists. They had been used to working alone, or with a few colleagues. Their knowledge was built on their own studies and research and on the steady flow of published information from other scientists. They were independent; this was the essence of academic life. The idea of physicists being organized into a national team and subject to a government bureaucracy was unthinkable to most of them. They were pure scientists, elite, aloof, alone in their pursuit of knowledge for its own sake. Their paths occasionally crossed those of their colleagues in the humanities or the social sciences, but politicians were at the opposite end of the professional spectrum.

Leo Szilard was one of those who knew that the gap between physicists and political leaders would have to be bridged. He insisted on an approach to the federal government to impress on political leaders the urgency of beating the Nazis to the development of nuclear bombs. He was able to convey some of this sense of urgency to Pegram, to Fermi, to Teller, and to Merle Tuve. Among his concerns was the huge supply of uranium ore in the Belgian Congo, a buried treasure that was certainly coveted by Germany. There were also substantial uranium ore deposits in Czechoslovakia.

―――――――――――

*Later in life Teller became a consistent foe of all scientific secrecy. See below.

Is it possible to establish an exact date for the beginning of this merger of science and government that was to become the greatest and most expensive military-industrial-scientific project of all time? Apparently there is a starting point, and it may have been unnoticed but for a "fit of housekeeping enthusiasm" by Laura Fermi more than ten years later. Mrs. Fermi found a copy of a letter to Admiral S. C. Hooper, Chief of Naval Operations, from George Pegram. It was dated March 16, 1939, the very day that Hitler's armies marched unchallenged into Czechoslovakia, where they immediately halted exports of Czech uranium ore. Mrs. Fermi published the letter in the biography of her husband, *Atoms in the Family*.[3]

Pegram reported to Admiral Hooper on the possibility of using uranium as an explosive a million times more powerful than any known explosive. "My own feeling is that the probabilities are against this," he wrote, "but my colleagues and I think the bare possibility should not be disregarded."

He then advised the Chief of Naval Operations that Fermi would be in Washington to lecture before the Philosophical Society and would be getting in touch with him.

Fermi did call on Hooper, accompanied by Merle Tuve of the Carnegie Institution, who was more Washington-wise than Fermi, only three months away from his escape from Italy.

Teller's recollection is that the two scientists were "thrown out" of Admiral Hooper's office. Their rejection was not quite that abrupt, but certainly the Navy was not impressed. Laura Fermi's own belief is that the hesitancy of the whole process—Pegram's lack of conviction, Fermi's dropping in because he was already in Washington—doomed the overture to failure.

Arnulf and Louise Esterer, in their biography of Szilard, speculate that Fermi was handicapped by being foreign born and by his heavy accent.[4] He was advised that the Navy would "keep in contact" with him, a little like the don't-call-us-we'll-call-you routine. Still, a contact had been made and there is evidence that at least one person, Dr. Ross Gunn of the Naval Research Laboratory, began to show some interest.

Fermi, Szilard, and their associates were now teamed up in planning a full-scale experiment to set up a controlled nuclear chain reaction. This would involve building a furnace or "pile" in which a mass of uranium would be deposited, mixed with a "moderator" that would slow the emitted neutrons from each fission to thermal speed so that the capture and fission of adjacent nuclei would be facilitated. There was considerable controversy over what substance would provide the best moderator. Water was considered, as well as "heavy" water, which is composed of oxygen and deuterium, an isotope of hydrogen. Eventually, however, Szilard concluded that pure graphite would be the best moderator, and Fermi agreed.

Unfortunately, Fermi and Szilard did not agree very often. "They didn't get along, you know," Laura Fermi reminded the writers. Fermi was methodical and even-tempered. Szilard was explosive and domineering. Perhaps Hungarian blood was thicker than scientists' water, but Szilard was constantly seeking help and counsel from two fellow Hungarians, Eugene Wigner at Princeton and Edward Teller at George Washington.

The one point Fermi and Szilard did agree on was that Teller should be invited to Columbia in the summer of 1939 to assist in the project. Both men were fond of Teller and perhaps saw him as a catalyst. For Fermi, however, the question of Teller's presence for the summer was figuratively as well as literally academic because in late June Fermi left Columbia to spend the summer lecturing at the University of Michigan in Ann Arbor. Pegram, as dean and head of physics, advised the unhappy Szilard that any further experimental work would have to await Fermi's return in the fall.

Meanwhile Edward and Mici temporarily abandoned their Washington house and moved to an apartment in New York on Morningside Heights. Teller's assignment was to lecture to graduate students as well as to consult and provide theoretical advice to the team that was planning the nuclear reactor. "We had a nice apartment near Columbia where the wind blew in one window and out the other, even though the two windows were in the same wall. I never understood the hydrodynamics of that, but it is a fact."

In June the American Physical Society held its annual meeting at Princeton. Szilard, watching the ominous development in Europe as Hitler became increasingly bellicose, made another appeal to the Navy. Ross Gunn, in his capacity as the Naval Research Laboratory advisor, was among those at the meeting. Szilard pleaded with him for Navy support of the uranium project. There was no doubt of the interest in uranium of the Navy's more sophisticated scientists, though more as a power source than as an explosive. Primarily through the efforts of Gunn, Admiral Harold G.

Bowen, director of the Naval Research Laboratory, had made a gesture to get a small research grant for investigation of uranium as a source of power. The research laboratory's hope was for a fuel for submarines that would not make the oxygen demands that limited the undersea time and the range of conventional power.

Szilard's frustration increased when, a few weeks later, Gunn wrote to him advising that, regretfully, the Naval Research Laboratory could not provide a grant for the experiment.

In desperation, Szilard went down to Princeton to discuss the situation with Wigner. It was then that Einstein's name came into the picture. Coincidentally, Einstein had a long-standing personal friendship with the Belgian royal family, especially with Elizabeth, Queen of the Belgians. Wigner and Szilard consulted with the patriarch of physics on the possibility of his writing a letter to the queen, warning her that the vast deposits of uranium ore in the Belgian Congo should not be allowed to fall into the hands of the Germans. Einstein consented, although all three agreed that the action would have to be approved by the U.S. State Department.

After their discussion with Einstein, Szilard began to have second thoughts about merely approaching the Belgians. It was more important, he believed, to get government support for nuclear research in the United States. Somehow, the President of the United States, Franklin D. Roosevelt, had to be reached. Through Lewis Strauss, later to become a dominant figure in the atomic establishment, Szilard had met a refugee Austrian economist, Gustav Stolper. Stolper told Szilard that Alexander Sachs, a New York banker and economist, was a personal friend of the President and could reach the White House directly. Sachs also happened to have a strong layman's interest in nuclear physics and had already pointed out to Roosevelt the significance of the new developments.

Szilard now redirected his efforts toward Sachs. The scientist and banker met in New York in late July. Sachs believed that the lack of a more positive approach on the part of Fermi and Pegram had been at least partly to blame for the lack of government interest in the efforts made up to that time. He agreed that a letter signed by Einstein, delivered by Sachs, would make the President sit up and take notice.

The subsequent events are an outstanding example of how honest men can differ in their recollections of an important event in history. There is no question that the basic outline of such a letter was agreed upon by Sachs, Szilard, and Wigner. There is no question that Szilard and Wigner visited Einstein at his rented summer home in Peconic, Long Island, on Sunday, July 30, 1939, driving out there in Wigner's car. According to the Esterer biography of Szilard, Einstein "then and there dictated a letter to Roosevelt, which Wigner took down in longhand."[5] On the other hand, Lewis Strauss, in his autobiography, reports that the letter was drafted in Sachs's office,[6] a version that is supported by evidence in the official history of the Atomic Energy Commission by Hewlett and Anderson.[7] However the letter was composed, Wigner's secretary typed it in Princeton the next morning.

The following Wednesday Teller was in his office in Columbia when Szilard appeared unexpectedly and asked if Teller could give him a lift out to Long Island. Wigner was not able to make the trip that day. "Where in Long Island?" Teller asked. "Wherever Einstein lives," said Szilard. Teller agreed.

Szilard could not drive at all and Teller was the owner of an aging 1935 Plymouth. Teller established roughly where Peconic was located and they set out, the typed version of the letter ready for the signature of the most famous scientist in the world. After what Teller describes as "one minor breakdown," they found the general vicinity of Peconic, but they couldn't zero in on Einstein's house, which was owned by a friend, Dr. Moore.

Teller recalls: "Finally we found a little girl about ten years old, with pigtails, but she couldn't help us when we asked for Dr. Einstein. Then Szilard said, 'You know—he's a man with long, flowing white hair.' That was enough—then she knew where he lived.

"We had the letter already typed, so Szilard just handed it to Einstein, who greeted us wearing old clothes and slippers. He gave us some tea and drank some himself while he read the letter. Then he signed it. His only remark was that this would be the first time that man exploits nuclear energy directly rather than indirectly through solar radiation, where the origin was nuclear in any case."

Who actually wrote one of the most famous letters in history? To Teller there is no question: "Szilard always represented the letter as written by Einstein. But I am convinced that Szilard was lying. The man who wrote that letter, in my opinion, was none other than Szilard, with some possible assistance from Eugene Wigner. Einstein did not impress me like the man who had written the letter, though he may have done so."

This is the letter that Einstein signed:

Albert Einstein
Old Grove Road
Nassau Point
Peconic, Long Island
August 2, 1939

F. D. Roosevelt
President of the United States
White House
Washington, D.C.

Sir:

Some recent work by E. Fermi and L. Szilard, which has been communicated to me in manuscript, leads me to expect that the element uranium may be turned into a new and important source of energy in the immediate future. Certain aspects of the situation which has arisen seem to call for watchfulness and, if necessary, quick action on the part of the Administration. I believe, therefore that it is my duty to bring to your attention the following facts and recommendations:

In the course of the last four months it has been made probable—through the work of Joliot in France as well as Fermi and Szilard in America—that it may become possible to set up a nuclear chain reaction in a large mass of uranium, by which vast amounts of power and large quantities of new radium-like elements would be generated. Now it appears almost certain that this could be achieved in the immediate future.

This new phenomenon would also lead to the construction of bombs, and it is conceivable—though much less certain—that extremely powerful bombs of a new type may thus be constructed. A single bomb of this type, carried by boat and exploded in a port, might very well destroy the whole port together with some of the surrounding territory. However, such bombs might very well prove to be too heavy for transportation by air.

The United States has only very poor ores of uranium in moderate quantities. There is some good ore in Canada and the former Czechoslovakia, while the most important source of uranium is the Belgian Congo.

In view of this situation you may think it desirable to have some permanent contact maintained between the Administration and the group of physicists working on chain reaction in America. One possible way of achieving this might be for you to entrust with this task a person who has your confidence and who could perhaps serve in an unofficial capacity. His task might comprise the following:

a) to approach Government departments, keep them informed of the further development, and put forward recommendations for Government action, giving particular attention to the problem of securing a supply of uranium ore for the United States;

b) to speed up the experimental work which is at present being carried on within the limits of the budgets of university laboratories, by providing funds if such be required, through his contacts with private persons who are willing to make contributions for this cause, and perhaps also by obtaining the cooperation of industrial laboratories which have the necessary equipment.

I understand that Germany has actually stopped the sale of uranium from the Czechoslovakian mines which she has taken over. That she should have taken such early action might perhaps be understood on the ground that the son of the German Under-Secretary of State, von Weizsäcker, is attached to the Kaiser-Wilhelm-Institute in Berlin where some of the American work on uranium is now being repeated.

Yours very truly,
Albert Einstein

Szilard returned the letter to Sachs and then, at Sachs's suggestion, added a memorandum making the point that a chain reaction using slow neutrons was a virtual certainty. A chain reaction with fast neutrons was less certain, but, if possible, would make atom bombs a probability. To complete the dossier, Sachs wrote his own covering letter.

Since the letter was to be hand-delivered by Sachs, he had to bide his time awaiting an opportunity for an appointment with the President. This proved to be more difficult than was first anticipated because Europe was moving rapidly toward war. On August 23 the German-Soviet nonaggression pact was signed, clearing the way for Hitler's planned invasion of Poland. In the early morning of September 1, 1939, the wires from Europe crackled with a three-word bulletin: "Germany invades Gdynia." A few minutes later came a second bulletin, datelined Berlin: "Hitler orders army to 'meet force with force.'" The years of threat and bluster and tension were over. World War II had begun.

Teller was among those who, through a refugee's firsthand experience, had been growing increasingly alarmed and pessimistic about any stable future for the world so long as the Nazis existed. "The actual beginning of the Second World War even came as a relief because I was convinced that in the end only the war could stop Hitler's takeover of the world."

On September 3 Great Britain and France declared war on Germany. On September 8 President Roosevelt declared a state of limited national emergency in the United States. It was impossible during this crisis period for Sachs to knock on the President's door.

Sachs finally got his appointment on October 11, more than two months after the Einstein letter was written. Also present at the White House meeting were Roosevelt's aide, General Edwin M. Watson, and two ordnance specialists summoned by Watson, Army Colonel Keith F. Adamson and Navy Commander Gilbert C. Hoover. As the meeting concluded, Roosevelt properly assessed the situation. "Alex," he said, "what you are after is to see that the Nazis don't blow us up." Then he told General Watson, "This requires action."[8]

Action, however, is seldom precisely that when dealing with the federal and military bureaucracy. The United States government had never had an effective continuing liaison with the nation's scientists, though various formal and ad hoc arrangements had existed since the Civil War when the National Academy of Sciences was formed to honor scientific scholarship and to advise the government on scientific matters.

Roosevelt's first step was taken almost immediately when he appointed an Advisory Committee on Uranium, which scheduled its first meeting on October 21. The chairman was Lyman J. Briggs, originally a soil physicist in the Department of Agriculture and in 1939 the director of the National Bureau of Standards. The other members were Colonel Adamson and Commander Hoover. Also invited were Fred L. Mohler of the Bureau of Standards and Richard B. Roberts of the Carnegie Institution. Roberts was substituting for his boss, Teller's friend Merle Tuve, who was out of town. Einstein was invited, but with his typical reticence in public affairs, he respectfully declined. At Sachs's suggestion, Leo Szilard was invited, and Szilard suggested that Eugene Wigner, Edward Teller, and Enrico Fermi be included.

Fermi included himself out. Though Szilard and Fermi were working together well as scientists, Fermi was distressed by Szilard's near-obsession with the urgency of the situation. Nevertheless, Szilard still wanted his Italian colleague at the meeting so he asked Teller to try and change Fermi's mind. Teller had returned to Washington from his summer in Columbia, but he considered it worth a trip to New York to persuade Fermi to attend.

"I told him he must come," Teller says, "but Fermi said he

won't, and when Fermi makes up his mind, then he has made up his mind." Then according to Teller's recollection, Fermi told him: "Edward, look. If I came, I know what I would say and I will tell you. You can speak for me."

Teller was amused at his role as Fermi's stand-in: "Having started my career in atomic energy as a chauffeur, I was now going to continue it as a messenger boy."

On October 21 the meeting got under way at the Bureau of Standards with an all-Hungarian triumvirate of academic physicists—Szilard, Wigner, and Teller.

As might be expected, Szilard dominated the meeting. He outlined the situation relative to the energy potential of fission. He was convinced that an atomic pile could be built if he and Fermi could obtain enough uranium oxide or uranium metal and enough pure graphite. The military ordnance experts were not impressed. They did not seem to comprehend that this was not just a question of a bigger explosion, but a new force beyond conventional imagination. The Esterers, in their Szilard biography, report that Colonel Adamson's comment—after he was told that 2.2 pounds of uranium would be equal to 20,000 tons of TNT—was that he had once been outside an ordnance depot when it blew up and it didn't even knock him down.[9]

Teller recalls a colonel (presumably Adamson) who said that he didn't "believe all this junk about complicated inventions; for instance, he had heard about a death ray and at Aberdeen Proving Ground [the Army's huge ordnance test area north of Baltimore] they have a goat tethered to a stake and they have offered $10,000 to anyone who could kill the goat with a death ray, but the goat is well and happy, thank you."

When the committee turned to Teller, he told them he didn't have anything to say for himself but that he had a message from Fermi. It was to the effect that in order to produce nuclear energy it would be necessary to slow down the neutrons in a schematic manner without absorbing them, then they would be absorbed in the rare isotope and there would be a good chance of making a nuclear reactor, which could then produce plutonium.

Then Teller, on his own, brought up the subject of money: "I said that this needed a little support. In particular we needed to acquire a good substance to slow down the neutrons, therefore we needed pure graphite, and this is expensive." Tuve had told Teller that the atomic pile project could be carried out for about $15,000. Teller settled for a more modest request—$2,000 for graphite and

$4,000 for everything else. The atomic age was to be launched for $6,000!

Colonel Adamson was still not convinced, and gave the scientists a lecture on the nature of war. It usually took two wars, he told them, before a new weapon could be fully developed and, besides, it was moral issues, not new arms, that brought victory.

Wigner was furious. If armaments were of so little importance, he suggested, why didn't the Army cut its budget by about thirty percent? Teller was equally indignant, although he didn't say what was on his mind—that the "moral superiority" of Hitler and Stalin had just smashed the Poles.

"I don't believe I was the only one with a little internal conflict when Adamson brought up that issue."

Adamson, facing the indignant scientists, retorted angrily, "All right, all right, you'll get your money."[10]

But they didn't get the money—not then, at least. There were to be four more months of bickering. The formal committee, which comprised only Briggs, Adamson, and Hoover, made a favorable recommendation to the President on November 1. Meanwhile Szilard continued his Gilbert-and-Sullivan partnership with Fermi, along with Herbert Anderson and others at Columbia. In Paris, Frédéric Joliot reported significant findings on the possibility of a controlled chain reaction with water as the moderator. Szilard, building from Joliot's work, now believed he would have an even better chance with graphite, and wrote another scientific paper to that effect.

The communications and negotiations continued, involving Einstein, Sachs, Pegram, Briggs, Szilard, and Admiral Bowen of the Naval Research Laboratory. No one seemed to be willing to go out on a limb and make a commitment. Eventually it was Sachs who put the pressure on Briggs's Uranium Committee. On February 20, 1940, the $6,000 appropriation was approved. It had taken four months to get what, even in 1940 dollars, was a tiny drop in the federal budget.

Soon afterward, intelligence reports reached Washington to the effect that the Kaiser Wilhelm Institute was initiating a full-fledged uranium fission research program.

The granting of that $6,000 was a symbolic turning point for Teller. He jokes that "I started as a chauffeur, I continued as a messenger boy, and at the Uranium Committee meeting I took on the stature of a financial genius." In truth, Teller was being wrenched from his academic involvement in physics, from his political innocence, into a new role as a scientific activist.

"To deflect my attention from physics, my full-time job which I liked, to work on weapons, was not an easy matter. And for quite a time I did not make up my mind. But this is one of the few instances when I can tell you, within an accuracy of twenty minutes, when I made up my mind."

After the Nazi war machine had invaded and devastated Poland, and annihilated a million Poles, World War II settled into the so-called phony war. Neither Britain nor France had the military forces to invade Germany and a stalemate set in. In the early spring of 1940 the Nazis marched, with very little resistance, into Denmark and Norway. Then there was a last pause before the total holocaust.

Early in April Teller received an invitation to the Eighth Pan American Scientific Conference to be held in Washington later in the spring, and to be keynoted by an address of President Roosevelt on May 10. Because of the anticipated size of the conference—several hundred people—Teller decided it would be more political than scientific. "I still wasn't really interested in politics and I had never seen Roosevelt. But I rather liked him as far as I understood his politics."

Teller accepted the invitation but was still inclined not to attend. Then, on May 8, Hitler's armies invaded the lowlands of Europe, the phony war was over and suddenly the Nazi menace cast a gigantic shadow across the world. The newspapers reported that the new phase of the war would be Roosevelt's topic. Teller decided to attend and hear what the President had to say.

Roosevelt, speaking to an audience of scientists from North, Central, and South America, deplored the invasion of Holland, Belgium, and Luxembourg. He pointed out that a free meeting of the type he was addressing could no longer take place in a large part of the world. He extolled the search for truth and the pursuit of progress through the conquering of disease, poverty, and discomfort. Then he continued:

> In contrast to that rather simple picture of our ideals, in other parts of the world teachers and scholars are not permitted to search for truth, lest the truth, when made known, might not suit the designs of their masters. Too often they are not allowed to teach the truth as they see it, because truth might make men free. . . .
> Today we know that until recent weeks too many citizens of our

American republics believed themselves wholly safe—physically, economically and socially from the impact of the attacks on civilization which are in progress elsewhere. Perhaps this mistaken idea was based on a false teaching of geography—the thought that a distance of several thousand miles from a war-torn Europe to a peaceful America gave us some kind of mystic immunity that could never be violated. . . .

You who are scientists may have been told that you are in part responsible for the debacle of today because of the processes of invention for the annihilation of time and space, but I assure you it is not the scientists of the world who are responsible, because the objectives which you held have looked toward closer and more peaceful relations between all nations through the spirit of cooperation and the interchange of knowledge. . . .

The great achievements of science and even of art can be used in one way or another to destroy as well as create; they are only instruments by which men try to do the things they most want to do. If death is desired, science can do that. If a full, rich, and useful life is sought, science can do that also. . . .

Can we continue our peaceful construction if all the other continents embrace by preference or by compulsion a wholly different principle of life? No, I think not.

Surely it is time for our republics to spread that problem before us in the cold light of day, to analyze it, to ask questions, to call for answers, to use every knowledge, every science we possess, to apply common sense and above all to act with unanimity and singleness of purpose.

I am a pacifist. You, my fellow citizens of twenty-one American republics, are pacifists too.

But I believe that by overwhelming majorities in all the Americas you and I, in the long run if it be necessary, will act together to protect and defend, by every means at our command, our science, our culture, our American freedom and our civilization.

Teller, the veteran of the oppression of Béla Kun, Admiral Horthy, and Adolf Hitler, was profoundly stirred by Roosevelt's message. As he interpreted it, the President was not suggesting something that scientists *may* do—"but something that was our duty and that we *must* do—to work out the military problems because, without the work of the scientists the war and the world would be lost.

"I had the strange impression," Teller recalls, "that he was talking to me. But my mind was made up and it has not changed since."

6

Prospects of Doomsday

THE call to Teller was not long in coming. In June 1940, a few weeks after Roosevelt's inspiring speech to the scientists, the Nazi war machine had subdued weak and demoralized France. The image of invincibility seemed to clothe the Germans and many feared they would quickly leap the English Channel and conquer the British.

Vannevar Bush, the lanky, amiable president of the Carnegie Institution, pressed Roosevelt to create a federal unit capable of facilitating the essential linkup between government and science. FDR responded in June 1940 with the creation of the National Defense Research Committee, headed by Bush and geared to applying science to the defense effort. The Uranium Committee was reconstituted as a part of the NDRC. Briggs was still the chairman, but he now reported to Bush. The new membership was composed of Pegram, Harold Urey, Jesse Beams, Tuve, and Gunn. Wigner, Fermi, Szilard, and Teller were named as consultants.

There were no foreign-born members of the Uranium Committee. Some officers of the Army and Navy, as well as many Congressmen (and probably many Americans) harbored an innate distrust of foreigners. This distrust created absurd, even comical situations. In 1940 neither Szilard nor Fermi had been in the United States long enough to acquire citizenship. At one point Alexander Sachs, himself a refugee, asked Uranium Committee chairman Briggs why Fermi and Szilard were not attending committee sessions. Briggs responded that it was a national security matter—the proceedings were *secret*. Sachs, in angry frustration, explained that the entire work of the committee was founded on the discoveries and expertise of the very scientists who were now being barred from it. Sachs's logic proved stronger than Brigg's bureaucratic instincts and the chairman relented. Szilard and Fermi were thenceforth allowed to discuss their own accomplishments, even to deal with their own secrets.[1]

There was no choice when it came to British scientists. Great Britain was the last Western European democracy not under the Nazi heel. British scientists were conducting investigations in fission research that paralleled the work in the United States and in many cases had uncovered new information that was indispensable to the whole nuclear development program. J. D. Cockcroft would soon be making important calculations on the potential of the man-made element plutonium as the material for a fission bomb. James Chadwick, whose discovery of the neutron had opened the door to the whole field, presented impressive new evidence for the use of uranium 235. He was convinced that U-235 could be separated from its heavier and more common isotope, uranium 238, and he foresaw that the separation could be accomplished by a gaseous diffusion process.

Because of the physical presence of Los Alamos, Oak Ridge, Hanford, and other bomb-building facilities in the United States, Americans are often inclined to think of the whole project as their own. Actually the British government and the scientists from Britain were intimately involved in the project throughout its history. So, in a lesser way, were the Canadians.

There were two focal points of research in the summer of 1940. First, there was the question of building and—its sponsors hoped—operating an atomic reactor or furnace that would sustain a nuclear chain reaction. This involved amassing a sufficient quantity of fissionable uranium so that the neutrons discharged from uranium nuclei in the mass would collide with other nuclei releasing more neutrons and continuing the process so as to cause a release of energy. There were basically two aspects to the problem—the propagation and absorption of *slow* or *thermal* neutrons, and the same potential with *fast* or *photo*neutrons. Thermal neutrons are neutrons that when emitted are slowed by passing through a moderator that limits the speed of their impact with the nucleus. Photoneutrons travel at nearly the speed of light and collide with a much greater impact. In general, it was assumed that a controlled nuclear reaction would be feasible with thermal neutrons, while a bomb would require photoneutrons.

In the summer of 1940 most of the research into the nuclear reaction had been based on thermal neutrons, and was leading toward the building of a "pile" or reactor. The work on fast neutrons was lagging far behind and so, presumably, was the theoretical research that could establish the feasibility of constructing an atomic bomb. In July the Carnegie Institution, with Teller participating, did some important research on the susceptibility of natural uranium to fast neutrons. Teller's tentative conclusion on the basis of the Carnegie work was that fast-neutron explosions were theoretically possible with natural uranium, but that it would require a sphere of uranium weighing about thirty tons, a highly discouraging assessment.[2]

The second major focal point of research was the quest for a means of separating U-235, or fissionable uranium, from U-238, or common uranium. In a mass of natural uranium only one atom in 140 was U-235. Trying to extract these U-235 atoms from the uranium haystack was a massive problem for which almost every physicist had proposed a solution. Every solution involved overwhelming complication and expense.

The chain reaction from the fission of U-235 had been established by the theoreticians with chalk and blackboard, but would it actually happen? It depended on what the physicists called the k or *reproduction* factor. That is to say, each time a neutron strikes a uranium nucleus, the number of neutrons released to perpetuate the process would have to be one or more. If the average number of neutrons freed by each collision was less than one, the reaction would not sustain itself, but would simply burn itself out like a few twigs that flare up and die out in a damp fireplace. If the number of neutrons freed was more than one the reaction would continue and accelerate, creating a hot atomic "fire," or if the reaction went fast enough, an explosion. So if k were greater than one, the chain reaction was a fact. If k were less than one, the "fire" would go out.

In 1940 and 1941 the most important center of nuclear research was at Columbia. Fermi was the presiding genius, but a great deal of the push and enthusiasm came from Szilard. Pegram, Urey, Anderson, Zinn, and others added their contributions and soon they were to be joined by Teller. The important thrust was toward the development of sustained slow-neutron reaction.

Meanwhile there was a significant new development at the radiation laboratory of the University of California at Berkeley.

Physics at Berkeley had been dominated for a decade by the powerful personality of Ernest O. Lawrence, inventor of the cyclotron. Lawrence, a promoter, a driver, and a unique experimentalist, devised a means of accelerating particles in a circular magnetic field, until, when they had reached a certain speed, they were shot off at a tangent into the target element. His first cyclotron was four inches in diameter, and developed energies of 80,000 electron volts. From then on Lawrence and his colleagues built bigger and bigger cyclotrons, which proved to be highly efficient tools for studying atoms by the process of smashing them with particles hurled from this powerful accelerator.

The physicists at Berkeley had used the cyclotron to repeat the Hahn-Strassmann fission experiment, but it remained for two of Lawrence's colleagues, Edwin M. McMillan and Glenn T. Seaborg, a chemist, to make another spectacular breakthrough. In the periodic table of elements, uranium was number 92, the heaviest natural element. Many physicists, Fermi included, had speculated that it might be possible to create heavier elements beyond uranium, known as *transuranic.* In irradiating uranium McMillan detected a different element which proved to be not a product of fission but something heavier than uranium. The uranium nucleus had absorbed an additional neutron. By the emitting of an electron, in the process known as *beta decay,* the new neutron turned into a proton that transformed the uranium into element 93, which he named *neptunium.* Then Seaborg discovered that in a few days the beta decay process continued for another step, creating another new proton and a more stable element, number 94, which he and McMillan called *plutonium.* The discovery earned McMillan and Seaborg the Nobel prize.

Like so many discoveries in the laboratory, the existence of transuranic elements had been predicted by the theoreticians as early as 1936. In the fall of 1939 Niels Bohr and John A. Wheeler not only foresaw the creation of plutonium, but predicted that, like U-235, it would be fissionable.

When McMillan proved their speculations to be correct, the quest for a sustained nuclear reaction and for an atomic bomb took a quantum jump forward. There were now two elements that potentially could be used to create a chain reaction. In theory, U-235 still was the most promising material, but the stupendous task of separating this isotope from common uranium still lay ahead. In 1940 no one was certain that U-235 could be separated in usable quantities. The discovery of plutonium opened the possibility of large-scale creation of fissionable material through an entirely different route. It appeared that plutonium could be produced in relatively large quantities by the neutron bombardment of ordinary uranium. There was a feasible alternative to the isotope-separation headache.

The excitement over the potential for uranium spurred new experimental work at Berkeley, where Glenn Seaborg, Emilio Segrè, a former colleague of Fermi's in Rome, and their associates, further substantiated the fission potential of plutonium. Almost simultaneously scientists in England, at Cambridge University's famous Cavendish Laboratory, were providing new information on the remarkable man-made element. By the spring of 1941, the usefulness of plutonium was assured beyond a reasonable doubt.

Despite the steady progress of nuclear research, Bush, Lawrence, and others were becoming concerned over the lack of clear direction of the Uranium Committee. It seemed to move with what Hewlett describes as "painful deliberation." The British were moving with a great deal more vigor, perhaps understandably; they were at war with their backs to the wall in a final struggle for survival. The United States was still at peace. Bush, who was not anxious to offend the committee, solved the problem temporarily by making the dynamic Lawrence a deputy to the methodical chairman, Lyman Briggs. Lawrence quickly persuaded the NDRC, on behalf of the Uranium Committee, to appropriate funds for plutonium research at Berkeley and for the separation of a small amount of U-235 with a mass spectrometer by A. O. Nier at the University of Minnesota.

For a longer-range assessment Bush decided to have the Uranium Committee's work reviewed by a special committee of the National Academy of Sciences. Academy president Frank B. Jewett selected a group headed by Arthur Compton, chairman of physics at the University of Chicago. It was Arthur Compton's brother, Karl, president of the Massachusetts Institute of Technology, who had been particularly restive about the Uranium Committee's apparent lassitude, especially when compared with the British. Lawrence was one of the review committee members.

After an exhaustive study, Compton submitted a report on May 17. Every possible use of fission was weighed, ranging from the relatively simple military use of dropping radioactive materials over enemy territory, to the development of controlled fission for power, to the ultimate weapon, the bomb. This involved further investigation of isotope-separation methods, more consideration of the best moderator to use in a controlled reaction (graphite, beryllium, or heavy water were most promising), and the potential of element 94, plutonium. The National Academy committee gave top priority to the development of a controlled chain reaction in natural uranium.

Bush was not entirely satisfied with the report, and its findings were then augmented by two industrial engineers to add some practical judgments to the assessments of the physicists. He wanted to know if and when a bomb could be built. The British group was already reaching that kind of conclusion; fortunately there was a continuous liaison between the two countries.

Briggs, apparently spurred on by the National Academy's scrutiny and the rapid British progress, proposed a budget of $167,000 for chain reaction study, mainly at Columbia, Princeton, and Chicago, and about $120,000 for studies of the gaseous diffusion and centrifuge methods of separating U-235 from U-238. Only $8,000 went toward further investigation of plutonium as a fissionable material.

By this time Roosevelt no longer needed to be sold on the necessity of a more powerful agency to centralize the organization of science for the defense effort. On June 28, 1941, he created a still higher level of scientific coordination—the Office of Scientific Research and Development, under his direct control and with authority over even the scientific laboratories of the military services. The NDRC was under the new OSRD. Bush was appointed director of the OSRD, the top job, while James B. Conant, the chemist-president of Harvard, became head of the NDRC.

At last the bureaucratic roadblocks to a total organization of the nuclear fission project had been removed. From the frail $6,000 begrudgingly granted the first Uranium Committee in February 1940, the nuclear fission quest had been moved to the center of the stage.

By March 1941 Edward and Mici Teller had been in the United States long enough to become citizens. With Merle Tuve and Ferdinand Brickwedde as sponsors, they swore allegiance to the United States in a ceremony in the federal court. Their commitment to America was now complete, and it may be that citizenship gave them a sufficient sense of permanence to buy their own home. After six pleasant years they gave up their rented house on Garfield Street and moved to their new residence in a development called Country Club Hills in the Virginia suburbs just outside Washington. Mici was especially pleased to be a homeowner, but the experience was to last only three months.

With very short notice, Teller was invited to seek a year's leave of absence from George Washington University and to spend a year in teaching and research at Columbia University. The invitation had come about at the urging of Hans Bethe. In the spring of 1941 Bethe had taken a one-semester leave from Cornell to teach at Columbia. When Bethe's short visit was nearly over Columbia urgently needed someone to take his place. Teller was Bethe's nomination.

Although Teller was asked to teach in the physics department, the invitation was based primarily on the need for more brains in the atomic pile project that was now occupying the full time of Fermi and Szilard. Perhaps, secondarily, the Columbia physicists still saw Teller as a peacemaker. Fermi and Szilard were not getting along any better in what Laura Fermi called "a strange collaboration." And yet the circumstances were such that they had to work together day after day in the now supercharged atmosphere of the Uranium Committee, now renamed the S-1 section.

In June the Tellers found tenants for their new house in Virginia and left Washington for another of their western vacations with Hans and Rose Bethe. It was the last relaxing vacation either scientist was to know for many years. Surprisingly, Mici did not resent having to give up their Washington life—"It was exciting to be moving to New York."

She and Edward rented an apartment at 88 Morningside Drive, at the top of the steep rise above the smoky expanse of Harlem. Just a short distance west was the cluster of Columbia and the physics department's Pupin Hall, where the foundations were being laid for the atomic era.

Fermi and Szilard both welcomed Teller enthusiastically. Although they couldn't tolerate each other, both were fond of their newest associate. "I certainly tried to make peace," says Teller, "but I believe I failed." Whether Teller could accept the credit or not, the fact is that Fermi and Szilard did manage to work together because they accomplished what they set out to do. Laura Fermi thinks Teller was one of the catalytic agents between the quiet, patient genius of Fermi and the brilliant, roughshod gusto of Szilard ("He was a wild man," says Bethe).

Although Fermi and Teller had worked together briefly in Rome in 1932 and had visited each other in Washington and New York, their professional and personal association did not reach its truly fruitful stage until Teller's arrival at Columbia in September of 1941.

It was one day during that pre-Pearl Harbor autumn that Fermi changed the direction of Teller's life.

Sometimes the most dramatic turning points in history are recognized only in retrospect. Enjoying a quiet lunch together it is doubtful that either Fermi or Teller was aware that the seed of an idea from the cosmos had been planted in the earth. They discussed the progress toward nuclear fission, and by this time they were reasonably confident that both a controlled chain reaction and an atomic bomb were feasible. Perhaps because they were good scientists with restless minds they were already looking beyond nuclear fission.

Both were thoroughly familiar with the discoveries of Gamow, Bethe, Charles Critchfield, and others that explained the source of the energy of the stars: intense heat that caused light nuclei, such as hydrogen, to fuse and in the process liberate incredible amounts of energy.

Perhaps it was possible, Fermi suggested, that the detonation of a nuclear fission (atomic) bomb would create heat on the earth comparable to that in the interior of stars. If so, that much heat in the presence of hydrogen atoms might cause them to fuse and the result would be such a release of energy as to overshadow even the colossal potential of nuclear fission.

In the realm of science, great ideas often spring forth from many minds in many places simultaneously. Perhaps others had perceived the possibility of nuclear fusion as a step beyond fission. But this moment, during a casual lunchtime conversation, is as close as recorded history can come to pinpointing the conception of a man-made hydrogen or *thermo*nuclear reaction, an idea that was to give birth ten years later to the hydrogen bomb.

"If my husband expressed an idea," Laura Fermi told us, "it vibrated in Teller and came back."

Indeed it did, as Fermi discovered. Teller was immediately fascinated. He listened as Fermi surmised that the nuclei of heavy hydrogen (deuterium) would be more easily subject to fusion than ordinary hydrogen. Deuterium exists as one part in 5,000 in natural hydrogen, but it was already known that the deuterium atoms could be separated out from the rest of the hydrogen fairly easily and inexpensively.

"At that time," Teller stated later, "physics had moved closer to the grim realities of war. Many of us had started to work on the fission bombs. It had become clear that these atomic bombs would be powerful, but expensive. If deuterium could be ignited, it would give a much less expensive fuel."[3]

So Teller had found an economic justification for pursuing the problem of a thermonuclear reaction. But, as Laura Fermi said, her husband considered Teller "scientifically the most congenial of the physicists, and the most stimulating." The chances are that it was a magnificent scientific puzzle, not tawdry economics that fueled Teller's brain.

At this stage, however, that brain miscalculated. Teller engulfed himself in the problem for weeks, computing, theorizing. At last he reached a conclusion: it wouldn't work.

"I decided that deuterium could not be ignited by atomic bombs. I reported my results to Fermi and proceeded to forget about it."[4]

Not really, of course. The idea rattled around in his subconscious and a few months later it would emerge in a different form and with a different conclusion. Meanwhile there were still immense problems to be solved in developing atomic fission, and the government considered these to be the first priority.

Mici thoroughly enjoyed New York. She had developed a close friendship with Laura Fermi. Often she and Edward visited the Fermis, who owned a house in Leonia, New Jersey. Sometimes they were joined by Fermi's associate Herb Anderson, or Art Kantrowics, a student of Teller. Szilard, then still a bachelor, visited the Tellers, but to Leo, Leonia was off-limits.

All in all, it was a pleasant sojourn in New York, especially in the fall of 1941. "At that time," Mici Teller recalls sardonically, "I still enjoyed the fact that Edward was famous." She did not enjoy the sudden sore throat she developed early in December. A well-meaning physician gave her a dose of the newly discovered wonder drug penicillin. Within hours she was seriously ill with a penicillin allergy and was hustled off to St. Luke's Hospital.

There in the misery of her hospital bed, an attendant told her the news. The Japanese had bombed Pearl Harbor.

The progress of the uranium project was almost as if both the government and the scientists knew the Japanese attack was coming. Only one month earlier the National Academy of Sciences review committee issued a third report on nuclear fission. This time, in contrast to the conservative assessment of the first two reports, the conclusions were sensational. The committee now believed that a fission bomb of fantastic destructive potential was feasible, could be built in three or four years, and could be used "to devastate Germany's military and industrial objectives."[5]

On Saturday, December 6, when the Japanese aircraft carriers were already steaming toward Pearl Harbor, Dr. Conant, speaking for Dr. Bush, head of the Office of Scientific Research and Development, called together the S-1 Section to announce an "all-out" effort to build a nuclear (atomic) bomb. This involved putting S-1 directly under OSRD, bypassing the National Defense Research Council (NDRC) headed by Dr. Conant. Nonetheless, Conant would serve as Bush's representative in the new group.

The other principal members were Briggs, chairman; Columbia's Pegram, vice-chairman, and three program chiefs: Arthur Compton, in charge of the chain reaction project (soon to be centered in Chicago instead of at Columbia); Harold Urey, in charge of the gaseous-diffusion and centrifuge methods of separating the U-235 isotope from U-238; and Ernest Lawrence, in charge of electromagnetic isotope separation and further studies of the potential of plutonium. E. V. Murphree was named chairman of the section's planning board. The areas of responsibility were not hard and fast—there was inevitable and necessary overlap.

On December 18, with the United States galvanized into action by the disaster to the Pacific fleet, with the Japanese tide sweeping over the Philippines and the East Indies, Conant called another meeting of the newly reorganized S-1 Section. Now, like the British, the American scientists felt the blast of war. The commitment was total, the effort unlimited. As H. D. Smyth reported later: "He [Conant] emphasized that such an effort was justified only by the military value of atomic bombs and that all attention must be concentrated in the direction of bomb development."[6]

The problems yet to be solved seemed almost endless. The separation of isotopes was not the most difficult in theoretical terms—it was essentially a technical trick. If, in uranium, one atom (U-235) is very slightly lighter than 140 other atoms (U-238), how is that lighter atom to be removed from the mixture? Ernest Lawrence, who invented the cyclotron, quite naturally saw his own toy as the solution, that is to extract that one atom in 140 electromagnetically. Another possibility was to use a centrifuge that would whirl gasified uranium at a fantastic speed, slinging the heavier atoms outward to be drawn off from the lighter ones. A gentle, slightly built physicist named Jesse Beams was identified with the centrifuge in much the way Lawrence was identified with the cyclotron. Beams presided over a huge centrifuge at the University of Virginia. His work was the principal hope of the centrifuge advocates.

But in the end it was the gaseous-diffusion process, directed by Harold Urey, that produced enough U-235 and produced it fast enough. This involved forcing uranium, in a gaseous mixture, uranium hexafluoride, through a porous barrier that admitted slightly more U-235 than U-238. But to reach the necessary concentration the process had to be repeated literally thousands of times. This, nevertheless, was what was done in the separation plant at Oak Ridge, Tennessee, which, for this one purpose, was as large as a plant assembling airplanes or tanks.

But all of this still depended on the scientists who were charged with solving the intricacies of a sustained chain reaction. This was still essentially pure physics, requiring the most sophisticated of both the theoreticians and the experimentalists. The bulk of the work was under Fermi at Columbia, with certain aspects under study at Princeton. The overall coordination was under S-1 Section Chief Arthur Compton, whose home base was at the University of Chicago.

In January 1942 Compton decided that the only way to coordinate the reactor project was to move all of the men and equipment to Chicago. This meant that the Columbia and Princeton contingents had to pull up stakes, often from well-established homes, and resettle in the Windy City. The migrants included Fermi, Szilard, Wigner, Wheeler, and Teller.

The actual shift took place over about six months. For Mici Teller it proved more difficult than she had expected. She discovered in June that she was pregnant. Almost immediately she had to leave New York for a month-long visit to Berkeley. Then she had to return to New York and, without Edward's help, pack up for a permanent move to Chicago in September. "He arrived from Berkeley just about the time I had everything packed," Mici recalls, with more humor than resentment.

Meanwhile, in attempting to keep up with the proliferation of the uranium project, the government was also pregnant with a new scheme. It was finally born as the Manhattan Project, the now legendary name for the Army organization that brought the nuclear program to its successful completion.

In May 1942 the S-1 Section, born as the Uranium Committee, underwent yet another revision. It became the S-1 Executive Committee of the Office of Scientific Research and Development. The personnel were the same, except that Pegram was dropped, Conant was chairman, and Briggs, for the first time since the old Uranium Committee was formed, held no rank other than membership on the committee.

Obviously the reorganization was to lay the groundwork for transfer of the project to military control. This was inevitable under the set of circumstances that had developed. First, it was clearer than ever that the project's military potential overshadowed all of its other possibilities. Second, as such, it had to be moved into the mainstream of military activities to assure priorities, manpower, and money. Last, the success of the United States venture led scientists and intelligence experts to believe that Germany might well be moving toward nuclear weapons at a comparable speed; it was essential that the United States not finish second best.

On June 13 the top military and civilian leadership heard the proposals of Bush and Conant. Vice President Henry A. Wallace, Secretary of War Henry L. Stimson, and General George C. Marshall, Army Chief of Staff, were present, and their conclusions were passed along to President Roosevelt. On June 18 Brigadier General W. D. Styer, staff chief for Services of Supply, ordered the creation of the Manhattan District under the Corps of Engineers to supervise the atomic bomb project. The project itself went by the code name of DSM (for Development of Substitute Materials), but in time the whole enterprise became generally known as the Manhattan Project.

After a brief period under the direction of Colonel J. C. Marshall, the Manhattan District and DSM were placed under a little-known colonel from the Corps of Engineers, Leslie L. Groves. At first Groves didn't even want the job. He was expecting, and preferred, an overseas assignment. He wasn't given the choice but he did get a promotion to brigadier general.

To most of the scientists the reasons for the selection of Groves were a mystery; more than that, the choice was an insult. He appeared to be everything that intellectuals dislike about military men—arrogant, autocratic, ignorant (from a scientist's point of view), and with all this his portly bearing was the caricature of the professional officer. There seemed to be no possibility that this man could command a collection of shaggy, multinational, multilingual, individualistic scientists, many of them on or close to the genius level, and with a fair amount of arrogance in their own ranks.

It is one of the paradoxes of the atom bomb project that this seemingly impossible relationship not only worked, but worked remarkably well. In many ways Groves was indeed ignorant, but he had an unexpected sixth sense that enabled him to give the scientists the latitude and the freedom they demanded. When it was all over, Teller could say of Groves:

"Well, with all of his shortcomings, his lack of technical knowledge, his lack of tact, he was a man of his word. He was industrious—he kept after the job and he made sure that everybody else did. And whatever else you might say about General Groves, he was capable of learning."

The summer of 1942 brought the first confrontation—a friendly one, for the present—between J. Robert Oppenheimer and Edward Teller. It is not generally realized today that for one who rose to the pinnacle of the bomb project Oppenheimer was relatively late in joining it. Immersed in his teaching and research at Berkeley, this ascetic, intellectual physicist was not even aware of the Uranium Committee and the secret fission project until September 1942. And even then he learned about it by accident when a British scientist discussed it with Lawrence in Oppenheimer's presence, under the mistaken assumption that the latter was privy to the secret. Actually what the scientist was suggesting was that Oppenheimer be brought more actively into the program.[7] Given Oppenheimer's qualities of leadership and scientific brilliance, it was inevitable that sooner or later his participation would be needed.

In late 1942 and early 1943 the theoretical physicist generally held in highest regard was Russian-born Gregory Breit of the University of Wisconsin. Breit, a consultant to the Uranium Committee, had been charged with theoretical studies of the fast-neutron potential that were necessary to a nuclear bomb. In January 1942 Compton, who seemed to have some kind of a personality clash with Breit, had brought Oppenheimer in to assist in the theoretical work. Breit was rankling his associates with an almost obsessive concern with secrecy—to the point of insisting that every page of research be listed and locked in a safe.[8]

Compton soon decided that Oppenheimer, not Breit, was the man he wanted to head the theoretical studies. The two physicists considered working out their differences, but principle and pride were involved. On June 1, 1942, Breit resigned from the fission program and Compton asked Oppenheimer to take over. Although Oppenheimer was concerned about his own lack of administrative background and experience in the laboratory, "I felt sufficiently informed and challenged by the problem to accept."[9]

The new theoretical chief's first important move was to summon the men he considered to be the top theoreticians to a summer conference at Berkeley. Their task was to deal with the ultimate theoretical barriers that, if removed, would clear the way for the building of the bomb.

The gathering at Berkeley was a monumental event not only for the cataclysmic questions that were discussed, but as an indication of which physicists Oppenheimer considered qualified to discuss them. The invited guests were Edward Teller, Hans Bethe, Felix Bloch, Robert Serber, Emil Konopinski, S. P. Frankel, Eldred Nelson, and J. H. Van Vleck. Not all of the names were household words, but in overall brilliance it was a collection of physicists reminiscent of the greatest days of Göttingen and Copenhagen.

Bethe's appearance was a tribute to the persuasiveness of Oppenheimer, an asset he was later to use in luring scientists to Los Alamos for the atom bomb project and—Teller would one day complain—in luring them *away* from the hydrogen bomb project.

Bethe had just taken a leave of absence from Cornell to join another war project. The radiation laboratory at the Massachusetts Institute of Technology needed physicists to work on radar, "which seemed to me far more important than nuclear weapons." He was settled in for the rest of the war, or so he thought, when Oppenheimer phoned. The caller said the work they would be discussing at Berkeley was far more important than radar. Bethe delayed a decision until he talked to his associates at M.I.T., who urged him to stay. "But frankly, I was curious, so I went," Bethe told us.

Edward and Mici Teller had just arrived in Chicago, where he was getting involved—too slowly for Teller—in the atomic pile project that Compton had uprooted from Columbia. Hans and Rose Bethe decided to stop off in Chicago en route to Berkeley for a briefing on the progress toward a sustained nuclear chain reaction.

The world's first atomic reactor would soon be taking shape on the squash court under the west stands of Stagg Field, the remnant of the days when the University of Chicago was known better for football. It was, of course, supersecret. The Chicago project had been given the code name of Metallurgical Laboratory, which quickly became the "Met Lab." Uranium was never called that; it was "tubaloy."

The goal of the reactor, or "pile" as it was generally known, was twofold. First, it was to sustain a nuclear chain reaction, proving that the value of k was more than one. Second, it was to bombard common uranium 238 with neutrons and thereby create the man-made element, plutonium, which was fissionable and could be used as an alternate to uranium 235 in the building of the bomb.

Teller was highly optimistic. He told Bethe there would be a chain-reacting pile in Chicago before the end of 1942 (he was right). Bethe was allowed to inspect the work under way and to talk to Fermi, Szilard, and Wigner. He sensed one particular stress developing. The OSRD and the Army, recognizing the ultimate vastness of the pile project, were already making plans to contract future reactors to major industrial firms. Wigner and Szilard didn't like this idea at all. They wanted the project kept within the government, under the control of the scientists.

The Tellers and the Bethes decided to join forces and take the train to Berkeley together, and when they arrived they jointly rented a house, shared also with Emil Konopinski.

On the train Teller told Bethe of his discussions with Fermi about the possibility of using an atom bomb as a trigger for a thermonuclear reaction—a hydrogen bomb. In New York, Teller had become fascinated with the concept and then had decided that it wouldn't work. In Chicago, restless because he hadn't yet been given any specific assignment, Teller's searching mind went back to theorizing on the hydrogen bomb. He broached the subject to Konopinski, who also had some spare time. Together they combed through Teller's original calculations and reached a new conclusion—it probably would work, after all. Deuterium (heavy hydrogen) could, in fact, be ignited by the heat of a nuclear explosion.

With this new conclusion Teller was able to present the Berkeley conference with convincing reason to give serious consideration to the building of a hydrogen superbomb, which the scientists were now beginning to refer to as the "super." This was one of two topics that disrupted the proceedings of the meeting, held under maximum security precautions in LeConte Hall on the Berkeley campus.

The other disruptive topic was a discovery far more terrifying. Like the first tremor of a California earthquake, its barely detectable rumbling spread unspoken alarm. Was this an inconsequential vibration or was there to be a cataclysm? It happened when Teller was explaining his calculations of the heat yield of a nuclear blast and why it would trigger fusion in heavy hydrogen. In the midst of the explanation it apparently was Oppenheimer who saw the apocalypse.

Would an atomic bomb instantly destroy the world?

The awesome possibility was implied in the heat buildup that Teller had correctly calculated. The intensity of the heat was such that Oppenheimer and some of the other scientists feared it could ignite the heavy hydrogen that naturally occurs in seawater, or start a reaction in the nitrogen that constitutes eighty percent of the atmospheric envelope surrounding the earth. The oceans and the heavens would catch fire. There would be nothing left.

The extent to which this fear was well founded is a matter of disagreement even among the physicists who were there. No one there considered the mathematical possibility higher than about one in three million. That would be a safe bet in any other enterprise, but such odds would be disturbingly low in the face of the consequences.

According to Nuel Pharr Davis in his dual biography *Lawrence and Oppenheimer,* the inability of any of the physicists to refute the implication of Teller's figures forced Oppenheimer to suspend the discussions until he could seek advice from Arthur Compton. At this time Compton was vacationing thousands of miles away near Otsego, Michigan. Davis's account follows:

> Oppenheimer reached him at the Otsego general merchandise store. In a distraught voice, Compton later reported to Pearl S. Buck, Oppenheimer spoke to him as follows: "Found something very disturbing—dangerously disturbing. . . . No, not to be mentioned over the telephone. . . . Yes, we must see each other. . . . Yes, immediately, without an hour's delay."
>
> By this time atomic leaders were forbidden to fly. Compton gave Oppenheimer directions for getting to Otsego by train and morning after next met him at the little station. Driving out to a deserted strip of beach, Compton listened to the story. He decided that the fission program would have to be abandoned unless Oppenheimer could definitely dispose of the heat question. "Better be a slave under the Nazi heel," he summed up, "than to draw down the final curtain on humanity."[10]

Both Teller and Bethe challenge Davis's version, though both concede that the possibility of a worldwide conflagration was discussed, as, quite naturally, it had to be so long as there was even the remotest possibility. "I recall that we were discussing this," says Bethe; "I recall also that we were very little concerned about it. But it was such a tremendous consequence that even if we were hardly concerned about it at all, it was important enough to take it seriously. Now I would have to put the chance of this at much lower than one in three million. I couldn't write down the number large enough to express it."

To Teller, "It never looked like anything you should expect, but this kind of thing had to be ruled out. I was concerned, along with some of my colleagues, and we furnished the answer that it couldn't happen."

Teller and Bethe each recall Oppenheimer's departure from the Berkeley meeting to consult with Compton. Bethe's recollection is that the principal Compton-Oppenheimer topic was whether the project should proceed directly to work on a thermonuclear bomb. Teller agrees but believes that the establishment of a new laboratory was also on their agenda.

Hewlett and Anderson in their official history of the Atomic Energy Commission confirm Bethe's recollection that the Oppenheimer-Compton agenda dealt primarily with the thermonuclear (hydrogen bomb) possibility. There had been discouraging findings on the amount of fissionable material necessary to produce a nuclear weapon. Now Teller and Konopinski had brought to Berkeley an idea that appeared to promise a bigger bang for the buck. All of a sudden the superbomb became a feasible goal. On the basis of Compton's recommendation a special meeting on the thermonuclear reaction was planned for late September.[11]

When Oppenheimer returned from his week-long visit to Compton's Michigan retreat, the meetings at Berkeley were formally reconvened. Apparently the fear of a nuclear Judgment Day had not been entirely dissipated. According to Davis, "They confronted each other in one of the high moments of science history."[12] They could not establish with certainty that the thermonuclear reaction would take place, but, according to Teller, they ruled out the end of the world in a nitrogen holocaust. "This kind of thing," Teller recalls, "had to be ruled out beyond a shadow of a doubt, and I think we did rule it out beyond a shadow of a doubt."

Despite Teller's reassurances, the slimmest shadow of a shadow of doubt must have remained, because two years later—on the eve of the first nuclear explosion—Teller himself was assigned by Oppenheimer to reconsider the doomsday threat. As Teller remembers it:

"A few months before the first nuclear explosion Oppenheimer gave me the very exciting job—me and this group—to look into the question how the nuclear explosive could work quite differently from the way it was supposed to work. In particular, there had been all kinds of wild speculation that the first nuclear explosion could set off a worldwide conflagration. And it was my job, if possible, to disprove that or, if not possible, to find out why it is—how this could happen.

"This of course did not merely relate to the question of the laws of physics as we knew them, but of the laws of physics that might be unknown to us—what phenomenon might exist that we haven't discovered as yet."

Then Teller reveals his total fascination for pure theoretical physics, even when dealing with such a macabre puzzle: "This was the kind of a job that was really delightful for me—to try to speculate in these wide ranges."

It is fair to extrapolate from these comments that Teller was not a Dr. Strangelove delighted by anything that is scientifically challenging even if it means the end of the world. His joy was based on the challenge to his wide-ranging imagination and his certainty that there was in fact no danger that water or nitrogen would be ignited by a nuclear blast.

By the early fall of 1942 the Manhattan Project had reached a terrible limbo between success and failure. Every stage had to proceed on the assumption that all of the other stages would be successful. The first atomic pile was taking shape under the grandstand at Stagg Field without any assurance that a chain reaction would take place; even worse, without positive assurance that it would not run out of control and blow up or irradiate a large section of Chicago.

The centrifuge method of separation of U-235 from U-238 had been abandoned as not feasible, and Lawrence's beloved electromagnetic separation system was downgraded to a standby. The S-1 committee had settled on a gaseous-diffusion plant—a fantastic, six-hundred stage Rube Goldberg colossus—in Oak Ridge, Tennessee, and no one knew yet that it would work. The pile project for the production of plutonium was thrust upon the Du Pont Company, almost against its better judgment. New finds from Chadwick in England cast doubt on the fission properties of plutonium unless it had far fewer neutron-absorbing impurities than the Chicago group had predicated.

It looked at first like the beginning of a bitter winter. American forces were now involved in the war and had launched their offensive in North Africa. England was enduring a daily Nazi air blitz. The German armies had penetrated deep into Russia and the two nations were now involved in a titanic, bloody, and exhausting land campaign.

General Groves had now taken full command, and if he had a surprisingly good relationship with Oppenheimer, he walked into trouble with the proud and powerful Ernest Lawrence. Groves, surveying his new empire, took a trip to Berkeley to investigate the magnetic isotope-separation process and the research on plutonium. As Teller described the incident to us, Groves had Lawrence gather the radiation laboratory staff together so he could meet them all and give them a little pep talk. When the talk was finished he turned to Lawrence and—according to Teller—reached his resounding conclusion:

"And so, Professor Lawrence, you'd better do a good job. Your reputation depends on it."

There was a stunned silence. People just didn't speak that way to Ernest Orlando Lawrence. But Lawrence chose to be a diplomat. Instead of responding directly, he invited General Groves to lunch at Trader Vic's restaurant, which happened to be Lawrence's favorite hangout.

There as Teller told it to us, "After consuming the appropriate number of catalytic agents," Lawrence looked General Groves in the eye and responded to the general's comment made in the laboratory.

"General Groves, you know—with respect to what you said to me—*my* reputation is already made. It is *your* reputation that depends on this project."

As Teller had said, Groves was capable of learning, and apparently after this exchange he not only accepted their relationship gracefully, but he learned a lot more about Lawrence. He was actually impressed enough to consider Lawrence as the chief of all the scientists, a job held de facto by Oppenheimer since his appointment by Compton as head of theoretical studies. Eventually Groves decided that Lawrence was too valuable in his work at the Berkeley lab to be moved away from it.

After the meeting of the theoretical scientists in Berkeley, Mici went back to New York to complete the final packing for Chicago. On arrival in Chicago she and Edward lived temporarily in the Fermis' apartment. Then they rented an apartment on Kimbark Avenue, near the university campus. Including the move to Berkeley and back, Mici had managed three geographic relocations while expecting her first child.

Mici admits it was a difficult time. Always possessed of a somewhat nervous temperament, she started smoking and soon was consuming cigarettes almost continuously. But she did manage to acquire the trappings of permanence once again. The old Congress Hotel in Chicago was auctioning off its furniture. Mici bought a rustic, oaken living room suite that still serves them well.

But the most important purchase was what she and Edward still affectionately call "the monster"—a concert grand Steinway piano. It cost them only $200 and went with them on all their subsequent moves—even to the limited confines of their tiny apartment in Los Alamos. The piano had become Teller's most satisfying form of relaxation. When the burdens seemed greatest he would sit down at the keyboard and coax forth the sounds of Mozart, Beethoven, or Bach. He and Mici also joined the Fermis occasionally for bridge—"Good friends, bad bridge players," is Laura Fermi's recollection.

As the birth of the Tellers' first child drew near, so did a major decision and a supreme event in the atom bomb project. The decision, in November 1942, was made jointly by Oppenheimer and Groves—to concentrate the widely dispersed research in a single laboratory. Isolation, not convenience, was the goal. The site selected was the remote campus of a private boys' school, the Los Alamos Ranch Academy, on a mesa between two mountain ranges twenty miles northwest of Santa Fe, New Mexico.

The selection of Los Alamos was like the other crucial decisions of the Manhattan Project. It was a commitment made in anticipation of a whole succession of scientific and technical promises that had not yet been fulfilled. In normal times such a procedure would be reckless—like General Motors producing a new type of engine for a fuel that hasn't been invented yet. But this was war, and time could be the difference between victory and defeat, between the survival and the destruction of Western civilization.

On December 2, 1942, the first of the great promises was

fulfilled. Fermi, Szilard, and their team—which included Teller—produced the world's first sustained nuclear chain reaction. In the giant "pile" under Stagg Field, composed of a latticework of graphite blocks and uranium bars, the value of that magic coefficient k became greater than one. Under a tense but methodical team of scientists, cadmium rods, which soak up neutrons like a sponge, were slowly withdrawn from the heart of the pile. With the cadmium no longer impeding their proliferation, the neutrons emitted from the nuclei of the atoms in the uranium bars began to collide with other nuclei, releasing more neutrons until the center of the pile became a roaring furnace of nuclear activity. The reactor was now "critical," as the graphs measuring neutron production showed more neutrons being freed than being absorbed—k was more than one. Nuclear power was a reality.

For two hours they allowed this new, elemental power plant to generate its heat. Above it stood two scientists with buckets of cadmium solution ready to pour it into the fire if the reaction started to run away and threaten a nuclear holocaust instead of a quietly humming furnace. The "suicide squad" was not needed. When Fermi was satisfied with his results, he ordered the cadmium rods slowly thrust back into the heart of the reactor, and as quietly as it had heated up, the nuclear fire went out. Eugene Wigner uncorked a bottle of good Italian Chianti, and he, Fermi, Szilard, Zinn, Anderson, Compton, and the rest of the crew toasted the dawning of the atomic age. Then Compton went to the telephone to give official notice to Conant at the OSRD in Washington—but he couldn't discuss a top secret openly. "The Italian navigator has set foot in the new world," said Compton. Fifteen years later the "Italian navigator," posthumously, and Leo Szilard, would be awarded a U.S. patent for the nuclear reactor.

Teller wasn't there for the great moment. He seems never to have had any particular yearning to be present on symbolic or ceremonial occasions. Once he was convinced that the reactor would work, the actual event seemed anticlimactic. It was comparable to the time back in January 1939 when he and Leon Rosenfeld observed the release of energy in the fission of the uranium nucleus in the Carnegie Institution laboratory. Rosenfeld was profoundly stirred while Teller found it a rather humdrum event because he knew it was going to happen.

Asked what he did that fall and winter of 1942 and 1943 in Chicago, Teller usually replies, "Odd jobs." Actually he completed a paper he had started at Columbia with some sophisticated calculations on the neutron "cross sections" (the scientist's term for what a layman might call probabilities or frequencies) in a nuclear reaction. The paper was widely used but Teller had neglected to put his name on it. Eventually it was published as the work of no identifiable author.

He also continued his theoretical research on the thermonuclear reaction with the active assistance of Konopinski, whom Teller was later to praise publicly as one of the most thorough and tireless investigators in this challenging field.

By January the War Department and Groves's Manhattan District were actively laying plans for a total move of the bomb project research and design to the lonely confines of Los Alamos. This time Oppenheimer would call on Teller for active assistance, along with John H. Manley, Serber, and McMillan.

Teller was now faced with a decision on whether to give his life over entirely to his country for the duration of the war, a commitment that would involve leaving his comfortable home in Chicago and moving himself and his family to a remote and isolated laboratory. It was physicist Harold Urey who helped Teller make up his mind. Urey's political views were, in Teller's opinion, too far to the left, but Teller nonetheless had immense respect for Urey, both as a physicist and as a man. So he went to Urey for advice, and it was straightforward. "You have to go," said Urey. "It's your duty."

By early February Teller, now totally involved, had his mind focused on organizing the Los Alamos crew. Mici, however, had a more pressing and irresistible concern. On the morning of February 10 the childbirth pangs began and she was transported to the University of Chicago Hospital. While Edward stood by (presumably pacing in the waiting room, although this is not documented), Mici gave birth to their first son. They named him Paul, and he was to grow up to be not a physicist but a philosopher.

Six weeks later Edward, Mici, and the infant Paul were on the train, bound for the uncertain and awesome future on the vast and empty mesa called Los Alamos.

7

Rebel on the Assembly Line

PHYSICIST Henry DeWolf Smyth described the mission of Los Alamos with beautiful simplicity in his now-famous "Smyth Report" that first put the chronicle of the atom-bomb project on the public record: "In our earlier discussion of chain reactions," says the Smyth account, "it was always taken for granted that the chain reacting system must *not* blow up. Now we want to consider how to *make* it blow up."*

When he set out for Los Alamos, Teller had a different idea. He supported the development of a nuclear bomb, but only as a way station en route to the thermonuclear bomb, the "super." Teller, according to Hans Bethe, "was not a team player."

"That's right, I wasn't," Teller readily concedes. If this were the fact, Teller suffered from only a slightly more advanced case of rugged individualism than most of his colleagues. The very essence of basic science implies the freedom of the scientist to follow his leads, choosing the paths, including those that branch off unexpectedly, that lead to new knowledge about the universe.

At Los Alamos there was a new concept. The greatest scientists in the world were there as mere operators in the assembly line leading to the final product. This is not to say that their labor didn't require the highest use of their imagination and genius; it did, but in a directed sense that none of them had known before. That they succeeded was to the credit of their foreman, J. Robert Oppenheimer, who somehow turned this babel into a chorus.

The basic scientific and technical problem to be solved was this: Fissionable material had to be placed within a container in suffi-

---

*The italics are the authors'. The full title of the government-published report is *A General Account of the Development of Methods of Using Atomic Energy for Military Purposes.*

cient quantity to become a "critical mass," that is to say, to produce enough flying neutrons to create an instant chain reaction (as contrasted with the slow reaction in Chicago). The fissionable material had to be assembled in such a way that it was segmented in separate portions that were *not* a critical mass until the desired time of detonation, at which point the subcritical portions would suddenly be brought together by some kind of mechanical device. By the time Los Alamos was established, the physicists were reasonably sure that pure uranium 235 or plutonium would produce a chain reaction rapid enough to result in a colossal explosion. What they had not figured out yet was the technical means of turning a subcritical mass into a critical mass. It was a lot more than just a mechanical puzzle. The best brains in theoretical and experimental physics were needed to solve bomb-assembly problems that, according to Smyth, were "staggering in their complexity."[1]

It was the threat of a virtual rebellion on the part of the scientists that quickly stifled plans to make Los Alamos a total military establishment, in which every scientist would be an officer in a full military chain of command with General Groves at the top. Conant favored it, or at least had no objections to it, and Oppenheimer went along with the idea. But, led by Robert Bacher and I. I. Rabi from M.I.T., the antimilitary faction won the day. Bacher and Rabi were concerned that in a military organization junior officers might be reluctant to challenge the scientific judgments of their superiors, and that scientific accomplishment—the only thing that really mattered—would be the loser.

The sustaining of civilian status for the scientists proved, in retrospect, to be one of the sound decisions in the Manhattan Project. Perhaps even more important was the selection of J. Robert Oppenheimer as the director of Los Alamos. To the conventional military mind, "Oppie" would seem to have had everything against him. He was the ultimate intellectual, he was occasionally arrogant and, worst of all, he had spent a large part of his life in sympathy with, and even in league with, communists. His brother was a communist; so was his ex-fiancée and so was his wife's late first husband. In his intellectual isolation at Berkeley, his awakening concern about social inequality in the world took the form of an almost naïve support of left-wing causes. On the basis of such a record, a gambler would lay heavy odds that a man like General Groves would have rejected Oppenheimer out of hand. In defying the odds, Groves took a personal risk and also proved himself to be capable of more discernment than would be assumed from his conventional and somewhat pompous military manner.

Oppenheimer's success in managing the project and managing the scientists is legendary and led to his apotheosis in the scientific community. The history of Los Alamos seems to indicate that the only important scientist he couldn't control was Edward Teller. To physicist Maurice Shapiro, Oppenheimer "commanded the profound respect and loyalty of nearly all of those who worked with him." To Joseph Volpe, a young officer with the Manhattan District and later General Counsel to the Atomic Energy Commission, Oppenheimer "had powers of advocacy that I had seldom seen."

Teller's assessment is, in part, just as extravagant. "On an intellectual level," Teller says of Oppenheimer, "in following the thousand things that were going on in the laboratory, understanding them all, influencing them all for the better, he did a truly magnificent job. Furthermore, he knew the character of every one of the people and he used his knowledge to get effects, to influence people."

But Teller had scarcely arrived at Los Alamos before he began to have reservations, or "subtle differences," in Teller's words. From these "subtle differences" was to grow a monumental struggle between two gifted and powerful men.

"Before I participated in the Manhattan Project, I was anything but an organization man," recalls Teller. "I worked on subjects that I liked because I liked them. I did not work on anything for the purpose, let us say, of my career. It never occurred to me, except for the simplest and most valid reason, to influence somebody around me. I was not and did not desire to become part of an organization."

But, Teller concedes, "one cannot work on something like atomic energy without becoming part of an organization. I had participated in the loose organization at Columbia and in a somewhat more tightly knit organization in Chicago. I have seen something of how Oak Ridge operated. But none of these organizations were run as systematically, with as much direction or with as much psychological finesse as Los Alamos, and this, to me, was deeply repulsive."

It is a wonder that any organizational structure could have been achieved on that remote New Mexico mesa, just from the sheer difficulty of getting there. It was connected to Santa Fe only by a narrow, winding, rutted road. Along this inadequate artery came the vehicles of the Army and the contractors carrying materials for the residence barracks that had to be erected in a matter of weeks. While the scientists had beaten down the proposal to make Los Alamos a military post, the Army had responsibility for physical construction, maintenance, and security.

Oppenheimer arrived on March 15 with an advance cadre of scientists and technicians, and most of the scientific staff moved in within the next two weeks. Hewlett and Anderson describe the chaos of that spring of 1943:

> Despite recurring difficulties, the people were ready before the housing on "the Hill." Scientists and their families crowded together in dude ranches near Santa Fe. Each day staff members had to reach the site over the miserable road. They could not yet obtain food there. They could communicate with the project office at Santa Fe only over a noisy Forest Service line. The laboratories were unfinished. Even the most basic equipment was not ready, and minor structural changes meant maddening delays. But soon the specialized equipment for nuclear research began to arrive. From Princeton came three carloads of apparatus, from Wisconsin two Van de Graaff generators, and from Illinois a Cockcroft-Walton accelerator. Harvard contributed a cyclotron. When the contractor laid the bottom pole piece of its magnet on April 14, the physicists could feel that a laboratory actually was in the making.[2]

So quickly was the formation of the Los Alamos laboratory taking place that the scientists arrived without any clear idea of their assignments. By the end of April fifty scientists were on the premises. Rabi and Bacher were both fresh from the radiation laboratory at M.I.T. and, according to Bethe, they persuaded Oppenheimer to divide the scientists into divisions, subdivided into groups, an organization plan that was working well at M.I.T. Oppenheimer set up four main divisions. Bethe was named to head the theoretical division, with Teller as one of his group leaders. Bacher was given command over the experimental physics division. Like Bethe, he had come from Cornell and had worked briefly at M.I.T. The most unusual choice was that of Joseph W. Kennedy to head the chemistry and metallurgy division. Kennedy, a student of Glenn T. Seaborg at Berkeley, had assisted Seaborg and McMillan in the work that led to the creation of plutonium, but in 1943 Kennedy was only twenty-six. The fourth division, ordnance, which included the engineering aspects of the project, was headed by Navy Captain William S. Parsons.

The evidence strongly suggests that Teller was somewhat of a malcontent the very day he started working at Los Alamos. On paper he seems to have had everything he needed, but the organization of the laboratory, the direction it was to go, and his own assignment were, in his mind, questionable. At the root of his dissatisfaction lay not only the interference with his free scientific spirit, but a feeling that he was deceived about the pursuit of the thermonuclear bomb.

"When Los Alamos was established as a separate entity from the Met Lab in Chicago," Teller contends, "one of the arguments was that we would work on the fusion bomb as well as on the fission bomb. We actually didn't, and this was certainly something that I was unhappy about. Furthermore, Bethe was given the job to organize the effort and, in my opinion, in which I well may have been wrong, he overorganized it. It was much too much of a military organization, a line organization."

Teller made positive and important contributions to the atomic bomb—all of his colleagues concede this. But his years on "the Hill" were marred by the friction with Bethe—painful to both of them in view of their long and close friendship—and by Teller's far more profound and ominous differences with Oppenheimer. Their clash was intensified by their own intrinsic qualities; both had a mixture of brilliance, knowledge, ambition, and ego, the stuff that giants are made of. At Los Alamos Teller was officially only a scientist with a third-rank authority, but the chances are that in his own mind—even if subconsciously—he saw himself as the director's equal.

Aside from basic problems such as supply of fissionable material—U-235 from the diffusion plant at Oak Ridge, and plutonium from the great uranium piles at Hanford—the large hurdle of the Manhattan Project was the problem of bomb assembly. This involved, as we noted above, the means of bringing together subcritical masses of uranium or plutonium and creating a critical mass which would instantly explode.

There were two approaches to this problem of triggering a bomb. Early priority was given to the so-called gun-type trigger. This involved, within a bomb housing, two subcritical masses, one of which would be literally a projectile fired into the other. The second kind of trigger was the *implosion* type. This system places subcritical masses of the fissionable material in the center of a sphere, surrounded by a conventional explosive, which is in turn surrounded by a strong metal shell. The detonation of the conventional explosive drives its force inward (hence *implosion* rather than *explosion*), concentrating the material into a critical mass which fissions into an atomic blast. The apparent physical and technical problems of the implosion trigger made it a second choice to the gun-type until its complexities began to be solved. In the end both kinds of trigger were put to use in the world's first and second atomic explosions.

Teller made significant contributions to the calculations necessary to the achievement of the implosion trigger, but if Bethe is to be believed, he made them reluctantly.

"The lab was organized, the theoretical division was formed, and I was made the division leader. I think it was from this moment on that Edward essentially went on strike," Bethe recalled, with some obvious bitterness, in his interview with the authors. Then he quickly added: "Well, he didn't literally; he continued to work, but from then on he seemed rather disinterested in working on the direct business of the laboratory. I am not sure whether I'm saying it exactly right, but I believe this was it. I believe maybe he resented my being placed on top of him. He resented even more that there would be an end to free and general discussion."

Recalling the meeting in Berkeley the summer before, where theoretical physicists let their hair down in open discussion, Bethe was willing to accept the tight security and the limited cross-talk of Los Alamos, but perhaps Teller was not.

"In Berkeley it was very much the style that Teller and Oppenheimer liked," says Bethe, "namely, that we talked constantly to each other. And this had to come to an end. We had to sit down in our offices and actually work something out, and this was against his style.

"He resented particularly that I was no longer available very much for discussions. I remember one occasion when I was terribly busy, and he came in to discuss some problem which sounded to me rather far away from our main problems, and so after an hour or so I looked rather conspicuously at my watch, which was one of those dollar watches you haul out of your pocket, and he didn't like that at all.

"He resented even more that he was removed from Oppenheimer. He had come to like discussions with Oppie very much, but Oppie was terribly busy. In the end an arrangment was made that Teller would see Oppenheimer once a week, for one predetermined hour—I think from ten to eleven on Monday morning or some such thing, and so that was that."

Bethe remembers what Teller himself concedes up to a point: "He objected to the laboratory being made very mission-directed, very purpose-directed. Experiments were agreed on in a very large group but then were carried out by each experimental group independently. There were meetings once a week of what was called a coordinating council. This was a group of fifty people, of which Teller was a member, but that wasn't the same thing as perpetual discussion."

At one point Bethe seems to have given up on Teller, whom he accuses of "more or less retiring into a corner." Later, knowing that Teller was enthusiastic about the development of the implosion trigger, Bethe says he specifically but unsuccessfully sought Teller's help. Von Neumann, probably the greatest mathematician of the century, periodically visited Los Alamos to apply his calculational skills to the project. Von Neumann was, according to Teller, "a mathematician who could descend to the level of a physicist." They were old friends, fellow Hungarians who had first met in Budapest in 1925. Teller's early bent toward mathematics helped to make them compatible and in Budapest he had briefly studied under a remarkable teacher named Lipot Feher who, a few years earlier, had taught von Neumann.

Various experimental and theoretical investigations eventually pointed toward the conclusion that while uranium 235 could be detonated with the gun-type trigger, the more complicated implosion type would be required to achieve fission in plutonium. Von Neumann reasoned that implosion would actually compress the plutonium and this compression would substantially increase the explosive force. The implication was that implosion could mean a larger yield from the available material—an important consideration when deliveries of plutonium were still only in minute quantities.

To Bethe, "This seemed terribly urgent and an extremely important problem. So when I asked Edward to undertake this problem with his group, and develop the theory of implosion hydrodynamics and all that—which seemed to me the most important task in the theoretical division—he refused."

Teller had worked with von Neumann on the implosion calculations and had become quite excited over the factor of compressibility. He denies that he flatly refused Bethe's request; in fact he claims not to recall this specific instance. "But it was a fact," Teller concedes, "that he and I did not work well together. He wanted me to work on calculational details at which I am not particularly good, while I wanted to continue not only on the hydrogen bomb, but on other novel subjects. He might have asked me to do some portion of the job that he had plenty of other people to do, but I don't recall a single instance like this, and if there was one it was certainly not major."

Teller's behavior, whatever the degree of his contrariness, is consistent with the pattern of his work. His mind is capable of coping with problems of immense scope and complexity. This quality, it will be recalled, prompted that high compliment from Eugene Wigner when he called Teller "the most imaginative person I ever met." This imagination was fired up by problems of cosmic importance, but when the theory had been confirmed, when the principle had been basically established, Teller was utterly bored by details, especially if he thought these details could be worked out by more routine minds. On this basis, Bethe could be accused of failing to understand Teller and use his abilities to full advantage, or Teller could be accused of being a prima donna unwilling to dirty his hands on the routine work.

Apparently Oppenheimer either understood Teller better or perhaps just made the best of a bad situation, because he moved Teller out of Bethe's theoretical group and gave him a nearly autonomous group of his own.

One way in which Oppenheimer showed his understanding of Teller had nothing directly to do with physics. He was designated the official greeter and guide for the new recruits to the staff—recruits who included the best scientists in the world. Teller enjoyed the task. His charges included von Neumann (one of the few who was permitted to contribute as a visitor rather than as a resident of the laboratory compound), Enrico Fermi, and even the great Niels Bohr. The genius of quantum mechanics had made a hairbreadth escape from Nazi-occupied Denmark in a small boat. It was inevitable that he would end up applying his knowledge at Los Alamos. But most of the young physicists were not aware of his proximity because he was required to use a false name, Nicholas Baker. His old friends, including Teller, jokingly called him "Uncle

Nick," a name that Teller continued to use in their correspondence to the end of Bohr's life. At Los Alamos the use that could be made of so famous an elder statesman was apparently limited. "He was the fifth wheel," says Teller, "or maybe the one thousand and first wheel" in that burgeoning city of scientists and technicians.

As the staff grew and the barracklike apartments were set up, Los Alamos began to acquire the characteristics of a small town. The sense of community was really forced upon them because security regulations were such that arrivals and departures were closely monitored. Wives were shut off from all knowledge of their husbands' classified work and theoretically many of them had no idea what they were there for.

When Mici and Edward Teller first arrived they brought their infant son, Paul, and two very large packing cases. One was Edward's beloved Steinway. The other was a rare item for that era, a Bendix automatic washing machine; useful at any time, but especially so when there are daily bundles of diapers to be washed.

The Steinway, except that it took up most of the sitting room, didn't present any security problem. There are, to this day, however, a few scientists who suggest its presence might have slowed down the Manhattan Project because Teller sometimes soothed his troubled mind by playing Mozart sonatas at three o'clock in the morning, at the expense of his neighbors' sleep.

The Bendix did present a security problem, to Mici's smoldering annoyance. There was no objection to her owning it, but none of the base plumbers was qualified to set it up, and the security officers balked at allowing a Bendix serviceman from Santa Fe into the supersecret surroundings. Meanwhile there was no public laundry and no diaper service. Mici pushed her complaint to the commanding general of the base. Here at last she found sympathy. It just happened that the general's wife also had a new baby and an unconnected Bendix. The red tape was cut very quickly and the Tellers, along with the general and his wife, were among the few families with their own automatic washing machine.

The attractive stone, log, and adobe buildings of the old Los Alamos Ranch School formed a nucleus of living and working headquarters. The main classroom building, known as Fuller Lodge, became the central dining room. The Arts and Crafts building became a home and office for Oppenheimer and his wife. The existing dormitory structures were adapted as apartments for the top-level scientists and Army officers. These quarters became known as "Bathtub Row" because they were the only apartments graced with bathtubs.

The new buildings thrown up by the Army proclaimed the inevitable ugliness of such emergency structures. The Tellers' apartment was serviceable—that was about all one could say for it. And it had no bathtub. Enrico Fermi did not arrive at Los Alamos until early 1944 and Teller recalls with pride that Fermi refused an apartment offered him on Bathtub Row, preferring to cast his lot with the bathless "troops" of ordinary physicists.

The Tellers and the Fermis reestablished their Chicago friendship. Laura Fermi has vivid recollections of Teller:

> Edward had become a prominent figure on the mesa by the time I arrived there. He was often seen walking absent-mindedly, with his heavy, uneven gait. His bushy eyebrows went up and down, as always when he was pursuing a new idea. He also helped his thought with uncoordinated motions of his arms, and the leather patches on his elbows came in sight. It was smart to be thrifty in wartime. Theoretical men wore their sleeves out at the elbows, and their wives prolonged the suits' lives with leather patches.
>
> Along with new ideas, Teller's mind produced doubts, scruples, uncertainties, changes of decision. His work, his duties toward it and toward his family, his responsibilities as a thinking citizen and as a scientist in wartime, all aroused questions in his mind, which mankind has not answered yet.
>
> When he could forget his worries, Edward delighted in simple pleasures. His favorite author was Lewis Carroll, and he started to read Carroll's stories and poems to his son, Paul, long before the child could understand them. Edward could be as playful and as naive as his little boy, and each day the two of them spent some time entertaining each other.[3]

The restrictions on social freedom could be quite depressing. The residents were allowed correspondence with a maximum of three families, and these letters were censored. They were not allowed to leave the compound more than twice a month and then were limited to trips to Santa Fe for entertainment and shopping. And obviously they could not discuss anything about the laboratory with anyone on the outside. To Mici, who knew nothing of the fate of her family in Hungary, and who had heard the gruesome stories of the Nazi persecution of Jews, the compound at Los Alamos sometimes was disturbingly suggestive of a concentration camp.

Mici had one great advantage over most of the wives. She worked part-time as a mathematician and was given a "Q" clearance which allowed her access to all but top-secret information. Edward could not tell her everything he was doing, but her knowledge of the nuclear potential from the early days before secrecy, plus her clearance, filled in a reasonably complete picture of what was going on.

Perhaps it was the restriction of freedom and the isolation that created a forced-draft kind of social life. There were lots of parties. There were amateur theater and musical groups. Picnics and hikes into the nearby mountains were permitted; even an occasional skiing expedition.

Teller's enjoyment of the gregarious side of life at Los Alamos was overshadowed by his feud with Bethe and then his growing irritation with Oppenheimer. For Teller there was not enough free discussion of their problems. The last time he had really enjoyed working with Oppenheimer had been in that summer meeting in Berkeley in 1942 when they had talked out all their problems in the manner to which Teller had been accustomed.

At Los Alamos it was different. Teller "deeply objected to the changes Oppenheimer was bringing about in the physics community.

"In the discussions to which I was accustomed, in Europe and in my first years in the United States, there was one fundamental postulate: If you did not understand, you said it. Anything that was unclear had to be brought out into the open; to look foolish is better than to remain foolish.

"Under Oppenheimer and among his students, I claim—although they may deny it—that this system of priorities was inverted. You do anything in order to avoid looking foolish. You talk as though you know, whether you know or don't know. This was a change in style to which I neither could nor would adapt myself."

There was an earlier occasion, just before they came to Los Alamos, on which Teller recalls Oppenheimer complaining about the "military spirit" of General Groves, which Oppenheimer said he could accept as "all right in wartime," and then, cryptically, had added, "This kind of military spirit will have to be resisted at some time. We physicists will have to do something about it—the time will come when that will be necessary."

These comments rubbed Teller the wrong way, and he remembers replying, "I doubt that I would ever want to be part of anything of that kind."

"From that day on," according to Teller, "my relations with Oppenheimer were distinctly less good—not on my part, but on his. I can't escape the impression that Oppenheimer was building up then and afterward an organization, a group of liberal-minded people with a common political aim. I think he wanted to recruit me for that organization, but in time he found out I was not ready to be recruited. Our friendship—which perhaps was real in its initial stages—now depended on my willingness to be recruited."

Whoever was responsible, it is obvious that an emotional fissure was opening between the two scientists. Sometimes, conscious of it and perhaps concerned about it, each would make overt gestures of friendship, but the gap continued to widen. Teller even concedes, "When I got to Los Alamos my friendship with Oppenheimer was already practically at a dead end."

But despite the strain between Teller and Oppenheimer, Teller feels that the director didn't want him to leave Los Alamos.

"Oppenheimer tried to keep me there. He tried to keep me happy, as he tried to keep everyone happy. He took his responsibilities as director quite seriously. Our connection was almost exclusively through my work, but he tried to make my work as rewarding as possible. He succeeded, I believe, and for that I should be grateful."

Among the ways in which Oppenheimer sought Teller's cooperation was his assignment of Teller to work first with his Hungarian compatriot, von Neumann, and, second, with Enrico Fermi, for whom Teller had almost unbounded admiration and affection. "Oppenheimer used me—and I didn't need much pushing—to explain to these people what was going on and to help bring them into the job."

But to Teller the relationship just didn't ring true. There was too much of the politician in Oppenheimer in the way he seemed to struggle to please even those he obviously didn't like—such as General Groves. Teller concedes, however, that this effort of the lab chief "need not mean more than that Oppenheimer was a director who used his political abilities to be a good director and work with people of very different kinds." But if Teller could rationalize Oppenheimer's behavior, viscerally he couldn't accept it: "To see a politician in action in this sense was a new and unpleasant experience for me."

Felix Bloch was another of that coterie of physicists who had fled from the clutches of Hitler and eventually donated their talents to the United States. In 1952 he was to win the Nobel prize, and ten years earlier he was one of those nine brilliant theoreticians who participated in that famous secret summer meeting with Oppenheimer at Berkeley. The following year Oppenheimer invited him to Los Alamos. Since Teller and Bloch had been close friends since their student days in Germany, Oppenheimer assigned them adjacent apartments at Los Alamos.

But Bloch soon became disillusioned with Oppenheimer's leadership, or perhaps with the whole Los Alamos experience. Unlike Teller, who found the experience rewarding despite its drawbacks, Bloch simply made up his mind to leave.

Oppenheimer, hearing about Bloch's disenchantment, was apparently fearful that he might persuade Teller to join him in an exodus from the laboratory. One evening when Oppenheimer was visiting the Tellers' apartment, he noticed a silly trinket hung on the wall. It was a plaque depicting a car trying to climb up a telephone pole. The inscription said KEEP SMILING.

"Guess who gave that to me," said Teller.

"Obviously Bloch," said Oppenheimer contemptuously.

Oppenheimer was right, but Bloch had found it impossible to "keep smiling," and soon announced his resignation. He asked Teller to take him to the railroad station at Lamy, an hour's drive from Los Alamos. After Teller had committed himself to the trip, he was surprised to receive an invitation to dinner with a small group at the Oppenheimers' house, scheduled at precisely the time he would have been driving Bloch to Lamy.

Teller often attended large parties at the Oppenheimers', but he rarely was invited to small gatherings, and this invitation made him highly suspicious. He felt reasonably certain that it had been extended so that he would not be able to drive Bloch to the railroad station—"Oppenheimer did not want me exposed to the evil influence of a deserter."

Teller solved the problem by asking permission to arrive late at the party and, as planned, took Bloch to the train. When he returned and joined the party, a late poker game was in progress. Teller joined in and nothing more was said about Bloch. But once again Teller found himself resenting Oppenheimer's tactics.

"I may be unjust," he says, "but the whole thing just looked like too much of a coincidence. He used friendships, he exploited friendships. Granted, he did not want me to leave Los Alamos, but obviously he manipulated people. In the physics community as I had known it, this just was not done." Begrudgingly Teller will concede that Oppenheimer's motivation may have been to keep the best people at the laboratory.

If Teller's relationship with Oppenheimer grew ominously colder, there were offsetting pleasures in his warm relationship with John von Neumann. "Johnny," as all his friends called him, was the only scientist of the era to whom the word "genius" was almost universally applied. He had an uncanny ability to handle complex mathematical calculations in seconds. When he was six years old he could divide one eight-digit number into another, entirely in his head.[4] At twenty-three, driven out of the University of Berlin by the Nazis, von Neumann came to America, first to teach at Princeton University and then as a professor at the Institute for Advanced Study. His genius attracted the military as World War II drew near and he became a consultant on such subjects as ballistics. Inevitably he was summoned to work for the Manhattan Project. Perhaps it was the nature of his own computerlike brain that enabled him to contribute some of the basic ideas that underlie electronic computers. And at Los Alamos his calculations were fundamental to the development of the implosion-type trigger.

According to Teller, the scientists used to say that it was possible to make two independent and true statements about Johnny von Neumann: (a) Johnny can prove anything, and (b) anything Johnny proves is correct.

Unlike most mathematicians, however, von Neumann was a man of broad cultural interests. This made him excellent company in any social gathering, and he had a particularly good rapport with Teller. They spent a great deal of time together and von Neumann, who had an eight-year-old daughter back in Washington (he only visited Los Alamos) took a shine to Teller's son Paul when the latter was about two years old. Johnny would lie on the floor and play with Paul's building blocks and they would scrap like equals when Paul tried to expropriate the blocks for himself.

Von Neumann was born a Jew, but converted to Catholicism. Whenever he was tempted to curse, he would stifle himself and announce, "Now I will have to spend two hundred fewer years in purgatory."

One day Teller and von Neumann went on a hike up to Lake Peak, one of the summits of the beautiful Sangre de Cristo mountain range, east of Los Alamos. Teller carried little Paul, "on my neck" most of the time. Von Neumann had packed a bottle of cool orange juice as his reward for braving the hot June sun. Finally they reached a pass and sat down to rest at the edge of a cliff overlooking the lake for which Lake Peak is named. Johnny brought out the bottle of orange juice as succor to this moment of intense thirst. He was about to put it to his lips when Paul cried out, "Paul want some!" With his characteristic generosity, von Neumann turned the bottle over to Paul, to offer him one small-boy-sized swallow. Paul took his sip and, before Johnny could prevent it, calmly poured the rest of the cool orange juice into the lake, three hundred feet below.

"The look Johnny gave my son made me tremble," Teller still recalls. But Johnny didn't say a word, thereby, Teller feels certain, sparing himself at least a billion years in purgatory.

When Teller had been removed from Bethe's supervision and was free to attack the problems where he thought he could make the best contributions, he began to enjoy himself at Los Alamos. He worked intensively with von Neumann on the implosion trigger, and in various areas with Fermi. Unfortunately, much of what Teller accomplished (in fact much of everything that was achieved at Los Alamos) is still classified by the federal government, under military or AEC regulations.*

From the earliest days of weapons research, Teller had to force himself to accept the new rule of scientific secrecy. Everything in his background and in his nature made secrecy abhorrent to him. His personality was gregarious, expansive, and talkative. He loved to learn new facts and to tell others about them. This was the secret of his success as a teacher and lecturer. He believed scientific investigation flourished and was more fruitful in an atmosphere of free and open discussion. He was convinced that the openness of the scientific community enhanced its appeal to the best young minds. So it was with extreme reluctance that Teller, during World War II, accepted the trappings of secrecy—classification, security checks, censorship—as necessary evils at best. In the intense struggle to create a nuclear weapon, he recognized that the Germans may well have been working toward the same end and that the United States could not afford to lose the race. But he has never given up the fight against secrecy and has come to believe that in the long run it has hindered science and has even had a negative effect on American weapons development.

*See Appendix I for Teller's own description of his work at Los Alamos.

Not long before the successful test of the first atom bomb, Teller was assigned to a mission to Oak Ridge to check out a potentially dangerous situation. The question was whether the accumulation of U-235 in the gaseous-diffusion plant might lead to a nuclear explosion. Under the compartmentalized research, each isolated facility was unaware of its part in the whole picture. Teller had to get the facts about the gaseous-diffusion plant without telling the personnel involved why he was doing it. Only through the cooperation of an enlightened engineer, Manson Benedict of M.I.T., was Teller able to accomplish the mission. Benedict was required to supply Teller with all the information he needed, but Teller could tell Benedict nothing. "He scrupulously avoided asking questions and showed complete understanding when I shut up." Teller completed the assignment convinced there was no danger of an explosion, but feeling inwardly explosive himself over his inability to explain the problem to the people most directly involved.

By the late spring of 1945 the long, weary, and desperate labors of the scientists, the engineers, the technicians, and the ordinary workingmen were nearing fruition. They had shed one burden— Germany had been defeated, ending the fear that Hitler's scientists could develop nuclear weapons before the United States. Actually, though the Americans could not know it, the Germans had never come close. Under the scientific direction of Werner Heisenberg, Teller's former teacher, the German physicists had reached approximately the stage that the American-British effort had reached in Chicago, just prior to the building of the first nuclear reactor. They had established the theoretical foundation, they had perfected the technical details, but they never carried them out. The usual assumption is that the Germans had neither the resources nor the inclination to build the massive industrial complex necessary to acquire sufficient amounts of U-235 or plutonium, and that this problem was compounded by the daily Allied bombing raids that harassed and eventually destroyed the German industrial establishment. This was confirmed in general terms by Heisenberg himself in an interview with the authors.

Teller believes there may be more to the story of the German failure. He was asked by the authors how, during the war, he reacted to the fact that in Germany his respected and beloved teacher, Werner Heisenberg, was working full-time to destroy the United States and Teller, too.

"Heisenberg wasn't," Teller immediately replied. He pointed out that Heisenberg protected a number of scientists who might otherwise have been killed by the Nazis. One of these was Fritz Houtermans, a first-rank nuclear physicist who fled to Russia after the Nazi takeover in 1933, only to be imprisoned by the Soviets. After the Soviet-German nonaggression pact of August 1939, and the brief rapprochement between the erstwhile enemies, Houtermans was released and sent back home, but the Nazis quickly incarcerated him again. He was released through the intercession of physicist Max von Laue as well as Heisenberg. Under their direction Houtermans produced some of Germany's most important studies of fast-neutron reactions and critical masses.

But, more important, Houtermans, according to Teller, presented Heisenberg with evidence that the better possibility for a fissionable material was in the man-made element number 94 (which the Americans had named plutonium), and Heisenberg seemingly ignored the advice. Why? Teller says, "This is to my mind the characteristic of a man who works on a project but does not want to work on it. In other words, I am not saying that he tried to destroy it. I am not saying either that he was sabotaging the Nazi effort. I am only saying that his was the behavior of a man who was working unwillingly."

David Irving, in his book *The German Atomic Bomb*, points out that after September 1941 there was "a great debate behind the scenes of German science. Many of the physicists were now beset with grave anxieties about the moral propriety of working on the uranium project—predominant among them being Heisenberg, von Weizsäcker, and Fritz Houtermans."[5] Significantly, Teller was acquainted with all three, and the first two would have to be considered among his close professional and personal friends.

The world's first nuclear explosion, a uranium bomb with an implosion trigger, was detonated at the top of a one-hundred-foot steel tower at Alamogordo, New Mexico, early in the morning of July 16, 1945. The test area was about two hundred miles south of Los Alamos, and not only the front-rank physicists of Los Alamos were there, but the entire military and managerial hierarchy of the Manhattan Project.

Almost every one of them has written his rhapsody, his treatise, or his lament on this event that changed mankind's status in the universe forever. It is not the authors' intention to add to this heavy volume of literature on the fiery dawn of the nuclear age. But Teller was also there and we asked him to describe it:

"There were two groups. One, those who were involved directly with the test, were in a bunker about ten miles away. Another group—and I was one of those—was twenty miles away.

"We went out at night and the test was to occur before sunrise. But it was raining—in the desert. For whatever reason, the test was postponed. Then it was put on again at dawn—it was just becoming a little light in the east. I was there at the countdown, of course. As I told you, I was involved with the predictions of what could happen, and I felt that we should be prepared for a bigger explosion than the one we had calculated, although I felt sure it would not be many orders of magnitude bigger.

"I must tell you that I took some personal precautions. I wore gloves, and on the exposed parts of my skin—on my face—I used suntan lotion. We were given a welder's glass, but in addition I put on dark glasses. Then I used the gloves to hold the welder's glass in such a manner that no light could reach my eyes, except through the welder's glass and the sunglasses.

"The countdown on the radio from the control center went down to minus five seconds. And then it stopped. Nothing happened. It seemed to me so long a time that I felt certain the shot had misfired.

"And then I saw a very faint light point which divided into three—that is, a high point and two side lobes, which was the beginning of the mushroom. I clearly remember a feeling of disappointment—'this is all?' Then I remembered—all of this was within a fraction of a second—that I had all these glasses between me and the event. So I tipped the welder's glass slightly to peek out the side.

"The impression I got was the one that you have if in a completely dark room you raise the curtains and the sunlight comes streaming in. That may have been a couple of seconds after the explosion and of course it was twenty miles away. And by that time, of course, I was impressed. It faded, I took off the glasses, and we saw the mushroom and the cloud developing that the wind blew in various directions."

The show over, the scientists boarded their buses to go back to Los Alamos. Teller took a last look at the golden cloud, now forty thousand feet high. The capricious wind had shaped it into a giant question mark.

8

Woe Without Warning

ON the eve of that first atomic explosion, one room at Los Alamos resembled a gaming hall at Monte Carlo. Some of the world's best experimental and theoretical physicists were gathered around a long table and they were placing bets. There was no roulette wheel; instead there was that famous floppy hat of J. Robert Oppenheimer, turned upside down. Its cavity was rapidly being filled with dollar bills.

There was an air not of excitement so much as tension. The question to be wagered had a certain doomsday quality, specifically, which scientist could most closely predict the force of the explosion to be unleashed the next day at Alamogordo. More was at stake for the scientists and for humanity than the mere value of their dollars.

With one exception, each physicist there had his own tout sheet, based on the myriad of factors that would combine to produce this man-made cataclysm. Their combined talents had conceived and designed an implosion charge that would detonate the bomb to be tested. But with all this carefully accumulated knowledge, none of these scientists could do more than make an educated guess as to the power of the monster they had created.

In general, the theoretical physicists guessed much higher than the experimentalists. The theoreticians' average estimates were in the range of ten to fifteen kilotons of TNT.* The experimental physicists' average predictions were much lower, generally around five kilotons.

Both of these well-informed groups were wrong. Only one scientist hit it on the nose, and he wasn't even on the Los Alamos staff. He was I. I. Rabi, a visiting fireman from Columbia. At that time Rabi was engaged in radar research, not bomb making, but he

*One kiloton is one thousand tons.

guessed the force would be equal to twenty kilotons of TNT, and he was right.

The apparent reason that the experimental physicists were so wide of the mark was that they were not sufficiently aware of the effect of the thermal radiation. When such a bomb is exploded, it sends out three successive waves of radiation. First is the radioactive gamma wave; next is the thermal radiation; and finally the shock wave.

The heat generated by the explosion is higher than the temperature at the center of the sun. This heat—thermal radiation—affects the shock hydrodynamics of the bomb. Depending on the nature of the material involved, the temperature, and other complex factors, the thermal radiation can give varying degrees of push to the shock wave.

The implosion bomb was designed for high efficiency in energy production and the thermal radiation was therefore able to push or accelerate the shock wave. Because physicist Robert E. Marshak played an important role in the calculation of the effect of thermal radiation, this form of radiation is now often known as the Marshak wave.

It was Marshak himself who recounted for us the story of the betting on the bomb, and Teller appended his own version. He disputes Marshak's contention that the theoretical physicists were not too far off in their predictions.

Teller's version is that there was the main betting pool but that he and some of the others, like seasoned gamblers, also made side bets. Rabi's bet was not based on his judgment so much as politeness—as a visitor he was making only an educated guess that did not put him in competition with his hosts. Teller went even farther, betting so high that "I was not betting in the field of what I considered probable; I was betting in the field of what others considered improbable, betting a long shot, so to speak. Thereupon, to my annoyance, one person bet even higher than I [Teller won't say who it was]. So I was much too high, somebody was higher than I, and Rabi, who was third highest, came closest."

Teller disputes Marshak's recollection that Rabi was exactly right. He believes he is confusing the main pool with the side bets.

What Teller claims to remember is that "on my side bets I made approximately nine bucks. I challenged anybody who would bet to guess the right result within a factor of two. In other words, if anybody guessed four he would win if the result was between two and eight. I made ten bets and won nine of them. All of them were low. The bet I lost was to Marshak. He bet ten kilotons and I paid off because the result was close enough to the double of ten. But in the pool he bet much lower than the ten."

But getting to the point, Teller concedes that "what follows from all this is that at the time we had badly underestimated. Even the official estimates were much lower than the actual result."[*]

There is something slightly chilling about the best scientists underestimating the potency of their own creation, but the short fall in the estimates seems to go back to the earliest days of the atom bomb project. When the possibility of an atomic explosion was still being considered, Oppenheimer felt confident that the effort would be justified if it produced a bomb with a force of just one kiloton.[1]

The final preparations and the actual testing of the first implosion-triggered plutonium bomb did not occur in a political vacuum. As the mighty Manhattan Project neared its successful completion, the statesmen were aware not only that they had a military weapon of horrifying power, but an atomic blackjack that was bound to be used in shaping the postwar world.

Teller at this time was still a comparative political innocent. His total lack of guile in matters of politics and statecraft led him to accept most of the decisions of his superiors so long as they did not deal with scientific verities. In his own realm he was self-assured, cocky, even domineering. Scientists learn and create by doubting and questioning. Scientific skepticism had become Teller's intellectual godfather.

Perhaps it was his Germanic training that enabled him at the same time to challenge and question scientific assumptions while accepting the dictates of the political power structure. J. Robert Oppenheimer was Teller's boss at Los Alamos. So when the time finally came that Teller found himself being edged toward political involvement, it was quite natural that he would seek the advice and approval of Oppenheimer.

In order to understand Teller's cautious testing of the waters be-

[*]On September 30, 1944, Bush and Conant had sent Secretary of War Stimson a memorandum predicting the bombs to be tested would have a force of between one and ten thousand kilotons, and that the date of demonstration would be prior to August 1, 1945. They were low on the yield, but accurate on the test date, which actually was only two weeks earlier than their prediction.

fore his first political plunge, we must first go behind the scenes in Washington and recount the fateful debate that preceded the first and only time the atom bomb was willfully used to destroy human life.

That decision, one of the monumental mistakes of human history, was destined to superimpose an additional level of fear and irrationality over all subsequent efforts to deal reasonably with both the constructive and destructive potential of atomic power.

In the days prior to the destruction of Hiroshima and Nagasaki, Teller was not aware that this awesome, yet almost cavalier decision was based at least in part not on military but political considerations. As late as the fall of 1973 he told us he was under the impression that the bombs were dropped on Japan "to save American lives." In 1945, however, even this assumption was not a conclusive one in Teller's mind and he had been examining alternatives to ending the war without incinerating masses of civilians.

Most significantly, Teller was not aware of the importance of the "Russian factor" in the final decision. Just as significantly, Oppenheimer did not share Teller's innocence. He was quite aware of most of the factors.

Oppenheimer knew, for example, that the first testing of the implosion bomb was tied in with the timing of the four-power Potsdam conference. He later testified, "We were under incredible pressure to get it done before the Potsdam meeting."[2] When the contractors supplying firing circuits and molds for casting the nuclear explosives were two weeks late in delivery,[3] the target date for the nuclear test was postponed, to the dismay of President Truman. This forced another delay in setting the Potsdam meeting date.

The coordination of the Potsdam parley with the bomb testing was to be Truman's second attempt to deter or prevent the extension of Soviet hegemony over Eastern Europe. His first tactic had been the abrupt canceling of the bountiful wartime lend-lease aid to Russia. This cancellation had done very little to deter Stalin's ambitions.

Truman's position had been made more difficult by two earlier events that had increased the friction between Russia and the United States. Franklin D. Roosevelt had been the strong figure who kept Churchill and Stalin from clawing each other apart. Like primordial enemies they could scarcely keep from each other's throats. Stalin bitterly remembered the British role in the Allied attempt to aid the White Guards in overthrowing the Bolsheviks after they had seized power in the communist revolution of 1917. Churchill's gift of historical perspective left little doubt in his mind that Soviet expansionism would reassert itself after World War II and he intended to do what he could to curb it. But he was not confident of success.

The Prime Minister soon discovered that the new American President shared his views, and the Soviets were shortly to realize the fact. Roosevelt's death, they felt, signaled a radical shift in American policy, a feeling that Truman's Secretary of State, Edward Stettinius, conceded was "understandable."[4]

It was not only understandable, it was to a point inevitable. The shotgun wedding that Hitler had forced on the reluctant Allies was no longer sanctified by the god of war. With peace, in Europe at least, neither Russia nor its western allies needed each other's arms or men for defense. Each side could revert back to its natural state of suspicion, fear, and hostility.

President Truman had discarded his predecessor's policy of cooperation with the Soviets (and one can only speculate on even Roosevelt's ability to sustain cooperation under postwar conditions) and replaced it with a powerful foreign policy aimed at reducing and, if possible, thwarting Soviet influence in Europe. If the Russians refused to cooperate in this cabal, this new order, "they could go to hell."[5]

The test of the new order came early when it was time to establish a new Polish government in Warsaw. There were two rival Polish groups planning to take over. One was a predominantly right-wing group in exile in London. The other was a pro-communist assembly appointed by the Russians and holding sway in Soviet-occupied Warsaw. Churchill and Truman supported the claims of the London Poles, who were predictably labeled by the Soviets as "fascists." The label was not justified. The Polish leaders in the West were men who had elected not to give in to the Nazis but to continue the fight against them. Their ranks included many Jews. The fall of these exiles from Soviet grace was the result of their anti-Russian and pro-Western orientation.

The Yalta Agreement, negotiated by Roosevelt, Churchill, and Stalin in January 1945, provided that the existing Soviet-sponsored government in Warsaw would be "reorganized and expanded to include pro-Western political leaders."[6] The vagueness of this language led to disagreements as to its meaning. Even without hazy verbiage, it was clear that each side would interpret the Yalta Agreement to its own advantage.

One of the most influential voices in the debate over postwar foreign policy was that of Averell Harriman, United States ambassador to the Soviet Union. Only eight days after Roosevelt's death, the ambassador explained his views on policy toward the Soviets to President Truman.[7] According to Harriman, the Soviets were following a dual program. First, they intended to cooperate with the United States and Great Britain and, second, while doing this they would attempt to extend their influence and control over neighboring states. In Harriman's view, Stalin believed that the Soviet government could "do as it pleased" in Eastern Europe without American interference.[8]

A few days earlier Harriman had insisted, "I am a most earnest advocate of the closest possible understanding with the Soviet Union." But he felt that the use of American economic muscle was the best way to insure Soviet cooperation. This kind of power would be language the Russians would understand; no translation would be necessary.[9]

Harriman felt that the risk of Soviet intransigence would be minimal.[10] He estimated that the Russians would need a six-billion-dollar loan to rebuild their war-devastated economy.[11] The Soviets were thus in no position to resist America's insistence on a free and democratic Eastern Europe. Truman expressed it simply: "The Russians needed us more than we needed them."[12]

Two weeks before V-E Day, President Truman decided to force the Polish issue to a showdown. In his view he held all the cards. The President was blunt. He acknowledged to Molotov that the Yalta Agreement was vague, but he insisted that the American interpretation must prevail.[13] He was contesting the Russian view that the Soviet-sponsored Warsaw leadership should hold four of the five seats in the new Polish government. Roosevelt, before his death, had challenged Stalin's interpretation of the Yalta Agreement. But he was somewhat flexible and had cautioned Churchill that "we placed, as clearly shown in the agreements, somewhat more emphasis"[14] on the Warsaw group than on the Western-oriented political leaders.[15]

Truman, asserting his authority in place of the fallen Roosevelt, got nowhere with Stalin, whose position was based on Russia's need for secure boundaries. The Soviet chief sent parallel messages to Truman and Churchill: "You evidently do not agree that the Soviet Union is entitled to seek in Poland a government that would be friendly to it. . . ."[16]

Stalin's rejection of Truman's demand was received in Washington one day before the German surrender on May 8, 1945. With the European war over, the American reaction to the Russian position was swift. The President's hammer struck hard; he signed an order that authorized the immediate cutback of lend-lease shipments to Russia.[17] Ships on the high seas bound for Russian ports were ordered to turn back. Cargoes destined for Russia aboard ships in American ports were unloaded.[18] Truman had made his point.

American public opinion was unprepared for this harsh action against a gallant wartime ally. Truman found himself under pressure to ease up a little. The order was modified so that ships at sea could continue their mission and ships in docks were allowed to continue loading their cargoes.[19]

But neither the original tough order nor its slight modification impressed Stalin. The Soviet dictator refused to accept the American position on the makeup of the Polish government, even under this threat of economic reprisal.

There was a swelling chorus of voices for a showdown with Stalin. Admiral Leahy, on May 14, urged a Big Three meeting. He warned that "the Polish issue has become a symbol of the deterioration of our relations with the Russians."[20] Churchill told his Foreign Secretary, Anthony Eden, "It is to this early and speedy showdown and settlement with Russia that we must now turn our hopes."[21] Both Ambassador Harriman and Joseph Grew, now acting Secretary of State, joined the chorus.[22]

It was in the shadow of crisis and showdown that the victorious wartime leaders made preparations to gather in Potsdam. The stage was set not only for a diplomatic poker party, but for a game in which—given just a little more time—the United States would possess a cataclysmic ace in the hole. The scientists, engineers, and technicians of the Manhattan Project were now racing the clock, working feverishly to assemble the planet's first atomic bomb.

Truman didn't have to risk a politically unpopular break with Russia. He felt that he could afford to wait. Then he could turn up that atomic ace, and who could top such a hand?

Secretary of War Stimson, a conservative Republican in the

"coalition" cabinet, agreed with the strategy of delay. He knew that "we shall probably hold more cards in our hands later than now."[23] Stimson, of course, was aware of the approaching zero hour at Los Alamos. The atomic clock was ticking.

Once it had been the fear that they were racing the Nazis that had spurred the men at Los Alamos. Now Germany was defeated, but the work, instead of slowing down, was intensified. Said Oppenheimer, "I don't think there was a time when we worked harder at the speed-up than in the period after the German surrender."[24]

By the end of June it was clear that the bomb would be ready for delivery in early August.[25]

"If it explodes—as I think it will—I will certainly have a hammer on these boys,"[26] said Truman at Potsdam, immediately prior to his first meeting with the Soviets. The conference opened on July 16, but formal talks did not begin until a day later because Stalin was late arriving. On the evening of July 16, Secretary of War Stimson, now joined by the new Secretary of State, James F. Byrnes, received a telegram:

OPERATED ON THIS MORNING. DIAGNOSIS NOT YET COMPLETE BUT RESULTS SEEM SATISFACTORY.

Truman now had his hammer.

To this he could add a pitchfork to jab the Russians, with three prongs: the first prong was the fact that the Emperor of Japan was seeking peace—which meant the United States no longer needed Russia's help in the war.[27] The second prong was the size of the American standing forces in Europe and the Pacific—nearly 12 million men. The third prong was American economic strength which could be used to tempt the Russians in their war-battered land.

But the key factor was the atomic "hammer." First, could it be made? The answer: Yes. Second, could it be made in time to affect the political outcome? Again, probably. Lastly, and most important, how and where in Japan should it be used in pursuit of military and political goals? That was the biggest question.

It was this last consideration that found Teller unaware and uninformed. Oppenheimer, in contrast, knew what was going on. He had been kept informed of the more sophisticated political and military considerations. He was later to testify that "much of the discussion revolved around the question raised by Secretary Stimson as to whether there was any hope at all of using this development to get less barbarous relations with the Russians."[28]

There was good reason for Oppenheimer to be aware of the deliberations on the bomb. The question as to whether it should be used against Japan had been discussed long before the new weapon was a reality. Roosevelt and Churchill had mulled over the question on Sunday, September 17, 1944, at Hyde Park, after their publicized meeting in Quebec the day before. The principals initialed an *aide-mémoire* which, in part, read, "It might perhaps, after mature consideration, be used against the Japanese, who should be warned that this bombardment will be repeated until they surrender."[29]

A few days later, on September 22, 1944, President Roosevelt questioned Vannevar Bush: Should the bomb actually be used against the Japanese or should it be tested in the United States and used as a threat? Bush felt that the question was premature, but should be discussed again when the United States was in a position to act. Roosevelt agreed.[30]

The energy equivalent of the bomb was still a matter of dispute. On Saturday morning, December 30, 1944, Groves briefed Roosevelt on the latest expectations. The general explained that by August 1, 1945, a uranium bomb with a gun-type trigger, with a yield of ten kilotons, would be available. This weapon would not require a full-scale test. In contrast, the work on the plutonium bomb, with its implosion trigger, was still plagued with scientific problems. The material could not be used as efficiently as the scientists had first hoped. The Los Alamos staff expected to have enough plutonium on hand by mid-July to produce an implosion bomb with a force equaling five hundred tons of TNT. As some of the problems were overcome, the lab hoped to raise the yield to twenty-five kilotons. Thus Groves expected to have what was then considered the more powerful gun-type bomb available for use on Japan if necessary. But the implosion bomb would also be used if it were ready.*[31]

Meanwhile a new question was intruding itself into the wartime nuclear bomb effort. At the University of Chicago, where the

---

*The gun-type uranium bomb exploded over Hiroshima, nicknamed "Little Boy," had a reported force of twenty kilotons, but actually was closer to thirteen. The implosion-type plutonium bomb used at Nagasaki, called "Fat Man," had a force of twenty kilotons.

"Metallurgical Lab" had achieved the first sustained nuclear chain reaction, the government was cutting back on the staff, and the scientists there were distressed. The cutback had begun early in 1944 and it was clear that Washington regarded the Chicago group as near the end of its assignment. The question that disturbed the scientists was whether this indicated a lack of commitment to peaceful as well as military nuclear research after the end of hostilities. Most of the scientists felt such a commitment was essential if the United States was to maintain its leadership.

Arthur Compton agreed, and assigned Henry D. Smyth to draft long-range plans that would encompass not only military goals, but civilian applications and basic research.[32] This was the dawn of the long-range planning for the use of atomic energy as a major power source.

Vannevar Bush was also worried about the lack of postwar planning, especially relating to the release of information on atomic energy. On September 19, 1944, he and Arthur Compton drafted a letter to Secretary Stimson. They foresaw the need, at the proper time, for legislation that would authorize the release of basic scientific information. They attempted to convince Stimson that the security of the United States would not long be served by trying to withhold its atomic secrets from the rest of the world. Russia, they believed, had the talent and resources to develop the bomb. Under these conditions, Compton and Bush felt, it would be better to start planning for an international atomic control agency, of which Russia would be a member.[33]

During this same period the voice of the venerable Niels Bohr was heard. The exiled Danish scientist called on President Roosevelt, and urged him at least to let the world know that the bomb was being built. He felt that international control was essential if the world was to head off a debilitating postwar nuclear arms race.

By early 1945 General Groves was involved in this dilemma. It was not in his province to worry about postwar atomic research or planning for international control. In a letter to Compton, Groves explained that he had to direct his limited resources and manpower to building the bomb that could win the war. This meant, for example, that projected engineering studies to establish the value of thorium as a nuclear fuel* had to be scrapped.[35] Compton protested, especially on behalf of work in Chicago. He felt the long-range

*In an interview with the authors in August 1974, Teller advocated the use of thorium as a substitute for uranium in nuclear reactors.

research must continue for the safety of the nation and to enable research projects to retain the commitment of the best scientists.[36]

The volatile Leo Szilard decided to act on his own, very much as he had done in 1939 in trying to alert Roosevelt to the need for a national effort to develop nuclear energy. In March 1945 he prepared a long memorandum urging international control. This, he argued, would be in the national interest because the United States was so vulnerable to an atomic attack. As soon as the new weapon was demonstrated, Szilard urged, the Soviets should be approached. Then he felt the United States should press on with development of not only the first stage of nuclear power—fission— but proceed as rapidly as possible with the "second stage."[37] By that Szilard meant nuclear fusion—the hydrogen bomb—but he was somewhat cloudy in his language. If international control proved not to be feasible, Szilard felt it would be a grievous error to delay work on the "second stage."

The argument and the ideas expressed in the Szilard memorandum were shared by his fellow Hungarian, Edward Teller. In many respects, during this period, they were in political agreement. Teller, however, claims he was reluctant to move into the political arena, to take the lead in a political confrontation. The irrepressible Szilard was not.

From the scientists' standpoint the disturbing question was whether or not Washington was listening to them. Stimson was certainly aware of their concern. After considerable prodding by Bush, Compton, Bohr, Szilard, and others, he finally agreed to ask Truman to appoint an advisory committee to deal with the ramifications of the atomic weapon that would stem from its testing and possible use.

The advisory group, which became known as an "interim committee" was appointed on May 2, 1945.[38] Stimson was chairman. The other members were Bush, Conant, Karl Compton, Under Secretary of the Navy Ralph Bard, Assistant Secretary of State William L. Clayton, and the President's special assistant, James F. Byrnes, a militant anti-Soviet who was soon to be Secretary of State.[39]

The interim committee was heavily weighted with government members, so to curb growing restlessness among the scientists, Stimson, on May 5 on Conant's recommendation, appointed a group called the Scientific Panel to advise the committee. The scientists who were invited to serve, and accepted, were Arthur

Compton, Ernest Lawrence, Robert Oppenheimer, and Enrico Fermi.[40]

Underlying these rather frantic activities in the last weeks before the test at Alamogordo was the question burning deep into the conscience of every scientist: How and where would the first bomb be used? And from this followed the second question: To what extent would the military leadership listen to the advice and the pleas of the men who built the bomb?

It was in this controversy that Teller, somewhat haltingly, finally became involved in attempting to influence government political and military policy.

The first meeting of the interim committee with the four members of its scientific panel took place on May 31, 1945, at 10 A.M. at the Pentagon. The importance of the gathering is underscored by the fact that General George C. Marshall, General Groves, and Harvey Bundy, Stimson's special assistant, were also there to lend their heavy weight to the decision-making process. *[41]

Obviously a key question was how long it would take for another country to build an atom bomb. Arthur Compton estimated that it would take six years. Once again the question of building a thermonuclear bomb was raised. Oppenheimer predicted that this task, if the United States should attempt it, would take three years.

During lunch the committee pursued the most critical question—the use of the bomb. Lawrence suggested the Japanese be invited to observe a demonstration of a nuclear bomb detonation. It would take place in an uninhabited area. No lives would be lost, but the message would be clear—surrender or else.

Oppenheimer disagreed with the proposal. There was, he felt, no demonstration sufficiently spectacular to convince the Japanese that further resistance was futile. Other objections to the demonstration idea were offered by various members. One of the greatest fears was a demonstration failure; suppose the bomb was a dud?

This challenge to Lawrence's proposal is difficult to understand.[42] It was true that the plutonium bomb, with its complicated implosion trigger, was not a sure thing and its future delivery prospects were still based somewhat on faith. The Los Alamos people, however, were all but certain that the uranium bomb, with its gun-type trigger, would work the first time. They were willing to use it

---

*An excellent, detailed account of the interim committee's deliberations is presented in *The New World,* by Richard G. Hewlett and Oscar E. Anderson, Jr.

against Japan without a test. It therefore seemed that there was no reasonable argument against a demonstration, unless there was concern by the military that there was an insufficient supply of weapon-grade uranium. By this reasoning a demonstration failure, granting this was a remote possibility, could leave the United States in the position of having its bluff called.

The rising voices of concern among the scientists, especially those at Chicago, could not be stilled by the government decision makers. It was Arthur Compton who recognized the importance of giving the scientists a sense of personal participation in the epochal events that were taking place. He established a series of committees to report on different aspects of their concern.[43] The most profound implications of weapons and nuclear research policy were to be explored by the Committee on Social and Political Implications, headed by James Franck, a Nobel prize winner and a long-time friend of Teller.

On June 11 the Franck committee completed its report, which was signed by Franck, D. Hughes, G. J. Nickson, E. Rabinowitch, Glenn C. Seaborg, Joyce C. Stearns, and Leo Szilard.

The most potent issue in the Franck report was its assertion that the United States would lose political support if it were to use atomic bombs on Japan without warning. It argued that atomic secrecy could not be effective and would not prevent a nuclear arms race. Therefore the only hope for safety lay in international control. To bomb Japanese cities would make the chance for international control much more remote. A demonstration over an uninhabited area, such as Lawrence had suggested, would probably be sufficient to end the war.[44]

On June 16, 1945, the Franck report was received at a meeting of the Scientific Panel. The members were in a terrible dilemma. They were in sympathy with the humanitarian instincts of their Chicago colleagues. Yet they were unable to conceive of any kind of technical demonstration that would be likely to end the war. As they reluctantly saw it, there was no alternative to direct military use.[45] They were willing, however, to advocate that the United States inform its principal allies—Britain, Russia, France, and China—before the bomb was used.

The Scientific Panel thus rejected the advice of the Chicago group. There was a bitter political fission between the two factions of scientists. Strangely, it was a break not along the lines that were to develop after the war when scientists seemed to be splitting into "liberal" and "conservative" camps. In 1945, Oppenheimer, a "liberal," endorsed military use of the atomic bomb. Lawrence, a "conservative," had, for a time at least, opposed it.

Similarly, Teller and Szilard, later to be identified with divergent political views, both were alarmed at the prospect of the use of the bomb on Japanese cities. They agreed that the use of the new weapon to protect the West from the Nazis might, at one time, have been acceptable. Both felt that using this weapon of terror against an enemy that was all but defeated was an unnecessary act of barbarism.

Szilard, in his characteristic way, swung into action.* In June 1945 he wrote to Teller, who was already brooding about how the bomb would be used. Said Teller:

"My apprehension reached a high plateau several months before Hiroshima when I received this letter at Los Alamos from Szilard. He asked my support for a petition urging that the United States would not use the atomic bomb in warfare without first warning the enemy."[46]

Teller agreed absolutely with the pleading of the Szilard petition and his intention was to circulate it among the scientists at Los Alamos. But he felt a loyalty and allegiance to the laboratory's highest authority.

"It was my duty," Teller wrote later, "first to discuss the question with the director, Dr. Oppenheimer. He was the constituted authority at Los Alamos; but he was more. His brilliant mind, his quick intellect, his penetrating interest in everyone in the laboratory made him our natural leader as well. He seemed to be the obvious man to turn to with a formidable problem, particularly political."[47]

It was at this point that perhaps Teller's Germanic respect for authority was stronger than his own conviction. In 1962 he wrote:

> Oppenheimer told me, in a polite and convincing way, that he thought it improper for a scientist to use his prestige as a platform for political pronouncements. He conveyed to me in glowing terms the deep concern, thoroughness and wisdom with which these questions were being handled in Washington. Our fate was in the hands of the

*Eventually Szilard got an audience with Secretary of State Byrnes. Several years later, Teller met Byrnes, who told Teller he hoped he wasn't the kind of Hungarian that Szilard was—"A terrible man; he told me precisely what I should do." Teller suspected that Byrnes was right: "Szilard told everybody what to do."

best, the most conscientious, men of our nation. And they had information which we did not possess.

Oppenheimer's words lifted a great weight from my heart. I was happy to accept his word and authority. I did not circulate Szilard's petition. Today I regret that I did not.[48]

The measure of Teller's acceptance of Oppenheimer's authority is revealed in the following letter to Szilard, dated July 2, 1945. It is noteworthy that he does not tell Szilard of his conversation with Oppenheimer.

Dr. Leo Szilard,
P.O. Box 5207,
Chicago 80, Illinois.

Dear Szilard:

Since our discussion I have spent some time thinking about your objections to an immediate military use of the weapon we may produce. I decided to do nothing. I should like to tell you my reasons.

First of all let me say that I have no hope of clearing my conscience. The things we are working on are so terrible that no amount of protesting or fiddling with politics will save our souls.

This much is true: I have not worked on the project for a very selfish reason and I have gotten much more trouble than pleasure out of it. I worked because the problems interested me and I should have felt it a great restraint not to go ahead. I cannot claim that I simply worked to do my duty. A sense of duty could keep me out of such work. It could not get me into the present kind of activity against my inclinations. If you should succeed in convincing me that your moral objections are valid, I should quit working. I hardly think that I should start protesting.

But I am not really convinced of your objections. I do not feel that there is any chance to outlaw any one weapon. If we have a slim chance of survival, it lies in the possibility to get rid of wars. The more decisive a weapon is, the more surely it will be used in any real conflict and no agreements will help.

Our only hope is in getting the facts of our results before the people. This might help to convince everybody that the next war would be fatal. For this purpose actual combat-use might even be the best thing.

And this brings me to the main point. The accident that we worked out this dreadful thing should not give us a responsibility of having a voice in how it is to be used. This responsibility must in the end be shifted to the people as a whole and that can be done only by making

the facts known. This is the only cause for which I feel entitled in doing something: the necessity of lifting the secrecy at least as far as the
broad issues of our work are concerned. My understanding is that
this will be done as soon as the military situation permits it.

All this may seem to you quite wrong. I should be glad if you
showed this letter to Eugene [Wigner] and to Franck who seem to
agree with you rather than with me. I should like to have the advice
of all of you whether you think it is a crime to continue to work. But I
feel that I should do the wrong thing if I tried to say how to tie the
little toe of the ghost to the bottle from which we just helped it escape.

With best regards.

Yours,
E. Teller

Teller's reasoning is open to question now, as it was then, and,
in fact, it is now questioned by himself. The letter also is one of the
earliest statements on behalf of one of Teller's crusades—the elimi-
nation of all secrecy in scientific research. Teller has consistently
believed secrecy is counterproductive in that it stifles research, in-
terferes with the free exchange of ideas—especially across national
boundaries—and deters the best scientists from entering government service.

The failure of Teller to tell Szilard of his discussion with Oppenheimer is one of the paradoxes of the letter. One physicist, Marvin
L. Goldberger, now chairman of physics at Princeton, seems to
doubt, by implication, that the Oppenheimer meeting took place
precisely as Teller has described it. During the war Goldberger and
his wife were both working at the Chicago Metallurgical Laboratory. He was in uniform, but she was a civilian. Because of his military status he decided not to sign an anti-bomb petition being circulated at the lab. His wife, however, did sign it.

In response to the authors' question about Oppenheimer's
blocking the petition at Los Alamos, Goldberger had this recollection:

"As far as the episode at Los Alamos involving Oppenheimer's
vetoing Teller's circulation of the petition, the only knowledge I
have of that is that I have heard Edward Teller state this repeatedly. I don't know anything more about it as to whether there is any
other substantiation of that statement. I am not doubting Teller's
word. I just have not heard anyone talk about it."

Among many other persons familiar with this period, and interviewed by the authors, three of them did corroborate Teller's version. These were Philip Morrison, Joseph A. Volpe, Jr., and General K. D. Nichols.

Then why didn't Teller, in his letter to Szilard, attribute his position to Oppenheimer's advice? "There was no need to," Teller says today. "It was my own decision."

Later he was to be furious about Oppenheimer's advice. The Los Alamos chief had skillfully persuaded Teller that scientists should not be involved in political decisions. Teller, after painfully searching his conscience, decided that he agreed with Oppenheimer. Then, after the blast at Hiroshima, he learned that Oppenheimer, the scientist, had not taken his own advice and had, in fact, participated in the decision to bomb Japan without warning. In defense of Oppenheimer, he did serve in an official capacity as a member of the advisory panel, and his advice was requested.

Teller, at the time, thought he understood the reason for the decision. As the years passed he came to look upon the Hiroshima and Nagasaki bombings as a critical mistake. In 1962 he wrote in *The Legacy of Hiroshima:*

> I am convinced that the tragic surprise bombing was not necessary. We could have exploded the bomb at a very high altitude over Tokyo in the evening. Triggered at such a high altitude, the bomb would have created a sudden, frightening daylight over the city. But it would have killed no one. After the bomb had been demonstrated— after we were sure it was not a dud—we could have told the Japanese what it was and what would happen if another atomic bomb were detonated at low altitude.
>
> After the Tokyo demonstration, we could have delivered an ultimatum for Japanese surrender. The ultimatum, I believe, would have been met, and the atomic bomb could have been used more humanely but just as effectively to bring a quick end to the war. But to my knowledge, such an unannounced, high altitude demonstration over Tokyo at night was never proposed.[49]

Actually there were numerous proposals from the highest authorities to end the war without bombing Japanese cities, but Teller was never made aware of them.

Among these authorities were General Carl A. Spaatz, later to be Air Force Chief of Staff; Lewis Strauss, later to become head of the AEC and Teller's close friend; General (and future President)

Eisenhower; Under Secretary of the Navy Ralph Bard; and, for a time, physicist Arthur Compton.

Spaatz had pioneered daylight precision bombing over Germany, had commanded the air forces that ruled the skies on D-Day, and then moved to command of the Strategic Air Force in the western Pacific. In this role he did not believe dropping the A-bomb over Japan was necessary to end the war or to save American lives. He urged a demonstration. Ironically, he had to command the missions over Hiroshima and Nagasaki.

Strauss, a wartime reserve admiral, wrote later: "I had made a suggestion to Secretary Forrestal that the power of the bomb be displayed as a warning in an uninhabited area. It seemed to me that a demonstration over a forest would offer impressive evidence to show the terrible effect of heat and blast."[50] Strauss was so familiar with Japanese terrain that he even suggested a specific location for the demonstration.

In mid-1945 General Eisenhower wrote to Stimson. He later recounted his feeling: "I told him I was against it on two counts. First, the Japanese were ready to surrender and it was not necessary to hit them with that awful thing. Second, I hated to see our country be the first to use such a weapon."[51]

Ralph Bard had been a member of the interim committee and first went along with the bombing proposal; then he had second thoughts. On June 27 he sent a memorandum to Stimson. It read, in part:

> During recent weeks I have also had the feeling very definitely that the Japanese government may be searching for some opportunity which they could use as a medium of surrender. Following the three-power [Potsdam] conference emissaries from this country could contact representatives from Japan somewhere on the China coast and make representations with regard to Russia's position and at the same time give them some information regarding the proposed use of atomic power, together with whatever assurances the President might care to make with regard to the Emperor of Japan and the treatment of the Japanese nation following unconditional surrender. It seems quite possible to me that this presents the opportunity which the Japanese are looking for.[52]

Arthur Compton, who served on the scientific panel to the interim committee, while his brother Karl served on the committee itself, also suggested the possibility of a demonstration that would impress the Japanese to the point where "they could see the uselessness of continuing the war."[53]

John J. McCloy, then Assistant Secretary of War, was one of the power brokers who spoke face to face with President Truman, just before Truman's departure for Potsdam. As McCloy later recalled it, he urged the President to inform the Japanese that the United States had a "terrifying destructive weapon," which would be used if they did not surrender.[54]

With opinions abundant from his highest aides, there is no doubt that Truman was aware of all the alternatives when he made the decision to drop the atomic bomb on Japan without warning. The question still remains as to whether the bombing was necessary to end the war, or to save American lives, and many of the highest authorities felt it was not.

Then why did Truman decide to use the bomb?

The great unknown political element might be described as the "Russian factor."

Richard G. Hewlett is the chief historian of the AEC.* With Oscar E. Anderson, Jr., he co-authored *The New World,* Volume I of *A History of the United States Atomic Energy Commission.* On a clear spring day in May 1974 we interviewed Dr. Hewlett on this and other questions in his office in the campuslike surroundings of the AEC in Germantown, Maryland.

We posed the suggestion that Japan was A-bombed not to win the war, which was already won, but to impress the Russians and make them more tractable after the war.

"This," Hewlett responded, "is an interpretation of a lot of the 'revisionist' historians. I think it wrong to say, as [historian] Herbert Feis did, that the Russian factor was never in the equation, that no one ever thought about the Russians.

"I had some interesting exchanges with people who were involved with Stimson in the War Department. I submitted some evidence that I thought, at the time, indicated that at least they were thinking about the Russian equation. The initial reaction was 'Oh, no, we never thought about that at all, that was never in our minds.' And then when I presented this piece of paper that had a somewhat ambiguous statement in it, the man said, 'By golly, I

---

*As of January 1, 1975, the Atomic Energy Commission became the Energy Research and Development Administration.

think you have something there. It is obvious that I wrote that; I must have written it. I don't remember anything about it—it really shocks me to see it. But I guess you are right. We must have been thinking about that to some extent.'"

In spite of this admission of the Russian factor, Hewlett believes the compelling reason for dropping the bomb was to win the war. But if it helped to keep the Russians off balance, this could have been a factor, too. He does not go along with the "revisionists," but believes that "all these things should be tested—and if we find out from their analysis or from other evidence which may come out that we should change our interpretation, by all means let us change it; I'm not wedded to one interpretation."

What evidence is there that Harry Truman knew that the Japanese were looking for a face-saving formula for surrender? And if he knew, how did he know?

Stalin didn't know—and of course neither did the Japanese—that the United States had broken the Japanese code early in the war. This enabled the Americans to intercept Tokyo's radio transmissions and monitor them. The most secret dispatches were available to Truman.

At Potsdam, when Stalin informed Truman and Byrnes that the Japanese had asked him to negotiate a peace, the Americans feigned surprise. Actually they had read the messages, chapter and verse. Stalin told Truman that he had given no definite reply since the Japanese were not yet ready to accept unconditional surrender.[55]

The Russian chieftain coupled this intelligence about the peace offer with an unsolicited promise that early in August the Red army would be ready to attack.[56]

Stalin may have had his own reasons for not jumping into the role of mediator too fast or too seriously. Like Pavlov's dog, he must have salivated at the thought of grabbing a hunk of Asian land mass from an already defeated Japan. If, by his inaction, he could prevent Japan from surrendering too soon, Stalin could move in for the kill and avenge the Japanese humiliation of Mother Russia in the War of 1905.

That same afternoon during a conversation between Truman and Stalin another hint of the Soviet tactics emerged. The Generalissimo informed the President that the Emperor of Japan, in a confidential message, requested that Prince Konoye be received as an emissary of peace. Stalin suggested ignoring the peace tender.

Truman put the ball back in Stalin's court and suggested that he do what he thought best.[57]

Meanwhile, starting late in June, another attempt had gotten under way in Switzerland to stop the now unequal battle, to save Japan from total ruin. The effort involved Lieutenant General Seigo Okamoto, a Japanese military attaché, and two Japanese bankers, Kojiro Kitamura and Kan Yoshimura, both officials of the Bank for International settlements at Basel. Per Jacobsson, a Swedish director of the bank, had excellent relations with influential Americans. At the urging of his Japanese associates Jacobsson made contact with Allen Dulles, one of America's supreme intelligence experts. Their discussions centered around the question of whether the Japanese would be allowed to keep their emperor.

Dulles wasn't authorized to send any formal assurances to General Okamoto on this point, but the general was convinced to the point that he decided to recommend to Tokyo that the war be ended. By this time the Potsdam Conference was under way. Dulles flew there and gave Stimson a firsthand report. [58]

Inasmuch as a promise to keep the emperor seemed to be the crucial issue, and Truman was aware of this, and the Japanese were eventually granted this concession, why were the bombs then dropped on Hiroshima and Nagasaki anyway? Why wan't the concession made and the war ended before such a holocaust?

Perhaps Oppenheimer, testifying nine years later at his own security hearing, provided an answer when he spoke of Stimson's concern over using the new weapons "to get less barbarous relations with the Russians."

The decision is history. The bombs, for whatever reason—to force a quicker surrender, to save American lives, to impress the Russians—were delivered over Japan, and the United States had demonstrated its willingness to kill a hundred thousand people in two cities with the most ghastly weapon ever devised.

When it was over, even the military men questioned the awesome decision. Admiral Leahy, the military advisor to Presidents Roosevelt and Truman, later said, "It is my opinion that the use of the barbarous weapons at Hiroshima and Nagasaki was of no material assistance in our war against Japan. The Japanese were already defeated and ready to surrender."[59] General Arnold and General LeMay agreed with Leahy.[60]

General Eisenhower, who emerged from the war as the most prestigious if not the most perceptive military leader, was deeply distressed by what he considered the destructive effect of the bombings on postwar United States-Soviet relations. In late 1945 he observed that "before the atom bomb was used I would have said, yes, I was sure we could keep the peace with Russia. Now, I don't know. . . . People are frightened and disturbed all over. Everyone feels insecure again."[61]

Unfortunately, for whatever the reasons, relations between the United States and Russia did deteriorate rapidly. The effect of this decay on Edward Teller was to trigger a complicated set of responses in his psyche and in his actions.

Teller's initial reactions were in the form of a concept of world government and the complete sharing of secrets—even atomic secrets—with the Soviets. Today he still believes in openness, but with the strict provision that both rival societies are open, that both parties are willing to dance to the same music.

With many others Teller has speculated on whether the course of history would have been different if an atom bomb had been demonstrated harmlessly over Tokyo.

"Would such a nighttime demonstration," Teller asked later, "have convinced the Emperor and the dissidents in his inner cabinet that they should seek peace immediately and unconditionally? Could we have avoided the tragedy of Hiroshima? Could we have started the atomic age with clean hands?"[62]

The answers will never be known, but the questions still trouble him, and the residual effects go on, thirty years later. And through those three painful decades, Teller knows, "Hiroshima has haunted many scientists and has distracted the judgment of quite a few policy makers."[63]

9

Flashback to Budapest

TELLER's decision, back in 1933, not to choose his native Hungary as a refuge from the oppression of Nazi Germany probably saved him from extermination. While he was emerging as a major physicist in the United States, his family was beginning the long, dark night of totalitarian horror. Commencing with the outbreak of war in 1939 the members of the Teller family—those who survived—were to endure two decades under the grinding heels of the Nazis and the communists. The love and devotion that had ennobled the lives of Max and Ilona Teller and their children were to be obscenely violated by the merciless agents of Hitler and Stalin.

There can be little doubt that the senseless privations visited upon his family contributed to the political conservatism of Edward Teller. Having experienced what happened under the Nazis when the most elementary rules of humanity broke down (as he had seen them break down in 1919), having learned of the excesses of Stalinist "reformers" who took over where Hitler left off, Teller seems to have formed definite ideas on the essential conditions for both freedom and security. The authors would summarize his views as follows: A nation lives by the rules laid down by lawful governments and changes the rules only by lawful processes.* Military strength keeps predator nations at bay (weak and divided Hungary could hold off neither the Germans nor the Russians). Economic strength undergirds military strength and an orderly society. A state-controlled economy is by its nature tyrannical; therefore the best hope for freedom in combination with strength lies in a vigorous and productive private capitalist business establishment. It is

---

*For example, Teller has for years actively opposed U.S. laws requiring secrecy in scientific research, yet he slavishly adheres to these laws "because you have to play by the rules."

not surprising that in the past two decades Teller has chosen many friends and has gathered his staunchest supporters from the captains of private industry.

In Hungary in the 1930s, under the regime of Admiral Horthy, Jews lived under some quotas and restrictions, but the constraints began to ease up somewhat during the closing years of the decade. Max Teller enjoyed an adequate law practice and even entertained hopes of becoming a law professor if the relations between Jews and gentiles continued to improve. He was now highly respected in legal circles.

In 1934 Emmi Teller, Edward's sister, married Andras Kirz, a successful lawyer who practiced mainly as the legal representative of a bank. Their only child, a son whom they named Janos, was born in 1937. Edward and Mici had returned to Hungary for a joyful reunion with their families in 1936. At the time no one realized that the onrush of the prewar disruptions would force them to cancel plans for another visit in 1938. After 1936 they never saw Hungary again.

With the commencement of the war in September 1939, the *modus vivendi* came to an end for Hungarian Jews. Hitler needed Hungary as a staging area for his operations against the Balkans and later for the attack on Russia. Hungary did not actually enter the war as a formal ally of Germany until June 1941, but the Nazis and their Hungarian admirers had effectively spread their political poison throughout the country. The Germans began to refer to Hungary as *verjudet*—full of Jews. New legal restraints were imposed on Jewish citizens. They were forcibly ghettoized by being allowed to live only in certain designated apartments.

By early 1944 it became evident that the Germans were losing their massive campaign against Russia. Hungary's government began to lose its stomach for the war. The Nazis reacted with further subversion and a violently stepped up anti-Jewish campaign. Even Admiral Horthy, despite his record of anti-Semitic acts and utterances, became a target of the Nazi hate machine. Propaganda minister Paul Joseph Goebbels wrote that

> Horthy and his family are strongly infected with Jewish blood, and they will continue to struggle against the solution of the Jewish problem. Horthy advances humanitarian arguments which, naturally, have absolutely no validity in the case of the Jews.[1]

In March 1944 Hitler's armored columns and troops advanced into Hungary, occupying the country to offset any inclination of the Hungarians to desert their German allies. Horthy became a virtual prisoner of the Nazis even though he nominally continued to run the country. With Germans or their Hungarian puppets in full command, the harassment of the Jews turned into total war.

Janos Kirz, though he was only seven, remembers the registering of Jews, who were required to carry a yellow card with a Star of David. Every few days the Nazis would invade the courtyards of the Jewish apartments and round up some of those who were young and healthy and haul them away to forced labor camps.

One day in the late spring of 1944 Andras Kirz was one of those selected for the labor camps. He was forcibly taken away from Emmi, his horror-stricken wife, and Janos. Deprived of husband and father, Emmi and Janos were forced to move in with her parents. Max and Ilona were spared for the present, apparently only because they were old.

In August of 1944 the Nazis stepped up their forced recruitment for the labor camps, taking women as well as men. At one point while the soldiers were rounding up young women of approximately Emmi's age, she slipped away and hid in a laundry room until the Nazi kidnappers had departed for the day.

After this experience the Kirz family and the Tellers concluded that the situation was going to get worse, not better, and decided that the protection of little Janos would have the highest priority. They managed to enroll him in a Red Cross home from October through December, a painful decision that separated him from his family, but assured him comparative safety for a while. Meanwhile the constant presence of the Nazis made the apartment living quarters of Emmi and her parents unbearable.

There was still some official mercy in Budapest, but it was foreign-born. Some of the few remaining neutral countries had taken selected apartment houses under their protection. Emmi's mother-in-law lived in such a small flat, and out of sheer desperation, she and Max and Ilona Teller moved in with Mrs. Kirz. It was horribly crowded—twenty-six people jammed into one small apartment, but it provided a temporary sanctuary, even at nine people to a room. In this last groping for safety, Emmi, who had been a teacher of English and German, managed to find a haven in a school that was protected by the Red Cross or some kind of international organization.

In October of that year, Andras Kirz was paradoxically released from his work camp in a remote section of Hungary. Apparently the release was permitted during a reorganization of the camp and was conditional on Kirz's assurance that he would voluntarily report back to a new location at a specified time. Andras walked all the way back to Budapest—a trek that took him four days. His reunion with his wife and Janos was a matter of a few sad days. Then he reported to the new camp and neither Emmi nor Janos ever saw him again. They learned later that he was shortly shipped away to Mauthausen, in Austria, where the Nazis maintained one of their lesser-known concentration camps. He was apparently murdered in the spring of 1945.

By December the Red Cross could no longer guarantee the safety of the children in the school where Janos was harbored. They were to be turned back into the ghettos or to anyone who could take care of them. At this time Janos was taken ill with a disease that caused his skin to break out into a rash, and he was sent to a hospital (the ailment later was diagnosed as a probable case of chicken pox). Emmi, learning that the school was being shut down, immediately started making inquiries as to her son's whereabouts. Nobody could shed any light on what had happened to Janos. Finally, after seven desperate days, she learned that he was in a ghetto hospital. By this time Jews were not even allowed to walk in the streets but Emmi, in her anxiety to be reunited with her son, defied the regulations and walked to the hospital, collected Janos, and added his presence to the already overburdened apartment.

In that fall of 1944 the Russians, having cracked the German advance, had mounted their own multipronged offensive and one column was marching toward Budapest. Horthy attempted to remove his country from what he knew was now a futile war. Instead, the Germans forced him out, ending the twenty-four-year rule of Europe's "first fascist." The leadership was taken over by a German puppet of the Nazis' choosing, the arch-nationalist Ferenc Szálasi, head of the Arrow-Cross party. Although his strength with the Hungarians lay in his superpatriotism, Szálasi was in many ways a little Hitler, and he measured up to German specifications. He may have been the most viciously anti-Jewish leader in all of Europe. Historian Emil Lengyel describes the death throes of Hungary under Szálasi:

What the Hungarist-Arrow Cross government did in these months of Hungarian agony belongs in a book on psychiatry. The Soviets were now deep in Hungary, racing toward the capital, held largely by crack German units. The Hungarian government decided that all streets in Budapest which were called after Jews should be renamed. Up to the last minute freight cars badly needed by the government for the prosecution of the war were filled with Jews to be shipped to German extermination camps. Boys of twelve and teen-agers carried rifles and shot down anybody whom they suspected of being Jews. In a frenzy of murder Arrow Cross men lined up Jews—women and children too—along the Danube banks so that their bodies should topple into the river, saving the inconvenience of digging graves.[2]

The Russian siege of Budapest began Christmas Day, 1945. By February 2 the Soviet army had completely surrounded the city, cutting off all supplies. Food disappeared. And yet the Nazis and the agents of Szálasi, despite their desperate situation, accelerated their slaughter of the Jews. Janos, for the first time in his life, was conscious of being hungry. Some Budapest residents literally starved to death.

Janos also remembers firsthand some of the horrors described by Lengyel. This was the period of total terror for Budapest's Jewish residents, now almost entirely sealed off from the rest of the community. The climax came during four successive days in January. At five thirty on each bitter cold morning the Nazis marched into the complex where Max, Ilona, and their grandson were living. Emmi was not there, having found a temporary haven in the school where she was teaching. The soldiers pounded on the apartment doors, routing all the occupants into the freezing darkness. They were herded by bayonets into a compound of a neighboring apartment. On each of the four days a portion of the Jews was separated from the others, like so many sheep from a flock. Amidst the helpless sobbing of friends and families, the separated Jews were marched away to the banks of the Danube. There, as Lengyel describes, they were machine-gunned into the black waters of the river, the Hungarian contribution to Hitler's "final solution."

The Nazi madmen disposed of thousands of Jews in a few days, but their subhuman efficiency was not swift enough to beat the arrival of the Russian army. The Pest side of the river, where the Tellers were living, fell to the Soviets on January 18, staying the executions of the Jews who were still alive. A few weeks later Buda also fell and the Nazis who had perpetrated the slaughter of the Jews were themselves slaughtered by the Russians.

Even today, the Tellers have no idea of the final fate of their family and friends. The casualties included Mici's brother, Suki Harkanyi, Edward Teller's closest childhood friend. No one knows how Suki, a warm and gentle young man, was put to death. Or perhaps, more accurately, no one asks.

Today Janos Kirz can say with deceptively cool objectivity, "The great surprise is not that my father was taken away, but that the rest of us survived."

In the simple terms of percentages, he is absolutely right. No one knows how many Jews were murdered by the Nazis in Hungary, but there were at least two-thirds of them, and perhaps as many as three-quarters of the approximately 800,000 who lived in Hungary in 1941. The sheer logistics of so many murders indicts the Hungarians as well as the Nazis. The task could not have been carried out by the exterminators without the enthusiastic cooperation of the psychopathic Szálasi government. "His Hungarian followers were as anti-Semitic as the Germans," according to Kirz.

With communist persecution still in the future in 1945, Kirz makes the ironic admission that his life and the lives of other members of his family were saved by the arrival of the Russians.

"If they had been slower, it is quite clear we would not be around," he says. The Jews who did survive, however, were mainly those who lived in Budapest. The large city provided more places to hide and more opportunity to mix with the surrounding gentiles, who were never quite sure who might have Jewish blood. The situation was nearly hopeless for the Jews in small towns. They were known and marked from the start, and hence were almost totally exterminated.

With the arrival of the Russians, Jews were at last able to come out of hiding, though food was in extremely short supply and, at least until the summer of 1945, whether a Hungarian ate often depended on what possessions he had to barter. Currency was all but worthless, and the luckiest were those who had something made of gold.

During the last two months prior to the conquering of Budapest by the Soviet army, Emmi was separated from her parents and her son and they did not know if she had survived, nor was she aware of their situation. In late January they were reunited after a period when fear and terror had left them shocked and numb.

"I remember the time when she first rejoined us," Janos Kirz says, "and then we went on our first walk through the city after the Russians had taken over—we were trying to go back to my Teller grandparents' home where, in fact, we were to live for the next five years. I remember as we walked, the situation in the streets—dead bodies, dead horses, and no windows left in the entire town. Most of the buildings were in absolute ruins."

The food shortage was so acute that Max Teller decided he would send Emmi and Janos off to visit Emmi's first cousin, Ilona Dobos, in Lugos, the once-happy refuge of Emmi's and Edward's childhood. Lugos was now under Romanian control and the food situation there was better than in Budapest. He was able to arrange for their transport there in a truck. They spent April and May in Lugos, a welcome respite from the nightmare of Budapest.

The war in Europe ended in May. The Russians occupied Hungary, but the four major powers established military missions in Budapest. Emmi Kirz, with her exceptional knowledge of both English and German, was able to obtain a good job as a translator and interpreter for the American mission. There seemed to be some hope of a return to a tolerable if not a stable existence. Max Teller even managed to reestablish the semblance of a legal practice.

But Max, with the same insight he had shown in the 1920s when Edward was weighing a future in Hungary, was not optimistic about the prospects of life under a Russian-dominated society. He was immediately correct about the economic situation. All bank deposits, currency, securities, bonds—any reserves in the form of paper—became worthless. The Germans had partially looted the country of gold and valuables and the Russians continued the process. The only recognized medium of exchange was gold, or something of concrete value, or food.

The Russian victory in the war had enshrined Joseph Stalin to an extent that he and his adherents, in all the countries under Russian domination, were stronger than ever. Janos Kirz points out that extremism seemed to flourish in Hungary. If Hungarian Nazis had been more vicious than the Germans they were emulating, the same was true of Hungarian-bred Stalinists.

The most critical domestic problem was a shortage of living space because so many buildings had been destroyed. Most apartments were partitioned to accommodate the problem. Max and Ilona Teller lived in half the space they had enjoyed before the war, and Emmi and Janos shared it.

One of the most encouraging aspects in the postwar situation for a brief period was the reopening of communication with the West. Edward Teller learned that his mother and father were still alive, that his sister had lost her husband. But letters dealt only with innocuous facts. It was many years before Edward learned the full story of the barbarities from the right or the left.

Anti-Semitism receded somewhat, but festered in the popular subsoil. Jews and communists shared a common hatred of the now-destroyed Nazis. To some extent, however, the situation of 1919 repeated itself. Just as Béla Kun came to power with strong Jewish adherents in that abortive coup at the end of World War I, so the Stalinists also counted many Jews among their numbers. Once again Christian Hungarians, especially those of the middle class, who longed for a return to capitalism, blamed the Stalinist Jews—and therefore Jews in general—for the latest threat of totalitarianism. But at least anti-Semitism was no longer official policy.

An Allied Control Commission under the United States, the Soviet Union, Britain, and France sponsored free elections in Hungary in late 1945. The Communist party won only 70 seats—just slightly more than one-sixth of the 409-seat parliament. The communist leader was Matyas Rakosi, a dedicated Stalinist, who, like his political antecedent, Béla Kun, soaked up communism as a Russian prisoner of war in World War I. He returned to Hungary with Kun, but was jailed by the Horthy regime when Kun was overthrown. He languished in a prison cell for most of the next twenty years. When he was released in 1940, he went immediately to Russia, and returned to his native country with the victorious Soviet army in 1945.

Even under the Control Commission, the Russian army was, by the Allied agreement, the occupying force in Hungary. Undoubtedly this armed presence gave aid and comfort to the communist political effort. By infiltration of the various political parties, by clever use of a bookful of subversive tricks, the Communist party systematically eliminated its opposition in Hungary. Hungary's brief experience with free democracy—its *only* such experience in a thousand years—was all but over by mid-1948. Freedom ended officially on May 15, 1949, when the communists, under the guise of the "Independent People's Front," won 95.6 percent of the votes in an outrageously rigged election. On August 20, which is Saint Stephen's Day, the most important national holiday in Hungary, a "Republic of Workers and Working Peasants" was proclaimed.

Max Teller was now seventy-eight, wearied by age and a failing heart. At about this time he told his family, with a touch of sardonic humor, that once he was denied a professorship because he was

too young, then because he was a Jew, and now because he was
not a communist. He had been thoroughly pessimistic about what
life would be like under Soviet domination, and his worst fears
were realized. When the iron grip of the Stalinists squeezed out
the last breath of freedom in Hungary, the will of this kindly, in-
sightful man was broken. In early 1950 he developed a severe case
of pneumonia. His tired heart could not withstand the ravages of
the disease. In his final agony, his thoughts were fixed on the dismal future to be faced by the wife and daughter at his bedside.
"What will become of you?" he said, and then, quietly, Max Teller
died.

His concern for the plight of Ilona, Emmi, and Janos proved to
be justified. Emmi's job with the American mission lasted until the
American military presence was discontinued in 1946. She then
worked for CARE, the American food relief organization. In 1948
she joined the staff of the American embassy, until 1950 when, under Russian pressure, the embassy staff was sharply reduced. The
only source of income left for the family was through Emmi's tutoring of students in German and English.

Apparently, Emmi's long association with American authorities
led the militant Hungarian communists to suspect her loyalty to
the regime. Or perhaps Edward's reputation was becoming known.
Actually she was an essentially uncomplicated person concerned
mainly with providing a living for her mother and her son. Nevertheless, in June 1951, at three o'clock in the morning, there was a
sudden pounding on the door of the Tellers' apartment.

Emmi opened the door to find the Budapest police on the
threshold. She was immediately served with a warrant which, one
of the policemen explained, necessitated their "deportation" from
Budapest within twenty-four hours. Why? Emmi wanted to know.
The policeman's reply was that because her father had been an
"industrialist," she and her family were adjudged to be "undesira-
bles."

What the communists had done, according to Janos Kirz, was to
resurrect a statute enacted back in the 1880s that allowed the police to force "undesirable" people out of the city. The original law,
however, had a specific purpose—to rid the city of prostitutes. The
communists now found the ancient statute a convenient way of
solving a lot of problems. It enabled them to rid Budapest of anyone they did not trust, or anyone who might seem even remotely
dangerous to the government. The practice also, every time it was

applied, freed an apartment for the communists' use. The vacated quarters were invariably turned over to government functionaries or to members of the secret police who could thereby watch over the vicinity.

The classification of the now-dead Max Teller as an "industrialist" seemed farfetched to his family, but it was apparently based on his one-time service on the board of directors of a corporation. In the short time that remained Emmi got in touch with a young lawyer, who had been a friend and admirer of Max, in the hope that he could appeal the deportation order. He tried but was unsuccessful. The order was being applied wholesale to some fifty thousand residents of Budapest.

When all hope had been lost, Ilona Teller and Emmi spent the remaining hours finding friends who were willing to keep the most valuable family possessions. Anything too large to carry, or to turn over to a neighbor—for example, all of the furniture—was simply confiscated by the communists.

Exactly twenty-four hours after the fateful knock on the door, Ilona, Emmi, and Janos were shoved into a truck and carted to the railway station, along with a hoard of other deportees. They were piled into a train that left Budapest on a rail line that headed ominously northeastward. The rumor spread that they were all headed for work camps in Russia. This proved not to be the case as the passengers were let off at various stations along the route. Emmi and her family were disembarked at a remote little town in northeast Hungary called Tallya.

Their home in exile proved to be the rude hut of a nearly illiterate peasant, a "kulak," who was considered equally undesirable by the government, apparently because he was still the private owner of some five acres of vineyards. The tiny house, with no running water, and an outhouse, was home not only to the kulak and his wife and the three Teller deportees, but also to another "undesirable" Budapest family of a husband, wife and teen-aged daughter. The peasant was surly and understandably resentful, but for eighteen months eight alienated people endured an acutely uncomfortable situation.

What was the real reason that Emmi, her mother, and her son were deported? Obviously the official reason, that the late Max Teller had been an "industrialist," was trumped up. It seems probable that Emmi's association with American agencies might have been a factor. But it is also probable that, for the first time, Edward

Teller's activities in the United States were affecting the lives of his family in Hungary. By this time the Soviets knew that he had played an important role in the atom bomb project and was now masterminding the American effort to build a hydrogen bomb—a project which was also being frantically pursued in Russia. But all of this, of course, is conjecture because the communists never chose to unveil their real reasons. Nor were Emmi and her family the most unfortunate. Many of their friends were deported at the same time and never appeared again. Stalin's followers were suffused with his paranoiac characteristics.

The situation in Tallya "was not particularly rosy," Janos recalls. Now fifteen years old, he worked in the peasant's vineyards, but his mother was not able to pursue any useful work. Their food came primarily from the peasant's garden. They were not allowed to leave the village. Most distressing to Janos was the lack of a local secondary school. Eventually he was able to catch up on his work with the help of a generous classmate back in Budapest who wrote to him every week, summarizing the week's work in school. With his friend's help, Janos pursued his school work avidly. At the end of the school year, in June 1952, he petitioned to be allowed to go to a neighboring village to take final examinations. His dedication to his studies was reminiscent of his uncle's experience a generation earlier.

"Remarkably enough," Janos told us, "I was given permission to go to a nearby town where there was a high school and take appropriate examinations. But when I arrived at the school and presented myself, they didn't dare to touch someone who had 'the plague,' so to speak. They were worried they might run into trouble." A short time later Janos was arrested when he bicycled to a neighboring village for a swim. He was haled before a local magistrate, but escaped with only a reprimand.

Emmi had repeatedly petitioned the authorities to be allowed to return to Budapest. Routinely, her pleas were turned down. Then, unexpectedly, in December 1952 she was advised that they were free to go back to the city. The reason they were allowed to return was just as unfathomable as the reason they were originally banished.

Their release from captivity may have been one of the early signs of growing popular pressure against the militancy of the hard-line Stalinist government. In March 1953 fate took a hand when Stalin died. The days of his adherent, the brutal Rakosi, were obviously numbered. Perhaps, in a desperate effort to change his image, he permitted the release of thousands more of the deportees from their rural exile. In July Rakosi was ousted and replaced by Imre Nagy, a communist, but also a man regarded as a Hungarian patriot. He reflected the resentment of the Russian yoke and the yearning for less oppression and an economic system with more emphasis on consumer goods.

As happy as Ilona, Emmi, and Janos were to return to Budapest, the experience brought new burdens. Their apartment had been confiscated. The same was true for most of the fifty thousand deportees who began to trickle back into Budapest. Only by a macabre stroke of luck did Emmi find a dwelling place. Max Teller's doctor, an old family friend, had a patient who died, making his apartment available. He notified Ilona and the three exiles moved in. They had to share the quarters with a total stranger. He, it turned out, was an informer for the secret police. He reported daily on the activities of his co-tenants.

Since the communist takeover, Edward Teller had not dared to attempt to communicate with his family, nor they with him. But both Edward from his end and Ilona and Emmi from Budapest, had kept in touch with Magda Hess, the onetime Teller family governess. Now Mrs. Jacob Schutz, she had moved from Budapest back to Chicago many years earlier. Mrs. Schutz became the relay point for information from both directions. The letters, however, were once again cautiously limited to the vaguest pleasantries about families and friends. Emmi, mainly from reading American newspapers during her days at the American embassy, was aware that her brother had become a major contributor to the development of nuclear weapons.

Reestablished in Budapest, Emmi once again found work as a private tutor and later the government apparently trusted her to the point where she was given various assignments as a translator. She was also assigned to teach employees of several foreign trade organizations that had offices in Budapest. Janos was allowed to return to school and was soon totally absorbed in his studies.

If any of them had any hopes of a return to a tolerable life, these hopes were quickly smashed. Emmi had been tutoring and teaching for a year or so after their return from exile when she received what seemed to be a routine request. The government asked her to accept a brief assignment as an interpreter in an industrial center outside Budapest. Innocently, she accepted the offer and was tendered a ride in an official car. It was ruse—she was put into the hands of the secret police and taken to prison.

For three ghastly days and nights, gentle, amiable Emmi Kirz was forced to sit up in a chair, with lights shining on her, while the communist police badgered her with questions. They wanted to know about her American associations at the embassy, her other American connections, but most of all they wanted to know about Edward Teller—where he was and what he was doing.

Emmi answered no questions because she had no answers. The more the police uncovered her apparent innocence, the more frustrated they became and the more they pressured her for information she did not have. At the end of the third day they gave up and let her sleep. On the fourth day they sent her home with stern warning never to tell what had happened. She was ordered thenceforth to meet regularly with the secret police and report on her activities.

Unable to talk about the terrible ordeal with her family, Emmi did take a chance and visit a lawyer friend, to whom she revealed the whole story. She told him the situation was so completely unbearable that she was seriously considering suicide in preference to relentless harassment by communist agents. The lawyer tried to steady her. He assured her that since she knew nothing useful to the communists they would probably not bother her again. His prediction, as it turned out, was correct. Undoubtedly, the police watched her, but they never pressed her for more information.

Meanwhile, the brightest part of the picture was that Janos was making good progress in school and in 1955 he was ready to go to the University of Budapest—if they would admit him. His prospects, on the face of it, did not look hopeful. The communist quota system allowed a certain proportion of peasants, workers, and other categories to move into higher education. But they were also realists, and Janos was bright and dedicated. The balance was apparently tipped in his favor by a professor who remembered and admired Edward Teller. Janos had first been denied even the opportunity to take entrance examinations, but when Ilona contacted the professor, the decision was reversed. Not only did Janos pass the examinations, but he did extremely well. He was admitted as a major in electrical engineering, a choice based on the predicted availability of jobs in that field.

While the communists appeared to be in firm command in Hungary, their apparent power was a veneer for seething unrest in many quarters. The old aristocracy had been wiped out, but some peasants, the suppressed bourgeoisie, and many intellectuals were kept in line only by the pervasive terror of the secret police. To many Hungarians, communism was an odious Russian import, and Russia was the historic enemy. They wanted, at least, a national communist, not a Soviet puppet, in command. The most popular choice was Imre Nagy, a moderate communist, but also regarded as a true Hungarian and a patriot. Nagy had served as Prime Minister from 1953 to 1955 in the wave of moderation that followed the death of Stalin. He was ousted when the hard-liners returned to power, putting Matyas Rakosi back in charge. Rakosi, presumably alarmed by popular uprisings against Russian influence in Poland, stepped down in June 1956. He was succeeded by another tough-minded communist, Erno Gero. Now the students in Budapest, taking their cue from Poland, were demanding the return of Imre Nagy, plus a series of political reforms based on liberal principles—such as freedom of speech—and a breaking of the Russian economic stranglehold on Hungary.

What had started as a peaceful demonstration broke into a bloody revolution when students tried to seize the Budapest radio station, closely guarded by the secret police. As the mob of students approached the station, someone started firing on them. When the shots rang out, they signaled the release of the pent-up fury of workers, peasants, and intellectuals, not just in Budapest but all over Hungary. It was not necessarily an anti-communist revolution; it was communists and anti-communists together in the greater cause of Hungarian nationalism, and against the domination of the Soviet Union.

As is so often the case in this kind of spontaneous uprising, the whole became greater than the sum of its parts. Many of those rebelling may have wished for a less violent and bloody solution, but the revolution had an internal momentum like a runaway locomotive. Thus Imre Nagy found himself thrust into power and at the throttle of this locomotive that was moving far too fast for him to control it. The direction became not just anti-Soviet, but to some extent anti-communist. Nagy repudiated the Soviet-sponsored Warsaw Treaty and declared Hungary to be a neutral nation, both steps which he may personally have wanted to avoid, but in the supercharged situation, he could only yield to the popular pressure.

The Russians feared that a successful Hungarian withdrawal from the Moscow orbit would trigger similar uprisings in the other satellite countries. By early November Russian tanks and troops already stationed in Hungary had seized strategic railroads and military outposts. Nagy appealed to the United Nations and the Russians supposedly agreed to "negotiate" the withdrawal of their forces. Actually, they had no such intention, and when the Hungarian and Soviet negotiators met in the town of Tokol, the seemingly successful proceedings were concluded with a banquet given by the Russians for their Hungarian guests. It was at its jovial height when the Soviet security police invaded the hall and arrested the Hungarian celebrants.[3]

Soviet tanks now rolled through the countryside and into Budapest. Under Soviet protection a new government was formed by Janos Kadar, a former Nagy ally, but a realist with no intention of allowing Hungary to leave the Russian orbit. He correctly observed that Nagy had lost control of the situation. Nagy eventually had to flee for his life and found sanctuary in the Yugoslav embassy. He left after a few days under an assurance of safe conduct to his home, but he underestimated Soviet treachery. As soon as he had left the embassy ground he was arrested and spirited away. The assumption is that he was executed.

In only two weeks the Hungarians, in their spontaneous uprising, had moved from Soviet-controlled communism, to national communism, to neutrality, to the hope of non-communist parliamentary democracy, and back under the Soviet heel again. The failure had cost them thousands of lives, millions of dollars in physical destruction, and hopeless resignation to orthodox communism for the foreseeable future.

If escape from communism can be considered a blessing, even if it means exile from one's native country, there were 200,000 lucky Hungarians, and Janos Kirz was one of them. He was a sophomore at the University of Budapest when the revolution erupted. In the midst of the chaos it became generally known in Budapest that the Austrian border was open, that escape was possible. On the other hand, self-imposed exile, while feasible, did not seem necessary during the brief period when it appeared that the revolution would succeed and that Hungary might even join the Western orbit of free nations. When this hope was smashed by the Russian tanks, Ilona Teller, Emmi, and Janos still entertained the idea that all three could leave together.

By the end of November, with the revolution over, and the Russians firmly in control, there was still a steady stream of escapees moving into Austria. Emmi's conclusion, however, was that her mother, now seventy-three, would be in no condition to attempt the exertions necessary to achieve a successful escape. The idea that either Emmi or Ilona would try to escape illegally was therefore abandoned.

After weighing the matter carefully, the mother, sister, and nephew of Edward Teller reached a painful decision. Possibly, they thought, because of Ilona's age, and because of Emmi's relative lack of essential skills needed by the government, there was a remote hope that they could eventually acquire passports and leave Hungary legally. But they knew that Janos, in training as an electrical engineer, and of military age, would never be allowed to emigrate. He was a prisoner in Hungary. The decision was that Janos should try to escape as soon as possible.

It was possible. For inexplicable reasons, the Russians were maintaining only minimal control over the Austrian border; almost as if they were willing to allow past and potential troublemakers to get out. But escape was still a hazardous undertaking—a certain proportion of the attempted escapes were failing, and the authorities dealt harshly with those who were caught.

Information about the various ways of escaping was being passed by word of mouth through Budapest. Janos, after weighing a number of possibilities, threw his lot in with a peasant who owned a farm on the Austrian border. He was making periodic trips to Budapest by train, rounding up small groups who wanted to escape, and then escorting them back to his farm, where he had developed a complex escape procedure.

The whole process could never have occurred without a great deal of sympathy and cooperation from a variety of Hungarians. For example, when the passengers boarded the train, the railroad authorities knew that many of them were traveling for the sole reason of hoping to escape. When the train neared the last station at the Austrian border, the train crew stopped in the farmlands a quarter of a mile short of the station. The potential escapees disembarked and vanished into the wheatfields. Then the train continued on its last quarter mile, to be greeted by Russian authorities who found no one aboard without legitimate business.

The peasant in charge of Janos's party led them to his house. There he provided them with dinner. When night fell he escorted them to the border, where the hospitable Austrian authorities took over. There Janos and his fellow exiles signed a receipt for the peasant which he took back to Budapest to collect his fee. The escape cost Emmi 5,000 Hungarian forints, or about $200.

The casualness with which Janos Kirz describes his own escape belies the extreme hazard of the undertaking. One week later, the same peasant, with a new consignment, was ambushed by the Russians. He was executed on the spot. His captured and thwarted refugees presumably were sent to prison. Janos had escaped by the grace of one week.

Janos had enough money to take a bus to Vienna, to the home of an old family friend who was already housing ten Hungarian refugees. He stayed with them for three weeks. His first attempt to contact Edward Teller was not made directly, but to Magda Hess Schutz in Chicago. He sent her a cablegram with the news that he was safe in Vienna. Mrs. Schutz telephoned Mici in Berkeley, where she and Edward were then living.

Teller immediately contacted some State Department officials to see if he could hasten Janos's trip to America. He was advised that by this time the refugee organizations were working so smoothly that any outside interference might only delay Janos's clearance to enter the United States. In early January, Janos was bused to Lansberg Air Force Base near Munich, from which he was flown directly to Camp Kilmer in New Jersey. The old World War I embarkation camp had been converted into a Hungarian refugee center.

From Kilmer, the first direct link was established between Edward Teller and the family he had left behind. Janos, whom Teller had never seen, telephoned, and arrangements were made to fly Teller's nephew immediately to Berkeley. He arrived there on January 15, 1957, which happened to be Edward's forty-ninth birthday. Two weeks later, a young man, not yet twenty, who had scarcely known a month in his life without fear, persecution, anxiety, or hunger, was a student at the University of California on the peaceful slopes above the blue Pacific Ocean.

Janos lived with the Tellers for two years. He fitted well into the family, and there was an immediate warm and mutual friendship between the refugee and his cousins, Paul and Wendy, though they were several years younger.

But joy in the presence of Janos as a link with the family back in Budapest was offset by the reality of the plight of Edward's sister and mother. Emmi was now separated from her only son. Ilona was growing old in a hostile and unstable country.

The means by which Emmi Kirz and Ilona Teller were freed

from their bondage is one of the bizarre episodes of Teller's life. After the death of his father and the communists' shutting off of Hungary from the West, Teller nevertheless made numerous appeals to the State Department to prevail on the Hungarian authorities to set his family free. In April 1956, just prior to the revolution, Teller sought the help of the powerful and influential Lewis Strauss, former chairman of the Atomic Energy Commission. Even Strauss was unable to turn the necessary wheels. It was a touchy situation. By that time Teller was known as the developer of the hydrogen bomb and was outspokenly distrustful of the Russians. The Soviets certainly felt that they owed this man no favors.

In truth, Edward was increasingly fearful that there might be retaliation against his mother and sister for allowing Janos to escape. Fortunately, with 200,000 Hungarians having fled the country during and immediately after the uprising, Janos Kadar's unsteady post-revolutionary regime was not in a position to seek additional revenge. Teller's family was not bothered again, but Teller had no way of knowing this.

"I tried all kinds of things, but nothing worked," he recalls.

It was a totally unexpected scheme that did work. One day, probably in late 1958, Teller, in a visit to Washington, bumped into his old friend Leo Szilard.

The bond between the two scientists was founded on an association that went back to their youth in Budapest, and had been strengthened through Teller's participation in Szilard's early efforts to convince the United States government of the potential of nuclear energy. Szilard was a domineering, even arrogant man, but Teller had always rolled with Szilard's intellectual punches and respected him just the same.

By 1958 there was, in theory, nothing to sustain their friendship; Szilard had moved politically leftward, while Teller had twined to the right. But physics and Hungarian blood were thicker than politics. Their only concession to formality was that each, in the Edwardian tradition, addressed the other by his last name.

"Szilard, won't you have dinner with me?"

"Teller, I'd be delighted."

At dinner, when they had caught up with each other's adventures and engaged in a little shop talk, Szilard took a chance and launched into politics. As Teller remembers the discussion, it went like this:

"Teller, you *must* come and visit Russia. If you'd only see—see them in *action*—you'd change your mind about them. You just *have* to see Russia."

Teller's response was curt. "I have no intention of visiting Russia."

"Why, why?" Szilard shook his chubby finger. "Don't be unreasonable."

"Look," said Teller, now leaning forward for emphasis. "There are many reasons, but one of them is this."

"Is what?"

"My mother and sister live in Hungary. Once I'm in Russia I don't know what the communists might do to force me into a situation which I don't like; try to extract information from me, whatever. They have kept these two women as hostages and this alone makes it *impossible* for me to visit Russia."

Szilard straightened up stiffly, almost in indignation.

"Teller, you are completely wrong. The Russians would never stoop to such methods. But I understand how you feel. Let me see what I can do about it."

What could Szilard do? Teller made no effort to press his friend on this cryptic response. But he knew Szilard had certain limited connections. These came about mainly because Szilard had attended the first Pugwash Conference. These meetings were the creation of the Canadian-born Cleveland industrialist Cyrus S. Eaton. Eaton had an almost idyllic belief in high-level coexistence. In this spirit he invited the top communist planners and scientists and some comparable American scientists, industrialists, and political leaders to a meeting at his summer playground in Pugwash, Nova Scotia.

If the Americans at Pugwash leaned a little toward the starry-eyed, Szilard was not of that ilk. As Teller learned the story, his Hungarian friend threw the first conference into confusion with an absurdly simple idea, "a characteristic Szilardian proposal," according to Teller.

Szilard's position was that there will never be real understanding between the capitalist and communist worlds unless each admits its weaknesses. There should be a thorough airing, in writing, of the shortcomings in each system. Further, Szilard contended, it should be the Americans who write about the mistakes of capitalism, and the weaknesses of communism should be admitted in writing by the Russians.

Szilard's proposal was answered with silence. There was no visible reaction, no discussion, according to Teller. It died aborning.

Soon after his chance meeting with Teller in Washington, Szilard left to attend the second Pugwash Conference. When he met the head of the Russian delegation, he recounted Teller's "absurd" story about his mother and sister being kept in Hungary against their wishes.

As Szilard relayed the conversation to Teller, the top Soviet representative feigned astonishment. "But why do you tell *me?*" he responded to Szilard. "Hungary is an independent country. I have nothing to do with what goes on in Hungary."

Nevertheless, just a half hour later the head of the Hungarian delegation approached the ex-Hungarian physicist. Szilard repeated the story of the plight of Teller's family. The Hungarian official listened politely, but made no commitments.

Three weeks later, in Budapest, Ilona Teller and Emmi Kirz were notified that they would be given passports to leave Hungary. Their forty-year vigil of turmoil and tragedy was about to end.

Why was Szilard able to accomplish what all of Teller's influential connections could not accomplish? For the outcome, Teller says, he is inclined to be both grateful and cynical. His analysis of the situation is that, first, the Hungarians realized that no purpose was served in keeping two harmless women in Hungary against their wishes. But Teller also believes that Szilard rather cleverly put them on the spot. He had defended the communists against Teller's harsh accusations that they were holding sister and mother as hostages. The communists did not want to lose the friendship of so influential a scientist as Szilard. But if they refused to respond to his pleas on behalf of Teller's family, they would, in effect, be admitting that Teller was right. Rather than alienate Szilard they decided to make the grand gesture of goodwill.

Regardless of how cynical the communists' motives might have been, the outcome was an extremely happy one. On January 18, 1959, a plane bearing the surviving members of the Teller family touched down at San Francisco airport. They were together again after twenty-three years.

10

Deuterium, Tritium, and Politics

AS the radioactive smoke from Hiroshima and Nagasaki drifted around the world, a new era in Teller's life began, as it did for many others, on a wild evening on August 14, 1945. He and Mici were at home in Los Alamos when, as Teller described it,

> the mountain quiet was shattered suddenly. . . . A wild racket broke upon the serenity of Jemez Mesa in a single instant, as if by a prearranged signal. Sirens whined, bells rang. Dozens of automobile horns blasted. I thought a giant traffic jam somehow had developed in the quiet streets. The cacophony was completed by the sounds of people running and shouting to each other. I rushed from my apartment to investigate the commotion, and soon discovered its cause: Japan had surrendered. The war was over.[1]

Just as the soldiers and sailors overseas wanted desperately to return to their homes and families, the euphoria of peace brought a similar reaction to the scientists of the Manhattan Project. Teller did not completely share the euphoria. He could understand and sympathize with the desire of his colleagues to put weapons work behind them and to return to the joy of pure science. Teller himself had such an opportunity. He had been invited to join the faculty of the University of Chicago, where he would work with his old friend Enrico Fermi. But events in the world gave Teller a visceral feeling that the danger was not over and he was distressed that not only servicemen and scientists, but even government officials in Washington wanted to get away from it all. "I knew that disintegration of the Los Alamos Laboratory could be a threat to America's future," he wrote later in *The Legacy of Hiroshima*.[2]

Hans Bethe, whose stature and influence were to continue to grow after the war, had a talk with Teller a few months after V-J Day. He recalled it for us:

"About New Year's of 1946 I had a long conversation with Edward about the future of Los Alamos. Oppie was leaving, or maybe had left already, so there was a question of succession.

"Edward asked whether I wouldn't take over from Oppie, which I didn't want to do at all. But I returned the compliment and said it would be a good thing if he took over because he was more interested in continuing this. 'Why don't you become the director?' I asked, but somehow he didn't like that."

At that time the leading candidate to succeed Oppenheimer was Norris Bradbury. In anticipation of Bradbury's accession, Bethe had another suggestion for Teller.

"I asked Edward, if Bradbury were to be the director, couldn't he be the leader of the theoretical division.

"And in this conversation, for the first time in my recollection, he expressed himself as terribly pessimistic about relations with Russia. He was terribly anti-communist, terribly anti-Russian. Now I knew that he had been anti-communist during the communist takeover in Hungary when he was about eleven, but now it came out in a much more forceful way.

"Teller said we had to continue research on nuclear weapons . . . it was really wrong of all of us to want to leave. The war was not over and Russia was just as dangerous an enemy as Germany had been."

Bethe couldn't agree. "I just couldn't go along with that. I thought it was more important to go home and get the universities restarted, to train young physicists again, and I was eager to get back to my own research. So we disagreed, but in a very friendly way at that time."

Meanwhile, back in Washington, the capital had generally accepted the comforting—and mistaken—belief that it would be at least twenty years before any other nation could develop an atom bomb. The military, of course, was thinking of Russia. Even as late as 1948 J. Robert Oppenheimer underrated the Soviets' technical ability and dedication. In a personal letter to the chairman of the General Board of the Navy he wrote:

> At the present time to the best of my knowledge the Soviet Union is not in a position to effectively attack the United States itself. Opinions differ and evidence is scanty as to how long such a state of affairs may last. One important factor may be the time necessary for the Soviet Union to carry out the program of atomic energy to obtain a

significant atomic armament. With all recognition for the need of caution in such predictions, I tend to believe that for a long time to come the Soviet Union will not have achieved this objective, nor even the more minor, but also dangerous possibility of conducting radiological warfare.[3]

Only a year later the Soviets were to prove that not only Oppenheimer but the Central Intelligence Agency knew little about Russian nuclear research. The CIA predicted as late as 1949 that the earliest the Soviet Union could produce an A-bomb would be sometime in the 1950s. The CIA was wrong, too.

Perhaps back on that night of August 14, 1945, Teller was one of the few that did not underestimate the potential of the Soviet Union. In any case, while others were rejoicing, Teller was worrying. He couldn't sleep. He didn't share the conventional assessment that denigrated Soviet science. Perhaps his childhood experiences had made him paranoid about the Russians.

The inviation to return to Chicago and teach physics was extremely tempting. In time, as Beth had suggested, Norris Bradbury, Oppenheimer's successor, invited Teller to be head of the laboratory's theoretical division.[4] This was tempting, too, but in Teller's mind the nation's atomic weapons project could afford no postwar lull.

He made his position clear to Bradbury: "I said I would remain only if the laboratory's intensive level of theoretical work could be maintained and channeled toward either of two goals—development of a hydrogen bomb* or refinement of atomic explosions." More specifically, Teller's demand was "a great effort to build a hydrogen bomb in the shortest possible time, or develop new methods of fission explosive and speed progress by at least a dozen tests a year."[5]

Bradbury's response, as Teller remembers it, gave him no hope at all. "I wish I could say that we will do one or the other, but the political conditions are such that I cannot promise you either." Bradbury was probably accurate in his assessment of the mood of the country. The war was over. Everyone wanted to go home. After so many years of battle and bloodshed, who could get enthusiastic about a crash program to build new weapons?

*The term "hydrogen," as applied to hydrogen fusion or a hydrogen bomb, actually refers not to ordinary hydrogen, but to one of the hydrogen isotopes, deuterium or tritium, sometimes referred to as "heavy hydrogen."

That evening there was a party at the home of Admiral William S. Parsons, who had headed up the Los Alamos engineering division. Oppenheimer was one of the guests. Despite the stresses in their relationship, Teller could still approach Oppenheimer as the most influential scientist in the country. He had only recently laid down the burdens of the directorship, but for many years he would continue to personify the electrifying success of Los Alamos.

Teller told Oppie of his discouraging conversation that afternoon with Bradbury. Perhaps the resigned director could still turn the tide. Teller's approach was direct: "This has been your laboratory, and its future depends on you. I will stay if you tell me that you will use your influence to help me accomplish either of my goals—that is, will you help enlist support for work toward a hydrogen bomb, or further development of the atom bomb?" Oppenheimer's response was curt: "I neither can nor will do so."[6]

Oppenheimer was undoubtedly speaking from his own convictions, but at that moment in history it is difficult to imagine any scientist giving Teller a different answer. To Teller it was clear that without the support and influence of Oppenheimer there was little possibility of firing up the government to push either project. Teller was not inclined to tilt at windmills. Within a few minutes he told Oppenheimer he had decided to accept the post at Chicago. Oppenheimer appeared to be pleased. He clasped Teller's hand, smiled, and told him, "You are doing the right thing." Later that same evening, as they were leaving Parsons's house, Oppenheimer again spoke to Teller. "Now that you have decided to go to Chicago, don't you feel better?"[7]

Teller did not feel better, but at least he had made up his mind. On February 1, 1946, the Tellers loaded the last of their belongings on a moving van and headed back to Chicago. Behind them on the mesa was the miracle city that had been home for three unbelievable years. Teller was to return often, sometimes fervently hoping to resurrect the superbomb program and other times finding even his own interest flagging as he was absorbed back into the academic climate of the University of Chicago.

The small theoretical group that remained at Los Alamos was headed by Robert Richtmyer. It is impossible, given the sudden slackening of the national muscle, to evaluate the performance of Richtmyer's group. But Teller took comfort that a few physicists were still there and working. As long as they kept the flame, there was a chance of a second coming.

During this period in neither the Soviet Union nor the United
States was there any significant public awareness or concern that
the hydrogen bomb was waiting to be discovered. Both nations
kept the secret stored in the scientific cupboard. A few times, outside Russia, the cupboard was opened briefly, but few representatives of the press or the public took notice. For example, the theory
of thermonuclear fusion was carefully explained at an open hearing of the Senate Special Committee on Atomic Energy in November 1945. Even when the transcript was published, it attracted little
attention.

The expert testimony was from Hans Bethe, who was called
upon to discuss the possibility of obtaining energy from atomic nuclei other than the nuclei of uranium or plutonium. Bethe, Teller's
old wartime Los Alamos boss, knew the subject as well as anybody.
Way back in 1938, at the Washington Conference on Theoretical
physics, his interest in the subject had been kindled by Gamow and
Teller. Bethe's theoretical findings were fundamental to subsequent discoveries.

Bethe emphasized to the Senate committee that "it is necessary
to make a clear distinction between the theoretical possibility of releasing atomic energy and the practical feasibility of doing so.
Theoretically, on the basis of the energy stored in the atomic nucleus according to Einstein's theory, energy could be obtained
from most atomic nuclei. For instance, the splitting of any of the
heavy nuclei into two or more parts, such as takes place in the
fission process, will release large amounts of energy if the splitting
can be accomplished. Likewise, the combination of two or more
light nuclei, such as hydrogen, into one will also release considerable energy—in this case the energy release is connected with a
building up of nuclei, not with a splitting. Only some medium-
weight nuclei such as iron are exceptions—no energy can be obtained from them either by splitting or by building up."

The problem, therefore, as emphasized by Bethe, "does not lie
in finding great stores [of energy] of atomic nuclei, but in finding a
way to release it." The laboratory transformations of atomic nuclei, either by splitting or building up, take place in only a few
atoms at a time and do release energy, but not enough to be of any
practical importance.

"How, then, can we ignite atomic nuclei?" Bethe asked. "In other words, how can we start a nuclear reaction which continues on
its own power and releases energy from the atomic nucleus in

practical amounts? There are only two known methods to obtain such a nuclear chain reaction. One of these is the nuclear fission on which the atomic bomb is based. The other involves the nuclear reactions which we believe take place in the interior of the stars, and which involve light nuclei.

"The sun's energy," Bethe continued, "is believed to be due to reactions between hydrogen nuclei on one side and carbon and nitrogen nuclei on the other. Each atomic nucleus has a positive electrical charge, therefore, they repel each other. It is difficult for two nuclei to get into contact and undergo a nuclear reaction. They can do this only if they move at each other with very high velocity. Then the velocity carries them together in spite of the repulsive forces."

The temperature at the center of the sun, as Bethe confirmed, is about 20 million degrees centigrade. This heat provides the high velocity necessary for a sustained and continuing thermonuclear reaction. Though Bethe didn't use the term, a kind of perpetual motion takes place in the sun and the stars because the high atomic velocities go on forever. In Bethe's terms, "The nuclear reaction can go on indefinitely and we have a self-sustaining reaction. The energy released from the nuclei produces the high temperature in the stars, and the high temperature in turn enables the nuclei to get together and release their energy."

After pointing out that "it seems almost impossible to create these conditions on earth," Bethe casually suggested the possibility of a hydrogen bomb as an example of a practical use of thermonuclear fusion. But, he explained, "In order to get the reactions accelerated to this extent, it would be necessary to have even higher temperatures than in the center of the sun."

Teller was not aware then, or later, of Bethe's testimony, or at least says he has no recollection of it. He was, of course, familiar with the subject. Surprisingly, at about this same time, the possibility of building a thermonuclear bomb, with a nuclear trigger, was broached in a commercially published book by Austrian physicist Hans Thirring. At some point Teller vaguely heard of Thirring's book, but never read it ("Perhaps I should have," he told us in 1974). The book was called *Die Geschichte der Atombombe* (The Story of the Atom Bomb).

Chapter 42 of Thirring's work was entitled "Die Superatombombe" and was remarkable in its understanding of the thermonuclear bomb principle, even if inaccurate in some of its forecasts.

Thirring begins his chapter with a discussion of the possibility of initiating a nuclear reaction by the use of a thermal process.* He suggests that the nuclear process so initiated might emit energy very rapidly, giving rise to a further increase in temperature, thus producing an explosive chain reaction. The fission of plutonium or uranium 235 offers the means to achieve the very high energies required for initiation of a thermonuclear process, according to the author.

Specifically, Thirring suggests that uranium 235 or plutonium be surrounded with a substance containing deuterium, for example, heavy water, paraffin, or lithium hydride. A second shell composed of a heavy substance would be required as a tamper in order to prevent this assembly from flying apart prematurely. At the moment of explosion, according to Thirring, fragments will be produced on the surface of the plutonium with energies of the order of 100 million electron volts, which will collide with the surrounding deuterium and transfer part of their energy. Though the transferred energy would be only a small fraction, it would be sufficient to promote the fusion reaction producing helium.

Thirring states that whether or not a chain reaction can be developed will depend, of course, on the feasibility of developing a suitable tamper which would defer the bursting of the bomb long enough so as to prevent rapid expansion with accompanying drop in temperature. Thus Thirring is clearly aware that the feasibility of developing a chain reaction involving fusion of light elements was open to question at that time.

The chapter closes with a discussion in which it is pointed out that the use of a fission bomb for triggering a fusion bomb would make it possible to produce a very much more powerful weapon, though it would not effectively decrease the amount of scarce U-235 or plutonium required for the production of a single bomb. Thirring, however, stressed again that the feasibility of the super-bomb is highly problematical even though the data he presents are believed to be reasonably sound.

Was Thirring a prophet or merely a good physicist? The subject he wrote about in 1946 was classified in the United States and remains so today. In 1974 the authors presented Teller with a copy of

---

*The authors are indebted to Dr. Manfred Mayer of the Johns Hopkins University for a summary translation of Chapter 42 of Thirring. The authors have further modified Dr. Mayer's translation.

this portion of *Die Geschichte der Atombombe* and asked him for a comment. Teller, though he disapproves of long-term classification, still believes in playing by the rules. His response was guarded. "The information contained in Thirring's book was known to people working in the field in 1946."

We pushed Teller a little more. Was Thirring correct in his theoretical description of a superbomb? "Thirring was not a fool," was Teller's reply, and nothing more.

As subsequent events bore out, Thirring's suggested technique was not quite feasible. He did, however, suggest the use of one substance, deuterium, that was later used with success. Teller used deuterium in combination with tritium in both of the two first U.S. detonations, the Greenhouse experiment and the Mike test. Thirring also suggested the use of lithium hydride as a fusion fuel. Once again, he was close. The Bravo test of the Castle series (which successfully detonated America's first H-bomb deliverable by aircraft) used lithium deuteride.

If Teller had read Thirring's little book in 1946, would the H-bomb have been developed sooner? Almost certainly not. The Austrian scientist's suggesting the use of liquid deuterium was sound, but deuterium needs tritium, another hydrogen isotope, in order to initiate a thermonuclear reaction. It is possible, however, that Hans Thirring's proposed use of solid lithium hydride could have served as an early alert to the feasibility of using a dry bomb and if this had happened sooner, it might have affected the outcome of the thermonuclear bomb race with the Russians.*

In 1946, while Thirring's book was being published in Vienna, Edward Teller had returned to his teaching and basic research at the University of Chicago. There were times, back in the surprisingly normal routine of the campus, when he almost forgot about weapons work, but seldom for long. He and Mici rented an apartment close to the campus, and visited the Fermis often, for bridge or Ping-Pong.

One of Teller's most promising students of this period was Mar-

---

*Actually there was some speculation as early as 1946 at Los Alamos on the possible application of lithium isotopes for weapons use. Robert D. Krohn, now a member of the Los Alamos Technical Information Group, recalls a discussion by physicist William Ogle on the possibility of separating lithium isotopes. Ogle predicted it would be easy to do because of the relatively large mass differences as compared with the small mass differences in uranium isotopes.

vin L. Goldberger, who was eventually to rise to the chairmanship of the physics department at Princeton. Ironically, he also became a severe and even bitter critic of Teller. Goldberger's opposition to Teller is based on a whole spectrum of differences. Goldberger disapproved of Teller's obsessive advocacy of the H-bomb. He believed (and still believes) that Teller's fear of the Russians borders on paranoia. In the eventual confrontation between Teller and Oppenheimer in the latter's security hearing, Goldberger was among the most vitriolic in his condemnation of Teller's testimony. At the same time, Goldberger has always acknowledged Teller's skill as a physicist. We asked Goldberger about his recollections and impressions of Teller in the postwar years in Chicago.

"After Dr. Teller joined the faculty at Chicago," Goldberger said, "he was involved in the selection of the first batch of graduate students to be admitted to the physics department at that time. I went to speak to him about the possibility of my doing graduate work at the University of Chicago. In some sense or other, he interviewed me for this.

"Subsequently, as a student at the university, I began to do my Ph.D. with Teller, but at a certain point he became so deeply involved with defense problems that he said he no longer had time to supervise thesis work and suggested that my colleague, Jeffrey Chew, and I should go to Enrico Fermi and ask him to take us on as students, which he did."

As a student remembering a professor, Goldberger's analysis of Teller's physics and politics differs in many ways from the judgment of other former students.

"First, in connection with his physics," Goldberger said, "he was doing, at the time I was in Chicago, virtually no research. Although he kept up with physics and interrelated strongly with people, and discussed problems with them, he himself was not doing anything of any particular significance. He had made a number of important contributions to physics as a younger man before the war, and I was quite familiar with his work. He did one piece of work, that I remember, in collaboration with Fermi on mu mesons which was very interesting and important.

"He was an extremely clever person, with deep physical intuition," Goldberger said, although differing with the assessment of other Teller associates in one particular respect: "He very frequently had difficulty in explaining his intuitions to others. I remember often during seminars when he would make a remark, and after he was finished, Fermi would get up and supplement Teller's comments with 'what Teller is trying to say is thus and such.'"

Another of Teller's students judged him somewhat differently. Harold Agnew, who was ultimately to become director of Los Alamos, also studied physics at Chicago.

To Agnew, Teller "was a wonderful lecturer for two types of individuals: those who knew absolutely nothing—in basic freshman courses he was a superb lecturer; or for those who knew everything. But for the in-between individual, it was very rough."

Actually, despite Goldberger's recollection, Teller did publish fourteen research papers during the several years he was in Chicago. Many of them were in collaboration with the most prominent physicists of that era. For example, there were three on mesotrons; one of the three was written with Fermi, another with Fermi and Victor Weisskopf, and another with McMillan. A paper on deuterium reactions was co-authored with Konopinski. Two papers were in collaboration with Maria Mayer, who was later to win a Nobel prize, and there were various others with such luminaries as Frederic de Hoffmann and Robert Richtmyer.

Goldberger belongs to the school that attributes at least part of Teller's fear and distrust of the Russians to the scars of early childhood. In this respect, Goldberger agrees with Hans Bethe.

"I became acquainted with his politics very early," Goldberger said, "and found that even during the period of late 1945, when the glow over U.S.-Soviet relations was rather widespread, that he already at that time expressed extreme apprehension about the Soviets and great concern over their growing military strength and their imperialist tendencies.

"It was known that his family had suffered seriously during the communist takeover in Hungary in 1919. He had a very deep hatred of the Russians." Goldberger didn't believe that in the post-World War II period Teller's fear was shared by his peers. "He was in a complete minority."

Goldberger was correct in asserting that only a minority of the scientists shared Teller's views, but it was a rather distinguished minority. John von Neumann was at least as anti-Russian, and Nobel Laureate Eugene Wigner was in Teller's political camp then and remains with him today. The reader can draw his own conclusions about the fact that von Neumann and Wigner were also Hungarians who had experienced both communism and fascism. Other scientists who concurred to some degree with Teller were

Ernest Lawrence, Luis Alvarez, David T. Griggs, and, at least in certain respects, Enrico Fermi.

Teller was still a consultant to Los Alamos. The work on the "super" was on the back burner, but there was some vigor in the work on the improvement of fission weapons. Hans Bethe was also a consultant at this time. "What remained," according to Bethe, "was the straightforward extension of the work on the fission weapon that we had done during the war. And on that Los Alamos did exceedingly well in the intervening years from 1945 to 1949."

"The main problem," Bethe remembers, "was to reduce the size of the weapon. The Nagasaki bomb was extremely clumsy, extremely big. It was a plutonium bomb and in the following three years there was a great refinement of the implosion techniques and thereby a reduction of the size of the weapon to something that could be carried even by fighter-bombers."

The implosion technique was also applied to the uranium 235 bomb. The gun-type trigger that had detonated the bomb over Hiroshima was largely abandoned in favor of the implosion that was first used only with plutonium.

In 1946 and 1947 Teller acquired two friends who were to influence and guide his life for many years thereafter. In the summer of 1946, when Edward and Mici were at Los Alamos, their second child, a girl, was born. Both parents admired the British actress Wendy Hiller and decided to name their daughter after her. Then Edward had some second thoughts—Wendy was a mere nickname. So to add respectability to it, they named their newborn girl Susan Wendy, but no one ever called her by her first name.

Between Edward Teller and Wendy there quickly developed that special affection that typifies the relationship between a father and his first daughter. He doted on her in her childhood and when she grew up they became friends with a mutual admiration. Wendy became a raven-haired beauty, with her father's dark coloring (but little else in physical resemblance), her mother's vivacity, and her paternal grandmother's features. She went to Wellesley, took a graduate degree in mathematics at Berkeley, and in 1971 married Alan Saleski, a mathematician on the faculty of the University of Virginia. In 1975 Wendy and her father were hard at work, collaborating on a popular book on physics.

Despite their closeness, Wendy assesses her father with both affection and detachment—"He is a frustrated man because his point of view is not popular . . . and he's a little bit vain." As for his position as head of the household: "He was away too much, but whenever he was home he always had time for Paul and me. My mother runs the household. My father doesn't have the slightest idea what's going on."

The other friend was Lewis L. Strauss.* Teller met him in 1947 and they eventually became devoted philosophical and political allies. Strauss had acquired a position of immense wealth and power through an incredible life in which he rose from poverty through dogged hard work, through devotion to Herbert Hoover during his rise to the presidency, and through an innate touch of financial genius that made him a millionaire investment banker before he was thirty. Although he had never been to college, he became fascinated with physics. This served him well during World War II when he joined the naval reserve as assistant to the chief of the Naval Bureau of Ordnance. He rose to the rank of rear admiral in a series of top-level jobs in the Navy Department.

In 1946 President Harry Truman named Strauss, recently returned to civilian life, a member of the first Atomic Energy Commission. At a meeting in April 1947, shortly after the new commissioners were confirmed by the Senate, Admiral Strauss addressed a memorandum to his new colleagues.

The memorandum questioned whether the Manhattan Engineer District Intelligence Division had engaged in continuous monitoring of the upper stratosphere for evidence of radioactivity.

> This would perhaps be the best means we would have for discovering that a test of atomic weapons had been made by another nation. It is to be presumed that any other country going into a large-scale manufacture of atomic weapons would be under the necessity of conducting at least one test to "prove" the weapon. If there is no such monitoring system in effect, it is incumbent upon us to bring up the desirability of such an immediate step and, in default of action, to initiate it ourselves at once.

Strauss's suggestion was unanimously approved, and he was assigned the task of implementing it.

Moving a gaggle of bureaucrats toward a common objective is never easy. To Strauss, at times, it must have felt like pushing on a slack string. If a monitoring system is to function effectively, there

---

*Strauss pronounced his name "straws."

must be centralized control. In this case that goal seemed un-reachable. The agencies involved included the Joint Chiefs of Staff, the Army, the Army Air Force, the Navy, Central Intelligence, the Joint Research and Development Board, the Department of State, and the Atomic Energy Commission.

But perhaps one of the agencies was already monitoring the atmosphere on its own—Strauss just didn't know. After several weeks of delay his first port of call was the office of the Secretary of the Navy, James V. Forrestal. When Strauss suggested that the United States apparently didn't have the capability to determine if the Russians were testing atomic weapons, Forrestal couldn't accept the reality. "Hell," he sneered, "we must be doing it!"[8]

"Well," Strauss replied, "you can be sure it isn't going on in the Navy or you would know it. Why not call Ken Royall and see if the Army or the Air Force is?"

Forrestal phoned Secretary of War Royall. The War Department had no such operation and no plans for one.

Strauss looked Forrestal squarely in the eye.

"Jim, if neither of the armed services takes on this responsibility, the commission will. If we do it, we'll have to buy planes and hire pilots. We'll have to get an appropriation for that. When we ask for the money, that will be the first time that Congress will know that monitoring hasn't been going on all this time."[9]

Strauss met Forrestal again on September 15, 1947, and by this time the latter had gotten the message. A few days later, on September 16, General Eisenhower, as chief of staff, ordered General Carl A. Spaatz and the Air Force to establish and operate a system that would have as its objective "the determination of the time and place of all large explosions which might occur anywhere in the world, and to ascertain in a manner which would leave no question, whether or not they were of nuclear origin."[10]

The plan was to have a monitoring system in operation by the spring of 1948. That was when a series of test nuclear shots, with the code name Sandstone, were to be staged in the Pacific Proving Grounds in the Marshall Islands. After the usual number of hitches and delays, the monitoring procedure was in operation, just in time for the Sandstone tests. It was clearly determined that atomic detonation in the atmosphere could be detected.[11]

Lewis Strauss was making a place for himself in the emerging postwar nuclear world, but he had yet to meet Edward Teller.

In that same spring of 1948, Teller's energies were branching off in some surprising new directions. The political liberalism that had dominated the Roosevelt era, and which Teller at one time more or less espoused, had not been entirely snuffed out by his suspicion of the Soviets. He still had dreams of nuclear blessings being shared by all of the nations on the earth under an international control system, and perhaps under a world government.

"I participated in the World Federalist movement for a short time," Teller confesses. "Then I found them to be unrealistic and I put the emphasis on Atlantic Union, which tries to have a more moderate aim of pulling together advanced democracies instead of trying to mix fire and water, or red and blue."

Not only did Teller support these causes, he was even willing to speak out for them. "After 1945," he remembers, "I got into bad habits, including the habit of public speaking. And perhaps even the worse habit of advocating some steps for the defense of the United States." Defense, in terms of Teller's early postwar thinking, included the attempt to form some kind of world federation.

"Today I would formulate these ideas in slightly more moderate terms, but I'm afraid I acquired those ideas in the late 1940s and I talked about them on many occasions."

As late as the spring of 1948—that same spring when Lewis Strauss was setting up his weapons-monitoring system—Teller accepted an invitation to speak on behalf of the World Federalists. The place was Temple Emanu-El in New York, an institution so well established that it was often called simply "the synagogue."

Teller, born a Jew, never practiced as one, and Mici, born a Jew, was actually raised as a Christian. The inside of a synagogue was not exactly familiar territory for either of them. Nevertheless, they were enthusiastically greeted by the rabbi.

The experience, immediately before the speech, proved difficult. The rabbi discovered that if Teller knew little of Judaism, his wife knew even less. "Mici displayed a remarkable ignorance about everything connected with the synagogue and the rabbi was visibly scandalized," her husband recalls.

But the show had to go on, and Teller made his speech. "I was told to talk for thirty minutes, precisely, and I am very proud of the fact that I spoke for thirty minutes, precisely."

Then there was another of those critical events in the shaping of Teller's life and thought.

"After I spoke some people came up to talk to me. One of them was a little old lady. She asked me what I thought of the Atomic

Energy Commission, which was then still quite newly established.

"I told her the AEC was very important and very hopeful, and I was glad it was established. She said this was very nice to hear because her son was working for the Atomic Energy Commission and she was worried about whether he was doing the right thing."

Would Teller like to meet her son? Of course, he would. The proud mother produced her boy. He was Lewis Strauss.

Teller and Strauss met at the foot of the bimah* and almost from that day on were drawn together emotionally. They were quite different; Strauss was shy for all of his wealth and power; Teller was effusive and gregarious. Both were Jews, but the religious comparison ended there. Strauss was an Orthodox Jew who prayed twice a day. Teller was religiously neutral. Years later Strauss would admit that his only disappointment in Teller was that the scientist so completely lacked a formal religious commitment.

In February 1948 the Soviet armies invaded Czechoslovakia. In April 1948 the Soviets blockaded the corridors to West Berlin, forcing the United States and its allies to feed and supply the city with a massive airlift. This was the same year that Alger Hiss, a former State Department official, then president of the Carnegie Endowment for International Peace, was accused of passing State Department documents to the Soviets. The tensions were growing. A substantial number of Americans saw a real danger of armed conflict with the Russians.

Up to this point the international situation still had not moved the superbomb off the back burner. Strauss and Kenneth Nichols, Groves's deputy in the Manhattan Project, were reported to have "joined in recommending that only the current level of effort be maintained in the thermonuclear program."[12] It was again a question of priorities. The theoretical calculations for a fusion bomb did not appear promising and there was work to be done in perfecting fission weapons.

Then, in the end of 1948, came a historic upset that moved Edward Teller close to his destined achievement. Defying all the pre-election predictions of pundits and pollsters, Harry Truman was elected President for a full term in his own right. The voters also surprised the experts by giving Truman a Democratic Congress.

---

*The bimah is the raised platform in the center of the synagogue on which is the desk for reading the Scroll of the Law.

This moved Connecticut Senator Brien McMahon into the chairmanship of the Joint Committee on Atomic Energy.

The previous June, Senator McMahon had invited William Liscum Borden to lunch. McMahon, who had never met his guest, arranged the meeting because he had been impressed by a book Borden had written about the possibility of developing nuclear-armed long-range rockets. Borden was offered and immediately accepted a job on the Senator's staff.[13] When McMahon assumed the atomic energy committee chairmanship, Borden moved on to the committee staff. There, five years later, he was to play a historic role in triggering the security hearings that led to Oppenheimer's disgrace. In the years after 1948, Teller had mixed feelings about Borden. He welcomed Borden's assistance in the political struggle to authorize research on the hydrogen bomb. But in 1954, when Oppenheimer was on the rack, Teller, despite his doubts and reservations about his former Los Alamos boss, was distressed at the agonizing sequence of events Borden had set off.

Even while McMahon and Borden were having their lunch in Washington, the Air Force's B-29s were carrying out their assigned monitoring task. The procedure went on day after day for well over a year. Then, on or about August 29, 1949, the vigilance of the monitoring crews was rewarded. Air samples collected near Japan were found to contain unexpected amounts of radioactivity. Further analysis confirmed that the radioactivity was the result of an atomic explosion. There had been no Allied nuclear tests. It appeared that after only four years, the United States monopoly of atomic power had ended.[14]

Truman appointed a special committee of scientists, chaired by Dr. Vannevar Bush, to review the evidence. The committee quickly came to the conclusion that the Soviets had indeed exploded an atomic bomb.[15] They dismissed any hopes that perhaps the explosion was an accident in some Russian laboratory. Beyond any question, the Soviets had joined the club.* This first Russian atomic shot became known as "Joe One."

Truman, however, was from Missouri. He had to be shown.[16] Patiently the scientists laid out the evidence. Years later, as a for-

---

*Dr. Bush had just completed a book, already at the printers, *Modern Arms and Free Men,* predicting it would be ten years before the first Soviet atom bomb would be ready for testing. The presses were stopped so Bush could change that part of the manuscript.

mer President, he told more of the story. "One of the planes operating in the long-range detection system collected an air sample
that was decidedly radioactive, and the entire detection machinery
at once went into high gear. The cloud containing the suspicious
matter was tracked by the United States Air Force from the North
Pacific to the vicinity of the British Isles, where it was also picked
up by the Royal Air Force, and from the first these developments
were reported to me by the CIA as rapidly as they became known."[17]

Truman now had to face a crucial question. Should the American people be informed? If so, should they be told the unvarnished
truth? He consulted State Department officials and the AEC. All
five AEC members urged him to tell everything. On Friday, September 23, the President reported the news to his cabinet, then released a public statement.

It read, in part:

> I believe that the American people, to the fullest extent consistent
> with national security, are entitled to be informed of all develop-
> ments in the atomic energy field.
>
> We have evidence that in recent weeks an atomic explosion oc-
> curred in the U.S.S.R.

The President went on to explain that "the eventual development of this new force by other nations was to be expected" and
"has always been taken into account by us."

The statement concluded with a call for "truly effective, enforceable international control of atomic energy."[18]

There was a paradox in Truman's statement. He was not persuaded himself that the Russians had exploded a bomb. Three
years later, as an ex-President, he said as much: "I am not convinced that the Russians have the bomb. I am not convinced that
the Russians have achieved the know-how to put the complicated
mechanism together to make an A-bomb work."[19]

This doubt that Truman felt personally—in defiance of all the
scientific evidence—is apparently why he referred to an atomic
"explosion" and not a "test" or a "bomb." He wasn't convinced that
the atomic blast might not have been an accident. His skepticism,
as late as 1953, is difficult to understand in the light of two subsequent Soviet detonations in October 1951.[20]

In the technology of building a hydrogen bomb, the trigger is an
atom bomb. The first Soviet atom bomb served as a symbolic trig-

ger in the political and technological fight that was to shake and divide the scientific community over the question of whether Americans should build an H-bomb. Was it scientifically possible? Was it necessary? Was it morally right?

For the most part, the scientists on both sides of this passionate argument were decent and honest men. But just as decent and honest politicians (and there are some) become devious and half dishonest in the heat of a political struggle, the H-bomb question brought out some of the same characteristics in scientists. They showed all the standard political weaknesses—overzealousness, unjustified questioning of the other side's motives, perhaps even a touch of demagogy. They had become so heavily courted for their opinions that some of them translated their scientific knowledge into self-assured political wisdom.

Neither Teller nor Oppenheimer could be accused of being flexible. Both were convinced they were right. Teller had briefly injected himself into politics in the earliest days of the uranium project in 1939 and 1940, and had attempted some involvement through the Szilard anti-bomb petition in 1945, but otherwise his role had been relatively passive. Oppenheimer was an old hand. He knew his way through the corridors of power. Both men quickly acquired important allies. At first it appeared that Teller was outclassed by the heavyweight scientist-politicians who backed up Oppenheimer. But, as the dialecticians are fond of saying, "the objective conditions" were on Teller's side. Teller's trump card was labeled Joe One.

A few months before that first Russian test shot, Teller had been invited back to Los Alamos by its director, Norris Bradbury. Relations between the two men were still good. Bradbury wanted to beef up his theoretical division and persuaded Teller to take a one-year leave of absence from Chicago.[21] As Teller explained to the authors in 1974, "I had no intention of working on the super. I did not make this request of Bradbury, nor did he suggest it. I was to work on the laboratory's regular weapons program."

Then the awful truth of Joe One changed the situation completely. Immediately upon learning the disturbing news, Teller telephoned Oppenheimer long distance for advice:

Teller: What do we do now?

Oppenheimer: Keep your shirt on.[22]

There were other physicists who were not so sanguine. A few days after the Truman announcement, three anxious scientists met at the faculty club on the Berkeley campus. Ernest O. Lawrence, Luis Alvarez, and Wendell Latimer were all aware that, in theory, a thermonuclear explosion was possible. Since they did not share Truman's contempt for Soviet scientific prowess, they assumed the Russians would take the next logical step and build an H-bomb. They saw it now as a race—if the United States did not develop a thermonuclear weapon first, the country could be subject to Soviet blackmail.[23]

They agreed that the first step was to touch base with Edward Teller. They were aware of his persistent interest in the superbomb and felt that he was the best-equipped scientist to bring them up to date on the state of the art. Teller, at a Los Alamos meeting, verified their fears that the thermonuclear program was on dead center. In 1954 during the celebrated Oppenheimer security hearing before the special Gray Board of the AEC, Latimer was to look back at the whole nuclear weapons project:

"In the period between 1945 and 1949," he testified, "we didn't get anywhere in our atomic program in any direction. We didn't expand our production of uranium much. We didn't really get going on any reactor program. We didn't expand to any appreciable extent our production of fissionable materials. We just seemed to be sitting by and doing nothing."[24]

But in 1949, Teller was optimistic. If the thermonuclear program were given a green light, it had a "good chance if there is plenty of tritium available."[25]

Meanwhile, back in Washington, Strauss was adding to his reputation as a powerful and active member of the AEC. On October 5, 1949, he sent a memorandum to his fellow commissioners "to raise a question for immediate consideration in the light of information as to progress which has apparently been made in Russia."

Strauss was afraid the American lead in numbers of fissionable weapons would, in time, shrink. He offered a proposal to anticipate such a development—a proposal that, not by design, played right into Teller's hands. Strauss wrote:

> It seems to me that the time has come for a quantum jump in our planning (to borrow a metaphor from our scientist friends)—that is to say that we should make an intensive effort to get ahead with the super. By intensive effort I am thinking of a commitment in talent and money comparable, if necessary, to that which produced the first atomic weapon. That is the way to stay ahead.

Strauss concluded, "I recommend that we immediately consult with the General Advisory Committee to ascertain their views as to how we can proceed with expedition."[26]

The memorandum, especially Strauss's words "as to how we can proceed," showed his misjudgment of the sentiment of the scientists and perhaps of the country as a whole. He seemed to assume that the GAC would support his proposal as a matter of course.

According to Latimer there was in fact little opposition to proceeding with the super bomb until the GAC itself began to mobilize the counterforces.

Latimer's conclusions were based on a trip that he, along with Lawrence and Alvarez, made to Washington after their conference with Teller at Los Alamos. Latimer spoke to AEC Commissioner Gordon Dean and to the chemists Dr. Kenneth Pitzer and Dr. Charles C. Lauritsen. On his way back to Berkeley, Latimer stopped off in Chicago to see Willard Libby and Harold Urey, both chemists. As Latimer later recalled, "I talked to everybody I could . . . I tried to build up pressure for it [the H-bomb]. I definitely tried to build up pressure for it."[27]

In spite of a favorable response at first, Latimer found the situation changing within a few weeks. "There had been a lot of back pressure built up; I think primarily from the [general] advisory committee. I don't remember now all the sources of information I had on it, but we very quickly were aware of the fact that the General Advisory Committee was opposed."[28]

Alvarez, a member of the party that went to Los Alamos and Washington, kept a diary in which he recorded the events of the several hectic weeks following Joe One. After the conference with Teller, Alvarez and Lawrence decided a heavy-water reactor must be built. This was important because in this kind of reactor, which uses heavy water rather than graphite between the lattice of uranium, some of the neutrons emitted by the uranium are absorbed by the deuterium nuclei in the heavy water, converting them into tritium. From Teller the Berkeley scientists learned that it was important to increase the supply of tritium. So their campaign to build a heavy-water reactor began in Washington.

On October 8, 1949, Alvarez wrote in his diary: "Arrived Washington after lunch. Went to AEC and talked with Pitzer, General McCormick, Latimer, and Paul Fine [Fine was the administrative assistant to Pitzer]. Told them what we planned to do (build a heavy-water reactor) and got good response."[29]

On successive days following, Alvarez recorded a meeting with Robert LeBaron, deputy secretary of defense for atomic affairs, who was "quite enthusiastic," then with Ralph Johnson, administrator of the AEC, to make arrangements to visit the Canadian heavy-water reactor at Chalk River. Surprisingly, the Canadians were far ahead of the United States in heavy-water technology.

When they had left Johnson, Alvarez and Lawrence visited Senator McMahon and Congressman Carl Hinshaw, told them of their plans, "and got good reactions," according to the Alvarez diary, which continued: "Stressed the need for cooperation between the British, Canadians, and ourselves."[30]

Next, Alvarez and Lawrence went to the chairman of the AEC, David Lilienthal. "Shocking" was the word Alvarez used in later testimony to describe Lilienthal's attitude: "He did not even want to talk about the program. He turned his chair around and looked out the window and indicated that he did not want even to discuss the matter. He did not like the idea of thermonuclear weapons, and we could hardly get into a conversation with him."[31]

On June 24, 1953, three and a half years after the visit from Alvarez and Lawrence, Lilienthal revealed his own thoughts concerning the super. He wrote in his journal:

> As I recall, the issue was: what to do about the fact that the Russians had exploded an atomic weapon. One view was that we should make an all-out effort to make a bigger weapon which has since been described in official statements, i.e., using a fission bomb to create pressures and temperatures that would set up a fusion of the light hydrogen atoms, particularly the isotopes of deuterium and tritium. Such an "H-bomb" was conceived as a huge business, in which any desired amount of hydrogen could be used in a single weapon.
>
> Another item on the program for testing at that time was a more efficient and much more powerful fission bomb.
>
> The question I raised before the final meeting of the NSC [National Security Council] Special Committee was the one I had raised throughout the discussions: Is this the best way to protect the security of the country? I urged that before we committed ourselves further to what had proved to be a "wasting asset" of super-bombs, we reexamine our whole national policy.
>
> It was clear at this time from conferences with General [Omar] Bradley, while I was a member of the Special Committee, that we had little else than atomic weapons for our defense. [The near-debacle of Korea soon after confirmed this.]

> In an early memorandum to the President, I expressed my views
> [at the same time that a majority of the AEC's General Advisory
> Committee expressed their disapproval for an all-out H-bomb pro-
> gram] in which I stressed the adverse political implications of going
> forward along this line, as increasing our emphasis on super-bombs
> as a policy for world peace.[32]

If Lilienthal was cool, Alvarez and Lawrence found a much
warmer reception when they met with the other four commissioners. They seemed to agree that the two scientists were on the right
track.

On October 11, 1949, the Berkeley pair flew to New York and
had planned to fly on to Ottawa and then to Chalk River. Unfortunately they were unable to get seats on a plane, so the Chalk River
trip was canceled. But while they were in New York they stopped
to see I. I. Rabi, later to become one of the chief opponents of the
thermonuclear program. At this point, however, Alvarez reported
Rabi to be sympathetic. In 1954 Alvarez paraphrased Rabi's comments as follows: "It is certainly good to see the first team back in.
You fellows have been playing with your cyclotron and nuclei for
four years and it is certainly time you got back to work, and I am
awfully glad to see you back in business." Alvarez got a definite impression that Rabi thought the hydrogen bomb was necessary.[33]

The next day Alvarez was back in Berkeley recruiting scientists
and engineers.[34] He approached Don Cooksey, associate director
of the University of California Radiation Laboratory; William Bro-
beck, assistant director and chief engineer; Nobel Laureates Edwin
McMillan and Glenn Seaborg; and a half dozen other Berkeley luminaries. Larry Hafstad, director of the AEC's reactor division,
flew in from Washington.[35] From the California Institute of Technology came David T. Griggs, professor of geophysics, and Robert
Christy, a Los Alamos veteran and an expert in neutron diffusion
and reactor technology.[36]

The scientists discussed the location of a heavy-water, tritium-
producing reactor, as well as its technology. The proceedings were
supposed to be top secret, but, somehow, small bits of information
leaked out.[37]

On October 16, 1949, columnist Drew Pearson informed the
American public that consideration of an H-bomb project was under way. It was the beginning, on the public level, of the emotional
upheaval that was to accompany the H-bomb question.[38]

Alvarez spent October 19 discussing the project with two very influential old friends, Lee DuBridge, president of Caltech, and Robert Bacher, the Caltech physicist who had contributed his expertise to the early organization of Los Alamos. "There was no doubt in my mind that they approved," Alvarez later testified.[39]

A few days later Alvarez telephoned Teller in Chicago, mainly in the hope of getting a reading from Fermi, whom Teller had just met at the airport after a trip to Italy. Fermi was too tired to react one way or the other. He told Teller he would count on Hans Bethe's judgment. Teller felt Oppenheimer was lukewarm to a thermonuclear project and Harvard President Conant was flatly opposed.[40]

Teller had misread Oppenheimer. The former Los Alamos boss, who was now chairman of the powerful General Advisory Committee, was not "lukewarm," but dead set against it. On October 21, 1949, Oppenheimer wrote a letter to Conant:

> Dear Uncle Jim,
>
> We are exploring the possibilities for our talk with the President on October 30. All members of the Advisory Committee will come to the meeting Saturday, except Seaborg who must be in Sweden, and whose general views we have in written form. Many of us will do some preliminary palavering on the 28th.
>
> There is one bit of background which I would like you to have before we meet. When we last spoke you thought perhaps the reactor program offered the most decisive example of the need for policy clarification. I was inclined to think that the Super might also be relevant. On the technical side, as far as I can tell, the Super is not very different from what it was when we first spoke of it more than 7 years ago: a weapon of unknown design, cost, deliverability and military value. But a great change has taken place in the climate of opinion. On the one hand two experienced promoters have been at work, i.e., Ernest Lawrence and Edward Teller. The project has long been dear to Teller's heart; and Ernest has convinced himself that we must learn from Operation Joe [the Russian explosion] that the Russians will soon do the Super and that we had better beat them to it.
>
> On the technical side, he [Lawrence] proposes to get some neutron producing heavy water reactors built; to this, for a variety of reasons, I think we must say amen [since there are three military applications other than the Super which these reactors would serve]*

---

*The portion of the text bracketed is as it was later paraphrased by Oppenheimer during the Gray Board Hearings for security purposes, at the government's request.

and many other things will all profit by the availability of neutrons.

But the real development has not been of a technical nature. Ernest spoke to Knowland and McMahon, and to some at least of the Joint Chiefs. The Joint Congressional Committee, having tried to find something tangible to chew on ever since September 23rd, has at last found its answers. We must have a Super and we must have it fast. A subcommittee is heading west to investigate this problem at Los Alamos and in Berkeley. The Joint Chiefs appear informally to have decided to give the development of the Super overriding priority, though no formal request has come through. The climate of opinion among the competent physicists also shows signs of shifting. Bethe, Teller, McCormack and LeBaron are all scheduled to turn up within the next 36 hours. I have agreed that if there is a conference on the Super program at Los Alamos, I will make it my business to attend.

What concerns me is really not the technical problem. I am not sure the miserable thing will work, nor that it can be gotten to a target except by ox cart. It seems likely to me even further to worsen the unbalance of our present war plans. What does worry me is that this appears to have caught the imagination, both of the Congressional and of military people, as the answer to the problem posed by the Russian advance. It would be folly to oppose the exploration of this weapon. We have always known it had to be done, and it does have to be done, though it appears to be singularly proof against any form of experimental approach. But that we become committed to it as the way to save the country and the peace appears to me full of danger.

We will be faced with all this at our meeting; and anything that we do or do not say to the President will have to take it into consideration. I shall feel far more secure if you have an opportunity to think about it.

I still remember my visit with gratitude and affection.

Robert Oppenheimer[41]

The letter exposes Oppenheimer's inner turmoil. He was agonizing over several problems. If he was convinced that the H-bomb was of "unknown . . . military value,"[42] then he did little to clarify the issue. In *The Oppenheimer Case,* author Philip Stern writes:

Oppenheimer, as a member of a Pentagon policy group, had argued against declaring a military need for the H-bomb since the AEC scientists had not yet declared it technically feasible; however, on the same day, sitting as an AEC advisor, he had discouraged expansion of technical research on the H-bomb on the ground that the Pentagon had failed to express any military need for such a weapon.[43]

It was true that on a purely technical level there had been little progress made in the last seven years. It was also clear that deuterium and tritium would be used as a fuel, but no facilities to produce tritium in large amounts had ever been planned. And since the scientists were talking about using the fuel in liquid form, refrigeration would be required; both deuterium and tritium in liquid form would otherwise simply boil away. The bulkiness of a refrigerated bomb explains Oppenheimer's doubt that "it can't be gotten to a target except by ox cart."

Even recognizing all these negative factors, it also was clear that Oppenheimer, in his letter, ignored the fact that almost no work had been done on the super bomb in those seven lean years. It is at least possible to understand Teller's frustration.

What would have happened if an all-out effort to build the super had been started years earlier? This hypothetical question was posed to Teller during the Oppenheimer security hearings in 1954 by Roger Robb, the AEC's counsel.

"Doctor," asked Robb, "it has been suggested here that the ultimate success on the thermonuclear was the result of a brilliant discovery or invention by you, and that might or might not have taken five or ten years. What can you say about that?"

Teller's response, in part, was, "I think it was neither a great achievement nor a brilliant one. It just had to be done. I must say it was not completely easy. There were some pitfalls. But I do believe that if the original plan in Los Alamos, namely, that the laboratory with such excellent people like Fermi and Bethe and others would have gone after the problem, probably some of these people would have had either the same brilliant idea or another one much sooner. In that case we would have had the bomb in 1947."[44]

It was at those same hearings that Robb tried to trip up Oppenheimer when the latter said he believed he had not expressed any view in opposition to the proposed H-bomb project to Conant, who was strongly opposed to it.[45] Then Robb brought out the letter to Conant and forced Oppenheimer to admit that his memory was wrong.[46]

The influence—or lack of influence—of Oppenheimer led to a controversy between Teller and Bethe that has never been resolved. Did Oppenheimer influence Bethe not to work on the super?

Teller visited Bethe at Ithaca in October 1949 and, as Bethe recalled the conversation, Teller tried to persuade him "to come to

Los Alamos full-time and to help evolve full-scale thermonuclear weapons."

"At the time Teller visited me," Bethe testified in 1954, "I had very great internal conflicts what I should do. Dr. Teller was presenting to me some ideas . . . which seemed to make technically more feasible one phase of the thermonuclear program. I was quite impressed with his ideas. On the other hand it seemed to me it was a terrible undertaking to develop a still bigger bomb, and I was entirely undecided and had long discussions with my wife."[47]

In November 1973 the authors interviewed Bethe at Cornell and he was more detailed about his recollections of those days in late 1949 and early 1950. He was surprised when Joe One was announced "and I must admit that I had a violent reaction that something more had to be done. Now I was hoping something more could be done in terms of nuclear reactors," Bethe continued, "which incidentally would produce more plutonium, and I offered my services to the director of the reactor division at Berkeley.

"Edward, however, decided this was the time to go into his beloved super. I was reluctant and quite uncertain, and I really didn't know which way I would go. I have told this story many times and it has also been published by the other side wrong, namely it has been presented that it was a question of money which was foremost in my mind.* That wasn't so at all, although I didn't want to lose income by doing this, but the prime question was the war question.

"It seemed to me then and it seems to me now that it was the wrong thing to do, that we should not have escalated. It seems to me now very clear that we should have developed the atomic bomb during the war when we had a desperate situation with the Nazis. But in 1949 vis-à-vis the Russians we still held all the cards, and we still held the card of greater production, greater delivery capability of the nuclear weapons. So I think the right direction would have been to say no, we are not going to do it. We may do some further research on it, but let's not make it a crash program. We really didn't need it, but when we embarked on it, I think it was one of the many examples of overkill that we indulged in in those days."

Bethe said his opinion "has not been changed by any of the

---

*Lewis Strauss later reported that he offered, out of his own pocket, to make up the difference between Bethe's salary at Cornell and what he would be paid at Los Alamos. Bethe, according to Strauss, refused the offer.

subsequent developments. I was dissuaded from joining the project by two people, namely Weisskopf, whom I mentioned before, and Placzek, who talked to me at great length, and made me visualize what the hydrogen war would mean. . . .

"So," Bethe continued, "Edward and I were on opposite sides at this point and remained so for a long time to come. (There is at present no issue on which we are on opposite sides.) I was then strongly convinced . . . that it would be evil for us to embark on this. Edward was strongly convinced of the opposite.

"Edward won the battle by enlisting first the Joint Congressional Committee on Atomic Energy, then some of the Atomic Energy commissioners, and, in the end, of course, President Truman gave the order to pursue."

While Teller was visiting Bethe, and trying to win him over, Bethe received a phone call from Oppenheimer. He suggested the two scientists visit him at Princeton. According to Teller's version, Bethe had decided, "after a somewhat strenuous discussion," that he would go to Los Alamos.

But a few days later when they met Oppenheimer in his office at Princeton he showed them a letter he had just received from Conant.

"I don't know whether he showed us the whole letter or whether he showed us a short section of it, or whether he only read to us a short section," Teller says. "Whichever it was, one phrase of Conant sticks in my mind and that phrase was *over my dead body,* referring to a decision to go ahead with a crash program on the thermonuclear bomb."[48]

Beyond that, as Teller recalls the meeting, Oppenheimer did not argue against a crash program. But when they left the office Teller was convinced that Bethe was intending to go to Los Alamos. Teller even remembers warning Bethe just prior to the meeting that "we are going to talk with Oppenheimer and after that you will decide not to come."

But Bethe didn't change his mind—according to Teller—because as they left Oppenheimer, Bethe smiled at Teller and said, "You see, you can be quite satisfied. I am still coming."

Teller doesn't know whether there was any later discussion between Oppenheimer and Bethe. Bethe says there was not.

But Teller recalls, "Two days later I called up Bethe in New York and Bethe said he had thought it over and he had changed his mind and he was not coming."

Bethe is adamant that "Oppenheimer did *not* persuade me against going to Los Alamos, and Oppenheimer seemed quite undecided at that point. It was these two other people [Weisskopf and Placzek] who persuaded me." In fact, Bethe insists, he, Weisskopf, and Placzek discussed how to persuade Oppenheimer himself to be against the super.

Regardless of the Bethe-Teller conflict on this issue, it does seem likely that Oppenheimer's reading of a letter from Conant, who enjoyed unique prestige in the academic world, must have had some effect on Bethe. Conant would not lightly use a phrase so compelling as "over my dead body."

The time for decision was drawing near. The General Advisory Committee, chaired by Oppenheimer, planned a meeting for late October. The committee's duty was to provide scientific and technical advice to the AEC and, on this specific issue, to recommend or not recommend a crash program to build a hydrogen bomb. The AEC leaned heavily on the expertise of the GAC.

Teller recalls a sense of foreboding as the meeting drew near. He was afraid that Oppenheimer's legendary powers of persuasion would spell doom for the H-bomb project.[49]

On October 29, 1949, eight troubled and somber men met in room 213 of the AEC headquarters on Constitution Avenue in Washington. In addition to Oppenheimer, they included Conant, who was president of Harvard; Enrico Fermi of Chicago; Lee DuBridge, president of Caltech; I. I. Rabi, chairman of physics at Columbia; Hartley Rowe, vice-president and chief engineer of the United Fruit Company; Cyril S. Smith, director of the Institute for the Study of Metals at the University of Chicago; and Oliver E. Buckley, president of the Bell Telephone Laboratories. One member, Glenn T. Seaborg, professor of chemistry at the University of California, was out of the country and could not attend.

Six of the eight members (all but Rowe and Buckley) had contributed to the development of the atom bomb that had culminated in the tragedies of Hiroshima and Nagasaki. The charred bodies of those devastated cities had been buried, but their stench was forever trapped in the consciousness of the scientists "who had known sin." They were doomed to recite the mourners' Kaddish for as long as they lived. There was a strong feeling among them that they were being asked to write the final act of man's tragedy.

Teller's apprehension was justified. The GAC reached its unanimous decision, and this was the heart of its statement:

We all hope that by one means or another, the development of these weapons can be avoided. We are reluctant to see the United States take the initiative in precipitating this development. We are all agreed that it would be wrong at the present moment to commit ourselves to an all-out effort towards its development.[50]

Even before he heard the news, Teller was resigned to the outcome. He knew the GAC members that well. It seemed now there would be no hydrogen bomb. But, as it turned out, the tormented members of the GAC did not have the last word.

11

The Capture of Washington

THE General Advisory Committee had turned thumbs down on the hydrogen bomb, and its parent agency, the Atomic Energy Commission, seconded the decision by a bare majority. Yet the bomb was built. In February 1975 we asked Edward Teller who was responsible for overruling such influential decision makers. With a half-smile, Teller responded:

"Senator Brien McMahon, Lewis Strauss, and Klaus Fuchs."

McMahon was the powerful chairman of the Joint Committee on Atomic Energy, Strauss was the most influential member of the AEC, and Klaus Fuchs was the brilliant and affable German-born British scientist who turned out to be a spy, passing the innermost secrets of Los Alamos along to the Soviets. He was exposed at the height of the H-bomb controversy.

As a fourth figure among the protagonists, Teller might have said "Teller," but preferred to be modest or await the evidence of history.

The GAC was no match for McMahon, Strauss, and Fuchs. But on that dreary day in Washington when it was reaching its futile decision, Oppenheimer was still acutely conscious of his committee's responsibility. He later spelled it out. First, the GAC was to decide whether the AEC "was doing what it ought to be doing." More specifically, was a crash H-bomb program "what it ought to be doing"?[1]

The October 29, 1949, meeting began as a joint session with the Atomic Energy Commission, plus a panel of top-level advisers. George F. Kennan, the Kremlin expert in the State Department, briefed the group on the political implications of the Soviet explosion. General Omar Bradley, chairman of the Joint Chiefs of Staff, and a group of officers discussed the military significance of Joe One. Members of the AEC staff were on hand, including Air Force

General James McCormack, chief of the AEC's military application division.

After the briefing, the AEC commissioners and the others retired from the room, leaving the GAC members alone with their thoughts. The deliberations began with a technical appraisal of a thermonuclear weapon by Enrico Fermi. The technicalities, of course, were not uppermost in the minds of the scientists there. The real question that began to surface in the discussion was whether the United States needed to build such a ghastly weapon.[2] On the drawing board the AEC had plans to build a gigantic atom bomb with a force equal to 500,000 tons of TNT. How much more destructive potential should the people of the world be exposed to? Were there enemy targets large enough to justify the use of megaton weapons? If this were the fact, the United States had larger concentrated centers of population than the Soviet Union. Then, assuming the Russians would, in time, match the United States, an H-bomb would be of greater value to them than a similar bomb in the American arsenal. Our cities were more vulnerable than theirs.

What were the arguments of the H-bomb advocates? The authors asked Richard Hewlett, chief historian of the AEC, to summarize them. He did, reminding us that the arguments were not necessarily his own views.

"First," Hewlett said, "it represented the next logical step in weapon development and many people were convinced that the Russians would take this step or were already working on it. It was a perfectly logical thing to do as a weapon, and as technology went on, it looked more and more possible to do this. The thermonuclear weapon represented such a great stride forward in weapon development, of such great importance for national security, that many people felt that you had to go ahead and find out if it could be done. You just could not wait. Strauss particularly felt this. I talked to him a good bit about it. I would also suspect that Teller agreed with this position."

The members of the GAC were neither military men nor politicians. To the military men the need for the H-bomb seemed to be part of a long-established thought pattern that if there were a better weapon available, or potentially available, you developed it and, if necessary, used it. If there could be an improved version of the M-16 rifle, even if it were more expensive, it was militarily logical that you employed it as soon as possible, and the thinking on the H-bomb seemed to be much the same. The scientists of the GAC could not accept the thinking of the generals and admirals, nor did they have the skepticism of politicians who base few decisions on a belief in the innate goodness of man. Militarily and politically, the prevailing mood was to be armed against the unpredictability of the Russian bear.

But even on a military basis there were logical reasons to question the necessity of a thermonuclear bomb. One of the principal anti-H-bomb arguments was that a cluster of fission bombs would be more efficient. Hewlett sees the question as more complex than that.

"The thermonuclear," he explained, "was not only a larger weapon—and this impressed many people—but it would have greater destructive power than anything we had at that time. Even more than that, it opened a whole new area of weapon technology. There were all kinds of possibilities that one could envision—for instance, more efficient weapons. Perhaps you could build weapons which were much smaller for a given yield than the fission weapons available at that time. Perhaps you could build a weapon which would be more efficient in the use of materials. At that time, for the fission weapons, you had to use plutonium or uranium 235. These were still relatively scarce materials.

"Then people started talking about fusion weapons where you were going to use deuterium. There are thousands of tons of deuterium in the sea. . . .

"You never know," Hewlett continued, "what all the possible results will be. Many people felt you could not neglect this area and say that we are not going to look at it at all, because there are all sorts of possibilities." In retrospect, Hewlett believes a great deal has been learned about weapon technology from the thermonuclear program.

Hewlett's judgment of Oppenheimer, based on a historian's perspective, sees factors at work in 1950 different from the first consideration of a thermonuclear reaction at that famous Berkeley meeting with Teller and other physicists back in 1942. At that time Oppenheimer was weighing a theoretical possibility. There were thermonuclear reactions in the universe and Oppenheimer foresaw the possibility of harnessing this power for weapons or energy.

"It seems to me that was somewhat different from what he was talking about in 1950 or 1951," Hewlett said. By that time, in Hewlett's judgment, Oppenheimer was objecting because he didn't think Teller's approaches would work, but also on purely moral grounds.

If Oppenheimer was trying to brake the drive toward an H-bomb, what about Teller, the scientist who was trying to make it go faster? Or if the event is to be viewed as a drama, what was the motivating force behind the man who was assuming the dual role of chief actor and writer of the script?

In one of many interviews for this book, the authors baited Teller. Why did he want to build an H-bomb? Wasn't it true that tremendous atomic bombs could be built and that there were no targets large enough to justify a thermonuclear weapon?

Teller was not offended by the question, and responded in a low and patient tone:

"I would argue that I am not omniscient. If there is a new possibility I would like to see it explored and developed. The use should be separated from the development. I cannot see the future. I did not know at that time that the thermonuclear explosive would lead to clean explosives and that these in turn could be used for the constructive, peaceful applications of Plowshare.

"But I did believe in science and in progress and in finding out what can be done. And I did have the confidence that there was at least a good possibility what we developed would be properly used rather than misused."

This was Teller's view in 1973. What was Enrico Fermi's view on that fateful October 29, 1949, when the GAC was deliberating? "The chances of success," Fermi later testified, were "of a somewhat better than even probability . . . in other words it was not a foregone conclusion by any means and we knew and we said it was not a foregone conclusion.

"On the other hand, it was to be expected that perhaps just with development and with some amount of technical luck the thing might be pushed through. That was the situation at that time . . . as far as I can recollect we all agreed with the situation." In other words, Fermi was saying that all of the members of the GAC felt it probably could be done, if the United States was set on doing it.[3]

But Fermi, like the other GAC scientists, had deeper concerns. He was worried that this new proposed program would interfere with conventional atomic weapons. He also hoped and felt that it would be easier to outlaw, by international agreement, a weapon that did not yet exist—"My opinion at that time was that one should try to outlaw the thing before it was born."[4]

At the GAC meeting, after Fermi had expressed his views, Oppenheimer asked each member to do the same. In general, they agreed with Fermi.

Hartley Rowe, for example, recalling his position in 1954 testimony, considered the A-bomb to be just another military weapon, and possibly even a deterrent to war. But the H-bomb was different; it had no place in a military campaign. If it were used, even in retaliation, "you are using it against civilization and not against the military." Then Rowe resoundingly added, "I don't like to see women and children killed wholesale because the male elements of the human race are so stupid that they can't get out of war and keep out of war."[5]

I. I. Rabi apparently changed his position during the meeting. Five years later he recalled Oppenheimer's stating that the question was "not whether we should make a thermonuclear weapon, but whether there should be a crash program. There were some people," Rabi continued, "and I myself was of that opinion for a time, who thought that the concentration on a crash program . . . was the answer. . . ."[6] Yet by the end of the meeting, which actually continued for three days, Rabi joined Fermi in condemning the H-bomb on moral grounds and in arguing that it was wrong for the United States to be the first nation to build the superbomb.

Why did Rabi change his position? It is impossible to know, exactly. He enjoyed a long-time, close friendship with Oppenheimer, although, testifying in 1954, Rabi did not recall any conversation on the issue between them prior to the meeting. He was also vague when questioned about his initial response to the enthusiastic H-bomb advocacy of Lawrence and Alvarez, when Rabi seemed to support them. "I think I may have been inclined towards their view on the basis of information they said they had from Dr. Teller."[7] In this same 1954 testimony, Rabi hedged when asked if he had ever been in complete agreement with Lawrence and Alvarez.

After each member of the GAC had made his separate statement, the committee adjourned for lunch. During the lunch break, Oppenheimer ran into Alvarez and Robert Serber, another physicist of the powerful Berkeley group. The three had lunch together and after the meal was over, Alvarez concluded that even at this early stage of the GAC meeting the H-bomb program was dead. Serber, who only a few days before had pledged his support for the program, now agreed with his former professor, Oppen-

heimer, who tried to persuade Serber that Russia would not build
an H-bomb unless the United States took the initiative.[8]

As chairman, Oppenheimer abstained from commenting at the
meeting until everyone else had spoken. He later reported that
"there was a surprising unanimity—to me very surprising—that the
United States ought not to take the initiative at that time in an all-
out program for the development of thermonuclear weapons."

For Oppenheimer it was a question of his judgment, his motives,
and his honor. When each member of the committee had spoken
his piece, he turned to them and made the personal issue clear.

"I am glad you feel this way, for if it had not come out this way, I
would have had to resign as chairman."[9]

A quarter of a century later, the complete text of the GAC report
still remains classified, for reasons that can be understood only by
security-obsessed bureaucrats. The main arguments of the majority and minority sections, however, have been declassified (both
majority and minority opposed a crash program, but for different
reasons).

It is known from various accounts, and from the report itself,
that the GAC carefully reviewed the current status of the A-bomb
before tackling the H-bomb question.[10] The committee also
looked with favor on the proposal of Lawrence and Alvarez to
build a heavy-water reactor. This was not necessarily because such
a reactor could be used to produce tritium (a hydrogen isotope
used in some versions of the H-bomb) but rather that the same
reactor could be programmed to produce plutonium. With more
plutonium available, a greater variety and number of fission bombs
could be turned out.

Having disposed of these preliminaries, the report moved into a
consideration of the proposed fusion, or thermonuclear, weapon.
It predicted that the H-bomb would be an expensive, unwieldy
weapon. (The assumption is that at that time the scientists were
thinking of a refrigerated bomb, in which case they were accurate
about its unwieldiness.)

Then the committee reached a rather surprising conclusion:
Unlike fission, with its power-generating potential, fusion research
was without any foreseeable peaceful application.[11] Even considering the state of the art in late 1949, such a viewpoint is difficult to
understand because within a few years scientists in a half dozen
laboratories were at work trying to harness thermonuclear energy
for peaceful purposes.

The report argued that the superbomb had a limited military

use. It could be used only to annihilate cities and their civilian populations. To initiate such a program would be politically damaging to America, tarnishing its image across the world.

The majority report, signed by Oppenheimer and all members except Fermi and Rabi, concluded with:

> We all hope that by one means or another the development of these weapons can be avoided. We are reluctant to see the United States take the initiative in precipitating this development. We are all agreed that it would be wrong at the present moment to commit ourselves to an all-out effort towards its development.
>
> In determining not to proceed to develop the Superbomb, we see a unique opportunity of providing by example some limitations on the totality of war, and thus eliminating the fear and raising the hopes of mankind.[12]

In their minority report, Fermi and Rabi pressed even more incessantly on the moral issue:

> The fact that no limit exists to the destructiveness of this weapon makes its very existence and the knowledge of its construction a danger to humanity as a whole. For these reasons, we believe it important for the President of the United States to tell the American people and the world that we think it wrong on fundamental ethical principles to initiate the development of such a weapon.[13]

The GAC's decision was kept under wraps, even for other scientists like Teller, for two weeks.[14] When he knew the decision had been reached, Teller was desperate for information, even though he was apprehensive. A few days after the decision he was en route from Los Alamos to Washington for a meeting with Senator McMahon. Perhaps, he thought, if he detoured via Chicago, his old friend Fermi might give him an inkling of the GAC verdict.

When Teller arrived in Chicago, Fermi was on the spot. The Italian scientist was aware of the intensity of Teller's concern. But the GAC report was classified and Fermi simply couldn't say a word about it.

He really didn't need to speak about the contents. Somehow the tone of Fermi's voice, his "body language," perhaps, told the story. "It was clear from the tenor of his remarks," Teller wrote later, "that certainly Fermi and possibly the entire GAC did not favor an all-out crash program."[15]

While Teller was in Fermi's office, trying to cope with his disappointment, he received an unexpected telephone call. The caller was John Manley, associate director of Los Alamos and secretary to the GAC. Manley suggested to Teller that he cancel his appointment with McMahon. Manley's argument was that the scientists should present a common front on the question of the superbomb. It would be unfortunate, Manley felt, if McMahon detected that the scientific community was not united on the issue.

Teller resented Manley's request and told the GAC secretary that he fully intended to keep his appointment with the Senator. To Teller this pressure was an unwarranted interference with his freedom of action. When Manley continued to press the issue, Teller offered to cancel the appointment, but to call McMahon and tell him exactly why he was doing so. Only then did Manley give up. "All right, you'd better see him," Manley said.[16]

When Teller arrived in Washington he was still not absolutely certain of the contents of the GAC report. But an angry Senator McMahon greeted him and, without specifically saying what the report contained, he sputtered at Teller, "I read this report and it just makes me sick."

Why did it make the Senator sick? Teller wondered aloud. He then told McMahon how essential he thought the thermonuclear weapon was to the nation's defense.

McMahon then all but told Teller the verdict of the GAC by promising his support "to make the thermonuclear bomb a reality."[17]

For the moment, Teller was heartened, but the euphoria was short-lived. When he returned to Los Alamos, Manley showed him the majority and minority versions of the GAC report. Teller couldn't see much difference between them, but concluded that the thermonuclear project was dead.

To Teller's surprise, some of the scientists at Los Alamos, particularly the younger ones, resented the implications of the GAC report. The immediate effect was to bring even the limited research on the thermonuclear weapon to a halt. Improvements to make fission weapons larger, more efficient, and more deadly were encouraged, while work in the field of fusion was prohibited.

This double standard made no sense to Teller. In interpreting their response, he wrote:

> The GAC report seemed to state the conflict rather bluntly. As long as you people work very hard and diligently to make a better atomic bomb, you are doing a fine job; but if you succeed in making real

progress toward another kind of nuclear explosion, you are doing something immoral. To this the scientists reacted psychologically. They got mad. And their attention was turned toward the thermonuclear bomb, not away from it.[18]

Teller was not the only one mystified by the moral distinction between fission and fusion and by the belief that the Soviets would abstain from the thermonuclear effort if the United States set a lofty example.

On Monday, October 31, 1949, Oppenheimer met in Washington with Secretary of State Dean Acheson. The GAC chairman had been given approval to report the committee's conclusions to Acheson. The Secretary of State heard Oppenheimer out with increasing puzzlement. Later he told his chief nuclear advisor, "You know, I listened as carefully as I know how, but I don't understand what Oppie is trying to say. How can you persuade a hostile adversary to disarm 'by example'?"[19]

There were still two more links in the chain of command before the final decision. The five AEC commissioners were not of one welded opinion; their fragmented advice would make life more difficult for the final judge—Harry S Truman.

When the AEC convened to consider the GAC report, Lewis Strauss suggested that the State and Defense departments be consulted prior to the commission's deliberations—all in the hope of presenting a united front to the President.[20]

Strauss's proposal was rejected, and the commissioners were more or less on their own, and their conclusions showed it. There were majority and minority reports. But to make their positions clear, each member also filed an individual statement.[21]

A majority opposed the crash H-bomb program. This consisted of Chairman David Lilienthal, Sumner Pike, and Henry DeWolfe Smyth, with Smyth urging delay more than rejection. Strauss and Gordon Dean, backing the H-bomb development, were in the minority.

Actually, in the initial stages, Strauss was the only convinced supporter of the thermonuclear weapon. After some hesitation, Dean joined up on Strauss's side. Smyth wanted to postpone a decision pending an immediate effort to try and reach an agreement with the Soviet Union to outlaw the menacing superbomb.

A harried President Truman was given little guidance. On November 10 he reached the conclusion that his decision had to be based not entirely on the AEC's report, but on political and military factors of concern to State and Defense.[22]

An indication of the arguments that persuaded the majority to turn thumbs down on the H-bomb was provided in 1954 by Sumner Pike in his testimony at the Oppenheimer security hearing. Pike recalled the main points he made in his memorandum:

> One of them was that we had no knowledge that the military needed such a weapon. Another one was that *the cost of producing tritium in terms of plutonium that might otherwise be produced looked fantastically high*—80 to 100 times, probably, gram for gram [authors' italics].
>
> The third one, and this sort of tied into the first, was, as we all know, that the damage power of the bomb does not increase with the size of the explosion, and it seemed that it might possibly be a wasted effort to make a great big one where some smaller ones would be more efficient.
>
> I think I put in another one: that as between the fission work we were doing and the fusion thing in question here, there were some good things about the fission things. Up to that time and up to the present [1954] nobody has brought up anything useful for mankind out of fusion.[23]

Pike's statement that it would cost eighty to one hundred times as much, gram for gram, to produce tritium as to produce plutonium seems to ignore the fact that tritium, which is extremely light, is needed in relatively small amounts, by weight, in comparison to plutonium, which is extremely heavy.*

Even with the majority decision of the AEC against them, the proponents of a crash program to build the super would not give up. It was in this connection that Teller attributed the ultimate adoption of the program to McMahon, Strauss, and Klaus Fuchs.

---

*In a letter to the authors, C. L. Marshall, director of the division of classification of the AEC, explained Pike's statement as follows:

"Both tritium and plutonium are produced in nuclear reactors as a result of interactions between the neutrons produced by the reactor and the materials that are placed in the reactor to be irradiated and in which the tritium or plutonium are generated. The statement that Mr. Pike made referred to the fact that it takes between 80 and 100 times the number of neutrons to produce a gram of tritium than it does to produce a gram of plutonium. All of the neutrons used for the production of tritium are unavailable to produce plutonium so that for each gram of tritium produced, plutonium production is reduced by 80 to 100 grams."

Fuchs, of course, contributed unwillingly when he was exposed as a spy who might have been slipping H-bomb secrets to Russia. But Teller was serious about the positive contribution of McMahon and Strauss.

It was certainly a fact that Teller's scientific assurance made him, if not a prime mover, at least a catalyst among prime movers. He was optimistic enough about eventual success to instill similar hope in those who came in contact with him. He had no doubt that it would require a great deal of hard work by dedicated, talented men, as had been the fact in the achievement of the atom bomb. He believed, along with Fermi, that "with some amount of technical luck the thing might be pushed through." The H-bomb, to Teller, never appeared to be an impossible dream.

The productive interaction between Teller and Strauss really began with their second encounter. Who initiated the meeting is not recorded, but Teller remembers discussing the event in advance with Oppenheimer. Teller had apparently forgotten his brief meeting with Strauss at Temple Emanu-El in New York because he asked Oppie, "What kind of man is Strauss?" Oppenheimer's reply was, "Very smart and very vain."

Strauss was also stubborn and persistent. He was not content to allow the commission's majority report to remain unchallenged.[24] On November 29, 1949, he wrote a letter to Truman that had a tone of desperation. In part, the letter said:

> I believe that the United States must be as completely armed as any possible enemy. From this it follows that I believe it unwise to renounce, unilaterally, any weapon which an enemy can reasonably be expected to possess. I recommend that the President direct the Atomic Energy Commission to proceed with the development of the thermonuclear bomb, at highest priority, subject only to the judgment of the Department of Defense as to its value as a weapon, and to the advice of the Department of State as to the diplomatic consequences of its unilateral renunciation or its possession. . . .[25]

The letter was accompanied by a memorandum that outlined Strauss's reasons for his recommendation that the President should make the H-bomb project a "highest priority." In essence, Strauss argued that the weapon was scientifically feasible, that the Russians had the technical competence to produce it themselves, and that "a government of atheists is not likely to be dissuaded

from producing the weapon on 'moral grounds.'" That self-right-
eously religious argument was backed up by a practical point—
Strauss was afraid the Russians might already be ahead of the
United States.

Having pressed the issue on President Truman, Strauss was not
one to leave any stone unturned. He moved next to Secretary of
Defense Louis Johnson, a former national commander of the
American Legion. Strauss seemed intuitively to know how to talk
Johnson's language. According to an account in *The Hydrogen
Bomb*, by James R. Shepley and Clay Blair, Jr., Strauss walked into
Johnson's office and said he was eager to get to the point.

"Mr. Secretary, isn't it an American tradition that we will never
accept the idea that we will be less armed than our enemies?" After
Johnson concurred with this rhetorical question, Strauss continued: "The AEC has just voted to reverse that tradition."

It was a long meeting, but when it ended, the Secretary of Defense was in complete agreement with Strauss.[26]

The pro-H-bomb forces were building strength. Senator McMahon was the titular leader, flanked on his symbolic charger by his
lieutenant, William Liscum Borden, the Joint Committee on
Atomic Energy's executive director. Strauss was his chief ally and
strategist. In early November the three men met in Strauss's hotel
room in Beverly Hills, California, to map their plans. McMahon
based his campaign primarily on Teller's optimistic evaluation of
the superbomb project, and the Senator was now more determined
than ever to see that all types of nuclear weapons were developed.
Even before his meeting with Teller he, like Strauss, had made a
direct, written appeal to the President.

McMahon told Truman that, in his view, there was no moral
distinction between a large weapon causing damage or a series of
small weapons inflicting the same results. Without free inspection
any agreement with the Russians not to proceed with the superbomb would be meaningless. He described the political hazards
the United States could be exposed to if the Russians won the thermonuclear race.[27]

From Los Angeles, McMahon and Borden traveled to Los Alamos for a meeting scheduled for Tuesday, November 15. In preparation for the meeting, several of the top scientists, Teller included, were invited to read the GAC report.

At the meeting Teller was silent for a while. Finally, after some
prodding, he "admitted his extreme disappointment that the distin-

guished scientists on the committee had not suggested a more imaginative response to the Soviet challenge."

At that time the distinguished mathematician Stanislaw Ulam was working at Los Alamos and was believed to be an advocate of the thermonuclear bomb. After reading the GAC report he wrote to fellow mathematician John von Neumann expressing his conviction that the report would delay but not kill the program. But Ulam was concerned that Teller's "insistent advocacy" might harm the program because he was getting on the nerves of some members of the committee.[28] (It is difficult for the authors to believe that any members of the GAC would have taken their position just to spite Teller. Even though they might have been faulted for their decision, it was not vindictive.)

During the afternoon of November 15, Teller presented a technical evaluation of the superbomb. He did not make any wild claims or promise success. As of that date, all work had been strictly theoretical. Until experiments were conducted it was impossible to be sure that nuclear fusion would take place. He offered a plan under which the first thermonuclear experiment could be conducted in 1951. This test would be only to prove a principle—that when deuterium and tritium (two isotopes of hydrogen) are ignited by the heat of an atomic blast, fusion will take place.

Even if this experiment were to be successful, Teller cautioned, it would not prove that an H-bomb could be built. He agreed with Fermi, however, that the chances of success were better than fifty percent. Some of the scientists did not agree with Teller's odds on success. Some even indicated that his scientific judgment was colored by his enthusiasm for the project.[29]

McMahon, on the other hand, was so encouraged by Teller's careful presentation that he decided to make another effort to see that Harry Truman understood the issue. To that end he instructed Borden to draft another letter to the President. The opening sentences in the completed version were foreboding:

"The profundity of the atomic crisis which has overtaken us cannot, in my judgment, be exaggerated. The specific decision that you must make regarding the Superbomb is one of the gravest ever to confront an American president." McMahon elaborated on his earlier arguments, and concluded his letter by stating: "If we let the Russians get the Super first, catastrophe becomes all but certain— whereas, if we get it first, there exists a chance of saving ourselves."[30]

In the inner circles of the political and defense establishments this was an extremely hectic time. But the media of information, hence the public, were very little involved in one of the most ominous decisions in the history of the human race. Even when hints of the deliberations reached reporters they were persuaded that it would be irresponsible to report the news. For example, Alfred Friendly of the Washington *Post* learned from confidential sources about the impending superbomb. He went to David Lilienthal to question the AEC chief further. Lilienthal urged Friendly not to publish anything at that time, and Friendly decided the responsible course would be to follow Lilienthal's advice.[31]

The first real breach of security came not from a reporter but from Senator Edwin C. Johnson of Colorado. Johnson was a member of the Joint Committee on Atomic Energy and was aware of the entire secret controversy. At about the time that Teller was conducting a secret technical briefing on the thermonuclear weapon, Johnson was interviewed on a national television program. In the course of the interview he revealed not only that American scientists had created an atomic bomb with six times the yield of the Nagasaki blast, but that they were working on a superbomb with one thousand times the explosive force of the first nuclear weapons.[32]

This unexpected disclosure from a knowledgeable Senator made it almost impossible to keep the lid of secrecy clamped down. Reporters were beginning to ask more searching questions: Just what was the United States really doing? The pressure on Truman for a decision was building up every day.

The moral issue was still at the forefront; it was very much on the conscience of the scientists who were critical of the H-bomb proposal. Teller also felt that it was difficult to divorce the weapon from its possible use, but he suggested a way in which the moral issue could be bypassed, or at least balanced against the question of American survival. If, after the United States announced its decision to proceed, the Soviet Union did not join in an international control concordat, the moral issue would be muted and the sin would be on the heads of the Russians. That was Teller's view; McMahon, in contrast, seemed to worry little about the moral issue. To the Connecticut Senator this was an academic question and we were living in a real world in which the United States was confronted with evil.[33]

On November 18, the same day that the Washington *Post* reported Senator Johnson's television indiscretion, President Truman convened a special committee of the National Security Council. This ad hoc group consisted of Secretary of Defense Louis Johnson, Secretary of State Acheson, and AEC chairman Lilienthal. Their responsibility was to evaluate further the political and military implications as well as the technical feasibility of a thermonuclear weapon.[34] The Joint Chiefs of Staff were consulted and they reinforced the now rapidly growing sense of urgency about a quick determination of the feasibility of the H-bomb. They looked upon it as a possible deterrent to war. Conversely, they also concluded that if the Soviets possessed the weapon "without possession by the United States" the situation would be intolerable.[35]

The military leadership's position closely paralleled that of Karl T. Compton, who at that time was chairman of the Research and Development Board of the Department of Defense. In a letter to the President dated November 9, he wrote, in part:

> Therefore, until an adequate international solution is worked out, it seems to me that our own national security and the protection of the type of civilization which we value, require us to proceed with the most powerful atomic weapons which may be in sight. We can "hope to God they won't work," but so long as there is a reasonable possibility that they may work, it seems to me essential that we proceed with research and development on such projects as long as possible enemies may be doing the same thing.[36]

As the semi-secret debate continued, the dike of secrecy was finally and totally breached by Drew Pearson in a radio broadcast on Sunday evening, January 15, 1950,[37] and two days later by James Reston in a front-page article in the New York *Times*.[38] Pearson's broadcast presented only the bare outlines of the controversy and he was not completely accurate. Reston, with the advantage of a newspaper's opportunity for presenting details, dealt in far greater depth than Pearson with the factual and philosophical issues involved.

Inexorably, the now almost plaintive protests of the GAC and the indecisiveness of a majority of the AEC were being snowed under by the powerful forces of the real leadership in Washington. The Joint Committee, under the gentle lash of Senator McMahon, was now fully committed to the super. The State Department had also fallen into line. In a policy memorandum the department argued that if the Soviet Union alone possessed thermonuclear weapons, this "would cause severe damage not only to our military posture but to our foreign policy position."[39]

Then came the Klaus Fuchs explosion. When, in 1975, Teller attributed the H-bomb to a triumvirate of McMahon, Strauss, and Fuchs, he was, of course, injecting some humorous irony by including Fuchs, the master spy, in company with a distinguished Senator and a determined member of the AEC.

But the fact is that in late January 1950, when Harry Truman was agonizing over the question of moving ahead with the H-bomb, he received news that Fuchs, one of the most distinguished physicists at Los Alamos in World War II and a man privy to the most profound nuclear secrets, had confessed turning over scientific information to the Soviet Union. As a result of a briefing session he attended at Los Alamos in 1946, Fuchs was fully informed on all of the information accumulated up to that time on the physics and technology of thermonuclear weapons.

It was doubly ironic that Teller and Fuchs had been friends at Los Alamos; he was often a visitor to the Tellers' apartment, and both Edward and Mici admitted enjoying his company. Teller first met Fuchs in June 1944, and recalls Fuchs with a surprising lack of resentment.

"He was by no means an introvert, but he was a quiet man. I rather liked him," Teller wrote later. "As a full-fledged member of the British team at Los Alamos, he was entitled to know everything we were doing. He had full access to the laboratory's secret work. He talked with me and others frequently in depth about our intensive efforts to produce an atom bomb. It was easy and pleasant to discuss my work with him. He also made impressive contributions and I learned many technical facts from him." Teller also said that "Fuchs was popular at Los Alamos because he was kind, helpful and much interested in the work of others."[40]

Like General Benedict Arnold in the Revolutionary War, who, some historians have argued, made contributions to the United States that exceeded the setback caused by his defection, a similar case might be made for Klaus Fuchs. His contributions to the atom bomb project might, historically, prove to be more important than the fact that he eventually gave some of them away. Like many members of his generation who grew up in Europe in the late 1920s and early 1930s, Fuchs felt he had to make a political choice between communism and fascism. In 1932, the year Chancellor Franz von Papen lifted the ban on Hitler's storm troopers, Fuchs,

only twenty-one, joined the Communist party. The next year he
fled to England. He was interned in Canada and, after screening to
learn whether he had Nazi sympathies, he was freed and returned
to England. As a first-rate physicist, he was in demand and was
soon working with Rudolph Peierls, another refugee and associate
of Bethe, and others. Fuchs became an expert on many subjects,
especially isotope separation by the diffusion process. Such expertise was desperately needed at Los Alamos.

When this "kind and helpful" man was arrested in England and
confessed to having spied for the Soviets, it was reasonable to expect that Edward Teller, the arch-anticommunist, would have exploded in anger. But he did not.

Teller later wrote:

> I neither defend nor excuse Fuchs' spying. But I am convinced
> that he spied because he thought he was doing the right thing for the
> country and for the political philosophy that commanded his alle-
> giance.
> Russia, however, found it difficult to believe that anyone would
> undertake the enormous risks of being a spy only to satisfy his con-
> science. Fuchs did what he arrogantly thought was right, but Russia
> refused to accept this as a contribution to world communism. Russia
> insisted on paying for this information. In the sordid story of Fuchs'
> spying, this payment was the most shameful episode.[41]

The Soviet agent had received only token amounts for his services. The largest single payment was $400—a mere symbolic ac-
ceptance in Fuchs's mind, but to cynical Russians this categorized
him as a hired spy and not a communist visionary.

Teller's reflections on Fuchs reveal a great deal about Teller. It
must be borne in mind that Fuchs's exposure came at time when
the people in the United States, in their postwar disillusionment,
were being stirred into an anti-communist frenzy. The safest and
most loudly proclaimed sentiment of small-bore politicians from
town councilmen to Senators was eternal hostility to the "menace
of Godless communism." Senator Joseph McCarthy was to ride
this frenzy to an absurd, if brief, peak of popularity. And yet Teller, presumably the arch-anticommunist, could detect the spark of
intellectual integrity in Klaus Fuchs, and for this integrity, however misguided and traitorous, Teller could not totally condemn
one of the most successful spies of the century.

Fuchs's confession was revealed in official United States circles on January 27, 1950. This meant the Russians were well versed in American thermonuclear progress at least through that briefing meeting in Los Alamos in 1946, and not an awful lot had been learned since then. The Russians, of course, had their own excellent physicists. They might have learned what Fuchs told them without any spying. But in these early days of 1950 there was now no question that one way or another they knew most of the essential facts about nuclear fusion and the potential of the thermonuclear weapon. They were not likely to sit back and do nothing.

If Fuchs's confession was perfectly timed to put the screws to Truman, there is still no evidence other than circumstantial that the Fuchs affair influenced the President's decision. The mounting political pressures had a head of steam even before the spy scandal added more heat.

On January 29, two days before Truman's announcement, Teller had gleaned enough information to be reasonably certain of what was coming. On that day he met Oppenheimer at an atomic energy conference. The former Los Alamos boss also suspected that the decision would go against the GAC recommendation. In that event, Teller asked Oppie, "Would you go to work on the hydrogen bomb?" Oppenheimer had a bitter, one-word reply: "No."[42]

Not all of the senior scientists, even some of the moderate ones, agreed with the GAC. One of the most quietly respected scientists in America was Nobel Laureate Harold C. Urey. In a speech on January 27 he made it clear that he was not in the GAC camp. Teller had gained an important ally.[43]

On Tuesday morning, January 31, the special committee of the National Security Council, Johnson, Acheson, and Lilienthal, gathered in a somber conference in the old State Department building. With their advisors and associates, they drafted the recommendation they would place in the President's uncertain hands later that day. Lilienthal argued for a delay in order to explore what he considered a basic weakness in the nation's defense policy—an unrealistic dependence on nuclear weapons. The other participants didn't challenge the AEC chairman's arguments but brushed them aside. They felt the irresistible need for a decision. Except for the mild differences with Lilienthal, the meeting was remarkably free of acrimony.[44]

At 12:35 P.M. the same day, the special committee was ushered into Truman's office. Secretary Acheson, as senior member, delivered the recommendation to the President. Lilienthal then made another plea for delay, as he had done in the morning meeting. President Truman was familiar with the AEC chief's point of view and interrupted him. In quiet times, the President said, a more detailed examination might have been possible. But Senator Johnson had already revealed so much that it was necessary to make a decision and to tell the American people.[45]

In a matter of minutes, the President's statement was ready to distribute to a hastily called press conference. It read:

It is part of my responsibility as Commander-in-Chief of the armed forces to see to it that our country is able to defend itself against any possible aggressor.

Accordingly, I have directed the Atomic Energy Commission to continue its work on all forms of atomic weapons, including the so-called hydrogen or super bomb.

12

Fusion and Confusion

TRUMAN had acted, but Teller was disturbed. The President's statement said he had directed the AEC to "continue" its work on all forms of atomic weapons. Teller, whatever his faults, has a genuine revulsion against intellectual dishonesty, especially when it emerges in spurious verbiage. He thought Truman was, perhaps unwittingly, guilty of a dishonest statement. "He gave the impression," Teller said later, "that we could produce a hydrogen bomb simply by tightening a few last screws. People understood from his announcement that the job was almost done.

"Actually, work had not begun," Teller pointed out. "We had eight years of thermonuclear fantasies, theories, and calculations behind us, but we had established no connection between theory and reality. We needed a thermonuclear test."[1]

The use of the word "continue" was not an accident. The President's statement had been drafted the evening before by Robert LeBaron, the Pentagon's liaison man with the AEC. The impression the White House sought to create was that the current slow pace of thermonuclear research would be speeded up.[2] There was to be no crisis-driven crash program. In that sense Truman's decision represented a compromise. Teller's victory was only partial.

The press, however, did not see it as a compromise. The news was generally treated at close to the sensational level. It is also doubtful that the Russians concluded the United States would only walk a little faster, instead of running to build an H-bomb.

After the Truman decision, Teller's critics did not offer to shake his hand and wish him well. Some, such as Oppenheimer, retired into a hostile and noncooperative silence. Others, like I. I. Rabi, were vocal in their continuing opposition. Bethe, later to count himself among the scientists who deeply regretted Truman's action, was not vocal in the early stages of the argument.

Rabi, like Teller, thought the President's announcement was

deceptive, but for different reasons. He put the blame for the deception not on Truman, but on the broad shoulders of Teller and Ernest Lawrence. To Rabi it was these two powerful scientists who had misled the military and the Congressional Joint Committee; Teller and Lawrence created the political pressures that forced the President's decision. "They had done an awful thing," in Rabi's opinion.

Rabi spoke with high emotion when we interviewed him in his office at Columbia University in May 1973.

"The differences of opinion were of a political sort, I thought, but later it developed they were deeply emotional. . . . Teller was going for it at all costs. It became doubtful that this thing would work or that it would be a weapon. This discussion went on in the context of very great advances in the art of making the fission bomb . . . to change to this other thing was very, very doubtful."

Rabi accused Teller of acting on "faith that somehow this could be made to work." Teller, according to Rabi, had no idea how to make it work, so he tried one thing after another "which, then, on examination, didn't turn out to be sound. In that context, I am sure he felt very much alone."

Thus, to Rabi, Truman's decision "was founded on a complete fallacy. It was a most terrible thing . . . the President made the decision—and announced it publicly—to go ahead . . . on a device where all the ideas we had were such that it would not work."

One of the results, he insisted, "was to lay down a challenge to the Soviet Union." Teller and Lawrence probably did not intend to deceive the President and Congress—"but they certainly made them embark on and announce a high priority in a field in which they did not know enough. It really constituted for a time, I thought, an extreme danger to the United States."

Why did Rabi consider it an extreme danger? "Because," he replied, "we put on the highest priority that we would make an object which would not work." In fact, Rabi added, it was proved "just about that time" that it would *not* work, by mathematicians Stanislaw Ulam and Cornelius Everett.

This comment could be interpreted as a serious charge against Teller and Lawrence. If "just about that time" meant that the two scientists knew the proposed superbomb wouldn't work, then they had intentionally misled the country. The exact chronology, however, vindicates Teller and Lawrence on this score. It was a few days *after* Truman's January 31 decision that Ulam made known his preliminary decision that there was a "fifty-fifty chance that the fusion reaction, once begun, would continue."[3] And Ulam's more pessimistic conclusion, that Teller's proposal was faulty, was not reached until March.

The opinions of Teller and Rabi were those of deeply committed men, but at this time neither was in the driver's seat. The matter was now on the table in Washington. The crucial problem was how to implement the President's decision. Would there really be a crash program? In the months ahead the question would be answered.

One of the influential figures of this period was Robert LeBaron, who served both as deputy to the Secretary of Defense for Atomic Energy, and chairman of the Military Liaison Committee to the Atomic Energy Commission. As one of those who felt an urgent need to get moving on the H-bomb project, LeBaron was in conflict with many of his former academic colleagues. LeBaron came into the military establishment with a background of scholarship. From 1913 to 1915 he was a graduate student and a faculty member in the chemistry department at Princeton. During World War I he served overseas as an Army artillery officer, then returned to Princeton to receive his master's degree in physics. For a year after the war he went to Paris to study physics in the Sorbonne under Madame Curie.

In 1950, LeBaron could still call H. D. Smyth, the Princeton physicist, an old colleague and friend, but now they had to cross swords. LeBaron saw the American scientific establishment as basically divided into two teams. One was at Berkeley, captained by Ernest Lawrence. The other was at Princeton, where Smyth, who told the story of the Manhattan Project in the esteemed "Smyth Report," was the field boss. The quarterback, ideologically speaking, was J. Robert Oppenheimer, but he stayed away from the line of scrimmage and avoided direct body contact.

With the exception of a few heavyweights like Eugene Wigner and John A. Wheeler, the Princeton group, as LeBaron saw them, just didn't want to play in the thermonuclear game. And they were confident that if they didn't play, there wouldn't be any game, or, if there were a game, they wanted a part in the coaching as well as the playing. This, at least, was LeBaron's assessment. He regarded Lawrence and Teller as allies, the former as the man with the political clout, the latter as the scientific genius who could get the job done. Teller, in retrospect, has some reservations about how LeBaron remembers the events of 1950.

At a meeting on February 2, 1950, the AEC commissioners met with the Military Liaison Committee to discuss the President's directive. A dispute quickly developed between LeBaron and Sumner Pike, who was then acting chairman of the AEC while David Lilienthal was preparing to give up the chairmanship. Pike argued that the AEC should be responsible for determining the new weapon's feasibility. Only after that should the Defense Department be brought in as a partner to determine the scale of the program.

LeBaron calmly but firmly dissented. He felt that the Pentagon and the AEC should co-author the program from its beginning. The planning for the development and testing of a thermonuclear weapon should be a joint effort. And LeBaron insisted that if the tests were successful, it was the commission's responsibility to be sure that enough tritium was available, not only for testing, but for immediate production of the H-bomb.[4]

A thread of distrust ran through the discussion. It was a power struggle such as constantly takes place between powerful government agencies. In this case, however, the military was especially suspicious of a commission that had J. Robert Oppenheimer as its chief scientific advisor.

The argument grew warmer, the words were sharper. LeBaron said he had learned from Lawrence and other scientists at Berkeley that the AEC's tritium program lacked direction and was not being pushed hard enough. This affront to Pike's integrity and competence riled tempers.[5]

Pike, stung by LeBaron's remarks, asked a few questions of his own, most pointedly "whether the military had actually established a requirement for a thermonuclear weapon." Was it a reasonable question? The military, after all, had fought for the thermonuclear program; therefore, they must have had a use for the weapon. The answer would have to be yes. But it wasn't. "No, not yet," was in effect what LeBaron replied. The Pentagon was waiting for a complete analysis that would reveal the cost of the program in terms of money and personnel, and particularly its effect on the existing fission program. The meeting ended with conciliatory words from Pike, who felt that cooperation between the two agencies of government was not only necessary, but possible.[6]

The military stance at the dawn of the H-bomb era was reminiscent of an earlier example of what might be called military inertia that was recounted by Teller in *The Legacy of Hiroshima*.

While Teller was at Chicago shortly after the end of World War II he went to Albuquerque for a conference with Air Force officials. The purpose of the meeting was to get the Air Force's opinion on the direction of atomic weapons development. The size of the bombs dropped over Japan had been determined by the carrying capacity and the space available in a B-29. The scientists needed the Air Force officers' guidance since it was the power of Los Alamos to develop a variety of weapons. Now they put the question to the military experts—should future bombs be bigger, smaller, more powerful, less powerful than the bombs dropped on Hiroshima? What did the Air Force want?

After a day of talking Teller could scarcely hide his annoyance. The only answer he could get from the supposedly knowledgeable Air Force men was "the bomb we have now is precisely what we need."[7] What they had was a Nagasaki-type bomb.

The military's contentment with the current state of the art was utterly unacceptable to Teller's restless Magyar soul. But then he had second thoughts about whether the military men were not so much apathetic as victims of the schism between scientists and soldiers. He decided that the Air Force officers did not necessarily lack intelligence, interest, or imagination, but only knowledge. His view was that "few of the military men involved in the conference had any notion of how an atomic explosive worked, and even fewer had any concept of what further atomic explosions could accomplish."

Teller came to realize that one of the principal causes of this military ignorance was unjustifiable secrecy.

> With secrecy preventing discussion of all new facts, it was only natural that the military men should accept, in our bizarre atomic world, only those changes they had to accept. The "bomb" was an unassailable fact and had to be accepted. But there was no opportunity, because of secrecy, and no incentive, because of inertia, to think farther ahead.[8]

If LeBaron could confess in 1951 that the military was "not yet" certain, perhaps a lack of information was again at fault. But the meetings with the AEC continued. The next day, February 3, the

Liaison Committee once again urged the commission to plan to produce enough tritium for both testing and production of thermonuclear weapons. The committee felt this should not interfere with plutonium production, and reactors to serve these dual objectives were suggested. In the meantime the committee recommended a scientific recruitment program.[9]

Teller was already doing just that, with messianic zeal, on his own. Almost immediately he was on a collision course with some of the nation's top scientists. Twelve of them, including Hans Bethe, stood up to criticize the new bomb project. They conceded the H-bomb of unlimited power was possible, in theory, but they couched their objections in the strongest moral terms:

> We believe that no nation has the right to use such a bomb, no matter how righteous its cause. The bomb is no longer a weapon of war but a means of extermination of whole populations. . . . We urge that the United States . . . make a solemn declaration that we shall never use the bomb first.[10]

Within a week a supporting statement came from the revered doyen of the world's scientific community, Albert Einstein.

> If [the H-bomb] is successful, radioactive poisoning of the atmosphere and hence annihilation of any life on earth has been brought within the range of technical possibilities. . . . In the end there · beckons more and more clearly general annihilation.[11]

Oppenheimer did not join his colleagues in public criticism of Truman's decision. Perhaps he felt that as chairman of the GAC he had no right to engage in public debate with the President. Then, too, dissent had its political risks. It was an era when dissent was sometimes equated with subversion, and Oppenheimer's past made him particularly vulnerable. As a prudent man he seemed to think it wise to keep his own counsel. When he did speak out on two occasions, he didn't oppose the substance of the decision but only the way it was reached.

Part of Teller's task was to reverse the "brain drain" that had occurred at Los Alamos since 1945. Years later, in 1962, he could look back to those days just before the bomb was dropped on Hiroshima and write glowingly of the team that was available:

A number of talented people joined our group. One of Bethe's students, Henry Hurwitz, proved that he had learned from his professor how to be systematic and ingenious. Two students from George Washington University, Geoffrey Chew and Harold Argo, interrupted their studies and came to Los Alamos to help us. Anthony Turkevich from Chicago contributed his knowledge of the theory of chemical reactions. Rolf Landshoff, a refugee from Germany, was the only one of the group who was going to stay at Los Alamos uninterruptedly from those days up to the present time. Two mathematicians, Stan Ulam and Jack Calkin, started to make calculations which even to a theorist seemed abstract. Nicholas Metropolis became interested in the use of computing machines, which in the later development turned out to be of great importance.[13]

Those were the new recruits involved in the thermonuclear project in 1945. Two of Teller's own students joined up—Harris Mayer and John Reitz. But there were older people from the Los Alamos group who were also involved—John Manley, Elizabeth Graves, Marshall Holloway, Charles Baker, and Egon Bretscher. In a special category because of their strong support of Teller were Marshall Rosenbluth and Frederic de Hoffmann. They were, over the subsequent years, to become Teller's close friends and collaborators. At this time Fermi was contributing; so was John von Neumann.[13]

When the war ended, this team, many of them heavy-laden with the burden of Hiroshima, dissolved. By 1946, Philip Stern points out in *The Oppenheimer Case*, there were only three scientists with postgraduate degrees working on the thermonuclear project.

How could reluctant scientists be summoned back to the service of their country's defense, especially with the moral doubts that pervaded their community? It wasn't just a question of attracting young talent. Men of the caliber of Bethe, Fermi, Oppenheimer, and Teller were needed not only for their acknowledged brilliance, but as an inspiration for the scientific troops. With the exception of Teller, scientific leadership just did not come forth.

Oppenheimer preferred to remain in Princeton as director of the Institute for Advanced Study, and in Washington as chairman of the GAC. Fermi was happy to be back in his laboratory at Chicago. Bethe stayed away for a while, but finally consented to occasional visits to Los Alamos as a kind of advisor.

Oppenheimer was not totally uncooperative. There is at least one instance where he helped Teller recruit an able scientist. In

Edward Teller's mother, Ilona Deutsch, at eighteen, before her marriage to Max Teller.

Edward's father, Max Teller, at about sixty.

Edward and Emmi Teller, age one and three.

Emmi Teller (left) at fifteen, with Edward (right), thirteen, and their governess, Magda Hess.

Edward Teller's high school graduation portrait.

Edward Teller as a student in Germany, about 1927.

Mici Teller and Edward Teller in 1935, the year after their marriage.

These were the participants in the fifth Washington Conference on Theoretical Physics, thrown into a turmoil when Niels Bohr (first row, fourth from left) interrupted the proceedings to announce that a month earlier, in Germany, the chemists Hahn and Strassman had split a uranium nucleus. The world was never the same again.

Stern, Carnegie Tech, Pittsburgh
Fermi, Rome, Columbia
Fleming, Carnegie Institution of Washington
Bohr, Copenhagen, Princeton
London, Duke, Paris
Urey, Columbia
Brickwedde, National Bureau of Standards
Breit, Wisconsin, Carnegie Institution
Silsbee, National Bureau of Standards
Rabi, Columbia
Uhlenbeck, Columbia
Gamow, George Washington
Teller, George Washington
Mrs. Mayer, Johns Hopkins
Bitter, Massachusetts Institute of Technology
Bethe, Cornell
Grayson-Smith, Toronto
Van Vleck, Harvard
Jacobs, Massachusetts Institute of Technology
Starr, Massachusetts Institute of Technology
Hebb, Duke
Squire, Pennsylvania
Kuper, U.S. Public Health Service
Mahan, Georgetown
Myers, Maryland

26 - Roberts, Carnegie Institution of Washington
27 - Critchfield, George Washington
28 - Baroff, U. S. Patent Office
29 - Bohr, Jr., Copenhagen
30 - Meyer, Carnegie Institution of Washington
31 - Herzfeld, Catholic University
32 - Lord, Johns Hopkins
33 - Inglis, Johns Hopkins
34 - Wulf, U. S. Department of Agriculture
35 - Wang, Peking, Carnegie Institution of Washington
36 - Johnson, Carnegie Institution of Washington
37 - Mohler, National Bureau of Standards
38 - Scott, National Bureau of Standards
39 - Vestine, Carnegie Institution of Washington
40 - Rosenfeld, Liege, Copenhagen, Princeton
41 - Seitz, Pennsylvania
42 - Diecke, Johns Hopkins
43 - Mayer, Johns Hopkins
44 - Hibben, Carnegie Institution of Washington
45 - Tuve, Carnegie Institution of Washington
46 - O'Bryan, Georgetown
47 - Hafstad, Carnegie Institution of Washington
48 - Cohen, Columbia
49 - Hoge, National Bureau of Standards
50 - Sklar, Catholic University
51 - Rossini, National Bureau

Teller at thirty-five, in 1943, with Mici just before their move to the Los Alamos laboratory.

A galaxy of famous physicists gathered in front of Princeton's Sayre Hall to celebrate the success of the Mike thermonuclear test in November 1952. Niels Bohr is second from the right in the front row (wearing a scarf). Hans Bethe is to Bohr's right. Immediately behind them on the right of the second row are George Gamow and I. I. Rabi. John A. Wheeler is behind Gamow, and Eugene Wigner is at the extreme left of the second row. Teller is partially obscured in the center of the next to last row.

Edward and Mici Teller and their children, Paul and Wendy, in 1957. (Jon Brenneis, Time-Life Picture Agency © Time Inc.)

Rear Admiral Lewis L. Strauss, Teller's close personal friend and political ally. Strauss was chairman of the AEC during the Oppenheimer hearing. This portrait was taken in 1959, when Strauss was Eisenhower's Secretary of Commerce designate, just before an embittered U.S. Senate refused to confirm his appointment.

EDWARD TELLER.
WAR CRIMINAL

■Worked on atomic bomb during WW2
■Father of Hydrogen bomb
■Largely responsible for establishment of the Livermore Rad Lab
■Leading advocate of arms race
■Leading advocate of nuclear blackmail
■Has acted as hawk advisor to Washington officials, including
   Nixon, since WW2

is living in our community:
1573 Hawthorne Terrace
848-8811

People in the community
have a responsibility to
challenge Teller on his   CAN YOU DIG IT?
activities. You can do this
by giving him a call or going
by to discuss them with him.

Circular distributed by Berkeley radicals prior to the "trial" of Edward Teller by a "war crimes tribunal" on November 23, 1970. The "trial" ended with a mob marching toward Teller's house, some of them threatening to burn it down.

Dr. John A. Wheeler, the celebrated Princeton physicist who was the first American to learn that German scientists had split a uranium nucleus, paving the way for the nuclear age. Wheeler has for many years been a colleague and defender of Teller.

Princeton Physics Professor Eugene Wigner, a Nobel prizewinner, fellow Hungarian, and friend and admirer of Edward Teller.

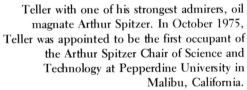

Teller with one of his strongest admirers, oil magnate Arthur Spitzer. In October 1975, Teller was appointed to be the first occupant of the Arthur Spitzer Chair of Science and Technology at Pepperdine University in Malibu, California.

Teller with his principal political patron, Vice President Nelson Rockefeller, and Mrs. Rockefeller at the new vice presidential mansion, October, 1975.

On December 2, 1963, exactly ten years after he was charged with being a security risk, J. Robert Oppenheimer received the prestigious Fermi Award from President Lyndon Johnson. After the White House ceremony, Teller, who had won the award in 1962, warmly congratulated his longtime rival. At the time the gesture seemed to symbolize the end of the long and bitter rivalry between the supporters of the rival scientists, but the ill feeling, though Teller and Oppenheimer may have personally made their peace, continued to divide the scientific world for at least another decade.

(Ralph Morse, Time-Life Picture Agency © Time Inc.)

It's usually standing room only when
Teller lectures at Tel Aviv University.
(Vivienne Silver.)

Edward Teller today (his
wife, Mici, is looking
through the window).
(Karsh, Ottawa)

1950 Conrad Longmire was at the Institute for Advanced Study. Teller desperately wanted him at Los Alamos, but Longmire was not willing to relinquish a prestigious post at the Institute. At Teller's suggestion, Oppenheimer gave Longmire the opportunity to accept the Los Alamos job with the proviso that he could return to his post at the Institute at any time. Longmire thereupon accepted the Teller offer and became a valuable member of the thermonuclear team.[14]

Otherwise there is some dispute about the degree to which Oppenheimer either helped or hindered Teller's recruiting efforts. AEC member Gordon Dean was especially concerned about Teller's need to hire the best personnel. In the spring of 1950 he urged Teller to make a direct appeal to Oppenheimer. Teller phoned the former Los Alamos chief and was told, as Teller remembers the conversation, "You know in this matter I am neutral. I would be glad, however, to recommend to you some very good people who are working here at the Institute."[15]

Oppenheimer mentioned a few names, Teller recalls, but "I wrote to every one of these people and tried to persuade them to come to Los Alamos. None of them came."[16]

Thus, with the exception of Longmire, Teller cannot recall any case in which Oppenheimer was helpful. At the same time, Teller admits that he knows of no documented case where Oppenheimer persuaded any scientist *not* to work on the superbomb. There was, on occasion, circumstantial evidence that Oppenheimer was obstructive, but hard evidence is still lacking.

There was one top-drawer physicist who did not turn Teller down, though recruiting him took some heavy persuasion. That was John A. Wheeler. Eleven years had passed since that famous day in January 1939 when Wheeler met Niels Bohr at a pier in New York and became the first person in America to know that an atomic nucleus had been split in Germany. In the subsequent decade Wheeler had become a famous physicist in his own right. He had been part of the A-bomb team, but had returned to Princeton after the war.

Wheeler recalled to the authors that even before the Soviets' first successful atomic test, Joe One, in 1949, Teller and John von Neumann had tried to persuade him to leave Princeton and join the H-bomb team. He had turned them down, but not without mixed feelings.

"Each time," Wheeler said, "I felt more strongly the importance of it because it was perfectly clear that our Soviet colleagues could make progress in developing a hydrogen weapon. Why should the United States be the second to get it?

"However," Wheeler continued, "the pressure did not really get hot until I had gone to France on sabbatical leave in June 1949. I intended to stay a year. During that fall [Joe One had been announced in September] the debate got hotter and heavier in the United States about whether we should go ahead with the hydrogen bomb project because the Soviets had exploded their first atomic weapon. Finally, Teller called, and there were transatlantic phone calls from members of the Atomic Energy Commission. Dr. Teller sent his trusted right-hand man, Frederic de Hoffmann, to meet me in France and explain (since it could not be done over the phone) the latest developments and the urgency. On that basis I made the decision to give up the work I was so excited about in my own research and came back to the United States to go to Los Alamos."

Wheeler was one of the first of the major physicists to come aboard. Gradually a crew was assembled under the leadership of Marshall Holloway, who was one of the top assistants to Los Alamos director Norris Bradbury. One of the important members of the team was Harold Agnew, who was later to succeed Bradbury as director. Eventually the team's responsibility was set forth—build a thermonuclear device, transport it to the Pacific, and fire it. The device, more often referred to as an "experiment," was known under the code word Greenhouse, a landmark name in the saga of fusion bomb development.

Agnew, still serving as the Los Alamos director, recalled for the authors the opposition, even within Los Alamos, after Truman's announcement ordering thermonuclear development.

"There were remnants," Agnew told us, "of this feeling that we shouldn't pursue these endeavors. I was not in sympathy with those individuals; in fact, I thought they were nuts. I just didn't understand them . . . they even got onto religious matters. They would quote the Bible. I thought they were quite off their rocker, frankly."

Agnew would not identify any of the individuals who offered this kind of opposition—"It was a long time ago. I don't know if their minds have changed. But there were people who were opposed. . . . My feeling was they ought to leave the place because we had a responsibility to the country to explore what could be done."

As the project picked up speed, Bradbury decreed a six-day work week at Los Alamos. The schedule was not popular, even with so dedicated a scientist as John Wheeler. At least not until the Bible, whose scriptures had been quoted by the opposition, came to Wheeler's rescue.

It was not long after the six-day decree that Wheeler arrived. "He was pooped from the long trip," Teller recalls. "We had dinner together with several others. He listened to a lot of complaints about the six-day week." But Wheeler was too tired to argue one way or another. "I just have to go to bed," he told the gathering.

The next morning Teller met a refreshed Wheeler, ready to go to work. "You know, Edward," he said (according to Teller's version) "you are so thoughtful. You had a Bible next to my bed. So before going to sleep I just happened to open it by chance and read, 'Six days shalt thou labor.'" Thenceforth Wheeler made tremendous contributions to the H-bomb project—six days at a time.

Teller now had Wheeler, Rosenbluth (who had then come from Stanford and was later to go to Princeton), and another colleague from the wartime era, Emil Konopinski, who took a leave from the University of Indiana.

The challenges that Teller faced in that year of 1950 were not just cosmic, but political. The essential problem was one of dialectic interaction between science and politics. Specifically, politicians weren't willing to provide money and manpower for a project until they were reasonably certain it was feasible. But without the funds to conduct a clear scientific demonstration of fusion on earth, the scientists could not prove it was feasible. A stalemate was threatened. It was the classic "Catch-22" situation.

How did Teller overcome it? Essentially what he seemed to do was first to appeal to the fear of Russia in McMahon, Strauss, and Borden, then to capture the imagination of scientists with a promise of high adventure, and parlay these emotions into a winning cause. The politicians were convinced that Teller's bomb would save America from Russian aggression, and the scientists were proud to march behind a man who was on the threshold of an epic breakthrough. If Teller's faith and determination did not move mountains, it did, in fact, obliterate an island.

That basic scientific problem was still there—to create on the surface of the earth a temperature high enough for fusion to occur. It was known that thermonuclear reactions taking place in the sun and the stars require nearly 20 million degrees Centigrade. The scientists had calculated that an even greater temperature would be needed for fusion to occur on earth.

In a letter to the authors, Hans Bethe explained why the required temperatures differed.

> The solution to the paradox is as follows: In the stars the nuclear reaction has to proceed slowly, taking a time of the order of 10 billion years. In a thermonuclear weapon the reaction must take place fast, taking a time of the order of one billionth of a second. The ratio of these times is about 10^{26}. In order to make the reaction go fast, one needs much higher temperature than for a slow reaction.
>
> In the projected thermonuclear power devices* the time for the reaction is not quite as short, but perhaps may be of the order of one second. But to compensate for this the density of the plasma in thermonuclear power producers is perhaps 10^{10} times slower than at the center of the sun.[17]

On February 23, 1950, the Military Liaison Committee met in Bradbury's office at Los Alamos. The director pledged a maximum effort on the thermonuclear weapon program, but assured the committee that promising fission weapons would not be neglected.

At this meeting, possibly for the first time, LeBaron and his committee understood the magnitude of the thermonuclear puzzle and the obstacles in the path of its solution. The central problem was finding a way to fuse the heavier isotopes of hydrogen and in doing so release energy. Deuterium is an isotope of hydrogen that is found in almost limitless quantities in sea water. During World War II an economical technique for its separation was developed. The joker, however, was that in theory the fusion of deuterium nuclei required a temperature of about 400 million degrees, far beyond the heating capacity of the atomic bomb.[18] This wide temperature gap had to be bridged before a thermonuclear reaction between hydrogen isotopes was possible.

The improved versions of the atomic bomb had been made far more powerful than in the days of Hiroshima and Nagasaki. The

---

*The thermonuclear power devices that Bethe refers to were a major area of fusion research when this letter was written in 1974, but had scarcely been conceived as a possibility in 1950.

wartime bombs created a temperature of about 50 million degrees for about 1.1 millionth of a second. As the power of the new generation of bombs increased, so did their temperature and the length of time of the explosion. These increases were sufficient to engender at least a hope that such a bomb could trigger a self-sustaining fusion reaction. The proposed method was to use the hydrogen isotope tritium in combination with the more common isotope deuterium. When the two isotopes were combined the best estimates were that they would fuse at about 80 million degrees.[19] Because deuterium occurs naturally in nature, it is relatively inexpensive. Tritium, which had to be created, was extremely rare and expensive. What was foreseen, however, was that tritium would reach fusion temperature more easily than deuterium and the tritium itself would then create the higher temperature needed for the fusion of tritium with deuterium.[20]

The cost of tritium became an operative economic factor in the planning for a thermonuclear experiment. This disturbed Teller, who felt the knowledge gained from the experiment justified its high cost. Bradbury, on the other hand, was more conservative and perhaps more realistic about the cost factor.

On March 2, eight days after the meeting in Los Alamos, Teller was back beating the bushes in Washington. He had dinner with William Liscum Borden, executive director of the Congressional Joint Committee on Atomic Energy.[21] Borden was one of the powerful conservatives on whom Teller built his political base. This awareness that men like Senator McMahon, Borden, and Lewis Strauss were behind him gave Teller the support to speak out and even to criticize his nominal bosses, the officials of the AEC. It is understandable that some of the commissioners were beginning to resent this free-wheeling, maverick scientist.

A development during the dinner with Borden was a perfect case in point. Teller was still concerned about his inability to recruit scientists. Borden was impressed with Teller's problem. He invited Teller to testify the next day, March 3, before the Joint Committee. It was only just before the hearing that Commissioner Henry D. Smyth received the unexpected news that Teller was about to testify.[22]

Teller is an impressive witness. He speaks without script or notes. His command of the English language is excellent, although his thick Hungarian accent requires a well-tuned ear. His thoughts are well structured, so that if his testimony is transcribed and printed, it reads well. He is confident in reporting past and current events but seldom makes any pretense about predicting the future. He is willing, even anxious to admit that he does not have all the answers. But his sincerity and his air of authority frequently convince his audience that he does.

Smyth was the only commissioner present at the hearing. This did not deter Teller from deploring the lost years when practically no work was done on thermonuclear reactions, certainly an implied criticism of the AEC. But Teller also blamed himself and others who had left Los Alamos. Now the lost time had to be made up, and somehow the scientific community must be persuaded of this. He did not guarantee success, but he believed the thermonuclear weapon was feasible. His call went beyond the shores of the United States. Despite the defection of one of Great Britain's star physicists, Klaus Fuchs, Teller thought there were several British scientists whose talents were needed.

Truman's directive of January 31 proved to be ambiguous. It was partly responsible for the infighting between the Department of Defense and the AEC. The President issued a clarifying order on March 10 that proved highly gratifying to Teller.[23] The two competing agencies were to be jointly responsible for planning the scope of production of hydrogen isotopes, particularly tritium. The AEC alone was given the task of arranging for quantity production of thermonuclear materials. And finally, the directive authorized a "feasibility test" to establish certain principles of the thermonuclear reaction.[24] This authorization, for the test to be called "Greenhouse," was what Teller had been advocating and hoping for.

As the project began to take form, the drumbeats of opposition grew louder. Truman's guidelines only amplified the crescendo. "Ban the H-bomb" signs appeared across the United States, some printed, some mere graffiti. There was hysterical talk about the power of such a bomb and not all the talk was exaggerated. Stories began to spread about the ghastly effects of radiation.

In March, Hans Bethe, Leo Szilard, and Frederick Seitz of the University of Pittsburgh participated in a Chicago round-table program that drew national attention. The question of the danger of radioactivity from an H-bomb blast was discussed, apart from the danger from the blast itself. Moderator Harrison Brown raised the issue:

BROWN: Will dispersal [of population] actually help if H-bombs are used not for blast but for radioactivity?

DR. SZILARD: In this case [dispersal] will not help at all.

DR. BETHE: You are certainly right when you emphasize the radioactivity. In the H-bomb neutrons are produced in large numbers. These neutrons will go into the air; and in the air they will make radioactive carbon fourteen, which is well known to science. This isotope of carbon has a half-life of five thousand years. It may well be that the number of H-bombs will be so large that this will make life impossible.

Szilard's subsequent statement indicated he was thinking of a different type of doomsday machine. Perhaps he was speculating on the theoretical possibility of building a cobalt bomb, a weapon that, in theory, would create a withering dose of severe radioactivity over thousands of square miles.

DR. SZILARD: Yes, that is true, Bethe, but that is not what I had in mind, because it would take a very large number of bombs before life would be in danger from ordinary H-bombs. What I had in mind was this: The H-bomb as it would be made would not cause greater radioactivity than that which is due to carbon; but it is very easy to rig an H-bomb on purpose, so that it should produce very dangerous radioactivity. . . . Let us assume that we make a radioactive element which will live for five years and that we just let it go into the air. During the following years it will gradually settle out and cover the whole earth with dust. I have asked myself: How many neutrons or how much heavy hydrogen do we have to detonate to kill everybody on earth by this particular method? I come up with about fifty tons of neutrons as being plenty to kill everybody, which means about 500 hundred tons of heavy hydrogen.[25]

Inasmuch as Bethe and Szilard were two of Teller's oldest and dearest friends, he was emotionally upset by their comments, especially because he felt they had exaggerated the danger of radioactivity. Trying to be rational, he told himself they had a right to be heard but he felt he should have the same privilege. As always, friendships meant a great deal to him; Bethe's and Szilard's comments must not be allowed to break the bond of many years.

But that was scarcely the beginning of the anti-H-bomb campaign. The prestigious *Scientific American* lent a substantial part of its March, April, and May editions to the opponents of the new bomb. Louis N. Ridenour wrote the first article on "The Theoretical Background of the Weapon," and reviewed "some questions it has raised in regard to our present policy of security."

Ridenour deplored the way the President had foisted the bomb upon the American people:

> A major issue of public policy, one quite possibly involving our national existence, was decided in a fully authoritarian way. Not without public discussion, to be sure, but without anything that could have been called informed public discussion. The public did not even know and still does not know what the actual questions at issue were.

Ridenour conceded that the H-bomb "can be made." He saw no limit to its size, and unlike fission, which has a peaceful, practical use in power reactors, "the fusion reaction offers no prospect at the present time of any use except in terms of an explosion." (Two decades later Ridenour was still right on this point, though research in controlled fusion as a source of cheap energy was progressing slowly but hopefully toward such a goal.)

Some of Ridenour's other objections were that the bomb's vast explosive power would be suitable only to the destruction of large targets, and thus would be more useful to the U.S.S.R. than the U.S.A.—"We have several large targets; the U.S.S.R. has only one or two." One of his principal conclusions was that "We are far more in need of means for the sure and accurate delivery of the bombs we already know how to make than we are of an improved and more destructive bomb."[26]

The April article, by Bethe, proposed "a first step towards international control of atomic weapons."

"I believe," Bethe wrote, "the most important question is the moral one. Can we who have always insisted on morality and human decency between nations as well as inside our own country, introduce this weapon of total annihilation into the world? . . . We would lose not only many lives but all our liberties and human values as well."

Bethe had an additional fear—that the President's decision could have spurred the Russians to doing the same.

"Our decision to make the H-bomb," Bethe reasoned, "which showed that we considered the project feasible, may well have prompted them to make the same decision. For this reason I think that our decision, if taken at all, should have been taken in secret." (Here Bethe disagreed with Ridenour, who had complained that decision was made without open public discussion.) But since the course had been set, Bethe believed, both the Soviet Union and the United States could benefit by some kind of mutual agreement.[27]

In one important respect Bethe disagreed with Robert F. Bacher, physicist and former AEC member, who concluded the *Scientific American* series in May 1950. Bethe noted that neutrons released in the air are captured by nitrogen nuclei which are thereby transformed into radioactive carbon 14. But he noted that carbon 14 has a half-life of five thousand years, hence its radioactivity is relatively weak. "Consequently," Bethe concluded, "even if many bombs were exploded it is not likely the carbon 14 would become dangerous."

Bacher was more alarmed. "If the neutrons escaped into the air," he wrote, "many of them would be absorbed by nitrogen and produce radioactive carbon. This material is most disagreeable as a radioactive contaminant since it has a half-life of many thousands of years."

Otherwise, Bacher questioned the H-bomb's usefulness as a weapon. "Would it really revolutionize warfare, as some say?" Overkill, Bacher contended, was already possible with improved fission bombs. He agreed with Ridenour that "from a military standpoint the solution of the delivery problem is vastly more important than exactly what kind of bombs would be carried if they could be delivered."[28]

Teller knew the attack was building and he was in print about the same time the first *Scientific American* article appeared. His article, "Back to the Laboratories," appeared in the March 1950 issue of the *Bulletin of the Atomic Scientists*. It was a period of frustration and risk for Teller and his mind must have been tortured by the looming possibility of failure. But he felt his critics had to be answered.

His article was an emotional appeal for support. It read like the extemporaneous Teller at his best. He was convinced of the justice of his quest. He did not attempt to mask his feelings. He was pained that his friends did not understand. He stood exposed, revealing, if not his warts, at least his freckles. The essay, however, was more than an emotional tract. It expressed in simple language Teller's scientific and political convictions.

> No one connected with the work on atomic bombs can escape a feeling of grave responsibility. No one will be glad to discover more fuel with which a coming conflagration may be fed. But scientists must find a modest way of looking into an uncertain future. The scientist is not responsible for the laws of nature. It is his job to find out how these laws operate. It is the scientist's job to find ways in which these laws can serve the human will. . . . It is not the scientist's job to determine whether a hydrogen bomb should be constructed, whether it should be used, or how it should be used. This responsibility rests with the American people and their chosen representatives.

Teller believes that scientists, like all citizens, must enjoy unhampered the right of free speech, of open criticism. He does not think any Hatch Act should restrict the scientist from taking a political position. And yet he seems to face an intellectual dilemma. He believes in free expression; he believes the nation must be defended against present and potential enemies. He would not sacrifice freedom or defense. If the public is sometimes misled, it is not the fault of the democratic system, but perhaps the concentration of opinion making in too few hands. In Teller's view, government censorship, in peacetime, is never an acceptable alternative.

He believes in the right of any scientist to engage in the research of his own choosing. He earnestly hopes, however, that of their own free will some of them will choose to work for the defense of freedom.

These views were reflected in a portion of his *Bulletin* article.

> To my mind we are in a situation not less dangerous than the one we were facing in 1939, and it is of the greatest importance that we realize it. We must realize that mere plans are not yet bombs, and we must realize that democracy will not be saved by ideas alone.
>
> Our scientific community has been on a honeymoon with mesons.* The holiday is over. Hydrogen bombs will not produce themselves. Neither will rockets nor radar. If we want to live on the technological capital of the last war, we shall come out second best. This does not mean that we should neglect research or teaching. If we get to work now, it will be sufficient to have perhaps one quarter of the scientists engaged in war work. The load could be lightened by rota-

tion. If we wait too long, not even the effort of all the scientists will suffice. . . .[29]

While there is no evidence that the AEC objected to Teller's article, the commission was beginning to chafe from the barrage of criticism. Most of the commissioners probably agreed with Teller's comments because they very nearly expressed what had become the official government position. The opponents of the H-bomb effort, on the other hand, were building up opposition to the project and were probably hampering recruitment. If scientists were to be attracted to the project, the criticism had to be stifled, or so the AEC believed.

On March 13, 1950, AEC General Manager Carroll L. Wilson sent a teletype dispatch to all managers of field operations:

> All AEC and contract employees working on AEC contracts are instructed to refrain from publicly stating facts or giving comment on any thermonuclear reactions of the commission's program of thermonuclear weapons development.[30]

This prior censorship was generally effective. Since most of the better universities held some kind of AEC research contract, many important physics professors were bound by the order and were silenced. It was soon apparent, however, that although they were prohibited from expressing themselves in print, their anti-H-bomb campaign continued in private. This influenced prevailing attitudes and probably recruiting as well.

The AEC's action certainly posed a constitutional question. Did the commission have the authority to abridge the right of free speech? In a free society did it have the authority to curb scientific dissent?

The authors posed these questions to Richard G. Hewlett, chief historian of the Energy Research and Development Administration (formerly the AEC). His response, in part, was this:

> The authority for the General Manager's order appears to have been a letter from President Truman to David E. Lilienthal, the AEC chairman on January 31, 1950, directing the AEC to proceed with the thermonuclear program. The President states in the letter:

*Referring to the great amount of basic research that was then under way on mesons, one of the subnuclear particles.

"I hereby direct that no official information be made public on it [the thermonuclear program] without my approval." The general manager's order on March 13, 1950, was the immediate result of a public statement made by an AEC headquarters employee. The statement was intended to remind all AEC and contractor employees of the importance of avoiding public statements on H-bomb development. The March 13 directive did not refer to the President's statement because it was still classified, but the commission was concerned about preventing any apparent violations of the President's instructions.[31]

The censorship effort was based on an extremely slender legal reed. Truman's letter had referred to the prohibition of "official information." This would not seem to have justified muzzling a scientist not directly employed by the AEC on the ground that his statements had "official" status.

Nearly twenty-five years after the AEC's partial success in muting the public H-bomb controversy, the authors asked Teller to comment on it in historical terms. Teller reread the 1950 *Scientific American* articles and offered these reflections in a letter to us:

What is most striking to me now is how little the effect of the hydrogen bomb was appreciated, even by experts. I may say that Ridenour and Bethe, whether I agree with them or not, are intelligent and well informed. Unfortunately, I cannot say the same about Bacher.

One must remember that the articles were written before intercontinental rockets were considered feasible (although Ridenour was probably closer to imagining such things than the others). I find it most interesting that the articles in 1950, at a time when we had relatively few atomic bombs, were already filled with the idea of "overkill." The point is that today, after the development of many years, I believe that this idea, when applied to our ability to damage Russia, is still not valid and as long as the Russians continue to take defense seriously, never will be (in my opinion, which may be a minority opinion). The point is that a country which is determined to survive can take very much more punishment than any of us, including myself, likes to think about.

I do not want to say that I saw coming events more clearly than the authors of the articles in the *Scientific American*. I was, I believe, less deluded about anybody's capability of predicting future events. At the same time I felt pretty certain about one development: That the Russians would have a hydrogen bomb in a short time. In that prediction I seemed to be justified.

Actually, one of my main reasons for working on the hydrogen bomb was its novelty. Not knowing how it would influence the future, I wanted both as a scientist and also for practical reasons to know how it would work. Some will perhaps consider this irresponsible because they pretend to be able to see into the future. If you realize that you cannot do so and if you are a little more modest about the influence that a scientist can have on the course of events, then I believe it is not irresponsible to try to work out those technical developments which can be worked out. . . .

At last I come to your original question. You were indeed right that already in the spring of 1950 the question of the radioactive by-products created by the H-bomb had been raised. I was not aware of that nor indeed had I seen at that time the articles in *Scientific American*. Among the arguments given there is one which is completely wrong—the one given by Bacher. In fact Bethe states that carbon-14 would be harmless and he is right. Bacher says carbon-14 is particularly nasty because its lifetime is long (which is a fact). But Bacher forgets two important points. Because the lifetime of carbon-14 is long, its activity at any one time is exceedingly small. The other and even more relevant fact is that the residence of carbon-14 in the biosphere is of short duration. As a general rule it finds its way into the oceans in ten years, and from there it is harmlessly deposited at the bottom of the ocean as limestone.

You will note that Bethe raised the question of radioactivity, but did not say the creation of big and dangerous amounts of radioactivity are necessarily connected if hydrogen bombs are detonated.

Actually, the technical content of the articles is both meagre and correct. . . .[32]

Despite Teller's published defense of his position in March 1950, his main energies were still directed to his research. His prime objective was to lay the theoretical foundation for what he considered would be the first thermonuclear reaction on the surface of our planet. But his sleep was disturbed by a horrible possibility: Were the Russians ahead in this race?

At Los Alamos, in early 1950, Teller delivered two staff lectures. With his typical Hungarian verve he outlined the possibility of releasing energy by fusing deuterium and tritium, with the required high temperatures being furnished by the atom bomb.[33] It was and is a simple theory that would eventually be translated into reality.

At this time, however, the doubts were almost overpowering. If fusion was started, could it be sustained? Were there unknown natural laws that foredoomed man's efforts to unlock the power of the stars? Teller seems never to have succumbed to the debilitation of doubt. He saw the obstacles, but he believed they would be surmounted.

Mathematics is the language of science and there was a need to talk faster and more accurately about the theory of the hydrogen bomb—if the project was to make sufficient progress. A computer was required to deal with the complex series of variables.

During World War II the first electronic computer was built at the Aberdeen Proving Ground in Maryland. It was known as the Electronic Numerical Integrator and Calculator, or ENIAC. It was a primitive, unwieldy device with more than 19,000 vacuum tubes. One of its uses was to plot the trajectory of a missile in flight. But it had no "memory," no ability to store and recall information.

In late 1944 or early 1945 Teller remembers learning about fast computers from John von Neumann. The probable father (though Teller does not think the biological term is appropriate) of the advanced electronic computer was von Neumann. Did von Neumann develop it?

In Teller's judgment, "I think it is fair to say that he was ahead of everybody else; that he made very great contributions; that probably the IBM company owes half its money to Johnny von Neumann and that Johnny perhaps did not get as high a compensation in either terms of money or in other terms as he deserved from this one great contribution alone.

"He introduced idea machines into our work," Teller explains, "and this was part of his achievement in getting electronic computers going and establishing a close connection between atomic energy research and fast computers."

Computer technology proved to be invaluable for fusion calculations. Early in 1950 von Neumann had designed a sophisticated computer known as MANIAC that was to be built at Princeton.[34]

To study a hydrogen bomb design based on one of Teller's ideas, a mathematical review was started on two fronts. In one case, information and instructions were being assembled for the ENIAC. Meanwhile mathematicians Ulam and Everett challenged the computers with slide rules, desk calculators, and tabular data. The two mathematicians used, as Ulam freely admitted, "unorthodox" procedures. They made visceral assumptions and tried to reduce the interrelated problems to their simplest form. Their hectic pace, in the early part of February 1950, began to yield hopeful signs.

Ulam at first felt there was a fifty-fifty chance that nuclear fusion, once started, would continue.[35]

While Ulam and Everett were engaged in manual labor, Teller was pouring forth his own torrent of ideas. So volatile and enthusiastic was Teller that laboratory director Norris Bradbury appointed a committee of the main division leaders with Teller as chairman. This committee would be formally responsible for the thermonuclear project at Los Alamos. Teller was now, in name as well as in fact, the project boss.[36]

As the Ides of March were approaching, Ulam went forth with his first prediction on the possibility of firing a thermonuclear reaction using a prescribed mixture of tritium and deuterium. It was a gloomy forecast: "The result of the calculations seems to be that the model considered is a fizzle."[37]

On April 17 Ulam met with von Neumann at Princeton to discuss the implications of Ulam's calculations. On April 21 they were joined by Enrico Fermi. Von Neumann concluded that the model must be changed if there was to be any chance of firing the mix. The amount of tritium must be increased. This was a challenging conclusion; tritium was both expensive and scarce.

Ulam was designated as the messenger to carry the ill tidings to Teller. When Teller heard the news—as Ulam reported to von Neumann—"he was pale with fury yesterday—literally, but think he is calmed down today."[38]

Teller's "fury," if the term is applicable, was not directed at von Neumann, whose scientific judgment and honesty he trusted, but toward Ulam. Teller was suspicious of Ulam's motives, as if he wasn't convinced that the mathematician really wanted the project to work. It was von Neumann who assured Teller that Ulam was only offering constructive criticism. The new suggested model might, after all, be a way station en route to a successful design. There is no question, however, that Ulam was pessimistic. On May 18, 1950, von Neumann received a note from Ulam, saying, "The thing gives me the impression of being miles away from going."[39]

How much faith could be put in Ulam's calculations? Hans Bethe reviewed them that summer in Los Alamos. He concluded that Ulam's figures would be confirmed when the computer results were available. Nevertheless, Bethe favored maintaining the schedule that called for the Greenhouse test in the spring of 1951.

A more optimistic view was taken by Marshall Rosenbluth, who also worked on the mathematics under von Neumann's direction.

"In fact," Rosenbluth recalled later, "the actual calculations, of which von Neumann was in general charge, were done by my wife and myself. And whereas they certainly did differ by some factors from the kind of rough ideas that Teller had, by and large they indicated that the lines he was following were completely correct and that something approximately as he described would behave approximately as he described and would constitute a successful design."

It was the communists themselves who created a renewed, though short-lived, sense of political unity in the United States. On June 25, 1950, communist North Korea's army crossed the 38th parallel and invaded South Korea. Truman felt the United States had to respond and immediately ordered naval and air forces to the defense of the poorly prepared and inadequately armed South Koreans. As the American and South Korean forces were being driven back to the southern end of the peninsula, a sense of urgency and alarm swept through the United States. In the national emergency, patriotism was on the rise and it became easier to recruit scientists for the thermonuclear effort. This was true even though there was a strong countervailing point of view. If the war were to spread beyond Korea (and in the critical early days of the conflict this seemed possible) more atomic weapons might be needed. Since the atom bomb already existed there was a serious question in the minds of military strategists as to whether Teller's fantasies should be fed with more scarce men and material. For immediate practical reasons a decision was urgently needed. DuPont was designing new reactors. Should they be built to produce tritium for thermonuclear tests or plutonium for conventional atomic bombs?[40]

It was to answer this question and others that the General Advisory Committee met in Washington on September 10. It received a progress report submitted by Teller and John Wheeler. Despite the brief upswing of interest that followed the outbreak of the Korean War, recruitment was still the most pressing problem; there was still a discouraging lack of qualified theoretical scientists. Under these conditions, and in the shadow of increasing tension with China over the Korean War, the GAC felt it necessary to warn Bradbury not to interfere with the development work on fission weapons.[41]

In late October the GAC met again, this time at Los Alamos. Von Neumann's MANIAC was not yet in operation. At Aberdeen the ENIAC had verified Ulam's discouraging conclusions about the thermonuclear potential, although the ENIAC lacked the sophistication to deal adequately with the complete problem.

Carson Mark, who was then head of the theoretical division at Los Alamos, reported to the GAC that Fermi and Ulam had concluded that if deuterium were ignited the fire would burn out before most of the material was consumed.[42] But for lack of sufficient accurate calculations the two scientists had to proceed on the basis of certain assumptions. Teller argued that more knowledge could reduce the uncertainty on which the assumptions were based and perhaps produce a different conclusion.

According to Hewlett and Duncan in *The Atomic Shield*:

> Teller took the floor to summarize the super. In his briefing he could offer little more than determination. He saw more theoretical work as essential. He thought Los Alamos lacked people to perform the detailed calculations and to carry on imaginative thinking. More than once he stressed how much more there was to explore. He admitted to von Neumann that the practicality of the super depended on the amount of tritium that might be needed and that the trend was unfavorable. He had no new ideas. In some way success would be grasped—how, he did not know. . . .[43]

Oppenheimer revealed himself to be in a growing state of tension vis-à-vis Teller. He did not share Teller's religious faith in creating thermonuclear fusion on the earth. He felt the forthcoming Greenhouse experiment made little technical sense, even though Bethe, Fermi, Teller, and Wheeler disagreed. Oppenheimer certainly believed that the fission program deserved a higher priority and that the superbomb was a distraction that was diverting attention from the "real" military needs of the nation.

But the clash went farther than that. If Teller was moved by a faith that he would succeed with the fusion bomb, Oppenheimer seemed to have a contrasting conviction that he would not. In December 1950 Wheeler concluded that if scientists were reluctant to go to Los Alamos, a broader scientific input could be obtained if a "satellite" thermonuclear program were set up in the more friendly academic atmosphere of Princeton. One of the chief goals would be to solve some of the still perplexing computer-programming problems. It was during a discussion of the feasibility of such an offshoot program at Princeton that one of the scientists told Wheeler that Oppie had said: "Well, it can't be done and even if it can be done it will cost too much; even if it doesn't cost too much it will take too much scientific manpower to make it; even if it doesn't cost too much in scientific manpower it will be too heavy to be delivered; even if it is not too heavy to be delivered it will be of more use to the Soviets than to us. So we should not go ahead and make it."

Oppenheimer's attitude added to Teller's frustrations because—as Teller is fond of saying—building an H-bomb is not a solo performance. In addition to the theoreticians, specialists in a wide variety of fields were essential. This was the period when a "wet" bomb was being developed, calling for knowledge of low-temperature and cryogenic physics.* One cryogenic physicist who worked with Teller during this period was Dr. Ferdinand Brickwedde, an old friend from the days in Washington in the 1930s.

Brickwedde had received his doctorate in physics in 1925 from Johns Hopkins. He first met Teller in 1935 at the Atomic Physics Colloquium in Washington. The Teller and Brickwedde families became close friends and the two scientists eventually published a joint paper dealing with the scattering of neutrons by liquid hydrogen.

Teller and Brickwedde met again in the summer of 1948 at Los Alamos. A cryogenics laboratory had been established there as part of the fledgling thermonuclear project. Earl Long was the first chief of the laboratory and Brickwedde was brought in as a consultant from the National Bureau of Standards.

When they worked together again in 1950, Brickwedde was sensitive to the intensity of Teller's concern, as he recalled those days for the authors:

"Well, he certainly was disturbed about it and very concerned and very unhappy about the way things were going, but I wouldn't say he was angry—I mean he didn't act like an angry man. He always seemed to me to be reasonable. He didn't say unkind things about other people. He was very, I would say, worried. He was concerned about the safety of our country and he believed it was

---

*A "wet" fusion bomb is designed to utilize deuterium and tritium in liquid form, which means the bomb assembly must have elaborate refrigeration equipment. Cryogenics is the branch of physics that deals with matter at very low temperatures, generally below the boiling point of liquid air, or minus 190 Celsius (Centigrade).

very important that we have this hydrogen bomb and have it early. . . . I'm pretty sure he felt the Russians would be working on it."

The collision course between the Teller and Oppenheimer forces was continuing. On December 29, 1950, an ad hoc panel, chaired by Oppenheimer, made one more effort to put the thermonuclear program on the back burner. It emphasized the importance of continuing work on fission weapons and since, at that point, there was as yet no practical H-bomb in sight, the report concluded:

> In fact, we believe that only a timely recognition of the *long-range* character of the thermonuclear program will tend to make available for the basic studies of the fission weapon program the resources of the Los Alamos laboratory. (Italics added)[44]

Just one month later, on February 1, 1951, Teller struck back. With the aid of Frederic de Hoffmann he produced a paper that offered a dramatic new concept for a hydrogen bomb. The very simplicity of it seem to change the picture, and suddenly many scientists who had doubts were converted.

But the new concept depended on the lessons to be learned by the interim experiment known as Greenhouse. So the planning for Greenhouse went on. Tentatively the date was sometime in May.

In Congress it is common practice to attempt to defeat a bill by loading it with amendments until it drowns of its own weight. This seems to be analogous to the ploy attempted by Teller's opponents prior to Greenhouse. In a letter to the authors, Teller wrote:

> When preparing for Greenhouse I was urged by friends of Oppenheimer to make a test which in their opinion would prove more than the test that was actually carried out. At that time it was my conviction that this suggestion was made in the hope that the test would fail, thereby terminating the program altogether.
>
> The decision of Greenhouse was indeed conservative because I knew that due to the opposition among scientists we could not permit a failure. At the same time it was my conviction that many things could go wrong. Up to that point all our calculations were on paper, and none was supported by experience.[45]

Years later Oppenheimer denied that he had predicted in the fall of 1950 that the impending Greenhouse test would fail. However, as noted, he felt that the test made little technical sense.[46]

Essentially, what was the Greenhouse test that was the root of so much controversy?

It was an experiment that was intended to demonstrate that liquid tritium and liquid deuterium would fuse when subjected to the heat of an atomic explosion. It was not a hydrogen bomb.

Deuterium and tritium were to be used in liquid form for practical reasons. In gaseous forms these two isotopes of hydrogen would require eight hundred times their volume in a liquid state. In order for deuterium or tritium to remain in a liquid state, they must be kept at an extremely low temperature. If either was poured into a cup or beaker at room temperature it would quickly boil away. The boiling point of water is 100 degrees Centigrade. The boiling point of hydrogen is minus 252 degrees.

Brickwedde explains that the method used to maintain the low temperature was to cool the apparatus with a flow of liquid hydrogen that in turn was prevented from boiling away by a high-vacuum insulation.

Brickwedde's laboratory was responsible for the cryogenic parts of the Greenhouse test, including the development of the vacuum insulation and the liquification of the tritium and deuterium, and then keeping the system cold until it was fired. At the Eniwetok site in the Pacific a plant had to be built for making liquid hydrogen, all of this falling on the shoulders of Brickwedde and a colleague, Harry Johnson.

The planning for Greenhouse on the faraway Eniwetok atoll was completed on January 15, 1951. Teller told his associates, in the words of a publisher when a manuscript is finished, to "put it to bed." On this date Teller knew what only a few of his fellow scientists also knew, that a theoretical breakthrough was about to occur that would put Greenhouse in its proper perspective and open the door to a test of a full-fledged hydrogen explosion.

What criteria establish the high point in a person's life? It depends not only on his own evaluation of his work, nor on the evaluation of his peers. Popular judgment sometimes selects the high point for him. It was Teller's successful design of an H-bomb that brought him worldwide recognition,[47] though in brilliance it did not compare with some of his other contributions to physics. In Teller's own assessment, his greatest contribution to his calling was his research in "the vibrations of polyatomic molecules," which Teller confesses is "less fashionable" than his achievements in nuclear energy. The layman knows what a hydrogen bomb is and what it can do, but he can hardly be impressed by the vibrations of polyatomic molecules.

The hydrogen bomb was an ingenious method of using natural forces—forces that were known—to achieve an objective. Even the method had been used in other areas. But the path is beaten to the door of the man who builds a better mousetrap, and Teller's design, if not an achievement in basic science, was nonetheless a great leap that gave the United States a good position in the home stretch of the thermonuclear race.

It was probably in late January 1951 that Teller walked into the next door office of his assistant, Frederic de Hoffmann. Twenty-three years later de Hoffmann still remembers it vividly:

> . . . there were a great number of things going forward which were not quite pointing the way. As I recall it, Edward came into my office and discussed an idea of his. . . . .

De Hoffmann and Teller both suspected that Teller had come up with something exciting, but the assistant told his boss that the best he could do then and there would be machine calculations:

> I then remember working a good portion of the night on it, and when Edward came in in the morning, we looked at it and—it's vivid in my memory—somehow the thing didn't quite go the way either of us expected it to be. And Edward, with his usual insight, simply looked at it—and I can't tell you now whether there was a factor of two or four or a pi, but I mean one factor was off—you know it was a quick calculation overnight—and as soon we had rectified that, the thing [seemed] solved, and we thought the thing was there.

Thus, apparently, in this casual discussion in de Hoffmann's office, was the hydrogen bomb born. But there were some disagreements and even some bitterness over whose contribution was critical.

For example, mathematician Stanislaw Ulam has claimed a major role in providing Teller with the fundamental idea that underlay Teller's invention, a role downplayed by the latter. De Hoffmann, in contrast, takes a much more generous view of Teller's relations with his associates:

> I might tell you a very human story about Edward [after the crucial H-bomb breakthrough]. Edward said, "Well, this is very nice,

Fred. Why don't we write up an internal report?" As internal reports were then set up, which I think was a terribly fair way to do it . . . it said on the left "Work done by" and on the right "Report written by." Because these things need not be the same—and you know it's become very fashionable to have all kinds of names appearing, and the poor guy who did the work with the brilliant idea appears as one of fourteen people. Well, so Edward said, "Let's be sure we have a joint paper." So I said, "Well, Edward, that's very nice of you, but I think if my facts serve me correct, it ought to say on the left "Work done by Edward Teller," and on the right "Report written by Fred de Hoffmann." And he said, "Absolutely not. It's going to be a joint report. You had these things ready. You did them overnight." And I said, "Well, Edward, we'll talk about this," and he said, "No. It's got to be a joint paper. That's absolute and final."

But de Hoffmann defied his boss's generosity, and when the report came out de Hoffmann took credit only as the writer, whereas it was Teller who was credited with "Work done by . . ." Twenty-four years later, the report is still classified.

Classification notwithstanding, a former chairman of the AEC, David Lilienthal later published a clue as to its contents. Lilienthal reported on a proposal to use a fission bomb "to create *pressures* and *temperatures* that would set up a fusion of the light hydrogen atoms, particularly the isotopes of deuterium and tritium [authors' italics]."[48] The emphasized words are probably the key to the fundamental nature of Teller's design. (The question of the bomb design will be discussed in more detail in the next chapter.)

Teller, in creating a theoretical model of a thermonuclear fusion device, had leapfrogged over the principles that were to be established in the upcoming Greenhouse test. But Greenhouse was still essential to the next step. Teller was optimistic that this pioneering test would add some experimental muscle to the new proposal, though the Greenhouse contraption was not a thermonuclear bomb or device.

Actually, Greenhouse was a series of tests subtitled Dog, Easy, George, and Item. The exact nature of all of them remains classified twenty-four years later, except that the third test in the series, Greenhouse-George, on May 8, was the crucial thermonuclear experiment.[49]

The vast construction and preparations for the tests at Eniwetok Atoll were carried out by an Air Force contingent called Task

Force Three, under General Elwood "Pete" Quesada. The project involved not only laboratories and workshops, but acres of living quarters. Teller and de Hoffmann did not fly out to the island until the day before the scheduled Greenhouse-George shot. On their arrival they inspected the array of equipment, dominated by the refrigeration machinery that was needed to keep the deuterium and tritium at the necessary low temperature. Finally they climbed the two-hundred-foot steel tower on which the explosive charges were mounted. When they were satisfied everything was in order, they returned to the living area, and relaxed by enjoying a cool swim in the peaceful lagoon. The shot was scheduled for dawn.

That night Teller took a walk with Bill Borden. He was obviously tense and uneasy. Then he revealed the reason for his inner turmoil: "This is more than just proof that a bomb will or will not work. This is a great scientific experiment. If it is a success it could mean that mankind has achieved a new means of obtaining energy, just as Enrico Fermi proved in 1942. It will mean that later all mankind can someday benefit from the immense power derived from fusion."[50]

An all-night rainstorm delayed the detonation for three hours. When the explosion took place Teller again watched with wonder another fireball and mushroom cloud. But to see the explosion meant nothing in terms of its success. The question was whether the fusion of the deuterium and the tritium had taken place. That required the interpretation of a plethora of data from recording instruments. Teller wrote later:

> That afternoon, to break the tension, Ernest Lawrence invited me to swim with him in the lagoon. When I came out of the water to stand on the white sands of the beach, I told Lawrence I thought the experiment had been a failure. He thought otherwise and bet me five dollars that we had been successful in igniting heavy hydrogen and producing a thermonuclear reaction.[51]

The next morning Teller learned from a colleague, Louis Rosen, that the preliminary evidence indicated the test was a smashing success. But he made Teller promise not to say anything until there was sufficient supporting evidence. But Lawrence was leaving that morning, before the additional readings could be assembled. Teller kept his promise and told no one:

. . . but when Lawrence left for the air strip, I could wait no longer. I ran after his jeep and silently handed him five dollars. It was worth it. I knew that success at Greenhouse ensured the successful construction of a hydrogen bomb along the lines detailed in the report to which de Hoffmann had signed my name two months earlier.[52]

But they didn't know what was happening in Russia.

13

Racing Through the Fog

THE Greenhouse success paved the way to further triumphs, but the joy of Teller and his associates might have been dampened had they been aware of momentous events in the Soviet Union. For the evidence is convincing that the Russians achieved not only the first experimental nuclear fusion on earth, but also produced the first deliverable hydrogen bomb.

To credit these achievements to another nation undoubtedly comes as a shock to most Americans, who have long taken it for granted that their country was first and that Edward Teller is "The Father of the H-Bomb." Teller, not surprisingly, detests that label of scientific paternity and insists, with a combination of real and false modesty, that it was "the work of many people." But *Life* magazine called the H-bomb "Edward Teller's magnificent obsession."

The fact that the Russians were first does not, however, downgrade the titanic achievement of Teller and his associates, because the scientists in each country worked in isolation, without the benefit of the other country's experience. It is doubtful that even the master spy Klaus Fuchs affected the outcome of the hydrogen bomb race. If there is a villain, it is the United States' obsession with secrecy, under which a few Americans kept other Americans from knowing what the Russians were doing.

Teller, without benefit of access to intelligence from the Soviet Union, simply did what he thought had to be done. He happened to be one of those scientists like Einstein, Oppenheimer, Bohr, and Heisenberg, whose imagination, even at an early age, engulfed the cosmos. To create nuclear fusion—the basic energy process of the stars—down here on the earth is consistent with the touch of destiny in his character. It is true that the challenge was presented at a time when Teller believed the free world was in mortal danger of being attacked by an implacable foe; a situation which seemed to provide moral justification for a terrifying weapon. This genuine fear was certainly part of his motivation. And yet, as we have come to know Teller, it is difficult to reject the notion that he was also motivated by the sheer majesty of the scientific achievement, like an architect with an opportunity to design the world's highest building.

Our firm belief that the Russians won the hydrogen bomb sweepstakes is not uncontradicted. The issue exemplifies the problems faced by biographers, journalists, and historians when they are confronted with conflicting testimony. Normally, the criterion is the witness's record of credibility. In the case of the thermonuclear project, however, statements from men of impeccable honesty differ widely—indicative, perhaps, that memories are fallible. Then, in addition, the effort to spotlight the truth is fogged over by that accursed governmental affliction known as "security." The surly guardians of military and scientific records have the truth under lock and key, and even a quarter of a century later they do not see fit to reveal it to the American people.

The alternative is to seek out the men and women who were associated with the H-bomb project in the years of its fruition. The authors interviewed or corresponded with more than a dozen of the survivors. Most of them were scientists, but the interviewees included a former Air Force officer, a former high Pentagon official, and the chief historian of the Atomic Energy Commission. (succeeded in 1975 by the Energy Research and Development Administration). Unclassified material was studied and information was requested from—and sometimes provided by—the AEC division of classification.

In one of the earliest interviews conducted for this book, on January 10, 1973, we confronted Dr. Marvin Goldberger, chairman of the department of physics at Princeton. One segment of the interview was as follows:

QUESTION: Did the Russians explode a hydrogen bomb before the Teller H-bomb was fired?

GOLDBERGER: Yes, that is a true statement.

QUESTION: What evidence is there for this?

GOLDBERGER: It is well known that we have a very elaborate system to monitor nuclear explosions in the atmosphere. And that system was in existence many years before the explosion of the Soviet thermonuclear weapon. It was on the basis of this collection system that the analysis was made, and the diagnosis was complete and incontrovertible.

Goldberger's answer was given without hesitation and with the assurance of a man who knows what he is talking about. It is possible only to speculate on how Goldberger knew. He did not work directly on the H-bomb and thus, under security rules, he had no "need to know." But he was a close friend of J. Robert Oppenheimer, who could have eventually been privy to this information.

It should be noted that the discussion dealt not with a "device" (that is, some kind of preliminary test) and that Goldberger used both the word "bomb" and the word "weapon."

Perhaps more important is the earlier, pre-weapon, stage. Which country exploded the first "device," which is to say, who achieved thermonuclear fusion first?

In searching out this question, our first solid evidence came from Major Theodore F. Walkowicz. In February 1945 Walkowicz returned from an overseas tour of duty to join the Scientific Advisory Group of the Air Force, a new unit set up by General H. H. Arnold, the Air Force's chief. The group was headed by Theodor von Kármánn, one of the world's supreme aerodynamicists and another of the amazing clique of Hungarian scientists who contributed so much to the United States' pursuit of nuclear and thermonuclear energy.*

Walkowicz received his master's degree in physics from Caltech. When he joined the Scientific Advisory Group he continued to work for his doctorate from M.I.T. Eventually, in 1948, he became the group's full-time executive officer.

Walkowicz, now president of the National Aviation Corporation, contributed some impressive testimony to the historical record of the Soviet-American competition. He told us of a mysterious occurrence, probably in early 1951:

WALKOWICZ: There was a Russian shot fired that we did not understand.

QUESTION: You mean an atomic explosion?

---

*There were so many brilliant Hungarian scientists that their colleagues at Los Alamos reached the conclusion that they possessed extraterrestrial intelligence and therefore were really agents from another planet. Quite commonly, Teller, Szilard, Wigner, von Kármánn, and von Neumann were referred to as "The Martians."

WALKOWICZ: Yes, it was a Soviet atomic explosion, and we did the usual thing of collecting air samples. A thing known as AFOAT One was in existence at that time. It flew airplanes all around the periphery of Russia and captured the debris after each one of the shots. These debris samples were analyzed, and from that there were deductions made as to the nature of the Soviet shot.

QUESTION: Why didn't you understand it?

WALKOWICZ: It was understandable only in terms of assuming that there had been a thermonuclear component to it. It wasn't a pure fission shot. There had to be fusion involved in it.

A special group of scientists was assembled to evaluate the air samples for the Scientific Advisory Board. Their collective wisdom earned them the nickname "the tree full of owls." One of them was John von Neumann.

"I remember his reporting to the Scientific Advisory Board," Walkowicz told us, "and to a lot of Air Force officers, that there was something chilly and strange in the debris samples. The implication was that it could be understood only in terms of there having been a fusion component in the shot."

That the Russians beat the United States to the first thermonuclear reaction may be a surprise, but it is consistent with their postwar accomplishments. Americans could not seem to shake loose from their minds the idea that the Russians were technically inept and, at best, "imitative." Even some military technicians and scientists adhered to this view—"They can't even manufacture a decent saucepan." On August 29, 1949, Joe One, the first Soviet atomic explosion, was detonated years ahead of even the pessimistic predictions of fearful American observers. They might have been even more surprised to know that within two weeks after Joe One, the Politburo issued an order to its scientists to build an H-bomb. The Soviet command recognized, as Teller and others had done, that the atomic trigger was now available and could be used to ignite thermonuclear components.

Walkowicz's contention that the Soviets achieved the first thermonuclear reaction has actually slipped into open literature.

In 1968 Harrison E. Salisbury wrote an introduction to a collection of essays by the dissident Russian physicist Andrei D. Sakharov, principal designer of the Soviet hydrogen bomb. Salisbury commented:

The measure of his achievement is underlined by the fact that while the Russians started far behind the United States in nuclear research, she was able to catch up and surpass the Americans in developing the hydrogen bomb. The first Soviet *experiment* in hydrogen fusion occurred months before those of the United States. Sakharov was responsible for this [our italics].[1]

According to Salisbury the breakthrough came in 1950:

This was the year in which he [Sakharov] and Dr. [Igor Y.] Tamm established the theoretical laws of controlled thermonuclear fusion—the means of harnessing the power of the hydrogen atom for the generation of electricity and other peaceful purposes. The work gave him a Stalin price and was part of the general body of research which won Dr. Tamm a share in the Nobel Prize for physics in 1958.[2]

Salisbury is thus in agreement with Walkowicz that the Soviets conducted their first nuclear experiment before the Greenhouse test of the United States, which didn't take place until May, 1951. Greenhouse was not, in official American accounts, a "true" thermonuclear reaction, while, apparently, the Russian shot was thermonuclear in the full definition of that term. In other words, by the accounts of Salisbury and Walkowicz the Soviet Union was first with any form of thermonuclear experiment and, by Goldberger's account, they were first with a deliverable bomb.

It was later revealed that theoretical work on fusion had been under way in Moscow's Lebedev Institute of Physics. Sakharov was only twenty-four when he began working at the institute as a student of Tamm. Neither Tamm nor his brilliant disciple, however, was primarily interested in fission. Tamm's field was quantum mechanics.

Sakharov could in many ways be compared with Teller. Both have a dual involvement in science and politics, though the Russian has gone much farther than his American counterpart in challenging the evils, as he sees them, in his own society. And Sakharov dwells in a country where such criticism is seldom tolerated.

Scientifically the two scientists have much in common. Both considered fission as only a way station en route to the goal of thermonuclear fusion. Each is considered the inventor of his country's hydrogen bomb. The date of Sakharov's initial interest in fusion is not certain. By 1948, however, he had published a paper that contained a hint that he was moving in that direction. It was a report on the temperature of excitation of plasma in a gaseous discharge.[3]

Teller doesn't recall being aware, at least until 1953, that the Russians were working on the H-bomb, an admission that makes the American security system seem dangerously inept. There is little doubt that Sakharov knew what Teller was doing. If through no other source, he would have known through the spying of Klaus Fuchs who, in 1950, confessed that he had passed classified information to the Russians. Fuchs had been at Los Alamos and was present at a top-secret conference when there was a review of all known facts about thermonuclear reactions.

Sakharov had advantages, other than exceptional intelligence, that Teller did not share. He was not burdened by having to take time out to fight political battles over the morality of his scientific endeavor. There appears to have been no Oppenheimer in his path. Sakharov had the full scientific resources of Mother Russia at his disposal. Even after Truman's famous H-bomb directive, Teller had to fight conflicting priorities.

Hence the sequence of events worked out as follows: In early 1951 the Soviet Union exploded a thermonuclear device, followed by the American Greenhouse test in May that may have been less advanced than the Russian shot. America's first true thermonuclear reaction was achieved in the Mike test of October 31, 1952. The first deliverable hydrogen bomb was detonated by the Soviet Union on August 12, 1953. The first American deliverable bomb, called Bravo, was set off February 2, 1954. It was probably a larger and more efficient bomb than the Russian version that preceded it. It will be noticed that the Soviet Union apparently skipped the intermediate stage of the American Mike test, going instead directly from the 1951 early test directly to the deliverable bomb in 1953. (Of course the Mike device, despite its sixty-five ton bulk, was not totally undeliverable. It could have been delivered in the hold of a ship. There was no aircraft then big enough to carry it, but General K. D. Nichols told us that it might possibly have been carried in a glider, towed by an airplane. Teller and his associates, however, did not build it for that purpose. It was conceived as a test of thermonuclear principles.)

If, as Walkowicz, Salisbury, and others have shown, the first Russian thermonuclear test preceded the first United States test (Greenhouse), an entirely different light is shed on the bitter conflict that preceded the inauguration of the American thermonuclear bomb project that was launched by Truman's announcement of January 31, 1950, and the steadfast opposition that continued from a large segment of the American scientific fraternity into 1952.

Did Oppenheimer and his cluster of supporters know about the Soviet thermonuclear shot when they were opposing the program advocated by Teller prior to the Greenhouse experiment of May 1951?

"They had to," Walkowicz insisted to us, "because Oppenheimer was on every committee. He blanketed every committee—he and his cohorts. And there were committees all over the place, you know, joint estimates, joint intelligence estimates and so forth. One of the committees was an AFOAT-One committee that worked, I think, also with the General Advisory Committee to the AEC. It worked on the assessment of debris from the Soviet test."

If Oppenheimer knew about the Soviet test, how is it possible to explain the prevailing sentiment among his supporters that if the United States didn't build an H-bomb, the Russians wouldn't?

"Why these guys still continued to fight our going ahead, I don't know," said Walkowicz. "Of course I couldn't understand most of the things they did."

Eugene Wigner, who shared the sense of urgency of Teller and Walkowicz for the thermonuclear effort, nonetheless disagrees with Walkowicz's contention that Oppenheimer "had to know" about the Soviet shot.

"I did not understand Oppenheimer's opposition to the H-bomb," Wigner said in April 1975, "but the man was not a traitor. I do not think he was aware of the Russian test."

As amazing as it might seem that Oppenheimer, the top scientific advisor to the AEC, didn't know about the test, there is evidence that Wigner is correct; that in the maze of security and politics, Oppenheimer was not informed. The evidence comes from Robert LeBaron, who, in 1951, was chairman of the Military Liaison Committee, the link between the Pentagon and the AEC.

LeBaron, whom we interviewed in April 1975, confirmed Walkowicz's statement that there was a hydrogen component in a Russian test in late 1950 or early 1951. This places the shot before Greenhouse. LeBaron recalled that the scientists who analyzed the debris reported only to a small group of six Air Force officers, plus LeBaron. It was passed on verbally to Secretary of State Acheson and to the President, but that was all. Even the secretaries of the various services were not informed.

During the interview the authors pressed LeBaron on the question of notification. He was asked, "Was the AEC, the GAC, Robert Oppenheimer, or Edward Teller aware of this intelligence?" LeBaron's reply was rather astounding:

"No, they were not notified. It was top secret. Any letter of transmittal would have gone over my desk and I did not sign such a letter."

A case can be made for secrecy in defense matters. But there is a bizarre, Alice-in-Wonderland quality about a security system so rigid that the very agency and the very scientists engaged in a scientific race—possibly for survival—with another country are denied access to information about that country's progress. It is comparable to a horse race in a fog, where no jockey ever knows if the other horses are ahead of him or trailing him.

Why, LeBaron was asked, was Teller, of all people, not informed? Although LeBaron could reply only that the information was "top secret," the very absurdity suggests it could have been sheer bureaucratic oversight. Teller, after all, had the "need to know" and was cleared for top-secret information.

Certainly, the Air Force leadership trusted Teller. He was on their side on the H-bomb controversy. But many Air Force men were deeply suspicious of Oppenheimer's motives, hence did not trust the GAC that he dominated, and they certainly had reservations about the AEC, primarily because of Oppenheimer's influence. On the other hand, if the Air Force had made it a point to inform Oppenheimer, this might have been an effective way to blunt his opposition. With his left-wing past, he would have been open to charges of disloyalty or irresponsibility if he had continued to oppose doing in the United States what the Soviet Union had already done.

When we confronted Edward Teller with this confusing story of the Soviet test that was detected but not announced, he first refused to discuss it at all. It is our guess that this was his first knowledge of such a possibility and that he was completely surprised. We suggested that he check with security to see if he could be permitted to comment. A week later he telephoned from Livermore. He told us that assuming our information was correct—and he was not saying that it was—then he had no knowledge of such a Russian thermonuclear test prior to Greenhouse.

It must have involved some convoluted reasoning to keep such vital information from Teller and possibly even from the AEC itself, though it was defensible to keep the news from the public. AFOAT One, the detection system of the Air Force, operated in secret until 1958; to publicize knowledge of the Russian test would have been to publicize the ability of the United States to detect it. But inasmuch as the system was not classified after 1958, the authors felt free to ask Richard Hewlett, the chief historian of the former AEC (now ERDA): Who set off the first thermonuclear explosion, the Russians or the United States?

"From all I have been able to see," said Hewlett, "we had it. The United States had the first thermonuclear explosion." He was then told about the apparent Air Force monitoring of a Soviet shot prior to the American detonation. Could Hewlett talk about it?

"I don't think I can," he said. "I don't know anything about it."

On November 29, 1974, we queried C. L. Marshall, director of classification of the AEC. His reply, in part, was:

> The United States detection system indicated that Soviet nuclear detonations occurred on the following dates:
>
> > August 29, 1949
> > October 3, 1951
> > October 22, 1951
> > August 12, 1953
> > August 23, 1953
>
> Joe 4, on August 12, 1953, was the first Soviet nuclear detonation in which debris was found to contain thermonuclear components. The previous tests were determined to have involved only fission devices.[4]

There is no reason to doubt the honesty of Marshall's letter. If LeBaron's statement is to be accepted, even the AEC has never been notified of the Russian shot of early 1951 and thus would have no record of it. And just as surprising, the tight little secret apparently never reached such H-bomb advocates as Senator McMahon, or his staff director of the Joint Committee on Atomic Energy, William L. Borden.

The latest and perhaps the most puzzling development in the whole weird security story did not occur until April 3, 1975, when the Defense Department quietly declassified a somewhat cryptic document. Dated February 16, 1950, only sixteen days after Truman launched the U.S. H-bomb project, it was a memo to Robert LeBaron from his assistant, H. B. Loper. The title was "A Basis for Estimating Maximum Soviet Capabilities for Atomic Warfare." It presented a series of assumptions on Soviet capability which should be "tested on the basis of adequate contrary evidence, rather than through lack of positive support before they are disregarded or modified. . . ." In this category the report assumed that Russian knowledge of basic physics was equal to American; that this may also be true for applied physics and chemistry; that the U.S.S.R. "has been determined since 1945 at the latest, to gain unquestioned superiority over the rest of the world in the atomic weapon field"; that "if there is conclusive evidence of a Russian shortage of uranium . . . it must be assumed that they have attempted to balance that shortage by the development of weapons of higher efficiency per ton of ore available, e.g. *a thermo-nuclear weapon* [authors' italics].

"Unless the above assumptions can be disproved," the memo presented conclusions on the Russians' "maximum position," which essentially assumed the Soviet Union was proceeding with "the same sense of urgency and disregard of costs as impelled our war effort."

And, finally, conclusions, "well within the realm of possibility," included one especially chilling consideration: "The thermonuclear weapon may be in actual production."

Teller told us in November 1975 that he never was aware of the memo. Apparently, neither was Oppenheimer nor any of the AEC scientists. Again, we can only raise the question: Why? and, a quarter of a century later, not expect a logical or authoritative answer.

The Russians themselves have shed a little light on the situation. In 1959 Eugene Wigner attended a nuclear physics conference with some Russian scientists present. Wigner later recalled for us that "a Russian boasted to me that they had the hydrogen weapon before we did and they did explode something that was probably a hydrogen weapon, not as good as Teller's, before we exploded one." This supported evidence that Wigner had already gleaned from intelligence that "they had exploded something you could call a hydrogen bomb, but it was a crude device; it was not very efficient. It was not as advanced as the one the United States exploded not much longer after that."

When Teller made his theoretical breakthrough on February 1, 1951, he felt confident that the bomb would become a reality. He wrote to Smyth: "It is now my conviction that the thermonuclear program is past its ignition point."[5] The smell of success gave him a rebirth of spirit. He had been nearly despondent until the puzzle was solved. Afterward he was the witty, ebullient Hungarian again. "During March and April of 1951," Teller wrote in *The Legacy of Hiroshima*, "I urged the feasibility of constructing a hydrogen bomb upon anyone who would listen. Early in March I discussed the report in detail with Norris Bradbury, the director of the Los Alamos Laboratory, with Carson Mark, head of our theoretical division, and others at the laboratory. In April I explained my ideas to Gordon Dean, chairman of the Atomic Energy Commission."

But there was trouble in Dean's office. "Dean seemed interested, but somehow distracted," Teller continued. "After leaving his office I discovered the reason for the distraction—the zipper of my trousers had failed and my fly was open. Dean remembered my open fly, not my ideas. Two months later, during another presentation, he seemed to be hearing the ideas for the first time. But in the meantime he had told a magazine reporter that I was a 'brilliant, if somewhat disarrayed scientist.' "[6]

Teller's new theoretical concept was confirmed, he felt, by the experimental shot that took place on May 8, 1951, at Eniwetok. This was the third of four detonations under the heading Greenhouse, and the only one designed as a stepping stone to a full-fledged hydrogen bomb.

The new concept involved a means of igniting liquid deuterium and tritium in a massive thermonuclear explosion, but it also pointed the way to a compact, deliverable bomb. This would be fueled not with impractical liquid isotopes of hydrogen, which must be refrigerated, but with lithium deuteride. The lithium deuteride version of the hydrogen bomb would have the double advantage of requiring no refrigeration and no expensive tritium.

In *Men Who Play God*, Norman Moss describes the physical and chemical nature of the lithium deuteride bomb:

> One way tritium is created is by bombarding lithium-6, an isotope of the metal, lithium, with neutrons. . . . The idea was to pack around the atom bomb not deuterium and tritium, but deuterium

and lithium-6, combined as lithium deuteride. The explosion of an atom bomb sends out a shower of low-energy neutrons, which would create tritium from the lithium. The tritium would fuse with the deuterium explosively at the same moment it was created.[7]*

The use of lithium to create a "dry" hydrogen bomb was apparently considered by Teller and others very early in the game. As early as February 3, 1950, a letter was sent by Harold J. Ness, president of the Lithium Company, to Carroll L. Tyler, manager, Santa Fe Operations, for the AEC at Los Alamos. The opening paragraph reads:

> We have noted that work has been approved on the hydrogen bomb, and we need not elaborate too much on the fact that this company is the only one, possibly in the world, that has broad industrial experience in connection with lithium, its production and its many applications. As you know, our company has been active in lithium for the past fifteen years.[8]

It is not known if the AEC accepted the proffer of the Lithium Company. But another clue that lithium was figuring in H-bomb plans very early is in a report from Oak Ridge National Laboratory, dated June 28, 1950, and stating: "The separation of the isotopes of lithium by chemical methods has been under investigation at ORNL for approximately nine months."

Letters in Los Alamos files indicating an interest in lithium for weapons are dated at leasst as early as October 5, 1950. There is also a letter from Teller to Darol Froman, dated June, 13, 1951, in which Teller points out some advantages of lithium 6 and urges that Oak Ridge give high priority to the construction of a separation plant. After mid-1951 there are numerous records of lithium isotopes being shipped to Los Alamos.[9]

If Gordon Dean was lukewarm about Teller's "new concept" for a hydrogen bomb, Hans Bethe was impressed. In April 1951, when Bethe came for one of his visits to Los Alamos, Teller couldn't wait to share the news of his breakthrough with his old friend. Teller offered to explain it with his mathematical evidence. Bethe didn't need the figures; he was an astute physicist and he knew it would work. John Wheeler also saw the light. The past is prologue in the sense that mistakes and blind alleys eliminate the unworkable and

---

*Moss was not correct concerning the bomb's configuration. See below.

invoke new directions. Wheeler explained that "all our ideas about how to create a fusion explosion were based on one premise. Within a fixed framework we went through unbelievably clever and subtle distortions to try to make it work, and we couldn't. This [Teller's] new idea changed the framework."[10]

But Teller, for all his acclaim, still seemed to be swimming against a tide of ill will. With the Greehhouse test apparently successful in proving certain principles, AEC Chairman Gordon Dean called a strategy meeting for June 19, 1951, at the Institute for Advanced Study in Princeton. Oppenheimer was the host. He was still chairman of the General Advisory Committee that had unanimously opposed the thermonuclear program. Other GAC members present were Enrico Fermi, Cyril S. Smith, I. I. Rabi, Lee A. DuBridge, Walter G. Whitman, and the committee's executive secretary, Richard Dodson. All the AEC commissioners were present—Dean, H. D. Smyth, Keith Glennan, Thomas Murray, and Summner Pike, along with three top staff members. Scientists from Princeton and Los Alamos completed the assemblage of luminaries. This group included Teller, Hans Bethe, Carson Mark, Darol Froman, Lothar Nordheim, John von Neumann, John Wheeler, and Norris Bradbury, the Los Alamos director.[11]

The agenda appeared to present one glaring omission. Out of dozens of persons invited to present their views, Teller was not included. As the author of the "new concept," he would have seemed to be the speaker most essential to the program. Instead, the program called for a presentation by Mark on the data from Greenhouse.

According to Hewlett, Bradbury was responsible for the agenda, an assignment that Bradbury denies was his.

> For one thing [he wrote the authors] the meeting was called by the GAC and/or the AEC and its agenda was not my business. It was desired that the laboratory present its assessment of the new proposals and its plans and needs for solving the problems foreseen. Since Teller and I had rather different ideas as to the most effective way to proceed, it would not have been appropriate to consider him "Laboratory spokesman" in these respects.

Bradbury's letter continued:

> So far as the great significance and prospects of the new approach were concerned, and the need for taking this very seriously, there

was no debate between Teller and myself. For me, personally, Teller's technical views were always of great interest and fully welcome. I cannot agree with Hewlett's dark implication that I tried to muzzle Teller.

Then Bradbury drove home his point about the nature of Edward Teller:

> I would have regarded [muzzling him] as highly inappropriate— and probably almost impossible. Edward was hardly known for shyness in such circumstances![12]

The record shows that Bradbury, though he may not have had ultimate responsibility for the agenda, did, on June 1, send a memo to Oppenheimer and on June 6 another memo to Froman and Mark. Both communications contained Bradbury's ideas for the Los Alamos part of the agenda. There was no mention of Teller.

Teller, by his own admission, was "furious." He was well aware that Bradbury seemingly was not fond of him. In fact, most of the Los Alamos scientists were conscious of an antipathy between the methodical Bradbury and the impetuous Hungarian. But Teller did head up the committee that was responsible for the fusion effort and presumably had a right to be heard. Bradbury must have been aware that both Bethe and Wheeler had hailed Teller's "new concept" as the breakthrough that had been so eagerly sought for more than eight years.

It almost seemed as if no one was on the side of the man who had accomplished the feat that made the meeting necessary. Gordon Dean had the right and possibly the duty to make sure Teller was heard, but he said nothing.

J. Robert Oppenheimer joined the ring of silence. A day or so before the June 19 meeting Teller met with Oppenheimer and explained his proposal. As Teller later recalled, Oppenheimer was enthusiastic. He was also host of the meeting and chairman of the GAC. Why didn't he insist that Teller be put on the agenda?

After the meeting got under way, a sullen and distressed Teller sat down to listen to the proceedings, consoling himself that someone familiar with his work would report on it. Then came Carson Mark's turn to speak. Teller listened, and waited. Then Gordon Dean spoke. Teller listened, and waited. Other scientists arose to make their reports, until Teller could stand it no more. He wrote about it later:

> I was amazed when Carson Mark, in his presentation, did not mention the hydrogen bomb report that I had handed him three months before. My amazement multiplied when Gordon Dean, still chairman of the AEC, spoke without mentioning the same report which I had explained to him two months earlier. My amazement approached anger as other scientists and officials who knew of the report spoke without referring to it.
>
> Finally, I could contain myself no longer. I insisted on being heard. My demand was met with spirited debate, but it was decided that I should be allowed to speak.[13]

It was H. D. Smyth, ideologically no friend of Teller's, who ended the debate by insisting that Teller be heard.

Teller, with the ponderous walk that only hints of his wooden foot, approached the blackboard "and again went through theory and calculation that already were familiar to half the men in the room."*

Apparently, by forcing his views on the meeting Teller won some grudging admiration. Three years later Dean's testimony recalled the event.

> Out of the meeting came something which Edward Teller brought into the meeting with his own head, which was an entirely new way of approaching a thermonuclear weapon. . . . It was just a theory at this point. Pictures were drawn on the board. Calculations were made, Dr. Bethe, Dr. Teller, Dr. Fermi participating the most in this; Oppy very actively as well. At the end of those two days we were all convinced, everyone in the room, that at least we had something for the first time that looked feasible in the way of an idea. I remember leaving the meeting impressed with this fact, that everyone

---

*John A. Wheeler, in February 1976, recalled for us a dramatic moment at the Princeton meeting. He and physicists John Toll and Kenneth Ford had been involved in calculations aimed at producing a mathematical model for the Teller concept under a project called Matterhorn. While Teller was explaining his idea they saw an opportunity to help him. Toll retrieved a chart they had made from computer tapes illustrating how the new super would burn, and detailing instant by instant the process. The chart was placed on the wall and its conclusions were self-evident. The calculations were applicable to both the cryogenic and the lithium deuteride bomb.

around the table without exception—and this included Dr. Oppenheimer—was enthusiastic. . . .[14]

One of the puzzling aspects of Dean's comments is that he
speaks as if he were learning of Teller's concept for the first time, as
if he had been uninterested or unconvinced when Teller had reported it to him two months before the Princeton meeting. There
is somewhat of a parallel in Oppenheimer's reaction. He knew
about the breakthrough before the meeting and did nothing to give
Teller a chance to speak about it. And yet, three years later, he
stated that the "new super"* was "technically so sweet that you
could not argue about that.

Today Teller will not discuss the technical aspects of the device
he described at Princeton. Once again, although he opposes
scientific secrecy, he will not violate it so long as the law is on the
books.

Many other sources are not so reticent. There are also some
false leads into the nature of the Soviet-American nuclear race. A
typical, oversimplified version is presented in Stern's *The Oppenheimer Case*:

> Edward Teller and others conceived the new approach that led to
> the first American H-bomb. Nevertheless, the Soviets were able to
> achieve their first thermonuclear explosion a scant eighteen months
> after ours, and with a far more sophisticated process, *one we later
> imitated* [authors' italics].[15]

A distinction must be made between what American scientists
knew in terms of thermonuclear technology and what they chose
to detonate. Stern is referring to the fact that the Mike test that
took place on October 31, 1952, seventeen months after Greenhouse, was a true thermonuclear detonation, but was an unwieldy,
refrigerated weapon. The Soviets' deliverable bomb, exploded on
September 12, 1953, was, in contrast, a compact lithium (dry)
bomb. As has been pointed out, however, the lithium concept had
been in the process of development in the United States long before the Soviet detonation.

If additional evidence is needed that Teller was not merely imi-

*"New Super" is a term used by AEC historians Hewlett and Duncan to de-
scribe Teller's device. The actual name is classified, presumably because it reveals
too much of the technical nature of the new concept.

tating Sakharov, it is available in *The Legacy of Hiroshima*, where Teller wrote of "our proof that a practical hydrogen bomb could be economically constructed."[16] He obviously was referring to the dry bomb because no one could consider the refrigerated bomb to be an economical weapon. Teller, in a different context, reluctantly told the authors that he discussed the lithium bomb with Gordon Dean prior to Greenhouse, which is to say prior to May 8, 1951.

To T. F. Walkowicz, there was no doubt at the Princeton meeting that Teller's revealed secret was "a brilliant invention which transformed overnight the possible thermonuclear technology from one that would involve very big, unwieldy weapons—so-called 'wet' weapons—to small, dry, highly efficient thermonuclear weapons."

Actually, Teller's contribution at Princeton was even broader than that. He established a method that could be most readily demonstrated with liquid deuterium and tritium, but he also made it clear that the same technology could be used to construct a compact, dry H-bomb by using lithium deuteride.

Since the exciting days in 1951 when the hydrogen bomb was taking shape there has been almost continuous controversy over whether Edward Teller or mathematician Stanislaw Ulam was the true "inventor." The overwhelming majority of observers has given Teller the credit, justifiably. There has been some bitterness, however, on the part of Ulam's associates and friends that he was never given his share of the honors. Up to now, most accounts have given Ulam credit for "triggering" the idea and Teller recognition for "inventing" the bomb. For example, John McPhee in his article "The Curve of Binding Energy," which appeared in *The New Yorker* of December 10, 1953, quotes physicist Ted Taylor as saying, "The secret, incidentally, is not a matter of materials. It is a matter of design." Then McPhee describes the origins of the idea:

> The design was hit upon by Stanislaw Ulam and Edward Teller in 1951. In the pages of a patent application they were described as the bomb's "inventors." After a long period of getting nowhere—an effort by many scientists, under considerable pressure from Washington—Ulam one day asked Teller to sit down in private with him and listen to an idea. They closed the door of Teller's office at Los Alamos and talked. Teller was much impressed with Ulam's idea and at once thought of a better way to do the kind of thing Ulam had in mind. The two men came out of the room with the answer to the problem of the hydrogen bomb.

A similar account of the genesis of the thermonuclear break-through is presented by Philip Stern in *The Oppenheimer Case,* and by Norman Moss in *Men Who Play God.* Moss wrote that "Ulam had an idea about a different kind of fusion process."[17] Ulam, in a letter to the authors, called Moss's account "terribly fragmentary since I did not talk about 'a different kind of fusion process,' but a different arrangement for enabling fusion to take place."[18]

Teller considers all these accounts about Ulam "triggering" his idea to be dead wrong. "Ulam triggered nothing," says Teller. "Stan Ulam came to me with an idea which was similar to the one on which I had been working. His idea did not seem to me to be practical. I told him what my opinion was and he kept insisting on his. To get him off my back I suggested we write a paper together. In actual fact I wrote the report and in this report both ideas were incorporated, together with arguments favoring the one which ac-tually worked out."

De Hoffmann confirms Teller's version. He recalls discussing the ideas with Teller, not with Ulam. "Edward really did have these ideas as far as I am concerned. That's where I heard them first," de Hoffmann told the authors. He felt he was in a position to know the sequence of events because "I worked with Teller in-tensely every day and, furthermore, I think he's always been more than fair when he assigns credit."

The situation is left permanently confused by the patent con-troversy. The government was willing to grant a patent for the hy-drogen bomb to Teller and Ulam jointly. Teller considered signing the patent papers "for the sake of peace. But I found that under the patent laws I had to make a statement under oath that Ulam and I invented this thing together. I knew that taking this oath would be perjury. I therefore refused to take out the patent and no patent was taken out."[19]

Teller's resentment of Ulam went farther than mere scientific disagreement. It was another manifestation of the basic conflict between the pro- and anti-bomb forces.

The antipathy, from Teller's standpoint, seemed to lie in his be-lief that Ulam was carrying water on both shoulders. On the one hand, in the critical weeks before the Princeton meeting, he seemed to be catering to the anti-bomb forces by predicting the project would fail. At the same time he appeared to be ready to take the credit if it should succeed. Teller, who had a record of willingness to assign credit, even when it was marginal, was distressed at Ulam's behavior.

Ulam has his staunch supporters, notably I. I. Rabi, whose opinions have usually carried great weight. Rabi, however, was surprised—or over the years had forgotten—when he was reminded by the authors that Oppenheimer testified in 1954 that "The principal inventor in all this business was Teller . . . it has not been quite a one-man show, but he has had some very, very good ideas, and they have kept coming."[20]

There was also bad blood between Teller and Bradbury. As early as April 4, 1951, two months before the acrimonious Princeton meeting, Teller had gone to Gordon Dean to argue for a whole new weapons laboratory, completely removed from Los Alamos. Teller's growing confidence in the thermonuclear effort was inversely proportional to his confidence in Bradbury. In the impatient Hungarian's opinion, the Los Alamos director was not moving fast enough. Teller had first proposed a new division at Los Alamos to deal exclusively with the "new super," but without success. Now he was asking Dean for a laboratory at Boulder, Colorado. He suggested a staff of 50 senior scientists, 82 junior scientists, and 228 assistants. Teller was not, as he freely admitted, a good manager, but he thought he had the ideal administrator in de Hoffmann.[21]

Dean wasn't sure what to do. He felt that he couldn't afford to lose Teller, but the enmity between Teller and Bradbury was exacerbating the situation at Los Alamos. But Dean wasn't concerned only with the loss of Teller's scientific genius. If Teller were to leave Los Alamos, it would set off a rumble of repercussions from his champions back in Washington—McMahon, Borden, Strauss, and LeBaron.

Perhaps, Dean found himself thinking, giving Teller his separate laboratory would be the best way out of the dilemma. The problem lingered into the summer of 1951, when Dean asked the other commissioners for their advice. On August 23 they reported back to the chairman. All anticipated a greater load on laboratory facilities but only Thomas Murray suggested the establishment of a second laboratory. H. D. Smyth and Keith Glennan were undecided.[22]

Teller was still fuming with impatience. He felt that the pace of preparations for the Mike test, tentatively scheduled for the fall of 1952, was agonizingly slow. There were recurring rumors that he was so disgusted he was about to resign. On September 11, he substantiated the rumors, writing a letter of resignation. De Hoffmann notified Dean that Teller was leaving. But Teller, under pressure from de Hoffman and others, reconsidered.[23]

The reconsideration proved to be only a temporary truce. Teller carried his problem to his former boss, Oppenheimer. The ex-Los Alamos chief reported to Dean that Teller would probably stay on if either Bethe, Fermi, or Oppenheimer himself would agree to direct the fusion program. For various reasons, both professional and personal, none of these three top-drawer physicists was willing to take on the job.[24]

Teller's unsatisfied demands were forcing him to a point of no return. He had furnished the basic concept for the new super. The project no longer required the kind of theoretical talent that he was best able to furnish. And yet he was constantly frustrated by Bradbury when he sought to speed up the preparations for the Mike test. He was convinced a second laboratory was needed, but was not in a position to lobby for it while he was on the staff of Los Alamos.

Then Bradbury appointed Marshall G. Holloway to coordinate theoretical work with engineering design and fabrication. Under Bradbury's plan, Teller would be responsible for all theoretical work and initial design. Holloway's responsibility would start where Teller's left off, and he would carry the test to completion.

The problem was that Holloway and Teller did not get along—they had frequently and openly clashed, usually on the issue of the test schedules. Bradbury must have known that the Holloway appointment would not be acceptable to Teller. Teller even entertained thoughts that the choice of Holloway was calculated to force him out of Los Alamos. The crucial clash between the two men came when Holloway insisted at least thirteen months of preparation was needed before the Mike test, while Teller insisted it could be done in nine months.

When Bradbury supported Holloway, Teller picked up his marbles and on November 1 he returned to his old post at the University of Chicago. Even under this stress, however, he could not completely forsake the thermonuclear program. He agreed to return to Los Alamos as a consultant, if he was needed.[25]

At least he was now free to lobby for a second laboratory. For the next several years his career would oscillate between physics and politics. The time was ripe to test his political clout in pushing the cause of the new facility. In a real sense he was not needed at Los Alamos. He had established the theoretical base; others could build on it. The real need now, he reasoned, was for a second laboratory to expand weapons development and to instill a degree of competition, something that Los Alamos had never known.

As he retrospectively explained his position—"Public accountability is not quite compatible with secrecy. And if you add technological complications to secrecy, then Los Alamos could pretend they were doing an excellent job and still stay way behind the Russians, for instance, forever. It is competition that keeps private enterprise honest. Since we did not have accountability, since we could not resort to the Russian measures of sending less than perfect scientific performers to Siberia, we better have some competition."

Teller expressed the same thoughts in slightly different form in *The Legacy of Hiroshima* :

> I knew that science thrives on friendly competition, on the fostering of different points of view and on the exchange of ideas developed in different surroundings. I knew, too, that a single group of scientists working together can easily become fascinated by special aspects of development—to the neglect of other hopeful approaches. My conviction grew that the safety of our country could not be entrusted to a single nuclear weapons laboratory, even though that laboratory were as excellent as Los Alamos.[26]

In Teller's campaign for a second laboratory, the troops took to the field in an almost predictable battle line. The grand marshal of Teller's forces was Senator Brien McMahon. On the other side of the field Oppenheimer's army stayed in its trenches and awaited yet another assault. It must have seemed to Teller to be a case of *déjà vu*—a reliving of the original fight to build the H-bomb. At least, in that battle, he had the unintentional assistance of Joe One and Klaus Fuchs. If he had known of the observed but unannounced Soviet thermonuclear test of late 1950 or early 1951, he would have had a powerful argument on his side. But, as was noted earlier, this intelligence was withheld from him, for reasons that pass all understanding.

Of course no one expected the Russians to stop testing after Joe One. On September 18, 1951, Walter F. Colby, the AEC's director of intelligence, informed Dean that there had been a second Soviet atomic test. The United States publicly announced it on October 3.[27] Even though these were not thermonuclear tests, they reinforced McMahon's determination to do whatever was necessary to hasten the United States' hydrogen project. He pressed Dean: "Couldn't you do more than you are doing to speed up the hydrogen program and improve the chances of ultimate success?"[28]

On October 11 the commissioners and the GAC met to discuss the problem, with Bradbury as the star witness. Understandably, Bradbury was on the defensive. He told the commission he felt that competition played no part in this kind of research. Rabi was concerned that a second laboratory would create too much competition for the few good people available. Only Willard F. Libby took the position that a second laboratory was a good way to relieve the workload at Los Alamos.[29] The General Advisory Committee, not surprisingly, withheld its support for another laboratory.

Bradbury was in a tough situation. Teller's continuing campaign implied a lack of confidence in both Los Alamos and its director. But Bradbury had a large contingent of scientific heavyweights in his corner to defend his prestige and honor.

Early in November Teller confronted Oppenheimer in his office at Princeton. The Hungarian's emotions were stirred; he minced no words. Los Alamos, he told Oppenheimer, was dragging its feet and he had little confidence in its ability to meet the Soviet challenge. The GAC should have supported the second laboratory. "Look," Teller said, "you never did give me a chance to talk to the GAC when it was deciding whether to go ahead with the hydrogen bomb. Please let me talk to the GAC now about setting up a second laboratory."

Teller's pressure seemed to have its effect. Oppenheimer agreed to let him address the General Advisory Committee meeting in Washington on December 13. But there was a condition that Teller didn't like. Oppenheimer suggested that Teller should address a closed session of the committee, without any other AEC people present.

This restriction didn't appeal to Teller at all; he saw it as wasting his ammunition. "No," he told Oppenheimer, "the more people from the AEC who hear what I have to say, the better I like it."[30]

Teller was finally afforded an opportunity to present his case before the audience that he really sought. He appealed to the high spirit of scientific "curiosity and adventure." He argued that there were enough unknowns to keep two laboratories busy and there were advantages in friendly competition.

When Teller completed his presentation he was in high spirits. "I came out of the meeting confident that my presentation had been a success, certain that I had made my points."[31]

His optimism turned out to be ill founded and once again he was thwarted. The GAC recorded another anti-Teller vote, this time in opposition to his second laboratory, though Teller didn't learn of the vote until sometime later. The rejection, according to Teller's information, was based on the predicted injury to the morale of scientists at Los Alamos. The committee felt that a vote for a second facility would amount to a vote of no confidence in Los Alamos.

The issue was really more complex than that. The AEC itself, in contrast to its advisory committee, was in general agreement that the criticism of Los Alamos by Teller and by its own Commissioner Thomas Murray was valid. There was a need to step up the pace of thermonuclear research. The AEC groped for a middle position between Teller's insistence on an entirely new laboratory and Bradbury's willingness to accept some organization changes. An obvious compromise would be to set up a semi-autonomous division at Los Alamos, devoted to thermonuclear projects and long-range goals. Such a solution, however, would demand that the head of the proposed division be someone acceptable to both Bradbury and Teller. Perhaps that is why this compromise never took shape.

The AEC meanwhile came up with another proposal. Los Alamos was laden with nonresearch activities, usually connected with emergency production problems. If these could be transferred to other facilities, Los Alamos could once again focus its energies on research, eliminating the need for another laboratory. This solution appealed to the commission, which then rejected the Teller plan for another facility on the basis that the proposed reorganization would take place. Only Commissioner Murray dissented.[32]

Once again Teller had been thwarted by the agency that employed him, and once again he bypassed the AEC and went directly to the Pentagon. He was still the favorite scientist of the armed forces. He was welcome in the corridors of military authority. The armed forces had funds for research and development and they trusted Teller's judgment.

Teller had an especially powerful ally in David T. Griggs, a bril-

liant geophysicist who was at this time chief scientist for the Air
Force. Griggs and Teller tended to think along the same lines.
Griggs did not have to be convinced of the need for a more aggres-
sive effort to build an H-bomb. So it was with renewed hope that
Teller called on the Air Force scientist at his Pentagon office. He
told Griggs his reasons for believing that a second laboratory was
essential to the nation's security, and he recounted his long tale of
frustrating failure at the hands of the GAC and the AEC itself.
Griggs didn't commit himself. But a short time later, at a meeting
in Florida of the Air Force's scientific advisory board, Griggs
passed Teller's story along to the colorful General James A. Doolittle, the legendary hero of the famous "Thirty Seconds over Tokyo." But Doolittle, with a doctoral degree in aeronautical engineering from M.I.T., was a pretty good scientist in his own right.
Under Griggs's prodding, he agreed to meet with Teller.

The Doolittle-Teller conference, probably in January 1952, gave
Teller a chance to explain his proposals to a man who had direct
combat experience in bombing as well as an understanding of the
potential of weapons. Teller told the general that it would be possible to design a whole arsenal of varied thermonuclear weapons "instead of concentrating on a single, big hydrogen bomb." The statement by Teller indicates that he was already aware of the flexibility
in weapon design that would be made possible by the use of the
"dry" lithium deuteride version of the H-bomb.

Doolittle listened carefully. Occasionally a hint of a smile
crossed his face. Teller was not sure whether the smile indicated
interest or amused skepticism. The general made no immediate
comment in support of Teller's proposals, but neither did he reject
them.[33]

In early 1952, while he was waiting for some kind of response, a
new opportunity was thrust before Teller, adding to the turmoil of
his life. Ernest Lawrence, the big man in high-energy physics, invited Teller to come out to visit him at the University of California.
On February 2 he and Lawrence went out to Livermore, site of a
former naval training base, in a beautiful valley forty miles west of
Berkeley. Lawrence had set up one of his particle accelerators at
Livermore, which had become an extension of the radiation laboratory on the Berkeley campus. That evening Lawrence took Teller to Trader Vic's. He had a proposition for Teller. He supported
the second laboratory. He wanted to see it established at Livermore and for Teller to resign from the University of Chicago and

accept a professorship at California. Then he could oversee the setting up of the new laboratory.

Teller was enthused about the idea, but his enthusiasm was tempered by a side issue, an ideological rift between himself and Lawrence that had surfaced two years earlier. At that time Teller had received an invitation to join the faculty of the University of California at Los Angeles (UCLA). This was 1950, the "year of the oath" in California. The California legislature had passed a law requiring all professors in public institutions to sign an oath of loyalty to the United States.

The personnel at Los Alamos were aware of it because the laboratory had a nominal academic affiliation with the University of California.

"Every month they sent us a fresh form to sign and it became quite a joke," Teller recalls. "None of us had any compulsion to sign it. I was upset about all this monkey business." There were actually some faculty members expelled because they refused to sign the oath—"and this made me worry," says Teller.

"What happened was this," Teller explains. "There was a meeting of the board of regents . . . at which the discharge of these professors was announced. At that meeting Regent Nyland made the statement that 'it makes no sense to claim that if these professors are expelled others won't join the University.' He mentioned, specifically, that I had just accepted an appointment. Nyland was for the oath and against the liberals.

"I did not know Nyland, nor did I know the kind of people who opposed the oath. It is my present opinion [Teller's comments were made in January 1975] that the opponents of the oath were not particularly good company, although those that were expelled, including the physicist John Carlo Wick, were good people. There was a big movement against the oath and all the real radicals kept in the background. The few idealists who were opposed got expelled and were used as martyrs.

"At that time," Teller continues, "my perception of the situation was that a real injustice had happened. And for that reason and only for that reason I decided to withdraw and not accept the invitation. That occurred after an interview with President Sproul [of the University of California]. He was very kind. He assured me—correctly, as I now know, but didn't know at the time—that this was a purely temporary thing, that these people will be invited back, which did happen. He said I shouldn't worry about it. However, his assurances were not good enough for me. I said I would not accept."

Although Teller had been spending a lot of his time at Los Alamos in 1950, he was still a member of the University of Chicago faculty and anticipated returning there on a full-time basis. It was Truman's January announcement about the hydrogen bomb that prompted Teller to stay, for a time, at Los Alamos.

Now, in 1952, Lawrence was asking him to come to the University of California at Berkeley, but Teller couldn't forget the turmoil over the loyalty oath two years before. In the meantime the Supreme Court of California had found the loyalty oath unconstitutional and all of the fired professors had since been invited to return. Not all of them did but, as Teller points out, at least they were asked.

Although Teller was, after 1950, in the process of moving politically to the right, and was supposedly a kindred spirit with Lawrence, he was distressed by Lawrence's attitude toward the loyalty oath. Teller learned that Lawrence was threatening to expose the scientists who refused to sign the loyalty oath by passing their names along to radio commentator Fulton Lewis, Jr. Lewis, who commanded a huge audience at the time, was politically far right and a defender of the infamous Senator Joseph McCarthy. Both, in Teller's opinion, were making irresponsible charges of subversion, and Teller deeply resented any semblance of cooperation between Ernest Lawrence and Fulton Lewis. A number of scientists that Teller knew had their jobs threatened as a result of the climate stirred up by Lewis and Joe McCarthy. In several cases Teller publicly defended accused scientists and probably saved their jobs for them. In one case he found a new and less sensitive job for a particularly beleaguered scientist. In an obvious understatement Teller recalls today that "I did not think Lawrence's threat was nice."

The loyalty oath issue is another example of how Teller's beliefs do not align themselves into any convenient category, such as "right wing" or "conservative." On certain issues he seems capable of leaping back across the fence to fight on the side of those who might roughly be described as civil libertarians.

Teller left Berkeley, after his visit with Lawrence, still uncertain as to where he was going. He returned to Chicago to learn that there was still no firm indication that the military would support a second laboratory. Then the first solid basis for hope came with a telephone call from Griggs at the Pentagon. The Air Force was definitely interested in the new laboratory concept. General Doolittle had been an effective advocate. Griggs had arranged an appointment for Teller with Thomas K. Finletter, Secretary of the Air Force. Teller recalls the interview:

"At first he listened in icy silence. But soon he warmed up to the theoretical possibilities and military practicalities of thermonuclear weapons."[34]

Finletter may have warmed up, but he didn't commit himself, at least not yet. But he immediately flew to Los Alamos to confirm in his own mind Teller's claim that "an arsenal of thermonuclear weapons" was feasible. Teller returned to Chicago only to receive another invitation to Washington, this time from none other than the Secretary of Defense, Robert A. Lovett.

While Teller waited nervously in Lovett's outer office, his confidence was severely shaken when Robert LeBaron, the military liaison with the AEC, joined him. "Edward," LeBaron said, "I've done everything I can, but it's a lost cause." With this discouraging assessment on his mind, Teller was ushered into Lovett's office, expecting to lose the battle. But LeBaron had either misjudged Lovett, or Lovett hadn't informed LeBaron of his decision. Teller remembers that "before I left the Secretary's office, I knew that I had won." Lovett agreed with Teller completely. The Air Force had laid plans for a laboratory under its own jurisdiction and had even begun negotiating for a site.

It was a decision made without the concurrence of the agency that should have been the prime mover—the Atomic Energy Commission. The pressure on the Air Force to make a unilateral decision came from powerful sources other than Teller—Lewis Strauss, Willard Libby, and the cold-war warrior Ernest Lawrence. But, according to Teller, the impending action of the Air Force stirred the AEC into facing up to the issue. "The Atomic Energy Commission at last became interested and began investigating possible locations for a second laboratory of its own."[35]

Teller now wanted the new laboratory to be established at the University of Chicago. Historically and symbolically this would be a good location. It was on the squash court under the stands of Stagg Field that the atomic age had begun in 1942. But since then many of Teller's colleagues, especially those in Chicago, had endured the shocks of Hiroshima and Nagasaki and had no more stomach for work on nuclear weapons. There was no popular movement among the Chicago scientists to grapple for their own laboratory.

The atmosphere was different in Berkeley. Lawrence, having developed the cyclotron, and having created at Berkeley a high-energy laboratory, was branching out into the old naval base at Livermore. His latest brain child was a tremendous linear accelerator at Livermore, designed to produce neutrons for generating plutonium or tritium. Lawrence was almost as excited about Teller's new super as was Teller himself. He saw a concept so challenging that he wanted to be a part of the effort. There were not only scientific worlds to conquer, there were forces out among the stars to explore.

Lawrence offered Teller bed and board if he would only use his influence to establish the second laboratory at Livermore. The California titan even agreed to be personally responsible for recruiting the necessary talent to man the laboratory. When Teller hesitated, Lawrence offered a compromise. Would Teller come out for a year, just to get the laboratory started?

Teller had reasons for hesitating. Two of his most respected colleagues were pulling him in the other direction. Fermi was violently opposed to Lawrence and his colleague, Luis Alvarez. To Fermi they were reactionaries. John von Neumann, despite his own strong anti-Soviet instincts, echoed Fermi's counsel. "Edward," he pleaded, "don't join those people—they are too reactionary."

In the final analysis, however, Teller had little choice. Livermore was where he could concentrate on his beloved new super, and be entirely welcome. He requested and received a one-year leave of absence from Chicago so that he could set up the thermonuclear program at Livermore. Rabi claims that as Teller bade farewell to his Chicago colleagues, he quipped, "I am leaving the appeasers to join the fascists." Teller denies having made such a statement.

The formal action that created the Livermore Laboratory was taken by the National Security Council in March and endorsed by the AEC a few days later. Like Los Alamos, the laboratory would be academically affiliated with the University of California but financed primarily by the commission.

In the weeks before his departure for Livermore Teller was kept busy with meetings in Washington. On April 1, 1952, he delivered a formal briefing for Secretary of State Dean Acheson, Deputy

Secretary of Defense William C. Foster, and AEC Chairman Gordon Dean.

Bradbury was now resigned to the fact of a partial transfer of power to Livermore. In May he spent two days at Berkeley, working out the details. He recommended that, for the time being, the new laboratory should concentrate on the new super and not go immediately into weapons testing.[36] The flaw in this plan was that without testing, the Livermore Laboratory would find it impossible to verify its theories.

The summer of 1952 was spent in drawing up plans and in the beginning of the first construction at Livermore. Teller moved his family to nearby Diablo on July 14.

Herbert York, a follower and, at that time, loyal colleague of Lawrence, was named the director of Livermore Laboratory. On September 8, Teller and Lawrence, accompanied by York, met with the commissioners. They were a confident trio, with ambitious plans for new weapons design. They expressed their determination to work in close cooperation with Los Alamos, but to avoid duplication of effort. Teller's intention, as he later told the authors, was set forth firmly: "I can tell you that from the very beginning, and to a great extent due to my insistence, we tried and did avoid those things in which Los Alamos was doing a decent job. We took seriously our role as competitors who had to open new avenues."

Within a few months the laboratory's business manager could report with pride that there were already 123 scientific people working on weapons at Livermore. They were housed in one of the buildings that had been constructed for the personnel attached to Lawrence's giant particle accelerator, which had been less than successful. The Livermore management projected an employment of about a thousand within two years.[37] The laboratory, so long sought by Teller, was off and running, but initially its track record would be spotty.

One of Teller's longtime friends, Ferdinand Brickwedde, would join Teller at Livermore later, but for the present he had to remain at Los Alamos as a consultant in cryogenics because the forthcoming Mike test would involve a cryogenic (low-temperature) device—a mixture of deuterium and tritium in liquid form.

The Mike detonation would be the first real test of Teller's new concept, even though it would be carried out by the Los Alamos crew, from which Teller had now withdrawn.

At this point it is well to recall again that John McPhee quoted physicist Ted Taylor in *The New Yorker* that design, not materials, was the secret to the fusion breakthrough.

Then what was Teller's design that, all at once, made the thermonuclear bomb feasible? The details are still classified, but Brickwedde explained the essence of the device's configuration for the benefit of the authors, allowing us, apparently, the first public description of the design that made the breakthrough possible.

The core of the device consisted of the thermonuclear fuel itself—in this case liquid deuterium and tritium. These two hydrogen isotopes were surrounded by liquid hydrogen that was the cooling agent to keep the deuterium and tritium in a liquid state. This core of thermonuclear fuel, plus hydrogen coolant, was then surrounded by fissionable material of the kind used in the existing atomic bombs. And, finally, the fissionable material was encased with a conventional explosive.

When the Mike device was detonated, the following sequence of events occurred: The conventional explosive drove the fissionable material inward, compressing it into a critical mass and creating an atomic explosion. This, in turn, compressed and heated the hydrogen isotopes (deuterium and tritium) to the point where thermonuclear fusion occurred, releasing unprecedented quantities of energy.

What Teller had done was to create a fission-fusion implosion bomb. The key was the fact that the fissionable material surrounded the fusion fuel, applying intense heat and pressure simultaneously. Before the Teller breakthrough, the stumbling block had been the inability to create sufficient heat for fusion to take place, and to continue once it had started. Even the new generation of atomic weapons, far more powerful than the bombs of 1954, did not produce the necessary temperatures for a long enough time. The fission-fusion implosion principle removed this one hurdle between man and thermonuclear fusion. No wonder that Oppenheimer would later describe it as "technically so sweet. . . ."

If the Teller concept seems simple, in essence it is. But its conception was not possible without years of theoretical work by diligent and curious scientists. Without their dedication and their faith that they could solve the problems, the United States may never have produced a hydrogen weapon. As Teller kept insisting, it was a joint effort by a group of remarkably talented men.

The engineers, as well as the scientists, could well take a large share of the credit. Brickwedde noted about the Mike shot, "It was at that stage of cryogenic engineering, I think, a remarkable feat. Today, of course, we have the cryogenic rockets, and large quantities of liquid hydrogen in the Saturn rocket. It doesn't seem to be as great an accomplishment now as it did back in those days. But the Mike test was the biggest low-temperature engineering development of that time."

There seems to be no reason not to accept Brickwedde's description of the Mike device's configuration and constituents as absolutely accurate. Nevertheless, the official spokesmen of the AEC dispute his assertion that the shot contained both deuterium and tritium. In a letter to the authors the AEC stated that "deuterium was the thermonuclear fuel used in Mike. We note therefore that part of the information you said you had received was inaccurate . . . the Ivy/Mike used only deuterium."[38]

This means there is a direct conflict between two reliable sources—Brickwedde, who was closely involved with construction of the Mike device, and the classification officers at the AEC, who were not. Because the conflict did not seem to involve security matters, but factual information, the authors called on Teller to clear up the disputed point. "I am sorry," he responded, "but I cannot discuss the matter."

Early in April 1975 the same question was put to Eugene Wigner, a Nobel prize winner and a scientist associated with nuclear physics for most of his career. "I really should not discuss the problem," he said, "because, as you know, I am not a weapons man, *but you certainly would not use deuterium by itself* [authors' italics]."

In the fall of 1952, the vast, cylindrical housing that contained the fuel and the refrigeration apparatus was being set up on the small island of Elugelab in the Eniwetok Atoll. The device plus its surrounding refrigeration equipment was so cumbersome that it was accurately described as "the sixty-five-ton monster." It was Teller's concept, but it was built by the men of Los Alamos. And the pressure of other work made it impossible for the inventor to watch the tests. Teller may have remembered the biblical story of how Moses wandered for forty years in the wilderness and was permitted to view the land of Canaan from a distance, but was not allowed to enter it. Teller's vantage point was a seismograph in a basement room on the campus at Berkeley.

At the last minute some official efforts were made to postpone or even cancel the test. Vannevar Bush, the wartime director of U.S. scientific research, was deeply disturbed by the timing of the event and, to some extent, he objected to its taking place at all. The timing was October 31, 1952, or two days before the national Presidential election. Later Bush explained his objections:

"I felt it was utterly improper—and I still think so . . . to confront an incoming President with an accomplished test for which he would carry the full responsibility thereafter. For that test marked our entry into a very disagreeable type of world."

Bush also "felt strongly that the test ended the possibility of the only type of agreement that I thought was possible with Russia at that time, namely an agreement to make no more tests. For that type of agreement would have been self-policing in the sense that if it was violated, the violation would be immediately known. I still think we made a grave error. . . ."[39]

Bush's comments, made in 1954, represent the earliest beginnings of the test-ban controversy which, within a few years, was to grow into a major national controversy in which Teller played a key role.

Gordon Dean was also concerned about the timing in relation to the election, and expressed his reservations to President Truman. Truman wanted to know the implications of delay. Dean explained that due to weather conditions, the delay could be a month or more. Under these circumstances, the President told him to go ahead with the test.[40]

The sixty-five-ton monster was ready to go, as scheduled. The closest observers, from the physical standpoint, were forty miles from Elugelab. But perhaps the closest observer, in terms of involvement, was Edward Teller, gazing at a seismograph in a gloomy basement room at Berkeley. Teller watched a tiny beam of light focused on a revolving drum of photographic paper.

> I waited with little patience [he later wrote], the seismograph making at each minute a clearly visible vibration which served as a time signal.
>
> At last the time signal came that had to be followed by the shock from the explosion, and there it seemed to be: the luminous point appeared to dance wildly and irregularly. Was it only that the pencil I held as a marker trembled in my hand?
>
> I waited many more minutes to be sure that the record did not miss any of the shocks that might follow the first. Then, finally, the film

was taken off and developed. By that time I had almost convinced myself that what I saw was the motion from my own hand rather than the signal from the first hydrogen bomb.

Then the trace appeared on the photographic plate. It was clear and unmistakable. It had been made by the wave of compression that had traveled for thousands of miles and brought positive assurance that Mike was a success.[41]

When the massive fireball had cleared, the scientists on the site could have no doubts. The entire island of Elugelab, one mile in diameter, was gone. There was just a deep hole in the ocean.*

In that terrifying explosion Teller achieved his triumph but, in a strange and ironic fashion, planted the seeds of his tragedy. Thermonuclear fusion was achieved despite the initial objections of the Atomic Energy Commission, the very agency that presumably should have pushed the experiment to its successful conclusion, and despite the unanimous objections of the commission's General Advisory Committee, headed by J. Robert Oppenheimer. It would be easy to say that Mike's fireball symbolized Teller victorious, Oppenheimer defeated, but it was not to be that simple.

In the official announcement the government did not use the word "bomb." And in the sense that the Mike device could not be carried in an airplane, it was not a bomb. The terse reference was only that "the test program included experiments contributing to thermonuclear research."[42] Several months later the new President, Dwight Eisenhower, referred to the test as "the first full-scale thermonuclear explosion in history."[43]

At this point Teller made no claim that a weapon had yet been created. He prepared a statement for this book, duly cleared by the AEC:

*Even today there is dispute as to the real power of the Mike shot, and the facts are still classified. John McPhee, in *The New Yorker* of December 10, 1973 (page 53), wrote as follows:

"The theoretical expectation for Mike was a few thousand kilotons—a few megatons. The fireball spread so far and so fast that it terrified observers who had seen many tests before. . . . The yield of the bomb was ten megatons. It so unnerved Norris Bradbury, the Los Alamos director, that for a brief time he wondered if the people at Eniwetok should somehow try to conceal from their colleagues back in New Mexico the magnitude of what had happened. Few hydrogen bombs subsequently exploded by the United States have been allowed to approach that one in yield."

The 1952 U.S. shot Mike had as its purpose the proving of a principle. No effort had been made at that time to get a deliverable weapon and the tested configuration was indeed not deliverable. However, it was perfectly clear to all of us that once the principle was proved, a deliverable weapon could be constructed, and all the basic design concepts necessary for its construction were available at that time. The actual test of a deliverable weapon occurred two years later and it worked essentially as we expected. In this whole development the Russian explosion that took place in the summer of 1953 had no effect on our state of technical knowledge or on our planning.[44]

But obviously the Russians considered it a thermonuclear race. On August 12, 1953, nine months after Mike, the Soviet Union exploded a deliverable hydrogen bomb. It was a "dry" lithium bomb, which is to say it did not require cumbersome refrigeration. Once again the sophistication of the Soviet technology was demonstrated. The United States did not have a comparable weapon, but (for reasons that will be discussed later) there was no panic in scientific circles or in the White House.

It was not until March 1, 1954, that the United States caught up with or, according to some scientists, surpassed the Russians in thermonuclear weaponry. In the Bikini Atoll of the Marshall Islands, the United States exploded a deliverable fusion bomb, using lithium deuteride. It was to cause worldwide consternation because of a misjudged aftereffect—fallout.

In the fall of 1952, however, all the United States had detonated was the cumbersome, sixty-five-ton Mike. The war in Korea was still seesawing. The United States, under the auspices of the United Nations, had won what seemed to be a relatively quick victory in 1950, only to be driven back when the Chinese armies came to the aid of North Korea.

In November of 1952, during the Thanksgiving holidays, Teller experienced what, by his account, was the most confusing and provocative incident in his multiple controversies with Oppenheimer. Teller, Oppenheimer, and Rabi were having lunch when, as Teller told us, Oppenheimer made an astounding statement.

"This is a story that I am sure Rabi will conveniently not remember," was the way Teller began his recounting of the incident. (In putting it this way Teller was, so to speak, protecting his flank, because when we confronted Rabi he, as Teller predicted, had no recollection of the event.) "During our lunch," Teller continued, "Oppenheimer said, 'Well, Edward, now that you have your

H-bomb, why don't you use it to end the war in Korea?' I answered him by saying: 'The use of weapons is none of my business. This is a political decision and I will have no part in it.' "

Is it possible that Oppenheimer was being sarcastic? "He didn't sound like it," says Teller. "I'm sure he was," insisted Hans Bethe when we reported the anecdote to him.

But Teller says the subject didn't end at Princeton. "I remember receiving a phone call from Oppenheimer shortly before Christmas. He said, 'Do you remember the conversation we had over lunch at Princeton? Well, I've been talking to some people in Washington and I just wanted to tell you that they are aware of the possibilities.' "

The story remains in the realm of the unprovable, but Teller is steadfast in insisting his recollection is correct. The authors, in attempting to track down other evidence of Oppenheimer's position vis-à-vis the use of nuclear weapons in Korea, found one article that, while far from confirming Teller's version, does indicate that the possibility had crossed Oppenheimer's mind. In July 1953, the lead article in *Foreign Affairs,* called "Atomic Weapons and American Policy," was written by J. Robert Oppenheimer. Advocating consultation and cooperation with the allies of the United States, he adds, "This does not mean that we should tie our hands." Then he goes on to say:

> It is not clear that the situation even in the Far East would be wholly unaffected. It is troublesome to read that a principal reason we should not use atomic weapons in Korea is that our allies would not like it. We need not argue here either that it is right or that it is wrong to use them there. In either case, our decisions should rest on firmer ground than that other governments, who know less than we about the matter, should hold a different view than ours.[45]

During the early weeks of 1953, there were recurring rumors in Washington that the newly elected President Eisenhower was threatening to use nuclear weapons to bring the Korean War to a close. But there was a great deal of difference between using nuclear weapons—that is, atomic bombs—and using a hydrogen bomb which, at that time, existed only as a design that involved sixty-five tons of undeliverable apparatus, as tested in the device known as Mike.

Teller, for his part, was puzzled and distressed by the seeming inconsistency of Oppenheimer's position. The man who fought the H-bomb because his dreams were troubled by the horror of Hiroshima and Nagasaki, now seemed—as far as Teller was concerned—to be urging the use of the ultimate weapon in another war. More and more, Teller found Oppenheimer "hard to understand." So, indeed, did many Americans, especially in the midst of the anti-communist neurosis of the early 1950s.

The actors were taking their places for one of the great dramas of the twentieth century.

14

Background for a Tragedy

THE accumulation of years of disagreement between Edward Teller and J. Robert Oppenheimer reached a critical point in 1954 when the ideologies each symbolized were in destructive political competition. Had the United States not been so deeply divided over the issue of communist subversion it is quite possible that the Teller-Oppenheimer rivalry might have remained an essentially intellectual struggle ending in a constructive compromise. But the bitterness of the discredited remnants of the depression-bred American left wing and the ferocity of the anti-communist right propelled the two scientific giants into a confrontation that neither had sought. Nor did either Teller or Oppenheimer fit into the political mold of those who claimed to carry their banners. Oppenheimer indeed had become a hero of the liberals and the political left, but many of his attitudes and opinions were unsympathetic to the communists. Teller had been embraced by the militant right, but he held many views that then and later could be classed as liberal. In short, both were strong individualists who could not be politically pigeonholed.

The issue, however, was not Teller versus Oppenheimer, but whether the latter was the proper man to hold a powerful position in the counsels of the defense establishment. President Eisenhower was becoming increasingly convinced that the ascetic physicist was in ideological bondage to Russia or, at best, a dupe of the communists. The President wanted Oppenheimer removed from his decision-making role.[1] Toward Teller, Eisenhower had no such reservations. In Teller's background, in Hungary, Germany, Denmark, England, and America, there was no hint that he ever had a shred of sympathy for communism. He remained suspicious of Russia even when the Soviets were the World War II ally of the United States. In 1954 such a record of steadfast anti-communism made Teller clean, while Oppenheimer was heavily tainted.

The national wrath that descended on Oppenheimer was a sub-climax in the philosophical conflict that had begun with the Russian Revolution in 1917. Most Americans welcomed the overthrow of the old regime of the czar in favor of the Western-liberal principles of the new government headed by Aleksandr Kerensky. In Russia, however, it was not a time for moderation, and Lenin's Bolsheviks, promising peace, bread, and land, and steeped in the techniques of violent revolution, swept Kerensky out of power and created panic in the old regimes of Russia's allies as well as her adversaries. To the dismay of her allies, Lenin, mindful of a starving and rebellious army, sued for a separate peace,

If the Treaty of Brest-Litovsk alarmed Russia's former friends, the long-term communist blueprint offended and frightened all of the capitalist nations. The Bolsheviks seized power with a pledge to socialize the means of production and to expropriate large land-holdings for distribution to the peasants. From there they would communize the rest of the world. To established capitalist regimes the dangers were clear. Foreign investments were threatened and communists were already spreading their gospel in Europe and the United States.

There was fascination in the new idea. Within Russia, Maxim Gorky's fight against his country's traditional anti-Semitism generated a sympathetic Jewish audience in the United States. Lincoln Steffens, a respected crusading reporter, visited Russia in 1919 and he was impressed. He wrote: "I have been over into the future, and it works."[2] If the intelligentsia led the cautious cheers for the new Russian regime, some trade unions were not far behind. Workingmen openly sympathetic to the communist idea formed "red" trade unions.* Departing from the pragmatic tradition of American labor, they not only pressed economic demands, but pledged their support to the struggle of the working class in the new Union of Soviet Socialist Republics.

Not surprisingly, there was a reaction to the wave of red sympa-

---

*The Workers Party of America, the successor to the underground Communist party, held a convention in New York City at the end of December 1922. Part of the party's adopted program was: "The labor unions must be revolutionized; they must be won for the class struggle against capitalism; they must be inspired with a new solidarity and united to fight a common battle. The existing craft unions must be amalgamated and powerful industrial unions created in each industry. . . ." The Trade Union Educational League was organized by the Workers party to lay the groundwork for industrial unions.

thy. Americans who equated freedom with private enterprise began to accuse their fellow Americans of disloyalty and even of treason. The accusations were not directed only to members of the Communist party. New terms were coined—"parlor pink" and "fellow traveler"—to describe Americans whose philosophy tilted leftward, or anyone who expressed even an openminded interest in the radically new kind of political system that had been implanted in Russia.

A genuine if groundless fear gripped many citizens that the Bolshevik idea was undermining America. Woodrow Wilson had been crippled by a stroke and his unrestrained Attorney General, A. Mitchell Palmer, led an anti-communist witch hunt that spread across the nation. The Palmer raids resulted in thousands of arrests. He reported to the Senate Judiciary Committee that 6,328 warrants for "alien anarchists" had been issued between July 1, 1919 and January 1, 1921.[3] He bragged to the Committee on the Civil Appropriations Bill for 1921 that "in the latter part of January 1920 our field reports indicate that 52 per cent of our work in the country was in connection with the so-called radical movement."

In battle-weary Europe, the communist emergence spawned the counterforce that was to be known as fascism, an apotheosis of patriotism and private power. Edward Teller had endured in rapid succession a cruel and fumbling Hungarian communist revolution and a militant reaction as Admiral Miklós Horthy, in November 1919, established the first fascist-type government in Europe. In Italy, on October 22, 1922, the bombastic Benito Mussolini led his followers in a march on Rome.

The appeal of his fascists (they were the first to use that word for a modern political movement) was irresistible; King Victor Emmanuel III made Mussolini premier with dictatorial policies. In a somewhat milder reaction to the same political stresses, Engelbert Dollfuss became chancellor of Austria in 1932 and, in 1934, Antonio de Oliveira Salazar brought more than three decades of fascist-type dictatorship to Portugal. All of these movements owed their popularity, at least in part, to fear of communism as the alternative. In absolute power and ruthlessness, however, they were all secondary to the forces of Adolf Hitler, who had become chancellor and dictator of Germany in January 1933.

In 1929 the October stock market crash in the United States had heralded the great depression that ended the postwar economic boom. Its effects spread quickly across the world, especially through the Western industrial countries. Whereas economic disillusionment strengthened fascism in Germany and drove brilliant men like Teller into exile, in the United States the trend was the other way. Herbert Hoover, symbol of the Republicans' immobility, was displaced in the landslide victory of Franklin D. Roosevelt, a popular-front President who immediately initiated a move leftward toward social reforms to offset the devastating effect of the depression on the common man.

In 1934 Roosevelt gave formal recognition to the now-entrenched communist government of Soviet Russia. The action gave a degree of respectability to domestic communists. Many leaders of the newly created Committee for Industrial Organization (later Congress of Industrial Organizations) professed communist, or, at least, left-wing leanings. In the depths of the worst economic depression in America's history, there was a legitimate reason to examine the philosophy of Marx in search of a remedy. The search was especially active on America's campuses where, sometimes leavened by expatriate Jews from Hitler's Germany, the spread of right-wing totalitarianism and militarism was deplored. Japan's brutal rape of Manchuria added fuel to the resentment. Then, in 1936, Mussolini, in a ruthless quest for imperial glory, bombed, invaded, and conquered Ethiopia, the proudest independent nation in Africa.

The climactic struggle for fascism came in Spain. In 1923 a military dictatorship replaced the monarchy. The dictatorship fell and was followed by a government that restored the monarchy in 1930, only to be replaced in 1931 by a shaky, anti-Catholic coalition of liberals and socialists. Upheavals from the left and right continued until 1936, when a strong left majority was elected to the Cortes, the Spanish parliament. The result was not order, but revolt by the Falangists (Spanish fascists), ostensibly in defense of the church, but reflecting the political schism across the world. The rebellion began with army units in Spanish Morocco which, joined by Moorish troops, invaded Spain from the south, while other revolutionary forces were building in the west. The leader was General Francisco Franco, who had been exiled to the Canary Islands by the republican government.

The European democracies remained officially neutral in the increasingly bloody Spanish conflict. President Roosevelt imposed an arms embargo. On balance, this hurt the Republican cause because Germany and Italy had commenced sending arms to Franco.

Russia, alone among the nonfascist powers, recognized the potential threat to socialist progress in Europe. Under Soviet direction an "International Brigade" was organized and attracted volunteers from all over the world to fight in Spain in a crusade against fascism. In the United States the Abraham Lincoln Brigade was formed as a division of the International Brigade.

Among the many Americans who gave their moral and financial support to the Abraham Lincoln Brigade was J. Robert Oppenheimer. In this same period Edward Teller was becoming increasingly alarmed at the spread of fascism, though he later recalled no awareness of either the International or the Lincoln Brigade: "I was simply not concerned with politics on a day-to-day basis." He was deeply involved in his theoretical work with George Gamow at George Washington University.

Oppenheimer's contributions were first made through a personal friend, Stanford professor Thomas Addis, and probably amounted to about $1,000 a year. In the winter of 1937–38, Addis suggested to Oppenheimer that the funds would be more effectively used if they were donated directly to the Communist party. Oppenheimer was steered to Isaac Folkoff, a Communist party official in the San Francisco area, and from then on made his contributions through Folkoff. Even after the cause of the Spanish loyalists was lost in 1938, Oppenheimer continued making donations to the party for various other projects.

These contacts, interlaced with personal friendships, laid the groundwork for the personal humiliation Oppenheimer was to endure fifteen years later. Between the idealistic era of the Lincoln Brigade, when fascism was the principal enemy of freedom, and 1953, when Senator Joseph R. McCarthy had whipped the nation into an anti-communist frenzy, anyone who had involved himself in joint effort with communist causes was suddenly caught with skeletons in the closet.

This was the lot of J. Robert Oppenheimer in 1953, despite the intervening years through which he had worked exhaustively in the service of his country. His admitted and sometimes seemingly naïve involvement in left-wing causes had provided a continuous security headache, especially for General Groves during the life of the Manhattan Project. In the postwar years Edward Teller believed that not only were Oppenheimer's political opinions disturbing, but sometimes strangely unpredictable.

The upshot of the known record of Oppenheimer's public and private commitments was that he wore entirely different masks, according to the segment of the nation that was judging his performance. To a majority of the scientific community he was one of the revered leaders of the age, a superb scientist and a selfless public servant, even though given to occasional outbursts of intellectual arrogance. To many Americans frightened by communism and obsessed with national security, he was the man who had shamelessly trafficked with the cold-war enemy, and his sins were emphasized in the mood stirred up by the demagogic Senator McCarthy.

If many scientists and government colleagues were willing to accept Oppenheimer's political views as the price of employing his brilliance, William Liscum Borden* was not. Borden had just resigned as staff director of the Joint Committee on Atomic Energy. He was an insider on questions of security. On November 7, 1953, he wrote his now-famous letter to J. Edgar Hoover, director of the FBI, stating that "more probably than not, J. Robert Oppenheimer is an agent of the Soviet Union."

Borden, a graduate of Yale University and its law school, had been a B-24 pilot in World War II, with thirty missions in the European theater. His confrontation with Oppenheimer was foreshadowed in 1946 when, on his release from war service, he wrote a book called *There Will Be No Time.* Essentially it was a plea for the development of nuclear weapons for tactical as well as strategic purposes. (Ironically, five years later, Oppenheimer would make a similar recommendation.) Borden's ideas impressed Senator Brien McMahon, who persuaded Borden to join his staff in 1948. After the 1948 election upset, when the Democrats unexpectedly gained control of Congress, McMahon assumed the chairmanship of the Joint Atomic Committee and soon moved Borden in as director. There Borden learned a lot about atomic weapons and, eventually, enough about the security record of J. Robert Oppenheimer to write his accusatory letter to Hoover.

What was the evidence that led Borden to make such a drastic

---

*When the authors interviewed Borden in January 1973 he was willing to discuss virtually all of his associations except with the Oppenheimer case, which he would not discuss at all.

charge against one of the world's great scientists? There were, of course, the prewar contributions to the Lincoln Brigade and the Communist party. There was the fact that Oppenheimer's wife, Katherine, his brother, Frank, and Frank's wife had all been members of the Communist party. Katherine Oppenheimer's former husband, also a communist, had died fighting in the Lincoln Brigade.

All of this, however, was known when Oppenheimer became director of Los Alamos. It worried the government, but his potential contribution was so important that the risk was taken. History proved the risk to be worthwhile. But in 1953 William Borden felt there was additional evidence that indicated Oppenheimer had crossed the line into treason.

At the forefront of Borden's suspicions was Oppenheimer's friendship with Haakon Chevalier,[4] an American-born instructor of French on the Berkeley campus. Chevalier's father was French and his mother was Norwegian. He spent his early years in the homelands of his parents. When he was eighteen he served for a year as a seaman, then came to Berkeley to study French literature. He published a book on Anatole France and translated some of the works of André Malraux.

At Berkeley he fell into the circle of left-wing intellectuals whose enthusiasms were stirred by the menacing rise of the Nazis in Germany. Chevalier met Oppenheimer in 1937 and, despite Oppenheimer's usual disdain for people not his intellectual equals—and Chevalier was not—the friendship persisted for many years. Philip Stern in *The Oppenheimer Case* speculates that the friendship fed on Chevalier's broad connections with activists of the left, which appealed to Oppenheimer's awakening social conscience.[5] It is also possible that Oppenheimer was flattered by Chevalier's unabashed hero worship.

History may have little noted the Oppenheimer-Chevalier relationship but for a quiet incident in the kitchen of Oppenheimer's house, on Eagle Hill, in Berkeley in January or February of 1943.[6] Chevalier and his wife were dinner guests. As Oppenheimer went into the kitchen to mix some martinis, Chevalier followed him. The two friends engaged in a brief conversation, casual, perhaps of no consequence, or perhaps a monumental edging toward the borders of treason.

Since only the two of them were present, what actually was discussed will never be certain. Their subsequent recollections were not precisely the same, and Oppenheimer damaged his own cause by altering his version on different occasions. They agreed, however, that they had discussed Chevalier's friend, George C. Eltenton, a native British chemical engineer who had once lived in Russia but was at that time working for the Shell Development Corporation in Berkeley. Eltenton had helped to organize a union of scientists and technicians at the Berkeley Radiation Laboratory.

Chevalier and Oppenheimer also agreed that Chevalier had informed Oppenheimer that Eltenton had made known to Chevalier that he had a means of getting technical information to the Russians. In subsequent testimony, Chevalier made it clear he had not made any request of Oppenheimer to provide the information; in fact, Chevalier testified that he had already rejected whatever Eltenton had proposed before that conversation in the kitchen. He was just reporting it to his friend, Oppenheimer. Oppenheimer in subsequent years presented three slightly varied versions of the kitchen conversation but, as Stern reported, "the crucial aspect is that in all the extant versions of the kitchen interlude Oppenheimer's immediate response to the notion of turning over information to the Russians was instantaneous and negative."[7]

For reasons never quite clear, however, Oppenheimer did not report the incident to security officers in Berkeley until August 25, 1943, when he urged Lieutenant Lyall Johnson to keep an eye on Eltenton.[8] This rather offhand suggestion by Oppenheimer seemed to arouse more curiosity about Oppenheimer than about Eltenton on the part of Lieutenant Johnson and his superior, Lieutenant Colonel Boris Pash, chief of counterintelligence for the Ninth Army Corps. Why did Oppenheimer finger Eltenton, who, incidentally, was already under surveillance? The two officers decided to summon Oppenheimer for an interview the very next day, August 26. It took place in Lieutenant Johnson's office in Durant Hall. What Oppenheimer did not know until eleven years later was that the interview was recorded on an early version of a tape recorder.[9]

After some bantering on security problems, Pash obliquely brought up the Eltenton matter, as evidence of "other groups" willing to transmit information about the atomic project to the Russians. Oppenheimer was cautious, he didn't want to involve people whose intentions were only to "make up, in other words, for the defects of our official communications" with "our allies," who were "battling for their lives."

"To put it quite frankly," Oppenheimer said, "I would feel friendly to the idea of the Commander in Chief informing the Russians that we were working on this problem. At least I can see there might be some arguments for doing that, but I do not feel friendly to the idea of having it moved out the back door."[10]

Oppenheimer made a distinction between those interested in transmitting information to the Russians and those who might deal with the Nazis. "With the Nazis it would have a somewhat different color." He made it clear that he did not agree with the arguments of those seeking to help the Russians "but . . . the guys involved evidently feel that what they were or are doing is consistent with government policy. After all, we share information with our ally, the British."[11]

Pash, the son of a Russian immigrant, and a former biology and physical education teacher, was quietly persistent in trying to establish what Oppenheimer was driving at and what he knew. Oppenheimer reported that two or three men, two of them at Los Alamos, told him they were contacted by an unnamed individual seeking to funnel information through Eltenton to the Soviet consul.[12]

Would Oppenheimer name the unnamed individual? No, he would not, though he was partially unmasked as a member of the faculty at Berkeley who was not on the atomic project. Oppenheimer said he was convinced that the channels no longer existed and it would serve no useful purpose to implicate persons who were contacted but did not get involved. "It is also my duty," he said, "not to implicate these people, acquaintances, or colleagues of whose position I am absolutely certain myself, and my duty is to protect them."[13] The interview ended with Pash regretting that Oppenheimer would not reveal information that security officers might not get otherwise if they were to "work a hundred years."[14]

It was all on tape, which Oppenheimer discovered to his shock years later when he told a different story. In 1943, however, the puzzle of Oppenheimer's behavior left Pash in a quandary. He had gone out of his way to implicate Eltenton, then had stubbornly refused to name Eltenton's contact. Was he protecting or accusing his friend Chevalier? Or was he shoring up his own security problem as the result of the Lomanitz case?

Giovanni Rossi Lomanitz was a precocious, gifted physicist, a protégé of Oppenheimer, who was only nineteen when he entered the graduate school of physics at Berkeley and, at Oppenheimer's urging, joined the staff of the Radiation Laboratory. Three years later, in 1943, Ernest Lawrence, director of the Radiation Laboratory, was so impressed with Lomanitz's work that he made him a group leader. That was on July 27, and three days later the young physicist was called up for a physical exam by his draft board.

He telephoned Oppenheimer in Los Alamos for help. Oppenheimer was aware that Lomanitz had joined various left-wing organizations but, apparently, had promised his mentor that he would curtail his activities if he went to work in the Radiation Laboratory. Oppenheimer wired the New York headquarters of the Manhattan District, saying, in effect, that Lomanitz was almost irreplaceable. The appeal ultimately went right to the top. General Lewis Hershey, director of the draft, would hear of no deferments. Lomanitz, the irreplaceable physicist, became a company clerk in the Army.[15]

General Groves's security aide, Lieutenant Colonel John Lansdale, called on Oppenheimer and, by implication, warned the top physicist that his defense of a man of such doubtful loyalty as Lomanitz was damaging to Oppenheimer. He also advised Oppenheimer that Lomanitz had not eased up on his political activities while working at the Radiation Laboratory, and Oppenheimer was furious that his protégé had broken a pledge.[16] But Lansdale insisted that his sole responsibility was to prevent the unauthorized transmission of information, not to interfere with a man's political or social beliefs. Surprisingly, Oppenheimer went farther. Stern reports that he told Lansdale that he didn't want any current members of the Communist party working for him at Los Alamos because party discipline always opened the "question of divided loyalty."

This would prove to be the last time Oppenheimer intervened in an attempt to assist a friend accused of left-wing activities or sympathies. The warning by Lieutenant Colonel Lansdale evidently had impressed him, and probably explains his devious and ambivalent response to the subsequent brush with Chevalier in the kitchen conversation. On the one hand, he recognized the importance of the Los Alamos project and his own indispensible role in it. On the other hand, he could not shut himself off from past convictions and loyalties. So he became, in relation to a friend like Chevalier, both an informer and a protector. It was the behavior of a man who knows that the security officers have two strikes against him already. Colonel Pash had speculated as much in a message to

General Groves, that Oppenheimer's involvement as protector of Lomanitz had prompted his turnabout in volunteering information about Eltenton and skirting an implication of Chevalier. Pash saw Oppenheimer's initiative in volunteering the Eltenton case interview as an effort "to retain the confidence of the Army personnel responsible for this project."[17]

Not all of the security officers were that sanguine about Oppenheimer. Captain Peer DeSilva, the local security officer at Los Alamos, interpreted Oppenheimer's failure to provide specific names as evidence that "J. Robert Oppenheimer is playing a key part in the attempts of the Soviet Union to secure, by espionage, highly secret information which is vital to the security of the United States."[18]

Eleven days after the Pash-Oppenheimer interrogation, intelligence officers intercepted a mysterious note[19] that further aroused their concern about Oppenheimer. The note was from a suspected communist, Joseph Weinberg, who had also been a student of Oppenheimer's, to "A. Flannigan." The note said:

> Dear A. Please don't make any contact with me, and pass this message to S and B, only don't mention any names. I will take a walk with you when this matter is all cleared up.

Since both the writer and the receiver were considered by Pash to be communists, and "since Weinberg had close contact and association with Dr. Oppenheimer" (as Pash later testified), he felt the letter was a result of Pash's meeting with Oppenheimer, though he couldn't prove any connection.

Lansdale was becoming increasingly alarmed by the web of security riddles that seemed to surround Oppenheimer. A Harvard law graduate and former Cleveland lawyer, Lansdale, on entering the Army, was assigned to counterintelligence in Washington. His first job was screening Army personnel to make sure they met the service's rather fuzzy loyalty criteria. He found an atmosphere in which G2 was more concerned about Russian than Nazi sympathizers, based on the belief that, in the long run, Russia, not Germany, would be the enemy. Lansdale concluded from his own study of communist theory that party members were intensely dedicated to the Soviet party line. He felt that this loyalty made them particularly willing to convey classified information to a nation that was, after all, an ally. By the time he became General Groves's aide on security matters, his fears were reinforced by actual evidence of this kind of treason.

In early September 1943, Oppenheimer, Groves, and Lansdale were together for sixteen hours on a train from Cheyenne to Chicago. Among other subjects, they discussed Oppenheimer's interviews with Pash. Oppenheimer told Groves he was still reluctant to reveal the identity of the professor that George Eltenton had used as an intermediary, but if General Groves ordered him to reveal the name, he would comply. The "sin," however, would then be on Groves's head, as Oppenheimer saw it. Groves decided not to press it, later explaining: "I was not going to make an issue of it because I thought it might impair his usefulness on the project."[20] Groves suspected that the unnamed contact might have been Oppenheimer's brother, Frank, which would explain Robert's reluctance to provide the identification.[21]

On September 12, a few days after the train ride, Lansdale, back in Washington, called on Oppenheimer, who was on a brief visit to the capital. Lansdale wanted to make another effort to extract the information that had eluded both Pash and Groves. The interview took place in Groves's office in the Pentagon. Once again there was a concealed microphone and a hidden tape recorder.

The interrogation began with pleasantries. Lansdale said, "You're probably the most intelligent man I ever met." Then they got down to business and Lansdale tried a bluff. He told Oppenheimer that he thought they now had identified Eltenton's contact. Lansdale wondered "if you feel you are in a position to tell me?"

The bluff didn't work. Oppenheimer balked, as he had with Pash. "It would be wrong," he said, since in his judgment the person he would not mention was not involved.

Lansdale was irritated. "I don't see how you can have any hesitancy in disclosing the name of the man who has actually been engaged in an attempt at espionage for a foreign power in time of war."

"I know," Oppenheimer responded. "It's a tough problem and I worried about it a lot."

After additional sparring Oppenheimer gave in to the point that he would agree to name the contact "if I had any evidence, or anything came to my attention which was indicative that something was transmitted."

Lansdale informed his target that information had been passed on to the Russians within the last week. Unfortunately he could not guarantee that the person who conveyed the information was the same one Oppenheimer had in mind. So Oppenheimer said nothing on that subject.

Foiled, Lansdale went off on a tangent and, unexpectedly, he got some answers. Lansdale's question was "Whom do you know on the project in Berkeley who are now—that's probably a hypothetical question—or have been members of the Communist party?"

"I know for a fact," replied Oppenheimer, "I know I learned on my last visit to Berkeley that both Lomanitz and Weinberg were members." Oppenheimer thought, but was not sure, that a secretary by the name of Jane Muir was a member of the party. With a few exceptions such as Steve Nelson and William Schneiderman, who were publicly known as party functionaries, Oppenheimer could not identify current members. Other past members he named included his wife, his brother (who, he believed, had not had any contact with the party for a long time), Bernard Peters, Mrs. Serber, and Jean Tatlock. Oppenheimer said he was not a communist and never had been one, though he had belonged to numerous communist-front organizations on the West Coast.

Then Lansdale asked about Chevalier, Oppenheimer's close friend. The response was to the point: "He is a member of the faculty and I know him well. I wouldn't be surprised if he were a member. He's quite a Red."[22]

Colonel Lansdale pressed further, and Oppenheimer's replies, published years later, sent a shudder through many of his defenders. Lansdale: "Could you get information about who is and who isn't a member of the party?" Oppenheimer: "I don't know whether I could now. At one time I could have. I never tried to." Lansdale: "Would you be willing to?" Oppenheimer: "Not in writing. I think that would make a very bad impression."

The physicist of course didn't know that he was in a situation in which he could incriminate himself as his words were "written" by the relentless turning of the tape recorder. Finally, the two-hour sparring match came to an end. Colonel Lansdale still didn't have the name of Eltenton's contact, but he put Oppenheimer on notice that the matter was not closed: "And don't think this is the last time I'm going to ask you because it isn't."

Actually, Lansdale did not ask again. Instead, he pressured General Groves to order Oppenheimer to reveal the elusive contact,

"Professor X." This time Groves decided he had no choice but to act. So on December 12, at Los Alamos, he ordered Oppenheimer to divulge the name of Eltenton's contact. And at last Oppenheimer complied, but what he said has since been a matter of dispute.[23]

As Oppenheimer recalled the episode at his security hearings he identified Haakon Chevalier as the contact. He said he told Groves that Chevalier approached only him, which differed completely from what he had told Pash four months earlier about three contacts in the atomic project. During the hearings he was to admit that the response to Pash was "a cock and bull story." When questioned as to why he lied, his only answer was "because I was an idiot."[24]

The day after Oppenheimer's encounter with Groves, three similar telegrams[25] to various security officials were sent by Colonel K. D. Nichols, then district engineer of the Manhattan District. One of the wires went to the Commanding Officer, United States Engineer Office, Santa Fe, New Mexico, attention Captain DeSilva, and read as follows:

> HAAKON CHEVALIER REPORTED BY OPPENHEIMER TO BE THE PROFESSOR AT RADLAB WHO MADE THREE CONTACTS FOR ELTENTON. CLASSIFIED SECRET. OPPENHEIMER BELIEVES CHEVALIER ENGAGED IN NO FURTHER ACTIVITY OTHER THAN THE THREE ORIGINAL ATTEMPTS.

If Oppenheimer's recollection of his conversation with Groves was correct, then he had committed a felony in his earlier response to Pash. Under Section 80, Title 18, of the United States Code, a felony is committed by anyone who "knowingly or willfully falsifies or conceals a material fact in any matter within the jurisdiction or agency of the United States." Years later a disillusioned and bitter Haakon Chevalier would claim that Oppenheimer had, in repeating Clevalier's alleged three contacts, both lied and exaggerated about his involvement with Eltenton.

Chevalier's ultimate disenchantment with Oppenheimer was shared by some of the physicist's colleagues, but not all of them. Teller was among those disillusioned when he was shown the evidence. On the other hand, a prominent physicist, commenting anonymously some nineteen years after the security hearings, thought Oppenheimer's apparent lies were unimportant. "Doesn't everyone lie to security officers?" he said.

Oppenheimer's naming of Chevalier didn't take the security

officers off his trail. They continued to press him about the political orientation and activities of some of his former students working at the Radiation Laboratory in Berkeley, particularly Bernard Peters.

Peters was a Bavarian Jew who was studying in Munich when Hitler took control of Germany. He was, naturally, anti-Nazi and, according to Oppenheimer, Peters had been a member of the German Communist party. In time he was arrested by the Nazis and was confined in the infamous Dachau extermination camp. Apparently a bribe arranged by his mother resulted in his being transferred to the Munich city jail. From there he escaped and fled to America. In New York he met and married a refugee from the Nazis. He worked for a time as a longshoreman so that his bride, Hannah, could attend medical school.

When Mrs. Peters received her medical degree the couple moved to California and Bernard, now supported by his wife, enrolled at Berkeley. His brilliance soon attracted the attention of Oppenheimer and before long, even though Peters lacked the usual academic credits, he was admitted, under Oppenheimer's sponsorship, to the graduate school in physics. There the teacher and the student developed a close professional and social relationship. The Oppenheimers and the Peterses often visited each other's homes and Hannah Peters occasionally administered to Robert's medical needs as his personal physician.

Thus it was quite natural in late 1942 when Oppenheimer was asked to head Los Alamos that he would invite Bernard and Hannah Peters to join him. Bernard's talents as a physicist could be utilized profitably and Hannah's services as a medical doctor were potentially useful. As Oppenheimer later described the offer he made to the couple, it was "an attractive deal" all the way around. For reasons that are not clear, however, they rejected it.[26]

Only a little more than a year after his offer to the Peterses, Oppenheimer was pressed by Captain DeSilva to name former students who would fall into the category of "truly dangerous." Surprisingly, Oppenheimer named Bernard Peters. He also mentioned David Bohm, Joseph Weinberg, "and somebody else." Given the background of friendship and collaboration between Oppenheimer and Peters, to have thus labeled him so soon afterward shocked some of Oppenheimer's colleagues when the story was revealed.

Captain DeSilva's memorandum of the conversation, dated January 6, 1944, revealed the extent of Oppenheimer's indictment of his friend. Whereas he felt both Bohm and Peters were "truly dangerous," Bohm's temperament and personality were dangerous only in the sense that he would be easily influenced by others. But Peters, in Oppenheimer's assessment, was a "crazy person," whose actions would be unpredictable. He described Peters as "quite a Red" with a background filled with incidents indicating his tendency toward "direct action."

The strange and tortuous double life that Oppenheimer was forced to lead during the Los Alamos period is indicated by the reports of the officers who kept him under constant surveillance. He had already put David Bohm in the "dangerous" category, and yet on March 12, 1944, intelligence agents made the following report:[27]

> 6:05 P.M.: Subject [J. R. Oppenheimer] and Frank [his brother] walked up and down Telegraph Avenue [in San Francisco] and in front of the hotel. Both engaged in earnest conversation with each other.
>
> 6:15 P.M.: David Bohm walked south on Telegraph Avenue and met the Oppenheimers in front of the hotel. J. R. Oppenheimer and Bohm engaged in conversation for five minutes but Frank stood about 10 feet away and did not participate in the conversation.
>
> 6:20 P.M.: Subject and Frank entered cab, license 53692, with Oppenheimer luggage and drove to Fisherman's Wharf, San Francisco.

According to Oppenheimer's account of the sidewalk conversation as he reported it to DeSilva ten days later in Los Alamos, Bohm wished to be transferred to Los Alamos. As a student at Berkeley, Bohm had idolized Oppenheimer and had wanted to follow his mentor to Los Alamos. Oppenheimer asked DeSilva if he had any objections to Bohm's transfer. DeSilva did object, so Oppenheimer dropped the matter.

One of the ironies of Oppenheimer's struggles with the security forces is that work at Los Alamos continued uninterrupted. As far as we have been able to learn, none of the scientific or technical staff at the laboratory, including Teller, knew anything about this ordeal behind the scenes of Oppenheimer's daily role as the Los Alamos chief.

These events, and many more of a similar nature, stirred the anxiety and resentment of William Liscum Borden in 1953 as he read Oppenheimer's security file. To Borden there was a *prima facie* case that a great administrator and scientist was also involved in espionage. He reached this conclusion on the basis of the security file then available to the Atomic Energy Commission. Borden did not have access to the dossier on Oppenheimer that had been accumulated over the years by the FBI.

The irony in Borden's accusation lay in the fact that conclusions reached by Borden in 1946 in his book *There Will Be No Time* were also reached by Oppenheimer in 1951 in the so-called Project Vista report. Borden described his thesis as "an argument for not viewing nuclear weapons as purely strategic, a point of view that was prevalent when the book was written. Rather, the book argues that the weapons could be and should be produced in quantity and available for tactical purposes, in the sense of the use against troops, against air bases in the event of a major war, as well as available for strategic purposes."

Borden's foresight eventually earned him his post as staff director of the Joint Committee on Atomic Energy. In contrast, Oppenheimer's similar outlook only intensified the case that was building against him. The Vista report stemmed from the growing concern in the Pentagon that the Russian army, never fully demobilized after World War II, had the capability of sweeping across Western Europe. The NATO forces there were outgunned and outmanned.

One answer would seem to be the development of tactical nuclear weapons that could be used against troops. The Air Force's concentration on large, strategic bombs limited the options of the United States and NATO in the event of war. If the Allied armies were overwhelmed by the Soviet forces it is true that in 1951 the United States could have used atomic bombs to wipe out Russian cities. By this time, however, Russia also had developed atomic weapons and the cities of Europe could have been hostage to any massive retaliation on the part of the United States Air Force.

The three military services commissioned a group of scientists at Caltech in Pasadena to study the problem of a more flexible response, adapting atomic weapons to conventional warfare.[28] When the Caltech scientists encountered problems in organizing and clarifying their views, Lee DuBridge, Caltech president as well as Vista chairman, invited Oppenheimer to help them out. After two days of review and discussion Oppenheimer, with the other scientists' assistance, prepared a revised report of Chapter 5, the most controversial part of the Vista findings. The recommendation was for a three-way allocation of fissionable materials, part to the Strategic Air Command of the Air Force, part for the development of smaller tactical weapons, and the remainder into a contingent reserve.

The proposal was viewed with alarm by the Strategic Air Command which, at this point, enjoyed the lion's share of the available nuclear materials. The concern was especially felt by David Tressel Griggs, a professor of geophysics at UCLA who had recently left his post to become Chief Scientist for the Air Force. Griggs's reservations were felt at least as strongly by Air Force Secretary Thomas Finletter. In addition, both were acutely aware of the damaging evidence in Oppenheimer's security file. They couldn't ignore their doubts. Did Oppenheimer conceive or support the Vista recommendations because he thought they were in the best interests of the United States? Or was he swayed by his ideological sympathy for the Soviet Union?

Griggs was later to testify that Finletter "had serious questions as to the loyalty of Dr. Oppenheimer." It was Griggs himself who was later to be attacked by the Alsop brothers for destroying Oppenheimer's reputation, though Teller believed Griggs was actually conveying Finletter's feelings.[29]

The case against Oppenheimer was accumulating in the mind not only of Borden, but in the minds of many Americans, including President Eisenhower.*

---

*On December 29, 1975, two news stories appeared that purported to shed new light on why Eisenhower took action against Oppenheimer. Both stemmed from a paper presented to the American Historical Association by Jack M. Holl, associate historian of the Energy Research and Development Administration. The Chicago Sun-Times, supplementing Holl's anecdote, said William Liscum Borden had prepared a secret report early in 1953 detailing H-bomb progress to that point. Physicist John A. Wheeler, according to the Sun-Times, was given a portion of the report but mislaid it on a Washington-bound train on which other passengers were said to include a group protesting the death sentence imposed on atom spies Julius and Ethel Rosenberg. Government officials apparently assumed that some of the passengers may have been communists, and that the secret report could have fallen into their hands. Eisenhower, according to the Sun-Times account, was furious at Borden for accumulating so much information in one place and at Wheeler for losing part of it. The President then became increasingly obsessed with the security issue. The Associated Press, in a dispatch also based on Holl's report, quoted Harold P. Green, a former AEC lawyer, as saying the key figure in the case was the late FBI director, J. Edgar Hoover, who, according to Green, bugged Oppenheimer's conversations with his attorneys throughout the AEC's investigations of its top scientist.

Added to this was the American state of mind in the early 1950s. The postwar disillusionment with Russia was at its peak, as was the fear of Soviet power and communist subversion. Senator Joseph R. McCarthy mounted this steed of fear and resentment and rode it wildly. On February 9, 1950, in Wheeling, West Virginia, he announced that he had a list of 205 known communists working in the State Department. The next day, in Denver, he changed "communists" to "bad security risks." The day after that he said the State Department employed "57 card-carrying communists." The number changed several more times, and McCarthy never produced the name of one subversive, but he had kindled fires of hate in the country.

The heady success of American forces in World War II had also generated a naïve belief in American omnipotence. Hitler had convinced the Germans in the early 1930s that they lost World War I not because of military weakness but from internal subversion. In the same way, McCarthy attributed the strength of Russia and the establishment of communism in China to traitors in America. Russia had acquired the atomic bomb only because treasonous Americans spied for the Soviets. The communists had taken over in China because traitors in the State Department had sold out the regime of Chiang Kai-shek. It was nonsense, but in the fever of the times, many Americans sincerely believed it.

After all, there *were* spies in the innermost councils of defense. On January 27, 1950, British scientist Klaus Fuchs had been arrested in London and had confessed to spying for the Soviet Union. Fuchs had been privy to America's most sophisticated information on nuclear weapons. He had contributed to the work on the thermonuclear bomb.

To William Liscum Borden it all added up to a case against J. Robert Oppenheimer. The clean-cut, Ivy League ex-pilot decided it was his duty to make a formal charge against the acknowledged leader of the American scientific community. His decision was to trigger events that profoundly altered the lives of Oppenheimer and Edward Teller, and created a schism that has never since been ended both among scientists and among citizens. This is what Borden wrote:

Dear Mr. Hoover:
This letter concerns J. Robert Oppenheimer.
As you know, he has for some years enjoyed access to various critical activities of the National Security Council, the Department of

State, the Department of Defense, the Army, Navy, and the Air Force, the Research and Development Board, the Atomic Energy Commission, the Central Intelligence Agency, the National Security Resources Board, and the National Science Foundation. His access covers most new weapons being developed by the Armed Forces, war plans at least in comprehensive outline, complete details as to atomic and hydrogen weapons and stockpile date, the evidence on which some of the principal CIA intelligence estimates is based, United States participation in the United Nations and NATO and many other areas of high security sensitivity.

Because the scope of his access may well be unique, because he has had custody of an immense collection of classified papers covering military, intelligence, and diplomatic as well as atomic-energy matters, and because he also possesses a scientific background enabling him to grasp the significance of classified data of a technical nature, it seems reasonable to estimate that he is and for some years has been in a position to compromise more vital and detailed information affecting the national defense and security than any other individual in the United States.

While J. Robert Oppenheimer has not made major contributions to the advancement of science, he holds a respected professional standing among the second rank of American physicists. In terms of his mastery of Government affairs, his close liaison with ranking officials, and his ability to influence high-level thinking, he surely stands in the first rank, not merely among scientists but among all those who have shaped postwar decisions in the military, atomic energy, intelligence, and diplomatic fields. As chairman or as an official or unofficial member of more than 35 important Government committees, panels, study groups, and projects, he has oriented or dominated key policies involving every principal United States security department and agency except the FBI.

The purpose of this letter is to state my own exhaustively considered opinion, based upon years of study, of the available classified evidence, that more probably than not J. Robert Oppenheimer is an agent of the Soviet Union.

This opinion considers the following factors, among others:

(a) He was contributing substantial monthly sums to the Communist Party;

(b) His ties with communism had survived the Nazi-Soviet Pact and the Soviet attack upon Finland;

(c) His wife and younger brother were Communists;

(d) He had no close friends except Communists;

(e) He had at least one Communist mistress;

(f) He belonged only to Communist organizations, apart from professional affiliations;

(g) The people whom he recruited into the early wartime Berkeley atomic project were exclusively Communists;

(h) He had been instrumental in securing recruits for the Communist Party; and

(i) He was in frequent contact with Soviet espionage agents.

2. The evidence indicating that—

(a) In May 1942, he either stopped contributing funds to the Communist Party or else made his contributions through a new channel not yet discovered;

(b) In April 1942 his name was formally submitted for security clearance;

(c) He himself was aware at the time that his name had been so submitted; and

(d) He thereafter repeatedly gave false information to General Groves, The Manhattan District, and the FBI concerning the 1939–April 1942 period.

3. The evidence indicating that—

(a) He was responsible for employing a number of Communists, some of them nontechnical, at wartime Los Alamos;

(b) He selected one such individual to write the official Los Alamos history;

(c) He was a vigorous supporter of the H-bomb program until August 6, 1945 (Hiroshima), on which day he personally urged each senior individual working in this field to desist; and

(d) He was an enthusiastic sponsor of the A-bomb program until the war ended, when he immediately and outspokenly advocated that the Los Alamos Laboratory be disbanded.

4. The evidence indicating that—

(a) He was remarkably instrumental in influencing the military authorities and the Atomic Energy Commission essentially to suspend H-bomb development from mid-1946 through January 31, 1950.

(b) He has worked tirelessly, from January 31, 1950, onward, to retard the United States H-bomb program;

(c) He has used his potent influence against every postwar effort to expand capacity for producing A-bomb material;

(d) He has used his potent influence against every postwar effort directed at obtaining larger supplies of uranium raw material; and

(e) He has used his potent influence against every postwar effort toward atomic power development, including the nuclear-powered submarine and aircraft programs as well as industrial power projects.

From such evidence, considered in detail, the following conclusions are justified;

1. Between 1929 and mid-1942, more probably than not, J. Robert Oppenheimer was a sufficiently hardened Communist that he either volunteered espionage information to the Soviets or complied with a

request for such information. (This includes the possibility that when he singled out the weapons aspect of atomic development as his personal specialty, he was acting under Soviet instructions.)

2. More probably than not, he has since been functioning as an espionage agent; and

3. More probably than not, he has since acted under a Soviet directive in influencing United States military, atomic energy, intelligence, and diplomatic policy.

It is to be noted that these conclusions correlate with information furnished by Klaus Fuchs, indicating that the Soviets had acquired an agent in Berkeley who informed them about electromagnetic separation research during 1942 or earlier.

Needless to say, I appreciate the probabilities indentifiable from existing evidence might, with review of future acquired evidence, be reduced to possibilities; or they might also be increased to certainties. The central problem is not whether J. Robert Oppenheimer was ever a Communist; for the existing evidence makes abundantly clear that he was. Even an Atomic Energy Commission analysis prepared in early 1947 reflects this conclusion, although some of the most significant derogatory data had yet to become available. The central problem is assessing the degree of likelihood that he in fact did what a Communist in his circumstances, at Berkeley, would logically have done during the crucial 1939–42 period—that is, whether he became an actual espionage and policy instrument of the Soviets. Thus, as to this central problem, my opinion is that, more probably than not, the worst is in fact the truth.

I am profoundly aware of the grave nature of these comments. The matter is detestable to me. Having lived with the Oppenheimer case for years, having studied and restudied all data concerning him that your agency made available to the Atomic Energy Commission through May 1953, having endeavored to factor in a mass of additional data assembled from numerous other sources, and looking back upon the case from a perspective in private life, I feel a duty simply to state to the responsible head of the security agency most concerned the conclusions which I have painfully crystalized and which I believe any fair-minded man thoroughly familiar with the evidence must also be driven to accept.

The writing of this letter, to me a solemn step, is exclusively on my own personal initiative and responsibility.

Very truly yours,

(Signed)William L. Borden,
(Typed) William L. Borden.

15

The Oppenheimer Noose

THE Oppenheimer hearing became a sort of historical imperative after William Liscum Borden's letter reached a President whose mood had evolved toward a passionate fear of communism. Still, the conspiracy theory of history dies hard, even in the hands of such an eminent historian as Arthur M. Schlesinger, Jr. In his view there was a political plot, a conspiracy hatched by unnamed scientists at the Livermore Laboratory, where Teller was the dominant figure.

In *A Thousand Days,* his history of the Kennedy administration, Schlesinger wrote:

> Livermore, in the spirit of Ernest Lawrence and Edward Teller, believed that American security rested on the unlimited development of nuclear striking power; in the jargon this was "infinite containment." Los Alamos, in the spirit of Robert Oppenheimer, believed that nuclear power should be only one component in a varied national arsenal; this was "finite containment." The bitterness of the time, early in the Eisenhower administration, when *the Livermore group had sought to destroy the Los Alamos position by branding Oppenheimer a security risk,* had to some degree abated. [italics ours][1]

Schlesinger did not document this accusation. In his foreword he wrote: "Every statement, I believe, has its warrant; but in order to protect confidential communications it has seemed better not to give a systematic indication of sources at this time."[2] Without any "indication of sources," Schlesinger's theory must remain suspect. General K. D. Nichols labeled it "nonsense."

Schlesinger is not alone in explaining history in terms of political conspiracy. Thomas W. Wilson, Jr., in his introduction to *The Great Weapons Heresy,* varied this proposition, but spoke with even greater passion:

Oppenheimer was convinced that the atomic age called for a renunciation of obsolete political and military traditions. He believed that the cause of the nuclear arms race would force a radical revision of the very way in which men thought about national security and international relations in the atomic age. What's more, he insisted that the secret issues should be debated publicly. . . .

The security risk heading in the matter of J. Robert Oppenheimer was an elaborate hoax; the government had something quite different in mind when it moved against Oppenheimer, something which had nothing at all to do with "loyalty," "associations," or "character." In one formulation, the issue was whether an open society could stand the shock of discovering it had become an unwilling but ironbound prisoner of the past. . . .[3]

If Wilson's theory is to be accepted, the fat was in the fire. Oppenheimer was against secrecy and this was seen as a threat to the power structure. In the prevailing mood of the cold war, secrets were of value and were not to be shared either with the American people or the reds under the beds. Actually Oppenheimer was not for total abandonment of security in relations with the Russians, but he went farther in this direction than most politicians and many scientists. In July 1953, only half a year before the hearings were ordered, he stated his position in *Foreign Affairs Quarterly,* commenting that "knowledge of the characteristics and probable effects of our atomic weapons, of—in rough terms—the number available, and the changes that are likely to occur with the next years. This is not among the things to be kept secret. Nor is our general estimate of where the enemy stands."[4]

He suggested "candor on the part of the officials of the United States government to the officials, the representatives, the people of their country. We do not operate well when the important facts, the essential conditions, which limit and determine our choice are unknown. We do not operate well when they are known, in secrecy and fear, only to a few men. . . ."[5]

In the light of their later confrontation, it is ironic that another powerful voice on record against secrecy belonged to Edward Teller. As far back as 1939, when the mere possibility of an atomic bomb was considered, Teller, along with Szilard, Fermi, and others, steeped in the academic tradition of openness, resisted the pressures to pull a curtain of secrecy around nuclear research. Only when they began to see the bomb project as a desperate race against the deadly might of fascism did the scientists reluctantly accept secrecy, first in the form of self-imposed regulations and later as official national security policy.

Teller accepted secrecy as a wartime necessity, but only a few months after the war was over, he was on the public record to minimize security regulations. He testified before the Special Committee on Atomic Energy of Congress in November 1945. By this time the so-called Smyth Report had been published, explaining in some detail the process of developing the bomb, and leaving only the mechanical details of bomb construction under wraps.

"All of the security regulations are irksome," Teller told the Congressmen. "Some seem to be unnecessary, especially since hostilities have ended, and some rules of secrecy are a serious hindrance to progress."

His goal was at least partial removal of secrecy. "Purely scientific data—that is, facts concerning natural phenomena—must not be kept secret," Teller testified. "If such secrecy is continued it will warp the entire research activity of any man who is involved on work in atomic power. He either has to sever relations with the scientific world not involved in the development of atomic power, or he has to acquire a split personality, remembering in certain parts of his work only certain parts of the information available to him."

Teller insisted that "scientific facts cannot be kept secret for any length of time. They are readily rediscovered. If we attempt to keep scientific facts secret it will certainly hinder us, but will hardly interfere with the work of a potential competitor."[6]

The only justifiable secrecy, in Teller's opinion, was that which dealt with technical details. And the policing of security regulations, he suggested, should be largely entrusted to the people who themselves engage in the work.

In 1946, aware of the rapidly chilling relationship between the United States and Russia, Teller made a proposal that, for its time, was almost heresy. It recalled in its political simplicity an earlier suggestion made in the prewar period by Russia's genial foreign minister, Maxim Litvinoff. He had argued that the way to disarm is to disarm. Such candor was viewed with suspicion. Litvinoff was ridiculed and his plan was dismissed.

Teller's suggestion, little noticed at the time, was for an open society with free communication jointly assured by the United States and Soviet Russia. In return, the United States would declassify all atomic secrets. This, Teller argued, would minimize the possibility of atomic war.

This was a sweeping proposal for a man who would subsequently be accused by scientific colleagues of harboring a paranoiac distrust of the Russians. He had not only urged that we turn over our atomic secrets to a potential foe, but even prepared a detailed blueprint for doing it.

"Every country," he said, "should be permitted to send to any other country as many agents as it pleases. These agents would be nominated by the country they represent and approved by the Atomic Development Authority, a proposed international agency. Their number would be determined by the country they represent and their expenses would be charged to that country; but they would be responsible only to the Atomic Development Authority. But these agents should have the right freely to enquire into any activity which may seem to them directed against their own country, or against world peace.

"It should be considered the duty of every citizen of every country to give full information to these agents of the Atomic Development Authority. International law—superior to any national legislation—should protect men who have given such information."

And, perhaps the heart of the plan, from Teller's standpoint, was embodied in the assertion that "as soon as it becomes effective all secrecy of information must cease."[7]

Teller did not believe that the removal of secrecy would destroy the American advantage in nuclear power. In 1945 the United States enjoyed an atomic monopoly, and even the best-informed leaders expected the advantage to last a long time. As late as 1948—a year before the first Russian nuclear device was detonated—Oppenheimer expressed the prevailing scientific opinion that the Soviet Union would not achieve nuclear weapons "for a long time to come."

Teller's 1945 proposal did not predict when the American monopoly would end, but he did say that "by giving full information to all comers we shall not lose our most essential advantage in atomic power. We shall retain our present installations and we shall retain our experience in production. The latter cannot be given away except by a process of education which is likely to take years. The real 'secrets' are exactly those production procedures which one cannot communicate readily but which must be learned by experience.

"On the other hand," Teller emphasized, "we shall have created an atmosphere of completely free discussion. In such an atmosphere alone it is possible to start with full energy and confidence the joint enterprise of exploiting atomic energy."

Teller's reputation as a realistic man, steeled by direct confrontation with Nazis and communists, was not well known in 1945. Consequently, his proposal may have been accepted as another idealistic fancy by an ivory-tower scientist. In 1945, however, Winston Churchill had not yet coined the term "Iron Curtain," and the Russians had not yet taken full control of the politics of Central Europe. There was still a large reservoir of sympathy in the United States for a valiant and courageous ally that had suffered terrible losses, in lives, lands, and cities, in the struggle against the Nazis. But the conflict of systems was beginning to surface; the Soviet leadership recognized, correctly, that the revolutionary wave had crested again in Hungary and the Balkans, and were prepared to take advantage of it. There was an equal and opposite response from the United States, and many intellectuals and scientists were alarmed as the cold war began to settle into the policies of both superpowers.

It is interesting to speculate on the course of world history if the Russians had taken Teller's ideas seriously. Certainly, if they had been receptive, there were elements in the Pentagon and the State Department that would have protested this "giveaway" of America's hard-won atomic secrets. Teller, had he been better known, might even have been accused of being "soft on communism."

Twenty-eight years later, in 1973, Teller's call for an open society would be sounded again under conditions fraught with coincidence. This time the call would come from Soviet Russia.[8] The author would be the brilliant and now defiantly dissident Soviet physicist Andrei D. Sakharov. Since his leading role in the creation of the Russian H-bomb in the early 1950s, Sakharov had become an outspoken critic of the suppression of political and personal freedom in the Soviet Union. His rebellion probably jeopardized his personal safety, but it won him the 1975 Nobel peace prize. This time, in 1973, his cause would be détente—an attempt to break the U.S.-Russian ice jam after a quarter century of cold war.

Sakharov's arguments for openness[9] are remarkably similar to those advanced in 1945, and repeatedly after that, by Edward Teller. This time, Arthur Schlesinger, defending Sakharov in the *Wall Street Journal* of September 27, 1973, found himself, perhaps unknowingly, on Teller's side when he concluded that "genuine and lasting détente requires a candid and open world."[10] The National Academy of Sciences had also joined the chorus, warning its Soviet counterpart that harassment of Sakharov would have "severe effects" on U.S. and Soviet scientific relations. The academy's cable cautioned the Russians that "were Sakharov to be deprived of his opportunity to serve the Soviet people and humanity, it would be extremely difficult to imagine successful fulfillment of American pledges of bi-national scientific cooperation."[11]

Teller's controversial 1945 position seemed at last to be vindicated in 1973. Simply stated, it warned the Russians that they cannot have it both ways. If there is to be détente, if there is to be real disarmament, then the United States and the Soviets must trust each other, and trust—the freedom from mutual fear—can be achieved only in an open society.

Recalling Teller's viewpoint, however, doesn't completely answer Schlesinger's undocumented charge that the Oppenheimer hearings were part of a political plot hatched by unnamed scientists at the Livermore Laboratory. And there had been comparable attacks from other quarters, notably the charge by Joseph and Stewart Alsop that Lewis L. Strauss, chairman of the Atomic Energy Commission, and a Teller ally, had been an instigator of the charges against Oppenheimer.

Beyond Borden's letter, which unquestionably tripped the mechanism that brought about the hearings, who were the real instigators? More specifically, was Teller one of them? The authors put the question to many of those close to the situation from both the scientific and political communities.

Marvin Goldberger, chairman of the Princeton department of physics and a strong critic of Teller's politics and his conduct at the hearing, nonetheless believes that Teller was not an instigator. Neither does Goldberger's Princeton colleague, physicist John A. Wheeler, though Wheeler is generally more sympathetic to Teller. Joseph Volpe, a lawyer and former Deputy General Counsel to the AEC, and a close friend of Oppenheimer, doesn't believe that Teller, or any scientists, had any part in instigating the hearings. Eugene Wigner, a Nobel Laureate, and professor emeritus of physics at Princeton, who shares many of Teller's political views, agrees with both of his Princeton colleagues, Goldberger and Wheeler.

Only I. I. Rabi, another Nobel prize winner, who is professor emeritus of physics at Columbia, is willing to believe that Teller may have been involved behind the scenes. "It could have been Teller or some other member of his clique," Rabi told us.

If Teller was not responsible, then who was? The prime candidate for this unenviable role, according to the Alsop brothers, was Strauss. Their conclusions were published in *Harper's* of October 1954 in an article entitled "We Accuse." The Alsops agreed that Strauss was not privy to the Borden letter. But "in any case, under the established procedures, the *lettre de cachet* set the whole ponderous security machinery in motion; and Strauss leaped into the driver's seat to make the wheels turn faster." It was Strauss, said the Alsops, "who hastened on the trial of the case."[12]

The Alsops' charges were, at best, exaggerated and, at worst, not true at all. The haste they attribute to Strauss doesn't seem to be supported by the facts of the prehearing procedure. Between December 23, 1953, and March 4, 1954, Oppenheimer's attorney Lloyd K. Garrison, on three occasions requested delays from AEC General Manager Nichols.[13] On each occasion the delays were granted with the concurrence of Strauss.[14] This was hardly the way "to make wheels turn faster."

The Alsops' attack on Strauss brought a quick and detailed response from C. A. Rolander, Jr., deputy director of the division of security of the AEC, in an office memorandum to General Nichols, dated October 25, 1954. Rolander had, in his own words, "spent full time as security representative and assistant counsel in the preparation for the conduct of the personal security clearance case of Dr. J. R. O." from January through June of 1954.

The memorandum continued:

> Recently I read the article, "We Accuse," by Joseph and Stewart Alsop. I am deeply concerned with the liberties taken with facts. I would feel that my obligation to you and the Commission would not be fulfilled were I not to call this to your attention.
>
> I have attached a list of excerpts from the article which appear to be most flagrant. I have also set forth in the attached enclosure what I believe to be "the facts" concerning these matters.[15]

In the fifteen-page rebuttal Rolander responsed to what he considered inaccuracies in the Alsop article. In part it is a defense of Lewis Strauss and in part it attempts to justify the accusations and decisions of the Gray Board.

For example, the Alsop brothers charged:

> On July 7, as Strauss proudly announced in his first press release on the Oppenheimer case, the new chairman "initiated the steps" that were to end with a heavy-handed squad of AEC security officers descending on Princeton to remove the classified documents which Oppenheimer had always been allowed to store in a specially guarded facility in his office.[16]

Rolander's version was quite different:

> Dr. Oppenheimer was notified that his clearance had been suspended on December 23, 1953. On December 24, two security representatives delivered a letter to Dr. Oppenheimer directing him to return all classified documents which had come from the AEC. They discussed with him when it would be convenient to turn over the material and it was agreed that the following Monday, the 28th, would be satisfactory to all concerned. From the 28th to 31st, *one* security man, *one* classification man and Dr. Oppenheimer's part-time assistant (former secretary) inventoried and effected the removal of the documents.[17]

There is still another version of this episode, as told to the authors by one of its principal participants, Bryan F. La Plante. He was chief of security for the Washington headquarters of the AEC. This is his recounting to us of the steps that followed the suspension of Oppenheimer's security clearance on December 23:

> I was asked, as we normally would do, to secure the files. Secure them until such time as arrangements would be made to transfer them back to headquarters. I visited Dr. Oppenheimer at his home in Princeton and told him what we were going to do. He knew why we were coming and what we were coming for. He was courteous and very helpful. We changed the combination on the locks and secured them by bars, until such time as they could arrange to be moved. JRO had said that he had never used them or had gotten into the vault.
>
> After we had completed this task, one evening we went over to Dr.

Oppenheimer's house, at his invitation, and talked with Dr. Oppenheimer and his wife, Kitty. He was perfectly friendly, affable, and very cooperative in every respect. There were no signs of bitterness on his part.

La Plante recalled an unusual side of their conversation:

Oppenheimer's wife Kitty [took] issue with the security people for having been rough on her friends, the Lesbians, at Los Alamos. Dr. Oppenheimer told her to hush up, be quiet, because he was irritated. . . . In those days and, I imagine, still today, the Lesbians and the Homos were considered criteria for security risks, for they were subject to blackmail. She (Kitty) was fighting the whole concept of security and cited these examples of fine people that we were particularly hard on. In her opinion it was a ridiculous thing for us to pick on those people.

Even if the security officers were not a "heavy-handed squad," as the Alsops described them, there is a disturbing insensitivity in the rebuttals of both Rolander and La Plante. Oppenheimer could hardly have defended his files with a shotgun. He was a civilized and intelligent man with little choice but to be "cooperative." He must have been bitter, whether he showed it or not.

William Liscum Borden had sent a copy of his famous November 7 letter not only to J. Edgar Hoover but also to the Joint Committee on Atomic Energy.[18] He had thus hung a serious problem around the neck of the Eisenhower administration. To ignore the Borden charges would be dangerous because, with the letter before the committee, there was the imminent possibility of a leak. If word of the charges were to leak out, the Eisenhower administration could be accused by the Democrats of harboring reds. There was the further danger that Senator McCarthy, still riding high on his personal witch-hunting crusade, might get wind of the Borden letter and use it to embarrass President Eisenhower.

On the other hand, the role of the scientific community could not be ignored. The nation depended on its scientists, and to a majority of them Oppenheimer was a symbol of sacrifice and dedication. The academics detested McCarthy and nursed the hope that Eisenhower would repudiate him and the climate of anti-intellectualism that was spreading across the land. The Republican President had indeed made some feinting gestures toward McCarthy, but the intellectuals were not convinced that Eisenhower had the fortitude to engage in open battle against the Senator from Wisconsin.

Their skepticism was to some extent reinforced by developments within the Republican administration. Ex-President Harry Truman, despite his anti-communist Truman Doctrine and other efforts to shore up the defenses against communism, was charged by Herbert Brownell, Eisenhower's attorney general, with promoting assistant Treasury Secretary Harry Dexter White to an important post after being advised by the FBI that White was a Soviet spy.[19]

In this troubled political climate the upcoming hearings on J. Robert Oppenheimer's security clearance could only be regarded by the liberal community as nothing more than political persecution. To support Oppenheimer, in the liberal view, was to oppose McCarthyism; to oppose Oppenheimer, regardless of motives, was to be written off as pro-McCarthy and an enemy of academic freedom.

It was a Hobson's choice that seemed to present no problems in the mind of President Eisenhower. On December 3, 1953, he ordered a "blank wall"[20] between Dr. Oppenheimer and any secret or top-secret information until a hearing had been completed. This was consistent with the President's earlier behavior. In April 1953 he had issued Executive Order 10450, "Security Requirements for Government Employment." Under the order's harsh new standards, emplyment was no longer a right but a privilege, and mere loyalty was not sufficient. A government employee had to be "reliable, trustworthy and of good conduct and character."

At the time of the Borden accusation Oppenheimer was part way through a one-year consultant contract with the Atomic Energy Commission that was due to expire on June 30, 1954. It was a renewal of an earlier annual contract. Most of his time during this period was spent at Princeton, where he was director of the Institute for Advanced Study. Among the institute's trustees was none other than Lewis L. Strauss and it was Strauss who had nominated Oppenheimer for the post of director.

Late in the afternoon of December 3, 1954, Strauss received an emergency summons from the White House. When he arrived he found a meeting already in progress in the Oval Office. In attendance, surrounding President Eisenhower, were Secretary of De-

fense Charles E. Wilson, Attorney General Brownell, Director of
Defense Mobilization Dr. Arthur S. Flemming, and General Robert Cutler, Special Assistant to the President for National Security
Matters. General Wilton Persons was also there, but did not participate in the conversation.[21]

The President was deeply disturbed about the Borden letter and
questioned Strauss as to whether the AEC, as the responsible
agency, had conducted a hearing on the charges as required by Executive Order 10450. Strauss replied that there had been no hearings since the order was promulgated, but the AEC was engaged
in applying the directive to all employees, and this "would include
contract consultants, such as Dr. Oppenheimer."[22]

At this point President Einsehower ordered Strauss to direct the
Atomic Energy Commission to proceed with the hearing.

How did Strauss react to this order that placed him in the forefront of the Oppenheimer matter? Did he, as Joseph and Stewart
Alsop had charged, "leap into the driver's seat to make the wheels
turn faster"?

Almost exactly twenty years later, on January 21, 1974, Lewis
Strauss died after a painful and prolonged bout with cancer. Four
days later, on a mild Friday afternoon in Washington, a memorial
service was held in the synagogue of the Washington Hebrew Con-
gregation. Among the gathering of family, dignitaries, and associates was an old friend, Edward Teller. After the service the authors, who were also present, drove Teller to Dulles Airport, where
he was to board a plane for Houston.

Teller was more subdued than usual, plainly reflecting on the
end of a long association. Finally he started to talk:

"At this time I think it would be appropriate to talk about Lewis."
He recalled, with sentiment and humor, some of his experiences
with Strauss, then he added this contribution to history:

"Here is a story which, perhaps wrongly, I feel free to tell you
now. I believe that I can now use my own judgment to violate
confidence which I have held for twenty years.

"On a day early in December, 1953, Lewis was just about to
leave for a conference between Eisenhower and the Prime Minister of England in Bermuda.*

---

*The Bermuda meeting was between Eisenhower, Prime Minister Churchill,
and Premier Laniel of France.

"I saw him in his office in Washington. Lewis was in a hurry and he told me: 'I just had a terrible piece of news. Please don't tell it to anyone. The President insists that we should open the case of the clearance of Oppenheimer. I hope there may be a way to avoid this, but I am afraid that we can't avoid it. It is very bad news and please don't tell anybody.'"

Teller's account of Strauss's reaction to the Eisenhower order was corroborated by several people who were close to the late AEC chairman.

General Nichols, AEC general manager under Strauss, told us, "Strauss had no other choice—he had to obey the orders of the President." Manuel Dopkin, who was scientific advisor to Strauss, confirmed the dilemma: "The admiral was a man who always performed his duty. He was a friend of Dr. Oppenheimer. After all, he recommended that Robert Oppenheimer be appointed, after the hearings, at an increase in salary, to the post of director of the Institute for Advanced Study. The whole episode was very painful to Admiral Strauss." Virginia Walker, Strauss's administrative assistant at the time, and an associate to the end of his life, recalled that Strauss was "horrified and deeply disturbed" when he returned from the historic meeting in the Oval Office.

Eisenhower's apparent determination to force confrontation with Dr. Oppenheimer has puzzled many observers, but Teller assessed the situation this way:

"For the President to disregard the Borden letter was not possible. At the same time, I have no access to any information that would tell me why Eisenhower made that decision, though I have a guess—a regret, as well as a connected guess.

"My regret is that Eisenhower did not decide simply not to consult Oppenheimer again—to exclude him from official consultations, but otherwise leave things unchanged.

"I think that indeed it may have been the behavior of a military man to have formal reasons to proceed and not simply to disregard Oppenheimer's opinion and exclude him from the innner circles. Had that been done there would have been less reverberation, nobody would have been hurt, with the possible exception of Oppenheimer being annoyed. People are annoyed when the President no longer consults them."

Teller realized, however, that perhaps the President did not feel he had this option.

"I was told that the president of Caltech [Dr. Lee DuBridge] wrote a letter to Eisenhower and said that we absolutely need Oppenheimer's advice and, in the interest of national security, it is necessary that Oppenheimer should continue to be consulted.

"Being faced with at least one document of this kind—and I'm pretty confident it was not the only one—the President felt that he did not heve the choice to make an informal decision. If he wanted to disregard Oppenheimer's advice, he needed a formal reason, at least this point of view has been suggested to me."

Teller made an unusual comparison between Eisenhower and Oppenheimer:

"It was a conflict between two unyielding people. One had the reputation for a lack of intelligence, the other for the highest intelligence. Yet they made the same mistake. It is generally believed—and I share this belief—that Oppenheimer was extremely intelligent. It is generally believed that Eisenhower was not particularly intelligent. He was an exceedingly nice person. He had many other virtues. High intelligence, however, was not one of them."

Eisenhower's mistake, in Teller's judgment, was insisting that the hearings proceed. Oppenheimer's error was in not accepting the alternative he was offered by Lewis Strauss.

That alternative to a formal hearing was tendered to Dr. Oppenheimer in a large, octagonal room in the Washington AEC headquarters on the afternoon of December 21, 1953. After Oppenheimer arrived, Strauss was joined by General Nichols, general manager of the AEC.

This was the offer: If Robert Oppenheimer would agree to tender his resignation as consultant to the AEC there would no longer by any reason to review his case. He was reminded that under Executive Order 10450 the files of all government employees that contained derogatory information had to be reevaluated, and since he knew that his file contained information in this category, he must realize that in due course his case would be reached.

Eight years later Strauss, in his autobiography, recalled Oppenheimer's dilemma:

> He said there might be some merit in resigning instead of having a hearing and asked me what I thought of the alternative. I felt unable to advise him. A resignation may carry connotations a hearing might dispel. On the spur of the moment it was not possible to be sure which course of action would have been the most prudent, and I am uncertain even now as to which would have been the wiser. Resignation would have left all the charges on the record.[23]

AEC Chairman Strauss took action to proceed with the charges against J. Robert Oppenheimer in compliance with Eisenhower's directive. The action was approved unanimously by other members of the commission. One of the most renowned members of the commission, Princeton physicist H. D. Smyth, was later to be the only commissioner to vote in favor of restoring Oppenheimer's clearance, but at this time he felt it would be unwise to ignore the Borden letter and to continue Oppenheimer's clearance. In a memorandum to Strauss he noted that "Borden's letter of accusation is important not because it brings forward new evidence of any consequence but because of the position he [Borden] has held as head of the staff of the Joint Congressional Committee on Atomic Energy."[24]

The AEC's general counsel, William Mitchell, was given the task of drafting a formal statement of charges against Oppenheimer. When he found himself in some difficulty—he had never handled a security case before—he requested and was granted the assistance of Harold P. Green, another lawyer on the commission staff.

Briefing Green, Mitchell explained that none of the commissioners was happy about proceeding against Oppenheimer. But Eisenhower's directive, coupled with the AEC's security regulations, left them with no other choice. Chairman Strauss, Mitchell reported, was particularly troubled by the case "and sought divine guidance as to the proper course of action."[25]

Mitchell was instructed by the commission not to include the fact that Oppenheimer had opposed the building of the H-bomb in the statement of charges, even though the FBI files supported these allegations. They felt it would be unfair to base a case on what, in essence, could be construed as a reflection of Oppenheimer's political convictions. The fact was that many scientists, including Hans Bethe, I. I. Rabi, and others were openly more critical of President Truman's decision to develop thermonuclear weapons than was Oppenheimer.

Mitchell advised Green on this stricture. But, as Philip Stern reported it, Green, in drafting the charges, did contrast Oppenheimer's original belief in the feasibility of the H-bomb with his later opposition. This, Green felt, was a measure of the scientist's veracity.[26]

The final draft of the charges was delivered to General Nichols, who approved it. Nichols explained, during an interview nearly twenty years later, that since the issue of Oppenheimer's alleged opposition to the H-bomb was included in the Borden letter, the commission had to deal with it.

On the fateful afternoon of December 21, 1953, in Strauss's office, the statement of charges was presented to Oppenheimer. Many of the allegations were old hat. Most of them were known to the AEC when Oppenheimer was cleared in 1947, and Admiral Strauss had been a member of the commission at that time.

Oppenheimer's earlier left-wing associations were certainly frowned on in 1947, but there was a different climate at the height of the cold war period in 1953. General Groves, who had cleared Oppenheimer—with some trepidation—in 1943, testified at the hearing that, under the requirements in 1953 of the Atomic Energy Act, "I would not clear Dr. Oppenheimer today if I were a member of the commission. . . ."[27]

Actually, of the twenty-four allegations in the statement of charges, twenty-three were a rehash of information available to the AEC in 1947. It was true, however, as the hearing board later commented, "Indeed, this is the only time that all of the available evidence regarding Dr. Oppenheimer has been correlated and presented in a package."[28]

There were some strange aspects of Oppenheimer's behavior even after all the suspicion and confusion dating back to 1943. For one thing, his friendship with Haakon Chevalier continued. He had been warned when Kenneth Nichols signed his 1943 security clearance that he must discontinue his left-wing associations. General Nichols told us he was greatly disturbed when Oppenheimer ignored the warning. After the war it was Admiral Strauss who, hoping to offer some friendly advice, repeated the same warning. But Virginia Walker, Strauss's executive assistant, recalled that "He [Oppenheimer] thought he was God and was not bound by security rules."

Now, on December 21, 1953, the period of forbearance was over. Oppenheimer knew the charges and he was given twenty-four hours to respond. A shaken Oppenheimer left Strauss and Nichols and went immediately to the office of Joseph Volpe, former general counsel to the AEC and a friend of Oppenheimer's from the Los Alamos days. Oppenheimer and Volpe, meeting at Volpe's office at 1700 K Street, were joined by another lawyer friend, Herbert Marks.[29]

They discussed how Oppenheimer should proceed but their

conversation, Volpe insisted to us, was bugged and taped. He based his charge on the fact that the AEC seemed to learn what transpired at the meeting. General Nichols vehemently denied the charge when we discussed it with him and, as general manager of the AEC, he was in a position to know. He doubted that any other agency, such as the FBI, might have bugged the meeting although he was not certain. He did insist, however, that the AEC was not aware of the conversation between Oppenheimer and the attorneys, Volpe and Marks.*

AEC Security Chief La Plante supported Nichols's denial. "This was peacetime," he told us, "and we did not go around bugging phones, surreptitiously listening to conversations; Joe is imagining things. If such a recording was made and if we had received it, it would be in the files and I would know it. There was nothing of that nature in the files."

Bugged or not, Oppenheimer had to make a decision—resign and lose his security clearance, or face his accusers. All during the next day Oppenheimer, his wife, Kitty, Volpe, and Marks considered the options. To resign would have left the charges standing, and this could be considered an admission of guilt. There was a new danger in a report that a Senate committee, headed by an extreme reactionary, Senator Edward Jenner, was now probing into Oppenheimer's past. The accusations were leaking out; it would be impossible to keep them from the public much longer.

A decision was reached. Oppenheimer would not resign. He would ask for a hearing on the charges.

It was a decision that was destined to change not only the life of J. Robert Oppenheimer, but also the life of Edward Teller. Two decades later an angry Teller spoke to us, bitterly, of Oppenheimer: "He wanted to be a martyr; he could have simply resigned."

Inasmuch as it was President Dwight Eisenhower who insisted on forcing the issue with Oppenheimer, it is interesting to learn more precisely what the President was thinking about the Soviets at that time. Eisenhower had just returned from the Bermuda conference with Churchill and Laniel. Lord Moran, the aging

---

*An Associate Press dispatch of December 29, 1975, provided evidence supporting Volpe's charge that his conversations with Oppenheimer were bugged. The AP quoted Harold P. Green, the AEC attorney who drew up the formal charges against the agency's top scientist, as saying the FBI bugged Oppenheimer's conversations with his attorneys throughout the investigation.

Churchill's personal physician, reported some revealing conversations with his patient, recorded on December 3.

> MORAN: But does Russia want war?
>
> CHURCHILL: I believe it is not in her interest to make war. When I meet Malenkov we can build for peace.
>
> MORAN: Then who is making difficulties?
>
> CHURCHILL: Ike. He doesn't think any good can come from talks with the Russians. But it will pay him to come along with us. I shall do what I can to persuade him. I might stay longer here than I meant, at any rate if I could persuade Ike to stay, too. He is the key man in this business.

Then there was this entry on December 5:

> The P.M. is less sure about things today. It appears that when he pleaded with Ike that Russia was changed, Ike spoke of her as a whore, who might have changed her dress, but who should be chased from the streets. Russia, according to Ike, was out to destroy the civilized world.
>
> "Of course," said the P.M., pacing up and down the room, "anyone could say the Russians are evil minded and mean to destroy the free countries. Well, if we really feel like that, perhaps we ought to take action before they get as many atomic bombs as America has. I made that point to Ike, who said, perhaps logically, that it ought to be considered. But if one did not believe that such a large fraction of the world was evil, it could do no harm to try and be friendly as long as we did not relax our defense preparations."
>
> I asked him how Ike had managed to retreat from his attitude toward Russia.
>
> "Oh, he hasn't," the P.M. put in. "But when we came out of the meeting he said there was a lot in what I said. Most people, when beaten in argument, become sulky. Ike is so selfless."[30]

It was clear that before and at least during the Los Alamos period Oppenheimer was sympathetic to causes espoused by the communists. The question was whether subsequently his ventures out into the world of politics had broadened him so that his reddish tinge had begun to fade. His postwar statements, particularly in December 1945 before the Senate Special Committee on Atomic Energy, and his later writing indicate a growing distrust of the Russians, sometimes remarkably like the views of Eisenhower.

Here are some excerpts from the testimony:

SENATOR BYRD (VIRGINIA): Are you going to use the bombs to bomb that nation out of existence, if we have any on hand, because they have broken the agreement and used the materials which they were allowed to use for the making of peacetime energy by converting that into a bomb? What would you do about it?

DR. OPPENHEIMER: If this situation arose, and it is clear from what I have said that I don't think it needs to arise, *I would use military measures of all kinds against the offending country.* [italics supplied][31]

Oppenheimer also equated the potential Russian threat with that of the Axis in the 1930s:

SENATOR MILLIKIN: If any important nation refuses full and free inspection, then all inspection would be useless, would it not?

DR. OPPENHEIMER: I think that if one important nation refuses, it would be a source of great concern about that nation. I think one would still wish to know and be glad to know what was going on in the rest of the world.

My view of it is this: One of the things which we now realize is that in the 1930s there was a growing and very visible threat of world war in the policies of the Axis nations, and that we in America were both inadequately informed and inadequately convinced by such information as was available that this threat was real.

I think there is no doubt that in the early thirties the military problem presented by the strength of the Axis was not a serious problem. It got to be serious only after many years of armament.

What I think we need is an indication that a threat of war begins to exist, and if you had a group of nations agreeing to atomic inspection and cooperation, of which one or two suddenly started to make barriers or started to two-time so that you were convinced that the information you were getting was unsound, this, I believe, would be a danger signal and would call for the declaration of an actual emergency.

SENATOR MILLIKIN: Let me put it this way, then: If one important nation refused the right of complete inspection, then the other nations would not be warranted in demobilizing, as far as atomic bombs are concerned?

DR. OPPENHEIMER: I would think it would be a very serious mistake to allow any nation to fail to cooperate in this point, if we had the power to prevent that.[32]

SENATOR MILLIKIN: When you speak about effective military defense I assume you are speaking in the passive sense. Military defense often

consists of aggression, of moving first, and I assume that you pre-
clude moving first—that you exclude moving first—from that proposition?

DR. OPPENHEIMER: The history of the American people shows that we
do not do that, and I am very proud that this is the case; but I think it
is one of the facts of life which must be taken into account in planning our future.

SENATOR HART: That is what is meant by "preventive war," in which
America has never participated?

DR. OPPENHEIMER: Well, we have after considerable persuasion.[33]

SENATOR BYRD: You speak of inspection. Suppose that government A
had an agreement they would not make any atom bombs. Suppose
we discovered government A breaking that agreement. What would
you do? Would you use bombs we had here to destroy the other nation by bombs, or what would you do about it?

DR. OPPENHEIMER: I don't know what the word "sanctions" means,
but I believe there is such a word and that it means any measures
which are necessary in order to cause that power to desist.[34]

On the afternoon of February 17, 1953, there was a meeting of
the Council of Foreign Relations. Oppenheimer had participated
in the work of its Soviet Study Panel. The panel's chairman, John
J. McCloy, later reported:

He was very concerned about the security position of the United
States. He pressed vigorously for not letting down our guard—. If
there was to be any negotiation, be certain that we were armed and
well prepared before we went to such a conference. Indeed, I have
the impression that he with one or two others, was somewhat, shall I
say, more militant than some of the other members of the group.[35]

Oppenheimer revealed his growing disillusionment with the Soviets in other remarks and writings. When the Baruch plan for the
internationalization of atomic controls failed, Oppenheimer commented that "openness, friendliness and cooperation did not seem
to be what the Soviet Union most prized on this earth." He saw no
early prospect of reviving proposals for nuclear cooperation because of the "peculiar obstacles presented by the programmatic
hostility and institutionalized secretiveness of communist countries." These views were remarkably similar to those expressed before and subsequently by Edward Teller.

To Oppenheimer, by 1953, the hope of agreement with the Soviets struck him as "irrelevant and grotesque; an acceptable, hopeful, honorable and humane agreement"[36] seemed beyond reach.

The question is, are Oppenheimer's political values to be judged by what he said or what he did? It was possible, Teller told us, that Oppenheimer's anti-Soviet public statements were uttered for the purpose of diverting suspicion from his earlier left-wing past. He knew that he was under constant surveillance. His serious writings, however, tended to support the belief that he had become thoroughly and sincerely disillusioned with Stalinist communism.

Teller, however, was becoming increasingly uncertain of Oppenheimer's motives.

"I did not understand him," Teller told us, "and since I did not understand Oppenheimer, I could not trust his judgment. All I know is that he was in favor of dropping the A-bomb, and then after the war he was in favor of dismantling Los Alamos. In the earlier years he was in favor of thermonuclear research. Then he opposed the building of the H-bomb. After it was built he suggested using it to end the Korean War." (Here Teller was reconfirming his belief that, at that famous lunch in Princeton in November 1952, Oppenheimer had seriously proposed using a hydrogen bomb in the Korean War.)

"He was a complex man, and I do not pretend that I understand him,"[37] said Teller, and he meant it.

These seeming contradictions would be probed and dark motives behind them would be alleged in the "trial" soon to follow.

The AEC decided that a three-man board would hear the charges. Oppenheimer's reputation demanded that his peers be of equal eminence. The chairman was to be Gordon Gray, the forty-five-year-old president of the University of North Carolina. Gray, a Democrat, was an Assistant Secretary of the Army in 1947, when Eisenhower was Chief of Staff.

The second member of what became known as the Gray Board was a sixty-six-year-old former North Carolinian, Thomas Alfred Morgan. Whereas Gray had been born into a wealthy family (his father was president of the R. J. Reynolds Tobacco Company), Morgan's father was a poor tobacco farmer. However, by an unusual set of circumstances and talent he acquired financial and social prominence and was by 1954 the retired board chairman of the Sperry Corporation.

A chemistry professor from Northwestern University was the third member of the board. Ward V. Evans was a staunch Republican, political conservative, and an explosives expert. At least the board included one scientist.

These were the men by whom J. Robert Oppenheimer would be judged. The full commission would then be charged with concurring or rejecting the board's "findings."

Roger Robb, assisted by Arthur Rolander, was to present the commission's case. Robb, a native Washingtonian, was known as a tough and successful prosecutor. As an attorney his clients spanned the political spectrum from Fulton Lewis, Jr., to Earl Browder. He was recommended for the assignment by the then Deputy Attorney General William P. Rodgers.

While the AEC was preparing its case, Oppenheimer, Volpe, and Marks were seeking legal talent. Both Joseph Volpe and Herman Marks felt that their former association with the AEC was a deterrent to the adequate representation of their friend Oppenheimer. Finally, after much debate, the mantle was placed upon the shoulders of a prominent New York lawyer, Lloyd K. Garrison. The mild-mannered attorney was a member of the board of trustees of the Institute for Advanced Study and of course was known to Oppenheimer. Unfortunately, for Oppenheimer, his attorney's reputation for integrity and erudition was not matched by experience in courtroom dog fighting.

Other lawyers had been considered. It was not easy to find, in the mid-fifties, the right attorney. Either they were tainted by having represented political subversives or they were clean and wanted to stay uninvolved in what promised to be a controversial case.

Joseph Volpe had argued for the retaining of a tough courtroom infighter, a battler who would enjoy slugging it out with Robb. It may be that before the hearings were over, Oppenheimer regretted not heeding Volpe's advice. Garrison's innate decency was hardpressed to match the opposition of a government reflecting the national hysteria over subversion. The scientific community may have been outraged by the treatment of Oppenheimer, but the people of America were not.

16

The Witness

THE proceedings *In the Matter of J. Robert Oppenheimer* before the Personnel Security Board of the AEC began at ten o'clock on the morning of April 12, 1954, under the chairmanship of Gordon Gray. Before the hearing had run its course and reached its climax on May 6, word of Oppenheimer's plight had reached the scientific community. The vast majority rallied to Oppenheimer's defense.

Until June 16, however, the outside world knew little of what had happened behind the closed doors of the Gray Board hearing room. On that date the AEC issued, for release at noon, the following statement:

> The Atomic Energy Commission is making public the attached transcript of the unclassified testimony presented to the Personnel Security Board in the Matter of J. Robert Oppenheimer. This release is made in advance of the time—later this month—when the commission will reach its decision.
>
> The wide national interest and concern in the matter make inevitable and desirable close public examination of the final determination.*
>
> AEC security clearance proceedings are conducted in privacy. The commission's personnel security regulations provide for closed hearings. The commission protects the privacy of the individuals concerned in such hearings if they so desire. In this instance, privacy was maintained for the hearings before the Board. However, Dr. Oppenheimer's attorneys, as was their privilege, have issued texts of some documents. In the present circumstances, release of the tran-

---

*This was not entirely the reason for the public release of the censored transcript. On June 11, AEC Commissioner Eugene Zuckert accidentally left his copy of the full transcript on a train. Fearing discovery, the AEC rushed the cleared version to press and released it. Ironically, Zuckert's copy was found, apparently unread, in the Boston lost-and-found office of the New Haven Railroad.

script, within the limits of security, will, in the opinion of the Commission, best serve the public interest.

When the text of the hearing was released, Edward Teller's testimony was exposed. A majority in the scientific community, already angry over what seemed to be political persecution of Oppenheimer, focused its anger on Teller. Whether Teller, or other scientists critical of Oppenheimer, were speaking from honest conviction did not matter. What mattered was that Oppenheimer was a symbol of the dedication, sacrifice, and intellectual freedom of so many scientists. Too many scientists—and ordinary citizens as well—were being cut down by the sickle of the "security" system. Teller was the most powerful and influential of the small minority of scientists who were willing to challenge Oppenheimer's influence on the national defense. Most of the scientists were aware that Oppenheimer was Teller's principal adversary in the latter's quest for support in the hydrogen bomb proposal. Some saw vindictiveness in Teller's testimony. Teller, therefore, was the villain.

The excitement over the case began even before the hearing when the New York *Times* published the charges and a statement by Oppenheimer. Shortly before the hearing the accused scientist and his attorney, Lloyd K. Garrison, met with *Times* reporter James Reston. "Dr. Oppenheimer," Reston wrote, "made the statement of charges and his reply available to The Times so that a record of the case could be written from actual documents."

When the *Times* story broke the next morning, University of Chicago physicist Marvin L. Goldberger was at Cornell as the guest of Hans Bethe. At four o'clock that afternoon "Murph" Goldberger was to participate in a seminar. He read the story and relayed the news to Bethe, who was stunned and angry. The seminar met as scheduled, but the physicists never got around to talking about physics; the only topic was the fate of J. Robert Oppenheimer. Goldberger recalls that the reaction at Cornell was typical—"the scientific community was filled with outrage and horror." He was thinking of Oppenheimer's contributions: The man who led the Los Alamos team was a lot more than that. He was, in a sense, the father of theoretical physics in the United States. He had done his utmost to bring about control of nuclear weapons. He was the author of the so-called Baruch proposal to put the control of nuclear energy under an international authority. He had continued his public service after the war by serving as chairman of the powerful General Advisory Committee of the AEC.

At Los Alamos, the huge scientific establishment conceived by Oppenheimer, the reaction was equally bitter. Physicist Marshall Rosenbluth, then working at Los Alamos, was president of the Federation of Atomic Scientists. He was one of the leaders in a campaign to collect signatures for a petition protesting the Oppenheimer hearings. His role had an added complexity because Rosenbluth was a former student and a friend of Teller. A Harvard graduate, he went to the University of Chicago in 1946 for postgraduate studies in physics. Teller was his thesis supervisor. At Teller's suggestion the young Rosenbluth spent his summers studying and working at Los Alamos. After he had received his doctorate, he joined the permanent staff at the atomic laboratory, serving there from 1950 to 1956. (He is now on the staff of the Institute for Advanced Study at Princeton.)

Despite the petition campaign on Oppenheimer's behalf, Rosenbluth didn't lose Teller's friendship.

"One thing, I think, one should say strongly in Teller's defense," Rosenbluth told the authors, "was that even though I disagreed with him on politics from the beginning, he was always a person with which one could still have personal friendship in spite of such disagreements. He has strong opinions, but he certainly respects the rights of other people to have other opinions."

In the course of the Gray Board hearing forty witnesses testified. The giants among the scientists included Hans Bethe, Enrico Fermi, Isadore Isaac Rabi, John von Neumann, and Teller. Rosenbluth strongly urged Teller not to testify—"but he felt, of course, that he had to. There was no way he could get out of it."

Oppenheimer's interrogators from Los Alamos, security officers John Lansdale, Jr., and Boris T. Pash, were also called as witnesses. Leslie R. Groves, Oppenheimer's old boss and protector from the war years, was asked to testify and did so.

Just as significant, however, were the names of those who did not testify. One of the key questions in the proceedings was whether Oppenheimer had lied when he denied his previous membership in the Communist party. This was one of the allegations in the statement of charges signed by Colonel K. D. Nichols notifying Oppenheimer of the suspension of his security clearance. There were seven key people who might have provided the answer, but they were never called to testify, hence the question of Oppenheimer's past membership in the Communist party was left hanging.

The paragraph in the Nichols charges relating to the Communist party membership was as follows:

> During the period 1942-45 various officials of the Communist Party, including Dr. Hannah Peters, organizer of the professional section of the Communist Party, Alameda County, California, Bernadette Doyle, secretary of the Alameda County Communist Party, Steve Nelson, David Adelson, Paul Pinsky, Jack Manley and Katrina Sandow, are reported to have made statements indicating that you were then a member of the Communist Party; that you could not be active in the party at that time; that your name should be removed from the party mailing list and not mentioned in any way; that you had talked the atomic-bomb question over with party members during this period; and that several years prior to 1945 you had told Steve Nelson that the Army was working on an atomic bomb.

Surprisingly, none of these seven individuals who were alleged to have fingered Dr. Oppenheimer as a Communist party member appears on the list of witnesses. The "defendant" was never given the opportunity to be confronted by his accusers. The question has subsequently been raised as to why Roger Robb, counsel for the Gray Board, did not produce the alleged accusers, or why Lloyd K. Garrison, Oppenheimer's attorney, did not challenge Robb on this issue. If Robb was convinced the allegations were true, why did he not subpoena the alleged informants?

In Robb's case, the question was answered in the course of an interview with him (he is now a federal appeals judge) in his chambers in Washington on April 4, 1974. His first response to our query about the failure to subpoena the seven persons mentioned was "I suspect that all of them probably would have refused to testify; I don't know. As far as I was concerned, what any of them said about Dr. Oppenheimer would not have meant too much."

We asked Judge Robb why, if the alleged informants were unreliable witnesses, did Nichols include their reported allegations in the statement of charges.

"Nichols's letter," Robb responded, "had stated that the informants had looked upon Oppenheimer as a member of the Communist party. These were only their spontaneous utterances. It is quite different from calling them up as witnesses and putting them under oath. In any event, I never considered calling any of them to testify. I did, however, send out an inquiry, a lead, to see if we could get a statement from George Eltenton. He flatly refused to talk to the FBI."

Haakon Chevalier, the friend from the famous kitchen conversation, had made a statement to the FBI that was in the file. But, as Robb recalls it, Chevalier was in France as preparations for the hearing got under way, and refused to make any more statements.

There was a similar impasse in regard to highly damaging statements by Paul Crouch, a former active member of the Communist party. The Nichols statement carried the charge by Crouch and his wife, Sylvia, that Oppenheimer hosted a closed meeting of a Communist party group in July 1941 at his Berkeley home.

If this charge were true, why didn't Robb nail Oppenheimer with Crouch's testimony? Robb explains it this way: "I did not interview Crouch. I did not call him because testimony concerning that episode that he would have testified about was pretty much in balance. He told the FBI that he thought he could identify the house. He described the living room where the meeting had taken place. The Bureau took Crouch into the living room after he had identified the house. He said, 'I'm sure that this is the house but the living room has changed since I was here.' Crouch had drawn the FBI a diagram of the living room. The FBI checked up and found the living room had been changed since the date of the meeting described. As it was . . . it fitted precisely Crouch's description [except that] a divider had been put in the living room since then.

"There was every reason to believe Crouch was telling the truth about that meeting. On the other hand, Oppenheimer produced witnesses who stated that he had been in New Mexico at that time. So there you were. You had Crouch's word against Oppenheimer's word and the alibi witnesses.

"It seemed to me that if Crouch had testified the evidence would have been evenly balanced. Furthermore, I knew that if the board found against Oppenheimer the findings would be attacked. And if that happened, I did not want to have the findings vulnerable to the charge that they found against Oppenheimer on the basis of the testimony of the 'disreputable' Paul Crouch. I am not saying that he was disreputable, but that is what would be said. That is why I did not call him in."

These then were Robb's reasons for not facing Dr. Oppenheimer with a select group of his alleged accusers. In the case of

Crouch, Robb was certainly aware of his questionable reputation for flights of fancy in dealing with important people, his court-martial and sentence as an Army enlistee for attempting to foment revolution in a Hawaii garrison, his trip to Russia, where, by his own account, he was advised of Soviet plans to penetrate the American armed forces, his about-face to a career as a U.S. government witness testifying against alleged communists, and the numerous examples of inconsistency in his testimony.

If Robb was unwilling, why didn't Oppenheimer's counsel, Garrison, call the accusers to the stand? The answer, of course, is that Garrison was in a box. He didn't know how damaging or how conclusive was the evidence of the informers. He dared not take the risk of calling on them to testify.

In the federal courts, under the so-called Jencks Act, the defendant is entitled to have, at the time a witness takes the stand, any prior witness statements he may have made, either before a grand jury, an investigating officer, or a prosecutor. This, of course, facilitates the opportunity of the defendant's counsel for cross-examination. There is, however, no requirement that a list of witnesses be furnished to the defense prior to the trial.

The difference in the Oppenheimer case was that it was not a trial but an administrative hearing or, as Garrison expressed it, "The purpose of this inquiry, which is not a trial, is to arrive at the truth as nearly as the truth can be arrived at."

So Oppenheimer's counsel was not entitled to prior disclosure of witness statements. Further, Garrison, in defending his client, was not entitled to review classified papers. Robb had received an "Emergency Q" security clearance for the hearing after only eight days of investigation. Garrison, after hemming and hawing, finally requested clearance in a letter to K. D. Nichols dated March 26, 1954, less than three weeks before the hearing began. The processing of his application was not yet completed before the hearing ended.

As the first day's testimony drew to a close, Gordon Gray requested a list of the witnesses Garrison intended to call in Oppenheimer's defense. Garrison immediately complied without discussion or argument. He might have been in a stronger tactical position if he had insisted that Robb release his witness list at the same time. In keeping with Garrison's posture of restraint and respectability in his defense of his client, he made no such demand on Robb—possibly to his later regret.

Not until the morning of April 20 did Garrison make his request to Gray for the board's witnesses. "Could you inform us as to who they will be?" Garrison asked, politely. Gray's inconclusive response was, "Yes, we can give you an indication. The board has not come to any final conclusion." Gray then explained that the decision as to whom they would call depended on Garrison's list. He had added a few names to his originally submitted list.

At one P.M. the next day Garrison again raised the question about the board's witnesses, again with great deference to the chairman. Gray avoided an answer: "I'm afraid that we will have to talk about that some at lunch, because I don't have anything new at the moment."

More and more the counsel for J. Robert Oppenheimer was flying blind. Without a chart, with even a simple mercator projection, it was impossible to lay out a course that would avoid the obstacles and traps that the wily Robb was constantly strewing in his path. An example of this was when no less than a former chairman of the AEC, testifying on behalf of Oppenheimer, stumbled very close to perjury.

By April 23 Garrison still did not know the identity of witnesses that would be called to testify against the interests of his client. Even a man as gentle as Garrison was, or appeared to be, could no longer shrink from a painful confrontation. He pleaded, "Mr. Chairman, I was informed by you yesterday afternoon that some witnesses would be called this coming week by the board. I had assumed from prior discussions that we would be informed of the names of these witnesses, but whether or not that assumption was correct, I asked you at the close of this session yesterday for the names of the respective witnesses in order that we might have time to prepare for cross-examination, if cross-examination seemed to be indicated with respect to one or more of them."

This plea for equity was not as completely innocent as it sounded. Garrison had a pretty good idea of the names of at least some of the witnesses to be called by the board, specifically those who represented Oppenheimer's scientific associates.

Before the hearing Robb and Arthur Rolander, the AEC's deputy security chief, had gone to Berkeley to interview Teller, Dr. Luis Walter Alvarez, Dr. Wendell M. Latimer, and Dr. Ernest Lawrence. Despite the secrecy surrounding the interviews, the word quickly spread around Berkeley and in fact throughout much of the American scientific community. As one Berkeley scientist put it, "What was said on the fifth floor reached the first floor in five minutes."

Robb had this recollection of his interview with Teller:

"I went out to see him. I remember that he came in from Livermore. We were waiting for him in his office in Berkeley. There was a green blackboard in the room, the kind all scientists seem to have. Finally, the door opened and Dr. Teller came in. He walked over to the blackboard and began to write something. I thought well, this is fine, no doubt he has thought of some extraordinary formula on his way in from Livermore and he is just putting it down on the board, and I will be here at the birth of a great idea.

"Then he stepped back and pointed to what he had written: 'I have just had a tooth out. Cannot talk, but you can ask questions.'"

As it turned out, however, Teller could talk a little and touched on what, years later, was to evolve as a bizarre story in the Oppenheimer saga.

Teller related a meeting with Oppenheimer when the latter was asked to join the atom bomb project at Los Alamos. As Robb recalls it, Oppenheimer told Teller, "'Well, you know, Edward, I had a few left-wing connections in my younger days.' Teller's response was routine: 'Well, if that is all there is to it, I wouldn't let it deter me at all.'"

Twenty years later, Teller had an entirely different recollection in recalling the incident for the authors. It went like this:

"One day, prior to Los Alamos, Oppenheimer and I were walking along the shores of Lake Michigan. Oppenheimer, without provocation, brought up his security problems.

"At that time we were on very good terms. I hadn't heard about that [his security problems] before—this was in the summer of 1942. Then he continued—'I have security problems because my wife has a cousin who is an officer in the Wehrmacht.'"

Teller was puzzled: "I thought, at that time, that it was a little peculiar that Oppenheimer would say that to me. I, of course, believed him. What he told me was probably true. But while it was true, it was also misleading."

This was another example where Teller, in his personal experience, found Oppenheimer's behavior puzzling and unpredictable. Inevitably these experiences must have accumulated into the kind of assessment of Oppenheimer that Teller ultimately formed in their climactic confrontation.

The authors confronted Robb with this entirely different version of Oppenheimer's security problems as related by Teller. Robb's recollection was that Teller told him Oppenheimer had worried about left-wing connections. Teller's story, related in 1974, was that Oppenheimer was worried, or appeared to be worried, about an in-law in the German Wehrmacht.

Robb seemed inclined to accept Teller's later version. The contradiction he analyzed this way: "Dr. Teller told me that Oppenheimer had some bad security connections, or something like that, and I just assumed this meant left-wing connections. Perhaps that is the explanation—I don't know."

Garrison continued his quest for the list of witnesses, but Robb's position was hardening. "Mr. Chairman," said the board's counsel, "unless ordered to do so by the board, we shall not disclose to Mr. Garrison in advance the names of the witnesses we contemplate calling."

Robb's refusal was not entirely unreasonable. He was concerned that disclosure of the witnesses would not be held in confidence, and he could point to the earlier leaking of information by Oppenheimer and Garrison to James Reston of the New York *Times.*

Robb tried to be tactful. "I think, furthermore, and I will be frank about it, that in the event any witnesses from the scientific world should be called, they would be subject to pressure. They would be told within twenty-four hours by some friends or colleagues what they should or should not say. I say, specifically and emphatically, I am not suggesting that this would be done by Dr. Oppenheimer, his counsel or anyone representing him. But I think the record abundantly shows here the intense feeling which this matter has generated in the scientific world. I think it perfectly reasonable to believe that should there appear here today that scientist Y was to testify, inside of twenty-four hours that man would be subject to all sorts of pressure."

Regardless as to whether Robb was being completely sincere, both sides had exerted varying degrees of pressure on both government officials and prospective witnesses.

The great Niels Bohr was among Oppenheimer's champions. Bohr protested about Oppenheimer's plight to Lewis Strauss, an incident which Strauss later recounted to Teller. As Teller remembers it, "Of course Lewis respected Niels Bohr very highly. Bohr said to Strauss, 'Now, Admiral Strauss, you may be right on a strictly legal basis. But in the case of such a remarkable person as Oppenheimer the strict legal considerations should not be applied; it is not proper to apply them in their literal sense.'"

Strauss, as Teller assessed him, was indignant. "Lewis was concerned that Niels Bohr should have advocated a different application of law to different people, and had apparently forgotten the basic issue, that the law sees no difference between various people. Incidentally, I am quite sure that he pointed that out also to Bohr. On this point, Lewis would not yield an inch."

I. I. Rabi also made a personal protest to Strauss. He told the AEC chairman of his "very grave misgivings as to the nature of the charge and the general public discussion which it has aroused, and the fear that as a result of such a discussion important security information absolutely vital to the United States may, bit by bit, inadvertently leak out."

One of the most crowded and dramatic days of the hearing was April 20. The procession of witnesses, mainly defenders of Oppenheimer, was a pantheon of scientific and governmental figures. Waiting to be called were Sumner Pike, one of the original AEC commissioners; Enrico Fermi, who remained one of the world's revered physicists; Jerrold R. Zacharias, director of the M.I.T. laboratory of nuclear science; Norman Ramsey of the Air Force Science Advisory Committee; James B. Conant, High Commissioner to Germany and former president of Harvard; George F. Kennan, one of the architects of postwar foreign policy; and David E. Lilienthal, first chairman of the AEC.

Kennan was Garrison's first witness. He was the anonymous author, the so-called "Mr. X" who wrote "Sources of Soviet Conduct," an article that appeared early in 1947 in *Foreign Affairs.* Since the article was critical of the Soviets, his anti-communist credentials were firmly established. His contacts with Oppenheimer were mainly during the physicist's chairmanship of the General Advisory Committee of the AEC. Herbert Marks, Oppenheimer's co-counsel, asked the crucial question of the witness: "What convictions, if any, did you form about him [Oppenheimer]?"

Kennan's reply was positive: "I formed the conviction that he was an immensely useful person in the councils of our government, and I felt a great sense of gratitude that we had his help. I am able to say that in the course of all these contacts and deliberations within the government I never observed anything in his conduct or his words that could possibly, it seemed to me, have indicated that he was animated by any other motives than a devotion to the interests of this country."

Later, Marks tried to draw more pro-Oppenheimer substance from Kennan by referring to the famous incident in 1943 when Oppenheimer apparently failed to report an effort by the Russians to secure information. Kennan again defended the accused. "I would also be inclined to bear in mind," he stated, "the fact that in 1943 the Soviet Union was hardly regarded by our top people in our government as an enemy; that great masses of American materials were being prepared for shipment to the Soviet Union, many of them, I assume, involving the transmission of official secrets."

The defense of Oppenheimer by so distinguished a scholar as Kennan seemed to expose the painfulness of the hearings to members of the Gray Board. Dr. Evans pleaded with Kennan, almost gratuitously, to appreciate the board's difficult position. "We all know Dr. Oppenheimer's ability," he told Kennan. "Nobody knows better than I do. This act mentions certain things—character associations and loyalty. It doesn't say in there anything about the outstanding ability which is mentioned here so much. You understand that point, don't you?"

Roger Robb couldn't do much to discredit the testimony of Kennan, but he was much more successful with Lilienthal. By the time the AEC's first chairman had left the stand, he was shaken, weary, and battered.

Oppenheimer's lawyers had counted on Lilienthal to be one of the best spokesmen for their client. His credibility and his credentials were the highest. He was a Harvard Law School graduate, one of the original directors of the Tennessee Valley Authority and its chairman from 1941 to 1946. In 1946 he became the first chairman of the Atomic Energy Commission. With Oppenheimer's input, Lilienthal and Dean Acheson drafted the so-called Acheson-Lilienthal report which became the basis for the Baruch plan for the international control of atomic energy. He was also Oppenheimer's friend, and he came to the hearing prepared to defend him.

Samuel J. Silverman, a member of the team of defense lawyers, carefully led Lilienthal through a recital of his government career and his relations with Oppenheimer. Robb observed Silverman's procedure with extra care because Robb regarded this defense lawyer as a particularly tough and effective adversary.

The circumstances of Oppenheimer's 1947 security clearance

were carefully examined. Under the grandfather clause in the Atomic Energy Act, persons already cleared under Manhattan District retained their clearance. On a continuing basis, however, the FBI was charged with the responsibility for reexamining and updating individual security files. If there was any new information that might change the picture the AEC had the obligation to decide whether to retain or remove clearance. In this process many cases were being reviewed.

On March 8, 1947, J. Edgar Hoover had delivered to Chairman Lilienthal the updated file on J. Robert Oppenheimer. On March 10, Lilienthal called together the AEC members—Dr. Robert F. Bacher, Sumner T. Pike, Lewis L. Strauss, and Wesley W. Waymack. Each was asked to review the file.

Their immediate reaction—or it may have been primarily his own—was expressed by Lilienthal in his testimony: "One of the first things that was observed was that although this file did contain derogatory information going back a number of years, it did not contain any reference, as far as I recall, or at least any significant reference to the work that Dr. Oppenheimer had done as a public servant."

By coincidence, just four days after that March 10, 1947, AEC meeting, Oppenheimer received the Medal of Merit from President Truman "in recognition of his outstanding public service."

Continuing his testimony, Lilienthal implied that the FBI report wasn't considered too alarming. It lacked balance. Still, as prudent men, he believed it was their duty to travel the last mile in evaluating Dr. Oppenheimer's loyalty. Dr. Vannevar Bush and Dr. James B. Conant were both in Washington at that time. The AEC invited them to come over to commission headquarters and inspect the file.

The support for Oppenheimer—in 1947—was nearly solid, according to Lilienthal in 1954. Bush and Conant expressed confidence in written memoranda. Secretary of War Robert P. Patterson, at the request of the commissioners, backed up Bush and Conant. So did General Groves in a written statement for Patterson, although Groves did urge that the commission "exercise its own independent judgment based on present circumstances."

Even President Truman was brought in. The General Advisory Committee to the AEC, chaired by Oppenheimer, was appointed not by the AEC but by the President. To further substantiate their judgment, Lilienthal and Bush called on Truman's counsel, Clark

Clifford, so that Clifford could make the President aware of the material in Oppenheimer's file. Lilienthal, recounting all of this seven years later, testified that "the President was advised and the President didn't express any views about what should be done. He did not express the view that the clearance should be cancelled or that he should remove Dr. Oppenheimer or anything of that kind."

Up to this point Lilienthal was calm and unruffled. His testimony was almost routine. Unfortunately for the former AEC chairman, Roger Robb was about to test the legal dictum that "cross-examination is the best known way to arrive at the truth."

At 12:30 P.M. the hearings recessed for lunch. At 2 P.M. they resumed and Lilienthal was given a rest while two other witnesses took the stand. Both were sympathetic to Oppenheimer. Dr. Conant, the Harvard president who became High Commissioner to Germany, had known Oppenheimer well since the dawn of the atomic era. They worked together on the Acheson-Lilienthal report, and they had been fellow members of the General Advisory Committee. To Conant, "Dr. Oppenheimer's appraisal of the Russian menace, of the Soviet situation, was hard-headed, realistic and thoroughly anti-Soviet." Then Conant added that the accused was "thoroughly loyal to the United States." Robb's cross-examination did not shake Conant's faith.

Fermi took the stand immediately after Conant. He was another former member of the General Advisory Committee who had worked for years with Oppenheimer. He was on the GAC when it took its historic vote in opposition to the development of the hydrogen bomb—an action overridden by the efforts of Teller and others. Fermi defended the committee because he felt that "One should try to outlaw the thing before it was born. I sort of had the view at that time that perhaps it would be easier to outlaw by some kind of international agreement something that did not exist. My opinion was that one should try and do that, and failing that, one should with considerable regret go ahead."

As Fermi remembered, there was little disagreement as to the technical feasibility of the H-bomb—"of somewhat better than even probability . . . perhaps just with development and some amount of technical luck the thing might be pushed through."

Fermi reminded the board that Oppenheimer, despite his opposition to H-bomb development, vigorously pushed for improvement of the United States' position in conventional atomic weapons, including new exploration for ores and expanding production of primary materials.

Robb addressed only a few minor questions to the witness, recognizing, perhaps, that there was no gain in attacking one of the most universally revered physicists.

Lilienthal was a different matter.

It was near the end of this long and tiring day when Robb stretched a snare across the trail. Lilienthal had been recalled to the stand and first was involved in this exchange with Garrison's lieutenant, Samuel Silverman:

> Q. How would you assess him [Oppenheimer] as a security risk?
>
> A. I did not so regard him up until the time my knowledge of the program ceased, and had no occasion to regard him as a security risk.
>
> Q. I think you already indicated that in March 1947 you consciously assayed the situation and came to the conclusion that he was not a security risk?
>
> A. Yes. At that time we had the file before us, and that was my conclusion, that in the light of the overall picture taking everything into account, the minus signs were very few indeed, and the plus signs were very great indeed, and I thought he was a contribution to the security of the country. I have had no occasion since that time to change that view.

Then, about 4:45, Robb began his cross-examination. For about an hour he pressed Lilienthal on the details of the GAC's recommendation of October 1949 that the United States not proceed with the development of the superbomb. There was the question of whether the Russians were capable of the same thing. Lilienthal, pressed by Robb, grew testy. Robb wanted to know exactly who assessed the Soviet capability. "I don't recall," said Lilienthal, "but I assume it would be scientists or intelligence officers. Probably the scientists, probably the GAC."

"Probably Dr. Oppenheimer?" Robb shot back.

"I'd rather you would not push me after I said I don't remember," snapped the angry Lilienthal.

The worst was yet to come. Lilienthal confirmed that on January 31, 1950, he wrote a classified memorandum and placed it in the AEC files. Between October 6, 1953, and November of that year Lilienthal requested the return of the manuscript and it was duly returned. It was a statement of the former AEC chairman's views and he was anxious for his "own protection" to have access to it.

Robb was concerned about the confidentiality of the classified memorandum. He asked Lilienthal, "I assume you kept this confidential?"

Lilienthal was momentarily full of assurance again. "Yes, and I have kept it in a safe and so on. I plan to return it to the commission now that I know you have a photostat."

There was a split second of silence, broken by Robb's "Beg pardon?"

Lilienthal still wasn't aware of the trap a few steps ahead.

"I think now that it is in the record and you have a photostat of it, it is probably just as well for me to return it to the commission or put it in a lock box."

"I see"—Robb was calm—"You thought when you got it back that this was the only copy."

"No," Lilienthal contested. "I knew it had been photostated."

At this point Gordon Gray, who was leaning forward intently, broke in. He felt it was his duty to point out to the witness that he had made conflicting statements. Earlier, in executive session, Lilienthal had said he did not know the memorandum had been photostated. "I am sorry to use the word 'perjury,'" Gray intoned, "but if at one point in the testimony the witness says one thing and at another point he says directly contrary, at one point the testimony is in error."

Lilienthal explained the discrepancy—he had learned "only yesterday" that there was a photostat. His troubles, however, were only beginning.

Robb, with the tension in the hearing room increasing, continued his interrogation by going over the events leading up to Oppenheimer's 1947 security clearance. This same ground had been covered by Silverman's questions, but Robb's plow went deeper, trying to turn up some darker hidden soil. After a series of sharp questions dealing with Lilienthal's receipt of Oppenheimer's file, Robb again tested the credibility of the witness.

Earlier the same day Lilienthal had testified that he had sought guidance in the White House from the President's counsel, Clark Clifford. Robb wanted more details.

Q. Did you suggest to Mr. Clifford that a special board be convened to review the material?

A. No, we did not.

Q. Was that ever discussed with Mr. Clifford?

A. No, I believe not.

Q. Are you sure of that?

A. I am not sure, but I have no recollection of it.

Robb—for the moment—didn't press the point and turned to other matters; a magician distracting his audience. Lilienthal's discussion with J. Edgar Hoover about the Oppenheimer brothers' files was examined.

Then Robb, like a sorcerer, exhumed a long-forgotten document. It was a memorandum of the Atomic Energy Commission's actions on March 10 and 11, 1947, prepared by Carroll Wilson, the AEC general manager at that time. Robb read it slowly, almost casually. Then after a long recital he reached a passage that he carefully emphasized:

"It was decided that the Chairman [Lilienthal] should confer with Dr. Bush and Mr. Clifford of the White House concerning the establishment of an evaluation board of distinguished jurists to make a thorough review and evaluation of the case."

Then farther along in the same memorandum, Robb read: "Dr. Bush and the Chairman met with Mr. Clifford and advised him of the circumstances in connection with this case and discussed with him the desirability of having a review of this case by a board of distinguished jurists or other citizens. The Chairman proposed that there be considered for membership on this board judges [sic] of the Supreme Court."

The memorandum recorded Clifford's strong objection to calling on members of the Supreme Court, but he agreed to discuss the matter with President Truman and report back to Lilienthal and Dr. Bush.

The reading completed, Robb put down the memo and addressed Lilienthal.

"You had forgotten that?"

The witness conceded that he had. Robb made the inevitable comparison between the proposal of 1947 and the hearing of 1954.

Q. But you would agree, would you not, sir, that in 1947 you and the Commission seriously considered, and were in fact of the view that a board should be impaneled to consider this matter?

A. It is quite evident from the memorandum that this was considered.

Q. And you thought enough of it to go to Mr. Clifford at the White House and so recommend?

A. That is right.

Q. In other words, you recommended in 1947 that the exact step which is now being taken, be taken then?

A. We suggested it, and I think perhaps that is the import of the memorandum as I recall, we suggested this to the White House.

Q. That step did not strike you as fantastic or unreasonable, did it?

A. No.

These startling admissions by a pro-Oppenheimer witness, this complete reversal of Lilienthal's testimony, certainly did not add to the credibility of the former AEC chairman, nor help the Oppenheimer cause.

In 1974 the authors asked Robb why he did not simply read the memorandum into the record, prior to his cross-examination of Lilienthal. Robb's response was that he didn't know at the start that it would be necessary to read the memorandum into the record.

Said Robb, "If I had made such a recommendation to Clark Clifford, I would have remembered it."

On April 22, 1954, Edward Teller was at Livermore, searching his own conscience as to his proper role in the hearing. He had already decided that it was his duty to testify. But he had worried about it, day after day. He felt a need to release the pent-up emotional pressure by talking about the Oppenheimer dilemma. Perhaps in the process of verbalizing he could clarify the torment in his own mind.

Teller has been so roundly condemned for his testimony, more often than not because his detractors inferred from his comments not an objective appraisal of Oppenheimer as an official voice in defense policy, but the welling up of Teller's resentment and frustration in coping with a voice of rival power and opposite persuasion.

But no one could read Teller's mind. And yet, in a remarkable document, apparently never noticed, Teller, on that April 22, revealed some of his innermost thoughts about the testimony that was to take place before the Gray Board six days later. The authors discovered the seemingly inconsequential memo among thousands of papers in Teller's files. It was marked "official use only."

Chester Heslep was working for the Atomic Energy Commission as a liaison officer with the United States Information Agency, which was seeking the advice of top scientists on President Eisenhower's Atoms for Peace program. Almost routinely, he stopped off at Livermore to discuss the question with Teller. But that is not what happened, as he related the event in a memo to his boss, Lewis Strauss.

Teller was interested only in discussing the Oppenheimer case. When I emphasized that my sole relationship with the Chairman [Strauss] was that of an information staffer assigned to assist in research and drafting of speeches, Teller said I should hear him anyway "so as to know what to look for" as the case unfolded.

You have requested that I record my recall of this conversation. While I listened attentively. I felt intuitively that this was none of my business and did not charge myself with making any notes then or later, especially since Teller indicated he would probably see you in Washington the following week. Rather, I got the idea—it may be erroneous—that Teller was, consciously or otherwise, rehearsing what he hoped to tell you personally.

Here are my general impressions of the conversation, which lasted more than an hour. (A copy is being sent Teller so that he may correct immediately any misinterpretations I may have made of his remarks.)

1. Teller regrets the case is on a security basis because he feels it is untenable. He has difficulty phrasing some of his assessment of Oppie's philosophy except a conviction that Oppie is not disloyal but rather—and Teller put this somewhat vaguely—more of a "pacifist."

2. Since the case is being heard on a security basis, Teller wonders if some way can be found to "deepen the charges" to include a documentation of the "consistently bad advice" that Oppenheimer has given, going all the way back to the end of the war in 1945.

3. Teller says what is needed, and the job is most difficult, was to show his fellow scientists that Oppie is not a menace to the program but simply no longer valuable to it.

4. Teller said "only about one percent or less" of the scientists know of the real situation and that Oppie is so powerful "politically" in scientific circles that it will be hard to "unfrock him in his own church." (This last phrase is mine and he agrees it is apt.)

5. Teller talked at length about the "Oppie machine" running through many names, some of which he listed as "Oppie men" and others as not being "on his team" but under his influence. He says the effort to make Conant head of the National Academy of Sciences

is typical of the operation of the "Oppie machine." He adds that there is no organized faction among the scientists opposing the "Oppie men."

6. Teller feels deeply that this "unfrocking" must be done or else—regardless of the outcome of the current hearing—scientists may lose their enthusiasm for the program.

7. Teller then orally documented a number of points to prove his contention of consistent bad advice. Since some of them go to the heart of the present controversy and some of them involve situations of which I have had no "need to know" in my duties with the commission and therefore have no perspective, I feel it would be unwise for me to attempt to recapitulate these points from memory. Teller can give them to you and by now may have done so.

The rest of the memo did not deal with the Oppenheimer case. It is doubly interesting in that after Heslep wrote it, he submitted it to Teller for his approval of its accuracy. Then it was sent on to Strauss, dated May 3, 1954, which was after Teller had testified. The Heslep memo turns out to be the most reliable evidence of Teller's state of mind before his fateful trip to Washington.

Of course prior to his own participation Teller had no knowledge of what had transpired behind the closed doors of the Gray Board. He did not know that Oppenheimer, confronted with that ten-year-old tape recording of his conversation with Los Alamos security officers, now admitted he had lied. He did not know that David Lilienthal had been cornered into admitting that a similar hearing on Oppenheimer's clearance had been considered back in 1947.

Prior to the opening of the hearing there was one other critical event that eventually influenced the course of Teller's testimony. Oppenheimer called on Teller for help. The actual date is not clear, but Teller recalls the occasion:

"My conversation with him was after Oppenheimer was asked to stop having anything to do with classified material and after he had asked that the hearings take place. I saw him—I believe it was in Rochester. There was a high-energy conference in Rochester at that time.

"When he saw me, he asked me, 'I suppose, I hope, that you don't think that anything I did has sinister implications.' I said I did not think that—after all, the word 'sinister' was pretty harsh. Then he asked if I would speak to his lawyer, and I said I would.

"I went and saw Mr. Garrison who trotted up something of a defense for Oppenheimer. I forget what the defense was, but since it consisted of things that I already knew, it left me entirely unimpressed. I did not make a point of it, but as far as I was concerned it was irrelevant. It did not change my mind.

"Actually, when I left for Washington I was prepared for the question that was going to be asked of me, namely: *Do I consider Oppenheimer a security risk?* And I was prepared to answer 'no' to that question."

Teller flew to Washington the day before his scheduled testimony. He arrived to find a message from Robb, asking to talk to Teller. At first Teller hesitated to see Robb. "I considered it not quite right. But considering that Oppenheimer had asked me to do the same thing, I felt that I could not say no to Robb."

As expected, Robb wanted to know how Teller would answer the crucial question.

"I told him," Teller remembers, "that I did *not* consider Oppenheimer a security risk.

"Whereupon, Robb showed me part of the testimony, showing that Oppenheimer had lied to a security person; that he admitted so lying, but that he could not now be prosecuted for what was a criminal offense because the statute of limitations had taken effect.

"When Robb showed this to me and gave me this argument, I said I guess that I cannot simply say that Oppenheimer is not a security risk. So in retrospect I am quite unhappy about this event.

"Had Oppenheimer not asked me to talk to *his* lawyer I would not have listened to Robb. I would have gotten into less hot water, personally. On the other hand, you may say that this brought out more of the actual facts."

When he ascended the witness stand in the drab hearing room of the Gray Board on April 28, 1954, Edward Teller was not aware that what he was about to say would profoundly and painfully change the future course of his life. He was the third and final witness during a long and tiring day. He had been preceded to the stand by Major General Roscoe Wilson, one of the Air Force's strong advocates of bigger nuclear bombs for strategic defense. He objected to the "pattern" of Oppenheimer's judgments because he believed a nuclear strike force was the "greatest deterrent to further Russian aggression." The next witness was Berkeley and Livermore chemist Kenneth Pitzer, who charged that Oppenheimer's lack of enthusiasm for the thermonuclear project "may have" discouraged other physicists from joining the program.

By this time Teller was a commanding figure in American

science. Whatever he was to say, it would have great weight, even if its intrinsic importance might be less than that of other witnesses. There was an exceptional tension in the room as he faced Robb for the first questions:

"Dr. Teller," said Robb, "may I ask you at the outset, are you appearing as a witness here today because you want to be here?"

Teller's reply was direct. "I appear because I have been asked to and because I consider it my duty upon request to say what I think in the matter. I would have preferred not to appear."

"I believe, sir," Robb continued, "that you stated to me some time ago that anything you had to say, you wished to say in the presence of Dr. Oppenheimer?"

"That is correct."

At Robb's request, Teller summarized his own academic background, his involvement in what he described simply as "war work," his postwar work for the AEC and his eventual assignment at the University of California. He recounted his relations with Oppenheimer. "I met him frequently, but I was not particularly closely associated with him, and I did not discuss with him very frequently or in very great detail matters outside of business matters."

Then very quickly the testimony reached its climax:

> ROBB: To simplify the issues here, let me ask you this question: Is it your intention in anything that you are about to testify to, to suggest that Dr. Oppenheimer is disloyal to the United States?
>
> TELLER: I do not want to suggest anything of the kind. I know Oppenheimer as an intellectually most alert and a very complicated person, and I think it would be presumptuous and wrong on my part if I would try in any way to analyze his motives. But I have always assumed, and I now assume, that he is loyal to the United States. I believe this, and I shall believe it until I see very conclusive proof to the opposite.
>
> ROBB: Now a question which is the corollary of that. Do you or do you not believe that Dr. Oppenheimer is a security risk?
>
> TELLER: In a great number of instances I have seen Dr. Oppenheimer act—I understood that Dr. Oppenheimer acted—in a way which for me was exceedingly hard to understand. I thoroughly disagreed with him in numerous issues and his actions frankly appeared to me confused and complicated. To this extent I feel that I would like to see the vital interests of this country in hands which I understand better and therefore trust more.
>
> In this very limited sense I would like to express a feeling that I

would feel personally more secure if public matters would rest in other hands.

These were the remarks that would come back to haunt Teller, but as his testimony continued, he made an actual assessment of what Oppenheimer's lack of support had cost the H-bomb project in time alone.

> It is my belief that if at the end of the war some people like Dr. Oppenheimer would have lent moral support—not even their own work, just moral support—to work on the thermonuclear gadget, I think we could have kept at least as many people in Los Alamos as we then recruited in 1949 under very difficult conditions.
>
> I therefore believe that if we had gone to work in 1945 we could have achieved the thermonuclear bomb just about four years earlier.

Teller's testimony continued for another hour under direct and cross-examination, but the remainder was merely postlude. He had at least partly blamed Oppenheimer and his followers for causing a four-year delay in the achievement of a successful hydrogen bomb. But even that was only a difference in policy, however passionately the conflicting opinions were defended. The important news that swept the halls of academe across the country was that Edward Teller had profaned J. Robert Oppenheimer in twenty-one words: . . . *I would like to see the vital interests of this country in hands which I understand better and therefore trust more.*

17

The Years of the Black Bugs

IN 1973, nearly twenty years after the Oppenheimer hearing, we questioned a world-renowned physicist about the long-term effects of the ordeal.

"Did it destroy Oppenheimer?" we asked.

"No," he replied, without hesitation. "I think it made Oppenheimer. I think it destroyed Teller."

Then, as if alarmed by his own frankness, he asked that we not quote him.

The terminal date of the Oppenheimer matter came on June 29, 1954. The United States Atomic Energy Commission, acting on the recommendation of its Personnel Security Board, declared J. Robert Oppenheimer to be a loyal citizen, but a security risk. To his defenders, Oppenheimer had now joined Socrates and Galileo in the pantheon of scientific martyrs.

A few weeks later Edward Teller arrived with Mici at Los Alamos for one of those frequent scientific meetings. By this time copies of the Gray Board testimony had been widely circulated among the scientists, especially at Los Alamos, where Oppenheimer was a living legend.

The gatherings like this one were usually jovial affairs, reunions of old friends as well as serious scientific sessions. The first large gathering of the meeting took place in the dining room of the central building. The Tellers were just about to sit down at their table when Edward spotted an old comrade, Bob Christy, nearby. They had known each other well since 1942 when both were at the University of Chicago. Briefly, during that period, the Tellers and the Christys had even shared an apartment. Subsequently Christy, a competent physicist, had moved to Los Alamos, where he made a significant contribution to the design of the Nagasaki bomb. Teller considered Christy a warm and good friend.

Spontaneously, Teller left his table, shouted cheery greetings to

Christy, and thrust out his hand. Christy looked icily at the hand and turned away.*

Teller was as stunned as if Christy had punched him. He staggered back to the table to rejoin Mici, trying desperately to sustain his composure. The shock was too great. He and Mici abruptly left the meeting and returned to their room, where Edward wept.[1]

This was the most dramatic and definite turning point in Teller's life. He was to endure this kind of rejection again and again for at least a decade because, in the minds of so many scientists, he had destroyed Oppenheimer. But no incident is so permanently branded on Teller's soul as this first rejected handshake.

On many occasions the authors attempted to elicit from Teller some expression of his personal suffering in the years after the Oppenheimer decision. Sometimes he was evasive, other times reluctant. Then, in an unguarded moment in August 1974, the bitterness poured forth:

"If a person leaves his country, leaves his continent, leaves his relatives, leaves his friends, the only people he knows are his professional colleagues. If more than ninety percent of these then come around to consider him an enemy, an outcast, it is bound to have an effect. The truth is it had a profound effect. It affected me, it affected Mici, it even affected her health."

The Oppenheimer storm that loosed the shower of hatred on Teller began with the release of the official rulings. The Personnel Security Board, by a vote of two to one, recommended to the AEC that Dr. Oppenheimer's security clearance not be reinstated. The affirmative votes were by Chairman Gray and Thomas Morgan, the self-made industrialist. The dissent was by the chemist and political conservative, Ward Evans.

The conclusions of Gray and Morgan were that:

1. We find that Dr. Oppenheimer's continuing conduct and associations have reflected a serious disregard for the requirements of the security system.

2. We have found a susceptibility to influence which could have serious implications for the security interests of the country.

3. We find his conduct in the hydrogen bomb program sufficiently disturbing as to raise a doubt as to whether his future participation,

---

*Questioned about this incident twenty-one years later (1975) Christy said it was a "spontaneous reaction of that moment." His bitter feelings toward Teller have mellowed over the years, he added.

if characterized by the same attitudes in a Government program relating to the national defense, would be clearly consistent with the best interests of security.

4. We have regretfully concluded that Dr. Oppenheimer has been less than candid in several instances in his testimony before this board.[2]

Evans's dissent was just as emphatic. The essence of his argument was that Oppenheimer was being punished on the basis of the same evidence under which he was cleared in 1947. He also insisted that if Oppenheimer had discouraged any scientists from working on the H-bomb, "it was because of his intellectual prominence and influence over scientific people and not because of any subversive tendencies."[3]

The Atomic Energy Commission of course supported the findings of Gray and Morgan, and the conclusion of AEC General Manager Nichols. The ruling of Commissioners Strauss, Zuckert, and Campbell was that "concern for the defense and security of the United States requires that Dr. Oppenheimer's clearance should not be reinstated." Commissioner Murray concurred in a separate statement.[4]

Only Henry De Wolf Smyth, the sole physicist on the commission, dissented, and his dissent was vigorous and bitter. "No gymnastics or rationalization allow me to accept this argument" (of the majority), Dr. Smyth intoned. "If in any recent instances Dr. Oppenheimer has misunderstood his obligation to security, the error is occasion for reproof but not for a finding that he should be debarred from serving his country. Such a finding extends the concept of 'security risk' beyond its legitimate justification and constitutes a dangerous precedent."[5]

In 1973 Smyth would not submit to a formal interview on the subject of Teller and the Oppenheimer hearings, but expressed his furious, unrelenting objection to Teller's 1954 testimony. Nor had time healed the resentment of I. I. Rabi or Marvin Goldberger or Hans Bethe, though Bethe's personal feelings toward Teller had mellowed slightly.

The question has been raised as to why the wrath of the academic community descended almost entirely on Teller. Why not on Borden, who triggered the whole affair with his charge that Oppenheimer was an agent of the Russians? Why not on Lewis Strauss, the chairman of the AEC? Why not on K. D. Nichols, whose compilation of charges laid the groundwork for the Gray Board proceedings?

The fact is that many of Oppenheimer's friends suspected, rightly or wrongly, that a power struggle between their champion and Teller had been building for many years. It dated back to Teller's dedication to building the super during the war when he was thwarted by Oppenheimer and Bethe, and reached its climax when Oppenheimer, as chairman of the powerful General Advisory Committee, had once more blocked Teller's favorite project in 1949. Teller won that battle by circumventing the GAC with a direct appeal to the military and to powerful leaders like Senator McMahon and Lewis Strauss, but—as the "Oppie men" saw it—Teller nursed a deep resentment against the one man who stood in his way.

Joseph Volpe, Jr., a lawyer for the Manhattan Project, and general counsel to the AEC from 1948 to 1951, knew most of the principals in the Oppenheimer controversy and formed some judgments of his own that may provide some insight into the anti-Teller explosion.

"My theory," he told the authors, "is that Teller, like the rest of us, is human and emotional. There came a time when he felt Oppenheimer had gotten too big for his breeches. There came a time when he felt that he knew more than Oppenheimer. There came a time when he felt his views on national defense were far better than Oppenheimer's. For many years he had taken a back seat to Oppenheimer, and now he had reached a point in his own career where he could challenge Oppenheimer and he challenged him."

The "challenge" that Volpe refers to is not the confrontation during the hearing, but the challenge of the GAC's decision against the H-bomb. Nevertheless, there is no question that many scientists felt that Teller regarded the confrontation before the Gray Board as another step in the challenge. Most of them did not interpret Teller's testimony as an intensely honest assessment of the role of Oppenheimer vis-à-vis national security, which Teller claims is all he intended.

Whatever Teller intended, the fact is that within a few days after the publication of the AEC's final ruling against Oppenheimer, Teller had serious second thoughts. Even before the trip to Los Alamos and his humiliation by Bob Christy he wrote a desperate letter to Lewis Strauss. He expressed his "relief" at the AEC's findings, but then revealed his alarm at his own conduct:

> I continue to feel that I made a grave mistake when I clearly im-
> plied that opinion of a man can make him a security risk. I did not
> say this, but, rereading my testimony, I see that I came extremely
> close to saying it. I therefore would feel very much happier if I could
> make a statement to the press in which I remedy as much of this
> damage as I possibly can. After a lot of headache and a waste of
> much paper, I arrived at this brief statement which I am attaching.
>   It seems particularly important for me to say something of this
> kind since my friends among the physicists attach very great impor-
> tance to this point. If I should lose their respect it would be an ex-
> tremely hard blow to me. . . .

And, of course, he did lose their respect. His plaintive after-
thought to the press was never released, partly on the advice of
Strauss, who wrote, "My general feeling is against it, but you are
perhaps under compulsions with which I am not completely in
touch." Teller decided he would only risk further complications
and the "clarification" was filed away and forgotten. This is what it
said:

> I am making the following statement in order to clarify a misun-
> derstanding about my testimony in the hearings of J. Robert Oppen-
> heimer.
>   I was asked to testify at the hearings and was asked to give my full
> opinion on Dr. Oppenheimer's advice. It was my duty to do so.
>   In my testimony I did not imply that the right to disagree should be
> limited. I consider that right as essential in a free society. That this
> question should have arisen in connection with my testimony is for
> me the most terrible part of the Oppenheimer case.
>   I am happy to see that the question of Dr. Oppenheimer's advice
> did not influence the determination of his clearance and that the
> Commission reaffirmed explicitly his right to voice his opinion.

For Teller there was a bitter irony in the whole experience. He
and Mici were gregarious people, but their companionship was almost entirely within the scientific community, with perhaps a
fringe of friends in other academic fields. It was a majority only in
this small pool of acquaintances that had resented the Oppenheimer testimony. In the broad ocean of public opinion, Edward
Teller was a national hero. He had carried the battle for a hydrogen bomb over the head of Oppenheimer's powerful General
Advisory Committee, over the heads of the AEC chiefs, and had

cleared the way for its successful creation. The military, especially the top brass of the Air Force, was deeply indebted to him.

In July 1954, shortly after the Oppenheimer ruling, *Life* magazine ran a major article by Robert Coughlin entitled "Dr. Edward Teller's Magnificent Obsession" and subheaded "Story behind the H-bomb is one of a dedicated, patriotic man overcoming high-level opposition." The article praised its subject lavishly:

> Teller's role nevertheless was unique, indispensible and decisive. Without it the chances are quite strong that the U.S. would not have the H-bomb in deliverable form today. In that event, in the well-informed judgment of President Eisenhower, "Soviet power would today be on the march in every quarter of the globe." Teller not only produced the brilliant idea which converted the H-bomb from a monstrous "gadget" to a versatile weapon. He also, by an almost fanatic determination, kept the idea of an H-bomb from dying of pure neglect.[6]

The *Life* article was followed two months later by a book, *The Hydrogen Bomb*, written by two Time-Life correspondents, James Shepley and Clay Blair, Jr. The authors purported to tell how the H-bomb came to be developed, but essentially they distilled the story into a titanic struggle between Oppenheimer and Teller. Shepley and Blair concocted a skillful and subtle hatchet job on Oppenheimer, and just as masterful a glorification of Teller. Their one caveat about the two scientists betrayed the posture of the authors and the anti-intellectual ferment of the McCarthy era. Both Oppenheimer and Teller, said Shepley and Blair, "are intellectual snobs."[7]

Despite his sensitive ego, the history of Teller's life tends to credit him with sincerity when he says, "I couldn't have cared less what the general public thought of me. Most people—certainly I—are much more influenced by what their friends think or, at any rate, what the people around them think."

Teller considered the *Life* account "insulting, since the same article blackened my friends. It was the source of the greatest possible embarrassment."

If he disliked what was said about him in *Life*, he was even more incensed by Shepley and Blair. First of all, *The Hydrogen Bomb* rubbed more salt into the wounds of the faithful troops behind Oppenheimer. Two decades later Hans Bethe could still charge that

"Surely this [book] was strongly inspired by people around Edward, perhaps not by Edward himself, who wanted to destroy not only Oppenheimer but also all his friends." Bethe, it must be recalled, had been Teller's loyal friend during the Washington era.

Teller came to despise the Shepley and Blair book so much that it turned his first meeting with young Senator John F. Kennedy into a disaster. In the Senate dining room, late in 1954, the physicist and the politician were introduced. Kennedy, according to Teller, "smiled a broad and beautiful smile, though perhaps not as beautiful as that of Eisenhower." Then the Senator from Massachusetts said precisely the wrong thing:

"I read so much about you in the Shepley-Blair book."

Teller remembers: "I got mad, I got really mad. That book did me a lot of damage. It abused Oppenheimer. It praised me to high heaven, and did it in less than a completely honest fashion. It caused a storm of protest and lost me many friends. I was tempted to comment on it, but everybody was commenting on it and usually their comments were even more mendacious. Under those conditions I thought I had better forget the whole mess."

The profound, almost irrational anger stirred in Teller by Kennedy's comment was probably a measure of the physicist's misery. He came to the conclusion that Kennedy, in assuming that Teller would appreciate a reference to *The Hydrogen Bomb*, misjudged him completely and even to bring it up was the mark of a dishonest man. Starting with this initial encounter, Teller developed a total distrust of John F. Kennedy—"and at that time I didn't even know he would someday be President."

But Teller had to respond politely, despite his bottled-up anger. He chose to sing, in *recitativo*, a line from *The Gondoliers* of Gilbert and Sullivan, to wit, "The things they have related, they are much exaggerated." Whereupon, according to Teller, "Senator Kennedy smiled again, perhaps a little less sweetly, and went away."

Coincidentally, it was only a short time later, in the midst of this most painful period, that Teller first met Richard M. Nixon, then Eisenhower's Vice President.

"I went to him because I was then, as now, very much interested in civil defense. One of Nixon's friends and supporters wanted to persuade him to push for a subway in Los Angeles. I thought that would be an excellent idea because that could help in establishing civil defense. So he arranged for me to see the Vice President.

"I came in and he asked me to sit down in a big leather armchair which immediately won my heart for the simple reason that my father, who was a lawyer, had a big leather armchair for his clients and I loved that chair. I, of course, right away had the wrong motivation. He sat me down in the big chair and without wasting a word about any book he may or may not have read, or anything he may or may not have heard about me, simply asked me what I had to say. Whereupon I spoke and he listened for twenty minutes. He did not interrupt. He did not *appear* to go to sleep. But after I had finished he started to ask me questions. And from the questions it was absolutely clear that he had listened, that he had understood what I was after. I had the impression of a fully reasonable contact."

This first meeting with Richard Nixon opened some doors to replace those that had been slammed shut by his scientific colleagues. The respect accorded to a beleaguered scientist by the ambitious Vice President, combined with their points of agreement in politics (at that time Nixon was second only to McCarthy as the herald of the menace of communism), established in Teller a loyalty to Nixon that was to endure to the last days of the discredited Nixon presidency twenty years later. Only when Nixon's tapes proved beyond doubt that he had participated in the Watergate cover-up did Teller concede any disenchantment with the political leader he had known since 1954.

What Teller was undergoing was a complete realignment of his friendships. Since he was now a prophet in the eyes of the military leadership, the adherents of the military's point of view loomed much larger in his life. Chief among these was Dave Griggs, who in 1954 was professor of geophysics at the University of California at Los Angeles. But Griggs's talents were far broader than his academic title. He was an expert on radiation and radar and served in numerous capacities as a science consultant to the Air Force during World War II. After the war he became a scientific intelligence advisor to General Douglas MacArthur in Tokyo and late in 1946 joined the Rand Corporation, the "think tank" set up by the Air Force to exploit its most productive brains. He eventually became head of Rand's nuclear energy division and remained a consultant there even after his appointment to UCLA in 1948. In 1951 and 1952 he was chief scientist of the Air Force, and a Teller ally in the H-bomb controversy. At the Oppenheimer hearing he was far more outspoken than Teller, testifying that the policy recommended by Oppenheimer's General Advisory Committee "could be a national catastrophe." He conceded he had impugned Oppenheimer's loyalty and that Oppenheimer had retorted by calling Griggs "a paranoid."[8]

Prior to Teller's painful confrontation with Christy, Griggs had been the only person to warn Teller that he might have blighted his friendships in the scientific community. The warning was delivered by Griggs immediately before Teller's ill-fated visit to Los Alamos. Los Alamos, of course, was still, by heritage, Oppenheimer territory. Livermore was the creation primarily of Teller and the conservative, business-oriented Ernest Lawrence. The climate was better there, though not without some friction. Herbert York, the director of Livermore, was sympathetic with Oppenheimer. Relations between York and Livermore's most celebrated scientist were decidedly cool.

"But with most of the other people—almost all of them—in the laboratory there was no trouble, certainly no serious trouble," Teller insists. "I think I knew them. I think they knew me."

Mici's recollection is that life went along very much as usual as long as she and Edward remained in the confines of their home neighborhood at Berkeley or when Edward was at Livermore. The problems arose when they made one of their frequent trips to scientific meetings. Mici still winces at the recollection that "people we had known for years and years suddenly didn't recognize us." Princeton physicist John Wheeler remembers walking with Teller in Los Angeles airport when they encountered two friends from Caltech. They shook Wheeler's hand and carefully avoided Teller.

Eventually the strain began to break Mici's normally robust health—she was afflicted with exhaustion and dizziness. Teller insists that the experience had no physical effect on him. He had suffered from a mild colitis for years and in 1956, two years after the Oppenheimer ruling, the condition became acute and forced him into a hospital. Inasmuch as colitis is generally recognized as an ailment closely tied in with emotional tension, the evidence is strong that Teller, despite his denials, was physically affected by the ordeal.

As the word of Teller's testimony spread across the land, it was almost possible to choose up sides between the pro- and anti-Teller factions. Lawrence was by long association and political inclination a man who sympathized with Teller. So was his colleague,

Luis Alvarez. Wheeler thought the hatred heaped on Teller was "out of proportion to his role in the whole affair." Princeton's Eugene Wigner, sharing Teller's acute distrust of the Russians, stood by his fellow Hungarian.

On the other side were such major physicists as H. D. Smyth, the scientist member of the AEC; I. I. Rabi (who had not liked Teller much even before the Oppenheimer case); Marvin Goldberger, later to be chairman of physics at Princeton; Cornell's Hans Bethe, once Teller's close personal friend; and Norris Bradbury, who succeeded Oppenheimer as director of the Los Alamos laboratory.

In this formidable array of defenders and detractors, Teller drew his greatest comfort from another group who played on neither team. These were the scientists who disagreed with what Teller said but defended his right to say it. In Teller's mind they are the truest of friends.

"You know," he told us one evening in Berkeley, "the Oppenheimer case had many unfortunate consequences for Mici and me. But it had one fortunate consequence. It made a sharp definition, a sharp division, between the many friends who turned out not to be friends at all, and the few friends who really were friends."

Teller's prime example was Szilard.

"Ideologically he was completely on Oppenheimer's side. But he never made the assumption—I don't think it ever entered his mind—that I said or did anything except what I believed was true and correct from my point of view."

The mutual respect of the two Hungarians persisted even though the effusive and sometimes officious Szilard was a chronic advice giver. For years he had attempted to direct Teller's activities, even to advising what plane or train Teller should take, and just as consistently, Teller had ignored Szilard's advice. "This should not have surprised him," said Teller, "because as a general rule his advice was not taken; in fact, he expected as much. I think Szilard was basically an exceedingly nice person, a good friend and, of course, an unusually intelligent human being."

Had not fate intervened, Enrico Fermi, like Szilard, might have eased Teller's post-Oppenheimer years. The peerless Italian also disagreed with Teller's assessment of Oppenheimer. He had been in Europe when the testimony and the ruling were released. He returned home to Chicago in September, but alarmingly weak and exhausted. After a cursory diagnosis he was admitted to a hospital for extensive tests. The verdict was cancer of the stomach. Fermi was going to die.

Teller was one of many friends who visited Fermi in the hospital. As Teller recalls the greeting, Fermi, stoically good-humored, said, "Well, they've played a dirty trick on me." His visitor, choking up at the frail appearance of such a vigorous man, could only attempt to be witty in return. "It's a dirty trick on your friends," Teller responded.

When Teller went to see Fermi he was struggling with a decision stemming directly from the Oppenheimer situation. Obviously Teller knew more than anyone else about the events leading to the development of a successful hydrogen bomb. He was already suffering from the barbs directed at him because of the embarrassing book by Shepley and Blair. Urged by his friends, Teller had written his own briefer version of the story. He had first entitled it simply "The Hydrogen Bomb," the same title as the Shepley-Blair book. Then Paula DeLuca, who was then his secretary at Berkeley, suggested that such a title to a piece written only by Edward Teller would make the author sound presumptuous. He changed the title to "The Work of Many People."

He discussed the long article with Fermi. Did Fermi think he should publish it?

"Do you have the manuscript here?" Fermi asked. Teller, hoping Fermi would be willing to read it, had brought it along. "Well, let me read it," said Fermi impatiently, just as if he were not mortally ill.

Teller sat quietly while Fermi read every word.

"I think you should publish it," was the sick man's firm conclusion.

Teller left the hospital grateful for Fermi's advice and with his mind almost made up. But he was saddened by the probability that he would never see his friend again. The impact of the visit went far beyond the surface discussion of whether an article should be published. The presence of the stricken Fermi moved Teller to one of his rare moods of serious religious contemplation. Discussing it with us twenty years later, he recalled his thoughts:

"I came away with a very peculiar feeling. Fermi, whether he believed in God or not, was a Catholic. In most religions a man who is dying confesses his sins. This now seemed to me to be the wrong way. If a man is dying, particularly if a good man is dying, you should confess *your* sins to *him*, because maybe he is going to see

God and maybe he can do something about your sins. In a completely irrational manner, that is how I felt about it. Fermi was a very wonderful man."

And Teller also felt certain, from the warmth of their final minutes together, that "what had happened had not disturbed our friendship."

A month later, the great Enrico Fermi, only fifty-three, was dead. His early death robbed the scientific world of one of its steadiest and most gifted performers. So great was his influence over his colleagues that, had he lived longer, and had he defended Teller, Fermi, more than anyone else, could have contributed to a reconciliation of the schism that divided the scientific world and has still not been closed, even today.

At about the same time that Teller was consulting Fermi on "The Work of Many People," he sent off a copy of the manuscript to Lewis Strauss. Like Teller, the AEC chairman was also in disrepute among most scientists because of the Oppenheimer ruling, though the fallout of resentment against Strauss did not reach its full intensity for several more years. Teller's letter said, in part:

> I am sending you my attempt at a manuscript. It is rather long and so I should hesitate to ask you to read it. It would be, however, exceedingly kind of you if you could do so. This is a matter of painful interest to me and I would appreciate your advice and guidance more than that of any other single person.

Teller went on to explain to Strauss that his colleagues were divided in the judgment as to whether or not he should publish it. Then he exposed more of his own turmoil:

> I agree with you completely that if I publish anything it will be used by some people to perpetuate the controversy. I have tried to avoid any provocation and, in particular, any reference to the book of Shepley and Blair, but I am quite sure that the other side will find weaknesses in what I say no matter how carefully I say it.

Teller set forth his reasons why he felt he should publish the article—"for the ninety percent of the physicists who are as yet uncommitted" and "to reach many of my friends in Los Alamos who will undoubtedly be influenced against me if I do not speak up," and "for some of the young scientists." Also "for the man in the street." Then he bitterly concluded:

Lastly I should like to write for anyone ten years from now who may want to look up the record of the present turbulent story and will find that the only thing I have said was the statement which I had to make in connection with the Oppenheimer case. I should like to have the privilege to be able to say something more kind than I said at that time and my best chance to say it is in connection with the excellent work of the many people who have collaborated in the development of the hydrogen bomb.

Strauss also approved, but Teller still was driven by a need to mend his broken friendships. Again he turned to Hans Bethe at Cornell, in a letter with a tone that indicates Teller's failure to grasp how completely he had alienated a close friend.

I have been working for quite some time now and with quite some intensity on a story of the hydrogen bomb. I do not yet have it in really final form nor am I sure what I will do with it. . . . I have tried to say only the kind and favorable things and I tried also in this respect to deviate from what seems to be general practice these days. I hope you approve of both tendencies.

Teller then made a hesitant sort of offer of the manuscript for Bethe's scrutiny, though whether Bethe ever saw it before publication is not certain. The letter concluded:

Hoping to see you sometime soon and also particularly hoping that we shall be again in a state where we can talk about the things we used to talk about. With best wishes to Rose.

Teller's plaintive effort to revive a once-valued friendship was completely unsuccessful. He was to try repeatedly for the next twenty years to reestablish the happy relationship of the 1930s, but Bethe apparently considered the damage beyond repair. They met a few times at scientific meetings and went through the motions of friendship, but on three separate occasions—the third in 1973—when Teller invited Bethe to come to Livermore, Bethe found reasons for declining the invitation or putting it off into the indefinite future. In 1975, Teller tried one more time. At last, Bethe accepted and made a brief appearance at Livermore. But it was the passage of healing time, not changes in attitudes, that partially restored this once solid friendship.

"The Work of Many People" could be seen as a conscious effort to bring scientists together again, although that was not Teller's ostensible purpose in writing the article. As it appeared in the February 25, 1955, issue of *Science,* it was the first public recounting of the scientific speculations and actual theoretical and laboratory work that led to the development of the hydrogen bomb. The specifics were limited by the restrictions of government classification, but overall, Teller presented a comprehensive and readable account of a towering scientific and technical achievement.

The article was true to its title—Teller credited no fewer than fifty-one scientists with various discoveries and specific tasks on the long road from theoretical musings in 1928 to the technical achievement of the deliverable bomb in 1954. He was neither modest nor outspoken about his own direct contributions. When Fermi suggested that deuterium (heavy hydrogen) rather than ordinary hydrogen might more readily be triggered by the heat of a nuclear bomb, Teller "after a few weeks of hard thought" decided it wouldn't work. Then, with the assistance of Chicago physicist Emil Konopinski, he reexamined his own conclusions and decided that, after all, it would work. And of course the second time he was right.

Once again, in "The Work of Many People," Teller raised the question of the physicists' concern that a thermonuclear reaction might ignite the atmosphere or the oceans, which is to say, wipe out the earth. He described how Konopinski and Cloyd Marvin, Jr. (the physicist-son of Teller's benefactor at George Washington University) established that this could not happen. Then, just to make sure, their findings were reviewed "by one of the most conscientious, meticulous and painstaking physicists, Gregory Breit. It was clearly necessary to prove this point beyond the shadow of any doubt, and it was so proved." The world could say amen.

There was not only a fascinating story but a hatchet-burying quality about "The Work of Many People." By this time Bethe, Bradbury, and Oppenheimer himself had presumably become Teller's unforgiving enemies. In return he praised them lavishly—and honestly, in that he gave their contributions the weight they deserved. In the search for the reactions that generate the energy of the stars, Teller stated that "the most remarkable part of the job was done by Bethe." And later—"his treatment of these reactions was so complete that in the next decade nothing useful could be added to his enumeration. Gamow had invented a new kind of game for the physicists, and Bethe proved to be the champion at it."

As for the A-bomb (the necessary trigger to the H-bomb) Teller, a few months after his Oppenheimer testimony, could write, "That it was done in time to have an influence upon the war was to a great extent due to the leadership of our director, Oppenheimer."

After the war when there was a possibility that Los Alamos might be abandoned altogether, Teller credited the survival of the facility to "a few determined people," among them, Norris Bradbury, the new director, "whose leadership was crucial."

Although it is easy to argue that Teller was trying to restore the friendships so agonizingly lost in the Oppenheimer affair, the evidence is that "The Work of Many People" was a straightforward account, written as he would have written it had there been no scientific schism. Throughout his life Teller seems to have been able to separate his scientific judgment of his colleagues from his assessment of their political or philosophical beliefs. His near-contempt for Oppenheimer, his disappointment in Bethe, his clash with Bradbury, all stemmed from nonscientific differences. The same is true for other "enemies," such as I. I. Rabi or Marvin Goldberger. The authors never heard Teller demean their achievements as physicists. Correspondingly, none of them has ever, in our presence, downgraded Teller's professional standing.

But whatever Teller's intentions when he wrote "The Work of Many People," it did not break the freeze that had descended around him. Even his children noticed the difference in his personality. Since childhood he had been given to moods of silent contemplation, but they seemed to become more frequent. There were times when Mici would warn the children, Paul, who was eleven at the time of the Oppenheimer hearings, and Wendy, who was eight, not to disturb their father. At these times Wendy would say, "Don't bother Daddy, he has black bugs in his head."

While Teller insists the aftermath did not affect his health, he readily concedes that "what the Oppenheimer case did to me was to make out of me a micro-politician." By that term he meant someone involved in the day-to-day currents of practical politics, rather than a disinterested scientist aware, at best, of only the sweeping, long-term trends in domestic or international affairs.

"And that happened," Teller explains, "when Bob Christy refused to shake hands with me. I had believed, and I still believe, that a physicist should be a physicist and not a politician, but I did become a politician, and I became one in self-defense. Now I know that self-defense, in some cases, justifies murder. Whether it ever justifies becoming a micro-politician, I don't know."

Teller had actually ventured into politics long before this era, but from the end of World War II his drift was inexorably to the right. Since he had acquired American citizenship in 1941 Teller had been a registered Democrat. He had admired Franklin D. Roosevelt and Harry Truman. "Believe it or not," he told us in 1974, "I was once a liberal." Certainly he did support international control of atomic energy, but only if the Russians would open up their closed society. Of course they didn't, and as Stalin tightened his grip on Eastern Europe, Teller's worst suspicions seemed justified. The communists seized Hungary in 1947 as ruthlessly as Béla Kun had captured it in 1918, but much more effectively. This fear fueled his belief in the need for the H-bomb and his frustration at those who seemed unwilling to face the danger of Soviets with thermonuclear weapons. He felt the growing admiration of such conservatives as Iowa's hawkish Republican Senator Bourke Hickenlooper. After the Oppenheimer case, Teller didn't have to abandon the liberals, they threw him out. This made it easier for him to ally himself with political conservatives and militant anti-communists.

After that uncomfortable meeting with John F. Kennedy in the Senate dining room in 1954, Teller nurtured a visceral dislike for the future President. A few years later he first met Nelson Rockefeller when the New York governor called on Teller as a consultant. The friendship became personal and lasting and more or less solidified Teller's affiliation with the Republican party.

There was a change in the direction of Teller the scientist, too. For reasons perhaps too profound to assess here, applied scientists seem to be more conservative than their theoretical colleagues, who tend to be political liberals. Teller was a theoretician, interested mainly in the riddles of pure science.

"As you know," he explained recently, "I am a social animal. I am interested in what people around me are interested in, I got into applied work when I felt that kind of work was needed, but I tried at the same time to pursue my work in pure science. The fact is that most of my friends have been pure scientists but after the

Oppenheimer case they avoided me. This—quite a bit to my regret—had an influence on me and I concentrated more on the applied field. This was not my intention, but it was a result."

As the experience of his ostracism recedes into the past, Teller is
capable of leavening his bitterness with some wit. His barbs are directed mainly at the self-righteousness of left-wing intellectuals:

"One of the things that happened to me," he could say in 1974,
"is not only that I lost my friends, but I believe I lost my status as
an intellectual. You know, an intellectual, as I found out to my
grief, is not necessarily a man who is intelligent, but a man who
agrees with other intellectuals. He is a man with whom it is acceptable for other intellectuals to associate. I lost my membership card
in the club."

Hans Bethe, that most poignant link to the happy days in Washington, could not, after two decades, forgive his friend Edward
completely. "Enough time has passed," said Bethe, "that I have
made peace with him, but I still think it was an awful thing to do."

18

The Era of the Falling Out

IF Teller's Oppenheimer testimony was "an awful thing" to many scientists, so were some of his other convictions to the liberals who dominated the laboratories and campuses. The H-bomb issue and Oppenheimer case had edged him toward the image of the kind of amoral and slightly unbalanced scientist who was soon to appear in a satirical movie as Dr. Strangelove. The issue of the 1950s was nuclear fallout—radioactive dust that was filtering down over the world as the result of the proliferation of American and Russian nuclear weapons test. There was a crescendo of demands for an end to open-air tests, for a U.S.-Soviet test-ban treaty.

Teller did not harbor any illusions. He knew that if he injected himself into the controversy as an opponent of a test ban, his Dr. Strangelove image would only be enhanced. His friend Lewis Strauss warned him that the fear of fallout radiation was increasing. Whether these fears were justified or not, the scientist—especially one with Teller's reputation—who opposed a test ban was walking into trouble.

In the beginning of the atomic age the issue was not fallout. The term itself was not generally used until at least 1950. The primitive nuclear weapons that obliterated Hiroshima and Nagasaki raised hardly a public whimper about radiation or fallout. And in truth the skin burns and internal damage were almost entirely confined to the hapless civilians of those doomed cities. There was not yet a recognized threat to the milk drunk by children in the American Middle West. The indignation was based on the nauseating fact that healthy white Americans had, by the push of a button, incinerated a practically defenseless yellow-skinned population. It was from this gruesome beginning of the nuclear age that the ban-the-bomb movement started. The immediate concern after the end of the war was that such weapons must never be used again. Protests and demonstrations to outlaw the atomic bomb erupted spontaneously in most Western countries. Mere tests, while they drew protests, were resented as provocations, not as a clear and present danger.

Then came the pathetic and disturbing story of a little Japanese tuna trawler with a cruelly ironic name, the *Lucky Dragon*. Early in the morning of March 1, 1954, the *Lucky Dragon*'s twenty-three crewmen suffered an ordeal that evoked worldwide pity and resentment. Suddenly nuclear testing and nuclear fallout were being damned as a direct and immediate threat to the peaceful citizens of the planet.

Teller would soon be in the forefront of the controversy. The Teller of this era—he was forty-six in 1954—was not ideally equipped to face the fray. His personal appearance did not help. As he grew older his always heavy eyebrows grew bushier, the most luxuriant in a celebrity since labor boss John L. Lewis. Lewis, of course, *wanted* to look ferocious, but Teller's brows gave him the shadowy, almost fierce countenance of the diabolical scientist. He tended, also, to be portly and his enemies must inevitably have made the comparison with the ascetic, gentle mien of J. Robert Oppenheimer.

This is not to say that Teller could not be gentle and even charming, but these qualities came across then—and still do—mainly to those who met and talked with him face to face. At times, in repose, his expression seems to reveal a deep inner sadness as if he is lamenting the disappearance of values and culture that, to him, are the essence of his beloved Western World.

In 1974 Teller told an interesting story that demonstrated the negative effect of his appearance. In 1959 a friend of his had watched the debate on CBS television between Teller and Lord Bertrand Russell on disarmament. Russell spoke with his chin thrust out, his voice cool and urbane. Teller tilted his head forward and talked with a deep, doomsday voice, through his eyebrows. The friend told Teller he concluded that Russell's arguments were the more persuasive. Then the friend read the transcript of the debate and changed his mind. Teller, he said, made the stronger argument. Apparently, Teller's forbidding appearance had damaged his case to the television audience.

This is not to say that a large segment of the public did not have a case against Teller. He was known to have contributed to the atom bomb. Very few people knew that Teller had attempted to forestall Hiroshima and Nagasaki in favor of a harmless demonstration of the bomb's effectiveness. But he never has been able to accept the thesis that there are forces in the universe that should never fall into the province of man's knowledge, forces that belong, so to speak, only to God. Teller believes it is man's destiny to explore and to learn. The forces unleashed in the process are neither good nor evil, only man can make them so. His determination to unlock the secret of thermonuclear fusion was viewed by his critics as the obsession of a warmonger tinged with paranoia. The public was not aware that in the Soviet Union physicist Sakharov had a parallel "obsession."

The test-ban debate was seeded by the fallout from the botched Bikini test and became a major issue during the 1956 presidential campaign. Adlai Stevenson was genuinely concerned about the effects of radiation on the living and the yet unborn. Many scientists were spreading the warning that as larger amounts of strontium 90, cesium 137, and other dangerous radioactive substances were released into the atmosphere, genetic accidents would multiply. In his own kind of flawless, nearly poetic prose, Stevenson called for a public airing of the issue, which he saw as a first step toward general disarmament. Stevenson's appeal was warmly welcomed by many members of the scientific community. But Teller, who had always voted Democratic, was repelled by what he considered Stevenson demagogy and his ignorance of the problem. Teller turned in his Democratic party card.

What Teller did not know was that influential members of the Eisenhower administration were privately in agreement with Stevenson but the public position of the administration was that the Democratic candidate was talking "catastrophic nonsense."[1]

The controversy, as was noted above, had been touched off by a tragic miscalculation at Bikini on March 1, 1954. But beyond that one event lay the larger question. Was this miscalculation a one-time occurrence or could it happen again as a risk of nuclear testing in the atmosphere? Did it happen because the United States was attempting to out-megaton the Soviet Union? Was the fission-fusion-fission bomb a political mistake and a scientific success? The official answers are still shrouded under that omnipresent cloak called security. Teller resents the cloak, but will not shed it so long as the law requires it. Other sources have been less reticent. The roots of the story go back to Los Alamos and Livermore in the early 1950s.

Teller admits his first year at Livermore was neither happy nor satisfying, even though he had fought for two years to get the laboratory established. Herbert York, the first director, had very little rapport with Teller, although they managed to muddle through together. It was Ernest Lawrence who provided the real moral support.

Even though Teller had "no reason to complain" about the situation at Livermore, he was still planning to return to the more academic climate of the University of Chicago. But Lawrence recognized that Teller was nearly indispensable. He knew that he had to offer an incentive. "Edward," he said, "if you stay here we can offer you a professorship."

Since Teller was already a full professor at Chicago (he was on leave of absence), Lawrence's offer was not necessarily irresistible. But there was another factor to be considered. "I happen to be married," Teller told us in recalling how he reached his decision. "Things of this kind I usually discuss with my wife."

And he did discuss it with Mici. She had no desire to return to the ice-cold winters of the Windy City. "You know," Teller said, "snow suits for the kids in Chicago, no snow suits in California."

On such profound issues did the thermonuclear future of the world depend. Teller stayed at Livermore for the next twenty-two years and his children never had to wear snow suits.

In September 1952, soon after Teller arrived at Livermore, he was joined by his old Washington friend and cryogenic expert, Ferdinand Brickwedde, who moved over from Los Alamos. The Brickweddes and the Tellers lived near each other in Diablo, twenty-five miles from Livermore. Every morning Brickwedde would give Teller a lift to the laboratory. The former's impression was that, despite the problems, Teller was a lot happier at Livermore than he had been at Los Alamos.

The first weapons tests under Livermore's jurisdiction were conducted in Nevada in the spring of 1953. They did not involve thermonuclear fusion, but even so they were less than successful. But still, as Teller pointed out, "We had enough data to understand in detail what had happened, and new knowledge in the life of a laboratory—even if that knowledge is disappointing—is most important. But we would have been happier if our first experiment had produced something of immediate value."[2]

As might be expected, Teller and his Livermore colleagues were subjected to "a heavy dose of ribbing" from their "rivals" at Los Alamos. The excellent work being done in the older laboratory must have been difficult for the still-fumbling scientists at Livermore to accept. But it was Teller, after all, who wanted the stimulus of competition—and now he had it.

Then Los Alamos and Livermore learned that they both had new and awesome competition in thermonuclear weaponry.

On August 20, 1953, the New York *Times* carried a dispatch, datlined Moscow, under the byline of Harrison E. Salisbury:

> The Soviet Government announced today that it carried out an experimental explosion of a hydrogen bomb within the last few days.
>
> The announcement said the experimental explosion had disclosed that the hydrogen bomb had a force much greater than that of an atomic bomb. It said the weapon was one of a variety of hydrogen bombs.
>
> The Soviet Government (said it) wished to emphasize that it was standing firm on its previous proposals for forbidding the use of atomic and other weapons of mass destruction within the framework of the United Nations and for a strict international control of this prohibition.*

Surprisingly, this was not the first announcement of the Soviet detonation of a hydrogen bomb. Four days *before* the test, Premier Georgi Malenkov had told a meeting of the Supreme Soviet that "the government deems it necessary to report to the Supreme Soviet that the United States has no monopoly on the hydrogen bomb."[3] Such a statement was an act of absolute confidence on Malenkov's part. It was practically an invitation for the United States to rev up the planes of AFOAT One and start collecting air samples. Their bomb, the Soviets seemed certain, would work.

The sequence of events also proved to be a propaganda coup for the Russians and showed, by hindsight, how the United States had blundered in not publicizing the Soviet thermonuclear test in 1951. The United States could easily have accused the Russians of starting the hydrogen bomb race, but the Pentagon kept silent. The Soviets must have been surprised and gratified when the United States kept their secret from a fearful world. Subsequently, the United States had announced its own Greenhouse and Mike tests, thereby proving that the capitalists had started this awful business.

---

*The Soviet concept of "international control" did not then and still does not include any form of on-site inspection.

The United States didn't officially announce the Russian shot, which apparently took place on August 12, until August 20, when AEC Chairman Strauss issued a statement. He conceded the Soviet test involved both fission and fusion, but noted, somewhat defensively, that "more than three years ago the United States decided to accelerate work on all forms of atomic weapons. Both the 1951 (Greenhouse) and 1952 (Mike) Eniwetok test series included tests involving similar reactions."[4]

The statement was approved by President Eisenhower, but the State and Defense departments referred all queries to the AEC. There never was any explanation as to why the American announcement was not made until a week after the Russian test.

What the American people were *not* told was that the Soviet Union clearly had fashioned a deliverable bomb. The United States, at that time, had no such weapon, although it was well along on the drawing boards. It was to be a "dry," lithium deuteride weapon, but was still many months away from an actual test.

In retrospect it is difficult to see what purpose was served by keeping the nature of the Russian weapon secret from all but those with a top security clearance. And even the blusterly old Secretary of Defense, Charles E. Wilson, still boasted that the United States had a three-year lead over the Russians in nuclear weapons. To Andrei Vishinsky, Russia's chief delegate to the United Nations, this boasting was patent nonsense. On November 27, Vishinsky, quite logically, called the Americans' bluff.

"Why," Vishinsky said, "don't you listen to your own specialists—chemists, physicists, etc.? What good is it to talk like this when the USSR possesses the atomic and hydrogen bomb, when the USSR in no way lags behind other countries, and those possibly do not even have all the weapons that the USSR has?"[5]

One possible reason for American complacency was the belief that the United States had ten times as many atomic bombs as the Russians. One strong piece of evidence is in *Churchill—Taken from the Diaries of Lord Moran*. On December 3, 1953, just a few months after the Russian thermonuclear bomb had been exploded, the Prime Minister of Great Britain went to Bermuda for a conference with President Eisenhower, On the eve of the first conference Moran recorded a conversation between Churchill and an unnamed professor:

P.M.: There was a time when the Western powers could have used the bomb without any reply by Russia. That time has gone. How many atomic bombs do you think the Russians have?

PROF: Oh, between three and four hundred. The Americans may have three thousand or four thousand.

P.M.: If there were war, Europe would be battered and subjugated; Britain shattered, but I hope not subjugated. Russia would be left without a central government and incapable of carrying on a modern war.[6]

Was the United States willing to lag in the fusion race in 1953 because of a quantitative superiority in all nuclear weapons? On June 20, 1974, the authors interviewed Harold Agnew, the director of Los Alamos, about the situation two decades earlier, including whether the Russians really did explode the first deliverable hydrogen weapon.

"I guess I really don't know," was Agnew's response. "I think from our understanding of what they did on their first device, that indeed it could have been delivered by existing airplanes at that time. I have a feeling that if we wanted to do the same thing and direct our efforts that way, we could have, too. It just depends on what your objectives are."

But why, Agnew was asked, didn't the United States develop a hydrogen bomb that could have been dropped from an airplane before the Russians did.

Once again the Los Alamos director began his reply with "I guess I don't know." Then he speculated: "We certainly followed it up with devices that could have been dropped. I think it's just the nature of our society and the way we operate. I don't think we've ever been interested in taking the offensive in that context. I don't think there was any reason for it. We did have fission bombs at the time. I may conjecture that at the time we had a bigger stockpile than the Soviets had, and one or two bombs one way or the other wouldn't make any difference. I think our energy or our efforts were more toward trying to understand the basic technology and, again, it's a matter of how one approaches these problems. The Russians might have been smarter. Somebody might have had a better idea, and they made something that looked like it would work smaller. Our first device, as you mentioned, the Mike device, was a big monster. We felt more comfortable with big things. It wasn't until much later that we found the technology was such that we could make things quite small."

What Agnew recalled and what Lord Moran reported was also confirmed by intelligence reports on Russian nuclear capability. They had made an H-bomb, but they did not have, nor were they likely in the near future to have, a stockpile of H-bombs. It was also comforting to know that even though they had mastered the lithium trick, the American-designed lithium deuteride bomb, soon to be tested, would prove to be much more destructive than the comparable Soviet model.*[7]

Teller's work at Livermore was mainly theoretical. Having acquired a University of California professorship, he was now also lecturing to graduate students on quantum mechanics. He had not lost his touch on the platform. His students found him to be an exciting and stimulating lecturer. The influence of Bohr's Copenhagen school was still strong in Teller's method. His students were told not to be afraid to ask "dumb" questions. If they did not understand, they were encouraged to say so. Teller insisted that "I try to teach my children to say they don't know what they don't know."

The two competing laboratories were, at the time of the Russian lithium shot in August 1953, preparing for their respective tests at Bikini. Los Alamos was planning to explode a deliverable H-bomb at the top of a tower. It was designed to be dropped from an airplane but the tower made possible more accurate measurement of the bomb's force. The expected yield was to be seven megatons, twice the originally predicted force of the Mike device.[9]

In line with Teller's belief that Livermore should not duplicate the work being done at Los Alamos, his laboratory decided to test the outer limits of usable thermonuclear power. Livermore built a bomb not designed to be deliverable—another cryogenic device like Mike. The test was to gain more experimental data. Its expected yield was calculated to be fifteen megatons—far more powerful than anything previously exploded.

The Los Alamos test—the deliverable weapon—was to be exploded first. It was detonated on March 1, 1954, in a test that proved to be a miscalculated experiment accompanied by blunder and tragedy. The actual yield of the bomb, code-named Bravo, was

---

*U.S. intelligence sources estimated the force of the Soviet H-bomb at one megaton.[8]

not seven megatons but a terrifying fifteen.[10] If the designers had realized it would be that powerful they would either have called off the test or cleared a far larger area of the Pacific of human habitation.

The meteorologists were also at fault. They had predicted that the wind would be blowing in a northeasterly direction from Bikini. And so it was, at the time of the explosion, but the direction suddenly changed and spread radioactive dust over an American destroyer. There were no injuries among the well-prepared sailors. When the dust clouds appeared the sailors went below decks while trained personnel washed away the radioactive debris with the ship's hoses.

The inhabitants of Uterik, Rongerik, and Rongelaap, three islands in the Marshalls nearly one hundred miles east of Bikini, were not so fortunate. The AEC announced that 26 American sailors and 236 inhabitants of these islands had been "unexpectedly exposed to radiation."[11]

The sailors were manning a weather station on Rongerik. They had been well briefed on fallout. When dust clouds appeared six hours after the explosion they donned protective gear and stayed in their tents. Exposed skin was quickly washed and the sailors suffered minor, if any, ill effects.

The natives had not been briefed. The word "radioactive" was not in their vocabulary. They watched in awe—and in ignorance—as the poisonous dust clouds blew over and the debris settled on their unprotected bodies. A few days after the explosion many of them fell ill—the first victims of the thermonuclear age. They were evacuated to a medical station at Kwajalein with itching skin, sores, and eventually uncontrolled vomiting. In a few days their hair began to fall out. None of them died, but it was three years before they could be returned to their island homes. Every year afterward they were examined to assess the long-term effect of their exposure.

One precaution that had been taken before the test was to send patrol planes out to scout the probable danger zone to make sure no ships were in the area. For unaccountable reasons, the planes did not sight the *Fuku Ryu Maru*—the *Lucky Dragon*. She was sailing east of Bikini, somewhere near the boundary of the prohibited area.[12] If the physicists had not underestimated the force of the explosion, it is possible that the *Lucky Dragon* would not have been within range of the fallout.

It was at 6:12 on the morning of March 1, 1954, that the twenty-three crewmen of the tuna boat saw a fiery glow on the western horizon. A few hours later a fine white ash drifted down on the men above deck. Like the Marshall Islanders, they had not been briefed on the danger of fallout. They took no precautions; they didn't go below, they didn't put on protective clothing, they didn't wash the dust from their skin or hair. Like the islanders, they became ill.

Two weeks passed before the *Lucky Dragon* berthed at Yaru, Japan. By that time several of the crewmen were seriously ill. The news spread, the world was shocked. It was the first acute realization of the terrible dangers of fallout. Anti-American demonstrations were held in the major cities of Japan. Bitter recollections were rekindled. Only nine years earlier a callous Uncle Sam had visited his wrath on Hiroshima and Nagasaki. Again, the culprit was the same and the victims were the same.[13]

With the secrecy lid clamped tightly in the United States the press and even members of Congress had difficulty in determining what had happened. The lack of information produced the usual result—speculation. One story was that the blast devastated everything within an eighty-mile radius.

President Eisenhower and AEC Chairman Strauss were finally forced to call a press conference. Strauss admitted the United States had miscalculated the force of the explosion. He was defensive, and told the press:

> The first shot has been variously described as "devastating," "out of control," and with other exaggerated and mistaken characteristics. I would not wish to minimize it. It was a very large blast, but at no time was testing out of control. The misapprehension seems to have arisen due to two facts. First, the yield was about double the calculated estimate—a margin of error not incompatible with a totally new weapon. . . .[14]

Strauss was accurate in describing the explosion as a "totally new weapon." Representative Cole, the Joint Committee on Atomic Energy Chairman, exulted that "we have passed another milestone. We now have a deliverable hydrogen weapon that can be dropped anywhere in the world." The Russians had achieved the same thing, but their weapon was different and smaller. It was a fusion bomb triggered by fission. American scientists had produced a fission-fusion-fission bomb.

As long as nuclear explosions produce by-products, scientists, by analyzing the debris, can usually determine the components of the bomb. The ash from the *Lucky Dragon* was analyzed by one of Japan's leading nuclear physicists, Dr. K. Kimura. To his surprise and puzzlement he found traces of an unusual uranium isotope, U-237. Since the nuclear trigger is composed of U-235, and the fusion fuel is lithium deuteride and tritium, what was the source of U-237?

In May, a mystified Kimura reported his findings to the Japanese Chemical Society. Soon there was an international search for the answer—Ralph Lapp in America, Mituo Tarketa in Japan, and Josef Rotblat in England. They reached similar conclusions. The U-235 triggered the fusion of lithium deuteride. The high-energy neutrons blasted away by the fusion created another explosion in a mass of natural uranium (U-238) that was the third stage of the bomb. The U-237 was a by-product of the last-stage explosion. The three explosions occurred almost simultaneously.[15]

In *Men Who Play God*, Norman Moss speculated:

> In the Bikini bomb there were probably several tons of [natural] uranium wrapped around the fusion bomb. The explosion by fission of this uranium probably contributed twelve megatons of the fifteen megatons of the bomb.[16]

The scientists at both Los Alamos and Livermore were alarmed by the miscalculations of the power of the three-stage bomb, despite the public reassurances of Lewis Strauss. Some of the laboratory people, aware of the underestimation of the bomb's force, began to worry about the possibility of a similar error in one of the shots scheduled for testing by the Livermore people.

There is still somewhat of a mystery surrounding the first Livermore tests in the Pacific. There was a Livermore shot, involving a cryogenic (low-temperature) device that went off as scheduled. Richard Hewlett, historian of the Energy Research and Development Administration (the former AEC), describes the first Livermore shot as "successful." Teller calls it a "disappointment." Official secrecy still hides the real facts.

In any case, the second Livermore shot, which was apparently of far greater experimental significance than the first, was canceled. Why was such a huge undertaking summarily scrapped? In *The*

Hydrogen Bomb, Shepley and Blair offer their own rather chilling explanation:

> The task force commander planned to follow the March 1 shot with a supergiant of all atomic bombs, which originally had been assigned a predicted force of 15 megatons. The new calculations pushed the giant bomb near the practicable limit of thermonuclear weapons, 45 megatons, 2,400 times the force of Hiroshima. The schedule of the tests was changed to put it last. The probability was that its mighty fireball and shock wave would destroy the entire chain of advance camps between Eniwetok and the "shot" island.
>
> Then at the last minute the task force commander and the Atomic Energy Commissioners decided that the bomb could not be fired without unacceptable risk to ships at sea and Marshall Island natives. It was postponed for a later test in a greater expanse of the Pacific.[17]

Hewlett, who is still bound by the limits of secrecy, states that "there is nothing in the record to reflect that there is any validity in these two paragraphs from the Shepley-Blair book. In other words I can say that no Livermore test was postponed because of Bravo; that we have no indication that Livermore ever had an estimated yield of either 45 megatons or 15 megatons for their test; and that no Livermore shot during Castle [the series that included Bravo and the Livermore tests] was moved to another site."[18]

Teller also challenges the version of Shepley and Blair and, at the authors' request, wrote his own account of the events, which has been cleared by classification officers:

> The workings of a laboratory such as Livermore depend on new concepts and on subsequent experiments which are wrongly called tests (a test verifies something which is presumed to be known, and an experiment attempts to make a longer step into the unknown). Livermore got off to a bad start by trying to make too long steps. Two small shots in Nevada led to disappointment.
>
> Two bigger shots (but, by far, not the biggest) were planned for the Pacific. The first of these was fired. It too was a disappointment. The second was to be a follow-on. One of my colleagues, Montgomery Johnson, a most careful and imaginative scientist, promptly figured out what was wrong with our planning and gave arguments as to why the second shot should not even be fired because its failure was predictable. Since we had to wait for the right weather and since each day spent in the Pacific costs great amounts of money, it seemed the

right decision to cancel the second shot. This appeared, of course, as a big disappointment to the Laboratory.

I went to Ernest Lawrence, explained the situation, and suggested that the shot be cancelled. He asked whether I had confidence and made a strong point of saying that I, myself, should be blamed for the failures of our initial attempts. He expressed full agreement of our policy of taking chances and my specific suggestion of cutting our losses at the moment. He suggested that I take the first plane to the Pacific and convince the people on the spot.

This action was characteristic of him. A decision made by him would, of course, have cancelled the shot. But he knew the people in Eniwetok were deeply involved in the planning activity and that his own knowledge was second hand. He wanted the people directly responsible for the shot, and in particular, Herb York, director of the Livermore Laboratory, to feel that the decision was made according to their own best convictions.

When I arrived I found that Herb York was reluctant to accept the suggestion to cancel the shot. But after detailed discussion of approximately one hour, he agreed that this should be done, provided others agreed. We then went through an exercise that took most of the day convincing our friends one-by-one and in groups that the shot should be cancelled. So you can see that the second shot (I believe it was called Echo) was cancelled (not postponed) and the cancellation had nothing to do with yield.

It was after this painful experience that we introduced the "premortem" committees for the purpose of a more thorough check on every planned experiment, which had the purpose of replacing the much less useful "post-mortem" discussions which had followed our first failures.

I do not know whether it was the bitter lessons or the pre-mortem committees that brought to a halt our string of bad luck in the test activities.

It should be particularly noted that the first shots planned by Livermore established a tradition to look for new fields, not just to produce bigger bangs.

The LASL shot of March 1, 1954, named Bravo, used an experimental thermonuclear device and had a yield of 15 megatons. I believe Lewis Strauss's comment to be correct, so a calculated yield of seven megatons is believable. Glasstone, as well as others, has referred to the functioning of a thermonuclear device as fission-fusion-fission.[19]

In *The Legacy of Hiroshima* Teller expressed the decision in a more colorful way: "If you have made a mistake in buttoning up your coat, you must undo the buttons and start all over again." He also conceded, "We had tried to do too much, and we had tried to do it in the wrong way."[20]

From the limited evidence available it does not appear that Teller was trying to blow up the world, nor was he in a megaton race with Los Alamos. It appears that he was seeking to test theories of fusion that were not yet understood.

This speculation is supported by Lowell Wood, a young protégé of Teller at Livermore. Wood, despite his youth, has worked close to Teller for many years. He is a tall redhead who sports a full beard, prompting Teller to refer to him affectionately as "the Hippie."

According to Wood, his boss tends to propose highly innovative systems (Wigner, after all, called Teller "the most imaginative physicist I have ever known").

"As a matter of fact," Wood told the authors, "he has proposed systems so radical that they still have to be experimentally evaluated. They are exceedingly difficult to even put to a test. They are in some respects like [Einstein's theory of] general relativity. General relativity has been around for fifty-five years and people are still groping to come up with reasonable tests for it. It's the same sort of thing with Edward. The U.S. has spent millions of dollars on some of his most notable designs in respect to nuclear explosives."

If Teller's theories are radical, the man himself "is a very conservative personality," according to Wood. "Edward just won't take any chances that he can possibly avoid. And, indeed, this kind of philosophy has been a guiding principle of, at least, the United States' nuclear explosives effort."

Wood contends that as a graphologist determines character from handwriting, a physicist's design for an experiment reveals the nature of the scientist. "The first [thermonuclear] devices were not hydrogen bombs, they were experiments to test the feasibility of hydrogen bombs. If you could see what they were and how people regard them today I think you would have a very considerable insight, a very deep insight into Edward Teller because of his experiments. I am afraid only one has received much attention in the public domain, so I really cannot comment on the other one. If you had a dozen prominent physicists lined up to view these devices and asked who was the most likely designer, the answer would be Edward Teller, pure and simple. They really carry the stamp, of, among other things, a very conservative person."

Another way to evaluate a man's personality is to interact with him over a long period of time. Lowell Wood first met Teller when the former was a sophomore at UCLA. Wood wrote:

> When you get to know him, the single most striking feature about Edward's life is the extreme difference between his public image and what he really is. The image that has been built up of him in the press, and I am afraid in the public mind, is that of a cold, calculating scientific superman. What he really is is a very warm, engaging, concerned human being.[21]

After fighting so long for a second laboratory, the series of mistakes at Livermore was particularly difficult for Teller to bear. But the mistakes had a positive value. The structure of the laboratory was reorganized. So, as Teller wrote:

> . . . we started again. But our efforts this time were led by a group of real experts. An expert, according to a favorite definition of Niels Bohr, is a man who by his own painful experience has learned all the mistakes that can be committed in a narrow field. We at Livermore had made all the mistakes that seemed possible. We were now experts, and each year from 1955 to 1958 the laboratory brought in a rich harvest of unexpected and practical results.[22]

One of Livermore's notable successes was the miniaturization of fusion weapons. In 1958 Teller's laboratory produced a thermonuclear warhead for the Polaris rocket.[23] Teller later received a Defense Department citation for the achievement.

The pace of work at Livermore was enhanced dramatically with the acquisition of a computer, UNIVAC-1, in 1953. After the weapons program gained momentum, the laboratory began to branch out and take on other assignments. By October 1955 some of the scientists were engaged in such futuristic pursuits as attempting to develop a nuclear propulsion system for space travel (a model of the space vehicle stands alone and forgotten on a windowsill in Teller's house in Berkeley). In January 1957 the lab began development work on a nuclear ram-jet for supersonic low-altitude missiles.

In July of that same year, Teller initiated a program for peaceful uses of atomic energy. It was named Project Plowshare.[24]

One month later the Soviet Union announced a successful series of tests of intercontinental ballistic missiles—IBMs. The assumption in the United States by that time was that the Russians had the means to deliver thermonuclear warheads to American targets. Teller held out the hope that someday both superpowers would beat their bombs into Project Plowshare, but meanwhile he feared that the Russians were gaining on the United States.

The public, however, seemed more concerned about the danger of fallout from continued nuclear testing. The debate on the test ban dominated the 1956 presidential campaign. In Teller's opinion, the danger from fallout was overrated. But he knew the public's fears were genuine and that the issue was politically explosive. As a result he came forth with his own proposal to reduce the amount of radioactivity in the atmosphere. In essence, it was a simple plan. The Russians and Americans would agree that in a given period of time they would not reintroduce into the atmosphere more than one half of the radioactive material that was disappearing due to natural decay.[25] Under this restriction, Teller believed that the scientists could then develop "clean" nuclear weapons.

No one paid much attention to this proposal during the 1956 campaign, but Teller revived it on March 20, 1958, in a letter he wrote to AEC Chairman Strauss.

> I think we could and should consider restricting the amount of radioactivity released in the atmosphere.
>
> There are obviously many ways in which to do this. We could agree to limit the amount of fission products we release. We might even go as far as to agree to release no future strontium after a set date—for instance, January 1, 1959. The latter possibility would hurt us, but it would not hurt us nearly as badly as a test moratorium.
>
> We could offer an agreement on a mutual basis or we could announce some unilateral restriction on the fission product released.

With some emotion, Teller then explained to Strauss why he favored his own kind of proposal to a test ban:

> In my opinion such a test moratorium would have disastrous consequences. The only military field in which we still possess superiority is that of nuclear explosives. A test moratorium would be a powerful tool in the hands of the Russians to deprive us of our last advantage. . . .[26]

Despite his proposal to Strauss, Teller recognized the growing influence of the test-ban advocates. He recognized that if development of nuclear fusion was to continue, two steps must be taken. One was to develop a "clean" bomb, the other was to accept the fact that sometime in the future all testing would be forced to move underground.

In 1957—the year before the proposal to Strauss—Teller and Lawrence appeared before a Senate subcommittee chaired by Senator Henry (Scoop) Jackson. The subject was to be the need for reactor products, but John H. Morse, special assistant to Strauss, recalls that Teller changed the subject.

"They [Teller and Lawrence] had just learned that Harold Stassen* was going to recommend a complete cessation of tests. So instead of addressing the issue for which the hearings had been arranged . . . they almost intuitively spoke of the great damage which would occur if all testing were stopped. . . . Senator Jackson found this to be such an impressive account of what would be denied by (an end to) testing that he arranged for the entire Joint Congressional Committee to hear from these eminent gentlemen the next day."

The two California scientists made their pitch to the entire committee, but it didn't stop there. During the course of the hearing Chairman Cole left the room. When he returned he asked Teller and Lawrence: "Could you gentlemen remain in Washington over the weekend? The reason I ask is that I have an appointment for you with the President on Monday."

They accepted, of course. Monday morning Strauss, Lawrence, Teller, and Mark Mills, one of Teller's principal assistants at Livermore, were ushered into the President's office. Morse recalls the meeting from accounts he heard later:

"The President seemed really interested in only one thing that they brought up, and that was the possibility of removing the radioactivity from large weapons; in other words, producing mostly fusion rather than fission reactions. And Dr. Teller made the statement, as he told me, that he thought over a period of time, if they worked hard at it, they could reduce the fission component of nuclear weapons to five percent, a very small proportion. The Presi-

*At that time Stassen was President Eisenhower's special assistant for disarmament.

dent was greatly interested in that as a peaceful application of nuclear explosions."

In 1962 Teller wrote of this 1957 meeting:

> One point was raised in the discussion which was and is of great
> importance. We can perfect "clean" nuclear explosives. These can
> be used in war to destroy an intended target without releasing radi-
> oactivity to be carried by the winds to do damage indiscriminately
> where no damage was intended. These "clean" explosives can also be
> used in peace as powerful workhorses in mammoth construction
> jobs.[27]

There were a lot of skeptics about the "clean" bomb proposal,
none more vehement than Senator Clinton Anderson of New
Mexico, who, later, was to be the nemesis of Lewis Strauss. On the
floor of the Senate, in the course of criticizing Strauss, Anderson
was sarcastic about the claims of Teller and Lawrence:

> Not only that, but on the day on which the chairman of the Atom-
> ic Energy Commission paraded Dr. Teller and Dr. Lawrence to the
> White House to talk about a cleaner bomb, they had come to Wash-
> ington to testify before the subcommittee on Military Applications of
> the Joint Committee on Atomic Energy, headed by the able Senator
> from Washington [Jackson]. In their testimony they said that this
> country needed more plutonium production. In the course of that
> testimony those witnesses made some voluntary observations about
> how to get a cleaner hydrogen bomb. When word of that testimony
> leaked out, Dr. Teller and Dr. Lawrence were rushed to the White
> House in order that a press release could be given out, in which they
> were labeled as great geniuses who were going to produce a vastly
> cleaner bomb.

Anderson was apparently being peevish when he referred to the
scientists as "great geniuses." It is a fact, however, that Livermore
did develop comparatively clean fusion weapons.

Underground testing was apparently first proposed in 1956 by
Teller's close friend, geophysicist David T. Griggs, who had been
scientific advisor to the Air Force. Griggs suggested to Teller that a
nuclear blast below the surface of the earth might produce valuable information about the earth's crust. And since radioactivity
would remain imprisoned in the underground cavity created by
the explosion, there would be no atmospheric fallout problem.
Shifting wind currents would no longer delay testing.

Teller liked Griggs's proposal; so did Gerald Johnson, who was in charge of Livermore's tests.[28]

On September 19, 1957, the United States detonated its first underground nuclear explosion. The bomb was a creation of the Livermore Laboratory and was code-named Rainier. As a starter, it was extremely small, in nuclear terms—a fission bomb of only 1.7 kilotons. It was exploded in a drilled hole nine hundred feet beneath the surface of a mesa in the Nevada desert. As Teller later described it—

> From an observation post a few miles away, a small group from Livermore watched the explosion. They saw much less than they would have seen in an atmospheric test.
>
> The mesa shivered and appeared to lighten in color. The top of it jumped upward nine inches, throwing up some sand that cascaded down the slopes. Then the earth fell back into place, apparently unchanged except for a few fissures. A slight shock was felt at the observation post. No trace of radioactivity escaped. The experiment was complete.[29]

What happened underground, and what was achieved by this first subterranean nuclear explosion? Initially the rock around the blast was vaporized and a cavity one hundred feet in diameter was created. The cavity was lined with four inches of molten radioactive rock, which, from the top, dripped into stalactites. Then, as the cavity began to cool, fissures broke in the molten rock and the hollow sphere collapsed. A chimney of rubble, four hundred feet high, was created. The radioactivity was monitored as it slowly crept underground. According to Teller, "It moved inches, feet, before it could reach any living thing it would decay."

A year later, the Rainier test was followed by other detonations with yields up to twenty kilotons. The scientists learned that explosives in the range of several hundred kilotons could be safely conducted underground in the Nevada test site. The experience would later be the basis of a Livermore proposal for underground nuclear explosions to loosen and retort oil shale, without disturbing the surface.

This was one of many ways in which Livermore scientists were interested in using nuclear weapons for peaceful purposes. By 1956 they had concluded that it would be more economical to move large volumes of earth by fusion explosives than by conventional explosives. With the reduction of the size of the fission trigger, thermonuclear blasts with much less harmful radiation were possible.

These proposals for peaceful uses were under the umbrella of Plowshare. The political trigger for what was to become Plowshare was the 1956 Suez crisis.[30] On October 29, the Sinai campaign was opened by Israel, Britain, and France, and by November 5 the Israeli army had occupied the entire Sinai peninsula. The Suez Canal was closed to shipping.

If the canal were to remain closed for a long time, it would seriously disrupt world trade. Harold Brown of Livermore envisioned the possibility of constructing a sea-level canal across Israel, bypassing the Suez. The new canal would be built with nuclear explosives.

In February of 1957 a secret meeting was held to explore the possibility. Scientists were on hand from Los Alamos, Livermore, and the Sandia Corporation laboratories. The discussion was not limited to the Israeli canal, however. A comparison of the costs of nuclear and conventional methods of building a sea-level canal across the Central American isthmus was also made. Another topic explored was the possibility of removing earth by nuclear means to facilitate open-pit mining of ore. The economics of this new genie would permit the construction of large harbors at relatively low cost. Oil production could be increased by fracturing underground rock formations, and underground furnaces—retorts—could be created in oil shale rock for the extraction of the kerogen (the crude-oil substance) from the rubbleized shale. These and other ideas were kicked around, but when the Suez Canal was reopened later in 1957, the urgency of the crisis disappeared.[31]

In July of 1957, Livermore's Harold Brown and Gerald Johnson, with strong support from Teller and Ernest Lawrence, formalized the proposals for peaceful uses by giving it a name. The name came from Nobel Laureate I. I. Rabi in a conversation with Brown. "So you want to beat your old atomic bombs into plowshares," Rabi said. Brown had his name—Project Plowshare.[32]

Long before the oil crisis of the winter of 1973-1974, caused by the Arab oil embargo after the Yom Kippur War, Teller had warned of the need for greater American self-sufficiency in fossil fuels. In an interview with the authors in 1973 he pointed out that it was intolerable for a great power's economy and defense to be dependent on the political whims of Arab sheikhs. He predicted that sooner or later the Middle Eastern oil merchants would realize they had a near monopoly and, knowing the buyers needed oil to survive, would charge what the traffic would bear.

American dependence on Arab oil seemed all the more ironic because on the slopes of the western Rockies 1.8 *trillion* barrels of oil are locked in oil shale. Many of the large oil companies had experimented, without real success, to find an economical way to extract it. The rock could be quarried and retorted in huge surface furnaces, but this is expensive and environmentally unacceptable. The oilmen have also considered setting off conventional explosives deep underground in the shale, and setting a subterranean fire to extract the oil substance. This is known as *in situ* retorting.

The Plowshare proposal was for *in situ* retorting, except that the furnace would be created by a nuclear explosion underground. The result would be a hollow column, loosely filled with rubble, as in the underground Nevada tests. But this rubble would be the oil shale that potentially could meet the United States' oil requirements for the foreseeable future. Set afire, it yields its kerogen (oil substance) which could then be pumped to the surface.[33]

This nuclear extraction proposal has never been tried. Despite its promise of leaving the surface of the mountains unblemished, the concept has seemed frightening and unacceptable to the public, and politicians have responded to their fears. Teller himself has been the butt of criticism and jokes by Colorado newspapers, specifically the Denver *Post*, for even considering the underground nuclear blasts.

Hence the proposal remains dormant. The Energy Research and Development Administration has reportedly been seeking private companies to furnish capital and serve as partners to the government. Nothing has happened. One possibility (suggested by the authors) is that the Navy, with a historical mandate to assure an adequate supply of fuel for its fleet, should be interested in an oil shale development contract with the Livermore Laboratory.

Nearly twenty years after it was conceived in the minds of Teller and his associates, the Plowshare program has gone nowhere. Teller believes that political considerations, augmented by environmental fears, have stopped it dead in its tracks. He cites one specific example: There are large coal deposits in Alaska near the Pacific coast that cannot be mined because of the lack of harbor facilities. One rich deposit is at Ogoturuk, south of Point Hope on the Arctic Ocean. But Ogoturuk has no deep-water harbor. In 1962 Teller wrote:

The harbor basin and the canal connecting it to the ocean would cost less than ten million dollars. Only four nuclear explosions, each with a yield of twenty kilotons, would be needed to dig a deep-water canal with a width of 250 to 300 yards. A turn-around harbor basin 600 yards in diameter could be dug at the end of the canal with a 200 kiloton nuclear explosion.[34]

In Teller's view, unjustifiable fears of the hazards of radiation have doomed this and other Plowshare projects.

The scientists in the Soviet Union evidently agree with Teller's contention that with care and proper safeguards nuclear earth moving can contribute to man's exploitation of the earth's resources. As early as 1949, shortly after the first Russian nuclear explosion, Andrei Vishinsky boasted:

> Right now we are utilizing atomic energy for our economic needs in our own economic interest. We are razing mountains. We are irrigating deserts. We are cutting through the jungle and the tundra. We are spreading life, happiness, prosperity and welfare in places wherein human footsteps have not been seen for a thousand years.[35]

It is difficult to accept Vishinsky's boast at face value. In 1949 the technology of nuclear explosives was still in a primitive state. And the "clean," relatively radiation-free, weapons were still far in the future. The extent to which nuclear engineering is being used in Russia is still clouded in official secrecy. But there have been frequent news reports that they are preparing to divert several rivers that now flow into the Barents Sea. By building a canal their waters could be redirected into the Volga River. The additional volume of water in the Volga would flow into the Caspian Sea, helping to raise it to its former level. In the past several years the Caspian's level has dropped about eight feet. Ports and fishing villages have been separated from the water and the sea's yield of fish has been cut in half. If this nuclear engineering task can be accomplished without danger to the environment, the fishermen of the Caspian Sea will undoubtedly be grateful.[36]

During the busy year of 1957 Teller wrote to Strauss that he had been asked to testify on civilian defense before the Military Operations Subcommittee on Government Operations on the morning of February 14.[37] The topic was civil defense. Both Teller and Wigner were concerned that the Soviet Union's first-strike capability (which is to say it could strike before the U.S. could respond) could inflict millions of casualties on American civilians. Teller's reasoning was that the very preparation for such an attack would lessen its probability. So he testified:

> The most essential requirement for a satisfactory defense for our population is an adequate system of shelters. This is not a new idea. It happens to be the best defense in a nuclear war as it was also the best defense in the older type of warfare.

The Soviets have a well-organized plan, in the event of a threatened nuclear strike, for the evacuation of all their major cities in forty-eight hours. Teller does not recommend a similar plan for the United States. In his testimony he explained why:

> In contrast, the evacuation of cities is not only self-defeating, but will endanger our war effort. I believe that this is a matter of great concern. If we prepare for mass evacuation of the cities and if we announce the fact, then we advertise to a potential enemy that a mere threat of mass attack will produce in this country a great degree of confusion. Thus, by the threat of an attack our military defenses can be weakened and so we will give an enemy an additional incentive to threaten or attack our population. If, instead, we should make it clear that we can protect our civilian population adequately and without interfering with the war effort, the purely military reason for an attack on our civilian areas will disappear.[38]

This testimony was delivered during the height of the cold-war period, when fears of Russia were at their highest. Today, in the spirit of *détente*, does Teller persist in his cold-war attitudes? During an interview in Tel Aviv in May 1972, the authors baited Teller. Most authorities, we suggested, believe peace is assured as long as there is mutual deterrent. Both the United States and Russia have "overkill" capacity. So why should the United States continue to build nuclear weapons?

"We do have a chance to destroy Russia," Teller responded, "if the Russians let us. But the Russians have devoted much more work to self-defense. I believe that within the near future the situation may arise that the Russians can wipe us out and we can do nothing to retaliate. The Russian leadership is extremely conservative—they are not going to attack us unless they have adequate defenses.[39]

Teller would not elaborate on what he meant by "adequate defenses." Can there be an adequate defense against an incoming thermonuclear missile? Can Moscow or Washington be defended against a MIRV (Multiple Independently-Targeted Reentry Vehicle—a missile with several warheads, each capable of being aimed to a specific target)? Again, the barrier of secrecy prevented Teller from explaining.

Perhaps he was aware of the "death ray" race. For years, science fiction and old radio horror dramas featured that old chestnut, the death ray. The death ray is no longer fiction. It exists today in the laser. In theory an earth-orbiting laser with enough energy can be programmed to intercept and destroy incoming missiles. In *The Soviet Conquest of Space*, Peter N. James wrote:

> The Soviets are developing a lethal laser weapon system for use in orbital space craft and space stations. Significant Soviet laser work is conducted in a secret laser facility built during the 1960s in the Steppes of Siberia.
>
> It is the Soviet objective to develop an orbiting defense network that can neutralize U.S. spacecraft and space stations, ICBMs and ABMs. If the Soviets continued on their present course and the United States executes its space and defense plans as outlined by the Secretary of Defense and the head of the National Aeronautics and Space Administration, it must be concluded without reservation that the Soviets will achieve clear-cut military, strategic and space superiority over the United States.[40]

James, who was employed by Pratt and Whitney, prepared assessments of Soviet capability for the Air Force. He undoubtedly knows his subject. It must be assumed, therefore, that the American intelligence has made defense officials aware of the Soviet development of laser interceptors. And it must be assumed further that the United States is engaged in a parallel research and development effort.* If this is the case, the world is shielded by Soviet

---

*The authors learned subsequently that the United States discontinued research on the orbiting laser in the spring of 1974. Then, early in December 1975 an alarm was sounded in the corridors of the Pentagon when both *Aviation Week* and ABC News reported that the Soviets were using ground-based lasers to "blind" U.S. observation satellites. These satellites are part of the early warning system designed to alert U.S. intelligence to any Soviet missile launch. A few days later, the new Secretary of Defense, Donald Rumsfeld, denied the existence of the Soviet lasers and reported that red glows reportedly seen on the Russian landscape resulted from a ruptured oil line that had caught fire.

and American secrecy from the knowledge of a new kind of arms race on which the future of the world may hang.

In March 1958, the director of Livermore, Herbert F. York, was asked to assume an important post in the field of his first love, space exploration. He left Livermore and went to Washington as Assistant Secretary of Defense for Research and Development. Lawrence and Teller had enthusiastically recommended York for the job but, according to Teller, "Herb got the job and within two weeks he sold us out. He was for nuclear weapons up to the day he went to Washington and never after. I said I did not understand Oppenheimer; I say I understand Herb York, but that does not make me respect him any more."

Teller, as usual, was worried about defense. He sensed a change in public opinion. Interest in nuclear projects seemed to be waning on the Hill.

"There was a clear movement," he explained later, "to change the Livermore Laboratory from its purpose to make nuclear explosions to the new field of space research. I opposed that. I wanted Livermore to continue doing the extremely important job that it started to do. And I thought, that in order to make sure, I should take over the directorship."

With Lawrence's support, Edward Teller was appointed director of the Livermore Laboratory in March 1958. Teller's intent was to keep the post for just one year. During his tenure, much of the ground was plowed for several decades of work in nuclear weaponry. He played an equally important role in the pursuit of peaceful uses of nuclear energy (Plowshare) and controlled fusion (Sherwood), that is, fusion used to produce heat energy.

Teller had already sought out and found an heir apparent, a young physicist named Mark Mills. Shortly before Mills was to assume the post, he was killed in a helicopter crash while flying from one island to another in the Eniwetok chain. Teller was shaken.

"Mark Mills's death was a dreadful blow—I felt lonely and lost. I had thought Mills and I would undertake the job jointly and that within a short time he would assume the full responsibility."[41]

In Washington the move toward an atmospheric test ban was gaining momentum. This put tremendous pressure on Livermore to complete a series of tests at the Pacific proving grounds in the summer of 1958. John Foster, Carl Haussman, Kenneth Street, and Duane Sewell worked with Gerald Johnson to perform as many tests as possible before the probable end to atmospheric detonations. The scientists pushed themselves almost beyond the limits of endurance. They worked twelve hours a day, seven days a week, for many weeks. They knew this might be their last chance to search for the kind of experimental evidence that could be obtained only from atmospheric testing.

Teller wrote of "surprises," "disappointments," and "successes surpassing our most optimistic expectations. We had to make last-minute adjustments. We sometimes had to act on guesses."[42]

From Teller's point of view, the rush was justified. Earlier in 1958 the Russians announced they would stop nuclear testing if the United States would. Responding to the Russian challenge, President Eisenhower proposed that scientists from the United States, Britain, and the U.S.S.R. meet to discuss the technical feasibility of detecting and thus policing nuclear tests. That summer, a conference of experts met and concluded that the detection of atmospheric tests would be relatively simple. Eisenhower invited the other two nuclear powers to a conference at Geneva to begin on October 31, 1958. The goal was to draft a treaty to end nuclear tests.

The day before the conference, the United States, as a sign of good faith, unilaterally announced a one-year suspension of nuclear testing. The Soviet Union continued atmospheric testing for just a few more days, then it, too, joined the voluntary moratorium.

During the one-year suspension the Eisenhower administration hoped to reach an enforceable agreement for a permanent test-ban treaty. The bitterest differences between the superpowers were on the issue of on-site inspection. Atmospheric testing is relatively easy to detect and, according to Teller, even detection of underground tests "is not exceedingly difficult, but identification and verification are. There are three chief obstacles to the policing of underground nuclear explosives: noise in the earth's crust may mean a test or an earthquake; a radioactive deposit is not easily located underground; and subsurface tests can be muffled."[43]

Seismology is an inexact art. Seismographs can establish the location of earth noises only within an area of about one hundred square miles. One approach to the detection of a suspicious earth movement would be to send in a team of inspectors. If radiation were found, only then would they know that a nuclear explosion had taken place. But, Teller cautions, "A one-megaton explosion, equivalent to one million tons of TNT, could be set off at a depth of 5,000 feet without leaving a trace of radioactivity on the surface. Seismographs could not tell inspection teams at what depth the suspicious disturbance had occurred."[44]

There are other obstacles to the detection of underground nuclear testing. It is established that explosives can be muffled. Instead of drilling a hole in the ground and inserting a nuclear device in the drilled hole to fracture the surrounding virgin earth, the nuclear device can be inserted in a prepared cavity. As Teller explains it, "If a twenty-kiloton bomb, with an explosive force equal to 20,000 tons of TNT, were set off in a hole nearly 500 feet in diameter located 3,000 feet below ground, it would be muffled so as to resemble an explosion of only seventy tons."[45]

It was because of this difficulty of underground detection that the United States demanded that a permanent test treaty be policed by on-site inspections of suspected violations.

Since Teller did not trust the Russians, he constantly illuminated methods by which they could cheat. I. I. Rabi criticized Teller for this attitude. He told us:

"I've never seen him take a position where there was the slightest chance in the interest of peace. I think he is an enemy of humanity. When it came to the first steps in arms control [the test ban] Teller was brilliant in inventing excuses and ways it could be circumvented, far beyond any reaches of common sense. We spent enormous fortunes trying to meet his objections."

Perhaps Rabi is right and Teller is paranoid about the Russians. Or it may be that the exposure of himself and his family to the communists compels him to view the Soviets with suspicion. He would probably paraphrase Murphy's law from "If anything can go wrong, it will," to "If the Soviets can cheat, they will." Teller remembers the Russians' denial that they had missiles in Cuba.

In 1960 Teller resigned as director at Livermore and was succeeded by Harold Brown. Two years earlier, Ernest Lawrence, mortally ill, made two requests of Teller shortly before Lawrence died on August 27, 1958. First, he asked that Teller remain as director as long as he could and, second, that when he was ready to step down, he could find no better successor than Brown.[46]

Teller, by 1960, felt that Brown and a new generation of young scientists were ready to take over the responsibility of running the laboratory. Lowell Wood, one of these younger scientists, tells a story about Teller that provided evidence that he had, first, a temper and, second, that he did not hold grudges. It happened shortly after Brown took over.

"This man was much younger," Wood recounted, "but he was almost as belligerently defensive as Edward is." It happened that the entire British Atomic Energy Commission and two U.S. Atomic Energy Commissioners were visiting the laboratory. Edward and this young man got into a mild disagreement. Neither one of them would give way in front of the visitors. Then the disagreement rapidly grew very sharp. They finally were shouting at each other at the top of their voices and they ended up stomping out opposite ends of the room.

"The young man just assumed that the argument meant he was dismissed and went to his office to clean out his desk. Then Brown came by, saw what he was doing, and assured him that Edward didn't have any hard feelings; that everything would be all right. Brown asked him, at least, not to resign on the spot—they would like him to stay."

And, as Wood explained, the "young man" stayed and became one of the laboratory's best scientists and has a distinguished record as a designer in nuclear explosives work.

Teller, however, never considered himself an administrator. He felt he could "best serve his country by returning to the classroom and the laboratory." On his resignation (he retained the title of associate director) he was appointed professor of physics at large in the University of California.

Actually there was more to Teller's relief at stepping down than his desire to teach and do research. As director he had to be overly cautious in making any public statements. His official position was inhibiting his need to speak his mind. "There were many things I wanted to say, things that I was convinced could be said effectively only if I were free of any official restraints. They could be said only if I divorced myself from government work."

He went back to the controversy over the test ban. On May 24, 1960, he wrote to British Rear Admiral Sir Anthony Wass Buzzard:

> I could probably convince you of the great advantage of nuclear weapons in a limited war.* . . . I am worried about our drifting to-

*In August 1975 there were rumblings of a new attack on South Korea by North Korea. Teller, asked to comment on reports that the U.S. might defend South Korea with tactical nuclear weapons, declared it might make sense from a military standpoint, but it still would be "a horrible mistake."

wards test suspension. It now has been conclusively demonstrated that underground tests and testing in interplanetary space are practical and that they can be concealed up to a considerable size. Tactical weapons can certainly be tested in a clandestine way. Therefore test cessation would be unilateral. Within a few years Russia could leave us far behind in its nuclear striking power, if they should decide to test in secret.[47]

Hans Bethe did not share Teller's distrust of the Russians. On April 25, 1960, he delivered a lecture before the Philosophical Society of Washington. His main point was:

> The Soviets consider their secrecy a great military asset, and will not easily give it up unless they get a lot in exchange. Test cessation is not enough. Because of the Russian secrecy the West has proposed that the verification of a test cessation agreement, and possibly of other disarmaments, should be primarily by physical methods, physical methods meaning less intrusion into the privacy of the Soviet Union.
>
> It is clear that the Russians have accepted the major premise, the major principle, that there should be a control system for test cessation agreement. This, in itself, is an important result of the negotiation and we must not jeopardize this achievement by breaking off the negotiations as some politicians have advocated, or by unreasonable demands that politicians have advocated, or by unreasonable demands that we know can't be fulfilled by Russia.

The question was how Bethe would define "unreasonable demand." Since small underground testing would be difficult to detect, the U.S. on February 11, 1960, proposed as a first step the banning of large nuclear explosions. As a means of policing compliance the Americans proposed a limit of twenty inspections a year on Soviet soil. In July 1960 the Russians agreed to on-site inspection—provided they were limited to not more than three per year.

While this debate was going on, Teller was urging the AEC to prepare for underground testing. He found himself facing opposition from an old adversary, Norris Bradbury, director of Los Alamos. To settle the controversy between Bradbury and Teller, the AEC called a special meeting. John Morse described for the authors what transpired at the meeting.

> Dr. Bradbury thought that it [underground testing] would cost too much; it would be too difficult to do; and that you could not get the

kind of results from a test standpoint that you should get. Also Dr. Bradbury thought that you would be restricted to very low yield tests underground. Dr. Teller took the opposite point of view on every issue, saying that he thought, if carefully done, you could get some better diagnostics on underground tests than you could on atmospheric tests. There were some aspects of tests you could not get underground, but you could get most of what you needed to know. He also thought that if you were careful and worked up to it progressively, we could probably test a megaton underground, and, as you m·'y know, we have tested five megatons underground. He also thought that it would be cheaper because the radioactivity problem released to the atmosphere would not exist. We would not have to be so careful about the weather. We would not have so many postponements of the tests because the winds were in the wrong direction, or some other problem of that sort.

The Atomic Energy Commission sided with Teller. Preparations were made for underground testing, when political conditions made such testing possible. In spite of Bradbury's earlier opposition, when underground testing was resumed in September 1961, Los Alamos, according to Teller, "did some very interesting and important work in the field."

During that same month, in the midst of negotiations on a test-ban treaty, the Soviet Union unilaterally returned to atmospheric testing, with thirty-two shots in two months. The Russian test series included the most powerful thermonuclear bomb ever to be detonated in the atmosphere. It had a reported yield in the range of fifty-five to sixty megatons, or 55 to 60 million tons of TNT.

Livermore was partially prepared to meet the Soviet challenge and to resume testing. The clearest picture of what happened is contained in a letter from Teller to Strauss, dated October 4, 1963. In part, it said:

> During all of the test moratorium Livermore was actively pressing to prepare for resumption of testing. We prepared for the resumption of underground testing which, in our opinion, had the greatest chance of being actually permitted. Our requests were only partially satisfied. In particular we were not permitted to proceed with some important details of the preparation, lest the Russians find out about these preparations and use them as evidence of bad faith on our part.[48]

The unilateral resumption of testing on the part of the Soviet

Union shook up public opinion in the United States. The Soviets had pledged that they would faithfully observe the moratorium as long as the British and the Americans did. In an article entitled "Teller Right from the Beginning," columnist Roscoe Drummond criticized both the Russians and the people who believed in their promises. Teller, of course, had been constant in his disbelief. Drummond hailed him and demanded that "the very least we can do is try to repair the unfairness of all the criticism which was directed for so long against one of nation's most distinguished and dedicated scientists. I refer to Edward Teller, who had to suffer the approbrium of being right from the beginning."

History proved Teller right in his fear that the uninspected test ban was a Soviet trap. But can his challenge to the prevailing fears of radiation be supported?

Teller admits that "too much radiation certainly is dangerous. Excessive amounts of radiation can cause painful burns and lesions on the skin, leave the body susceptible to cancer or leukemia, cause the mutation of unborn children, or result in death."[49]

Teller also agrees that in the event of all-out nuclear war that (in addition to the obvious horrors) people would be exposed to dangerous radioactive fallout. But radiation from test fallout, he contends, is another matter.

> . . . it is very small. Its effect on humans is so is little that if it exists at all it cannot be measured. Radiation from test fallout might be harmful to humans. *It might be slightly beneficial* [our italics]. It might have no effect at all. The smallest doses producing noticeable effects in animal experiments, approximately one tenth of one roentgen unit per week, are more than a thousand times as great as world-wide fallout. These experiments produced a slight increase in the incidence of animal tumors—and a lengthening of the animals' average life. The living organism is so complicated and the intertwining of cause and effect is so intricate that we may never know the biological effect of so small a cause as world-wide fallout.[50]

If fallout in amounts produced by nuclear testing is not harmful to the living what is its effect on the unborn? Can it produce genetic accidents? Will it produce mutations and abnormalities in future generations? According to Teller: "World-wide fallout can be expected to influence heredity." Then he raises a paradoxical question: "But are abnormalities harmful?"[51] Without genetic abnormalities the human race would not have evolved into its present state. Still, Teller conceded he would be concerned if there were a notable increase in the rate of mutations. But, he claims, such a rate has not been observed.

During his lifetime, by Teller's calculations, an individual receives fifty times more radiation from natural sources than he does from fallout.

There are other causes of genetic abnormalities. As the temperature of the male sperm increases so does the statistical chance of mutations. "Our custom of dressing men in trousers causes at least a hundred times as many mutations as present [1962] fallout levels." Teller suggests the hazard might be reduced if men wore kilts.

Background radiation varies with geography and particularly with altitude. The citizens of Denver are exposed to nearly double the normal natural radiation. In the high mountains of Peru the natural radiation is twice that at sea level. Statistically an airline hostess should have a greater chance of bearing an abnormal child than the girl at the ticket counter.

Even at sea level, Teller points out, background radiation varies with the kind of soil. For example, thorium is radioactive. It is found in both monazite sands and in thorite. There are large deposits in Brazil, India, East Africa, South Africa, Idaho, and the Carolinas. People living in these regions are exposed to more than the normal natural radiation. To Teller's knowledge, no good statistical studies exist to evaluate the effect, if any, on the tens of thousands of people living in villages, for generations, on this radioactive soil.

One of Teller's favorite stories deals with the relative radiation hazard of sleeping with your wife as opposed to the dangers of leaning against a Dresden III-type nuclear reactor for a year. All humans, he points out, emit radioactivity from their bodies.

"One young employee of the AEC asked a friend of mine a question: From what do you get more radiation—from leaning up against a reactor for a full year or from sleeping each night with your wife? My friend did not know the answer. The young man from the AEC made some calculations and sent around a notice which said: 'I have calculated that, and actually you get a little more radiation if you lean up for a full year against the Dresden III reactor than from your habit of sleeping each night with your wife. I am not going to initiate a campaign for a regulation that all married couples must sleep in twin beds. However, I must warn, from the point of view of the radiation hazard, that if you sleep each night with *two* girls you will get more radiation than from leaning up for a full year against the Dresden III reactor.'"

In early August 1963, years of meetings, deadlocks, breakdowns, and reconcilations finally yielded a limited test-ban treaty that was initiated by the representatives of the United States, the Soviet Union, and Great Britain. In the United States the proposed treaty had the full backing of Secretary of Defense Robert McNamara and the Joint Chiefs of Staff. On August 9 President Kennedy submitted it to the Senate for ratification.

More than six weeks of debate followed. On August 23, Teller appeared before the Preparedness Investigating Subcommittee of the Senate Armed Services Committee. He told the Senators that the test ban would not make it more difficult for Russia to "catch up" (as some of its proponents had claimed) because "it is by no means certain that the United States is ahead of the Soviet Union in the field of nuclear explosives." In other words, the Russians would not need to catch up if they were already ahead. He felt the ban could not be policed and that, for example, the Russians might test in distant space where detection would be impossible. Teller also worried about the wording of the treaty; he believed it excluded common ballistic missile defense arrangements with the NATO allies of the United States. He summed it all up with the comment that "I feel it is my duty to conclude by the statement that ratification of the treaty would have grave consequences for the security of the United States and the free world. . . ." Later, after the completion of his prepared remarks, his emotions overflowed. If the Senators voted to ratify the treaty "you will have given away the future safety of our country and increased the dangers of war."[52]

Teller's testimony was widely publicized. When Kennedy was asked his reaction, the President sneered, "It would be very difficult to satisfy Dr. Teller in this field."[53]

The New York *Times,* in a feature story published the day after Teller's testimony, called him "the last of the unreconstructed nuclear scientists of World War II." All of the other influential scientists of that period, the *Times* pointed out, were either dead or had joined the ranks of test-ban proponents.

"What government officials cannot forget, however," the *Times* said, "is that the Hungarian-born physicist was right in consistently pushing, over formidable opposition, for development of a hydrogen bomb. The weapon has been critical to maintaining the nuclear balance of power in the world."[54]

Teller's persuasiveness was not sufficient. The Senate ratified the nuclear test-ban treaty on September 23, 1963, by the overwhelming vote of 80 to 19.* Although Britain and the Soviet Union had not yet formally ratified the document, there was no doubt that they would. Nuclear tests in the atmosphere, under water, and in space were thenceforth prohibited. The only country with nuclear capability that did not sign was France. The nuclear successes of China and India were still in the future.

By the time the treaty was ratified, Teller was resigned to the fact that it was going to happen. But when President Kennedy hailed the achievement in a broadcast statement, Genevieve Phillips, Teller's loyal secretary since 1956, went out to her car to listen. She didn't want him to have to hear the President in his Livermore office. When Mrs. Phillips returned to her desk, distressed at Kennedy's note of triumph, Teller consoled her. "Gen," he said, "you knew it was going to happen. Why do you think I've been brooding for weeks?"

Then Teller left the room, and Genevieve Phillips put her head down on the desk and cried.

*The only Senator not voting was Clair Engle, Democrat, of California. Seriously ill in a hospital, Engle nonetheless sent word that he would have voted with the majority for the treaty.

19

There Is No Peace

BY assuming an active role in the test-ban controversy, Teller had finally accepted without qualification his moral duty, as he saw it, to become directly involved in matters of national interest. He immersed himself in consulting, advising, even cajoling public and private men of power. Not all of his friends approved.

"His is a wasted life, scientifically speaking," said Laura Fermi in an interview with us in 1973. Since 1938 the Tellers and the Fermis had been close friends. Enrico had died in 1954, but his widow had kept in touch with Edward and Mici. Laura Fermi became no mere echo of Enrico. She carried on as a writer of several books, including a biography of her husband and a book on famous immigrants to America. She was not a scientist, but through her husband acquired a good working knowledge of physics. On the basis of Enrico's judgment, she knew Teller had been a great physicist.

But Teller's life of the past two decades has left Laura Fermi puzzled and disappointed. "To me—I am no scientist so I can't really say—but it seems to me that this restlessness and traveling is an attempt to make up for lack of achievement in the traditional sense. From what my husband said about him, I would have expected something more scientifically important. He never seems to settle down to do some serious work, somehow. I don't think that in the beginning he had this need to be important, to be with important people, that I seem to sense."

Laura Fermi's analysis of Teller may be too harsh, even lacking in sufficient insight as to his motivation. The editors of *Time* did not agree with her. In 1957, after the Soviets had startled the United States by rocketing the first two man-made satellites into orbit, *Time,* in the aftershocks of Sputnik I and Sputnik II, did a cover story on the state of science in the United States. On the front of the issue of November 18, 1957, was the shaggy countenance of "Scientist Edward Teller." He was presented, in a four-page story inside, as the shining example of American science at its best. There were secondary tributes to such Teller allies as Lawrence, Seaborg and Alvarez, and to Teller adversaries Rabi and Oppenheimer. Teller was selected as the first among American scientists because, in the opinion of *Time,* he, more than any of his colleagues, had recognized the accelerating pace of Russian scientific achievement, and had done the most to persuade the United States to stay ahead.[1] In terms of popular recognition, winning the front cover of *Time* was the zenith of Teller's career.

Laura Fermi's objective facts about Teller are accurate. Since the middle 1950s Teller has been incessantly on the run. In a typical work week, he has been known to work two days at Livermore, attend a meeting in Washington, make a speech in Miami, visit Nelson Rockefeller in New York, make a social visit to Dallas, and attend a consulting session in Los Angeles. In busier weeks he has consulted in Tel Aviv or Bangkok, or other foreign capitals, usually on energy problems or on peaceful uses of nuclear power.

During the past twenty years Teller has been a paid consultant to at least ten private corporations and an unpaid board member, advisor or consultant to more than a dozen government or non-profit agencies. One of the most time-consuming was his taking personal charge of interviews of students seeking grants from the John Hertz Foundation, a project which his wife, Mici, played an equal part.

Teller will not divulge how much he was paid for any of his corporate consultantships on grounds that this would be a violation of a private contractual agreement. Most of the corporations are defense contractors.

The late columnist Drew Pearson, a longtime critic of Teller, did not miss the opportunity to cast doubt on his intellectual honesty. On September 25, 1963, Pearson wrote a vitriolic column on Teller in the wake of his unsuccessful opposition to the test-ban treaty. According to Pearson, Senators Stennis, Thurmond, and Henry Jackson "have long thought the sun rose and set on Teller. When other senators diagnosed his objectiveness, however, they found that Teller had served as a consultant for various big defense contractors at fees of $1,000 a day."

Teller's sardonic response to us was, "I wish he had been right." In a letter he explained: "My main source of income has always been with the University of California. In all consultations with

Federal agencies, including the military, I have served without remuneration."

The assumption that Teller was always paid for his advice or testimony gave him the last laugh on one occasion. In 1967 he voluntarily testified at a public hearing in New York on a proposed Storm King Mountain reservoir for Consolidated Edison's hydroelectric plant. The reservoir was opposed by an environmental group which also had a battery of consultants ready to testify. In the midst of his testimony Teller was challenged by the environmentalists' lawyer as to how much he was being paid to support Con Edison. Teller responded that he was paid nothing. At the next session of the hearings, most of the opposing consultants failed to appear, apparently embarrassed by the possibility of having to answer the same question.

Since Teller will not reveal his earnings, including his fees for consulting, it is impossible to say what his net income has been or to gauge his net worth. The available evidence indicates he is not a wealthy man. The house on Hawthorne Terrace in Berkeley where he and his wife have lived for twenty years, is relatively modest. When he retired from the Livermore Laboratory in June of 1975 he expressed doubt that he could keep his house. "We may not be able to afford it," he told us.

A cynic might say that any man will justify, on moral grounds, that which fattens his pocketbook. To pass such a judgment on Teller is to ignore his capacity to fight for causes whch pay him nothing or, equally significant, his capacity to fight for friends who have been loyal to him.

In early 1959 President Eisenhower nominated Teller's close friend, political mentor, and H-bomb ally, Lewis L. Strauss, to be Secretary of Commerce. On the basis of historical precedent, Strauss should have been confirmed by the Senate almost automatically. Only four Presidents in history had ever had cabinet appointees rejected and in each case under extraordinary circumstances. But the political climate had changed drastically from the McCarthyist hysteria that had prevailed during the AEC's Oppenheimer security hearing in 1954. The resentment over the Oppenheimer findings swept through the scientific community immediately, and Teller was the first to feel it. It was five years after the Oppenheimer explosion before the fallout descended on Strauss, who had been chairman of the AEC. He was now widely blamed for the Oppenheimer affair, even though he had very little part in initiating it. Strauss was a brilliant, ex-investment banker who made a million dollars, then devoted most of his life to public service. Like Teller he opposed the test-ban treaty, but unlike Teller he was often arrogant about his convictions. And Strauss was a practicing Jew.

At Strauss's request, Teller testified on his behalf before the Senate Committee on Interstate and Foreign Commerce. His statement was essentially simple. He detailed Strauss's contributions to science and defense as one of the founders of the Office of Naval Research and as a member and chairman of the AEC. He especially emphasized the AEC's involvement in peaceful uses of nuclear energy.

It is probably an indication of Teller's essential nature at this time in his life that his loyalty to a friend overcame his awareness of the sentiment of the vast majority of his fellow scientists. In the midst of the hearings, the secretary of the American Physical Society invited Strauss to be the main speaker at its annual banquet in Washington. A large number of the physicists, probably a majority of them, were furious. The attack was led by Edward U. Condon, a former director of the National Bureau of Standards and a past president of the APS. Condon wrote a letter to the society's governing council announcing that he would not be present, and detailing a litany of charges against Strauss in the form of rhetorical questions:

> Is not Strauss the man who long fought against the policy of allowing even the scientists of allied nations to have minute quantities of radioactive materials for medical research or the therapeutic relief of human suffering? . . .
>
> Is not Strauss the man who sought to exercise one-man dictatorial control over all atomic energy matters in America by ingeniously combining his role as chairman of the Atomic Energy Commission with that of scientific advisor to the President in atomic energy matters, using this double role to justify keeping his fellow commissioners in ignorance of atomic energy affairs which they needed to know to do their duties as commissioners? . . .
>
> Is not Strauss the man who long misled the President and misinformed the public about the fall-out dangers of large scale nuclear testing?
>
> Is not Strauss the man who was principally responsible for direct-

ing the security persecution of our former [APS] president, J. R. Oppenheimer?

Moved by Condon and others, a group in the APS created "The Last Strauss Committee," which sent a letter to every member of the society for his signature. The committee had "no objection to the appearance of controversial figures before the Society," but wanted to make it clear that his appearance did not constitute an endorsement by the APS as he awaited Senate confirmation as Secretary of Commerce. A substantial proportion of the society's members signed the letter.

Teller's public defense of Strauss before the Senate committee came only five days after the APS dinner. Five weeks later the full Senate, by a narrow margin, stunned Eisenhower by rejecting the nomination. It was a bitter blow to Strauss, who had regarded himself, justifiably, as a dedicated public servant. He returned to private life and never accepted another public post.

After the rejection Teller immediately wrote a letter to Strauss expressing his regrets. Strauss's reply was poignantly brave:

> You were good to write me as you did . . . and I shall always treasure your letter. You and I have stood shoulder to shoulder on many battlefields, and I think that time is abundantly vindicating the causes for which we contended. As for the enemies whom we have made, history will accord us the more respect because of them.
>
> Be of good cheer and let us be sure to keep in touch with each other. . . .

On July 1, 1959, Teller received a letter from President Eisenhower:

> I personally and deeply appreciated your testimony before the Senate committee on behalf of Admiral Strauss and, as you know, I share your feeling of shock and resentment concerning his ultimate rejection by the Senate itself. He has been an invaluable public servant whom I shall greatly miss both personally and in the conduct of the business of government.

In the midst of the Strauss controversy Teller was, for the second time in his life, hospitalized for ulcerative colitis. It was not to be his last attack. Coincidentally, this was the same affliction which eventually killed Ernest Lawrence, a death that Teller felt deeply. He was at the time of his life when he would, with sad regularity, endure the passing of his best friends from the scene. Fermi had died in 1954 at fifty-three; von Neumann in 1957, also only fifty-three. Szilard was sixty-six when he died in 1964; Gamow, who had moved to the University of Colorado, died in 1967 at sixty-three.

In 1957, when Teller was fighting off an almost continuous bout with colitis, Lawrence was seriously ill. Teller wrote to Strauss, joking about his own affliction: "On my last medical check up it was found that I have the same trouble as Ernest. It is a good thing to imitate him, but it seems I am carrying it too far. I have resigned from many of the things I am now doing and will have to lead a more quiet life."

Fortunately, Teller did not carry his imitation "too far." In the summer of 1958 Lawrence, already weakened by colitis, was appointed, along with Robert Bacher and James Fisk, as an American scientific representative to the Atoms for Peace Conference at Geneva. Teller had been worried that Lawrence was in no condition to take on such a responsibility. His worry was justified; in midsummer Lawrence became so weak that he had to come back home to California. By mid-August, the tireless, dictatorial inventor of the cyclotron, the greatest of the high-energy physicists, was mortally ill. He died on August 27, 1958. Despite their occasional personality clashes, Lawrence and Teller were essentially kindred spirits. When he died, Teller had lost another of his champions. In honor of the departed physicist, the Berkeley radiation laboratory was renamed the Lawrence Berkeley Laboratory, and Livermore, which they had sired together, became the Lawrence Livermore Laboratory.

In 1962 and 1963 Teller was to go through two emotional ordeals—the first offset with some humor, the second a heart-rending resurrection of the pain of the past. In 1954 Congress had created a special award to be presented annually by the Atomic Energy Commission to a scientist who had made outstanding contributions to nuclear physics. The candidate for the honor is recommended by the AEC's General Advisory Committee on the basis of an advisory poll of scientists. The official nomination is then made by the AEC and approved by the President of the United States. The first award was made to Enrico Fermi when he was terminally ill. On his death, the prize appropriately was renamed the

Enrico Fermi award. Subsequent winners included Lawrence, Seaborg, and Bethe.

On November 15, 1962, Teller received formal notice that he would receive the Fermi award in a White House ceremony on December 2. His selection was "in recognition of his contribution to chemical and nuclear physics . . . his leadership in thermonuclear research . . . and his efforts to strengthen national security."

Teller brooded over what he should say in response to the award and finally wrote a speech that, although its text no longer exists, apparently reviewed the H-bomb controversy in such a way that his friends felt he was stirring up old animosities. But it was forwarded anyhow to the AEC and the Pentagon, probably for security clearance. En route to Washington Teller and his wife stopped off overnight at White Sulpher Springs, West Virginia, where they were the guests of their old friend Ted Walkowicz. He is the aeronautical engineer who had been executive officer of the Air Force's Scientific Advisory Group and later moved into private industry.

At an unreasonable 6:30 A.M. on the day Teller was to receive the award from the President, Walkowicz was awakened by the jangling telephone in his room. It was Harold Brown, the director of research and engineering at the Pentagon. Walkowicz recalls the sequence of events:

"Hello, Teddy," said the voice on the phone, "this is Harold."

"Harold, how are you?"

"Fine, Teddy. How are things?"

"Fine, but why the hell are you calling me at six-thirty in the morning?"

"You haven't seen Edward recently, have you?"

"You know goddamn well he's sleeping right down the hall."

"Well, how do you like his speech for the Fermi Award?"

"I haven't seen it yet, but I guess *you* don't like it."

Brown then pleaded with Walkowicz to persuade Teller to tone the speech down. "Let's not reopen old wounds," said Brown.

"Okay," said Walkowicz, "I'll see what I can do." And he rolled over to go back to sleep, only to have the phone ring again.

"Hello," said Walkowicz, now getting exasperated.

"Hello, Teddy old boy."

"Who's *this*?"

"Mack McHugh." It was General Godfrey McHugh, Air Force aide to President Kennedy. "Have you seen Dr. Teller recently?"

Walkowicz muttered an obscenity. "You've got the same thing on your mind, haven't you?"

Indeed, he had. Once again Walkowicz agreed to try and persuade Teller to modify the speech.

By this time, there wasn't much point in trying to sleep. Walkowicz got dressed and went down to the dining room. Edward and Mici were already having breakfast. Edward looked like a thundercloud, and "he and Mici practically had their backs to each other." Walkowicz sat down.

"What's the matter?"

"Teddy," Mici pleaded, "tell him not to do it."

Teller was stone-faced. Finally he sputtered at his wife, "Be quiet. I do what I want to do."

Mici looked at Walkowicz again. "He wants to make a stupid speech and reopen all that argument."

"Let me see the speech," said Walkowicz. There was not a sound as he read it carefully. When he had reached the last page, Walkowicz moaned, "This is terrible, terrible."

Teller snatched the speech out of Walkowicz's hand. "It's none of your business," he said—according to Walkowicz's recollection.

"Of course it's none of my business," Walkowicz agreed. "If you want to make a horse's ass out of yourself, go ahead!"

The meeting of the threesome dissolved into the kind of total disorder that can be achieved only by two feuding Hungarians. Walkowicz finally brought the situation to a focus by admitting he had gotten the protesting telephone calls.

"See, Edward," said Mici, "even Harold Brown thinks you are crazy."

And so, according to Walkowicz, he and Mici edited the speech, "with Edward fighting like a lion over every word and phrase. We finally turned it into something very innocuous. And he agreed to sit still for just a word of appreciation for the award."

Walkowicz believes in all seriousness that Teller's original version of the speech, with references to things that Fermi said on his deathbed, would have badly exacerbated the schism that had existed since the Oppenheimer hearing.

"Edward," Walkowicz warned him, "remember that the most important thing is to get invited back to the White House." This advice was delivered when the Tellers and their companion landed at Washington National Airport. "Remember, don't insult the President in his own home."

What Walkowicz underestimated was Teller's dislike of John F. Kennedy. Consequently, Teller did not take his friend's advice.

About six o'clock that evening the latest recipient of the Fermi Award phoned Walkowicz at his home.

"How did it go?" Walkowicz inquired.

"Well, almost okay."

"What do you mean, *almost* okay?"

"Well," said Teller, "I think I made one small mistake."

This sounded ominous to Walkowicz. What had happened was that under the Plowshare program the scientists at Livermore had proposed building a second Panama Canal to be excavated with nuclear explosives. After the formal presentation of the award to Teller and after Teller's acceptance speech (all of which had gone smoothly), Kennedy took Teller aside to learn more about the possibility of a canal produced in such a radically different way. The President wanted to know a lot of things. He especially wanted an estimate on how long it would take to do all the geological research, the survey work, the soil sampling, and the economic calculations and the nuclear calculations.

"While he was asking me all these questions," Teller reported later, "I interrupted. I said 'Excuse me, Mr. President. All *that* will take less time than it will take you to make the right political decision.'"

Although Teller's affable nature is such that he does not normally take any pleasure in overt insults, he had come very close with Kennedy. He had tossed the President a non sequitur that, under the circumstances, left Mr. Kennedy nonplussed. He gave what Teller described as "a sour grin" and went off to talk to somebody else.

Exactly one year later the Fermi award ceremony was endured again but one year had made the circumstances dramatically and tragically different. Oppenheimer had now lived for ten years as a near-recluse—a martyr to the cold war. Teller had endured his own kind of ostracism, but had come out of the shadows somewhat when he received the Fermi award in 1962. Since many scientists rarely thought of Teller without complementary thoughts of Oppenheimer, it was not surprising that the nominee for the 1963 Fermi award was that "security risk" of a decade earlier. Oppenheimer had continued to hold the exalted academic post of director of the Institute for Advanced Study. But just as Teller was a hero to the public and a turncoat to many academics, Oppenheimer, conversely, was a villain to much of the public, and virtually a saint to a segment of academia.

Although Teller was not one to wobble on his convictions about national defense, it is obvious from his letters and statements over the decade since Oppenheimer was first accused that he desperately wanted to end the scientific and political rift that had blighted the lives of both men. Consequently, when the General Advisory Committee polled the scientists on the 1963 Fermi award nominee, Teller cast his vote for Oppenheimer. He was genuinely delighted when he received official word in April from the AEC that the man who had steered the atom bomb team had been selected. Teller, as a former winner, was invited by President Kennedy to be present at the ceremony on December 2, 1963.

Only ten days before the scheduled presentation, John F. Kennedy was gunned down in Dallas. In the confusion there was some concern over when and where the Fermi award ceremony would take place. But Lyndon Johnson, who had assumed the presidency with laudable assurance, quickly notified Oppenheimer and the invitees that the presentation would be made at the White House as scheduled.

When Oppenheimer appeared at the White House, many of the guests had not seen him for some years. Once remarkably youthful for his years, he was now, at fifty-nine, painfully thin, gray, and wearied. Teller, despite his regular bouts with colitis, was hale and heavy by comparison.

The December 2 date was, by design, the twenty-first anniversary of the first achievement of a controlled nuclear reaction by Enrico Fermi and Leo Szilard on December 2, 1942. Not by design, it was the tenth anniversary of the date that Oppenheimer had been advised that the Atomic Energy Commission had declared him to be a security risk.

The guests at the brief ceremony included Oppenheimer's wife, Kitty, their two children, Peter, twenty-two, and Katherine, nineteen; Glenn Seaborg, then chairman of the AEC; physicist H. D. Smyth, who, back in 1954, had been Oppenheimer's only defender on the AEC; Edward Teller; and a large contingent of important scientists.

President Johnson had been quietly advised before the presentation that since Oppenheimer had been Kennedy's choice for the award, the AEC would understand if the new President preferred not to make the presentation personally, since it was fraught with political pitfalls. To Johnson's credit, he insisted on carrying out the wishes of his murdered predecessor, calling it "one of President Kennedy's most important acts." A gaunt but smiling Oppenheimer accepted the award and a $50,000, tax-free check. His response was Oppenheimer at his best.

"I think," said the prize winner, "that it has taken some charity and some courage for you to make this award today. That would seem to me a good augury for all our futures."[2]

When the formal ceremony was over, it was Teller's turn to try and bind the wounds that had subjected both men to ten long years of pain. Graciously, and without an apparent sense of tension or embarrassment, he stepped forward and offered Oppenheimer his hand. Oppenheimer accepted it with equal grace, and their clasp was firm and convincing. Several photographers memorialized the apparent reconciliation.

Unfortunately for Teller, his gesture, whatever his motives, was seen in its worst light by some of his unforgiving colleagues. One of them contended that Kitty Oppenheimer "walked away in disgust." At least one of the photographs, however, shows her looking on, though not sharing her husband's smile. Another witness sarcastically insisted that "Teller waited until the cameramen were around before he shook Oppenheimer's hand."

Comments such as these seem to overlook some obvious aspects of the situation in which Teller found himself. First, although Teller was not going to back down on his sincere convictions about national security, he continued to nurse the belief that he could restore the personal friendships that once transcended scientific or political opinions. Second, as the previous year's winner of the Fermi award, it seemed fitting that he be present. And, last, being present, it would have been the height of boorishness *not* to shake Oppenheimer's hand.

Life magazine, in a highly emotional recounting of the Teller-Oppenheimer controversy,[3] saw in their handshake a hope for an end of the ten-year fissure between two camps of scientists. It was not to happen, except by the slow, binding forces of still more time. The arguments were never settled, but raging passions are eventually stilled when they become aging passions.

If there were die-hards against Teller on the left, there was comparable intransigence on the right. Senator Bourke Hickenlooper, ranking Republican on the Joint Atomic Energy Committee, called the Fermi Award ceremony "revolting," and no Republican committee members showed up for it. Oppenheimer was not to rankle them much longer. His health was failing. A little more than three years later, he was dead.

Perhaps it is possible to place too much emphasis on the "climate of opinion" as a factor in the way the actions of men are evaluated. But if there is such a factor, Dr. Oppenheimer seems to have exemplified it like few great men of his century. A typical case can be made by reviewing editorial comments in the Baltimore *Sun* papers of 1954 and 1963. In both of those years, these newspapers were renowned for perceptive editorial judgments.

On June 30, 1954, *The Evening Sun* made this comment on the AEC's finding that Oppenheimer was a security risk:

> It is probable that this conclusion will be long debated by many persons. But this much is certainly clear to everyone: Dr. Oppenheimer had the fullest and fairest of hearings . . . it is clear that the two groups who have reviewed the evidence have done so in an eminently dispassionate and judicious manner. Even that part of the public which will recognize the real personal tragedy that is involved for Dr. Oppenheimer will feel that those who have formally found against him have done so out of a high sense of justice and responsibility.

On April 6, 1963, the day after Oppenheimer's selection for the Fermi award, an editorial in *The Sun,* called "Climate's Victim," said, in part:

> So dangerously short is memory that we find it hard today to recall the atmosphere that hung over this country a decade ago when Dr. Oppenheimer's security clearance was reviewed and then withdrawn. . . .
>
> The witch-hunters could ride high for a while because the atmosphere arose more fundamentally from a national worry, a national self-distrust. . . . To blame it on the Russians or on the eternal imperfections of human affairs would not suffice. Within our own society we had to find sacrificial victims, ritual scapegoats. We were sick in the head.
>
> Dr. Oppenheimer was one of the scapegoats. His long record of distinguished, loyal service to the nation was brushed aside because of a minor indiscretion. Ruthlessly, under a cloak of mealy-mouthing that sounded sort of legal but wasn't, and rang sort of reasonable but was disgracefully irrational, the dagger was thrust. . . .
>
> The public value of the action [the Fermi award] is that a measure

of justice has been done, an unfairness tardily and partially corrected; and that we are reminded that such a climate can darken this
country's spirit and will, and did darken them not so long ago.

The Baltimore *Sun* papers can be forgiven only to the extent
that they, like many newspapers and millions of Americans, saw
Oppenheimer in two different eras in different climates. What was
"a high sense of justice and responsibility" in 1954 was "disgraceful-
ly irrational" looking back from 1963, but this was no more nor less
than the prevailing popular view in each of those years.

For most of his life Teller has shown no interest at all in religion,
a gap that often disturbed his friend Lewis Strauss, who was an intensely devout Jew. The neutrality of Teller's religious life reaches
far back into his childhood. The intellectual community of Budapest was indifferent to formal religion, and well mixed between
those who were nominally Jewish or Christian. Mici's family,
though Jewish by origin, adopted Christianity, but little of either
faith rubbed off on her. The two children of Edward and Mici,
Paul and Wendy, were likewise raised with little or no religious
training. And yet in the middle 1960s when Wendy was a student at
Radcliffe, her father learned from her brother, Paul, that Wendy
had been steadily dating one young man for a while. When Teller
phoned his daughter, with a typical father's anxiety, he wanted to
learn something about the suitor.

"I was absolutely shocked," Wendy said, "when my father's first
question was 'Is he Jewish?' He had never asked that kind of thing
before. I only knew in the vaguest terms that I was Jewish. I had
not been brought up as a Jew and I had no idea that it made any
difference."

Teller's surprising question to his daughter may have had no
particular significance, or it may have been an indication of his
awakening sense of his own role as a Jew in a world where the future of Judaism was still precarious and where one country, Israel,
had become an outpost of Western values. Whatever the basis for
his interest, Teller began to pay increasing attention to the struggle
of Israel and by the late 1960s had finally allowed himself to become directly involved in the new country's fortunes. There was
an additional factor: Teller's aunt, cousin, and other members of
his family, as well as his close friend Ferenc von Körosy, had mi-
grated to Israel after World War II.

It is certain that Teller's first overt interest in Israel came about through his professional association and personal friendship with Yuval Ne'eman, a native Israeli who became one of the world's premier theoretical physicists. Ne'eman received most of his scientific training in London and his Ph.D. thesis in 1960 was so impressive as to give him immediate prominence among physicists. He returned to Israel to head up the atomic energy establishment there. In 1963 he came to the United States and served for two years as a visiting professor at Caltech.

After his departure from Caltech, Ne'eman returned to Israel, where he created the physics department at the university of Tel Aviv. It shortly became one of the five or six outstanding centers in the world for the study of particle physics. In 1972 he became president of the university. In 1969 a Caltech physicist, Murray Gell-Man, was awarded the Nobel prize for work nearly identical with Ne'eman's, specifically the classification of subnuclear particles. The same year, Ne'eman won the Einstein prize for his contribution to the same subject.

Teller and Ne'eman first met at a party in Berkeley during the period when the latter was teaching at Caltech. They knew of each other's work and developed an immediate friendship. But Ne'eman's interest in Teller went beyond physics. The Israeli saw in the American physicist a man who recognized the necessity of maintaining the strength of the Western World. Many Israelis, according to Ne'eman, consider the attitude of Americans toward Western defense as dangerously naïve—"perhaps because for us the memory of Hitler is overwhelmingly present." Israel, he believes, cannot afford to relax. In short, the attitude of Israel is a microcosm of what Teller feels ought to be the posture of the United States. And the people of Israel feel they are more secure because of Teller's successful development of the hydrogen bomb.

There had been that one prelude to Teller's active interest, the Plowshare Project, launched back in 1956, partially as a result of the Sinai campaign of that year. The possible closing of the Suez Canal spawned the idea of a second canal through Israel, excavated with nuclear explosives.

In 1966, when he met Ne'eman in Berkeley, the Plowshare Project was still faltering—it had not yet resulted in a single earth-moving task. Teller was still interested in the prospects of Plowshare in Israel. This time Ne'eman was able to persuade Teller to visit Israel to have a look. The Plowshare concept still didn't move, but Teller was obviously captivated with the industrious little country. "He was ready to become involved in something having to do with Israel," Ne'eman deduced—correctly.

With Ne'eman's guidance and support, Teller urged the governors of the University of Tel Aviv to consider the creation of an applied science department. "He helped correct the bias that made the university leadership feel they should be involved only in basic science," Ne'eman told us. The upshot was that, through Teller's urging, not only was a school of applied science established but also a school of engineering.

Within two years Teller had been elected to the university's board of governors and became, to Ne'eman, "probably the most important scientific member of the board."

Teller has since visited Israel an average of twice a year, "and every one of his visits has been useful for something," Ne'eman contends. He has not only advised, but taught, especially on the semi-popular level where Teller's ability as a lecturer shines so brightly. In 1970 Teller gave a series of ten lectures. A five-hundred-seat lecture hall proved to be not large enough and the sessions were moved into a thousand-seat auditorium. There were still people turned away.

From this activity within the University of Tel Aviv, Teller branched out to be an advisor to the university and to the government of Israel on science-based industries. He suggested various ways in which the university, by supplying the right courses, and the industries, by taking advantage of university talent, could achieve the most successful collaboration. In 1973 he formally assumed chairmanship of a committee on the board of governors on science-based industries, specifically directed toward development of a Tel Aviv industrial park.

On one of Teller's visits he and Ne'eman were having lunch with one of the ministers of the Israeli government. Ne'eman was at that time involved in pure theoretical physics, work that adds to basic knowledge, but often is incomprehensible to government functionaries who want immediate practical applications.

"Is anything good ever going to come out of your work?" the politician asked Ne'eman.

Teller, who had put up with this question many times himself when he was involved in basic physics, was somewhat annoyed at hearing it again.

"Why don't you give the answer that Faraday gave to Gladstone," he advised Ne'eman. The Israeli scientist had not heard the anecdote, so Teller recounted it for him.

It seems that Faraday was lecturing in London shortly after he had invented the dynamo—which produced electricity by rotating a coil in a magnetic field. He had his working model with which he demonstrated how to produce a small electric current. This particular evening the hall was graced by the presence of Prime Minister William Gladstone. At the end of the lecture, Gladstone approached Faraday and offered his congratulations, but then asked, "Is anything practical ever going to come out of it?"

"Well, sir," Faraday replied, "I'm not sure yet what can be done with it, but of one thing I'm certain—someday you'll find a way to tax it." Today, many a utility company will confirm Faraday's prowess as a prophet as well as an inventor.

In 1958 Teller won the Einstein prize (an annual physics award established and financed by his friend Lewis Strauss) as a sort of prelude to his winning the more prestigious Fermi award in 1962. The Nobel prize, which eventually was bestowed on most of his closest scientific colleagues, has thus far eluded Teller. And yet he has written and published scientific papers in collaboration with no fewer than eleven eventual Nobel prize winners. In addition, one of Teller's students from his postwar years in Chicago won the Nobel prize in physics in 1957 at the remarkably young age of thirty-four. He is Chen Ning Yang, who came from China in 1946, studied under Teller in Chicago until he earned his doctorate in 1948, then moved on to the Institute for Advanced Study. His Nobel prize, for findings on the behavior of subatomic particles, was awarded in collaboration with another Chinese immigrant, Tsung-Dao Lee.

Of all the Nobel prizes among Teller's associates, however, the one awarded to Maria Goeppert-Mayer seemed to please him the most. She was born in Silesia (then part of Germany, now Poland) and was eventually to become, though her father's family, the seventh generation to produce a university professor. She grew up in Göttingen (her father was a professor of pediatrics) and, despite the prejudices against women in science, entered the University of Göttingen in 1924 and won her doctorate in physics in 1930. She had left Göttingen before Teller arrived, but he met her on several of her return visits. Maria married Joseph E. Mayer, an American student of chemical physics at Göttingen. In 1930 they went to Baltimore, where her husband joined the faculty of the Johns Hopkins University.

Maria was not on the faculty; she was a housewife and in fact had two children while she was living in Baltimore. But she continued to work at physics for the joy of it. After Teller came to George Washington University in 1935 he reestablished contact with the Mayers, and he and Mici visited them often in Baltimore. Teller was extremely fond of both of them.

In 1939 the Mayers went to Columbia when Joseph was hired as a professor. Maria taught one year at Sarah Lawrence College, then found more challenging work in the laboratory of Harold Urey at Columbia. Coincidentally, Teller also came to Columbia before moving on to Chicago and Los Alamos. At one point when he was at Los Alamos he persuaded Oppenheimer to let him hire Maria Mayer to do some important calculations on uranium.

Once again their paths crossed in Chicago when Joseph Mayer was summoned there in 1946 as a professor of chemical physics. This time, however, his wife's achievements had become equally well known and she was assigned to her own professorship in Chicago's Institute of Nuclear Studies. Admittedly not a nuclear physicist, she got a crash course from Teller. In 1949 Teller and Maria Mayer co-authored a paper entitled "On the Origin of the Elements." From this beginning in nuclear physics, Maria Mayer began to develop some theories on the structure of the nucleus, specifically pertaining to the shell-like arrangement of subnuclear particles.

Maria Mayer did not receive the Nobel prize until 1963, when she was chronically ill. She shared it that year with Teller's lifelong friend Eugene Wigner and with J. Hans D. Jensen. In her Nobel lecture, in a halting voice, she paid special tribute to Teller. For him it was a bitter-sweet event, to see a beloved friend finally recognized in the sunset of her life.

Whereas the United States before World War II was extremely weak in theoretical and pure science, fantastic strides were made during and immediately after the war. This was true to the point that the roles of Europe and the United States were reversed. In the 1920s, and the early 1930s, the greatest physicists were in Germany, especially in Göttingen; in Denmark in the remarkable circle around the great Niels Bohr; with other circles around Fermi in Rome and Rutherford at Cambridge. America was a mere colony;

its most ambitious scientists had to study in Europe. By the 1950s the situation had reversed. Hitler had driven the best talent out of Germany. Then the pressure cooker of war had developed scientists, and especially physicists, at an accelerated rate. The centers of science shifted from the old universities of Europe to new centers at Princeton, Harvard, Columbia, Chicago, Berkeley, Caltech, and a dozen other campuses. I. I. Rabi recalled in 1957 that "when I went to Europe a quarter of a century ago I was provincial. When I went to Europe after the war, it was Europe that had become provincial."[4] The Nobel statistics tell the same story. From 1901 through 1930, only five Nobel prizes in science were awarded to Americans. Since 1930, the United States has collected eighty-two, almost as many as the rest of the world combined.

The excellence of the United States in basic science was pleasing to Teller, but he actually began to worry about a loss of interest in technology on the part of bright American students. In response to this need he and Ralph W. Chaney, a paleontologist, created in 1963 at Livermore a department of applied science, similar to the program he was later to promote at the University of Tel Aviv.

"This education had been, to a greater and greater extent, neglected, starting from the Second World War," Teller explained to us in 1974. "Our young people are losing interest in applied science. If they lose that we are going to lose our leadership in technology. In weapons, the writing is on the wall, because the Russians are getting ahead of us. In the peaceful economy, the same can be said. We are losing out to Western Europe, particularly to Germany and Japan. If our interest is replaced by a slogan that claims to want to take us back to nature, we won't go back to nature, we'll just go back to the Middle Ages."

The department of applied sciences at Livermore now enrolls about a hundred University of California graduate students, working on controlled fusion, properties of materials, lasers, and other highly technical fields. "We are doing something in a neglected and badly needed portion of education," Teller insists. Through June 1975, when he retired from Livermore, he was one of the principal teachers of the applied science courses, a task which he obviously relished.

Teller has joined a large number of physicists in beginning to question what is probably the most spectacular branch of scientific research, the so-called high-energy physics. This is the study of particles, particularly subnuclear particles, through the use of gigantic cyclotrons and accelerators, some of them costing hundreds of millions of dollars. They are designed to accelerate subatomic or subnuclear particles to fantastic speeds so as to smash apart the nucleus of the target element. The cyclotron, an accelerator that swirls the particle in a circle in order to build up speed, was invented by Ernest Lawrence, the Berkeley colossus of physicists, and his associates.

The accelerators came into being at a time when, as Teller explained to us, "the atom was understood because it is held together by electromagnetic forces. The nucleus was really not understood. The forces that hold the nucleus together are both very much stronger than the forces that hold an atom together and they are, to this day, unknown in their very nature." (Of course in the practical sense they were well enough known to build nuclear weapons.)

"It was unavoidable in the development of science that physicists should turn to the elucidation of nuclear forces as their number one problem. This is where the trouble started. This understanding of nuclear structure [greatly advanced by Maria Mayer and Wigner, according to Teller] which continued to develop continued also to be incomplete because it was still based on a crude idea of nuclear forces. So you go ahead and look for them.

"If you look for a detailed microscopic behavior you have to look into exceedingly small linear dimensions. In fact, you want to look into linear dimensions which are not more than one millionth of the dimension of the atom. This, according to the laws that govern all microscopic matter, cannot be done, except by using very big energy packages.

"This, in turn, had two consequences: To produce these big energy packages, which in fact have been produced, you need great investment in money, in scientific manpower and in ingenuity. This has been done; the effort has absorbed one half—and I would say the better half—of the effort of the physicists since World War II.

"The other point is, however, that when you use these big chunks of energy, without which the fine spacial structure cannot be investigated, *you deliver enough energy to change the object you are looking at.*"

Here Teller is hearkening back to one of the basic principles of quantum theory—that the atomic or nuclear behavior being observed is changed by the very fact that it is being observed. It is a concept developed primarily by Bohr and Heisenberg.

"What happened," Teller explained to us, "was that indeed we started to change the kinds of thing we were looking at. In the course of using these high-energy packages we managed to produce a profusion of new entities, of new particles. . . . In other words, we open the world, but it is practically not interacting with the world in which we live. . . . We create our own particles. Probably we will never understand nuclear forces until we have understood this new creation. And in this understanding we have made, in more than a quarter of a century, exceedingly little progress. In high-energy physics we have an increasing number, but still a limited number, of isolated observations, each of which has cost mega-bucks and the sweat of scores of highly educated people. Whenever a new observation is produced, you then have it followed up by a dozen explanations, mutually contradictory to each observation, which are usually published even before the observer has time to say 'I'm sorry, the observation wasn't quite right.'

"This is the kind of situation I described when I said that high-energy physics is at a dead end. I believe that in the end, in the real end, the contradictions will be somehow clarifed, and as a by-product, nuclear forces will be explained. . . . But if you would ask whether it is more likely that we shall have the answers ten years from now, or one thousand years from now, I will tell you I will bet for the one thousand years."

In the late 1950s Teller met Governor Nelson Rockefeller of New York and commenced an association that was to install Teller as a powerful behind-the-scenes force in federal policy, especially relating to energy. Rockefeller first summoned Teller when the former was seeking advice on the formation of a group of scholars to prepare a report on the American future. The commission was formed with Teller as an advisor. It produced a book called *Prospects for America.*

Teller minimizes his contribution to this first project for Rockefeller. "I sat in on many of the meetings and made some comments," he told us. "One of my contributions was to convince Nelson that we should do something about civil defense. He followed this up for quite a few years before abandoning it as politically unfeasible at that time. But he really worked hard on it and I was impressed by his willingness to pitch in on an unpopular cause."

Political realists might charge that *Prospects for America* was really designed to test Rockefeller's prospects for the presidency. Whatever its direct effects were on the governor's political fortunes, its side effect was to cement a firm and lasting friendship between Rockefeller and Teller. At Rockefeller's request, Teller traveled about the country delivering speeches in support of increased attention to civil defense—"making people mad, as I usually do." Briefly, in the early 1960s, Teller, having made his connections with the family, went to work for Lawrence Rockefeller, Nelson's banker brother, as an advisor on the structure of small companies.

The great northeast power blackout of 1965 launched Teller into what was to amount almost to a new career as an expert in all forms of energy. Alarmed by the massive electrical failure, Governor Rockefeller called on Teller to advise him on energy problems. In attacking the problem, Teller found himself for the first time giving major consideration to environmental problems—"Through Nelson I became an environmentalist before that was popular."

In 1970 it was probably Rockefeller's influence that prevailed on President Nixon to appoint Teller to the President's Foreign Intelligence Advisory Board, on which Rockefeller also served. The name of the board describes its function even though Teller's unfriendly colleague, physicist Marvin Goldberger of Princeton, describes it as "a 'think' outfit that doesn't do anything." In 1975 the board came under some press and congressional criticism for its alleged lack of surveillance of the CIA's possible abuses of its power. Oversight of the CIA is supposedly one of the responsibilities of the Foreign Intelligence Advisory Board, and evidence of the CIA's misdeeds was breaking out all over.

From Teller's standpoint, "One of the real attractions of the board to me was that Nelson was on it." At the monthly meetings the physicist and millionaire-politician saw each other regularly and their mutual respect was further enhanced. The upshot was that on Labor Day 1973 Rockefeller, who was about to resign as governor of New York, asked Teller to serve as one of the forty-two members of a new Rockefeller creation, the Commission on Critical Choices for Americans.

Once again many Rockefeller watchers saw in this new commission a continuing part of the Rocky-for-President campaign. If so, it was a grander design than anything that had preceded it. The ex-officio members included Nelson himself, Senate Majority Leader Mike Mansfield, and Minority Leader Hugh Scott, House Majority Leader Thomas P. O'Neill, Jr., and Minority Leader John Rhodes, and last but far from least, Secretary of State Henry Kissinger.

Other members included city planner Edward J. Logue, Clare Boothe Luce, Daniel Patrick Moynihan, consumer advocate (and ex-Miss America) Bess Myerson, CBS President William S. Paley, Marina von Neumann Whitman (an economist and daughter of the late John von Neumann), Lawrence Rockefeller, and a host of comparable notables.

Six panels were set up. The first was on energy, the second on food, health, and population, the third on raw materials, industrial development, and world trade, the fourth on international trade and monetary systems and inflation, the fifth on change, national security, and peace, and the last on the quality of life.

Rockefeller himself was chairman of all the panels. As the energy panel's work progressed, however, Teller emerged as the dominant member. So intensely did he devote himself to the task of writing a report on energy that for most of the summer of 1974 he lived in a guest house on the Rockefeller compound in Pocantico Hills, near Tarrytown, New York. When the report was released to the public on April 2, 1975, it was entitled *Energy—A Plan for Action,* and subtitled "A Report by Edward Teller to the Energy Panel of the Commission on Critical Choices for Americans." In other words, it was officially presented not as the panel's report or the commission's report, but as Teller's report.

Teller's treatment of the energy system, citing specific goals for 1985 and targets for the end of the century, is thorough and feasible. Unlike the pie-in-the-sky proposal of President Nixon in 1974 proclaiming "energy independence by 1980," Teller sees no hope for energy independence in the United States, "but interdependence whereby the U.S. will be in the position to make a positive contribution to the world economy."

He advances some of his favorite ideas. One is the extraction of oil from oil shale by the use of underground nuclear explosions which permits the whole extraction process to take place deep beneath the earth's surface wth a minimum of environmental disruption. Another Teller idea is the use of thorium as an inexpensive substitute for uranium as a nuclear power fuel.

An appendix contains a list of "recommendations for urgent action." These include a grab-bag of proposals, including heavy federal taxes on automobiles that consume excessive amounts of gasoline, a fifty-five-mile-an-hour speed limit, minimum insulation requirements in home-building codes, tax credits or loans for industries that improve fuel efficiency, the labeling of equipment and appliances to indicate average annual cost of operation, and requiring minimum lifetimes for appliances and easy repairs with a guaranteed supply of spare parts. There is a series of recommendations for the protection of the environment, including (another favorite Teller idea) a requirement that nuclear power plants be built underground or under water.

The automobile industry takes a much more severe beating from Teller in the report than the oil and utilities industries. He seems sympathetic to the financial and production problems of the energy suppliers, but he shakes his admonishing finger at the motor tycoons: "Too little progress has been made in improving the engines in our automobiles to make them compatible with environmental standards or to improve fuel economy . . . a change in the 'life style' of our Detroit factories is long overdue."

But for one particular recommendation, and a political turnover, the energy report might have been filed and forgotten. Despite the time and effort that Teller put into it, it was poorly organized and when it was released it was a public relations dud. It engendered some news wire stories and some minor television mention, but seemed to go unnoticed by Congress.

Teller, however, is extremely realistic on one aspect of the development of energy sources—he believes the goals will not be achieved without expenditures of huge sums of money. He foresees a need for expending $80 billion a year, or $840 billion by 1985, on capital development. This is more than four times the average annual expenditure in the years immediately preceding 1975. This $840 billion, he believes, "must be stimulated both by direct and indirect government action." In his appendix he proposes "an Energy Trust Fund with provisions controlling the expenditures of funds in a manner similar to the Highway Trust Fund. Disbursements from this fund should be made only to increase the supply of energy."

In the summer of 1974 while Teller was absorbed in the report, the bubbling Watergate caldron boiled over and a scandal-plagued Richard Nixon resigned from the presidency. Soon after Gerald Ford assumed the office, he nominated Nelson Rockefeller to be his Vice President. After weeks of stormy confirmation hearings, Rockefeller was confirmed by the Senate and Teller had a close friend just outside the White House.

The pressure on President Ford to deal with the long-term prospects for energy was coming from all directions. But the conservative President's posture was that government ought not to interfere in the marketplace. His economic advisors eschewed any dramatic, direct government commitment to energy expansion, such as Teller had proposed in his recommendation for an Energy Trust Fund.

Probably no one knows who changed Ford's mind, and Nelson Rockefeller may or may not have had a hand in it. Certainly the President was under pressure to take some action, or to accept the image of a do-nothing leader, the Herbert Hoover of the 1970s. Suddenly in late September of 1975 he did a turnabout and proposed a billion-dollar Federal Energy Independence Authority to finance the development of synthetic fuels and nuclear power through 1985.

It was almost precisely what Teller had proposed, even with a different name. Conservatives charged that Ford had repudiated his own policy in advocating such a huge government involvement in private-capital projects. Teller saw the hand of Rockefeller at work, and perhaps a connection with his own report.

"There is obviously a connection," he explained to us, "in that Rockefeller figured in one and figures now in the other." Perhaps it was modesty that made Teller add, "But in no way is there a close connection because Nelson does not force his opinion on anybody else."

Does Teller approve of a federal investment of that one-hundred-billion-dollar magnitude for the long-term development of energy?

His answer to us was emphatic: "I don't approve of it, I think it's absolutely necessary. I think the people who are opposing it are out of their minds. We either do something about energy or we don't. If we won't help private industry to do something about it, then we either ration energy, or make long strides toward regulating the energy industry and in the end quite possibly nationalizing it. I dislike both of these. The concept proposed here is similar to the one that was used to build up the artificial rubber industry during the Second World War; to put in government funds to be handled under the auspices of private industry, making it possible to use their skills, and have enough control through the loan mechanism so that nothing happens that can be called improper. With the present uncertainties in the general situation, it is very difficult to expect private industry to invest big chunks of money when the next government regulation may push them into bankruptcy."

By late 1975 Ford's energy proposal faced tough opposition if not outright rejection in Congress, but the concept of some kind of government underwriting of the huge capital needs of the energy industry seemed likely to survive in one form or another. Whatever the outcome, the idea and the pressure it generated is probably, to date, the most fruitful result of the strong bond between Teller and Rockefeller.

One might speculate how such a fast friendship between an urbane and somewhat arrogant millionaire-politician and a brilliant immigrant physicist ever was established in the first place. Certainly there is the chemistry of compatible personalities, but above the personal level there are obvious reasons why Teller would look to Rockefeller as his political ideal. It must be recalled that Teller was a registered Democrat and a self-described liberal until the presidential campaign of 1956, when he objected violently to what he considered was Adlai Stevenson's politicizing of the test-ban issue. Teller could not make the full jump to the political right (though in a strictly pragmatic way he admired Nixon), but Rockefeller, who in those days was the archetypical Republican liberal, represented a point on the political spectrum where the color was agreeable. At that time both still shared some golden hopes for international control of nuclear energy, and both felt that the closed society of the Russians was the barrier to peace. Both were (and still are) intensely distrustful of the Soviets, hence both believe in a strong weapons development program and extensive measures to improve civil defense in the United States. On his retirement from Livermore in June 1975, Teller accepted, for the first time, a paid consultantship to Rockefeller. It is difficult to imagine his becoming involved in this way with any other political leader.

In the 1960s, as the American involvement in the Vietnam war escalated, the student radical movement began to build momentum in the campuses across America. The earliest version of this radicalism was relatively benign—in one quarter the southern lunch-counter sit-ins in peaceful protest over the rights of black citizens, in another quarter the so-called hippies, young people in rebellion over the frenetic pace of the industrialized, automated society. Then the lack of progress in the civil rights movement and the increasing ferocity of the Vietnam war transformed many young people into militants, even revolutionaries, who had lost faith in the capitalist system and the democratic process. The peaceful protests of the early sixties became ugly and violent.

In the 1950s and early 1960s if Teller was damned, it was usually by academics still harboring a profound resentment over his contribution to the government's findings against J. Robert Oppenheimer. This resentment has never died in the hearts of most of the scientists who remember it, but by the middle sixties, that generation of scientists was no longer dominant. The relatively isolated Oppenheimer incident was unknown or blurred by time to the younger scientists and students whose principal preoccupation was with racial injustice, the Vietnam war, and the arrogance of American power.

Consequently Teller found himself in a new spotlight, though its glare was just as harsh as the now-dimming Oppenheimer beam. But as the hippies were at first unobtrusive flower children, so Teller's first experience with student radicals was more humorous than threatening.

It happened in 1967 when the Atomic Energy Commission attempted to stimulate the release of natural gas with an underground nuclear blast near Rulison, in western Colorado. Teller was present as one of the supervising scientists. This is his version of the incident, as he recounted it to us.

"Well, you know the local people in western Colorado near Grand Junction were told in detail what would happen, and they were for the shot. The environmentalists brought suit, but the judge ruled for us.

"In the end five characters who looked like the wild west, but came from New York, went into the excluded area, sat down on the ground over the bomb, and said, 'You can go ahead and shoot; you'll blow us up.'

"I offered to go and sit with them. You see, it was not all that dangerous because the bomb was to be exploded at sea level while they were sitting quite a bit higher with 8,000 feet of rock formation between them and the bomb.

"But I wasn't allowed to go in there. Instead a helicopter was sent in and offered to help them come out. Three of the five chickened out.

"Since the two others were left, they were given advice that at shock time they should bend their knees. That advice was not given for religious reasons, but rather because the environmentalists among our ancestors did not do a very good job at that truly critical time when our ancestors took the first big step away from nature and stood up, so that our spinal column is in an unnatural vertical position. Of course all our backaches date from that period and, indeed, the spinal column is the most vulnerable portion of the human anatomy.

"Now we told these two people that when the shock from the nuclear explosion arrives it will be felt on the soles of their feet and it might conceivably hurt their backbone, but if they bend their knees so that there is a bit of tether between the soles of their feet and their backbone, then there won't be any damage.

"Well, nothing happened. Or at least we don't know what happened. It may be that the Devil took the two environmentalists but if he took them, he left no hide nor hair nor hoof nor cleft. They just vanished.

"If, on the other hand, you make the assumption that they survived and that, at any rate, their bodies, in whatever state, remained on the surface of the earth and walked away, I am very sure they did not suffer any hardship, because if they had suffered any hardship we would have heard about it."

Subsequent brushes with dissident groups could not be treated so lightly by Teller. He watched the development of the so-called Free Speech Movement in Berkeley with considerable alarm. Later he wrote that "within a year there was no longer free speech in Berkeley. Within a year a vice president of the university was shouted down by the students when he reminded them that if they insist on free speech they must grant the right of speech to those who happen to disagree with them."

The Free Speech Movement, which coincided with the spreading civil rights militancy all over the country, was refueled by the Vietnam war, or so it is generally assumed. Teller, however, had his own theory, and the war, as he saw it, was only one factor. He called it the "forest fire analogy." The conditions for a forest fire, he pointed out, were a dry forest, a first flame, and a wind to spread the conflagration. In 1971 he reflected on this analogy.

The dry forest is our barren academic atmosphere. In 1945 we had three and one half million students, most of them eager to study. Now we have eight and one half million, most of them attending college because it is 'the thing to do.' They have been lured into academia with the biblical words, 'knowledge will make you free.' They are the words of the serpent. Knowledge in the modern world is most important, but knowledge alone will not suffice. The bulk of the young people at the universities are aimless, disappointed, and confused. They are ripe for any radical solution."

The "first flame," in Teller's view, was ignited by what he calls "Third World Communism." The student agitators, he contended, no longer venerate the Russian bureaucracy, but Che Guevara and "the anti-intellectual Mao Tse-tung, who ridicules learning."

"The extremists," Teller wrote, "preach destruction and postulate that an unspecified future will certainly be better than the rule of the present establishment."

As for the wind that spreads the flames, Teller has his answer—television. "The news media have always loved the sensational and the violent. But now we have the picture—better than a thousand words—flashed by satellites across the world."

If Teller, writing this in 1971, overlooks the sense of outrage American students felt at the Cambodian invasion of 1970, he does claim a reason. The radical movement, he declares, is global in scope, not just American and, kindled by academic disillusionment, lighted by "Third World Communism," and spread by television, it exists apart from specific acts of the United States government: "It is all too easy for us to see the causes as they appear only in our country."

There may be merit in Teller's argument, but there is also ample evidence to show that the pursuit of the Vietnam war and specifically the Cambodian incursion ordered by President Nixon focused the radical movement at Berkeley and gave it a target. The target was Teller himself, and for the first time in his forty-year academic career he was threatened with physical danger.

In early November 1970, a flyer was widely circulated on the Berkeley campus. In large black letters across the top it exclaimed: EDWARD TELLER—WAR CRIMINAL. In the center was a crudely reproduced photograph of the "war criminal" that made him look particularly dark, unshaven, and evil. The flyer enumerated its charges:

Worked on atomic bomb during WW2.
Father of hydrogen bomb.
Largely responsible for establishment of Livermore Rad Lab.
Leading advocate of arms race.
Leading advocate of nuclear blackmail.
Has acted as hawk advisor to Washington officials, including Nixon, since WW2.

The message continued with the information that "He is living in our community: 1573 Hawthorne Terrace 848-8811."

At the bottom of the sheet was a suggestion: "People in the community have a responsibility to challenge Teller on his activities. You can do this by giving him a call or going by to discuss them with him. CAN YOU DIG IT?"

And, lest there be any doubt about how to reach Teller, there was a small map showing how to find his house.

The "war criminal" accusation stemmed from the so-called War Criminal Trials that had been conducted in Sweden under the leadership of Lord Bertrand Russell (in 1959 Teller and Russell had debated disarmament on a CBS television program). Russell's proceedings were based on the Nuremberg War Crimes Tribunal conducted by the victorious Allies to charge, try, and, if guilty, punish the Nazi perpetrators of World War II. In Berkeley the cause was taken up by a radical commune known as the Red Family. The commune included a number of faculty members as well as students among its followers. Their particular concern was military research under the jurisdiction of the University of California and the radicals knew that the largest of the university's military research establishments was the Lawrence Livermore Laboratory. Among the founders of the Red Family was Thomas Hayden, the husband of the actress and antiwar activist Jane Fonda.

A week or so in advance, the Red Family, plus a group called the Center for Participant Education and other campus organizations, announced their intention to hold a "War Crimes Tribunal" on November 23, 1970, in the Pauley Ballroom on the Berkeley campus. The event was well publicized by the *The Daily Californian*, the campus newspaper, which at that time was dominated by the radicals. The "defendants" were Teller; Charles Hitch, president of the University of California; Glenn Seaborg, physicist and former Berkeley chancellor and former chairman of the AEC; John Foster, former director of Livermore; John O. Lawrence, physicist and brother of the late Ernest Lawrence; and Michael May, director of the Livermore Laboratory in 1970.

The "tribunal" was scheduled to start at 7:30 P.M. on November 23. That afternoon a Berkeley physicist, Hardin Jones, became alarmed at the virulence of the attacks on Teller being circulated on the campus prior to the meeting. At 3:30 P.M. he telephoned Berkeley Chancellor Roger Heyns to warn him that the gathering was violence-prone. He was concerned, he later reported, about "criminally-motivated commando types." He wanted the administration to deny the "tribunal" the use of the Pauley Ballroom.

Jones was told that Heyns was not available. He asked then for Vice-Chancellor Robert Connick; he also did not come to the phone. At 4:30 Jones called Chancellor Heyns again, and was still not able to talk to him. He told the chancellor's secretary that the call was urgent. She told him Connick would call after 5 P.M. Connick did not call, but Robert Kerley, Vice-Chancellor for Administration, called for him. Jones, now desperate, pleaded with Kerley to deny the radicals the use of university facilities. He warned that the safety of Edward and Mici Teller was in the balance. Kerley told Jones he could not interfere with a meeting sponsored by a legitimate campus organization.

Hardin Jones was so furious and frustrated at the administration's apathy that at 7 P.M., a half hour before the "trial" was convened, he typed out a memo detailing his futile efforts to force the cancellation of the event, and predicting that it would end in violence.

The "War Crimes Tribunal" went off as scheduled. The entire proceeding was tape-recorded. Its mood was set within a few minutes when Jack Nicholl of the Red Family reported that on December 1, the Vice Premier of South Vietnam, Nguyen Cao Ky, would speak to the Commonwealth Club in San Francisco. "We don't even need to hold a hearing about Ky . . . he deserves to die," said Nicholl.

A long succession of speakers detailed the excesses and outrages of the Vietnam war (many of their criticisms were accurate and justified) and reviewed the legal definitions of a war criminal. Among the speakers were Charles Schwartz, a member of the Berkeley physics department. He was the first to zero in on Teller as the radicals' number one culprit. Teller, he said, exemplified "the cold-war philosophy that holds the Russians . . . the great evil on earth."

The proceedings went on for more than three hours. Teller was called "a leading sparkplug . . . for an even greater military nuclear arsenal" and "a paranoid anti-communist"; the Lawrence Livermore Laboratory was "a scientific whore-house."

Near the end of the session, Nicholl raised his voice again.

"I would like to ask a question of the audience," he said. "What are you people going to do when you go home tonight? You know, are you going to go home and off these labs and off these people, or are you just going to sit there and listen to this crap, huh? What are you going to do, huh? I'm gonna try and off these labs. You want to get some guns, we will do it."

Robert Cahn, another Red Family member, then spoke up. "So we have to talk, I think, a little bit; I mean the testimony is so apparent—what are we going to do?"

With that a general cry arose from the audience—"Let's get Teller. We want Teller."

Someone from the tribunal, never definitely identified, responded with "Let's get Teller *tonight*."

A woman's voice from the audience echoed, "Let's go. People outside and in front are ready to go. We want to get this to them. We got a responsibility to expose these people to the community and not let them live in the same way any longer. Let's go!"

"What's the address?" someone shouted. It was supplied.

At this point, perhaps in fear that the crowd was becoming a mob, Robert Cahn attempted to cool the passion somewhat. "I don't think you're going to accomplish a lot by marching down to Edward Teller's home . . . I think you will have to organize for a longer range than for the next half hour."

But as Cahn attempted to advocate "a whole bunch of things we can do in terms of the war crimes hearing for more investigation," the audience began to move toward the exits. Hardin Jones claims that at this point they were shouting, "Break Teller's windows, burn his house, kill him."

Edward and Mici were at home in their Spanish-style house on tree-shaded Hawthorne Terrace. Someone—they are not sure who—telephoned to warn that the tribunal was being worked up into a frenzy. Then Teller's young colleague Lowell Wood, who had heard about the threat to his boss, arrived at the house to offer assistance. Teller called the police. Both campus and Berkeley city police responded, the latter in riot gear. One contingent surrounded the house, which rests on a knoll about fifty feet back from the road. Another contingent cordoned themselves across Hawthorne Terrace at its intersection with Cedar Avenue, about a half-block from the house. When about fifty militants from the "tribunal" arrived, the police were ready. The Tellers, and their house, were saved. The mob burned him in effigy at the intersection.

Radicals, who had disrupted Teller's life as a small boy, and had made hostages of his family after World War II, had struck again. Some of their friends urged them to move away from their comfortable home on Hawthorne Terrace. They stayed, but now live behind a high chain-link fence with an alarm system. The yard is guarded by a huge dog. Otherwise Teller has not changed his routine nor his beliefs except to the extent that they have been altered or modified by the passage of time and the changing of circumstances.

He continues to believe that scientific secrecy should be abolished and has written and spoken publically on the issue for twenty years. But until the Russians open their society he believes the United States must continue to expand its nuclear weapons arsenal, though critics like physicist Marvin Goldberger ask, with some logic, "Why don't Teller and his associates talk about the end of the absolute madness of this arms race? Where does their scenario come to an end?"

Wherever it might end, Teller shows no signs of knuckling under to his critics. He belongs to the American Security Council, which he freely describes as "an association of right-wing people with whom I have joined. Most of them are retired armed forces officers [actually many are also major industrialists] organized by a man by the name of John Fisher. In one connection—the debate on the ABM—he and his publication were effective."

Teller's contention, however, is that he belongs to the American Security Council only because he believes in its overall goals. That does not exempt the council from his criticism. "One thing Fisher is habitually doing appears to me objectionable. He is conducting public opinion polls by sending out slanted questionnaires. I have protested that on more than one occasion—without effect. I have, however, not left the organization."

In 1972 Teller was accorded one of the highest honors of his career, an honor which he accepted with enthusiasm, only to turn it back less than two years later. In Boulder, Colorado, a University of Colorado political scientist, Dr. Edward J. Rozek, created a postgraduate institution called the Center for the Study of Democracy and Communism. Rozek is a remarkable man who endured a catalog of privations in World War II. He was a Polish soldier who fought the Nazis, was wounded and hospitalized, then escaped, lived underground, was caught and thrown into a Hungarian concentration camp. He escaped again and crawled by night all the way to the French coast and thence to England, where he joined the Polish army in exile. He fought in France, was wounded, recovered, and, with the war's end, emigrated to America. He worked as a farm laborer and a used-car salesman in Illinois, stashing away enough money to pay his own tuition at Harvard. He graduated *magna cum laude,* then stayed on to get a doctorate in political science. His first professorship was at Boulder, where he eventually founded his postgraduate center.

For all his acknowledged brilliance, Rozek was nonetheless regarded by some of his colleagues as a right-wing extremist and a paranoiac anti-communist. Perhaps his political leanings attracted him to Teller, whom Rozek admired as a patriotic American and a man who recognized the menace posed by the Soviet Union. In the summer of 1972 Teller presented a series of lectures at the center. They went deeply into Teller's political philosophy, but in sum were campaign speeches for Richard Nixon.

About this time Rozek made connections with Arthur Spitzer, a millionaire oil tycoon who, in escaping from Romania, had undergone privations almost as severe as Rozek's. While Rozek aspired to academic achievement, Spitzer aspired to business success. Starting with one gas station near Los Angeles in 1953, he expanded his holdings into a chain and eventually into the largest block of stock in the Tesoro Petroleum Corporation.

The two men found they shared gratitude to the United States for their opportunities, unbounded admiration for Edward Teller, and unbridled horror of totalitarianism, especially the Russian version. In October 1972 Spitzer provided the financial underpinning for a new institution, officially named the Edward Teller Center for Science, Technology and Political Thought. Unlike its predecessor, the Teller center had no formal connection with the University of Colorado. Spitzer envisioned a western version of Princeton's Institute for Advanced Study. A prestigious advisory board was recruited. It included such national figures as Lewis Strauss, Senator Henry M. Jackson, Frank Shakespeare, the broadcasting executive who had been President Nixon's chief of the United States Information Agency, a sprinkling of conservative businessmen, and a host of Teller's scientific comrades (those who stuck with him after the Oppenheimer fiasco), including Harold Agnew, the director of Los Alamos, Frederic de Hoffmann, Alfred Sklar, Ted Walkowicz, and Eugene Wigner.

The Edward Teller Center, in addition to lectures and courses at Boulder, conducted two national conferences on energy in January and June of 1974. Teller chaired both, and both received national press and broadcasting coverage. Meanwhile, Rozek had invited Teller to leave Berkeley and move to Boulder to become professor-in-residence at the center that bore his name.

In early 1975 Teller suddenly and summarily severed his connections with the Edward Teller Center. He would not discuss his reasons except to say they were not based on any objections to the right-wing leanings of Rozek or Spitzer; the latter remains a good friend. He would only concede that the situation was "embarrassing," and that "it is something I should not have gotten involved in."

Having rejected one honor that might have physically memorialized him beyond the grave, in what light will Teller now be remembered? That will depend to a great extent on the kind of world that is left to remember him. He is physically memorialized now in every nuclear weapons silo, on every Polaris submarine, in the aresenal of the United States, which, to a great extent, means the arsenal of the Western World. Most of those missile warheads, whether they be small and tactical or large and strategic, are now thermonuclear—hydrogen—bombs. They are all physical manifestations of the ideas generated by Teller as far back as 1942, and the concept that sprang from Teller's brain in early 1951. Of course, many others contributed, but even Oppenheimer spoke of "Teller's invention of the H-bomb."
ler's invention of the H-bomb."

If the state of the world degenerates into a nuclear Armageddon, those who survive may regard Teller as the real incarnation of the fictional Dr. Strangelove. If the nations open the doors of their scientific cupboards and share their discoveries for the benefit of all mankind, Teller may be remembered as one of the bravest and strongest advocates of an open society. If, through mutual recognition of strength, the nuclear powers seek détente, then agreement, and, finally, peace, Teller's magnificent obsession with thermonuclear power may be recalled as a monumental contribution to a world without war.

But all of this depends on an unpredictable set of circumstances. The achievement that no one can take away from Teller is recognized mainly by other scientists. He is a great physicist and a great teacher of physics. Not even his bitterest political enemies or his scientific rivals ever contested this as we wrote his biography. His study of the vibrations of polyatomic molecules, which he describes as "not very fashionable" physics, is now considered invaluable to other physicists, especially one important theorem that is commonly known as the Jahn-Teller Effect.

Few scientific colleagues were closer to Teller than physicist Frederic de Hoffmann, who was his principal aide during the early 1950s when Teller was desperately seeking the key to thermonuclear fusion. These are some of de Hoffmann's comments to us:

"I was honored that at one time I could work with him. I am sure that everybody who did this is deeply grateful to him for how much one learns from him because one learns a great, great deal about how to solve physical problems—how to attack things, how to think things through. This is a trait that he has given freely to the physics community around the world. I am sure that all of the people that you've interviewed about Edward's teaching will tell you he's a marvelous teacher. He honestly tells people what he has to say, and if they are opposed to him he listens to what they have to say on the subject.

"Edward has always taken too little credit. There is a whole host of people that has worked with Edward over the years, there was usually a joint paper with Teller and the other person. I venture to say that in most of these papers (this is a guess of mine, obviously, rather than a provable fact) Edward was the driving intellectual force behind the idea. That doesn't mean that the other people didn't contribute because he worked with some awfully good people in his life. But Edward is a man who understands physics in the deepest sense of the word."

On June 16, 1975, Teller retired from the Lawrence Livermore Laboratory, where, for twenty-three years, he had been both the leading scientist and a father figure to a generation of younger colleagues. It was not altogether a happy occasion. The people closest to Teller know his power and his occasional irascibility, but they also know him as warm friend, a sentimental musician, and the head of a family who dotes on his wife, his son, his daughter, and his grandchildren. And they know also that he is a strangely restless and vaguely unhappy man, seemingly traveling about the earth in the quest of some elusive and formless Holy Grail.

His colleagues gave him a farewell banquet at which Teller made what he described as "my last un-retired speech." Within that speech Teller encapsulated much of the humor, ambition, frustration, fear, and sadness that has been the mark of his character for most of his life. His remarks, as usual, were delivered without text or notes.

"I think," he began, "I am known to a few of you as an excellent listener who, however, is at his very best when listening to himself." The audience laughed heartily.

"I believe that the story that has been told here of national defense, of the Atomic Energy Commission, of the Lawrence Laboratory, ranks among the very best that a considerable number of people could accomplish and did accomplish in the United States, and I'm proud of having been a part of it.

"But, at the end of this story of success we are left in second place, behind the Russians. I, for one, don't want to be first—but I want to survive." At this point, Teller's tone was somber.

"I said to a few of my friends that I have to mention this tragic situation in which we find ourselves. And at least one of them told me, with a little emphasis, 'Edward, you cried "wolf" once too often. Nobody is going to listen to you.' He was wrong. He forgot that *I* am a good listener." The solemnity was broken. Once again his colleagues roared.

"I did not cry 'wolf' too often." Teller was serious again. "I did not say the Russians are ahead of us. I said the Russians are going to be ahead of us. And now, they are.

"They are very cautious. They are conservative, and they know that five years from now they will be much *farther* ahead of us. This is the situation in which this country finds itself. You don't hear that often because people on the left say the United States is all-powerful and misuses its power. People on the right say, 'If we made only a little effort we would rectify everything in no time at all.'

"The Russians are today ahead of us and they are going to *stay* ahead of us for years to come. This means danger. This means hardship. This is not unconnected with the energy shortage, which, in itself, is a tremendous problem, and which is a part of the problem of this laboratory.

"At this time of real crisis, of national crisis, of worldwide crisis, this laboratory—which is a good one—is not as young as it used to be, is not as good as it used to be."

Teller then recounted the story of how Livermore was set up to provide competition for Los Alamos which, in 1952, he felt was not as good as it had been during the war years. "For a human organization, it is not easy to remain useful, and it is particularly difficult if public opinion is not for technology, not for defense, or if the budget is cut, if the directives push us toward the routine rather than toward the new."

Teller likened the struggle of Livermore and Los Alamos to get public and financial support to the struggle to deal with the energy crisis. He bewailed the "undeservedly unsupported program for new initiatives on energy."

Remembering failures of the earliest nuclear tests planned by the Livermore Laboratory, Teller suggested an aphorism: "Without occasionally overextending yourself, you will get nowhere."

"What is all this about? Inside the laboratory, in the United States, in the Free World, I claim that what it *is* about is freedom. And there are only two freedoms which, to me, matter. Number one—and everybody knows it—is freedom of speech. Number two is the freedom to make your own mistakes. If you don't have the freedom to make mistakes, you will never do anything.

"One of my good friends here hinted something about the end of the world. Nothing of the kind is in sight. The world will last. People will last. Humankind will last. This is one of the biggest crises, as was the case with every historical crisis because every historical crisis in its time was the biggest.

"The terrible situation which we face today is not a question of the end of the world. It may be a question of the end of the freedom of speech and the freedom of making our own mistakes. But as long as we can safeguard those freedoms, we can make the future better than was the past."

APPENDIX

Appendix I

Mr. Stanley Blumberg
4200 Hayward Avenue
Baltimore, MD 21215

Dear Stanley:

This is a review of what I did in Los Alamos during World War II. It is, of course, severely restricted by requirements of classification.

My first activity in Los Alamos was to indoctrinate the people who came to the Laboratory. I was by that time connected with atomic energy for four years, whereas most of the recruits to Los Alamos were newcomers. The indoctrination happened in seminars and also occasionally in individual talks. That activity persisted throughout my whole stay at Los Alamos. It was particularly enjoyable to tell Fermi what we were doing when (I believe about 1944) he came to the Laboratory. It should be noted that due to the policy of compartmentalization, Fermi, who up to that time worked in Chicago, could not be informed about details while he was in Chicago.

The most fruitful of the exercises in indoctrination was that of Johnny von Neumann. He occupied a rather peculiar position, being the only scientist who *visited* Los Alamos frequently and who had complete access to everything we were doing. Others who had similar privileges like, for instance, Drs. Tolman and Conant, exercised a supervisory activity and did not contribute.

I had, of course, met Johnny von Neumann many years before, for the first time in 1925 in Budapest. While we had talked about scientific topics at earlier times, our discussions at Los Alamos were the real beginning of thorough cooperation. It was also the beginning of the most significant part of the implosion program. It actually happened within the first few months of our work in Los Alamos.

Johnny was quite interested in high explosives. In my discussions with him some crude calculations were made. The calculation is indeed simple as long as you assume that the material to be accelerated is incompressible, which is the usual assumption about solid matter. If one accelerates a solid shell inward the area through which the shell has to move decreases as r^2, as you approach the center. If the material is incompressible then the necessity that the same amount of material must pass through a smaller area leads to the conclusion that the velocity must increase as $1/r^2$. It is not difficult to show that this in turn means that the acceleration must vary as $1/r^5$, and that in order for this to happen the pressure must change as $1/r^4$. In materials driven by high explosives, pressures of more than 100,000 atmospheres occur. (A point with which Johnny was familiar, but I was not.) If a shell moves in one-third of the way toward the center you obtain under the assumption of an incompressible material a pressure in excess of eight million atmospheres. This is more than the pressure in the center of the earth and it was known to me (but not to Johnny), that at these pressures, iron is not incompressible. In fact I had rough figures for the relevant compressibilities. The result of all this was that in the implosion significant compressions will occur, a point which had not been previously discussed.

The importance of this point is obvious. At higher densities the amount of material needed for a nuclear explosion is decreased. This, of course, had decisive consequences on the time scale needed for the accomplishment of our task since materials were expected to remain in exceedingly short supply.

Bethe was in charge of the theoretical work. It was a fact that he and I did not work well together (as he stated to Gwinn). He wanted me to work on calculational details at which I was not particularly good, while I wanted to continue not only on the hydrogen bomb, but on other novel subjects.

In the end, Oppenheimer resolved the difficulty by moving me out of the theoretical division and giving me a group of my own. At a later time we reported to Fermi, an arrangement that worked very well.

Most of the new topics on which I worked remain classified. There are, however, a few which I can mention.

One was the question of opacities. At the very high temperatures expected in nuclear explosions rapid heat transport by radiation was to be expected. This is a phenomenon well known to astrophysicists. However, heat transport in a heavy material like uranium had its great intricacies. It was judged that this work could be performed outside the Laboratory without telling people what it was needed for. I got permission to work on this with Dr. Maria Mayer at Columbia University, and with two of her graduate students. In the long run this topic turned out to be of great importance; the results were declassified. In fact the material on which the two students, Boris Jacobson and Harris Mayer,* worked were first used as classified Ph.D. theses, but later were published. Both Maria Mayer and Boris Jacobson have died. Harris Mayer is now at the Institute of Defense Analysis in Arlington, Va. You might want to talk with him about our collaboration.

Another topic was quite marginally connected with nuclear explosives. The question arose whether the gas diffusion plant for separating nuclear isotopes could lead to accumulation of U 235 and cause a nuclear explosion. Due to the compartmentalization the people working on the diffusion plant could not be given the appropriate data. I was supposed to review the blueprints but it soon turned out that in this way I could not get enough information to make the relevant decisions for safety. Collaboration was therefore established between Manson Benedict and myself (Manson is now an eminent nuclear engineer at M.I.T. He is a great believer in the fast breeder and after many years of friendship we now have our disagreements. You might want to interview him.) This exercise again made it necessary for me to visit in New York. Actually, I was one of the rather few people who were allowed to leave Los Alamos quite frequently on business trips.

Another topic was, of course, further calculations concerning the hydrogen bomb or "Super." I have never completely abandoned this subject during the Los Alamos days. One phase which has been unclassified might amuse you. This was the clarification of the question whether or not it was conceivable that an H-bomb when and if it could be detonated, might give rise to a propagating nuclear explosion in the earth. It soon turned out that the only case where an argument for such a propagation could be made was

*Not a relative of Maria Mayer.

propagation in air. Actually, nitrogen nuclei can react with other nitrogen nuclei as has been later experimentally verified in considerable detail. A few of us (Marvin, Konopinski, and myself) made detailed and conclusive calculations showing that such a propagation could not occur.

This led to a further activity. Oppenheimer asked me to look into the question of the possibility of a fission bomb leading to some unexpected big effects due to any novel but imaginable law of nature. Such a law, of course, had to be of the kind as to escape observation up to that time. This was a most challenging and most welcome task. Since a lot of imagination was needed it was understood that I should shop around and ask everyone in Los Alamos if there would be any trouble. As you well know, we could find no trouble and none was, of course, ever observed. The fact that the explosion was bigger than originally expected was due to the incomplete and conservative nature of the calculations and the result was, as you also know, by no means unexpected to me.

Even this incomplete list might give you the impression that I was not unemployed in Los Alamos. Neither was I really missed in the calculational effort. Really excellent people, including Victor Weisskopf, Klaus Fuchs, and Richard Feynman, to mention only a few, were ready and willing to do the job. It is conceivable that even Bethe might admit that I had not wasted my time.

Sincerely,

ET:oc

Edward Teller

Appendix II

A PETITION TO THE PRESIDENT OF THE UNITED STATES

Discoveries of which the people of the United States are not aware may affect the welfare of this nation in the near future. The liberation of atomic power which has been achieved places atomic bombs in the hands of the Army. It places in your hands, as Commander-in-Chief, the fateful decision whether or not to sanction the use of such bombs in the present phase of the war against Japan.

We, the undersigned scientists, have been working in the field of atomic power. Until recently we have had to fear that the United States might be attacked by atomic bombs during this war and that her only defense might lie in a counterattack by the same means. Today, with the defeat of Germany, this danger is averted and we feel impelled to say what follows:

The war has to be brought speedily to a successful conclusion and attacks by atomic bombs may very well be an effective method of warfare. We feel, however, that such attacks on Japan could not be justified, at least not unless the terms which will be imposed after the war on Japan were made public in detail and Japan were given an opportunity to surrender.

If such public announcement gave assurance to the Japanese that they could look forward to a life devoted to peaceful pursuits in their homeland and if Japan still refused to surrender our nation might then, in certain circumstances, find itself forced to resort to the use of atomic bombs. Such a step, however, ought not to be made at any time without seriously considering the moral responsibilities which are involved.

The development of atomic power will provide the nations with new means of destruction. The atomic bombs at our disposal represent only the first step in this destruction and there is almost no limit to the destructive power which will become available in the

459

course of their future development. Thus a nation which sets the precedent of using these newly liberated forces of nature for purposes of destruction may have to bear the responsibility of opening the door to an era of devastation on an unimaginable scale.

If after this war a situation is allowed to develop in the world which permits rival powers to be in uncontrolled possession of these new means of destruction, the cities of the United States as well as the cities of other nations will be in continuous danger of sudden annihilation. All the resources of the United States, moral and material, may have to be mobilized to prevent the advent of such a world situation. Its prevention is at present the solemn responsibility of the United States—singled out by virtue of her lead in the field of atomic power.

The added material strength which this lead gives to the United States brings with it the obligation of restraint and if we were to violate this obligation our moral position would be weakened in the eyes of the world and in our own eyes. It would then be more difficult for us to live up to our responsibility of bringing the unloosened forces of destruction under control.

In view of the foregoing, we, the undersigned, respectfully petition: first, that you exercise your power as Commander-in-Chief, to rule that the United States shall not resort to the use of atomic bombs in this war unless the terms which will be imposed upon Japan have been made public in detail and Japan knowing those terms has refused to surrender; second, that in such an event the question whether or not to use atomic bombs be decided by you in the light of the considerations presented in this petition as well as all the other moral responsibilities which are involved.

Notes

CHAPTER 1

1. Nicholas M. Nagy-Talavera, *The Green Shirts and the Others: A History of Fascism in Hungary and Rumania.* Stanford, Calif., Hoover Institution Press, Stanford University, 1970, p. 40.
2. Ibid., p. 41.
3. Rudolf L. Tokes, *Bela Kun and the Hungarian Soviet Republic.* Published for the Hoover Institution on War, Revolution and Peace, Stanford University, Stanford, Calif., by Frederick A. Praeger, New York, Washington, 1967, p. 203.
4. Emil Lengyel, *1,000 Years of Hungary.* New York, John Day, 1958, p. 205.

CHAPTER 2

1. Edward Teller and Albert L. Latter, *Our Nuclear Future . . . Facts, Dangers and Opportunities.* New York, Criterion Books, 1958, p. 19.
2. George Gamow, *Thirty Years That Shook Physics: The Story of Quantum Theory.* Garden City, N.Y., Doubleday, 1966, p. 4.
3. Ronald W. Clark, *Einstein, the Life and Times.* New York, Avon Books, 1971, p. 415.
4. Ibid., p. 573.
5. Ibid., p. 571.

CHAPTER 3

1. Ruth Moore, *Niels Bohr, the Man, His Science, and the World They Changed.* New York, Alfred A. Knopf, 1966, p. 152.

CHAPTER 4

1. Philip M. Stern with Harold P. Green, *The Oppenheimer Case: Security on Trial.* New York, Harper & Row, 1969, p. 10.
2. Robert Coughlin, "The Tangled Drama and Private Hells of Two Famous Scientists," *Life,* December 13, 1963, p. 5.

CHAPTER 5

1. Ruth Moore, *Niels Bohr, the Man, His Science, and the World They Changed.* New York, Alfred A. Knopf, 1966, p. 236.
2. Lewis L. Strauss. *Men and Decisions.* Garden City, N.Y., Doubleday, 1962, p. 172.
3. Laura Fermi, *Atoms in the Family, My Life with Enrico Fermi.* Chicago, University of Chicago Press, 1954, p. 162.
4. Arnulf and Louise Esterer, *Leo Szilard, Prophet of the Atomic Age.* New York, Julian Messner, 1972, p. 69.
5. Ibid., p. 74.
6. Strauss, p. 177.
7. Richard G. Hewlett and Oscar E. Anderson, Jr., *A History of the United States Atomic Energy Commission,* Vol. 1, 1939-1946, *The New World.* Springfield, Va., National Technical Information Service, U.S. Department of Commerce, 1972, p. 16.
8. Ibid., p. 17.
9. Esterer, p. 82.
10. Hewlett, p. 20.

CHAPTER 6

1. Arnulf and Louise Esterer, *Leo Szilard, Prophet of the Atomic Age.* New York, Julian Messner, 1972, p. 85.
2. Richard G. Hewlett and Oscar E. Anderson, Jr., *A History of the United States Atomic Energy Commission,* Vol. 1, 1939-1946, *The New World.* Springfield, Va., National Technical Information Service, U.S. Department of Commerce, 1972, p. 32.
3. Edward Teller, "The Work of Many People," *Science,* Vol. 121, February 25, 1955, p. 267.
4. Ibid., p. 268.

5. H. D. Smyth, *A General Account of the Development of Methods of Using Atomic Energy for Military Purposes.* Washington, D.C., Atomic Energy Commission, 1945, p. 50.

6. Ibid., p. 55.

7. Arthur Compton, *Atomic Quest.* New York, Oxford University Press, 1956, p. 178.

8. Nuel Pharr Davis, *Lawrence and Oppenheimer.* New York, Simon and Schuster, 1968, p. 126.

9. Ibid., p. 127.

10. Ibid., p. 131.

11. Hewlett, p. 104.

12. Davis, p. 131.

CHAPTER 7

1. H. D. Smyth, *A General Account of the Development of Methods of Using Atomic Energy for Military Purposes.* Washington, D.C., Atomic Energy Commission, 1945, p. 155.

2. Richard G. Hewlett and Oscar E. Anderson, Jr., *A History of the United States Atomic Energy Commission,* Vol. 1, 1939-1946, *The New World.* Springfield, Va., National Technical Information Service, U.S. Department of Commerce, 1972, p. 233.

3. Laura Fermi, *Atoms in the Family.* Chicago, University of Chicago Press, 1954, p. 221.

4. Clay Blair, Jr., "Passing of a Great Mind," *Life,* Feb. 25, 1957. p. 90.

5. David Irving, *The German Atomic Bomb.* New York, Simon and Schuster, 1967, p. 102.

CHAPTER 8

1. *In the Matter of J. Robert Oppenheimer.* Transcript of Hearings before Personnel Security Board, Washington, D.C., April 12, 1954 through May 6, 1954. Washington, D.C., U.S. Government Printing Office, 1954, p. 30.

2. Ibid., p. 31.

3. Richard G. Hewlett and Oscar E. Anderson, Jr., *A History of the United States Atomic Energy Commission,* Vol. 1, 1939-1946,

The New World. Springfield, Va., National Technical Information Service, U.S. Department of Commerce, 1972, p. 375.

4. James F. Byrnes, *Speaking Frankly.* Westport, Conn., Greenwood Press, reprint 1974, p. 104.

5. Harry S. Truman. *Memoirs,* Vol. 1, *Years of Decision.* Garden City, N.Y., Doubleday, 1958, p. 77.

6. Gar Alperovitz, *Atomic Diplomacy: Hiroshima and Potsdam.* New York, Simon and Schuster, 1965, p. 20.

7. Truman, p. 76.

8. Ibid., p. 70.

9. Herbert Feis, *Churchill, Roosevelt, and Stalin.* Princeton, N.J., Princeton University Press, 1957, p. 598.

10. Truman, p. 70.

11. James V. Forrestal, *The Forrestal Diaries,* Walter Mills, ed. New York, Viking, 1951, p. 41.

12. Truman, p. 71.

13. Herbert Feis, *Between War and Peace.* Princeton, N.J., Princeton University Press, 1960, p. 105.

14. Feis, *Churchill, Roosevelt, and Stalin,* p. 575.

15. Alperovitz, p. 21.

16. Ibid., p. 34.

17. Truman, p. 228.

18. Ibid.

19. Alperovitz, p. 56.

20. William Daniel Leahy, *I Was There.* New York, Whittlesey House, 1950, p. 367.

21. Winston Churchill, *The Second World War,* Vol. 6, *Triumph and Tragedy.* Boston, Houghton Mifflin, 1953, p. 503.

22. Alperovitz, p. 40.

23. Ibid., p. 41.

24. *In the Matter of J. Robert Oppenheimer,* pp. 32-33.

25. Hewlett and Anderson, pp. 374-380.

26. Jonathan Daniels, *Man of Independence.* Philadelphia, Pa., J. B. Lippincott, 1950, p. 266.

27. Ray S. Cline, *Washington Command Post.* Washington Office Chief of the Military, History Department of the Army, 1951, p. 343.

28. *In the Matter of J. Robert Oppenheimer,* p. 34.

29. Hewlett and Anderson, p. 327.

30. Ibid., p. 328.

31. Ibid., p. 334.

32. Ibid., pp. 322-323.

33. Ibid., p. 326.

34. Ibid.

35. Ibid., p. 333.

36. Ibid., pp. 340-341.

37. Ibid., p. 342.

38. Ibid., p. 345.

39. Ibid., p. 344.

40. Ibid., p. 345.

41. Ibid., p. 356.

42. Ibid., p. 358.

43. Ibid., p. 366.

44. Alperovitz, p. 154.

45. Hewlett and Anderson, p. 367.

46. Edward Teller with Allen Brown, *The Legacy of Hiroshima.* Garden City, N.Y., Doubleday, 1962, p. 13.

47. Ibid.

48. Ibid., pp. 13-14.

49. Ibid., p. 14.

50. Lewis L. Strauss, *Men and Decisions.* Garden City, N.Y., Doubleday, 1962, p. 193.

51. *Newsweek,* November 11, 1963, p. 107.

52. Strauss, p. 192.

53. Arthur H. Compton, *Atomic Quest, A Personal Narrative.* New York, Oxford University Press, 1956, pp. 238, 239.

54. Strauss, p. 193.

55. John Toland, *The Rising Sun, The Decline and Fall of the Japanese Empire 1936–1945,* Vol. 2. New York, Random House, p. 948.

56. Ibid.

57. Ibid., p. 950.

58. Ibid., pp. 932, 933, 951.

59. Leahy, p. 441.

60. Fletcher Knebel and C. W. Bailey, *No High Ground.* New York, Harper & Row, 1960, p. 111.

61. Edgar Snow, *Journey to the Beginning.* New York, Random House, 1959, p. 357.

62. Teller, p. 19.

63. Ibid., p. 20.

CHAPTER 9

1. Emil Lengyel, *1000 Years of Hungary.* New York, John Day, 1958, p. 227.
2. Ibid., p. 242.
3. Ibid., p. 237.

CHAPTER 10

1. Edward Teller with Allen Brown, *The Legacy of Hiroshima.* Garden City, N.Y., Doubleday, 1962, p. 21.
2. Ibid., p. 22.
3. *In the Matter of J. Robert Oppenheimer:* Transcript of Hearings before Personnel Security Board, Washington, D.C., April 12, 1954 through May 6, 1954. Washington, D.C., U.S. Government Printing Office, 1954, p. 47.
4. Teller, p. 22.
5. Ibid.
6. Ibid., p. 23.
7. Ibid.
8. Lewis L. Strauss, *Men and Decisions.* Garden City, N.Y., Doubleday, 1962, pp. 201, 202.
9. Ibid., p. 203.
10. Ibid., p. 204.
11. Ibid.
12. *U.S. News & World Report,* December 24, 1954, p. 101.
13. Philip M. Stern with Harold P. Green, *The Oppenheimer Case: Security on Trial.* New York, Harper & Row, 1969, p. 113.
14. Strauss, p. 216.
15. Stern, p. 133.
16. Norman Moss, *Men Who Play God: The Story of the H Bomb and How the World Came to Live With It.* New York, Harper & Row, 1968, pp. 24-25.
17. Harry S. Truman, *Years of Trial and Hope.* Garden City, N.Y., Doubleday, 1956, p. 306.
18. Moss, pp. 24-25.
19. Truman, p. 307.
20. Strauss, pp. 205-206.
21. *In the Matter of J. Robert Oppenheimer,* p. 714.
22. Moss, p. 26.

23. Ibid., p. 25.

24. *In the Matter of J. Robert Oppenheimer*, pp. 658-659.

25. Ibid., p. 775.

26. Strauss, p. 217.

27. *In the Matter of J. Robert Oppenheimer*, p. 659.

28. Ibid.

29. Ibid., p. 776.

30. Ibid., p. 777.

31. Ibid., pp. 777-778.

32. David E. Lilienthal, *Journals,* Vol. 3, *Venturesome Years 1950-1955.* New York, Harper & Row, 1966, p. 406.

33. *In the Matter of J. Robert Oppenheimer*, p. 778.

34. Ibid.

35. Ibid., p. 779.

36. Ibid.

37. Ibid.

38. Ibid., p. 780.

39. Ibid., p. 781.

40. Ibid., p. 783.

41. Ibid., p. 242.

42. Ibid., p. 243.

43. Stern, p. 179.

44. *In the Matter of J. Robert Oppenheimer*, p. 714.

45. Ibid., p. 231.

46. Ibid., p. 243.

47. Ibid., p. 328.

48. Ibid., p. 715.

49. Teller, p. 43.

50. Moss, p. 21.

Chapter 11

1. *In the Matter of J. Robert Oppenheimer.* Transcript of Hearings before Personnel Security Board, Washington, D.C., April 12, 1954 through May 6, 1954. Washington, D.C., U.S. Government Printing Office, 1954, p. 76.

2. Ibid., p. 77.

3. Ibid., p. 397.

4. Ibid., p. 395.

5. Ibid., p. 513.

6. Ibid., p. 453.

7. Ibid., p. 461.

8. Ibid., pp. 246-247.

9. Philip M. Stern with Harold P. Green, *The Oppenheimer Case: Security on Trial.* New York, Harper & Row, 1969, p. 143.

10. Norman Moss, *Men Who Play God: The Story of the H Bomb and How the World Came to Live with It.* New York, Harper & Row, 1968, p. 20.

11. Lewis L. Strauss, *Men and Decisions.* Garden City, N.Y., Doubleday, 1962, p. 218.

12. Moss, p. 21.

13. Moss, p. 20.

14. Edward Teller with Allen Brown, *The Legacy of Hiroshima.* Garden City, N.Y., Doubleday, 1962, p. 45.

15. Ibid., p. 44.

16. Ibid.

17. Ibid., pp. 44-45.

18. Ibid., p. 45.

19. Stern, p. 147.

20. Strauss, p. 218.

21. *In the Matter of J. Robert Oppenheimer,* p. 304.

22. Harry S. Truman, *Years of Trial and Hope.* Garden City, N.Y., Doubleday, 1956, p. 307.

23. *In the Matter of J. Robert Oppenheimer,* p. 432.

24. Strauss, p. 219.

25. Ibid., p. 220.

26. James R. Shepley and Clay Blair, Jr., *The Hydrogen Bomb.* New York, David McKay, 1954, pp. 80-83.

27. Strauss, pp. 222-223.

28. Richard G. Hewlett and Francis Duncan, *A History of the United States Atomic Energy Commission,* Vol. II, 1947-1952, *Atomic Shield.* U.S. Atomic Energy Commission, 1972, p. 392.

29. Ibid., p. 393.

30. Ibid., pp. 393-394.

31. Stern, p. 152.

32. Washington *Post,* November 18, 1949, p. 1.

33. Hewlett and Duncan, p. 402.

34. Ibid., p. 394.

35. Ibid., p. 395.

36. Strauss, p. 440.

37. Drew Pearson, transcript of radio broadcast, January 15, 1950.

38. James Reston, New York *Times*, January 17, 1950, p. 1.

39. Hewlett and Duncan, p. 403.

40. Teller, p. 28.

41. Ibid., p. 29.

42. Ibid., p. 46.

43. New York *Times*, January 28, 1950, p. 1.

44. Hewlett and Duncan, p. 407.

45. Ibid., p. 408.

CHAPTER 12

1. Edward Teller with Allen Brown, *The Legacy of Hiroshima.* Garden City, N.Y., 1962, p. 46.

2. Philip M. Stern, with the collaboration of Harold P. Green, *The Oppenheimer Case: Security on Trial.* New York, Harper & Row, 1969, p. 154.

3. Richard G. Hewlett and Francis Duncan, *A History of the United States Atomic Energy Commission,* Vol. II, *Atomic Shield.* Washington, D.C., Atomic Energy Commission, 1947-1952, pp. 439-40.

4. Ibid., p. 411.

5. Ibid., p. 412.

6. Ibid.

7. Teller, p. 31.

8. Ibid.

9. Hewlett, pp. 412-13.

10. James R. Shepley and Clay Blair, Jr., *The Hydrogen Bomb.* New York, David McKay, 1954, p. 105.

11. Ibid., p. 106.

12. *Science,* February 25, 1955, p. 27.

13. Ibid.

14. Trans., p. 83.

15. Ibid., p. 719.

16. Ibid.

17. Letter from Hans Bethe to the authors, January 6, 1975.

18. Hewlett, p. 414.

19. Norman Moss, *Men Who Play God.* New York, Harper & Row, 1968, p. 45.

20. Hewlett, p. 415.

21. Ibid., p. 416.

22. Ibid.

23. Ibid., p. 417.

24. Ibid.

25. Shepley and Blair, p. 108.

26. *Scientific American,* March 1950.

27. *Scientific American,* April 1950.

28. *Scientific American,* May 1950.

29. Edward Teller, "Back to the Laboratories," *Bulletin of Atomic Scientists,* March 1950.

30. Shepley and Blair, p. 110.

31. Letter from Richard C. Hewlett to the authors, March 27, 1955.

32. Letter from Edward Teller to the authors.

33. Hewlett, p. 438.

34. Ibid., p. 439.

35. Ibid.

36. Ibid.

37. R. G. Marshak, ed., *Perspectives in Modern Physics: Essays in Honor of Hans A. Bethe.* New York, Interscience Publishers, 1966, pp. 593-98.

38. Hewlett, p. 440.

39. Ibid.

40. Ibid., p. 527.

41. Ibid., p. 528.

42. Ibid., p. 529.

43. Ibid., p. 530.

44. Ibid., p. 531.

45. Letter from Edward Teller to the authors, December 28, 1973.

46. Trans., pp. 951-52.

47. Ibid., p. 714.

48. David E. Lilienthal, *Journals,* Vol. 3, *Venturesome Years.* New York, Harper & Row, 1966, p. 406.

49. Letter from C. L. Marshall to authors, December 31, 1974.

50. Hewlett, Appendix 4.

51. Teller, p. 520.

52. Ibid.

CHAPTER 13

1. Harrison E. Salisbury, Introduction to *Progress, Coexistence and Intellectual Freedom* by Andrei D. Sakharov. New York, W.W. Norton, 1968, p. 11.

2. Ibid.

3. Ibid., p. 12.

4. C. L. Marshall, Director, Division of Classification, United States Atomic Energy Commission, Washington, D.C. Letter to authors, November 29, 1974.

5. Richard G. Hewlett and Oscar E. Anderson, Jr., *A History of the United States Atomic Energy Commission,* Vol. I, 1939-1946, *The New World.* Springfield, Va., National Technical Information Service, U.S. Department of Commerce, 1972, p. 542.

6. Edward Teller with Allen Brown, *The Legacy of Hiroshima.* Garden City, N.Y., Doubleday, 1962, p. 51.

7. Norman Moss, *Men Who Play God.* New York, Harper & Row, 1968, p. 60.

8. Harold J. Ness, President, Lithium Company, Newark, N.J. Letter to Carroll L. Tyler, Manager, Santa Fe Operations, U.S. Atomic Energy Commission, Los Alamos, New Mexico, February 3, 1950.

9. Robert D. Krohn, Technical Information Group, Los Alamos, New Mexico. Letter to Arthur D. Thomas, Classification Officer, Lawrence Livermore Laboratory, Livermore, California, December 11, 1974.

10. Moss, p. 52.

11. Hewlett and Anderson, p. 544.

12. Norris E. Bradbury, former director, Los Alamos Laboratory, Los Alamos, New Mexico. Letter to authors, May 14, 1975.

13. Teller, pp. 52-53.

14. *In the Matter of J. Robert Oppenheimer.* Transcript of Hearings before the Personnel Security Board, Washington, D.C., April 12, 1954 through May 6, 1954. Washington, D.C. U.S. Government Printing Office, 1954, p. 305.

15. Philip M. Stern with Harold P. Green, *The Oppenheimer Case: Security on Trial.* New York, Harper & Row, 1969, p. 491.

16. Teller, p. 51.

17. Moss, p. 52.

18. Stanislaw M. Ulam, Gainesville, Florida. Letter to the authors, May 13, 1975.

19. Edward Teller, Lawrence Livermore Laboratory, Livermore, California. Letter to authors, July 5, 1974, plus interview comments, May 26, 1975.

20. *In the Matter of J. Robert Oppenheimer,* p. 80.

21. Hewlett and Anderson, p. 541.

22. Ibid., p. 554.

23. Ibid., p. 555.

24. Ibid., p. 556.

25. Ibid.

26. Teller, p. 54.

27. Hewlett and Anderson, p. 558.

28. Ibid., p. 559.

29. Ibid., p. 562.

30. Teller, p. 58.

31. Ibid., p. 59.

32. Hewlett and Anderson, p. 571.

33. Teller, p. 59.

34. Ibid., p. 61.

35. Ibid.

36. Hewlett and Anderson, p. 583.

37. Ibid., p. 584.

38. Letter from C. L. Marshall, Director of Classification, United States Atomic Energy Commission, to authors, December 31, 1974.

39. *In the Matter of J. Robert Oppenheimer,* p. 562.

40. Moss, p. 59.

41. *Science,* February 25, 1955, p. 274.

42. Moss, p. 60.

43. Ibid.

44. Letter from Edward Teller, Lawrence Livermore Laboratory, Livermore, Calif., declassified statement to authors, June 4, 1973.

45. J. Robert Oppenheimer, "Atomic Weapons and American Policy," *Foreign Affairs Quarterly,* July 1953.

CHAPTER 14

1. Lewis L. Strauss, *Men and Decisions.* Garden City, N.Y., Doubleday, 1962, p. 262.

2. Lincoln Steffens, *Autobiography of Lincoln Steffens.* New York, Harcourt & Brace, 1931, Chapter 18.

3. Anthony Bimba, *History of the American Working Class,* 3rd edition. New York, International Publishers, 1936, p. 288.

4. Philip M. Stern with Harold P. Green, *The Oppenheimer Case: Security on Trial.* New York, Harper & Row, 1969, p. 15.

5. Ibid.

6. *In the Matter of J. Robert Oppenheimer.* Transcript of Hearings before the Personnel Security Board, Washington, D.C., April 12, 1954 through May 6, 1954. Washington, D.C., U.S. Government Printing Office, 1954, pp. 14, 130-131, 135, 142. And Haakon Chevalier, *Oppenheimer: The Story of a Friendship.* New York, George Braziller, 1965, pp. 52-55.

7. Stern, p. 44.

8. *In the Matter of J. Robert Oppenheimer,* pp. 813, 845-853.

9. Ibid., p. 813.

10. Ibid., p. 864.

11. Ibid., p. 865.

12. Ibid., p. 819, 845.

13. Ibid., p. 848.

14. Ibid., p. 852.

15. Ibid., p. 123.

16. Ibid., p. 276.

17. Ibid., p. 816.

18. Ibid., p. 274.

19. Ibid., p. 824.

20. Ibid., p. 277.

21. Ibid., p. 168.

22. Ibid., pp. 871-886.

23. Ibid., pp. 153, 889.

24. Ibid., p. 137.

25. Ibid., pp. 152-153.

26. Ibid., pp. 150-151.

27. Ibid., p. 150.

28. Ibid., pp. 521-584.

29. Ibid., p. 749.

CHAPTER 15

1. Arthur M. Schlesinger, Jr., *A Thousand Days: John F. Kennedy in the White House.* Boston, Houghton Mifflin, 1965, p. 457.

2. Ibid., Foreword.

3. Thomas W. Wilson, Jr., *The Great Weapons Heresy*. Boston, Houghton Mifflin, 1970, Introduction.

4. J. Robert Oppenheimer, "Atomic Weapons and American Policy," *Foreign Affairs Quarterly*, July 1953, p. 532.

5. Ibid., p. 530.

6. Edward Teller, Testimony before Special Congressional Committee on Atomic Energy, November 1945, p. 277.

7. Edward Teller, "A Suggested Amendment to the Acheson Report," *Bulletin of the Atomic Scientists*, Vol. 1, No. 12 (June 1, 1946), p. 5.

8. Henry M. Jackson, "First Human Détente," New York *Times*, September 9, 1973, Op Ed page.

9. Arthur M. Schlesinger, Jr., "The Price of Détente," *Wall Street Journal*, September 27, 1973.

10. Ibid.

11. *The Sun*, Baltimore, Maryland, September 16, 1973, editorial page.

12. Joseph and Stewart Alsop, "We Accuse," *Harper's*, October 1954, p. 29.

13. C. A. Rolander, Jr., Deputy Director, Division of Security, AEC, office memorandum to K. D. Nichols, October 25, 1954, p. 5.

14. Ibid.

15. Ibid.

16. Joseph and Stewart Alsop, p. 29.

17. Rolander, p. 3.

18. *In the Matter of J. Robert Oppenheimer*, Transcript of Hearings before the Personnel Security Board, Washington, D.C., April 12, 1954 through May 6, 1954. Washington, D.C., U.S. Government Printing Office, 1954, p. 837.

19. Pittsburgh *Post Gazette*, November 7, 1953, p. 1.

20. Dwight D. Eisenhower, *The White House Years: Mandate for Change*. Garden City, N.Y., Doubleday, 1963, p. 311.

21. Lewis L. Strauss, *Men and Decisions*. Garden City, N.Y., Doubleday, 1962, p. 267.

22. Ibid., p. 268.

23. Ibid., p. 277.

24. Ibid., p. 275.

25. Philip M. Stern with Harold P. Green, *The Oppenheimer Case: Security on Trial*. New York, Harper & Row, 1969, p. 223.

26. Ibid., p. 227.

27. *In the Matter of J. Robert Oppenheimer,* p. 171.

28. Rolander, p. 2.

29. Stern, p. 231.

30. Lord Moran, *Churchill, Taken from the Diaries of Lord Moran.* Boston, Houghton Mifflin, 1966, pp. 537, 538.

31. U.S. Senate, Special Committee on Atomic Energy, U.S.1, Senate. Washington, D.C., December 5, 1945, p. 199.

32. Ibid., p. 190.

33. Ibid., p. 192.

34. Ibid., pp. 198-199.

35. *In the Matter of J. Robert Oppenheimer,* p. 734.

36. Oppenheimer, "Atomic Weapons and American Policy," p. 536.

37. *In the Matter of J. Robert Oppenheimer,* p. 470.

CHAPTER 16

All material in this chapter is derived from interviews by the authors or from the transcripts of the hearing *In the Matter of J. Robert Oppenheimer.*

CHAPTER 17

1. Robert Coughlan, "The Tangled Drama and Private Hells of Two Famous Scientists," *Life.* December 13, 1963 (Reprint), p. 11.

2. *In the Matter of J. Robert Oppenheimer.* Transcript of Hearings before Personnel Security Board, Washington, D.C., April 12, 1954 through May 6, 1954. Washington, D.C., U.S. Government Printing Office, 1954, p. 1019.

3. Ibid., p. 1021.

4. Ibid., p. 1052.

5. Ibid., p. 1065.

6. Robert Coughlan, "Dr. Edward Teller's Magnificent Obsession," *Life,* July 13, 1954, p. 61.

7. James R. Shepley and Clay Blair, Jr., *The Hydrogen Bomb.* New York, David McKay, 1954, p. 26.

8. *In the Matter of J. Robert Oppenheimer,* p. 758.

CHAPTER 18

1. Arthur M. Schlesinger, Jr., *A Thousand Days: John F. Kennedy in the White House.* Boston, Houghton Mifflin, 1965, p. 451.

2. Edward Teller with Allen Brown, *The Legacy of Hiroshima.* Garden City, N.Y., Doubleday, 1962, p. 64.

3. Norman Moss, *Men Who Play God.* New York, Harper & Row, 1968, p. 63.

4. New York *Times,* August 20, 1953, p. 1.

5. Moss, p. 85.

6. Lord Moran, *Churchill, Taken from the Diaries of Lord Moran, The Struggle for Survival, 1940–1965.* Boston, Houghton Mifflin, 1966, p. 535.

7. Moss, p. 85.

8. James R. Shepley and Clay Blair, Jr., *The Hydrogen Bomb.* New York, David McKay, 1953, p. 155.

9. Moss, p. 86.

10. Ibid., p. 87.

11. Ibid.

12. Ibid., p. 89.

13. Ibid., p. 90.

14. Shepley and Blair, p. 160.

15. Moss, pp. 92-93.

16. Ibid., p. 94.

17. Shepley and Blair, p. 161.

18. Richard G. Hewlett, letter to the authors, June 1975.

19. Edward Teller, letter to the authors, June 1975.

20. Teller, p. 66.

21. *Newsline,* Lawrence Livermore Laboratory, University of California, September 1972, p. 11.

22. Teller, p. 66.

23. Moss, p. 74.

24. *Newsline,* pp. 14-15.

25. Teller, p. 68.

26. Edward Teller, letter to Lewis Strauss, March 20, 1968.

27. Teller, p. 68.

28. Ibid., p. 82.

29. Ibid., p. 83.

30. "Engineering with Nuclear Explosives," Proceedings of the Third Plowshare Symposium, U.S. Atomic Energy Commission, April 21, 22, 23, 1964, p. 4.

31. Ibid.

32. Teller, p. 82.

33. Stanley A. Blumberg and Gwinn Owens, "Oil Shale: Will It Yield Its Treasure to a Nuclear Blast?" *The Evening Sun,* Baltimore, Maryland, December 12, 1972, editorial page.

34. Teller, p. 84.

35. Ibid., p. 86.

36. *Evening Sun,* Baltimore, Maryland, A. P. Dispatch, April 24, 1975, p. A3.

37. Edward Teller, letter to Lewis Strauss, February 9, 1957.

38. Edward Teller, prepared statement before the Military Operations Sub-Committee, February 14, 1957.

39. Stanley A. Blumberg, "Physicist Teller Sounds Alarm," *News American,* Baltimore, Maryland, June 18, 1972, p. 3A.

40. Peter N. James, *Soviet Conquest from Space,* New Rochelle, N.Y., Arlington House, 1974, p. 30.

41. Teller, p. 71.

42. Ibid.

43. Ibid., p. 192.

44. Ibid., p. 193.

45. Ibid., p. 194.

46. Ibid., p. 73.

47. Edward Teller, letter to Rear Admiral Anthony Wass, May 24, 1960.

48. Edward Teller, letter to Lewis Strauss, October 4, 1963.

49. Teller, p. 107.

50. Ibid., p. 180.

51. Ibid., p. 181.

52. New York *Times,* August 14, 1963, p. 6.

53. New York *Times,* August 24, 1963, p. 18.

54. New York *Times,* August 14, 1963, p. 18.

CHAPTER 19

1. *Time,* November 18, 1957, cover story.

2. Philip M. Stern, *The Oppenheimer Case,* New York, Harper & Row, 1969, p. 456.

3. Robert Coughlan, "The Tangled Drama and Private Hells of Two Famous Scientists," *Life,* December 13, 1963.

4. *Time,* November 18, 1957, p. 21.

Index